THE GERMAN ORDER OF BATTLE
WAFFEN SS
AND
OTHER UNITS
IN WORLD WAR II

THE GERMAN ORDER OF BATTLE

WAFFEN SS

AND

OTHER UNITS

IN WORLD WAR II

George F. Nafziger

COMBINED PUBLISHING

Pennsylvania

PUBLISHER'S NOTE

The headquarters of Combined Publishing are located midway between Valley Forge and the Germantown battlefield, on the outskirts of Philadelphia. From its beginnings, our company has been steeped in the oldest traditions of American history and publishing. Our historic surroundings help maintain our focus on history and our books strive to uphold the standards of style, quality and durability first established by the earliest bookmakers of Germantown and Philadelphia so many years ago. Our famous monk-and-console logo reflects our commitment to the modern and yet historic enterprise of publishing.

We call ourselves Combined Publishing because we have always felt that our goals could only be achieved through a "combined" effort by authors, publishers and readers. We have always tried to maintain maximum communication between these three key players in the reading experience.

We are always interested in hearing from prospective authors about new books in our field. We also like to hear from our readers and invite you to contact us at our offices in Pennsylvania with any questions, comments or suggestions, or if you have difficulty finding our books at a local bookseller.

Combined Publishing
P.O. Box 307
Conshohocken, PA 19428
E-mail: combined@combinedpublishing.com
Web: www.combinedpublishing.com
Orders: 1-800-418-6065

Cataloging-in-Publication Data is available from the Library of Congress.

ISBN 1-58097-058-3

Printed in the United States of America.

Contents

CONTENTS

CONTENTS

CONTENTS

Introduction

The German army had a number of special forces, most of which are best described by the French term *hors de ligne*, that is "outside of the regular army." Foreign troops have always fallen into this category in every army and the Germans certainly ended up with a tremendous force of foreign soldiers fighting in their uniforms. However, the Germans had three other non-traditional forces in their army.

The first, the Waffen SS, sprang from Hitler's personal bodyguard and much like many other Guard forces in the world's long military history, developed into a completely independent army all unto itself. Though not intentionally, it most assuredly falls into a category quite similar to that held by Napoleon's Imperial Guard, whose roots also are found in a dictator's personal bodyguard. Unlike the Imperial Guard, which was Napoleon's favored children, the SS belonged not to Adolf Hitler, but to Heinrich Himmler, Reichs-führer der SS. It was not only a field force, but a tool in the internal political struggle between Hitler's cronies.

The SS also, like Napoleon's Imperial Guard, contained large numbers of foreign troops. In contrast to Napoleon's Imperial Guard, however, the SS went on a massive recruiting effort among foreign nationals in an effort to make it as large as possible. And, also unlike Napoleon's Imperial Guard, the German portions of the SS were subjected to an ideological mania for racial purity that was frequently swept aside when it was convenient. Large portions of the SS contained non-Germanic troops. Much of the SS fought with a stead-fastness that was found in Napoleon's Old Guard, while some parts formed with foreign nationals had very poor reputations that included mass desertions, mutiny, and atrocity.

The second portion of forces *hors de ligne* in the German army was the Luftwaffe ground troops. The German division of operations between the army, navy, and air force was contorted by personalities and the political power base on which the Reich was formed. Hermann Göring claimed and was given anything that had any involvement with flying. As a result, the German paratroopers or *fallschirmjägers*, were part of the Luftwaffe. Operationally they were handled by the Army, but they were Göring's toys to play with as he wished. Like the SS, however, they also developed a ferocious reputation as fanatical fighters and were greatly feared and respected by their enemies.

Unlike the *fallschirmjägers*, the Luftwaffe also produced a number of Luftwaffe Field Divisions. These units were a second line formation at best, though they frequently ended up in the front lines and invariably took a terrible pounding for their troubles. They were underequipped and undertrained for frontline duties, though eventually they developed reasonable combat skills. They were produced as Hermann Göring attempted to garner favor from Hitler by producing a series of divisions to block the advance of the Russian armies in the winter of 1941/2.

The third force *hors de ligne* was a small number of naval divisions that were raised very late in the war. The surface navy had been so torn up by the Allies that it had very little use. Those ships that were operational continued to retain full use of their crews, but those crews whose ships were gone, those support people who were suddenly without function, found themselves swept up and rifles shoved in their hands in an effort to stem the flow of the Russian hordes westward into the Fatherland.

The last force is the traditional forces *hors de ligne* and those are the multitude of completely foreign forces that fought alongside the Germans. The largest single group of foreigners in the German army were former citizens of the Soviet Union. They started out as small numbers of volunteers that simply joined up with the Wehrmacht as it pushed through Russia. They were deserters from the Soviet army and they were enthusiastic citizens who came forward and wanted to fight against their communist oppressors. It is believed that fully 25 percent of the German army at the end of the war were former citizens of the Soviet Union.

Germany also obtained a large number of foreign troops from the various puppet states that it established. The largest force was probably the Italians. After the Allies invaded, Italian society tore itself in half. The diehard fascists remained true to Mussolini and the Germans, forming a number of divisions and a large number of support units that fought until the end of the war.

Germany also established a puppet state in Slovakia, which provided three infantry divisions, a mechanized division, and a security division, all of which fought on the Russian front. Then there is the puppet state of Croatia, which was as much an endlessly bleeding ulcer to the Nazis as was Spain to Napoleon. In order to deal with this, and perhaps following Frederick the Great's opinion that the entire Balkans was "not worth the bones of one Pomeranian grenadier," Hitler encouraged Croatia to form an army that would be entirely committed to fighting the Serbian and communist partisans in Yugoslavia.

There is an amazing spectrum of performance and quality to be seen as one examines the combat record of these forces. Most of the SS and the *fallschirmjägers* were surely the most aggressive and hardest fighting units in the German army. The SS was frequently used as the fire brigade rushing from one emergency to another, plugging the line and beating back Russian, American or British breakthroughs. The *fallschirmjägers* more often found themselves put into the critical positions in the line and simply refused to be pushed out of them. The Luftwaffe Field and Naval Divisions were stopgap measures of varying military prowess that were never used to lead any assault. The foreign troops, like the SS, ran the spectrum of quality from extremely good to most often of modest value. They are also one of the most interesting and saddest portions of the history of World War II. They were frequently motivated by nationalism and the desire to liberate themselves from one oppressor, only to find themselves oppressed by yet another.

Glossary of Terms

AC	Armored car	OKH	Oberkommando des Heeres (Supreme Army Command)
AOK	Armeeoberkommando (Command of an army in the field)	PAK	Panzerabwehrkanone (anti-tank gun)
Arko	Artillerie Kommando (brigade level staff)	plat	platoon
AT	anti-tank	Pz I	Panzer Mk I, Sd Kfz 101
btry	battery	Pz II	Panzer Mk II, Sd Kfz 121
btrys	batteries	Pz III`	Panzer Mk III, Sd Kfz 141 L/45
co	company	Pz III (50)	Panzer Mk III, Sd Kfz 141 L/42 with 50mm gun
col	column	Pz III (lg)	Panzer Mk III J, Sd Kfz 141/1 L/60 50mm gun
cos	companies		
Feldersatz	Replacement	Pz IV	Panzer Mk IV, Sd Kfz 161 L/24 short 75mm gun
fG	freie Gliederung (unit with a variable role, not strictly regulated)	Pz IV (lg)	Panzer Mk IV, Sd Kfz 161 L/43 long 75mm gun
FK	Feldkanon (field gun)	Pz VI	Panzer Mk VI, Sd Kfz 181 L/56 88mm gun
HMG	heavy machine gun		
hvy	heavy	PzBu39	light anti-tank rifle Model 39
Inf Sup Plat	Infantry support platoon	PzBu41	heavy anti-tank rifle Model 41 (28mm)
KwK	Kampfwagenkanone (tank mounted gun; the main tank armament)	regt	regiment
		sFH	heavy howitzer (generally the 150mm K18)
kz	kurz (short); short-barreled gun		
leFH	105mm light field howitzer	sfl	selbstfahrlafette (self-propelled gun carriage)
leIG	75mm light infantry support gun		
lFK	light field gun (generally 75mm lFK)	sIG	150mm heavy infantry support gun
lg	lang (long); long-barreled gun	SP	self-propelled
LMG	light machine gun	sPzB	schwere Panzerbüchse (heavy anti-tank rifle)
lt	light		
maint	maintenance	std	standard
Mk	Mark (equipment model designator)	StuG	Strumgeschütz (assault gun)
mot	motorized	StuK	Sturmkanone (assault gun mounted cannon)
motZ	fully motorized		
Mrs	Mörser or 210mm howitzer assigned at the army level	sup	supply
		tmot	teil motorisiert (partially motorized)
mtg	mounting (as in weapons mounted on a half-track)	z.b.V.	zur besondere Verwendung (for special purposes)
Nebelwerfer	multiple-barreled rocket launcher		

1
Waffen SS
Divisions and Brigades

The SS (Schütz Staffel or Defense Squad) was a political formation and much like its earliest predecessor, the Praetorian Guard, it took on both a military and a political role during its life. It was also a political tool used both by Adolf Hitler and by its commander, Heinrich Himmler, for political purposes. Hitler used it to control the country, while Himmler used it in the interminable squabbles between the Nazi upper echelons as such men as Göring and Himmler fought for Hitler's favor and the destruction of their enemies.

On 30 January 1933 Adolf Hitler became Chancellor of Germany. He did not feel that he could rely on either the Reichswehr or the police guards appointed by the state to provide for an adequate defense of his person. As a result he turned to his close friend and political associate, SS-Gruppenführer 'Sepp' Dietrich, and directed him to form a bodyguard.

Dietrich began the process of handpicking a force, which by 17 March 1933 contained 120 volunteers and a few members of the older Stosstrupp Adolf Hitler, forming them into the nucleus of what was called the "SS Stabwache Berlin" (SS Staff Watch Berlin). Their arms were limited to rifles and they were housed in the Alexander Barracks, not far from the Reich Chancellery, Hitler's official residence. The Stabwache underwent almost continual growth and reorganization thereafter. By May it had become the SS Sonderkommando Zossen and contained three companies. These companies had their instructors drawn from the army and the police, rather than the Allgemeine-SS. They were trained not only in military drill, etc., but also in police and antiterrorist work. In June three more companies were recruited and organized into the SS Sonderkommando Jüterbog. By September 1933 both forces were joined into a single formation that was renamed the "Adolph Hitler Standarte." On 9 November these men took an oath of personal loyalty to Hitler and the entire unit was renamed the "*Leibstandarte-SS Adolph-Hitler*" or which was commonly abbreviated "LAH."

Though theoretically under the control of Heinrich Himmler, commander of the SS, Hitler began to display his micro-managerial style and intervened personally in the direction of their activities. This led to its commander, Sepp Dietrich, evolving into a position of power quite independent of Himmler, which he exploited to the fullest. By 6 March 1934 the Leibstandarte contained 986 men. On 24 May 1934 Himmler responded positively to Dietrich's request that the LAH be allowed to use army, rather than SS formation terminology, abandoning "Sturmbann" and "Sturm" for "Bataillon" and "Kompanie," but the rank titles remained those of the SS.

On 30 June 1934 the LAH stepped out of the role of a bodyguard and into the pages of history as a political force when it became the principal executioner in the "Night of the Long Knives." Ernst Röhm and his SA had become an embarrassment to Hitler and in order to both consolidate his power and establish good relations with the army, Röhm had to go. The executions lasted for three days and resulted in a major change in the role of the LAH and its position within the Allgemeine-SS. The first overt change was the replacement of the SA-Feldjägerkorps and Allgemeine-SS sentries outside Gestapo headquarters with members of the LAH. Other important sentry positions were similarly shifted to the SS. The SS was, as a result of the "Night of the Long Knives," the instrument by which Hitler removed his principal rival for power in Germany, and began his process of subjugating the Wehrmacht to his will. Though the "Night of the Long Knives" was an act of appeasement, it was the first step towards the collapse of the Wehrmacht's ability to control its own destiny.

The LAH was motorized in October 1934. By early 1935 the LAH had risen to regimental strength—2,551 men—and contained a staff, three motorized infantry battalions, a motorcycle company, a mortar company, a signals platoon, an armored car platoon, and a regimental band. Its training had become more military and less police related and it adopted the army's *feldgrau* (field gray) uniforms. A company of the LAH marched with the army into Saarbrücken during the reoccupation of the Saarland on 1 March 1935. It participated in the occupation of Austria and served as the guard of honor for Hitler in his triumphant reentry into Vienna. During that operation it covered 600 miles in 48 hours, bringing recognition by the army in general and General Heinz Guderian in particular. In October 1938 it also participated in the occupation of the Sudetenland.

A second element of the SS had begun forming when Hitler rose to power as well. Because of his fear of insurrection and counterrevolution Hitler ordered that SS detachments be formed all across Germany. "Kasernierte Hundertschaft" of 100 men were organized and consolidated into company and battalion-sized Politische Bereitschaften (Political Reserve Squads). Some of these units also played a role in the "Night of the Long Knives." On 24 September 1934 Hitler ordered that these Politische Bereitschaften were to be brought together and organized into the SS-Verfügungstruppe or SS-VT. They were a political force that were to be at the disposal of the Nazi regime. They were formed on the basis of *standarten* which was the equivalent of an army infantry regiment. Each *standarten* was to contain three battalions, a motorcycle company, and a mortar company. Signals units were raised as well and the entire force was placed under the command of Reichsführer-SS Heinrich Himmler. In peacetime it was to control the state, but in time of war it was to be transferred to the army. In 1935 in Munich three sturmbanne were merged to form the SS-Standarte 1/VT, given the title "Deutschland," and equipped like an army horse-drawn regiment. At the same time the same process occurred in Hamburg forming the SS-Standarte 2/VT "Germania" and in Nürnberg forming the 3/VT "Germania." The SS-VT was recruited solely from party members of Aryan blood and was subjected to a very severe set of physical and mental regulations.

On 1 October 1936 Hausser was promoted to the rank of SS-Brigadeführer and made Inspector of the Verfügungstruppe. He organized a divisional staff and began the formation of the SS-VT into an operational division. The formation was soon joined by a flood of veterans from World War I, including SS-Sturmbannführer Felix Steiner, who brought with him a background in shock troop tactics from the trenches of France. He was given command of the SS-VT Standarte "Deutschland" and began training them in those tactics. He replaced the army weapons used by "Deutschland" with the submachine gun and hand grenades and began a rigorous training program that soon attracted considerable attention and approval.

When Austria was occupied by Germany a new Standarte was organized from Austrian personnel and given the title "Der Führer." Prior to the reoccupation of the Sudetenland in October 1938 both "Germania" and "Deutschland" were mobilized to the army and partici-

pated in the operation. By late 1938 all of the SS-VT Standarten were organized into motorized regiments. In May Hitler authorized the SS-Verfügungstruppe into a full division and the SS Regiment z.b.V. "Ellangen" (an artillery regiment), the SS-Sturmbann "N" (a pioneer battalion), a reconnaissance battalion, an antiaircraft machine-gun battalion, an ersatz or replacement battalion, and an anti-tank battalion were organized.

There was also a third element of the SS forming at the same time, the "Totenkopfverbände." These were the notorious concentration camp guards. They dated from December 1935 and by July 1937 they were grouped into three regiments, totaling 4,500 men.

The Totenkopfverbände were initially formed solely to guard the concentration camps and to control the civil population if riots should erupt when Hitler invaded Poland, but their role was to expand.

A total of five formations were raised initially: Oberbayern, Elbe, Sachsen, Ostfriesland, and Brandenburg. However, by 1937 they were reduced to three: Oberbayern, Brandenburg, and Thuringen. When Austria was annexed into the Reich the "Ostmark" Totenkofverband was organized.

Between the occupation of Austria, the Sudetenland, and Czechoslovakia and 1939 a further 12 regiments were raised. In addition, after Danzig was occupied, ethnic Germans were used to organize the "Heimwehr" Danzig SS Totenkopf verband.

By 1939 the SS-VT had grown to include five standarte, a medical battalion, an anti-tank demonstration company, a motorized signals platoon, and a tmot or semi-motorized pioneer detachment. On 17 August 1939 Hitler authorized them to be used as police reinforcements within the framework of the Wehrmacht, that is, they were to be used to garrison the rear areas of the war zone that had been conquered by the army. With the outbreak of war eminent, on 31 August 1939 the SS-Totenkopf Division stood ready, mobilized for war on the Polish border.

When the Polish campaign was completed, the SS-Verfügungstruppen were withdrawn to Germany and underwent a major reorganization. The three SS-Verfügungstruppen Regiments were reorganized into the SS-Verfügungsdivision, and the Leibstandarte was expanded into a fully motorized infantry regiment. The members of the 1st, 2nd, and 3rd Totenkopf Regiments were merged with a cadre drawn from the SS-Verfügungstruppen and some police reservists to form the SS Division, "Totenkopf."

Yet another division was formed by drafts from the "Ordnungspolizei" (national, rural, and local police). They were joined by elements from the Totenkopf Regiments and organized into the Polizei Infantry Division.

By the time France was invaded, the SS had been reorganized into three divisions and a number of smaller formations:

SS Leibstandarte "Adolf Hitler"
SS Verfügungsdivision
SS Totenkopfdivision
SS Polizeidivision
Independent Totenkopf Regiments
SS Junkerschule (officers' School) "Braunschweig"
SS Junkerschule (officers' School) "Bad Tölz"
SS Artzliche Akadamie (Medical School) "Graz"
SS Verdaltungsführerschule (Administration School)

It was in early 1940 that the term Waffen-SS came into use, but not until July 1940 was it a term known to the general German public.

In addition to the Totenkopf regiments already in the field, a further eight were recruited and dispatched to police the various non-German cities in occupied Europe. To provide a continuous supply of replacements for the field units, Ersatzeinheiten (Replacement Units) were organized.

In April 1940 the SS Regiment "Nordland" was formed from Danish and Norwegian sympathizers. In June 1940 a similar unit, SS Regiment "Westland" was formed from the Belgians and Dutch. On 20 November 1940 these two regiments and the 5th SS Artillery Regiment were organized to form the "Germania" Division. At the same time the Verfügungs Division was renamed the "Deutschland Division," which was soon changed to "Reich" and shortly later to "Das Reich."

The name changing didn't stop there and "Germania" was renamed the "Wiking" Division. The 6th and 7th Totenkopf Regiments were joined with a number of other SS support troops and designated the SS Kampfgruppe "Nord." This would eventually become the SS Gebirgs-Division "Nord" (SS Mountain Division "North").

The remaining Totenkopf Regiments were organized into two brigades. The 8th and 10th Totenkopf Regiments became the 1st SS (mot) Brigade and the 4th and 14th became the 2nd SS (mot) Brigade.

When June 1941 and the invasion of Russia arrived, the Waffen-SS had expanded to:

SS Leibstandarte	SS Division Wiking
"Adolf Hitler" Brigade	SS Gebirgs-Division Nord
SS Division Das Reich	1st SS (mot) Brigade
SS Division Totenkopf	2nd SS (mot) Brigade
SS Polizei Division	SS Cavalry Brigade

As the war in Russia progressed the need for troops continued to expand and the SS began to open up its ranks. First they opened up to the Volk Deutsch (ethnic Germans) of the western and eastern Europe and finally all pretense of Aryan blood would be dropped as a requirement for entry into the SS.

The first of such units was the Finnish Volunteer Battalion, which was a purely mercenary formation. They were followed by the "Nordwest" Volunteer Regiment of Dutch-Belgian nationals. Various legions were organized and led by German officers and NCOs. Later foreign nationals rose to positions of authority in these formations.

The western volunteers developed a very good fighting reputation, as good as the German SS units. However, they were too few for the needs of the SS. The solution to the manpower needs was the Volkdeutsche that lived all over eastern Europe. In 1939 it was estimated that in Rumania, Hungary, and Yugoslavia there were 1,500,000 Volkdeutsche. In the spring of 1940 the recruiting began among the Rumanian Volkdeutsche. After the conquest of Yugoslavia in 1941 it was proposed that a division of Yugoslavian Volkdeutsche be raised and that formation became the SS-Gebirgs Division "Prinz Eugen." Manpower, however, continued to be an ever-escalating problem and as the reserves of Volkdeutsche dwindled attention turned to eastern non-Germans. When the July 1944 bomb plot against Hitler failed, Himmler was given tremendous powers and he took advantage of them to recruit non-German easterners, specifically Balts, Armenians, Caucasians, Turkestani, Cossack, and Georgian volunteers from the various foreign legions of the German army into the Waffen-SS. The Balts lived up to the modest expectations held for them and were assigned to defending their homelands. Others, like the Bosnians of the 13th "Hanschar" Division fought well for a while. And yet others were considered little more than cannon fodder. These non-German easterners were denied the status of full SS membership. They were denied various privileges and their uniforms were such that they could not be identified as "real" Waffen-SS personnel.

The loyalty of these non-German easterners was always suspect and their behavior was frequently horrific. That behavior was such that there were frequent demands for them to be withdrawn from the line by senior SS commanders in the fall of 1944. The result was that several units were disbanded and some of their leaders were court-martialed and executed.

Non-German nationals eventually would form 57 percent of the Waffen-SS. Around 400,000 Reich Germans would serve in the SS uniform by war's end. So did about 137,000 western Europeans, 200,000 eastern Europeans, and 185,000 Volkdeutsche. The breakdown by nationality of the non-Germans was as follows:

Hungarian Volkdeutsche	80,000	Spaniards/Swiss/Swedes Luxemburgers/British	4,000
Dutch	50,000	Albanians	3,000
Cossacks	50,000	Bulgarians	1,000
Czech Volkdeutsche	45,000	Finns	1,000
Latvians	35,000	Scandaniavan Volkdeutsche	775
Ukrainians	30,000	Russian Volkdeutsche	100
Croatian Volkdeutsche	25,000	France Volkdeutsche	84
Flemings	23,000	British Volkdeutsche	10
Italians	20,000	American Volkdeutsche	5
Estonians	20,000	Brazilian Volkdeutsche	4
Croatians	20,000	Chinese Volkdeutsche	3
Western European Volkdeutsche	16,000	South-West Africa Volkdeutsche	3
Walloons	15,000	South-East Africa Volkdeutsche	2
Serbians	15,000	South American Volkdeutsche	2
Beylorussians	12,000	Spanish Volkdeutsche	2
Danes	11,000	Palestinian Volkdeutsche	2
French	8,000	Japanese Volkdeutsche	2
Turkestanis	8,000	Sumatran Volkdeutsche	2
Rumanian Volkdeutsche	8,000	Mexican Volkdeutsche	1
Norwegians	6,000	Australian Volkdeutsche	1
Rumanians	5,000	Indian Volkdeutsche	1
Polish Volkdeutsche	5,000	New Guinean Volkdeutsche	1
Serbian Volkdeutsche	5,000		

This listing may not be complete in that it does not indicate the Bosnians, unless they are included in the Croatian figure.

By the end of 1942 the Waffen-SS had risen to a strength of 190,000 officers and men. Its growth would continue as division after division was formed. However, by 1945 some of these divisions were divisions in name only.

In 1943 the Wehrmacht French Volunteer Sturmbrigade Regiment was transferred to the Waffen-SS and became the SS "Franzosisches' Freiwilligen Standarte." This would become the SS Freiwilligen Sturmbrigade "Charlemagne," then the SS Waffen-Grenadier-Brigade Charlemagne (1st French) and finally the 33rd Waffen SS Grenadier Division "Charlemagne" (1st French).

A similar transfer occurred when the Belgian "Rexist" Walloon Legion was formed into the SS Freiwilligen Sturmbrigade "Wallonie." Latvians, Letts, and Estonians flowed into the SS as they joined the Germans in liberating their homelands. By the end of 1943 the SS contained the following formations:

General Kommando I SS Panzer Korps Leibstandarte
General Kommando II SS Panzer Korps
General Kommando III (Germanisches) SS Panzer Korps
General Kommando IV SS Panzer Korps
General Kommando V SS Gebirgs Korps General Kommando VI (Lettisches) SS Freiwilligen Armee Korps

General Kommando VII SS Panzer Korps
1. SS Panzer Division Leibstandarte "Adolf Hitler"
2. SS Panzer Division Das Reich
3. SS Panzer Division Totenkopf
4. SS Panzergrenadier Division Polizei
5. SS Panzer Division Wiking
6. SS Gebirgs-Division Nord
7. SS Freiwilligen Gebirgs Division "Prinz Eugen"
8. SS Kavallerie Division
9. SS Panzer Division "Hohenstaufen"
10. SS Panzer Division "Frundsburg"
11. SS Freiwilligen Panzergrenadier Division "Nordland"
12. SS Panzer Division "Hitler Jugend"
13. SS Freiwilligen b.h. Gebirgs Division (Kroatisches)
14. Galizisches SS Freiwilligen Infantry Division (n.A.)
15. Lettisches SS Freiwilligen Infantry Division (n.A.)
16. SS Panzergrenadier Division "Reichsführer SS"
17. SS Panzergrenadier Division "Götz von Berlichingen"
I SS Freiwilligen Grenadier brigade (mot)
II Lettisches SS Freiwilligen Grenadier Brigade
III Estniches SS Freiwilligen Grenadier Brigade
IV SS Freiwilligen Panzergrenadier Brigade "Nederland"
V SS Sturmbrigade "Wallonien"
VI SS Sturmbrigade "Langemarck"
SS Freiwilligen Ski Regiment "Norge"
Franzosisches SS Freiwilligen Regiment
SS Kommando Obersalzburg
1 SS Flak Abteilung Kommando Stab RFSS

11 SS Flak Abteilung Kommando Stab RFSS
Begleitbataillon (Escort Battalion) RFSS
Landsturm Nederland

Documents indicate that, around this time, the Waffen-SS contained 246,717 men, of whom 156,438 were combat troops, 64,311 were maintenance, supply and special duty troops, and 25,968 were staff and administrative troops. A letter from the SS Führungshauptamt dated 10/11/44 shows the SS as having the following units:

General Kommando I SS Panzer Korps Leibstandarte
General Kommando II SS Panzer Korps
General Kommando III (Germanisches) SS Panzer Korps
General Kommando IV SS Panzer Korps
General Kommando V SS Gebirgs Korps
General Kommando VI SS Armee Korps der SS (Lettisches)
General Kommando VII SS Panzer Korps
General Kommando IX Waffen Gebirgs Korps der SS (Kroatisches)
General Kommando XI SS Army Korps
General Kommando XII SS Army Korps
General Kommando XIII SS Army Korps
General Kommando XIV Kossack Kavallerie Korps
 1. SS Panzer Division Leibstandarte "Adolf Hitler"
 2. SS Panzer Division Das Reich
 3. SS Panzer Division Totenkopf
 4. SS Panzergrenadier Division Polizei 5. SS Panzer Division Wiking
 6. SS Gebirgs-Division Nord
 7. SS Freiwilligen Gebirgs Division "Prinz Eugen"
 8. SS Kavallerie Division
 9. SS Panzer Division "Hohenstaufen"
10. SS Panzer Division "Frundsburg"
11. SS Freiwilligen Panzergrenadier Division "Nordland"
12. SS Panzer Division "Hitler Jugend"
13. SS Freiwilligen b.h. Gebirgs Division (Kroatisches)
14. Galizisches SS Freiwilligen Infantry Division (n.A.)
15. Lettisches SS Freiwilligen Infantry Division (n.A.)
16. SS Panzergrenadier Division "Reichsführer SS"
17. SS Panzergrenadier Division "Götz von Berlichingen"
18. SS Freiwilliger Panzergrenadier Division "Horst Wessel"
19. SS Grenadier Division der SS (lettische Nr. 2)
20. SS Grenadier Division der SS (estnische Nr. 1)
21. Waffen Gebirg Division der SS "Skanderbeg" (albanische Nr. 1)
22. SS Freiwilliger Kavallerie Division
23. Waffen Gebirgs Division der SS "Kama" (kroatische Nr. 2)
24. Waffen Gebirgs (Karstjäger) Division der SS
25. Waffen Grenadier Division der SS (ungarische Nr. 1) "Hunjadi"
26.

27. SS Freiwilliger Grenadier Division "Langemarck" (flämische Nr. 1)
28. SS Freiwilliger Grenadier Division "Wallonien"
29.
30. Waffen Grenadier Division der SS (russische Nr. 2)
31. SS Freiwilliger Grenadier Division
 1. Kossack Kavallerie Division
 2. Kossack Kavallerie Division
SS Freiwilliger Panzergrenadier Brigade "Nederland"
Franzosische Brigade der SS
Waffen Gebirg Brigade der SS (tartarische Nr. 1)
Waffen Gebirg Brigade der SS (italienische Nr. 1)
Sturmbrigade "Dirlewanger":
Freiwilliger Grenadier Brigade "Landstorm Nederland"
Waffen Grenadier Brigade der SS "Charlemagne" (französische Nr. 1)
Kommando Stab RF SS
SS Kommando Obersalsberg
 I. SS Flak Abtielung/Kommandostab RF-SS
 II. SS Flak Abtielung/Kommandostab RF-SS
Begleit Betaillon RF SS
SS Feldgendarmerie Kompagnie/Kommadnostab RF SS
 1. SS Panzergrenadier Führer Begleit Kompagnie "LSSAH"
 2. SS Panzergrenadier Führer Begleit Kompagnie (armored) "LSSAH"
Waffen Grenadier Regient der SS (rumänisches)
Osttürkischer Waffen Berband der SS
Waffen Grenadier Regiment der SS (bulgarisches)

501st Heavy SS Panzer Battalion
502nd Heavy SS Panzer Battalion
503rd Heavy SS Panzer Battalion
505th SS Reconnaissance Battalion
509th SS Reconnaissance Battalion
509th SS Panzerjäger Battalion
501st SS Heavy Artillery Battalion
501st SS Observation Battery
502nd SS Heavy Artillery Battalion
502nd SS Observation Battery
503rd SS Heavy Artillery Battalion
503rd SS Observation Battery
504th SS Heavy Artillery Battalion
504th SS Observation Battery
505th SS Heavy Artillery Battalion
505th SS Observation Battery
506th SS Observation Battery
507th SS Observation Battery
508th SS Observation Battery
509th SS Mountain Artillery Regiment
500th SS Nebelwerfer Battery
502nd SS Nebelwerfer Battalion
503rd SS Nebelwerfer Battalion
504th SS Nebelwerfer Battalion

505th SS Nebelwerfer Battalion
521st SS Multipul Nebelwerfer Battalion
522nd SS Multipul Nebelwerfer Battalion
505th SS Flak Battatlion
506th SS Flak Battatlion
509th SS Flak Battatlion
SS Jagdverbände
500th SS Jäger Batalion
600th SS Fallschirmjäger Battalion (former 500th Bn)
501st SS Signals Battalion
500th SS Observation Battalion
509th SS Mountain Pioneer Battalion
& various supply and medical units

As the war was winding down in 1944 and 1945 the last of the small, independent regiments and battalions were absorbed into the larger brigades and divisions. Only the shattered remains of these large formations would remain when the end finally came.

The Waffen-SS was noted for its fanatic resistance in battle and its hard-hitting ferocity. It also developed a reputation for atrocities, which cannot be denied. It had some excellent commanders and some miserable ones, whose only claim to command was their political connections.

The Waffen-SS was an army within an army. It was outside the Wehrmacht, yet utilized its equipment and tables of organization. Indeed, it generally had first choice of all the equipment and if a new weapons system was available it would generally be found in the SS first. On the other hand, life in the Waffen-SS was not soft. They were expected to perform and found themselves serving as fire brigades, regularly charging into the thick of battle to try to stem the flow of enemy forces. They were also picked as the shock troops to lead the attack. They were to pay a heavy price for their being designated the elite of Nazi Germany in terms of blood and equipment.

What follows is a quick history of each division and brigade, identifying as best as can be the major organizational changes. That is followed by a few selected organizational tables that provide the detailed internal structure and weapons allocations of the SS formations.

Leibstandarte SS Adolf Hitler

Established on 9/3/33, on 8/15/38 it had four battalions (each of one machine-gun and three rifle companies), an infantry gun (13th) company, an anti-tank (14th) company and a motorcycle (15th) company. In addition it had an armored car platoon, a pioneer platoon, a motorcycle messenger platoon, a regimental signals platoon, a music platoon, and a light infantry column. An ersatz battalion was organized on 8/26/39. On 1/21/40 the 16th (Infantry Gun) Company was organized and on 3/2/40 an unnumbered pioneer company was established in the LSSAH. On 4/17/40 the 4th Battalion, SS Artillery Regiment was assigned to the LSSAH. It contained a survey troop, a signals platoon, the 10th, 11th, and 12th Batteries (105mm leFH), and a light artillery column. This resulted in the LSSAH being redesignated the Reinforced Leibstandarte SS Adolf Hitler. On 4/29/40 the Panzersturmbatterie (Sturmgeschütz Battery) was added. It was formally incorporated on 7/16/40. For the war with France it had:

3 Infantry Battalions (4 companies per battalion)
13th (Light Infantry Gun) Company
14th (Anti-tank) Company
15th (Motorcycle) Company
16th (Heavy Infantry Gun) Company
Pioneer Company
Sturmgeschütz Company (forming)

Motorcycle Reconnaissance Platoon
Armored Car Platoon
Artillery Battalion (3 105mm leFH batteries & light artillery column)
Signals Platoon
Supply Column Battalion

On 10 May 1940 the SS Leibstandarte Adolf Hitler Division was organized and equipped as follows:

Brigade
1 Headquarters
1 Divisional/Brigade Band
3 Battalions, each with
1st, 2nd, & 3rd (mot) Infantry Companies, each with 18 LMGs, 2 HMGs & 3 50mm mortars
1 (mot) Support Company, with
1 (mot) Panzerjäger Platoon (3 50mm PAK 38 & 2 LMGs)
1 (mot) Panzerjäger Platoon (3 37mm PAK 36 & 1 LMG)
1 (mot) Engineer Platoon (2 HMGs & 3 LMGs)
1 (mot) Mortar Platoon (6 80mm mortars)
4th Battalion
2 Motorcycle Companies (3 50mm mortars, 4 HMGs & 18 LMGs)
1 Armored Car Company (8 20mm & 16 LMGs)

1 (mot) Support Company, with
  1 (mot) Panzerjäger Platoon (3 37mm PAK 36 & 2 LMGs)
  1 (mot) Engineer Platoon (3 LMGs)
  1 (mot) Mortar Platoon (6 80mm mortars)

5th Battalion
1 Self Propelled Flak Battery (16 37mm guns)
1 Self Propelled Battery (6 75mm guns, probably StuGs)
1 Self Propelled Panzerjäger Company (9 47mm guns & 3 LMGs)
  1 (mot) Infantry Support Gun Company (4 150mm sIG)
  1 (mot) Infantry Support Gun Company (8 75mm leIG)

LSSAH Artillery Regiment, with
1 (mot) Staff Battery, with
  1 Signals Platoon
  1 Weather Detachment
1 (mot) Battalion
  1 (mot) Signals Platoon
  1 (mot) Calibration Section
  3 (motZ) Batteries (4 105mm leFh 18 howitzers & 2 LMGs ea)
  1 Light (mot) Supply Column
1 (mot) Battalion
  1 (mot) Signals Platoon
  1 (mot) Calibration Section
  2 (motZ) Batteries (4 150mm sFH 18 howitzers & 2 LMGs ea)
  1 (mot) Flak Battery (4 88mm & 2 20mm guns)
  1 Light (mot) Supply Column

LSSAH Signals Group
1 (mot) Radio Company
1 (mot) Telephone Company

LSSAH Pioneer Battalion
3 (mot) Pioneer Companies (9 LMGs ea)
1 (mot) Bridging Train
1 Light (mot) Engineering Supply Column

LSSAH Supply Train
4 Light (mot) Supply Columns
1 Heavy (mot) Fuel Supply Column

LSSAH Commissary Troops
1 (mot) Bakery Platoon (later Company)
1 (mot) Butcher Platoon (later Company)
1 (mot) Medical Company
1 (mot) Field Post Office

On 8/19/40 the LSSAH was reinforced and built up to the strength of a brigade in Metz. A brigade staff was established with a divisional mapping detachment and a field gendarmerie troop. The three infantry battalions were reorganized and expanded such that each had three rifle companies, one machine-gun company and one heavy company with an armored car platoon.

On 8/19/40 the 4th (Wach) Battalion was organized with the 16th through 20th Companies. It was organized the same as the other three battalions. The 5th (Heavy) Battalion was organized in Metz at the same time. It was organized with the 13th (leIG) and 16th (sIG) Companies being redesignated as its 1st and 2nd Companies, a new 3rd Company or self-propelled 47mm PAK guns drawn from the T-Division, and a 4th Company organized from the sturmgeschütz company. In September the 5th Battalion incorporated the former 14th (Panzerjäger) Company and equipped it with 50mm PAK 38 guns.

In October 1940 a 37mm Flak company was added to the brigade. On 8/19/40 the artillery battalion was expanded into a two battalion regiment. The 1st (105mm leFH) Battery was drawn from the Verfügungstruppe, the 2nd and 3rd Batteries were the former 12th and 10th Batteries. The 2nd Battalion was organized with the 4th and 5th (sFH) Batteries and the 6th (88mm) Flak Battery, which came from the Artillery-Ersatz-Regiment.

On 8/19/40 the armored car and motorcycle reconnaissance units were expanded into a full battalion with two motorcycle companies and an armored car company. In addition, the pioneer company was expanded into a full battalion with three companies, two bridging half platoons and a pioneer supply column. The signals platoon became a two company battalion and the supply and fuel transportation units were expanded. It is not known when they were added, but on 4/13/41 there is reference to two platoons of 20mm flak guns being assigned to the brigade. Similarly, by 5/9/41 the brigade was being called the SS Division LSSAH.

German records from 1 January 1941 indicate that the division had undergone some further modifications. It was, at that time, organized and equipped as follows:

Division Staff
1 (mot) Signals Platoon
1 Divisional Band
1st, 2nd & 3rd (mot) Infantry Battalions, each with
  3 (mot) Infantry Companies (18 LMGs, 2 HMGS & 3 50mm mortars ea)
  1 (mot) Machine Gun Company (12 HMGs)
  1 (mot) Support Company
    1 Mortar Platoon (6 80mm mortars)
    1 Panzerjäger Platoon (4 50mm PAK 38 & 1 LMG)
    1 Pioneer Platoon (3 LMGs & 2 HMGs)
5th Battalion
1 Self Propelled Panzerjäger Company (12 50mm PAK 38 & 6 LMGs)

1 Self Propelled Panzerjäger Company (9 47mm guns & 3 LMGs)
1 (mot) Infantry Gun Company (8 75mm leIG)
1 (mot) Infantry Gun Company (4 150mm sIG)
1 Sturmgeschütz Battery(6 75mm StuGs)
1 Self Propelled Infantry Flak Battery (16 37mm flak guns)

Reconnaissance Battalion
2 Motorcycle Companies (3 80mm mortars, 4 HMGs & 18 LMGs)
1 Armored Car Company (8 20mm guns & 16 LMGs)
1 (mot) Heavy Company
1 Mortar Platoon (6 80mm mortars)
1 Panzerjäger Platoon (4 37mm PAK 36 & 1 LMG)
1 Pioneer Platoon (3 LMGs)

(mot) Artillery Regiment
Regimental Staff
1 (mot) Weather Detachment
1 (mot) Signals Platoon
1 (mot) Battalion
1 (mot) Calibration Detachment
1 (mot) Signals Platoon
3 Batteries (4 105mm leFH 18 & 2 LMGs ea)
1 (mot) Light Supply Column
1 (mot) Battalion
1 (mot) Calibration Detachment
1 (mot) Signals Platoon
2 Batteries (4 100mm K 18 & 2 LMGs ea)
1 Battery (4 88mm flak guns &)
1 Battery (2 20m flak guns)
1 (mot) (36 ton) Light Supply Column

(mot) Pioneer Battalion
3 (mot) Pioneer Companies (9 LMGs ea)
1 (mot) Brüko K Bridging Train
1 (mot) Light Pioneer Supply Column

(mot) Signals Battalion
1 (mot) Radio Company
1 (mot) Telephone Company

Supply Command
4 (mot) (30 ton) Light Supply Columns
1 (mot) Heavy Fuel Column
1 (mot) Supply Platoon
1 (mot) Maintenance Company

Other
1 (mot) Divisional Administration
1 (mot) Bakery Platoon
1 (mot) Butcher Platoon
1 (mot) Medical Company
596th (mot) Field Post Office

Leibstandarte participated in the invasion of Greece and when the invasion began on 5 April 1941, the division was organized and equipped as follows:

Leibstandarte SS Adolf Hitler
Divisional Staff
Divisional Staff (2 HMGs)
1 (mot) Signals Platoon
1 Divisional Band
1 (mot) Infantry Regiment
1st–4th (mot) Battalions, each with
3 Infantry Companies, each with (18 LMGs, 2 HMGs, 3 50mm mortars)
1 (mot) Heavy Machine Gun Company (12 HMGs)
1 Support Company with
1 Engineer Platoon (3 LMGs & 2 HMGs)
1 Panzerjäger Section (4 50mm PAK 38 & 1 LMG)
1 Mortar Platoon (6 80mm mortars)
5th Battalion
1 (mot) Infantry Gun Company (8 75mm leIG)
1 (mot) Infantry Gun Company (4 150mm sIG)
1 Self Propelled Panzerjäger Company (9 47mm & 3 LMGs)
1 Self Propelled Flak Company (16 37mm flak guns)
1 Sturmgeschütz Battery (6 SdKfz 142 StuGs)

Leibstandarte SS Adolf Hitler Reconnaissance Battalion
2 Motorcycle Companies, each with (18 LMGs, 4 HMGs, 2 80mm mortars)
1 Armored Car Company (8 20mm & 16 LMGs)
1 (mot) Support Company, with
1 Engineer Platoon (3 LMGs)
1 Panzerjäger Section (4 50mm PAK 38 & 1 LMG)
1 Mortar Platoon (6 80mm mortars)

Leibstandarte SS Adolf Hitler Artillery Regiment
Regimental Staff
1 (mot) Signals Platoon
1 (mot) Weather Platoon
1st (mot) Artillery Battalion
1 (mot) Signals Platoon
1 (mot) Calibration Platoon
3 (motZ) Batteries (4 105mm leFH & 2 LMGs ea)
1 (mot) Light Supply Column
2nd (mot) Artillery Battalion
1 (mot) Signals Platoon
1 (mot) Calibration Platoon
2 (motZ) Batteries (4 150mm sFH & 2 LMGs ea)
1 (motZ) Heavy Flak Battery (4 88mm guns & 2 20mm guns ea)
1 (mot) Light Supply Column

Leibstandarte SS Adolf Hitler Signals Battalion
1 (mot) Radio Company
1 (mot) Telephone Company

Leibstandarte SS Adolf Hitler Pioneer Battalion
3 (mot) Pioneer Companies (9 LMGs)
1 (mot) "K" Bridging Train
1 (mot) Light Supply Column
Commissary
1 Division Administration
1 (mot) Butcher Company
1 (mot) Bakery Company
Supply Train
4 (mot) (30 ton) Light Supply Columns
12 (mot) Heavy Fuel Supply Column
1 (mot) Maintenance Company
1 (mot) Light Supply Company
Medical
1 (mot) Medical Company
Other
596th (mot) Field Post

However, records of the 6th Army from 2 May 1941, show the support company of the four infantry battalions contained:

1 (mot) Mortar Platoon (6 80mm mortars)
1 (mot) Panzerjäger Platoon (4 37mm PAK 36 & 1 LMG)
1 (mot) Panzerjäger Platoon (3 50mm PAK 38 & 2 LMGs)
1 (mot) Pioneer Platoon (3 LMGs & 2 HMGs)

Those same records indicate that the panzerjäger battalion still was equipped with 37mm guns, not the 50mm indicated above for April. The 12 heavy fuel columns were reduced to one by 2 May. Apparently the number had been increased for the purposes of the campaign. Otherwise, the April organization is the same as that shown for 2 May 1941. Between 16 May 1941 and 15 October 1942 the organization of the Leibstandarte SS Adolf Hitler Division seems to have settled down and consisted of:

Divisional Staff
Divisional Staff (2 HMGs)
1 (mot) Mapping Platoon
2 (mot) Infantry Regiments, each with
1 (mot) Regimental Staff Company, with
1 Engineering Platoon
1 Signals Platoon
1 Motorcycle Platoon
3 (mot) Battalions, each with
1 (mot) Staff Platoon
3 Infantry Companies, each with (18 LMGs, 4 HMGs, 2 80mm mortars & 2 flamethrowers)
1 Support Company with

1 Engineer Platoon (4 LMGs)
1 Panzerjäger Section (3 50mm PAK 38)
1 Infantry Support Gun Platoon (2 75mm leIG guns)
1 (mot) Infantry Gun Company (2 150mm sIG & 6 75mm leIG guns)
1 Self Propelled Flak Company (2 Quad 20mm Flak guns & 8 20mm Flak guns)
1 Self Propelled Panzerjäger Company (6 75mm PAK 40 & 6 LMGs)
Leibstandarte SS Adolf Hitler Sturmgeschütz Battalion
1 (mot) Battalion Staff Company
3 Sturmgeschütz Batteries (7 StuGs ea)
Leibstandarte SS Adolf Hitler Armored Troop, with
1 Armored Staff Company
1 Medium Armored Company
2 Light Armored Companies
1 Armored Maintenance Platoon
Leibstandarte SS Adolf Hitler Motorcycle Battalion
1 (mot) Staff Section
2 Motorcycle Companies, each with (18 LMGs, 4 HMGs, 2 80mm mortars & 3 anti-tank rifles)
1 Half Track Company, with (3 37mm PAK 36, 56 LMGs, 4 HMGs, & 6 80mm mortars)
1 Light Armored Car Platoon (3 LMGs)
1 (mot) Support Company, with
1 Engineer Platoon (4 LMGs & 2 flamethrowers)
1 AT Section (3 75mm AT guns, 3 anti-tank rifles & 2 LMGs)
1 Infantry Support Gun Section (2 75mm leIG guns)
1 Flak Section (4 20mm Flak guns)
Leibstandarte SS Adolf Hitler Artillery Regiment
Regimental Staff
1 (mot) Staff Battery
1 (mot) Observation Battery
1 Panzerjäger Section (1 50mm PAK 38 & 2 LMGs)
1 (motZ) Nebelwerfer Battery (6 launchers)
1st–2nd (mot) Artillery Battalions, each with
1 (mot) Battalion Staff Battery
2 (motZ) Batteries (4 105mm leFH & 2 LMGs ea)
1 (motZ) Battery (4 150mm sFH & 2 LMGs)
3rd (mot) Artillery Battalion
1 (mot) Battalion Staff Battery
2 (motZ) Batteries (4 150mm sFH & 2 LMGs ea)
1 (motZ) Battery (4 100mm K18 guns & 2 LMGs)
4th (mot) Flak Battalion
1 (mot) Battalion Staff Battery
2 Self Propelled Flak Batteries (9 20mm Flak guns)
3 (motZ) Flak Batteries (4 88mm guns & 3 20mm guns ea)

Leibstandarte SS Adolf Hitler Panzerjäger Battalion
- 2 Self Propelled Panzerjäger Companies (Marder) (9 75mm PAK 40 & 6 LMGs)
- 1 (mot) Panzerjäger Company (9 50mm PAK 38 & 6 LMGs)

Leibstandarte SS Adolf Hitler Signals Battalion
- 1 (mot) Radio Company
- 1 (mot) Telephone Company
- 1 (mot) Light Signals Supply Column

Leibstandarte SS Adolf Hitler Pioneer Battalion
- 3 (mot) Pioneer Companies (9 LMGs & 2 flame-throwers ea)
- 1 (mot) Light "K" Bridging Train
- 1 (mot) Light Supply Column

Commissary
- 1 (mot) Division Administration (2 LMGs)
- 1 (mot) Butcher Company (2 LMGs)
- 1 (mot) Bakery Company (2 LMGs)

Supply Train
- 12 (mot) Light Supply Columns
- 3 (mot) Heavy Supply Columns
- 3 (mot) Light Fuel Supply Columns
- 3 (mot) Maintenance Companies
- 1 (mot) Light Supply Company

Medical
- 2 (mot) Medical Companies (2 LMGs ea)
- 1 (mot) Field Hospital (2 LMGs)
- 3 Ambulance Companies (2 LMGs ea)

Other
- 1 (mot) Military Police Company
- 1 (mot) Field Post
- 1 (mot) SS "KB" Platoon

On 6/5/41 the motorized brigade began expanding into a full division. The former 5th (heavy) Battalion was now designated the Heavy Battalion. The 37mm flak battery was detached to the newly forming flak battalion. The flak battalion was organized with two 37mm flak batteries and one 20mm flak battery. The sturmgeschütz company and the 47mm self-propelled anti-tank companies were detached to the Schönberger Battalion. The Heavy Battalion now contained a 75mm leIG company with eight guns, a 150mm sIG company with four guns, and a 50mm PAK 38 company with twelve guns. The artillery received a 7th Battery organized with 88mm guns. On 6/15/41 a survey battery was organized. On 6/30/41 the Leibstandarte had:

- 1/,2/,3/,4/Leibstandarte SS Adolf Hitler Infantry Regiment (5 companies each)
- 1/,2/Leibstandarte SS Adolf Hitler Artillery Regiment (3 batteries in 1st Bn, 4 in 2nd Bn, plus 1 battery, plus 1 survey company, 1 flash ranging platoon and a sound ranging platoon)

- Leibstandarte SS Adolf Hitler Heavy Battalion (3 companies)
- Leibstandarte SS Adolf Hitler (Schönberger) Panzerjäger Battalion (1 sturmgeschütz battery & 1 47mm self-propelled PAK battery)
- Leibstandarte SS Adolf Hitler Reconnaissance Battalion (4 companies)
- Leibstandarte SS Adolf Hitler Flak Battalion with 2 37mm flak companies (9 guns ea) & 1 20mm flak (12 guns)
- Leibstandarte SS Adolf Hitler Pioneer Battalion (3 companies)
- Leibstandarte SS Adolf Hitler Signals Battalion (1 radio & 2 phone companies) Leibstandarte SS Adolf Hitler Supply/Admin Troops

By 7/1/41 the infantry battalions were reorganized and strengthened. Each battalion now had five companies. The first three were rifle companies, the fourth was a machine gun company, and the fifth company was a heavy weapons company containing an 80mm mortar platoon, an anti-tank platoon and a pioneer platoon. The reconnaissance battalion was expanded again and a heavy company was added to the armored car and two motorcycle companies.

On 8/11/41 the 8th Battery (100mm guns) was organized and assigned to the 2nd Artillery Battalion. It joined the 2nd Battalion on 9/23/41 in the Crimea. About the same time the flak battalion was reequipped and all three companies had 37mm guns.

On 12/20/41 the 3rd (Armored Car) Company LSSAH was newly organized and re-equipped. In July it was added to the LSSAH Reconnaissance Battalion as the 4th (Armored Car) Company LSSAH. On 1/1/42 the heavy company of the reconnaissance battalion was reinforced by the addition of one heavy infantry gun platoon (t o 150mm sIG guns).

On 2/1/42 a three company panzer battalion was added to Leibstandarte. Its staff contained two Panzer Mk III command tanks and three Panzer Mk II tanks. Each company contained three Panzer Mk II tanks and ten Panzer Mk IV tanks. On 2/21/42 Hitler ordered the reorganizing of the LSSAH. A 5th Infantry Battalion was added, as was a heavy panzerjäger battalion, and a sturmgeschütz battalion formed from the Schönberger Battalion.

On 2/23/42 the sturmgeschütz battery of the Schönberger Battalion was reorganized as the Sturmgeschütz-abteilung LSSAH and contained:

Staff and Staff Battery
1st Sturmgeschütz Battery (7 StuGs)
2nd Sturmgeschütz Battery (7 StuGs) (from SS Wiking Division)
3rd Sturmgeschütz Battery (7 StuGs)

On 3/1/42 a division staff escort company was established. At the same time a staff for the artillery battalion was established and the battalion was expanded to include two 105mm leFH batteries, one 150mm sFH battery, and one nebelwerfer battery. On the same date a panzerjäger battalion was organized with three companies. It was equipped with captured 76.2mm guns mounted on Panzer Mk II chassis (SdKfz 132 Marders). It joined the division near Stalino in June 1942.

On 4/1/42 the 3rd (Light Half Track) Company was organized in the Reconnaissance Battalion. It had four platoons, 36 SdKfz 250, and a total of 58 light machine guns, 4 heavy machine guns, 4 80mm mortars, and 3 37mm PAK 36 guns mounted on the half tracks. On 4/25/42 a self-propelled 20mm flak platoon was organized in the Reconnaissance Battalion.

On 6/21/42 the heavy mortar platoons of the heavy companies were equipped with 75mm leIG guns. The heavy mortars were then assigned to the machine gun companies. On 7/5/42 the two infantry regiments were reorganized as follows:

1/1st Infantry Regiment (former 1/LSSAH)
2/1st Infantry Regiment (former 3/LSSAH)
3/1st Infantry Regiment (former 6/LSSAH)

1/2nd Infantry Regiment (former 5/LSSAH)
2/2nd Infantry Regiment (former 2/LSSAH)
3/2nd Infantry Regiment (former 4/LSSAH)

Each battalion had three schützen companies, a machine-gun company (12 heavy machine guns, & 6 80mm mortars), and a heavy company (3 50mm PAK 38 and 2 75mm leIG). Each regiment organized a 16th (self-propelled) Flak Company (12 20mm guns), a 17th (Infantry Gun) Company (6 150mm sIG), and an 18th (Panzerjäger) Company (9 self-propelled anti-tank guns).

On 7/5/42 the former heavy battalion/LSSAH was disbanded. Its staff was assigned to the newly forming panzerjäger battalion and the infantry gun companies and panzerjäger companies were divided up between the battalion heavy companies and the 17th and 18th Regimental Companies.

On 7/5/42 a new staff and two further 105mm leFH batteries were organized. By the end of July 1942 the artillery regiment underwent a major reorganization. It now had:

Staff
  Observation Battery (from the former Survey Battery)
  Flak Platoon
1st Battalion

Staff
1st Battery (4 105mm leFH)
2nd Battery (4 105mm leFH)
3rd Battery (4 105mm leFH)
2nd Battalion
Staff
4th Battery (4 105mm leFH) (newly formed)
5th Battery (4 105mm leFH) (newly formed)
6th Battery (4 105mm leFH) (newly formed)
3rd Battalion
Staff
7th Battery (4 150mm sFH)
8th Battery (4 150mm sFH) (newly formed)
9th Battery (4 150mm sFH) (newly formed)
4th Battalion
Staff
10th (Nebelwerfer) Battery
11th Battery (4 105mm leFH) (former 4th & 5th Batteries)
12th Battery (4 100mm K18) (former 8th Battery)

In mid-July the panzerjäger battalion was reequipped with Marder II (SdKfz 138) which had a 75mm PAK 40 mounted on the chassis of a 38(t) tank. Each panzerjäger company had nine Marders.

On 7/30/42 a 4th (Heavy) Company was established in the pioneer battalion. It contained an anti-tank platoon, a heavy machine-gun platoon, a mortar platoon, and Ladungswerfer Platoon. It appears to have been dissolved in April 1943.

In July 1942 the 3rd (20mm) Flak Battalion was disbanded and merged with the flak companies of both infantry regiments. A new flak battalion was organized with:

1st (Heavy) Battery (88mm guns)
2nd (Heavy) Battery (88mm guns)
3rd (Heavy) Battery (4 self-propelled 88mm guns)
4th (Medium) Battery (9 self-propelled 37mm guns)
5th (Medium) Battery (9 self-propelled 37mm guns)
6th (Light) Battery (six self-propelled quad 20mm flak guns and four self-propelled 20mm flak guns)

On 10/14/42 the panzer battalion was expanded into a full, two battalion regiment. The 1st–3rd Companies were in the 1st Battalion and the 5th–7th Companies were in the 2nd Battalion. In addition there was a 9th Panzer Pioneer Company. The formation of a 4th Company in the 1st Battalion was anticipated, hence the numbering. The 4th Company was raised on 10/15/42 and equipped with Panzer Mk VI (Tiger) Tanks. On 11/24/42 Leibstandarte became a panzer grenadier division.

1st SS Panzergrenadier Division Leibstandarte SS Adolf Hitler

Formed on 11/24/42, it had:

1/,2/,3/1st Panzergrenadier Regiment LSSAH (plus 16th Flak Company, 17th IG Company, & 18th Anti-Tank Company)

1/,2/,3/2nd Panzergrenadier Regiment LSSAH (plus 16th Flak Company, 17th IG Company, & 18th Anti-Tank Company)

1/Panzer Regiment LSSAH (1st–3rd Companies)

2/Panzer Regiment LSSAH (5th–7th & 9th Companies)

1/,2/,3/,4/Artillery Regiment LSSAH included a survey battery 1st & 2nd Bn 3 105mm leFH btrys ea, 3rd Bn 3 150mm sFH btrys, 4th Bn 1 100mm & 2 150mm sFH btrys)

Reconnaissance Battalion LSSAH (1 light schützen panzer company, 2 VW reconnaissance companies, 1 armored car company & 1 heavy company)

Panzerjäger Battalion LSSAH (3 companies)

Sturmgeschütz Battalion LSSAH (3 batteries)

Flak Battalion LSSAH (3 88mm & 2 37mm batteries)

Pioneer Battalion LSSAH (3 companies)

Armored Signal Battalion LSSAH (2 companies)

Divisional (Einheiten) Support Units

The 3/2nd Panzergrenadier Regiment was equipped with half tracks in its one heavy and three schützen companies. On 11/25/42 the 3rd Company of the pioneer battalion was transferred to the LSSAH Panzer Regiment as its 9th Company and a new 3rd Company was organized.

The 17th Company in each regiment had an unusual organization. It contained two platoons equipped with 75mm leIG and three platoons equipped with 150mm sIG. On 5/1/43 the 14th (Machine Gun) Company, 2nd Panzergrenadier Regiment was disbanded, which resulted in a renumbering of the remaining three regimental support companies: 15th (Flak), 16th (Infantry Gun), and 17th (Panzerjäger).

On 1/11/43 the 3/2nd Panzergrenadier Regiment was equipped with Flammenwerfer 41 (flamethrowers). In addition, the 1st Panzergrenadier Regiment was ordered to form a 19th (Reconnaissance) Company. For some reason it couldn't be formed, so an 18th (Reconnaissance) Company was organized in the 2nd Panzergrenadier Regiment.

In April 1943 the Staff of the 4th Artillery Battalion, and the 5th, 6th, and 7th Batteries were transferred to the 12th SS Panzer Division "Hitler Jugend" as a cadre for its artillery. The 2nd Artillery Battalion was then rebuilt from new drafts. The 2/Artillery Regiment LSSAH was reequipped with two batteries of armored,

self-propelled 105mm Sd Kfz 124 Wespe and its third battery with 150mm Sd Kfz 165 Hummels. The heavy companies of the reconnaissance battalion and the 3/2nd SS Panzergrenadier Regiment LSSAH were reequipped with the 150mm heavy infantry guns mounted on the Panzer 38(t) known as the Bison. The staff of the 4th Battalion was not reestablished. It was also in April 1943 that the 1/LSSAH Panzer Regiment LSSAH transferred all its tanks to the 2/Panzer Regiment LSSAH. The 1/Panzer Regiment LSSAH assumed that little equipment would be available for reestablishing it on the home front, so collected from the battlefields of Russia and took with it four damaged Panzer Mk IVs, two damaged Panzer Mk III, two drivable T-34s, forty cows and 12 Hiwi's to help maintain the vehicles. Earlier, in February the regiment's armor inventory and organization was as follows:

1/,2/1st SS Panzer Regiment
  1 Regimental Staff Signals Platoon
  1 Regimental Staff Light Panzer Platoon
  Each Battalion had:
    1 Panzer Staff Company
    3 Medium Panzer Companies
  4th Heavy Panzer Company

Mk II	12
Mk III (lg)	10
Mk IV (lg)	52
Mk VI	9
Cmd	9

On 5/1/43 the LSSAH Panzer Regiment was ordered to reorganize. Personnel from the 1/LSSAH were sent back to Germany. Of these men, 328 were then sent to form the 12th Panzer Regiment of the 12th SS Panzer Division "Hitler Jugend." The remainder were used to form a new 1/LSSAH Panzer Regiment that was to be equipped with Panzer Mk V (Panther) Tanks. This new 1/LSSAH Panzer Regiment was then organized with a staff company with eight Panzer Mk V tanks, and four companies with 22 Panzer Mk V tanks each. It was not fully equipped until mid-July and did not participate in Operation Citadel. The remaining 2/LSSAH Panzer Regiment was raised to four companies, each of which had 22 Mk IV tanks. The Tiger Company of the division was authorized to have 15 Tiger Tanks, including one command tank.

On 5/15/43 the 1st and 2nd Panzergrenadier Regiment finally formed the 19th (Reconnaissance) Company and the 20th (Pioneer) Company using the pioneer platoons of the heavy companies. On 5/16/43 the heavy mortar platoons were detached from the machine-gun companies and reattached to the battalions' heavy companies.

Shortly before the battle of Kursk, on 7/1/43, the division's panzer forces were organized and equipped as follows:

2/1st SS Panzer Regiment
  1 Regimental Staff Signals Platoon
  1 Regimental Staff Light Panzer Platoon
  Each Battalion had:
    1 Panzer Staff Company
    4 Medium Panzer Companies
    13th Heavy Panzer Company

Mk II	4
Mk III (kz)	3
Mk III (lg)	10
Mk IV (lg)	67
Mk VI	13
Cmd	9

Records show that on 7/4/43 it also had 18 (motZ) PAK 75mm, 21 75mm self-propelled anti-tank guns, and 34 sturmgeschütz. Documents indicate that the Tiger tanks were assigned to the 13th Company of the LSSAH Panzer Regiment.

After Kursk the division was withdrawn from the front and sent into Austria where it was rebuilt and refitted. The 1/Panzer Regiment LSSAH rejoined the division and was now equipped with Panzer MkV (Panthers) Tanks. On 9/7/43 the division had 23 Panzer Mk VI and four under repair, 65 Panzer Mk V and six more under repair, 51 Panzer Mk IV and three under repair, and 8 command tanks with two more under repair.

In August 1943 the former Observation Battery was reorganized as a Nebelwerfer Battery and added to the artillery regiment as the 11th (Werfer) Battery.

On 10/7/43 an armored flak platoon was organized in the 3/2nd Panzergrenadier Regiment.

1st SS Panzer Division Leibstandarte SS Adolf Hitler

On 10/22/43 the 1st SS Panzergrenadier Division Leibstandarte SS Adolf Hitler was renamed as the 1st SS Panzer Division Leibstandarte SS Adolf Hitler. Its assigned units were:

1/,2/,3/1st SS Panzergrenadier Regiment LSSAH
1/,2/,3/2nd SS Panzergrenadier Regiment LSSAH
1st SS Reconnaissance Battalion LSSAH (6 companies)
1/,2/1st SS Panzer Regiment LSSAH (13 companies)
1st SS Panzerjäger (Battalion LSSAH (3 companies)
1st SS Sturmgeschütz Battalion LSSAH (3 batteries)
1/,2/,3/,4/1st SS Artillery Regiment LSSAH included a survey battery
1st SS Flak Battalion LSSAH (5 batteries)
1st SS Pioneer Battalion LSSAH (4 companies)
1st SS Armored Signal Battalion LSSAH (2 companies)
1st SS Projector (Werfer) LSSAH (raised 9/44)
1st SS Replacement (Ersatz) Battalion LSSAH (raised 10/44)
1st SS Divisional (Einheiten) Support Units

On 10/22/43 the panzerjäger battalion was renamed the SS-Panzerjägerabteilung 1/LSSAH. This formation suffered heavy casualties and in early 1944 only one weak company, with 17 percent of authorized strength remained. It was then transferred to the 12th SS Panzer Division "Hitler Jugend." In addition, the sturmgeschütz battalion was renamed the SS-Sturmgeschützabteilung 1.

In early November 1943 the 1st SS Panzer Regiment had been brought back to nearly full strength and was organized as follows:

1/,2/1st SS Panzer Regiment
  1 Regimental Staff Panzer Company
  Each Battalion had:
    1 Panzer Staff Company
    4 Medium Companies

Mk IV (lg)	95
Mk V	96
Cmd	9

    1 Heavy Panzer Company

Mk VI	27

The bulk of the division was withdrawn from combat on 12/4/43 and a kampfgruppe was organized that remained in combat. The 1st SS Panzer Regiment was reduced to a battalion of three companies, one each of Mk IV, Mk V and Mk VI tanks. On 4/11/44 the kampfgruppe was withdrawn from combat and transferred to OB West where it was reincorporated into the reforming division and rebuilt. The 1/1st SS Panzer Regiment was subsequently rebuilt with four companies, each with 17 Panther tanks. The 2/1st SS Panzer Regiment was rebuilt with four companies, each with 22 Mk IV tanks.

On the same date the reconnaissance battalion was renamed the SS-Panzer-Aufklarungsabteilung

1/LSSAH. On the same date flak battalion was renamed the SS-Panzer-Flakabteilung 1/LSSAH. In November the 6th Flak Battery was detached to the corps staff of the I SS Panzer Corps as a flak company. An interesting chart in T-78, Roll 417 shows that eight Mk VI Tiger Tanks were dispatched from the factory in December 1943 to the division, despite no organizational charts indicating the assignment of a Tiger tank detachment. On 4/28/44 the division was organized as follows:

Division
Division Staff
Divisional Escort Company
Motorcycle Platoon (6 LMGs)
Self Propelled Flak Platoon (4 20mm guns)
Self Propelled Anti-Tank Platoon (3 LMGs & 3 75mm PAK 40)
Infantry Gun Platoon (2 75mm leIG)
Mixed Panzergrenadier Platoon (4 HMGs, 6 LMGs, & 2 80mm mortars)
1st SS Panzer Regiment
Regimental Staff
Self Propelled Flak Platoon (6 20mm guns)
1st Panzer Battalion
(1–4th Companies) (Mk V Panthers)
Panzer Maintenance Platoon
2nd Panzer Battalion
(5–8th Companies) (Mk IV Panzers)
1 Halftrack Pioneer Company (40 LMGs & 6 flamethrowers)
1 Panzer Maintenance Company
1 (mot) Panzer Supply Column
1st SS Panzergrenadier Regiment
Regimental Staff
1st Battalion
1–3rd Companies (4 HMGs, 18 LMGs, 2 80mm mortars & 2 flamethrowers)
4th Company (12 HMGs & 6 80mm mortars)
5th Company
1 Pioneer Platoon (3 LMGs)
1 Panzerjäger Platoon (3 50mm PAK 38)
1 Infantry Gun Section (2 75mm leIG)
2nd Battalion (6–10th Companies) (same as 1st Battalion)
3rd Battalion (11–15th Companies) (same as 1st Battalion)
16th (self-propelled flak) Company (12 20mm & 4 LMGs)
17th (self-propelled infantry gun) Company (6 150mm sIG & 7 LMGs)
18th (self-propelled panzerjäger) Company (9 75mm PAK 40 & 9 LMGs)
2nd SS Panzergrenadier Regiment
same as 1st SS Panzergrenadier Regiment

1st SS Reconnaissance Battalion
Battalion Staff
1 Armored Car Company (18 20mm & 24 LMGs)
1 Armored Car Company (16 20mm & 25LMGs)
2 (halftrack) Companies (4 HMGs, 56 LMGs, 2 80mm mortars & 3 37mm PAK 36)
1 (halftrack) Company
1 Pioneer Platoon (13 LMGs & 1 75mm gun)
1 Panzerjäger Platoon (9 LMGs & 3 75mm PAK 40)
1 Infantry Gun Section (2 75mm leIG & 4 LMGs)
1 Gun Section (8 LMGs & 6 75mm guns)
1 (mot) Reconnaissance Supply Column (3 LMGs)
1st SS Panzerjäger Battalion
Battalion Staff
2 Self Propelled Panzerjäger Companies (6 75mm PAK 40 & 10 LMGs ea)
1 Self Propelled Panzerjäger Company (6 88mm & 10 LMGs ea)
1st SS Sturmgeschütz Battalion
Staff
1–3rd Sturmgeschütz Batteries (11 StuG & 2 LMGs ea)
1st SS Panzer Artillery Regiment
1st (Self Propelled) Battalion:
Staff & (self-propelled) Staff Battery (6 LMGs)
2 Self Propelled leFH Batteries (6 SdKfz 124 Wespe with 105mm leFH ea)
1 Self Propelled sFH Battery (6 SdKfz 165 Hummel with 150mm sFH)
2nd Battalion
Staff & Staff Battery (2 LMGs)
4th, 5th & 6th (motZ) Batteries (4 105mm leFH & 2 LMGs ea)
3rd Battalion
Staff & (mot) Staff Battery (6 LMGs)
7th, 8th, & 9th (motZ) Batteries (4 150mm sFH & 2 LMGs ea)
Attached
1 (motZ) Battery (4 100mm K18 & 2 LMGs)
1 (motZ) Nebelwerfer Battery (6 150/210mm launchers)
1st SS Flak Battalion
Staff & Staff Battery
3 (motZ) Heavy Flak Batteries (4 88mm, 3 20mm & 2 LMGs ea)
2 Self Propelled Medium Flak Batteries (9 37mm & 4 LMGs ea)
1 (motZ) Searchlight Platoon (3 600mm searchlights)
1st SS Panzer Pioneer Battalion
Staff (2 LMGs)
1 (halftrack) Pioneer Reconnaissance Platoon (2 LMGs)
1 (halftrack) Pioneer Company (43 LMGs, 3 heavy anti-tank rifles, 2 80mm mortars & 6 flamethrowers)

2 (mot) Pioneer Companies (2 HMGs, 18 LMGs, 2
80mm mortars & 6 flamethrowers)
1 (mot) Heavy Panzer Bridging Train (4 LMGs)
1 (mot) Pioneer Supply Column (1 LMG)
1st SS Panzer Signals Battalion
1 (mot) Telephone Company (5 LMGs)
1 Panzer Radio Company (35 LMGs)
1 (mot) Signals Supply Column (4 LMGs)
1st SS Supply Troop
1/,2/,3/,4/1st SS (mot) 120 ton Transportation Companies (8 LMGs ea)
5/1st SS (mot) Heavy Supply Column (4 LMGs)
7,8/,9/,10/1st SS (mot) heavy Fuel Columns (4
LMGs ea)
1st SS (mot) Workshop Company (4 LMGs)
1st SS (mot) Supply Company (8 LMGs)
1st SS Truck Park
1/,2/,3/1st SS (mot) Maintenance Companies (4
LMGs)
1st SS (mot) 75 ton Heavy Maintenance Supply
Column
Medical
1/,2/1st SS (mot) Medical Companies (2 LMGs ea)
1/,2/,3/1st SS Ambulances
Administration
1st SS (mot) Bakery Company (6 LMGs)
1st SS (mot) Butcher Company (6 LMGs)
1st SS (mot) Divisional Administration Platoon (2
LMGs)
1st SS (mot) Field Post Office (2 LMGs)

In the spring of 1944 the 10th and 11th (Werfer)
Batteries/LSSAH Panzer Artillery Regiment were
equipped with 150mm and 210mm nebelwerfer
launchers. They were organized into a Werfer Battalion,
becoming the 2nd and 3rd Batteries. The 1st Werfer
Battery was newly raised.

In May 1944 the division was in Belgium where the
3rd Pioneer Company of the pioneer battalion was
equipped with half tracks. It was also in May that a
feldersatz battalion was organized in Turnhout, Belgium. In June 1944 the 17th (Infantry Gun) Company,
1st Panzergrenadier Regiment and the 16th (Infantry
Gun) Company, 2nd Panzergrenadier Regiment were
reequipped with self-propelled 150mm infantry guns.
Their infantry guns were distributed to the battalions'
heavy companies.

On 7/1/44 the machine-gun companies and the
reconnaissance companies of the panzer grenadier regiments were disbanded. The remaining companies were
renumbered as follows:

1/1st SS Panzergrenadier Regiment
1–3rd Panzergrenadier Companies
4th Heavy Company

2/1st SS Panzergrenadier Regiment
5–7th Panzergrenadier Companies
8th Heavy Company
3/1st SS Panzergrenadier Regiment
9–11th Panzergrenadier Companies
12th Heavy Company
13th (leIG) Company (formerly 17th Company)
14th (Flak) Company (formerly 16th Company)
15th (Pioneer) Company (formerly 20th Company)
16th (Panzerabwehr) Company (formerly 18th
Company)
1/2nd SS Panzergrenadier Regiment
1–3rd Panzergrenadier Companies
4th Heavy Company
2/2nd SS Panzergrenadier Regiment
5–7th Panzergrenadier Companies
8th Heavy Company
3/2nd SS Panzergrenadier Regiment
9–11th Panzergrenadier Companies
12th Heavy Company
13th (leIG) Company (formerly 16th Company)
14th (Flak) Company (formerly 15th Company)
15th (Pioneer) Company (formerly 19th Company)
16th (Panzerabwehr) Company (newly organized)

In July 1944 the panzer regiment and its tank inventory
were as follows:

1/,2/1st SS Panzer Regiment
1 Panzer Staff Company
1 Battalion
1 Panzer Staff Company
4 Medium Panzer Companies (Mk V)
1 Battalion
1 Panzer Staff Company
4 Medium Panzer Companies (Mk IV)
Mk IV (lg)   98
Mk V   89
Flakpz38   12

In August 1944 the SS Panzer Artillery Regiment
LSSAH was completely reorganized. It now had:

SS Panzer Artillery Regiment LSSAH
Regimental Staff
Regimental Staff Battery
Self Propelled 20mm Flak Battery
1st Battalion
Battalion Staff & Staff Battery
1st (armored) Battery (105mm Wespe) (former
4th Battery)
2nd (armored) Battery (105mm Wespe) (former
5th Battery)
3rd (armored) Battery (150mm Hummel) (former
6th Battery)

2nd Battalion
  Battalion Staff & Staff Battery
  4th (motZ) Battery (6 105mm leFH)
  5th (motZ) Battery (6 105mm leFH)
3rd Battalion
  Battalion Staff & Staff Battery
  6th (motZ) Battery (6 150mm sFH)
  7th (motZ) Battery (6 150mm sFH)
  8th (motZ) Battery (4 100mm K18 guns)

The 10th and 11th Nebelwerfer Batteries were detached from the artillery regiment's structure, but remained with the division. At the end of August 1944 LSSAH organized, in Germany, a panzer flak company with two platoons of self-propelled quad 20mm flak guns (Mk IV chassis) and one platoon of self-propelled 37mm flak guns. After Normandy the division was reorganized with a single panzer battalion organized with two companies, each with 14 Mk V Panther tanks and two companies with 14 Mk IV tanks.

The division suffered severe damage in the destruction of German forces in the Falaise pocket. The survivors were withdrawn to Sieburg where the division was rebuilt.

In November 1944 the 16th (Panzerjäger) Company, 1st Panzergrenadier Regiment was disbanded. In April 1945 the heavy companies of the battalions were disbanded and the platoons in the regimental companies were combined, i.e. into infantry gun companies, panzerjäger companies, etc. The rifle companies were renumbered 1st–3rd, 5–7th, and 9–11th companies.

It was also in November that the 10th (Panzer Flak) Company joined the LSSAH in the field. In addition, the remains of the SS-Sturmgeschützabteilung 1. was used to organize a new SS-Panzerjägerabteilung 1 LSSAH. This battalion contained a staff and staff Company, 1st Company (10 Jagdpanzer IV), 2nd Company (10 Jagdpanzer IV), and 3rd Company (12 75mm PAK (motZ). On 11/7/44 a new organization was mandated for the division. It was ordered organized and equipped as follows:

Division Staff
  1 Divisional Staff
  1 (mot) Mapping Detachment
  1 (mot) Escort Company
    1 Machine Gun Platoon (4 HMGs & 6 LMGs)
    1 Motorcycle Platoon (6 LMGS)
    1 Self Propelled Flak Platoon (4 20mm flak guns)
  1 (mot) Military Police Detachment (15 LMGs)
1st SS Panzer Regiment
  1 Panzer Regimental Staff & Staff Company
    1 Panzer Signals Platoon

  1 Panzer Platoon
  1 Panzer Flak Platoon (8 20mm flak guns)
  1 (halftrack) Panzer Pioneer Company (2 HMGs, 43 LMGs, 2 80mm mortars & 6 flamethrowers)
  1 Panzer Maintenance Company (4 LMGs)
1st Battalion
  1 Panzer Battalion Staff (1 LMG)
  1 Panzer Battalion Staff Company (5 LMGs & 3 20mm Flak guns)
  4 Panzer Companies (22 Panther Mk V Tanks ea)
  1 (mot) Supply Company (4 LMGs)
1st Battalion
  1 Panzer Battalion Staff (1 LMG)
  1 Panzer Battalion Staff Company (4 LMGs & 3 20mm Flak guns)
  4 Panzer Companies (22 Mk IV Tanks ea)
  1 (mot) Supply Company (4 LMGs)
1st SS Panzergrenadier Regiment
  1 Panzergrenadier Regimental Staff (2 LMGs)
  1 (halftrack) Panzergrenadier Regimental Staff Company
    1 Staff Platoon (1 LMG)
    1 Signals Platoon
    1 Motorcycle Platoon (4 LMGS)
1st Battalion
  1 Battalion Staff
  1 (mot) Supply Company (4 LMGs)
  3 (halftrack) Panzergrenadier Companies (3 HMGs, 30 LMGs 2 80mm mortars, 7 20mm & 2 75mm guns)
  1 (halftrack) Panzergrenadier Mortar Company
    2 Infantry Gun Platoons (2 LMGs & 6 75mm guns)
    2 Heavy Mortar Platoons (2 120mm mortars ea)
  1 (mot) Supply Company (4 LMGs)
2nd Battalion
  1 Battalion Staff
  1 (mot) Supply Company (4 LMGs)
  3 (mot) Panzergrenadier Companies (4 HMGs, 18 LMGs & 2 80mm mortars)
  1 (mot) Heavy Panzergrenadier Company
    1 Panzerjäger Platoon (3 75mm PAK & 3 LMGs)
    2 Heavy Mortar Platoons (2 120mm mortars ea)
  1 (mot) Supply Company (4 LMGs)
3rd Battalion
  same as 2nd Battalion
1 Self Propelled Infantry Gun Company
  (6 150mm sIG & 8 LMGS)
1 Self Propelled Flak Company
  (12 20mm & 2 LMGs)
1 (mot) Pioneer Company
  1 (mot) Staff Platoon (1 LMG)
  1 (mot) Platoon (12 LMGs, 1 20mm & 6 flamethrowers)

1 (mot) Platoon (8 LMGs & 12 flamethrowers)
1 (mot) Platoon (2 HMGs & 2 80mm mortars)
1 (mot) Platoon (6 LMGs & 6 flamethrowers)

2nd SS Panzergrenadier Regiment
same as 1st SS Panzergrenadier division

Panzerjäger Battalion
1 Battalion Staff & Staff Platoon (3 jagdpanzers)
2 Jagdpanzer Companies (13 Jagdpanzer IV ea)
1 (motZ) Panzerjäger Company (12 75mm PAK & 12 LMGs)
1 (mot) Supply Company (4 LMGs)

1st SS Panzer Reconnaissance Battalion
1 Panzer Reconnaissance Battalion Staff (2 LMGs)
1 (mot) Reconnaissance Battalion Staff Company
1 (mot) Signals Platoon (3 LMGS)
1 **Armored Car Company** (16 20mm & 25 LMGs)
1 **Half Track Reconnaissance Company** (2 75mm, 2 80mm mortars & 44 LMGs)
1 **Half Track Reconnaissance Company** (2 75mm, 7 20mm, 2 80mm mortars, 3 HMGs & 30 LMGs)
1 **Half Track Reconnaissance Company**
1 Staff Platoon (1 LMG)
1 Panzerjäger Platoon (6 75mm & 2 LMGs)
1 Mortar Platoon (2 LMGs & 6 80mm Mortars)
1 Pioneer Platoon (13 LMG)
1 (mot) Supply Company (4 LMGs)

1st SS (mot) Flak Battalion
1 Staff & (mot) Staff Battery (2 LMGs)
3 (motZ) Heavy Flak Companies (6 88mm, 3 20mm & 3 LMGs ea)
2 (motZ) Medium Flak Companies (9 37mm & 4 LMGs ea)
1 Self Propelled Flak Platoon (3 quad 20mm guns)
1 (mot) Searchlight Platoon (4 searchlights)

1st SS (mot) Nebelwerfer Battalion
1 Staff & (mot) Staff Battery (1 LMG)
3 (motZ) Nebelwerfer Batteries (6 150mm launchers & 2 LMGs ea)
1 (motZ) Nebelwerfer Battery (6 210mm launchers & 2 LMGs)
1 (mot) Supply Company (3 LMGs)

1st SS Panzer Artillery Regiment
1 Regimental Staff & (mot) Staff Battery (2 LMGs)
1 Self Propelled Flak Battery (4 quad 20mm guns)
1 Observation Battery

1st Battalion
1 Battalion Staff & (mot) Staff Battery (2 LMGs)
1 Flak Platoon (2 mountain 20mm flak guns)
1 Self Propelled Battery (6 150mm sFH Hummels SdKfz 165 & 4 LMGS)
2 Self Propelled Batteries (6 105mm leFH Wespe SdKfz 124 & 4 LMGs ea)

2nd Battalion
1 Battalion Staff & (mot) Staff Battery (2 LMGs)
1 Flak Platoon (2 mountain 20mm flak guns)
2 (motZ) Batteries (6 105mm leFH & 4 LMGs ea)

3rd Battalion
same as 2nd Battalion

4th Battalion
1 Battalion Staff & (mot) Staff Battery (2 LMGs)
1 Flak Platoon (2 mountain 20mm flak guns)
1 (motZ) Battery (6 105mm leFH & 4 LMGs)
2 (motZ) Batteries (6 150mm sFH & 4 LMGs ea)

1st SS Panzer Pioneer Battalion
1 Battalion Staff
1 (halftrack) Battalion Staff Company (9 LMGs)
1 (halftrack) Reconnaissance Platoon (8 LMGs)
2 (halftrack) Pioneer Platoons (2 HMGs, 43 LMGs, 2 80mm mortars, & 6 flamethrowers)
2 (mot) Pioneer Companies (2 HMGs, 18 LMGs, 2 80mm mortars & 6 flamethrowers)
1 (mot Light Panzer Bridging Train (3 LMGs)

1st SS Panzer Signals Troop
1 Panzer Telephone Company (11 LMGs)
1 Panzer Radio Company (19 LMGs)
1 (mot) Supply Platoon (2 LMGs)

1st SS Feldersatz Battalion
5 Companies

Supply Troop
1 (mot) Supply Battalion Staff
1 (mot) Supply Battalion Staff Company
6 (mot) 120 ton Transportation Companies (8 LMGs ea)
1 (mot) Maintenance Company (4 LMGs)
1 (mot) Supply Company (8 LMGs)

Maintenance Troops
2 (mot) Maintenance Companies (5 LMGs ea)
1 (mot) Maintenance Company (4 LMGs)
1 (mot) Heavy Maintenance Supply Column

Other
1 (mot) Butcher Company (4 LMGs)
1 (mot) Bakery Company (5 LMGs)
1 (mot) Divisional Administration Company (4 LMGs)
2 (mot) Medical Company (4 LMGs ea)
1 (mot) Medical Supply Company (4 LMGs)
1 (mot) Field Post Office

On 11/17/44 the 101st Corps Heavy Panzer (Tiger) Battalion, now known as the 501st Heavy Panzer (Tiger) Battalion was temporarily assigned to the division.

On 12/1/44 the 2nd (Motorcycle) and 4th (Armored Car) Companies, LSSAH Reconnaissance Battalion, were disbanded. The battalion retained its staff (six armored cars), the 1st (VW) Company, 2nd (light half track) Company, 3rd (heavy) Company, and its supply company.

On 12/3/44 the tank inventory and organization of the 1st SS Panzer Regiment were as follows:

1/1st SS Panzer Regiment
1 Panzer Staff Company
1 Panzer Flak Platoon
1 Panzer Battalion
  1 Panzer Staff Company
  2 Medium Panzer Companies (Mk V)
  2 Medium Panzer Companies (Mk IV)
    Mk IV (lg)   37
    Mk V   42
    FlakpzIV (2V)   4
    FlakpzIV (37)   4
501st Heavy Panzer Battalion
  1 Panzer Staff Company
  3 Heavy Panzer Companies (Mk VI)
    Mk VI   45

On 2/1/45 the tank inventory and organization of the 1st SS Panzer Regiment were as follows:

1/,2/1st SS Panzer Regiment
1 Panzer Staff Company

1 Panzer Flak Platoon
1st Battalion
  1 Panzer Staff Company
  4 Medium Panzer Companies (Mk V)
2nd Battalion
  1 Panzer Staff Company
  2 Medium Panzer Companies (Mk IV)
  2 Sturmgescütz Companies (StuG IV)
  StuG   28
  Mk IV (lg)   19
  Mk V   34
  FlakpzIV (37)   8

On 3/1/45 the 1st and 12th SS Werferabteilung were transferred to the Special Units of the RFSS and became the 501st and 502nd Werferabteilung of the 6th Panzer Army Oberkommando. The 3/501st Werferabteilung was disbanded in early April 1945 and its troops absorbed into the 2/501st. At the end of April the 2/501st was dissolved and absorbed into the 1/501st and Division Escort Company.

1st SS Brigade Reichsführer

Formed on 4/24/41 from the SS-Totenkopfverbände, it contained:

1/,2/,3/8th SS Infantry Regiment Reichsführer
1/,2/,3/10th SS Infantry Regiment Reichsführer
Radio & Signals Troops

It was not originally intended as a combat unit, but was to serve as a line of communications security brigade with a police mission. However, by June 1941 it was expanded and thrown into the line. It was equipped with Czech guns and French vehicles. At that time it contained:

Headquarters
1 Brigade Headquarters
1 (mot) Signals Detachment
1 Motorcycle Platoon (3 LMGs)
8th & 10th SS Reichsführer Infantry Regiments
(mot) Infantry Regiment Headquarters
(mot) Headquarters Company
  Company Headquarters
  Signals Platoon
  Motorcycle Platoon

Pioneer Platoon (3 LMGs)
13th (mot) Infantry Gun Company
  3 Light Infantry Gun Platoons (6 75mm leIG)
  1 Heavy Infantry Gun Platoon (2 150mm sIG)
14th Light (mot) Panzerjäger Company (4 LMGs & 12 37mm PAK 36)
Motorcycle Platoon (3 LMGs)
3 (mot) Infantry Battalions
  1 (mot) Battalion Headquarters
  3 (mot) Infantry Companies (12 LMGs & 3 50mm mortars)
  1 (mot) Machine Gun Company (12 HMGs & 6 80mm mortars)
51st SS Artillery Battalion
Battalion Headquarters
1 (mot) Signals Platoon
1 (mot) Calibration Section
2 (motZ) Batteries (2 LMGs & 4 105mm Czech howitzers ea)
1 (motZ) Battery (2 150mm Czech howitzers & 2 LMGs)
51st Reconnaissance Detachment
1 Motorcycle Company (3 50mm mortars, 4 HMGs & 18 LMGs)

Armored Car Platoon (4 Sd Kfz 222 & 3 Sd Kfz 223 armored cars)
51st (mot) Flak Company
1 (motZ) Light Flak Battery (12 20mm flak guns)
1 Self Propelled Light Flak Platoon (3 37mm flak guns)
51st Panzerjäger Company (12 37mm PAK 36 & 4 LMGs)

51st Pioneer Company (9 LMGs)
51st Signals Company

On 9/1/41 it was renamed the 1st SS (mot) Infantry Brigade.

1st SS (mot) Infantry Brigade

Formed in May 1941 as the SS-Brigade (mot). However, on 9/1/41 it was renamed the 1st SS (mot) Infanterie Brigade. In May 1941 it had:

8th Infantry Regiment RFSS
1st Battalion (1–4th Companies)
2nd Battalion (5–8th Companies)
3rd Battalion (9–12th Companies)
13th Company
14th Company
Light Infantry Column

10th SS Infantry Regiment RFSS
same as 8th Infantry Regiment
Medical Company
Transportation Platoon
Signals Company
Maintenance Platoon

During the course of 1941 it was expanded to:

Staff
Military Police Troop
Field Post Office
8th SS Infantry Regiment (15 companies)
Signals Platoon
Motorcycle Messenger Platoon
Regimental Band
1st Battalion (1–4th Companies)
2nd Battalion (5–8th Companies)
3rd Battalion (9–12th Companies) 13th Company
14th Company
16th Company
Light Infantry Column
Medical Company
Ambulance Platoon
Signals Company
Work Station Company
10th SS Infantry Regiment (16 companies)
1st Battalion (1–4th Companies)
2nd Battalion (5–8th Companies)
3rd Battalion (9–12th Companies)
13th Company
14th Company

16th Company
Light Infantry Column

At times the 8th and 9th Flak Batteries and the 1st Field Howitzer Battery, Heavy Artillery Battalion were apparently attached. During the course of 1942 the 16th Company of the 10th Regiment was disbanded. On 11/12/43 it was reorganized as follows:

1st SS Infantry Brigade
1/,2/,3/39th SS Grenadier Regiment
1/,2/,3/40th SS Grenadier Regiment
51st SS Artillery Battalion
51st SS Motorcycle Company
51st SS Panzerjäger Company
51st SS Flak Company
51st SS Signals Company
51st SS Panzergrenadier Replacement (Ersatz) Battalion

The brigade was to add the 41st SS Grenadier Regiment and be reorganized into a full division. On January 1944 this new force was organized into the 18th SS Panzergrenadier Division "Horst Wessel."

SS Waffen-Grenadier-Brigade Charlemagne (1st French)

Formed between 8/28/44 and 9/30/44 in the SS Truppenübungsplatz Westprussen with the French SS Freiwilligen (Volunteer) Sturmbrigade as the first grenadier regiment. On 8/10/44 it was reinforced with troops drawn from the French Legion (Légion Volontaire Francaise) and the 638th Infantry Regiment, which became the second grenadier regiment. On 10/1/44 the two regiments in the French brigade were renumbered as the 57th and 58th Regiments and the brigade units assumed the number 57.

57th SS Grenadier Regiment
58th SS Grenadier Regiment

SS 57th Artillery Battalion
SS 57th Panzerjäger Battalion
SS 57th Pioneer Company
SS 57th Signals Company
SS 57th Field Replacement company
SS Grenadier Training and Replacement Battalion

In February 1945 it was reorganized as the 33rd Waffen SS Grenadier Division "Charlemagne" (1st French).

Waffen SS Mountain Brigade (1st Tartar)

Formed 7/8/44 in Hungary from Tartars recruited in the Crimea. It contained Waffen the Gebergsjäger Regiment (Tartar Nr. 1). On 10/11/44 the brigade units were intended to receive the number 58. It was disbanded on 1/1/45 in Slovakia.

SS Waffen Grenadier Brigade (1st Italian)

After Otto Skorzeny's rescue of Mussolini on 12 September 1943, 1,500 Italian officers and men volunteered for service in the Waffen-SS. They were sent to Münsingen where they were organized into the Italienische Freiwilliger Verband. They were formed into the SS Legion "Italia" and sent to northern Italy for training.

On 9/7/44 the *Milizia armata* was formed into the 1st and 2nd Infantry Regiments, an artillery battalion, a panzerjäger battalion, an ersatz battalion and an officer battalion. It was renamed the 1st Italienisch Freiwilligen-Sturm Brigade Milizia armata (Pol) in February 1944. It was formed from the Miliz Regiment de Maria, which had been formed in December 1943 from Italians loyal to Mussolini. Both infantry regiments were numbered the 81st and 82nd Regiments and the brigade units were given the number 59 on 10/11/44. In February 1945 it was renamed the 29th Waffen SS Grenadier Division (1st Italian).

1st SS Polizei Jäger Brigade

Formed on 4/15/45 in Stettin with the 1/,2/,3/8th SS Polizei Regiment, the 1/,2/,3/50th SS Polizei Jäger Regiment, and two companies of the 9th SS Panzergrenadier Ersatz (Replacement) Battalion, a signals company and a panzerjäger company. Both regiments were Ordnungs Polizei. The Brigade formed part of 610th Division z.b.V. in the Oder Corps during April 1945. During the Soviet thrust into Berlin it was roughly handled and withdrew with the 46th Panzer Corps. On 4/24/45 its remains were 20 miles northwest of Angermünde.

SS Division Verfügungstruppe (SS-VT)

The division was formed on 4/1/40 from the independent SS Verfügungstruppe Leibstandarte Adolph Hitler and the SS Standarte "Germania," both of which had served in Poland. To them was added the SS Standarte "Deutschland," which had not seen combat. The SS Verfügungstruppe Leibstandarte Adolph Hitler consisted of:

SS Verfügungstruppe Leibstandarte Adolph Hitler
1 (mot) Signals Platoon
1 Motorcycle Messenger Platoon
1 Regimental Band
1/,2/,3/LSSAH (mot) Infantry Battalions,
   3 (mot) Rifle Companies (9 LMGs, 2 HMGs & 3 50mm mortars ea)
   1 (mot) Machine Gun Company (8 HMGs & 6 80mm mortars)
   1 (mot) Pioneer Platoon (3 LMGs)
   1 Motorcycle Company (9 LMGs, 2 HMGs & 3 50mm mortars)
   1 (mot) Infantry Gun Company (8 75mm leIG)
   1 (mot) Panzer Abwehr Company (12 37mm PAK 36 & 6 LMGs)
   1 Armored Car Platoon (4 20mm & 8 LMGs)

Once formed the division contained:

   1/,2/,3/SS Standarte Deutschland, Germania, & Der Führer
   1/,2/,3/SS Artillery Standarte (3 batteries each)
   4/,5/SS Artillery Standarte (3 batteries each, formed in 1940)
   SS Reconnaissance Battalion (3 companies) (replaced in 1940 by a SS Motorcycle Battalion— 4 companies)
   SS Pioneer Truppe (3 companies)
   SS Signals Truppe (2 companies)
   SS Replacement Truppe (4 companies)

Each Standarte contained three battalions, each with three motorized companies (9 LMGs, 2 HMGs & 3 50mm mortars ea), a motorized machine gun company (8 HMGs & 6 80mm mortars). In addition, there was a motorized pioneer platoon (3 LMGS), a motorcycle company (9 LMGs, 2 HMGs, & 3 50mm mortars), a motorized infantry gun company (8 75mm leIG), a motorized panzerjäger platoon (12 37mm PAK 36 & 4 LMGs), an armored car platoon (4 20mm & 8 LMGs), and a motorized light infantry supply column. Later the following were raised:

SS-VT Panzerabwehr (Anti-Tank) Battalion (3 companies)
SS-VT Flak Battalion (2 batteries—raised to 3 batteries when the heavy company of the reconnaissance battalion was assigned to the battalion)

On 10 May 1940 the division was organized and equipped as follows:

Division Staff
   1 Division Staff
   1 (mot) Signals Platoon (2 HMGs)
1st, 2nd & 3rd Polizei Regiments, each with
   1 Staff Company
      1 Signals Platoon
      2 Engineer Platoon (3 LMGs)
   3 Infantry Battalions, each with
      3 Infantry Companies (12 LMGs ea, later added 3 50mm mortars)
      1 Heavy Company (12 HMGs & 6 80mm mortars)
   1 Panzerjäger Company (12 37mm PAK 36 & 4 LMGs)
   1 Mounted Company
   1 Bicycle Company
   1 Infantry Support Gun Company (initially 8 75mm leIG later 2 150mm sIG & 6 75mm leIG guns) (company added later)
   1 Light (horse drawn) Supply Column (deleted later)
Panzerjäger Battalion
   1 Staff Company
      1 (mot) Signals Platoon
   3 (mot) Panzerjäger Companies (12 37mm PAK 36 & 6 LMGs)
Reconnaissance Battalion
   1 Staff Company
      1 (mot) Signals Platoon
   2 Bicycle Companies (9 LMGs) (later added 3 50mm mortars & 2 HMGs)
Artillery Regiment
   1 Staff Battery
      1 (mot) Signals Platoon
      1 (mot) Weather Platoon
   1st, 2nd & 3rd Battalions, each with
      1 Staff Battery
         1 (mot) Signals Platoon
      3 (motZ) Batteries (4 105mm leFH 18 & 2 LMGs)
   4th Battalion, with
      1 Staff Battery
         1 (mot) Signals Platoon
      3 (motZ) Batteries (4 150mm sFH 18 & 2 LMGs)

Signals Battalion
   1 (tmot) Telephone Company
   1 (mot) Radio Company
   1 (mot) Light Signals Supply Column
Pioneer Battalions
   3 Pioneer Companies (9 LMGs ea)
   1 Light (mot) Engineering Supply Column
Service Troops
   300th Bakery Platoon
   300th Butcher Platoon
   300th Division Administration
   300th Field Post Office
   300th (mot) Military Police Platoon

300th Veterinary Company
1/,2/300th Ambulance Columns
300th Field Hospital
1/,2/300th Medical Companies

During the fall of 1940 the 4th Sturmbann of the Artillery Standarte became the 1/Leibstandarte Artillery Regiment. On 11/20/40 the SS Standarte Germania was transferred to the SS Division Germania, which later became 5th Wiking SS Panzer Division. On 12/21/40 the division was renamed the Reich SS (mot) Division.

Reich SS (mot) Division

When the division was formed on 12/21/40, it had:

   Division Staff
      Motorcycle Platoon
      Mapping Platoon
      Operations Platoon
      Military Police Detachment
   Deutschland SS Regiment
      1st Battalion (1–4th Companies)
      2nd Battalion (5–8th Companies)
      3rd Battalion (9–12th Companies)
      13th (Infantry Gun) Company
   Der Führer SS Regiment
      same as Deutschland
   11th SS Infantry Regiment (disbanded in 1942)
      same as Deutschland
   Reich SS Panzerjäger Battalion (3 companies)
   1/,2/,3/Reich SS Artillery Regiment (9 batteries)
   Reich SS Pioneer Battalion (staff & 3 companies)
   Reich SS Flak MG Battalion (staff & 2 companies)
   Reich SS Signals Battalion (2 companies)
   Reich SS Supply Troops

This organization was very transient. The organization continued to grow and expand as combat proved an expanded organization was desirable. Among the first things added were a panzerjäger company and a flak company to each of the infantry regiments. There are also indications that a motorcycle reconnaissance company was added. On 10 May 1940 the SS Das Reich (mot) Division was organized and equipped as follows:

Division Staff
   1 Divisional Staff (2 HMGs)
   1 (mot) SS Divisional Mapping Detachment

3 (mot) Infantry Regiments (Der Führer, Deutschland & 11th SS Regiment), each with
   1 Regimental Staff Company, with
      1 (mot) Signals Platoon
      1 (mot) Engineer Company (9 LMGs)
      1 Light Armored Car Platoon (2 HMGs & 4 LMGs)
      1 (mot) Motorcycle Platoon (4 LMGs)
      1 Regimental Band
   3 (mot) Battalions, each with
      3 (mot) Infantry Companies, each with 12 LMGs & 3 50mm mortars
   1 (mot) Machine Gun Company (12 HMGs & 6 80mm mortars)
   1 Motorcycle Company (3 50mm mortars, 2 HMGs & 9 LMGs)
   1 (mot) Infantry Support Gun Company (2 150mm sIG & 6 75mm leIG guns)
   1 (mot) Panzerjäger Company (12 37mm PAK 36 & 6 LMGs)
   1 Light (mot) Supply Column (later eliminated)
SS Das Reich Infantry Gun Battery
   6 self-propelled sIG
SS Das Reich Panzerjäger Battalion
   1 (mot) Signals Platoon
   1 Battalion Band
   3 (mot) Panzerjäger Companies (9 37mm PAK 36, 2 50mm PAK 38 & 6 LMGs)
   3rd AT Company later equipped with (3 50mm PAK 38, 8 37mm PAK 36 & 6 LMGs)
SS Das Reich Reconnaissance Battalion
   1 (mot) Signals Platoon
   1 Battalion Band
   2 Motorcycle Companies (3 50mm mortars, 2 HMGs & 18 LMGs ea)

1 Light Armored Car Company (6 HMG & 20 LMGs)
1 (mot) Support Company, with
1 Panzerjäger Platoon (2 37mm PAK 36 & 2 LMG)
1 Mortar Platoon (6 80mm mortars)
1 Engineer Platoon (3 LMGs)
SS Das Reich Artillery Regiment
1 (mot) Signals Platoon
2 (mot) Weather Detachments
3 (mot) Battalions
1 (mot) Signals Platoon
1 (mot) Calibration Detachment
3 (motZ) Batteries (4 105mm leFH 18 howitzers & 2 LMGs)
1 (mot) Battalion
1 (mot) Signals Platoon
1 (mot) Calibration Detachment
3 (motZ) Batteries (4 150mm sFH 18 howitzers & 2 LMGs)
SS Das Reich Flak Battalion
1 Battalion Band
2 (motZ) Flak Batteries (12 37mm guns ea)
SS Das Reich Signals Battalion
1 (mot) Radio Company
1 (mot) Telephone Company
1 Light (mot) Signals Supply Column
SS Das Reich Feldersatz Battalion
3 Companies
SS Das Reich Pioneer Battalion
3 (mot) Pioneer Companies (9 LMGs ea)
1 (mot) "B" Bridging Train
1 Light (mot) Engineering Supply Column
Supply Train
1st–5th Light (mot) Supply Columns
6th–7th Heavy (mot) Supply Columns
13th–15th Light (mot) Supply Columns (added later)
10th–12th Heavy (mot) POL Supply Columns
1st, 2nd, & 3rd (mot) Maintenance Companies
SSDR (mot) Supply Company
Commissary
SSDR (mot) Bakery Platoon (later Company)
SSDR (mot) Butcher Platoon (later Company)
SSDR (mot) Division Administration
Medical Service
1st–3rd SSDR Ambulance Columns
SSDR (mot) Field Hospital
1st & 2nd SSDR Medical Companies
Other
SSDR (mot) Military Police Platoon
SSDR (mot) Field Post Office

Das Reich participated in the invasion of Greece and when the invasion began on 5 April 1941, the division was organized and equipped as follows:

Das Reich SS (mot) Division
Divisional Staff
1 Divisional Staff (2 HMGs)
1 (mot) Mapping Detachment
3 (mot) Infantry Regiments, each with
1 (mot) Staff & Staff Company, with
1 Signals Platoon
1 Motorcycle Platoon (6 LMGs)
1 (mot) Engineering Platoon (9 LMGs)
1 Armored Car Platoon (2 20mm & 4 LMGs)
3 (mot) Battalions, each with
3 (mot) Infantry Companies (9 LMGs, 2 HMGs, 3 50mm mortars ea)
1 (mot) Heavy Machine Gun Company (8 HMGs & 6 80mm mortars)
1 Motorcycle Company (3 50mm mortars, 2 HMGs & 9 LMGS)
1 Infantry Gun Company (8 75mm leIG)
1 Panzerjäger Company (12 37mm PAK 36 & 4 LMGs)
1 (mot) Light Infantry Column
SS Das Reich Reconnaissance Battalion
1 Armored Car Company (6 20mm & 24 LMGs)
2 Motorcycle Company (2 50mm mortars, 4 HMGs, & 9 LMGs)
1 (mot) Company, with
1 Engineer Platoon (3 LMGs)
1 Panzerjäger Section (2 37mm PAK 36 & 2 LMGs)
1 Mortar Platoon (80mm mortars)
SS Das Reich Panzerjäger Battalion
1 (mot) Signals Platoon
1 Battalion Band
3 (mot) Panzerjäger Company (11 37mm PAK 36 & 6 LMGs)
SS Das Reich Artillery Regiment
Regimental Staff
1 (mot) Staff Battery
1 (mot) Signals Platoon
1 (mot) Weather Detachment
1 Regimental Band
1st–3rd (mot) Artillery Battalions, each with
1 (mot) Battalion Staff Battery
3 (motZ) Batteries (4 105mm leFH 18 & 2 LMGs)
4th (mot) Artillery Battalion
1 (mot) Battalion Staff Battery
2 (motZ) Batteries (4 150mm sFH 18 & 2 LMGs ea)
1 (motZ) Battery (4 100mm K18 guns & 2 LMGs)
SS Das Reich Sturmgeschütz Battery
(6 StuGs)
SS Das Reich Flak Battalion
2 (mot) Light Flak Batteries (12 20mm guns ea)

SS Das Reich Signals Battalion
1 (mot) Radio Company
1 (mot) Telephone Company
1 (mot) Light Signals Supply Column
SS Das Reich Pioneer Battalion
3 (mot) Pioneer Companies (9 LMGs)
1 (mot) Brüko B
1 (mot) Light Supply Column
Administration
1 (mot) Division Administration
1 (mot) Butcher Company
1 (mot) Bakery Company
Supply Train
1/,2/,3/,4/,5/(mot) Light Supply Columns
6/,7/(mot) Heavy Supply Columns
9/,10/(mot) Light Fuel Supply Columns
1/,2/,3/(mot) Maintenance Companies
1 (mot) Light Supply Company
Medical
1/,2/(mot) Medical Companies (2 LMGs ea)
1 (mot) Field Hospital (2 LMGs)
1/,2/,3/Ambulance Companies (2 LMGs ea)
Other
1 (mot) Military Police Company
1 (mot) Field Post

Between 16 May 1941 and 15 October 1942 the division was organized as follows:

Divisional Staff
1 Divisional Staff (4 HMGs)
1 (mot) Mapping Detachment
2 (mot) Infantry Regiments, each with
1 (mot) Regimental Staff Company, with
1 Signals Platoon
1 Motorcycle Platoon (6 LMGs)
1 Panzerjäger Platoon (3 50mm PAK 38 & 2 LMGs)
3 (mot) Battalions, each with
3 Infantry Companies, each with
(18 LMGs, 4 HMGs, 2 80mm mortars & 2 flamethrowers)
1 Support Company with
1 Engineer Platoon (4 LMGs)
1 Panzerjäger Section (3 50mm PAK 38 guns)
1 Infantry Support Gun Platoon (4 75mm leIG guns & 3 28mm anti-tank guns)
1 (mot) Infantry Support Company (4 75mm leIG)
SS Das Reich Armored Troop, with
1 Armored Staff Company
1 Medium Armored Company
2 Light Armored Companies
1 Armored Maintenance Platoon

SS Das Reich Motorcycle (Volkswagen) Regiment
1 (mot) Staff & Staff Company, with
1 Signals Platoon
1 Motorcycle Platoon (6 LMGs)
1 Panzerjäger Platoon (3 50mm PAK 38 & 2 LMGs)
2 (mot) Battalions, each with
1 (mot) Staff Platoon
3 (mot) Infantry Companies (18 LMGs, 4 HMGs, 2 50mm mortars ea)
1 (mot) Heavy Machine Gun Company (12 HMGs & 6 80mm mortars)
1 (mot) Support Company, with
1 Engineer Platoon (4 LMGs)
1 Panzerjäger Section (3 50mm PAK 38 & 2 LMGs)
1 Infantry Support Gun Section (2 75mm leIG guns)
SS Das Reich Artillery Regiment
Regimental Staff
1 (mot) Staff Battery
1 (mot) Observation Battery
1st–3rd (mot) Artillery Battalions, each with
1 (mot) Battalion Staff Battery
3 (motZ) Batteries (4 105mm leFH 18 & 2 LMGs)
4th (mot) Artillery Battalion
1 (mot) Battalion Staff Battery
2 (motZ) Batteries (4 150mm sFH 18 & 2 LMGs ea)
1 (motZ) Battery (4 100mm K18 guns & 2 LMGs)
5th (mot) Flak Battalion
1 (mot) Battalion Staff Battery
1 Self Propelled Flak Battery (8 20mm Flak & 2 quad 20mm guns)
1 Self Propelled Flak Battery (9 37mm guns)
1 (mot) Flak Battery (4 88mm guns & 3 20mm guns)
1 Light (mot) Supply Column
SS Das Reich Reconnaissance Battalion
1 Armored Car Company (18 20mm & 24 LMGs)
1 Light Armored Car Platoon
1 Motorcycle Company (2 80mm mortars, 4 HMGs, & 18 LMGs)
1 (mot) Company, with
1 Engineer Platoon (4 LMGs)
1 Panzerjäger Section (3 50mm PAK 38 guns)
1 Infantry Support Gun Platoon (2 75mm leIG guns)
SS Das Reich Panzerjäger Battalion
1 Self Propelled Panzerjäger Co (Marders) (9 75mm PAK 40 & 6 LMGs)
1 (mot) Panzerjäger Company (9 75mm PAK 40 & 6 LMGs)

1 (mot) Panzerjäger Company (9 50mm PAK 38 & 6 LMGs)

SS Das Reich Signals Battalion
1 (mot) Radio Company (4 LMGs)
1 (mot) Telephone Company (4 LMGs)
1 (mot) Light Signals Supply Column (2 LMGs)

SS Das Reich Pioneer Battalion
3 (mot) Pioneer Companies (18 LMGs & 2 flamethrowers ea)
1 (mot) Light "B" Bridging Train (2 LMGs)
1 (mot) Light Supply Column

Commissary Service
1 (mot) Division Administration (2 LMGs)
1 (mot) Butcher Company (2 LMGs)
1 (mot) Bakery Company (2 LMGs)

Supply Train
12 (mot) Light Supply Columns (2 LMGs ea)
3 (mot) Light Fuel Supply Columns (2 LMGs ea)
3 (mot) Maintenance Companies (2 LMGs ea)
1 (mot) Light Supply Company (2 LMGs)

Medical
2 (mot) Medical Companies (2 LMGs ea)
1 (mot) Field Hospital (2 LMGs)
3 Ambulance Companies (2 LMGs ea)

Other
1 (mot) Military Police Company
1 (mot) Field Post

1 (mot) SS "KB" Platoon

The division was ordered refitted on 2/23/42. In Prague the 2/,3/Deutschland Infantry Regiment were raised anew. The motorcycle battalion was re-formed in Bergen, the two (mot) artillery battalions were re-formed in Dachau, the panzerjäger company was re-formed in Hilversum, and a pioneer company was formed in Dresden and Arolsen.

The Langemark (mot) Grenadier Regiment was formed on 4/20/42. The staff and 2nd Battalion were formed from the remains of the 4th SS Infantry Regiment and the 1st Battalion was formed from the Motorcycle Battalion, SS Das Reich. It was organized as a "fast" regiment and equipped with Volkswagen Kubelwagens. The flak machine-gun battalion (20mm guns) was converted into a flak battalion (20mm, 37mm, and 88mm guns). A panzer battalion was formed on 2/15/42 in Wildflecken with three companies. On 4/18/42 it became the 5th SS Panzer Battalion and was used in the organization of the Wiking Division. On 4/20/42 the 2nd SS Panzer Battalion was raised and assigned to the division.

On 10/15/42 the division's name was changed to "Das Reich" and on 11/9/42 its name was changed to "SS Panzergrenadier Division Das Reich."

2nd SS Panzer Division "Das Reich"

Formed on 11/9/42 in France as the SS Panzergrenadier Division "Das Reich" from the SS (mot) Division "Das Reich." On 24 April 1942 it contained:

Division Headquarters
1 Headquarters LMG Section
1 (mot) Mapping Section

Deutschland & Der Führer (mot) Infantry Regiments, each with
Headquarters
1 (mot) Signals Platoon
1 Motorcycle Platoon (6 LMGs)
1 (mot) Panzerjäger Platoon (3 50mm PAK & 2 LMGs)

1st–3rd Battalions, each with
3 (mot) Infantry Companies (18 LMGs, 4 HMGs, 2 50mm mortars and 2 flamethrowers ea)
1 Heavy Weapons Company, with
1 Engineer Platoon
1 Panzerjäger Section (3 50mm PAK & 2 anti-tank rifles)

1 Infantry Support Gun Section (4 75mm leIG)
1 (mot) Infantry Support Gun Company (4 150mm sIG)

SS Das Reich Panzer Battalion: regimental staff & 2nd battalion
Staff Panzer Company
1 Medium Panzer Company
2 Light Panzer Companies
1 Armored Maintenance Company

SS Langemark Regiment
Headquarters Section
(mot) Headquarters Heavy Weapons Company, with
1 Motorcycle Platoon (6 LMGs)
1 Signals Platoon
1 Panzerjäger Platoon (3 50mm PAK & 2 LMGs)

1st Battalion
1 (mot) Staff Section
1 (mot) Headquarters Heavy Weapons Company, with

1 Reserve Platoon
1 Signals Platoon
1 Panzerjäger Platoon (3 50mm PAK & 2 LMGs)
1 Infantry Support Gun Section (2 75mm leIG)
1 (mot) Machine Gun Company (12 HMGs & 6 80mm mortars)
3 (mot) Infantry Companies (18 LMGs, 4 HMGs, & 2 50mm mortars ea)

2nd Battalion
1 (mot) Staff Section
1 (mot) Headquarters Heavy Weapons Company, with
1 Reserve Platoon
1 Signals Platoon
1 Panzerjäger Platoon (3 50mm PAK & 2 LMGs)
1 Infantry Support Gun Section (2 75mm leIG)
1 (mot) Machine Gun Company (12 HMGs & 6 80mm mortars)
3 (mot) Infantry Companies (18 LMGs, 4 HMGs, & 2 50mm mortars ea)

SS Das Reich Artillery Regiment
1 (mot) Staff Platoon
1 (mot) Observation Platoon

1st Battalion
1 (mot) Staff Platoon
3 (motZ) Batteries (4 105mm leFH 18 & 2 LMGs ea)

2nd Battalion
1 (mot) Staff Platoon
3 (motZ) Batteries (4 105mm leFH 18 & 2 LMGs ea)

3rd Battalion
1 (mot) Staff Platoon
3 (motZ) Batteries (4 105mm leFH 18 & 2 LMGs ea)

4th Battalion
1 (mot) Staff Platoon
2 (motZ) Batteries (4 150mm sFH 18 & 2 LMGs ea)
1 (motZ) Battery (4 100mm guns & 2 LMGs)

Flak Battalion
1 (mot) Staff Platoon
1 Self Propelled Battery (2 quad 20mm & 8 20mm guns)
1 Self Propelled Battery (9 37mm guns)
1 Battery (3 self-propelled 20mm & towed 4 88mm)
1 (mot) Light Supply Column

SS Das Reich Signals Battalion
1st (mot) Telephone Company (4 LMGs)
2nd (mot) Radio Company (4 LMGs)
1 (mot) Light Signals Supply Column (4 LMGs)

SS Das Reich Pioneer Battalion
3 (mot) Pioneer Companies (18 LMGs & 3 flamethrowers ea)
1 (mot) Light Engineering Supply Column (2 LMGs)
1 (mot) "B" Bridging Column (2 LMGs)

SS Das Reich Reconnaissance Battalion
1 (mot) Signals Platoon
1 (mot) Heavy Weapons Company
1 Panzerjäger Platoon (3 50mm PAK & 2 LMGs)
1 Engineer Platoon (4 LMGs)
1 Infantry Support Gun Section (2 75mm guns)
1 Motorcycle Company (18 LMGs, 4 HMGs, & 3 50mm mortars ea)
1 Light Armored Car Company (18 HMGs & 24 LMGs)
1 Light Armored Car Supply Column

SS Das Reich Panzerjäger Battalion
1 (mot) Staff Section
1 (mot) Signals Platoon
1 Self Propelled Panzerjäger Company (9 75mm PAK & 6 LMGs)
2 (mot) Panzerjäger Companies (9 50mm PAK & 6 LMGs ea)

SS Das Reich Administrative Service
1 (mot) Bakery Company (2 LMGs)
1 (mot) Butcher Company (2 LMGs)
1 (mot) Divisional Administration (2 LMGs)

SS Das Reich Medical Service
1st SS (mot) Medical Company (2 LMGs)
2nd SS (mot) Medical Company (2 LMGs)
1st SS (mot) Field Hospital (2 LMGs)
1st SS Ambulance Company (2 LMGs)
2nd SS Ambulance Company (2 LMGs)
3rd SS Ambulance Company (2 LMGs)

SS Das Reich Supply Service
12 SS (mot) Light Supply Columns (2 LMGs ea)
2 SS (mot) Heavy POL Company (2 LMGs ea)
1 SS (mot) Supply Company (2 LMGs)
3 SS (mot) Maintenance Companies (2 LMGs ea)

Other
SS (mot) Field Post Office
SS (mot) Military Police Company

The Das Reich Panzer Battalion was expanded into a regiment in November 1942 with the organization of a staff and 2nd Battalion. The division underwent some substantial equipment changes and was equipped as follows:

Division Headquarters
1 Division Staff
1 (mot) Mapping Section
1 (mot) Escort Company

1 Motorcycle Platoon (6 LMGs)
1 Infantry Gun Section (2 75mm leIG)
1 Self Propelled Flak Platoon (4 20mm guns)
1 Self Propelled Panzerjäger Platoon (3 75mm PAK 40)
1 Heavy Infantry Platoon (2 80mm mortars, 2 HMGs & 6 LMGs)

Der Führer Panzergrenadier Regiment
Headquarters
1 (mot) Signals Platoon
1 Motorcycle Platoon (6 LMGs)
1 (mot) Panzerjäger Platoon (3 75mm PAK 40 & 2 LMGs)

1st & 2nd Battalions, each with
3 (mot) Panzergrenadier Companies (18 LMGs, 4 HMGs, 2 80mm mortars and 2 flamethrowers ea)
1 Heavy Weapons Company, with
1 Mortar Platoon (6 80mm mortars)
1 Panzerjäger Platoon (3 75mm PAK 40)
1 Panzerjäger Platoon (3 anti-tank rifles)
1 Infantry Support Gun Section (4 75mm leIG)

3rd Battalion
3 Panzergrenadier Companies (4 HMGs, 34 LMGs, 2 80mm mortars & 2 flamethrowers)
1 Heavy Company
1 Infantry Gun Section (4 75mm leIG)
1 Panzerjäger Platoon (3 75mm PAK 40)
1 Anti-Tank Rifle Platoon (3 heavy anti-tank rifles)
1 (motZ) Infantry Support Gun Company (4 150mm sIG)
1 Self Propelled Flak Company (12 20mm guns)
1 Motorcycle Company (4 HMGs, 18 LMGs 2 80mm mortars & 3 75mm PAK 40)
1 (motZ) Infantry Support Gun Company (4 150mm sIG)

Deutschland Panzergrenadier Regiment
Headquarters
1 (mot) Signals Platoon
1 Motorcycle Platoon (6 LMGs)
1 (mot) Panzerjäger Platoon (3 50mm PAK & 2 LMGs)

1st–3rd Battalions, each with
3 (mot) Infantry Companies (18 LMGs, 4 HMGs, 2 50mm mortars and 2 flamethrowers ea)
1 Heavy Weapons Company, with
1 Engineer Platoon
1 Panzerjäger Section (3 50mm PAK & 2 anti-tank rifles)
1 Infantry Support Gun Section (4 75mm leIG)
1 (mot) Infantry Support Gun Company (4 150mm sIG)

SS Das Reich Panzer Battalion
Regimental Staff

1st Battalion
Staff Panzer Company
1 Heavy (Tiger) Panzer Company
1 Medium Panzer Company
2 Light Panzer Companies
1 Armor Replacement Company
2nd Battalion
Staff Panzer Company
1 Medium Panzer Company
2 Light Panzer Companies
1 Armor Replacement Company

SS Langemark Reconnaissance Regiment
1 (mot) Staff Company
1 Signals Platoon
1 Panzerjäger Platoon (3 75mm PAK 40 & 3 LMGs)
1 Motorcycle Platoon (6 LMGs)
1 Self Propelled Flak Platoon (4 20mm guns)
1 Armored Car Copany (18 20mm & 24 LMGs)
1 (mot) Light Reconnaissance Suply Column
2 Reconnaissance Battalions, each with
2 (mot) Reconnaissance Companics (2 80mm mortars, 4 HMGs, 18 LMGs & 3 heavy anti-tank rifles)
1 (mot) Support Company
1 Pioneer Platoon (4 LMGs)
1 Panzerjäger Platoon (3 75mm PAK 40 & 3 LMGs)
1 Infantry Gun Platoon (4 75mm leIG)

SS Das Reich Flak Battalion
1 (mot) Staff Company (1 LMG)
1 Self Propelled Medium Flak Company (9 37mm guns)
3 (motZ) Heavy Flak Batteries (4 88mm, 3 20mm & 2 LMGs)
1 (mot) Light Flak Supply Column

SS Das Reich Artillery Regiment
1 Regimental Staff
1 Regimental Staff Battery
1st Battalion
1 Battalion Staff
1 Battalion Staff Battery (6 LMGs)
3 Self Propelled leFH Batteries (6 105mm leFH SdKfz 124 Wespe ea)
2nd & 3rd Battalion
Staff & Staff Battery (6 LMGs)
2 (motZ) Batteries (6 105mm leFH & 2 LMGs ea)
4th Battalion
Staff & Staff Battery (6 LMGs)
2 (motZ) Batteries (6 150mm sFH & 2 LMGs ea)
1 (motZ) Battery (6 105mm sK 18/40 guns & 2 LMGs ea)

SS Das Reich Signals Battalion
1st Panzer Telephone Company (6 LMGs)

2nd Panzer Radio Company (35 LMGs)

1 (mot) Light Signals Supply Column (4 LMGs)

SS Das Reich Pioneer Battalion

1 (halftrack) Pioneer Company (40 LMGs & 6 flamethrowers)

2 (mot) Pioneer Companies (18 LMGs & 2 flamethrowers ea)

1 (mot) Light Engineering Supply Column (2 LMGs)

1 (mot) "K" Bridging Column (2 LMGs)

1 (mot) Light Pioneer Supply Column (4 LMGs)

SS Das Reich Panzerjäger Battalion

1 (mot) Staff Section

1 (mot) Signals Platoon

1 Self Propelled Panzerjäger Company (9 75mm PAK & 6 LMGs)

2 (mot) Panzerjäger Companies (9 75mm PAK & 6 LMGs ea)

SS Das Reich Administrative Service

1 (mot) Bakery Company (4 LMGs)

1 (mot) Butcher Company (4 LMGs)

1 Divisional Administration (4 LMGs)

1 (mot) Field Post Office

SS Das Reich Medical Service

1st & 2nd SS (mot) Medical Company (2 LMGs)

1st SS (mot) Field Hospital (2 LMGs)

1st–3rd SS Ambulance Company (2 LMGs)

SS Das Reich Supply Service

9 SS (mot) Heavy Supply Columns (4 LMGs ea)

4 SS (mot) Heavy POL Company (4 LMGs ea)

1 SS (mot) Supply Company (2 LMGs)

1 SS (mot) Maintenance Company (2 LMGs)

SS Das Reich Maintenance Battalion

3 SS (mot) Maintenance Companies (2 LMGs ea)

1 SS (mot) Heavy Replacement Col (4 LMGs)

Other

SS (mot) Military Police Company

In February 1943 it was organized and equipped as follows:

1/,2/2nd SS Panzer Regiment
  1 Regimental Staff Signals Platoon
  1 Regimental Staff Light Panzer Platoon
  Each Battalion had:
    1 Panzer Staff Company
    1 Medium Panzer Company
    2 Light Panzer Companies
  4th Heavy Panzer Company

Mk II	10
Mk III (lg)	81
Mk IV (lg)	21
Mk VI	10
Cmd	9

On 5/1/43 the Das Reich Panzer Regiment was ordered to send men from one battalion back to Germany to form a new battalion equipped with Mk V Panther Tanks. One of the remaining battalions was organized with two medium and two light panzer companies. The third battalion was organized with two companies of captured T-34 tanks and one light panzer company. The Tiger company was authorized to have 15 Tigers. For the battle of Kursk the division had 104 tanks and 33 assault guns. Also included was a company of 14 Tiger tanks. On 7/1/43 the panzer inventory and organization of the panzer regiment were as follows:

2/2nd SS Panzer Regiment
  1 Panzer Staff Company
  2 Medium Panzer Companies
  2 Light Panzer Companies
2nd SS Panzerjäger Battalion
Heavy Panzer Company

Mk II	1
Mk III (lg)	62
Mk IV (lg)	33
Mk VI	14
T-34	25
Cmd	10

In August reinforcements arrived in the form of:

1/2nd SS Panzer Regiment
  1 Panzer Staff Company
  4 Medium Panzer Companies

Mk V	71

During the summer of 1943 the SS Schützen Regiment Langemark was disbanded. The 1st Battalion was used to strengthen the reconnaissance battalion to five companies and the 2nd was used to form a new Feldersatz Battalion. On 10/22/43 the division was renamed the 2nd SS Panzer Division "Das Reich."

1/,2/,3/3rd SS Panzergrenadier Regiment "Deutschland"

1/,2/,3/4th SS Panzergrenadier Regiment "Der Führer"

At the same time the other units in the division were given the number 2. The bulk of the division was withdrawn from combat on 12/4/43 and a kampfgruppe was organized that remained in combat. The 2nd SS Panzer Regiment was reduced to a battalion of three companies, one each of Mk IV, Mk V and Mk VI tanks. On 4/11/44 the kampfgruppe was withdrawn from combat and transferred to OB West where it was reincorporated into the re-forming division and rebuilt. The

1/2nd SS Panzer Regiment was equipped with four companies, 17 Panther tanks each. The 2nd Battalion was a mixed battalion, having two companies with 22 Mk IV tanks and two with 22 sturmgeschütz each. The 2nd battalion was restructured in June 1944 and one sturmgeschütz company was reequipped with Mk IV tanks. In May 1944 Das Reich was organized as follows:

Division
Division Staff
Divisional Escort Company
Motorcycle Platoon (6 LMGs)
Self Propelled Flak Battery (4 20mm guns)
Self Propelled Anti-Tank Platoon (3 LMGs & 3 75mm PAK 40)
Infantry Gun Platoon (2 75mm leIG)
Mixed Panzergrenadier Platoon (4 HMGs, 6 LMGs, & 2 80mm mortars)
2nd SS Panzer Regiment
Regimental Staff
Self Propelled Flak Battery (6 20mm guns)
1st Panzer Battalion
(1st–4th Companies) (68 Mk V Panthers total)
1 Panzer Maintenance Platoon
2nd Panzer Battalion
(5th–8th Companies) (66 Mk IV Panzers & 22 StuGs total)
1 Panzer Maintenance Company
1 Halftrack Pioneer Company (40 LMGs & 6 flamethrowers)
1 (mot) Panzer Supply Column
3rd "Deutschland" SS Panzergrenadier Regiment
Regimental Staff
1st Battalion
1st–3rd Companies (4 HMGs, 18 LMGs, 2 80mm mortars & 2 flamethrowers)
4th Company
1 Mortar Platoon (2 LMGs & 4 120mm mortars)
1 Panzerjäger Platoon (3 LMGs & 3 75mm PAK 40)
2 Infantry Gun Sections (1 LMG & 2 75mm leIG ea)
2nd Battalion (6th–10th Companies) (same as 1st Battalion)
3rd Battalion (11th–15th Companies) (same as 1st Battalion)
16th (self-propelled flak) Company (12 20mm & 4 LMGs)
17th (self-propelled infantry gun) Company (6 150mm sIG & 7 LMGs)
18th (mot) Pioneer Company (2 HMGs, 12 LMGs, 6 flamethrowers & 2 80mm mortars)

4th "Der Führer" SS Panzergrenadier Regiment
same as 3rd SS Panzergrenadier Regiment
2nd SS Reconnaissance Battalion
Battalion Staff
Heavy Platoon (6 SdKfz 234/3 with 75mm KwK & 6 LMGs)
1 Armored Car Company (18 20mm & 24 LMGs)
1 (halftrack) Armored Car Company (16 20mm & 25 LMGs)
2 (halftrack) Companies (49 LMGs, 2 80mm mortars & 3 75mm guns)
1 (halftrack) Company
1 Pioneer Platoon (13 LMGs & 6 flamethrowers)
1 Panzerjäger Platoon (8 LMGs & 3 75mm PAK 40)
1 Infantry Gun Section (2 75mm leIG & 4 LMGs)
1 Gun Section (8 LMGs & 6 75mm guns)
1 (mot) Reconnaissance Supply Column (3 LMGs)
2nd SS Panzerjäger Battalion
Battalion Staff
3 Self Propelled Panzerjäger Companies (14 75mm PAK 40 & 14 LMGs ea)
2nd SS Panzer Artillery Regiment
1 Regimental Staff & Staff Battery (2 LMGs)
1 Self Propelled Flak Battery (4 quad 20mm guns & 2 LMGs)
1st (Self Propelled) Battalion
Staff & (self-propelled) Staff Battery (6 LMGs)
2 Self Propelled leFH Batteries (6 105mm leFH SdKfz 124 Wespe & 2 LMGs ea)
1 Self Propelled sFH Battery (6 150mm sFH SdKfz 165 Hummel & 2 LMGs)
2nd Battalion
Staff & Staff Battery (2 LMGs)
2 (motZ) Batteries (6 105mm leFH & 2 LMGs ea)
3rd Battalion
same as 2nd Battalion
4th Battalion
Staff & Staff Battery (2 LMGs)
2 (motZ) Batteries (6 150mm sFH & 2 LMGs ea)
1 (motZ) Battery (6 105mm sK 18/40 guns & 2 LMGs ea)
2nd SS Flak Battalion
Staff & Staff Battery
3 (motZ) heavy Flak Batteries (4 88mm, 3 20mm & 2 LMGs ea)
1 (motZ) Medium Flak Batteries (9 37mm & 4 LMGs ea)
1 (motZ) Searchlight Platoon (4 600mm searchlights)
2nd SS Panzer Pioneer Battalion
Staff (2 LMGs)
1 (halftrack) Pioneer Company (2 HMGs, 46 LMGs, 3 heavy anti-tank rifles, 2 80mm mortars & 6 flamethrowers)

2 (mot) Pioneer Companies (2 HMGs, 18 LMGs, 2
80mm mortars & 6 flamethrowers)
1 (mot) Heavy Panzer Bridging Train (5 LMGs)
1 (mot) Light Panzer Bridging Train (3 LMGs)
2nd SS Panzer Signals Battalion
1 Panzer Telephone Company (14 LMGs)
1 Panzer Radio Company (20 LMGs)
1 (mot) Signals Supply Column (1 LMG)
2nd SS Feldersatz Battalion
5 Companies
2nd SS Supply Troop
1–7th/2nd SS (mot) 120 ton Transportation Companies (8 LMGs ea)
5/2nd SS (mot) 20 ton Light Flak Supply Column
2nd SS (mot) Workshop Company (4 LMGs)
2nd SS (mot) Supply Company (8 LMGs)
2nd SS Truck Park
1/,2/,3/2nd SS (mot) Maintenance Companies (4
LMGs)
2nd SS (mot) 75 ton Heavy Maintenance Supply
Column
Medical
1/,2/2nd SS (mot) Medical Companies (2 LMGs ea)
1/,2/,3/2nd SS Ambulances
Administration
2nd SS (mot) Bakery Company (6 LMGs)
2nd SS (mot) Butcher Company (6 LMGs)
2nd SS (mot) Divisional Administration Platoon (2
LMGs)
2nd SS (mot) Military Police Troop (5 platoons) (15
LMGs)
2nd SS (mot) Field Post Office (2 LMGs)

Before the June 1944 allied landings in Normandy the
2nd SS Panzer Regiment and its panzer inventory were
as follows:

2nd SS Panzer Regiment
1 Panzer Staff Platoon
1 Panzer Flak Platoon
1 Battalion
1 Panzer Staff Company
4 Medium Panzer Companies (Mk V)
1 Battalion
1 Panzer Staff Company
4 Medium Panzer Companies (Mk IV)

Mk IV (lg)	78
Mk V	79
StuG	13
Flakpz38	12

The division was heavily damaged in Normandy during
June–July 1944. It was later withdrawn and rebuilt in
October/November 1944. On 12/10/44 the panzer
inventory and organization of the 2nd SS Panzer Regiment were as follows:

1/,2/2nd SS Panzer Regiment
1 Panzer Staff Company
1 Battalion
1 Panzer Staff Company
4 Medium Panzer Companies (Mk V)
1 Battalion
1 Panzer Staff Company
2 Medium Panzer Companies (Mk IV)
2 Sturmgescütz Companies (StuG)

StuG	28
Mk IV (lg)	28
Mk V	58
FlakpzIV (2V)	4
FlakpzIV (37)	4

The division surrendered to the Americans in 1945.

2nd (mot) Brigade Reichsführer SS

This brigade was formed on 1 May 1941 form the 4th,
5th, and 14th Totenkopf Regiments. It was intended as
a line of communications, security unit. It was reorganized into a combat formation on 5/7/41. On 1/10/41
the brigade was organized as follows:

Headquarters
1 Motorcycle Messenger Platoon
4th & 14th (mot) SS Infantry Regiment, each with
Headquarters
1 (mot) Signals Platoon
1 Motorcycle Messenger Platoon

1 (mot) Pioneer Platoon (3 LMGs)
1 Regimental Band
1st, 2nd & 3rd Battalions, each with
3 (mot) Rifle Companies (9 LMGs, 2 HMGs &
2 50mm mortars ea)
1 (mot) Machine Gun Company (8 HMGs & 3
80mm mortars)
1 (mot) Infantry Gun Section (2 75mm leIG)
1 (mot) Panzerabwehr Company (12 37mm PAK
36 & 4 LMGs)
1 (mot) Flak Company (12 20mm flak guns)
1 (mot) Light Infantry Column

1 (mot) Mixed Signals Company
1 (mot) Maintenance Platoon
1 (mot) Medical Company
1 (mot) Ambulance
1 (mot) Military Police Detachment
1 (mot) Field Post Office

On 6/25/41 it was assigned to the XXXXII Corps, 9th Army. The brigade had:

Headquarters
1 Brigade Headquarters
1 (mot) Signals Detachment
1 Motorcycle Platoon (3 LMGs)
4th, 5th, & 14th SS Reichsführer Infantry Regiments
(mot) Infantry Regiment Headquarters
(mot) Headquarters Company
  Company Headquarters
  Signals Platoon
  Motorcycle Platoon
  Pioneer Platoon (3 LMGs)
(mot) Infantry Gun Company
  3 Light Infantry Gun Platoons (2 75mm leIG guns ea)
  1 Heavy Infantry Gun Platoon (2 150mm sIG guns)

Light (mot) Panzerjäger Company (4 LMGs & 12 37mm PAK 36)
Motorcycle Platoon (3 LMGs)
2 (mot) Infantry Battalions
  1 (mot) Battalion Headquarters
  3 (mot) Infantry Companies (12 LMGs & 3 50mm mortars ea)
  1 (mot) Machine Gun Company (12 HMGs & 6 80mm mortars)
52nd SS Artillery Battery (6 150mm sFH)
52nd SS (mot) Flak Company (12 20mm flak guns)
52nd SS Pioneer Company (9 LMGs)
52nd Signals Company

The 14th Regiment was disbanded in the summer of 1941. The 5th Regiment was disbanded in the winter. On 6/30/41 the brigade was disbanded. In December 1941 the 4th Regiment was redesignated as the SS Infantry Regiment Langemark and absorbed into the "Das Reich" Division.

The brigade was re-formed in 1942 with the SS Freiwilligen Legion Nederlande, Flanders, and Begleit (Escort) Battalions RFSS. Later it was renamed the 2nd SS (mot) Infantry Brigade. On 18 May 1943 it became the Lettish SS Freiwilligen Brigade.

Lettish Freiwilligen Legion

Formed on 2/26/43 for all Lettish SS Freiwilligen Units, on 18 May it was organized into the Lettish SS Freiwilligen Division and the Lettisch Freiwilligen Brigade. It had:

1/,2/,3/1st Lettish SS Freiwilligen Regiment (former 4th Regiment)
1/,2/,3/2nd Lettish SS Freiwilligen Regiment (former 5th Regiment)
1/,2/,3/3rd Lettish SS Freiwilligen Regiment
1/,2/,3/4th Lettish SS Freiwilligen Regiment
1/,2/,3/5th Lettish SS Freiwilligen Regiment
Lettish SS Bicycle Battalion, Lettish Legion (became 15th SS Bicycle Battalion, Lettish Division)
1st Lettish SS Artillery Regiment, Lettish Legion (became 15th SS Artillery Regiment)
Panzerjäger Battalion, Lettish Legion (became 15th SS Panzerjäger Battalion)
Signals Battalion, Lettish Legion (became 15th SS Signals Battalion)

Pioneer Battalion, Lettish Legion (became 15th SS Pioneer Battalion)
Medical Battalion, Lettish Legion (became 15th SS Medical Battalion)
Supply Troop, Lettish Legion (became 15th SS Supply Troop)

The 1st Lettish Regiment was to become the 1st Regiment of the Lettish Division, then the 32nd SS Freiwilligen Grenadier Regiment. The 2nd and 3rd Regiments went through the same evolution and eventually became the 33rd and 34th SS Freiwilligen Grenadier Regiments. The 4th and 5th Regiments would become the 1st and 2nd Regiments of the Lettish Brigade, respectively, then the 42nd and 43rd SS Freiwilligen Grenadier Regiments, respectively.

2nd Lettish Freiwilligen-Brigade

Reorganized on 10/22/43 with:

Brigade Staff
  1 Motorcycle Platoon (6 LMGs)
  1 (mot) "KB" Platoon
42nd Lettish SS Freiwilligen Grenadier Regiment
  (former 1st)
  1 Regimental Staff
  1 Regimental Staff Company
    1 Signals Platoon
    1 Pioneer Platoon (3 LMGs)
    1 Bicycle Platoon
  1st, 2nd & 3rd Battalion, each with
    3 Rifle Companies (12 LMGs, 2 heavy anti-tank rifles, 2 80mm mortars ea)
    1 Machine Gun Company (12 HMGS & 4 120mm mortars)
    1 Infantry Gun Company (2 150mm sIG & 6 75mm leIG)
    1 (motZ) Anti-Tank Company (9 75mm PAK 40 & 6 LMGs)
    1 Pioneer Company (9 LMGs & 2 80mm mortars)
43rd Lettish SS Freiwilligen Grenadier Regiment
  (former 2nd)
  same as 1st Regiment
Flak Battalion
  1 Staff & (mot) Staff Battery (1 LMG)
  1 Self Propelled Light Flak Company (12 20mm flak guns)
  1 Self Propelled Medium Flak Company (9 37mm flak guns)

  1 (motZ) Heavy Flak Company (4 88mm guns, 3 20mm guns & 3 LMGs)
Artillery Battalion
  1 Battalion Staff & Staff Battery
  3 Batteries (4 105mm leFH & 2 LMGs ea)
Support Units
  1 (mot) Signals Company
  1 (mot) Medical Company (2 LMGs)
  1 (mot) Ambulance (1 LMG)
  1 (mot) Military Police Troop (2 LMGs)
  1 (mot) Field Post Office
  1 (mot) 120 ton Transportation Company (8 LMGs) (replaced by (horse drawn) Heavy Supply Column)
  2 (horse drawn) Heavy Supply Column
  1 (mot) Maintenance Company
  1 Veterinary Company

The brigade support units were numbered 52. In the winter 1943/44 the brigade organized two training regiments:

1/,2/,3/1st Ausbildung (Training) Regiment
1/,2/,3/2nd Ausbildung (Training) Regiment

On 1/7/44 the 2nd Lettish SS Freiwilligen Brigade was reorganized into the 19th (Lettish) SS Freiwilligen Division.

SS Totenkopf Division (SS-TK)

Formed on 10/16/39 in Dachau, it contained:

1st SS Totenkopf (mot) Infantry Regiment
  1st Battalion (1–4th Companies)
  2nd Battalion (5–8th Companies)
  3rd Battalion (9–12th Companies)
  13th–14th Companies
2nd SS Totenkopf (mot) Infantry Regiment
  1st Battalion (1–4th Companies)
  2nd Battalion (5–8th Companies)
  3rd Battalion (9–12th Companies)
  13th–14th Companies
3rd SS Totenkopf (mot) Infantry Regiment

  1st Battalion (1–4th Companies)
  2nd Battalion (5–8th Companies)
  3rd Battalion (9–12th Companies)
  13th–14th Companies
SS Totenkopf Reconnaissance Battalion
  (2 motorcycle companies & 1 armored car platoon)
SS Totenkopf Panzerabwehr (Anti-Tank) Battalion
  (3 companies)
1/,2/,3/SS Totenkopf Artillery Regiment (3 batteries per battalion)
SS Totenkopf Pioneer Battalion (3 companies)
SS Totenkopf Signals Battalion (2 companies)

During the winter the division added the 4/SS Totenkopf Artillery Regiment, which was a heavy battalion. Among the other things added were a panzerjäger company and a flak company to each of the infantry regiments. There are also indications that a motorcycle reconnaissance company was added. In 1942 it added the SS Totenkopf Feldersatz Battalion and the SS Totenkopf Flak Battalion. On 5/10/40 the SS Totenkopf (mot) Division was organized and equipped as follows:

Division Staff
  1 Divisional Staff (2 HMGs)
  1 (mot) SS Divisional Mapping Detachment
3 (mot) Infantry Regiments, each with
  Regimental Staff Company, with
    1 (mot) Signals Platoon
    1 (mot) Engineer Platoon (3 LMGs)
    1 (mot) Motorcycle Platoon (4 LMGs)
  3 (mot) Battalions, each with
    3 (mot) Infantry Companies (12 LMGs & 3 50mm mortars ea)
    1 (mot) Machine Gun Company, with
      (12 HMGs & 6 80mm mortars)
    1 (mot) Infantry Support Gun Company (2 150mm sIG & 6 75mm leIG)
    1 (mot) Panzerjäger Company (12 37mm PAK 36 & 6 LMGs)
    1 Light (mot) Supply Column (later eliminated)
SS Totenkopf Panzerjäger Battalion
  1 (mot) Signals Platoon
  3 (mot) Panzerjäger Companies (9 37mm PAK 36, 2 50mm PAK 38 & 6 LMGs)
  3rd Panzerjäger Company later equipped with (3 50mm PAK 38, 8 37mm PAK 36 & 6 LMGs)
SS Totenkopf Reconnaissance Battalion
  1 (mot) Signals Platoon
  2 Motorcycle Companies (3 50mm mortars, 2 HMGs, & 18 LMGs ea)
  1 (mot) Support Company, with
    1 Light Armored Car Platoon (1 HMG & 3 LMGs)
    1 Panzerjäger Platoon (3 37mm PAK 36 & 1 LMG)
    1 Mortar Platoon (6 80mm mortars)
    1 Infantry Support Gun Section (2 75mm leIG guns)

  1 Engineer Platoon (3 LMGs)
SS Totenkopf Artillery Regiment
  1 (mot) Signals Platoon
  2 (mot) Weather Detachments
  3 (mot) Battalions, each with
    1 (mot) Signals Platoon
    1 (mot) Calibration Detachment
    3 (motZ) Batteries (4 105mm leFH 18 & 2 LMGs)
  1 (mot) Battalion
    1 (mot) Signals Platoon
    1 (mot) Calibration Detachment
    3 (motZ) Batteries (4 150mm sFH 18 & 2 LMGs)
SS Totenkopf Signals Battalion
  1 (mot) Radio Company
  1 (mot) Telephone Company
  1 Light (mot) Signals Supply Column
SS Totenkopf Feldersatz Battalion
  3 Companies
SS Totenkopf Pioneer Battalion
  3 (mot) Pioneer Companies (9 LMGs ea)
  1 (mot) "B" Bridging Train
  1 Light (mot) Engineering Supply Column
Supply Train
  1st–5th Light (mot) Supply Columns
  6th–7th Heavy (mot) Supply Columns
  13th–15th Light (mot) Supply Columns (added later)
  10th–12th Heavy (mot) POL Supply Columns
  1st, 2nd, & 3rd (mot) Maintenance Companies
  SST (mot) Supply Company
Commissary Service
  SST (mot) Bakery Platoon (later Company)
  SST (mot) Butcher Platoon (later Company)
  SST (mot) Division Administration
Medical Service
  1st–3rd SST Ambulance Columns
  SST (mot) Field Hospital
  1st & 2nd SST Medical Companies
Other
  SST (mot) Military Police Platoon
  SST (mot) Field Post Office

On 22 April 1941 the division contained:

1st SS Infantry
  1st–3rd Battalions
  13th Company
  14th Company
  15th Company
  16th Company
2nd SS Infantry
  1st–3rd Battalions
  13th Company
  14th Company
  15th Company

Regiment Reconnaissance Battalion
Artillery Regiment
  1st (light) Battalion
  2nd (light) Battalion
  3rd (light) Battalion
  4th (heavy) Battalion
Regiment Sturmgeschütz Battery
Panzerjäger Battalion
Flak Battalion
Pioneer Battalion
Signals Battalion

3rd SS Infantry Regiment
   1st–3rd Battalions
   13th Company
   14th Company
   15th Company
   16th Company

Supply Troop
Divisional Administration
Medical Service
Intendant Service
Military Police Detachment
Field Post Office

On 5/16/41 a new organization was issued for the division that remained in effect until 10/15/42. That organization was as follows:

Divisional Staff
   1 Divisional Staff (4 HMGs)
   1 (mot) Mapping Platoon
2 (mot) Infantry Regiments, each with
   1 (mot) Regimental Staff Company, with
      1 Signals Platoon
      1 Motorcycle Platoon (6 LMGs)
      1 Panzerjäger Platoon (3 50mm PAK 38 & 2 LMGs)
   3 (mot) Battalions, each with
      3 Infantry Companies, each with (18 LMGs, 4 HMGs, 2 80mm mortars & 2 flamethrowers)
      1 Support Company with
         1 Engineer Platoon (4 LMGs)
         1 Panzerjäger Section (3 50mm PAK 38 guns)
         1 Infantry Support Gun Platoon (4 75mm leIG & 3 28mm sPzBu 41 guns)
   1 (mot) Infantry Support Company (4 75mm leIG)
SS Totenkopf Armored Troop, with
   1 Armored Staff Company
   1 Medium Armored Company
   2 Light Armored Companies
   1 Armored Maintenance Platoon
SS Totenkopf Motorcycle (Volkswagen) Regiment
   1 (mot) Staff & Staff Company, with
      1 Signals Platoon
      1 Motorcycle Platoon (6 LMGs)
      1 Panzerjäger Platoon (3 50mm PAK 38 & 2 LMGs)
   2 (mot) Battalions, each with
      1 (mot) Staff Platoon
      3 (mot) Infantry Companies (18 LMGs, 4 HMGs, 2 50mm mortars ea)
      1 (mot) Heavy Machine Gun Company (12 HMGs & 6 80mm mortars)
      1 (mot) Support Company, with
         1 Engineer Platoon (4 LMGs)
         1 Panzerjäger Section (3 50mm PAK 38 guns & 2 LMGs)
         1 Infantry Support Gun Section (2 75mm leIG)
SS Totenkopf Artillery Regiment
   Regimental Staff

1 (mot) Staff Battery
1 (mot) Observation Battery
1st–3rd (mot) Artillery Battalions, each with
   1 (mot) Battalion Staff Battery
   3 (motZ) Batteries (3 105mm leFH 18 & 2 LMGs ea)
4th (mot) Artillery Battalion
   1 (mot) Battalion Staff Battery
   2 (motZ) Batteries (3 150mm sFH 18 & 2 LMGs ea)
   1 (motZ) Battery (3 100mm K18 guns & 2 LMGs)
5th (mot) Flak Battalion
   1 (mot) Battalion Staff Battery
   1 Self Propelled Flak Battery (8 20mm & 2 quad 20mm AA)
   1 Self Propelled Flak Battery (9 37mm guns)
   1 (motZ) Flak Battery (4 88mm guns & 3 20mm guns)
   1 Light (mot) Supply Column
SS Totenkopf Reconnaissance Battalion
   1 Armored Car Company (18 50mm PAK 38 & 24 LMGs)
   1 Motorcycle Company (2 80mm mortars, 4 HMGs, & 18 LMGs)
   1 (mot) Company, with
      1 Engineer Platoon (4 LMGs)
      1 Self Propelled Section (3 50mm PAK 38 guns)
      1 Infantry Support Gun Platoon (2 75mm leIG)
   1 (mot) Light Reconnaissance Supply Column
SS Totenkopf Panzerjäger Battalion
   1 Self Propelled Panzerjäger Company (9 75mm PAK 40 & 6 LMGs)
   2 (motZ) Panzerjäger Companies (9 75mm & 6 LMGs)
SS Totenkopf Signals Battalion
   1 (mot) Radio Company (4 LMGs)
   1 (mot) Telephone Company (4 LMGs)
   1 (mot) Light Signals Supply Column (2 LMGs)
SS Totenkopf Pioneer Battalion
   3 (mot) Pioneer Companies (18 LMGs & 2 flamethrowers ea)
   1 (mot) Light "B" Bridging Train (2 LMGs)
   1 (mot) Light Supply Column
Commissary
   1 (mot) Division Administration (2 LMGs)

1 (mot) Butcher Company (2 LMGs)
1 (mot) Bakery Company (2 LMGs)

Supply Train
12 (mot) Light Supply Columns (2 LMGs ea)
3 (mot) Light Fuel Supply Columns (2 LMGs ea)
3 (mot) Maintenance Companies (2 LMGs ea)
1 (mot) Light Supply Company (2 LMGs)

Medical
2 (mot) Medical Companies (2 LMGs ea)
1 (mot) Field Hospital (2 LMGs)
3 Ambulance Companies (2 LMGs ea)

Other
1 (mot) Military Police Company
1 (mot) Field Post
1 (mot) SS "KB" Platoon

Apparently during the combat in Russia it was very heavily committed early in the campaign. On 6/28/41 one of the two infantry regiments was so heavily damaged in combat around the Dünaburg bridgehead that it was temporarily disbanded. On 3/6/42 it was organized like the SS Das Reich Division, the 3rd SS Tank Regiment was formed, as was the SS Totenkopf Motorcycle Battalion. The motorcycle battalion was formed from the 3/9th SS Infantry Regiment. On 24 April 1942 the division was organized and equipped as follows:

Divisional Staff
1 Divisional Staff (4 HMGs)
1 (mot) Mapping Platoon

2 (mot) Infantry Regiments, each with
1 Signals Platoon
1 Motorcycle Platoon (6 LMGs)
1 Panzerjäger Platoon (3 75mm PAK 40 & 2 LMGs)
3 (mot) Battalions, each with
3 Infantry Companies, each with (18 LMGs, 4 HMGs, 2 80mm mortars & 2 flamethrowers)
1 Support Company with
1 Engineer Platoon (4 LMGs)
1 Panzerjäger Section (3 75mm PAK 40 guns)
1 Panzerjäger Section (3 28mm PzB 41 guns)
1 Infantry Support Gun Platoon (4 75mm leIG)
1 (mot) Infantry Support Company (4 105mm sIG)

SS Totenkopf Armored Troop, with
1 Armored Staff Company
1 Medium Armored Company
2 Light Armored Companies
1 Armored Maintenance Platoon

SS Totenkopf Motorcycle Battalion
1 (mot) Staff
3 (mot) Reconnaissance Companies (2 80mm mortars, 4 HMGs, & 18 LMGs)
1 (mot) Machine Gun Company (6 80mm Mortars & HMGs)

1 (mot) Reconnaissance Company
1 Infantry Gun Platoon (2 75mm leIG)
1 Panzerjäger Platoon (3 75mm PAK 40 & 2 LMGs)
1 Pioneer Platoon (3 LMGs)

SS Totenkopf Artillery Regiment
Regimental Staff
1 (mot) Staff Battery
1 (mot) Observation Battery
1st–3rd (mot) Artillery Battalions, each with
1 (mot) Battalion Staff Battery
3 (motZ) Batteries (3 105mm leFH 18 & 2 LMGs ea)
4th (mot) Artillery Battalion
1 (mot) Battalion Staff Battery
2 (motZ) Batteries (3 150mm sFH 18 & 2 LMGs ea)
1 (motZ) Battery (3 100mm K18 guns & 2 LMGs)

SS Totenkopf (mot) Flak Battalion
1 (mot) Battalion Staff Battery
1 Self Propelled Flak Battery (8 20mm & 2 quad 20mm AA)
1 Self Propelled Flak Battery (9 37mm guns)
1 (motZ) Flak Battery (4 88mm guns & 3 self-propelled 20mm guns)
1 (mot) Light Flak Supply Column

SS Totenkopf Reconnaissance Battalion
1 (mot) Signals Platoon
1 Armored Car Company (18 50mm PAK 38 & 24 LMGs)
1 Motorcycle Company (2 80mm mortars, 4 HMGs, & 18 LMGs)
1 (mot) Company, with
1 Engineer Platoon (4 LMGs)
1 Panzerjäger Section (3 75mm PAK 40 guns)
1 Infantry Gun Platoon (2 75mm leIG)
1 (mot) Light Reconnaissance Supply Column

SS Totenkopf Panzerjäger Battalion
1 Self Propelled Panzerjäger Company (9 75mm PAK 40 & 6 LMGs)
2 (motZ) Panzerjäger Companies (9 75mm & 6 LMGs)

SS Totenkopf Signals Battalion
1 (mot) Radio Company (4 LMGs)
1 (mot) Telephone Company (4 LMGs)
1 (mot) Light Signals Supply Column (2 LMGs)

SS Totenkopf Pioneer Battalion
3 (mot) Pioneer Companies (18 LMGs & 2 flamethrowers ea)
1 (mot) Light "B" Bridging Train (2 LMGs)
1 (mot) Light Supply Column (2 LMGs)

Commissary
1 (mot) Division Administration (2 LMGs)

1 (mot) Butcher Company (2 LMGs)
1 (mot) Bakery Company (2 LMGs)
Supply Train
 12 (mot) Light Supply Columns (2 LMGs ea)
 3 (mot) Light Fuel Supply Columns (2 LMGs ea)
 3 (mot) Maintenance Companies (2 LMGs ea)
 1 (mot) Light Supply Company (2 LMGs)
Medical
 2 (mot) Medical Companies (2 LMGs ea)
 1 (mot) Field Hospital (2 LMGs)
 3 Ambulance Companies (2 LMGs ea)

Other
 1 (mot) Military Police Company
 1 (mot) Field Post
 1 (mot) SS "KB" Platoon

On 8/1/42 it added the Thule Schützen Regiment as a fast regiment. After heavy losses in Russia, it was moved to France for refitting. On 11/9/42 it was reorganized into the SS Totenkopf Panzergrenadier Division.

3rd SS Panzer Division "Totenkopf"

Formed on 11/9/42 in South France by the 1st Army as the "SS Panzergrenadier Division "Totenkopf" from the SS Totenkopf (mot) Division. When organized it consisted of:

1/,2/,3/1st SS Panzergrenadier Regiment "Totenkopf"
1/,2/,3/3rd SS Panzergrenadier Regiment "Totenkopf"
1/,2/3rd SS Panzer Regiment "Totenkopf" (from the battalion formed in the Summer of 1943).
SS Totenkopf Reconnaissance Battalion (4 companies)
1/,2/,3/,4/SS Totenkopf Artillery Regiment
SS Totenkopf Panzerjäger Battalion (3 companies)
SS Totenkopf Flak Battalion (4 batteries)
SS Totenkopf Sturmgeschütz Battalion (4 batteries)
SS Totenkopf Pioneer Battalion (3 companies)
SS Totenkopf Signals Battalion (2 companies)

The Thule Schützen Regiment was absorbed into the 1st SS Panzergrenadier Regiment "Totenkopf." The two panzer grenadier regiments were named the 1st SS Panzergrenadier Regiment "Thule" and the 3rd SS Panzergrenadier Regiment "Theodor Eicke." In February 1943 the 3rd SS Panzer Regiment was organized and equipped as follows:

1/,2/3rd SS Panzer Regiment
 1 Regimental Staff Signals Platoon
 1 Regimental Staff Light Panzer Platoon
 Each Battalion had:
  1 Panzer Staff Company
  1 Medium Panzer Company
  2 Light Panzer Companies
 4th Heavy Panzer Company

Mk III (lg)	71
Mk III (75)	10
Mk IV (lg)	22
Mk VI	9

On 5/1/43 the 3rd SS Panzer Regiment was reorganized such that its battalions each had two medium and one light panzer company. In the summer of 1943 the reconnaissance battalion was reinforced to six companies and the panzer regiment was reinforced to eight companies. For the battle of Kursk the division had 114 tanks and 28 assault guns. Included was a company of 11 Tiger tanks. On 7/1/43 the panzer inventory and organization of the 3rd SS Panzer Regiment was as follows:

1/,2/3rd SS Panzer Regiment
 1 Regimental Staff Signals Platoon
 1 Regimental Staff Light Panzer Platoon
 Each Battalion had
  1 Panzer Staff Company
  2 Medium Panzer Companies
  1 Light Panzer Company
 9th Heavy Panzer Company

Mk III (lg)	63
Mk IV (kz)	8
Mk IV (lg)	44
Mk VI	15
Cmd	9

On 10/21/43 the division was reorganized by the order of the Führer as a Panzer Division. On 10/22/43 the division was given the number 3 and the panzer grenadier regiments were renumbered the 5th SS Panzergrenadier Regiment "Thule" and the 6th SS Panzergrenadier Regiment "Theodor Eicke." All other portions of the division were numbered "3rd." In December 1943 the Panzerjäger Battalion was disbanded and the sturmgeschütz battalion was rebuilt.

5th SS Panzergrenadier Regiment "Thule"
 1st Battalion (1–4th Companies)
 2nd Battalion (5–8th Companies)

3rd Battalion (9–12th Companies)
13th Company
14th Company
16th Company
6th SS Panzergrenadier Regiment "Theodor Eicke"
same as 5th SS Panzergrenadier Regiment
3rd Panzer Regiment
1st Battalion (1–4th Companies)
2nd Battalion (5–8th Companies)
Heavy Company
Pioneer Company
3rd Artillery Regiment
1st (self-propelled) Battalion (1–3rd Companies)
2nd Battalion (4–6th Companies)
3rd Battalion (7–9th Companies)
4th Battalion (10–12th Companies)
3rd Reconnaissance Battalion (5 companies)
3rd Sturmgeschütz Battalion (4 batteries)
3rd SS Flak Battalion (4 batteries & observation battery)
3rd Pioneer Battalion (3 companies)
3rd Signals Battalion (2 companies)

In July 1944 the division was organized and equipped as follows:

Division Staff
1 Divisional Staff (2 LMGs)
1 Divisional Band
1 (mot) Mapping Detachment
(mot) Military Police Detachment (15 LMGs)
1 (mot) Escort Company
1 Self Propelled Flak Battery (4 20mm flak, 4 HMGs & 6 LMGs)
1 Motorcycle Platoon (6 LMGs)
Totenkopf SS Panzer Regiment
1 Regimental Staff & (mot) Staff Company
1 Panzer Signals Platoon
1 Panzer Platoon
1 Panzer Flak Battery (8 37mm flak guns)
1 Panzer Maintenance Company (4 LMGs)
1st Panzer Battalion
1 Battalion Staff (1 LMG)
1 Battalion Staff Company (11 LMGs)
4 Panzer Companies (22 Mk V Panther Tanks ea)
1 (mot) Supply Company (4 LMGs)
2nd Panzer Battalion
1 Battalion Staff (1 LMG)
1 Battalion Staff Company (11 LMGs)
4 Panzer Companies (22 Mk IV Tanks ea)
1 (mot) Supply Company (4 LMGs)
1st Totenkopf SS Panzergrenadier Regiment
1 Regimental Staff & (mot) Staff Company
1 Staff Platoon (1 LMG)

1 Signals Platoon (7 LMGs)
1 Motorcycle Platoon (4 LMGs)
1st (halftrack) Battalion
1 Battalion Staff (6 LMGs)
1 (mot) Supply Company (4 LMGs)
3 (halftrack) Panzergrenadier Companies (4 HMGs, 29 LMGs, 2 80mm mortars, 6 20mm & 2 75mm leIG)
1 (halftrack) Heavy Panzergrenadier Company
1 Mortar Platoon (2 LMGs & 4 120mm mortars)
1 Gun Platoon (6 75mm & 4 LMGs)
2nd Battalion
1 Battalion Staff
1 (mot) Supply Company (4 LMGs)
3 (mot) Panzergrenadier Companies (4 HMGs, 18 LMGs & 2 80mm mortars)
1 (mot) Heavy Panzergrenadier Company
1 Mortar Platoon (2 LMGs & 4 120mm mortars)
1 Gun Platoon (6 75mm & 4 LMGs)
3rd Battalion
same as 2nd Battalion
1 Self Propelled Heavy Infantry Gun Company
(6 150mm sIG)
1 Self Propelled Flak Company
(12 20mm & 2 LMGs)
1 (mot) Pioneer Company
1 (mot) Pioneer Staff Platoon (1 LMG)
1 (halftrack) Pioneer Platoon (12 LMGs, 1 20mm & 6 flamethrowers)
1 (mot) Pioneer Platoon (8 LMGs & 12 flamethrowers)
1 (mot) Pioneer Platoon (2 HMGs & 2 80mm mortars)
1 (halftrack) Pioneer Platoon (6 LMGs & 6 flamethrowers)
2nd Totenkopf SS Panzergrenadier Regiment
1 Regimental Staff & (mot) Staff Company
1 Staff Platoon (1 LMG)
1 Signals Platoon (7 LMGs)
1 Motorcycle Platoon (4 LMGs)
1st (mot) Battalion
1 Battalion Staff
1 (mot) Supply Company (4 LMGs)
3 (mot) Panzergrenadier Companies (4 HMGs, 18 LMGs & 2 80mm mortars)
1 (mot) Heavy Panzergrenadier Company
1 Mortar Platoon (2 LMGs & 4 120mm mortars)
1 Gun Platoon (6 75mm & 4 LMGs)
2nd & 3rd (mot) Battalions
same as 1st Battalion
1 Self Propelled Heavy Infantry Gun Company
(6 150mm sIG)
1 Self Propelled Flak Company
(12 20mm & 2 LMGs)

1 (mot) Pioneer Company
(2 HMGs, 12 LMGS, 2 80mm mortars & 18 flamethrowers)

Totenkopf SS Panzerjäger Battalion
1 Battalion Staff & Staff Platoon (1 LMG & 1 jagdpanzer IV)
2 Jagdpanzer Companies (14 Jagdpanzer IV)
1 (motZ) Panzerjäger Company (12 75mm PAK & 12 LMGs)
1 (mot) Supply Company (3 LMGs)

Totenkopf SS Panzer Reconnaissance Battalion
1 Battalion Staff (3 LMGs)
1 Battalion Staff Company
   1 Armored Car Platoon (3 75mm, 13 20mm & 16 LMGs)
   1 (mot) Signals Platoon (7 LMGs)
1 Armored Car Company (16 20mm & 25 LMGs)
1 (halftrack) Reconnaissance Company (2 75mm, 2 80mm mortars, & 44 LMGs)
1 (halftrack) Reconnaissance Company (4 HMGs, 29 LMGs, 2 80mm mortars, 6 20mm & 2 75mm guns)
1 (halftrack) Reconnaissance Company
   1 Staff Platoon (2 LMGs)
   1 Panzerjäger Platoon (6 75mm, 2 LMGs)
   1 Platoon (2 LMGs & 6 80mm mortars)
   1 Pioneer Platoon (13 LMGs)
1 Supply Company (4 LMGs)

Totenkopf SS Artillery Regiment
1 Regimental Staff & (mot) Staff Battery (2 LMGs)
   1 Self Propelled Flak Battery (4 quad 20mm guns)
1st Self Propelled Battalion
   1 Battalion Staff & Staff Battery (2 LMGs)
   2 Self Propelled Batteries (6 150mm sFH SdKfz 165 Hummel)
   1 Self Propelled Battery (6 105mm leFH SdKfz 124 Wespe ea)
2nd & 3rd Battalions, each with
   1 Battalion Staff & Staff Battery (2 LMGs)
   2 (motZ) Batteries (6 105mm leFH & 6 LMGs ea)
4th Battalion
   1 Battalion Staff & Staff Battery (2 LMGs)
   2 (motZ) Batteries (6 150mm sFH & 6 LMGs ea)
   1 (motZ) Battery (6 105mm K & 6 LMGs ea)

Totenkopf SS Flak Battalion
1 Battalion Staff & Staff Battery (1 LMG)
3 (motZ) Heavy Batteries (4 88mm, 3 20mm & 4 LMGs)
1 (motZ) Medium Battery (9 37mm & 4 LMGs)
1 (mot) Searchlight Battery (4 600mm searchlights)

Totenkopf SS Pioneer Battalion
1 Battalion Staff (2 LMGs)
1 (mot) Battalion Staff Company (6 LMGs)
1 (halftrack) Reconnaissance Platoon (8 LMGs)
1 (halftrack) Pioneer Company (2 HMGs, 46 LMGs, 6 flamethrowers, & 2 80mm mortars)
2 (mot) Pioneer Companies (2 HMGs, 18 LMGs, 6 flamethrowers, & 2 80mm mortars ea)
1 (mot) Light Panzer Bridging Train (3 LMGs)

Totenkopf SS Signals Battalion
1 Panzer Telephone Company (14 LMGs)
1 Panzer Radio Company (20 LMGs)
1 (mot) Supply Column (1 LMG)

Feldersatz Battalion
2–5 Companies

Supply Troop
1 (tmot) Supply Battalion Staff (2 LMGs)
6 (mot) 120 ton Transportation Companies (8 LMGs ea)
1 (mot) Supply Company (8 LMGs)
1 (mot) Ordnance Company (4 LMGs)
2 (mot) Maintenance Companies (5 LMGs ea)
1 (mot) Maintenance Company (4 LMGs)
1 (mot) Maintenance Supply Column (4 LMGs)

Other
1 (mot) Bakery Company (5 LMGs)
1 (mot) Butcher Company (4 LMGs)
1 (mot) Divisional Administration Platoon (2 LMGs)
2 (mot) Medical Companies (4 LMGs ea)
1 (mot) Decontamination Company
3 Ambulances (1 LMG ea)
1 (mot) Field Post Office (2 LMGs)

The division capitulated to the Americans by Linz in 1945.

3rd Estonian SS Freiwilligen Brigade

Formed on 10/22/43 as the SS Estonian Freiwilligen Brigade with the 1st and 2nd SS Freiwilligen Grenadier Regiments. They were renumbered. The brigade stood as follows:

Brigade Staff
1 (mot) "KB" Detachment
1 Motorcycle Messenger Platoon (6 LMGs)

45th SS Freiwilligen Grenadier Regiment
1 Regimental Staff

1 Regimental Staff Company
1 Signals Platoon
1 Bicycle Platoon
1 Pioneer Platoon (3 LMGs)
3 Battalions, each with
3 Grenadier Companies (12 LMGs, 2 heavy anti-tank rifles & 2 80mm mortars ea)
1 Machine Gun Company (12 HMGs & 4 120mm mortars)
1 Infantry Gun Company (2 150mm sIG & 6 75mm leIG)
1 (motZ) Panzerjäger Company (9 75mm PAK 40 & 6 LMGs)
1 Pioneer Company (9 LMGs & 2 80mm mortars)
46th SS Freiwilligen Grenadier Regiment
same as 45th SS Freiwilligen Grenadier Regiment
53rd SS Flak Battalion
1 (mot) Battalion Staff
1 Light Self Propelled Flak Company (12 20mm guns)
1 Medium Self Propelled Flak Company (9 37mm flak guns)
1 (motZ) Heavy Flak Company (4 88mm, 3 20mm & 2 LMGs)

53rd SS Artillery Battalion
1 Staff Battery
3 Light Howitzer Batteries (4 105mm leFH & 2 LMGs ea)
53rd SS Signals Company
Supply Troop
1 (mot) (120 ton) Transportation Company (8 LMGs)
1 (mot) Maintenance Company
2 (horse drawn) Heavy Supply Columns (6 LMGs ea)
Other
1 (mot) Medical Company
1 (mot) Ambulance Company
1 (mot) Military Police Detachment (2 LMGs)
1 (mot) Field Post Office

The 53rd SS Panzerjäger Battalion and 53rd SS Feldersatz Battalion were added later. In January 1944 the brigade was expanded into the 20th Estonian SS Freiwilligen Division.

SS Polizei Division

Formed on 10/1/39 with troops drawn from the Ordnungs Polizei, as the Polizei Division. It contained:

1/,2/,3/1st Polizei Schützen Regiment
1st Battalion (1–4th Companies)
2nd Battalion (5–8th Companies)
3rd Battalion (9–12th Companies)
13th–14th Companies
1/,2/,3/2nd Polizei Schützen Regiment
1st Battalion (1–4th Companies)
2nd Battalion (5–8th Companies)
3rd Battalion (9–12th Companies)
13th–14th Companies
1/,2/,3/3rd Polizei Schützen Regiment
1st Battalion (1–4th Companies)
2nd Battalion (5–8th Companies)
3rd Battalion (9–12th Companies)
13th–14th Companies
Polizei Bicycle Squadron
Polizei Panzerabwehr (Anti-Tank) Battalion (3 companies)
Polizei Pioneer Battalion (3 companies)

The army assigned the 1/,2/,3/,4/228th Artillery Regiment, the 300th Signals Battalion (2 cos), divisional supply troops, and various administrative troops. On 4/1/40 the 228th Artillery Regiment was redesignated the 300th Artillery Regiment. Also, a number of the supply and support troops of the division had their numbers changed. Those changes were: 2/354th and 4/260th Light Supply Columns became the 2/,3/300th; the 2/,3/4/625th Supply Train became the 4/,5/,6/300th; the 8/300th Fuel Column became the 7/300th; the 625th Supply Commander became the 300th; the 3/2nd Maintenance Company became the 300th; the 300th Supply Company was established; the 571st Field Bakery and 571st Butcher Platoon were redesignated the 300th; the 625th Field Hospital became the 300th; the 1/,2/522nd Vehicle Maintenance Platoons became the 1/,2/300th; and the 521st Field Post Office became the 300th Field Post Office.

In early 1940 the 300th Artillery Regiment and the 300th Signals Battalion were sent back to the army and the following were formed:

1/,2/,3/,4/Polizei Artillery Regiment (formed on 5/6/40)
Polizei Signals Battalion (formed on 6/23/40)
Polizei Reconnaissance Battalion (formed on 4/28/40)

The 300th Administrative Troops remained with the division. In 1941 the division formed a three company flak battalion. On 22 April 1941 the division contained:

1st SS Polizei
    1st–3rd Battalions
    13th Company
    14th Company
2nd SS Polizei Regiment
    1st–3rd Battalions
    13th Company
    14th Company
3rd SS Polizei Regiment
    1st–3rd Battalions
    13th Company
    14th Company
Reconnaissance Battalion
Panzerjäger Battalion

Regiment Flak Battalion
Artillery Regiment
    1st (light) Battalion
    2nd (light) Battalion
    3rd (light) Battalion
    4th (heavy) Battalion
Pioneer Battalion
Signals Battalion
Supply Troop
Divisional Administration
Medical Service
Veterinary Service
Military Police Detachment
Field Post Office

Between 5/16/41 and 10/15/42 the division was organized and equipped as follows:

SS Polizei Infantry Division
Divisional Staff
    1 Divisional Staff (2 LMGs)
    1 (mot) Mapping Detachment
1st, 2nd & 3rd SS Polizei Regiments each with
    1 Signals Platoon
    1 Pioneer Engineer Platoon (3 LMGs)
    3 Battalions, each with
        3 Infantry Companies, each with (12 LMGs, 3 anti-tank rifles, 3 50mm mortars)
        1 Heavy Infantry Company (12 HMGs & 6 80mm mortars)
        1 Infantry Support Company (2 150mm sIG & 6 75mm leIG)
        1 Panzerjäger Company (2 50mm PAK 38, 9 37mm PAK 36 & 5 LMGs)
SS Polizei Panzerjäger Battalion
    3 (mot) Panzerjäger Companies (6 50mm PAK 38, 4 37mm PAK 36 & 8 LMGs ea)
SS Polizei Bicycle Battalion
    2 Bicycle Companies, each with (3 50mm mortars, 2 HMGs, 12 LMGs, 3 anti-tank rifles)
    1 (mot) Support Company, with
        1 (mot) Engineer Platoon (3 LMGs)
        1 Infantry Gun Platoon (2 75mm leIG)
        1 Self Propelled Panzerjäger Company (3 37mm PAK 36 & 2 LMGs)

SS Polizei Artillery Regiment
    Regimental Staff Battery
    1–3rd Artillery Battalions, each with
        1 Signals Platoon
        1 Calibration Detachment
        3 (motZ) Batteries (3 105mm leFH 18 & 2 LMGs ea)
    4th Artillery Battalion
        1 Signals Platoon
        1 Calibration Detachment
        3 (motZ) Batteries (3 150mm sFH 18 & 2 LMGs ea)
SS Polizei Signals Battalion
    1 (mot) Radio Company
    1 (tmot) Telephone Company
    1 (mot) Light Signals Supply Column (2 LMGs)
SS Polizei Pioneer Battalion
    1 (mot) Pioneer Company (9 LMGs & 3 anti-tank rifles)
    2 Pioneer Companies (9 LMGs & 3 anti-tank rifles ea)
    1 Light Engineering Supply Column (2 LMGs)
300th Divisional Supply Troop
    1/,2/,3/300th (mot) Light Supply Columns
    4–6/300th (mot) Light Supply Columns
    8–10/300th (mot) Light Supply Columns
    7/300th (mot) Light Fuel Column
    300th (mot) Maintenance Company
    300th Supply Company
    300th Divisional Administration Platoon
    300th (mot) Butcher Company

300th (mot) Bakery Company
1/,2/Polizei Medical Company
1/,2/300th Ambulance Companies
300th Field Hospital
300th (mot) Military Police Company
300th (mot) Field Post
300th Veterinary Company

On 2/24/42 the Polizei Division and the assigned army support units became SS units. On 10/15/42 the "Polizei Schützen Regiments" became "SS Polizei Infantry Regiments" and on 2/1/43 they were renamed "SS Polizei Grenadier Regiments." On 1 January 1943 the division had:

Divisional Staff
1 (mot) Mapping Detachment
1 Divisional Staff (2 LMGs)
1st & 2nd SS Polizei Infantry Regiment, each with
Regimental Staff
Staff Company
1 Engineering Platoon
1 Signals Platoon (3 LMGs)
1 Bicycle Platoon (3 LMGs)
1st Infantry Battalions
3 Infantry Companies (18 LMGs & 3 50mm mortars)
1 Heavy Weapons Company (14 HMGs & 6 80mm mortars)
1 Infantry Support Gun Company (2 150mm sIG & 4 75mm leIG)
1 Panzerjäger Company (2 50mm PAK 38, 10 37mm PAK 36, 4 LMGs)
2nd Infantry Battalion
3 Infantry Companies (18 LMGs & 3 50mm mortars)
1 Heavy Weapons Company (14 HMGs & 6 80mm mortars)
1 Infantry Support Gun Company (2 150mm sIG & 4 75mm leIG)
1 Panzerjäger Company (2 75mm PAK 40, 2 50mm PAK 38, 9 37mm PAK 36, 4 LMGs)
Bicycle Reconnaissance Battalion
2 Bicycle Companies (3 80mm mortars, 3 50mm mortars, 11 LMGs, 2 HMGs ea)
1 (mot) Heavy Weapons Company
1 Infantry Support Gun Section (2 75mm leIG)
1 Engineer Platoon (4 LMGs)
1 Panzerjäger Platoon (3 37mm PAK 36)
SS Polizei Artillery Regiment
Regimental Staff Battery
1 Signals Platoon
1 (mot) Calibration Platoon

1st Battalion
1 Battalion Staff Battery
1 Signals Platoon
1 Calibration Platoon
3 (motZ) Batteries (3 105mm leFH 18 & 2 LMGs ea)
1 (motZ) Battery (2 122mm Russian howitzers & 2 LMGs)
2nd Battalion
Battalion Staff Battery
1 Signals Platoon
1 Calibration Platoon
2 (motZ) Batteries (3 105mm leFH 18 & 2 LMGs ea)
1 (motZ) Battery (2 105mm leFH 18 & 2 LMGs)
1 (motZ) Battery (1 76.2mm Russian gun)
3rd Battalion
1 Battalion Staff Battery
1 Signals Platoon
1 Calibration Platoon
3 (motZ) Batteries (3 105mm leFH 18 & 2 LMGs ea)
1 (motZ) Battery (2 150mm sFH 18 & 2 LMGs)
4th Battalion
Battalion Staff Battery
1 Signals Platoon
1 Calibration Platoon
1 (motZ) Battery (2 150mm sFH 18 & 2 LMGs)
1 (motZ) Battery (3 150mm sFH 18 & 2 LMGs)
1 (motZ) Battery (3 220mm French Mortars & 2 LMGs)
SS Polizei Flak Battalion
1 (mot) Signals Platoon
1 (motZ) Battery (14 20mm guns, 4 searchlights, & 2 LMGs)
1 (motZ) Battery (12 37mm guns, 4 searchlights, & 2 LMGs)
1 (motZ) Battery (4 88mm guns & 2 LMGs)
SS Polizei Panzerjäger Battalion
1st (motZ) Company (2 75mm PAK 40, 8 37mm PAK 36 & 6 LMGs)
2nd (motZ) Company (2 75mm PAK 40, 8 37mm PAK 36 & 6 LMGs)
3rd (motZ) Company (2 76.2mm, 8 37mm PAK 36 & 6 LMGs)
SS Polizei Signals Battalion
1 (mixed mobility) Telephone Company (6 LMGs)
1 (mot) Radio Company (4 LMGs)
1 (mot) Light Signals Supply Column (1 LMG)
SS Polizei Pioneer Battalion
1 (mot) Pioneer Company (7 LMGs & 2 anti-tank rifles)
2 Pioneer Companies (7 LMGs & 2 anti-tank rifles)
1 (mot) Light Signals Supply Column (1 LMG)

Supply Units
1/,2/,3/,4/,5,6/300th (mot) Light Supply Columns (2 LMGs ea)
8/,9/,10/SS Polizei (mot) Light Supply Columns (2 LMGs ea)
7/300th (mot) Light Fuel Supply Column (2 LMGs)
300th (mot) Maintenance Company
SS Polizei Supply Company (2 LMGs)

Medical Units
1/SS Polizei (mot) Medical Company
2/SS Polizei (mot) Medical Company
SS Polizei (mot) Field Hospital
1,/2/300th Ambulance Companies
300th Veterinary Company

Other
300th (mot) Bakery Company
300th (mot) Butcher Company
300th Administration Company
300th (mot) Field Post Office
300th (mot) Military Police Platoon

On 6/6/43 the three infantry regiments were redesignated SS Polizei Panzergrenadier Regiments. The division detached a kampfgruppe for special operations. It was later reunited with the division in northern Greece. In February 1944 the division was organized and equipped as follows:

Divisional Staff
1 (mot) Mapping Detachment
1 Divisional Staff (2 LMGs)
1 Divisional Band

7th SS Polizei Infantry Regiment, each with
Regimental Staff
1 (mot) Staff Company
1 Signals Platoon (3 LMGs)
1 Panzerjäger Platoon (3 75mm PAK 40 & 3 LMGs)
1 Motorcycle Platoon (6 LMGs)

1st–3rd (mot) Infantry Battalions
3 Infantry Companies (4 HMGs, 18 LMGs & 2 80mm mortars)
1 Heavy Weapons Company (6 HMGs, 6 80mm mortars, 4 75mm leIG,3 75mm PAK 40)
13th (mot) Infantry Support Gun Company (4 150mm sIG)
14th (mot) Flak Company (12 20mm & 4 LMGs)
16th Pioneer Company (19 LMGs, 3 anti-tank rifles & 6 flamethrowers)

8th SS Polizei Infantry Regiment, each with
Regimental Staff
1 (mot) Staff Company
1 Signals Platoon (3 LMGs)

1 Panzerjäger Platoon (3 75mm PAK 40 & 3 LMGs)
1 Motorcycle Platoon (6 LMGs)

1st–3rd (mot) Infantry Battalions
same as 7th SS Polizei Regiment
Mountain Pack Howitzer Battery (4 65mm 216 (i)
13th (mot) Infantry Support Gun Company (4 150mm sIG)
14th (mot) Flak Company (12 20mm & 4 LMGs)
16th Pioneer Company (19 LMGs, 3 anti-tank rifles & 6 flamethrowers)

Motorcycle Reconnaissance Battalion
1 Armored Car Company (ordered formed)
2 Motorcycle Companies (2 80mm mortars, 4 HMGs & 18 LMGs)
1 Motorcycle Company (ordered formed)
1 (mot) Heavy Weapons Company (ordered formed)
1 (mot) Light Supply Column (ordered formed)

SS Polizei Artillery Regiment
Regimental Staff Battery (ordered formed)
1 Signals Platoon
1 (mot) Calibration Platoon

1st Battalion
1 Battalion Staff Battery (6 LMGs)
3 (motZ) Batteries (4 105mm leFH 18 & 2 LMGs ea)

2nd Battalion (ordered formed)
Battalion Staff Battery
3 (motZ) Batteries (4 105mm leFH 18 & 2 LMGs ea)
1 (motZ) Heavy Battery (4 150mm sFH & 5 LMGs)

SS Polizei Flak Battalion
1/,2/4th (motZ) Battalion (4 88mm guns, 3 20mm & 2 LMGs)
1 (motZ) Search Light Battery

SS Polizei Signals Battalion (ordered formed)
1 (mot) Telephone Company
1 (mot) Radio Company
1 (mot) Light Signals Supply Column

4th SS Polizei Pioneer Battalion
1 (mot) Staff Company
2 (mot) Pioneer Companies (2 HMGs, 16 LMGs 2 50mm mortars & 2 80mm mortars)
1 Pioneer Company (2 HMGs, 34 LMGs 2 50mm mortars & 2 80mm mortars)
1 (mot) Reconnaissance Platoon (8 LMGs, 1 80mm & 1 50mm mortar)
1 Brüko K (2 LMGs)
1 (mot) Light Signals Supply Column (2 LMGs)

Supply Units
4/,5/4th SS (mot) (90 ton) Transport Companies (2 LMGs ea)

Medical Units
 1/,2/4th SS Polizei (mot) Medical Companies
 1/,2/4th SS (mot) Ambulance Companies
Other
 4th SS (mot) Bakery Company
 4th SS (mot) Butcher Company
 4th SS Administration Company
 4th SS Maintenance Company
 1/,2/4th SS Vehicle Maintenance Company
 4th SS (mot) Military Police Platoon (3 LMGs)
 4th SS (mot) Field Post Office

By May 1944 the division had undergone another significant reorganization. At that time it contained:

Divisional Staff
 1 (mot) Mapping Detachment
 1 (mot) Escort Company
  1 Motorcycle Platoon (3 LMGs)
  1 Infantry Gun Section (2 75mm leIG)
  1 Self Propelled Flak Platoon (4 20mm guns)
  1 Self Propelled Panzerjäger Platoon (3 75mm PAK 40)
  1 Heavy Infantry Platoon (2 80mm mortars, 2 HMGs & 6 LMGs)
7th SS Polizei Infantry Regiment
 Regimental Staff
 1 (mot) Staff Company
  1 Signals Platoon (3 LMGs)
  1 Panzerjäger Platoon (3 75mm PAK 40 & 3 LMGs)
  1 Motorcycle Platoon (6 LMGs)
 1st–3rd (mot) Infantry Battalions
  3 Infantry Companies (4 HMGs, 18 LMGs & 2 80mm mortars)
  1 Heavy Weapons Company (6 HMGs, 6 80mm mortars, 4 75mm leIG, 3 75mm PAK 40)
  13th (mot) Infantry Support Gun Company (4 150mm sIG)
  14th (mot) Flak Company (12 20mm & 4 LMGs)
  16th Pioneer Company (2 HMGs, 12 LMGs, & 6 flamethrowers)
8th SS Polizei Infantry Regiment
 same as 7th SS Polizei Infantry Regiment
4th SS Polizei Panzer Battalion
 1 Panzer Battalion Staff Company (6 20mm & 21 LMGs)
 3 Sturmgeschütz Companies (14 StuGs & 16 LMGs)
 1 Panzer Maintenance Company (2 LMGs)
4th SS Reconnaissance Battalion
 1 (half track) Reconnaissance Company (2 20mm, 2 HMGs & 18 LMGs)
 3 (mot) Reconnaissance Companies (2 HMGs & 18 LMGs)

 1 (mot) Heavy Reconnaissance Company
  1 Panzerjäger Platoon (3 75mm PAK 40)
  1 Infantry Gun Platoon (3 75mm leIG)
  1 Pioneer Platoon (4 LMGs & 6 flamethrowers)
  1 (mot) Light Supply Column (3 LMGs)
4th SS Polizei Artillery Regiment Regimental Staff Battery
 1 Regimental Staff Battery (6 LMGs)
 1 Self PRopelled Flak Platoon (4 20mm & 2 LMGs)
 1st & 2nd Battalions, each with
  1 Battalion Staff Battery (6 LMGs)
  3 (motZ) Batteries (4 105mm leFH 18 & 2 LMGs ea)
 3rd Battalion
  Battalion Staff Battery (6 LMGs)
  3 (motZ) Batteries (4 150mm sFH 18 & 2 LMGs ea)
4th (mot) SS Polizei Flak Battalion
 1/,2/,3/4th (motZ) Battalion (4 88mm guns, 3 20mm & 3 LMGs)
 1 Self Propelled Flak Battery (9 37mm guns)
 1 (mot) Light Flak Supply Column
 1 (motZ) Search Light Battery
4th SS Polizei Signals Battalion
 1 (mot) Telephone Company (6 LMGs)
 1 (mot) Radio Company (6 LMGs)
 1 (mot) Light Signals Supply Column (1 LMG)
4th SS Feldersatz Battalion
 3 Companies
4th SS Polizei Pioneer Battalion
 1 (mot) Staff Company (3 LMGs)
 3 (mot) Pioneer Companies (2 HMGs, 16 LMGs 2 50mm mortars & 2 80mm mortars)
 1 Brüko K (2 LMGs)
4th SS Divisional Supply Troop
 3 SS (mot) (120 ton) Transport Companies (8 LMGs ea)
 3 SS (mot) (90 ton) Transport Companies (6 LMGs ea)
 1 (mot) Supply Company (8 LMGs)
Medical Units
 1/,2/,3/4th SS Polizei (mot) Medical Companies
 1/,2/4th SS (mot) Medical Supply Companies
Other
 4th SS (mot) Field Bakery (6 LMGs)
 4th SS (mot) Butcher Company (4 LMGs)
 4th SS Administration Company (2 LMGs)
 4th SS Maintenance Company
 1/,2/4th SS Vehicle Maintenance Company
 1 (mot) Heavy Replacement Supply Column (4 LMGs)
 4th SS (mot) Military Police Platoon (3 LMGs)
 4th SS (mot) Field Post Office

In July the reconnaissance battalion appears to have converted the half track reconnaissance company into an armored car company. The artillery regiment added an independent (motZ) 105mm gun battery to the 3rd Battalion. The medical forces were reinforced by a third (mot) supply company and a (mot) decontamination company. In the supply troops, the supply company was not equipped with 12 LMGS, 2 heavy anti-tank rifles and 2 20mm guns. In addition, the non-motorized part of the division was disbanded in July 1944.

4th SS Polizei-Panzergrenadier Division

The division was formed on 6/1/43 as the Polizei Panzergrenadier Division, while the SS Polizei Division was still with the 18th Army in Russia. A motorized infantry battalion had already been formed, and on 10/31/42, two further battalions were forming in the SS Troop Training Center Heidelager (Debicz) by Cracow. The division contained 1st, 2nd and 3rd Polizei Panzergrenadier Regiments. Each regiment had three battalions. The 3rd Polizei Panzergrenadier was never completed.

The third regiment was disbanded, the 2/3rd became the 1/2nd, and the 3/3rd became the 3/1st. An artillery regiment (six batteries), a reconnaissance battalion (six companies), a flak battalion (two batteries), a sturmgeschütz battalion (three batteries) and a signal battalion were raised. The division was serving in Greece in 1943 and was not concentrated, but had portions of it deployed to different regions. On 10/22/43 the division was renumbered as the 4th SS Polizei Panzergrenadier Division. In early 1944 the 1st and 2nd SS Polizei Grenadier Regiments were renumbered the 7th and 8th SS Polizei Panzergrenadier Regiments respectively. In April 1944 the Kampfgruppe, then operating in Russia, joined the rest of the division in Greece. In July 1944, the division was organized and equipped as follows:

Division Staff
1 Divisional Staff
1 Divisional Band
1 (mot) Mapping Detachment
(mot) Military Police Detachment (9 LMGs)
1 (mot) Escort Company
  1 Self Propelled Flak Battery (4 20mm flak, 4 HMGs & 6 LMGs)
  1 Motorcycle Platoon (6 LMGs)
7th SS Panzergrenadier Regiment
1 Regimental Staff & (mot) Staff Company
  1 Signals Platoon
  1 Motorcycle Platoon (6 LMGs)
1st Battalion
3 Panzergrenadier Companies (4 HMGs, 18 LMGs & 2 80mm mortars)
1 Heavy Panzergrenadier Company

1 Mortar Platoon (6 80mm mortars)
1 Panzerjäger Platoon (3 75mm pAK & 3 LMGs)
1 Support Platoon (1 LMG & 4 75mm leIG)
2nd & 3rd Battalions, each with
same as 1st Battalion
1 (motZ) Heavy Infantry Gun Company (6 150mm sIG)
1 (motZ) Flak Company (12 20mm & 2 LMGs)
1 (mot) Pioneer Company (2 HMGs, 12 LMGS, 18 flamethrowers & 2 80mm mortars)
8th SS Panzergrenadier Regiment
same as 7th SS Panzergrenadier Regiment
4th SS Panzerjäger Battalion
1 Battalion Staff & Staff Platoon (1 LMG & 3 jagdpanzer IV)
2 Jagdpanzer Companies (14 Jagdpanzer IV & 2 LMGs ea)
1 (motZ) Panzerjäger Company (12 75mm PAK & 12 LMGs)
1 Panzer Flak Company (12 self-propelled 20mm flak guns)
1 (mot) Supply Company (3 LMGs)
4th SS Flak Battalion
1 Battalion Staff & Staff Battery (1 LMG)
3 (motZ) Heavy Batteries (4 88mm, 3 20mm & 4 LMGs)
1 (motZ) Medium Battery (9 37mm & 4 LMGs)
1 (mot) Searchlight Battery (4 600mm searchlights)
4th SS Panzer Reconnaissance Battalion
1 Battalion Staff
1 Armored Car Company (18 20mm & 24 LMGs)
1 (mot) Reconnaissance Companies (4 HMGs, 18 LMGS & 2 80mm mortars)
1 Heavy Company
  1 Pioneer Platoon (4 LMGs & 6 flamethrowers)
  1 Panzerjäger Platoon (3 75mm PAK & 3 LMGs)
  1 leIG Platoon (1 LMG & 2 75mm leIG)
1 Supply Company (4 LMGs)
4th SS Artillery Regiment
1 Regimental Staff & (mot) Staff Battery (6 LMGs)

1st Battalion
 1 Battalion Staff & Staff Battery (2 LMGs)
 2 (motZ) Batteries (6 105mm leFH & 6 LMGs ea)
2nd & 3rd Battalions, each with
 same as 1st Battalion
4th Battalion
 1 Battalion Staff & Staff Battery (2 LMGs)
 2 (motZ) Batteries (6 150mm sFH & 6 LMGs ea)
 1 (motZ) Battery (6 105mm K & 6 LMGs ea)
4th SS Pioneer Battalion
 1 Battalion Staff (3 LMGs)
 1 Battalion Staff Company (3 LMGs)
 3 (mot) Pioneer Companies (2 HMGs, 18 LMGs,
  6 flamethrowers, & 2 80mm mortars ea)
4th SS Signals Battalion
 1 (mot) Telephone Company (6 LMGs)
 1 (mot) Radio Company (7 LMGs)
 1 (mot) Supply Column (1 LMG)
Feldersatz Battalion
 2–5 Companies
Supply Troop
 1 (tmot) Supply Battalion Staff (2 LMGs)
 3 (mot) 120 ton Transportation Companies (8
  LMGs ea)
 3 (mot) 90 ton Transportation Companies (6
  LMGs ea)
 1 (mot) Supply Company (8 LMGs)
 1 (mot) Ordnance Company (4 LMGs)
 1/,2/4th SS (mot) Maintenance Companies (5
  LMGs ea)
Other
 8th SS 8th (mot) Butcher Company (4 LMGs)
 8th SS (mot) Bakery Company (5 LMGs)
 8th SS (mot) Divisional Administration Platoon (2
  LMGs)
 1/,2/8th SS (mot) Medical Companies (4 LMGs ea)
 8th SS (mot) Decontamination Company
 1/,2/,3/8th SS Ambulances
 8th SS (mot) Medical Supply Company (4 LMGs)
 1/,2/8th SS Veterinary Company (6 LMGs)
 8th SS (mot) Field Post Office (2 LMGs)

On 15 August 1944 the entire division was organized and equipped as follows:

Division Staff
 SS Polizei (mot) Mapping Detachment
 SS Polizei (mot) Staff Company
  Infantry Platoon (2 HMGs, 11 LMGs & 2 80mm
   mortars)
  (motZ) Panzerjäger Platoon (3 75mm PAK 40)
  Self Propelled Flak Battery (1 20mm flak guns)
  Motorcycle Platoon (3 LMGs)
 Divisional Band

7th SS Polizei (mot) Grenadier Regiment
 (mot) Regimental Staff Company
  Signals Platoon
  (motZ) Panzerjäger Platoon (3 75mm PAK 40)
  Motorcycle Platoon (6 LMGs)
 1st (mot) Battalion
  3 (mot) Companies (4 HMGS, 18 LMGs, 2
   80mm mortars & 1 (motZ) 47mm PAK ea)
  1 (mot) Heavy Company
   1 Mortar Platoon (6 80mm mortars)
   1 (motZ) Panzerjäger Platoon (3 75mm PAK 40
    & 6 LMGs)
   1 Panzerjäger Detachment (3 anti-tank rifles)
   1 (motZ) Infantry Gun Platoon (4 75mm leIG)
 2nd & 3rd (mot) Battalions, each with
  3 (mot) Companies (4 HMGS, 18 LMGs, 2
   80mm mortars ea)
  1 (mot) Heavy Company
   1 Mortar Platoon (6 80mm mortars)
   1 (motZ) Panzerjäger Platoon (3 75mm PAK 40
    & 6 LMGs)
   1 Panzerjäger Detachment (3 anti-tank rifles)
   1 (motZ) Infantry Gun Platoon (4 75mm leIG)
 13th (motZ) Infantry Gun Company (6 150mm
  sIG)
 14th (motZ) Flak Company (12 20mm & 4 LMGs)
 16th (mot) Pioneer Company (2 HMGS, 16 LMGs
  & 3 flamethrowers)
8th SS Polizei (mot) Grenadier Regiment
 1st, 2nd, & 3rd (mot) Battalions, each with
  3 (mot) Companies (4 HMGS, 18 LMGs, 2
   80mm mortars ea)
  1 (mot) Heavy Company
   1 Mortar Platoon (6 80mm mortars)
   1 (motZ) Panzerjäger Platoon (3 75mm PAK 40
    & 6 LMGs)
   1 Panzerjäger Detachment (3 anti-tank rifles)
   1 (motZ) Infantry Gun Platoon (4 75mm leIG)
 13th (motZ) Infantry Gun Company (6 150mm
  sIG)
 14th (motZ) Flak Company (12 20mm & 4 LMGs)
 16th (mot) Pioneer Company (2 HMGS, 16
  LMGs & 3 flamethrowers)
4th SS Polizei Reconnaissance Battalion
 1 Armored Car Company (17 LMGs & 3 20mm
  guns)
 3 (mot) Light Reconnaissance Companies (2
  80mm mortars, 4 HMGs, & 18 LMGs ea)
 1 (mot) Heavy Reconnaissance Company
  1 (motZ) Panzerjäger Platoon (3 75mm PAK 40)
  1 (motZ) Infantry Gun Company (2 75mm leIG)
  1 (mot) Pioneer Platoon (4 LMGs)
 1 (mot) Supply Company (3 LMGs)
 1 Flak Detachment (4 20mm flak guns)

4th SS Polizei Sturmgeschütz Battalion
- 1 Staff Sturmgeschütz Company
  Flak Detachment (2 quad 20mm self-propelled flak guns)
- 2 Sturmgeschütz Companies (14 StuGs ea)
- 1 Sturmgeschütz Company (13 StuGs)
- 1 Armored Maintenance Company (2 LMGs)

4th SS Polizei (mot) Artillery Regiment
- 1 (mot) Staff and Staff Battery (4 LMGs)
  - 1 Flak Detachment (2 quad 20mm self-propelled flak guns)
- **1st Battalion**
  - 1 (mot) Battalion Staff & Staff Battery (6 LMGs)
  - 1–3rd (motZ) Batteries (4 105mm leFH & 5 LMGs ea)
- **2nd Battalion**
  - (mot) Battalion Staff & Staff Battery (6 LMGs)
  - 4–6th (motZ) Batteries (4 105mm leFH & 5 LMGs ea)
- **3rd Battalion**
  - (mot) Battalion Staff & Staff Battery (6 LMGs)
  - 7–9th (motZ) Batteries (4 150mm sFH & 5 LMGs ea)
  - 10th (motZ) Battery (4 100mm guns & 5 LMGs)

4th SS Polizei Flak Battalion
- 1 (mot) Battalion Staff & Staff Battery
- 1–3rd (motZ) Batteries (4 88mm, 3 20mm & 3 LMGs ea)
- 4th Self Propelled Battery (9 37mm flak guns & 4 LMGs)
- 1 (mot) Light Flak Supply Column
- Searchlight Battery (4 600mm searchlights)

4th SS Polizei (mot) Pioneer Battalion
- 1 Staff & Staff Company (6 LMGs total)
- 3 (mot) Pioneer Companies (2 HMGs & 18 LMGs ea)

- 1 (mot) Bridging Column (3 LMGS)

4th SS Polizei Signals Battalion
- 1 (mot) Telephone Company (7 LMGs)
- 1 (mot) Radio Company (7 LMGs)
- 1 (mot) Light Supply Column (3 LMGs)

4th SS Polizei Feldersatz Battalion
- 1 Company (4 LMGs)
- 1 Company (1 75mm PAK 40, 1 20mm flak, 2 heavy anti-tank rifles & 4 LMGs)
- 1 Company (6 HMGS, 12 LMGs & 2 75mm leIG)

4th SS Polizei Supply Troop
- 3 (mot) 120 ton Transportation Companies (5 LMGs ea)
- 2 (mot) 90 ton Transportation Companies (6 LMGs ea)
- 1 (mot) Supply Company (2 20mm guns, 2 heavy anti-tank rifles & 12 LMGs)

4th SS (mot) Polizei Administration Battalion
- Staff Company (6 LMGs)
- 1 (mot) Bakery Company (7 LMGs)
- 1 (mot) Butcher Company (7 LMGs)
- 1 (mot) Administration Company (7 LMGs)

4th SS Medical Battalion
- 2 (mot) Medical Companies (6 LMGs ea)
- 3 (mot) Supply Medical Companies (1 LMG ea)

Other
- 1 (mot) Ordnance Company (3 LMGs)
- 1/,2/4th SS Maintenance (4 LMGs ea)
- 1 (mot) Heavy Maintenance Supply Column
- 4th SS Polizei (mot) Military Police Troop (3 LMGs)
- 4th SS Polizei Field Post Office (2 LMGs)

The division was captured by the Russians in 1945.

4th SS Freiwilligen-Panzergrenadier Brigade "Nederland"

Formed on 10/23/43 in Thüringia from the SS Freiwilligen Legion Niederlande as its 1st Regiment and a newly formed 2nd Regiment, becoming the 1st and 2nd SS-Nederland Freiwilligen Panzergrenadier Regiments. A reconnaissance company, panzerjäger battalion, an artillery regiment with two battalions, a pioneer battalion, a signals company, a feldersatz battalion and supply troop were also formed. The 1st Company of the Freiwilligen Nederlander Legion was given the name of "General Seyffardt" as an honorary title on 2/9/43. On 10/21/43, when the SS was renumbered, the two regiments changed numbers to 45th and 46th, which lasted until 11/12/43 when they became the 48th and 49th.

- 1/,2/,3/48th SS Freiwilligen Panzergrenadier Regiment "General Seyffardt"
- 1/,2/,3/49th SS Freiwilligen Panzergrenadier Regiment "De Ruiter"
- 54th SS Reconnaissance Company
- 54th SS Panzerjäger Battalion
- 1/,2/54th SS Artillery Regiment
- 54th SS Pioneer Battalion
- 54th SS Signals Company
- 54th SS Feldersatz Battalion
- 54th SS Supply Troop

OKH records show the brigade organized and equipped as follows from 3 January to May 1944. The 2nd Artillery

Battalion and the Reconnaissance Company shown below existed earlier, but were missing by January 1944.

Brigade Staff
1 Brigade Staff (4 HMGs & 2 LMGs)
1 Self Propelled Flak Company (4 20mm & 1 LMG)
54th (mot) Mapping Detachment
54th (mot) Military Police Detachment (2 LMGs)

48th "Gen. Seyffard" SS Panzergrenadier Regiment
1 Regimental Staff
1 (mot) Regimental Staff Company
1 Signals Platoon
1 Pioneer Platoon (4 LMGs)
1 Panzerjäger Platoon (3 LMGs & 3 75mm PAK 40)
1 Motorcycle Platoon (6 LMGs)

1st & 2nd Battalions
3 (mot) Panzergrenadier Companies (4 HMGs, 18 LMGs, 2 80mm mortars, & 2 flamethrowers)
1 (mot) Heavy Company (4 75mm leIG, 3 LMGs, 3 75mm PAK 40, & 6 80mm mortars)
1 Self Propelled Infantry Gun Company (6 150mm sIG & 7 LMGs)
1 Self Propelled Flak Company (12 20mm & 4 LMGs)

49th "De Rutter" SS Panzer Greandier Regiment
same as 48th Panzer Greandier Regiment

Divisional Fusilier Battalion
54th SS (mot) Company
1 Armored Car Platoon (6 20mm & 6 LMGs)
1 Panzerjäger Platoon (3 LGMs & 3 75mm PAK 40)
1 Panzergrenadier Platoon (2 80mm mortars, 4 HMGs & 18 LMGs)

54th SS Panzerjäger Battalion
1 Battalion Staff (2 LMGs)
1 Self Propelled Panzerjäger Company (10 75mm PAK 40 & 14 LMGs)
1 (motZ) Flak Battery (4 88mm, 3 20mm & 2 LMGs)
1 Sturmgeschütz Battery (10 StuGs & 2 LMGs)

54th SS Artillery Regiment
1 Regimental Staff & Staff Battery (6 LMGs)
1 Self Propelled Flak Battery (4 quad 20mm & 2 LMGs)

1st & 2nd Battalions, each with (2nd Battalion not present in 1944)
1 Battalion Staff (1 LMG) & Staff Battery (6 LMGs)
2 (motZ) Batteries (4 105mm leFH & 2 LMGs ea)
1 (motZ) Battery (4 150mm sFH & 2 LMGs)

54th SS Pioneer Battalion
1 Battalion Staff (4 LMGs) & (mot) Staff Company (3 LMGs)

2 (mot) Pioneer Companies (2 HMGs, 18 LMGs, 6 flamethrowers & 2 80mm mortars)

54th SS Panzer Signals Detachment
54th SS Panzer Radio Company (25 LMGs)
54th SS (mot) Light Supply Column (1 LMG)

54th (mot) SS Reconnaissance Company (not present in 1944)
1 Armored Car Platoon (6 20mm & 6 LMGs)
1 Panzerjäger Platoon (3 75mm PAK 40 & 3 LMGs)
1 Mixed Panzergrenadier Platoon (2 80mm mortars, 4 HMGs & 18 LMGs)

54th SS Feldersatz Battalion
5 Companies

54th SS Supply Troop
1/54th SS (mot) 120 ton Transportation Company (8 LMGs)
2/54th SS (mot) Heavy Supply Column (4 LMGs)

Truck Park
54th SS (mot) Maintenance Company (4 LMGs)

Other
54th SS (mot) Administration Company (combined admin, bakery & butcher functions) (10 LMGs)
54th SS (mot) Medical Company (4 LMGs)
54th SS (mot) Decontamination Company
54th SS (mot) Field Post Office (2 LMGs)

On 3/10/44 the panzerjäger battalion is shown to have been organized and equipped as follows. The date of this change is not known.

54th SS Panzerjäger Battalion
Self Propelled Battalion HQ
2 Towed Batteries (4 88mm, 3 20mm, & 2 LMGs each)
1 Sturmgeschütz Battery (10 StuG & 2 LMGs)
1 Self Propelled Panzerjäger Battery (10 Marders & 14 LMG)

On 7/26/44 the Nederland Brigade suffered very heavy casualties in combat on the Russian front. As a result, on 8/1/44 the brigade was reorganized and both regiments now had only two battalions each. The 1/48th and 3/49th were disbanded, the 3/48th became the 1/48th. The 54th SS Panzerjäger Battalion had two companies with Jagdpanzer IV with 10 tanks. In August the artillery regiment formed a 3rd Battalion. On 10/11/44 the Brigade number was dropped and it became known as the Freiwilligen Panzergrenadier Brigade "Nederland." On 2/10/45 it was used to form the 23rd SS Freiwilligen Panzergrenadier Division Nederland.

SS Division Wiking

Initially the division was known as the "Germania Division." It was formed on 11/20/40, but on 3/8/41 it was renamed the SS Division Wiking and all non-regimental units had their names changed from Germania to Wiking. The division had:

1/,2/,3/Germania SS (mot) Regiment
1/,2/,3/Nordland SS (mot) Regiment
1/,2/,3/Westland SS (mot) Regiment
Wiking SS Reconnaissance Battalion
Wiking SS Panzerjäger Battalion
Wiking SS Flak Machine Gun Battalion
1/,2/,3/,4/Wiking SS Artillery Regiment
Wiking SS Flak Battalion
Wiking SS Pioneer Battalion
Wiking SS Signals Battalion
Wiking SS Feldersatz Battalion

On 10 May 1940 the division was organized and equipped as follows:

Divisional Staff
Divisional Headquarters (2 HMGs)
1 (mot) SS Divisional Mapping Detachment
3 (mot) Infantry Regiments, each with
Regimental Staff Company, with
1 (mot) Signals Platoon
1 (mot) Motorcycle Platoon (4 LMGs)
3 (mot) Battalions, each with
3 (mot) Infantry Companies (12 LMGs & 3 50mm mortars ea)
1 (mot) Machine Gun Company (12 HMGs & 6 80mm mortars)
1 (mot) Infantry Support Gun Company (2 150mm sIG & 6 75mm leIG guns)
1 (mot) Panzerjäger Company (12 37mm PAK 36 & 6 LMGs)
1 (mot) Engineer Platoon (3 LMGs)
1 Light (mot) Supply Column (later eliminated)
SS Wiking Panzerjäger Battalion
1 (mot) Signals Platoon
3 (mot) Panzerjäger Companies (9 37mm PAK 36, 2 50mm PAK 38 & 6 LMGs)
3rd Panzerjäger Company later equipped with (3 50mm PAK 38 8 37mm PAK 36 & 6 LMGs)
SS Wiking Reconnaissance Battalion
1 (mot) Signals Platoon (2 LMGs)
1 Motorcycle Company (3 50mm mortars, 2 HMGs & 18 LMGs)

1 Light Armored Car Company (10 HMGs & 25 LMGs)
1 (mot) Support Company, with
1 Panzerjäger Platoon (3 37mm PAK 36)
1 Infantry Support Gun Section (2 75mm leIG guns)
1 Engineer Platoon (3 LMGs)
SS Wiking Artillery Regiment
1 (mot) Signals Platoon
2 (mot) Weather Detachments
3 (mot) Battalions, each with
1 (mot) Signals Platoon
1 (mot) Calibration Detachment
3 (motZ) Batteries (4 105mm leFH 18 & 2 LMGs)
1 (mot) Battalion
1 (mot) Signals Platoon
1 (mot) Calibration Detachment
3 (motZ) Batteries (4 150mm sFH 18 & 2 LMGs)
SS Wiking Signals Battalion
1 (mot) Radio Company
1 (mot) Telephone Company
1 Light (mot) Signals Supply Column
SS Wiking Flak Battalion
3 Self Propelled Batteries (12 20mm guns ea)
SS Wiking Feldersatz Battalion
3 Companies
SS Wiking Pioneer Battalion
3 (mot) Pioneer Companies (9 LMGs ea)
1 (mot) "B" Bridging Train
1 Light (mot) Engineering Supply Column
Supply Train
1st–5th Light (mot) Supply Columns
6th–7th Heavy (mot) Supply Columns
13th–15th Light (mot) Supply Columns (added later)
10th–12th Heavy (mot) POL Supply Columns
1st, 2nd, & 3rd (mot) Maintenance Companies
SS Wiking (mot) Supply Company
Commissary Service
SS Wiking (mot) Bakery Platoon (later Company)
SS Wiking (mot) Butcher Platoon (later Company)
SS Wiking (mot) Administration Detachment
Medical Service
1st–3rd SS W Ambulance Columns
SS Wiking (mot) Field Hospital
1st & 2nd SS W Medical Companies
Other
SS Wiking (mot) Military Police Platoon
SS Wiking (mot) Field Post Office

On 22 April 1941 the division contained:

SS Infantry Regiment "Deutschland"
  1st–3rd Battalions
  13th Company
  14th Company
  15th Company
  16th Company
SS Infantry Regiment "Der Führer"
  1st–3rd Battalions
  13th Company
  14th Company
  15th Company
  16th Company
11th SS Infantry Regiment
  1st–3rd Battalions
  13th Company
  14th Company
  15th Company
  16th Company

Reconnaissance Battalion
Artillery Regiment
  1st (light) Battalion
  2nd (light) Battalion
  3rd (light) Battalion
  4th (heavy) Battalion
Sturmgeschütz Battery
Panzerjäger Battalion
Flak Battalion
Pioneer Battalion
Signals Battalion
Supply Troop
Divisional Administration
Medical Service
Intendant Service
Military Police Detachment
Field Post Office

The records of the 6th Army indicate that on 2 May 1941 the division was organized and equipped as follows:

SS Wiking (mot) Infantry Division
  Divisional Headquarters (2 HMGs)
  1 (mot) SS Divisional Mapping Detachment
3 (mot) Infantry Regiments, each with
  Regimental Staff Company, with
    1 (mot) Signals Platoon
    1 (mot) Motorcycle Platoon (4 LMGs)
  3 (mot) Battalions, each with
    3 (mot) Infantry Companies (12 LMGs & 3 50mm mortars ea)
    1 (mot) Machine Gun Company (12 HMGs & 6 80mm mortars)
  1 (mot) Infantry Support Gun Company (2 150mm sIG & 6 75mm leIG guns)
  1 (mot) Panzerjäger Company (12 37mm PAK 36 & 4 LMGs)
  1 (mot) Engineer Platoon (3 LMGs)
SS Wiking Panzerjäger Battalion
  1 (mot) Signals Platoon
  3 (mot) Panzerjäger Companies (8 37mm PAK 36, 3 50mm PAK 38 & 6 LMGs)
SS Wiking Reconnaissance Battalion
  1 (mot) Signals Platoon (2 LMGs)
  1 Motorcycle Company (3 50mm mortars, 4 HMGs & 18 LMGs)
  1 Light Armored Car Company (10 HMGs & 25 LMGs)
  1 (mot) Support Company, with
    1 Panzerjäger Platoon (3 37mm PAK 36)
    1 Infantry Support Gun Section (2 75mm leIG)

  1 Engineer Platoon (3 LMGs)
SS Wiking Artillery Regiment
  1 (mot) Signals Platoon
  2 (mot) Weather Detachments
  3 (mot) Battalions, each with
    1 (mot) Signals Platoon
    1 (mot) Calibration Detachment
    3 (motZ) Batteries (4 105mm leFH 18 & 2 LMGs)
  1 (mot) Battalion
    1 (mot) Signals Platoon
    1 (mot) Calibration Detachment
    3 (motZ) Batteries (4 150mm sFH 18 & 2 LMGs)
SS Wiking Signals Battalion
  1 (mot) Radio Company
  1 (mot) Telephone Company
  1 Light (mot) Signals Supply Column
SS Wiking Flak Battalion
  3 Self Propelled Batteries (12 20mm guns ea)
SS Wiking Feldersatz Battalion
  3 Companies
SS Wiking Pioneer Battalion
  3 (mot) Pioneer Companies (9 LMGs ea)
  1 (mot) Brüko B (Bridging Train)
  1 Light (mot) Engineering Supply Column
Supply Train
  1–8/Wiking SS Light (mot) Supply Columns
  12–14/Wiking SS Light (mot) Supply Columns
  9–11/Wiking SS Heavy (mot) Fuel Supply Columns
  1st & 2nd (mot) Maintenance Companies
SS Wiking (mot) Supply Company

Commissary Service
  SS Wiking (mot) Bakery Platoon (later Company)
  SS Wiking (mot) Butcher Platoon (later Company)
  SS Wiking (mot) Administration Detachment
Medical Service
  1st–3rd SS W Ambulance Columns
  SS Wiking (mot) Field Hospital
  1st & 2nd SS W Medical Companies
Other
  SS Wiking (mot) Military Police Platoon
  SS Wiking (mot) Field Post Office

The division continued to grow and by late May 1941 the Wiking SS Artillery Survey Battalion was added. During the summer of 1942 the division formed the Wiking SS Panzer Battalion (from the Reich Panzer Battalion). From 16 May 1941 to 15 October 1942 the division was organized and equipped as follows:

Divisional Staff
  Divisional Staff (4 HMGs)
  1 (mot) Mapping Platoon
2 (mot) Infantry Regiments (1st-Germania & 2nd Nordland), each with
  1 (mot) Regimental Staff Company, with
    1 Signals Platoon
    1 Motorcycle Platoon (6 LMGs)
    1 Panzerjäger Platoon (3 50mm PAK 38 & 2 LMGs)
  3 (mot) Battalions, each with
    3 Infantry Companies, each with (18 LMGs, 4 HMGs, 2 80mm mortars & 2 flamethrowers)
    1 Support Company with
      1 Engineer Platoon (4 LMGs)
      1 Panzerjäger Section (3 50mm PAK 38 guns)
      1 Infantry Support Gun Platoon (4 75mm leIG & 3 28mm sPzBu 41 guns)
  1 (mot) Infantry Support Company (4 75mm leIG guns)
SS Wiking Armored Troop, with
  1 Armored Staff Company
  1 Medium Armored Company
  2 Light Armored Companies
  1 Armored Maintenance Platoon
SS Wiking Motorcycle (Volkswagen) Regiment
  1 (mot) Staff Staff Company, with
    1 Signals Platoon
    1 Motorcycle Platoon (6 LMGs)
    1 Panzerjäger Platoon (3 50mm PAK 38 & 2 LMGs)
  2 (mot) Battalions, each with
    1 (mot) Staff Platoon
    3 (mot) Infantry Companies (18 LMGs, 4 HMGs, 2 50mm mortars ea)
    1 (mot) Heavy Machine Gun Company (12 HMGs & 6 80mm mortars)

1 (mot) Support Company, with
  1 Engineer Platoon (4 LMGs)
  1 Panzerjäger Section (3 50mm PAK 38 & 2 LMGs)
  1 Infantry Support Gun Section (2 75mm leIG guns)
SS Wiking Artillery Regiment
  Regimental Staff
  1 (mot) Staff Battery
  1 (mot) Observation Battery
  1st–3rd (mot) Artillery Battalions, each with
    1 (mot) Battalion Staff Battery
    3 (motZ) Batteries (4 105mm leFH 18 & 2 LMGs ea)
  4th (mot) Artillery Battalion
    1 (mot) Battalion Staff Battery
    2 (motZ) Batteries (4 150mm sFH 18 & 2 LMGs ea)
    1 (motZ) Battery (4 100mm K18 guns & 2 LMGs)
  5th (mot) Flak Battalion
    1 (mot) Battalion Staff Battery
    1 Self Propelled Flak Battery (8 20mm & 2 quad 20mm AA)
    1 Self Propelled Flak Battery (9 37mm AA guns)
    1 (motZ) Flak Battery (4 88mm guns & 3 20mm guns)
    1 (mot) Light Supply Column
SS Wiking Reconnaissance Battalion
  1 Armored Car Company (18 50mm PAK 38 & 24 LMGs)
  1 Light Armored Car Platoon
  1 Motorcycle Company (2 80mm mortars, 4 HMGs, & 18 LMGs)
  1 (mot) Company, with
    1 Engineer Platoon (4 LMGs)
    1 Panzerjäger Section (3 50mm PAK 38 guns)
    1 Infantry Support Gun Platoon (2 75mm leIG guns)
SS Wiking Panzerjäger Battalion
  1 Self Propelled Panzerjäger Co (Marder) (9 75mm PAK 40 & 6 LMGs)
  1 (motZ) Panzerjäger Co (9 75mm PAK 40 & 6 LMGs)
  1 (motZ) Panzerjäger Co (9 50mm PAK 38 & 6 LMGs)
SS Wiking Signals Battalion
  1 (mot) Radio Company (4 LMGs)
  1 (mot) Telephone Company (4 LMGs)
  1 (mot) Light Signals Supply Column (2 LMGs)
SS Wiking Pioneer Battalion
  3 (mot) Pioneer Companies (18 LMGs & 2 flamethrowers ea)
  1 (mot) Light "B" Bridging Train (2 LMGs)

1 (mot) Light Supply Column
Commissary Service
  1 (mot) Divisional Administration Platoon (2 LMGs)
  1 (mot) Butcher Company (2 LMGs)
  1 (mot) Bakery Company (2 LMGs)
Supply Train
  12 (mot) Light Supply Columns (2 LMGs ea)
  3 (mot) Light Fuel Supply Columns (2 LMGs ea)
  3 (mot) Maintenance Companies (2 LMGs ea)
  1 (mot) Light Supply Company (2 LMGs)
Medical
  2 (mot) Medical Companies (2 LMGs ea)
  1 (mot) Field Hospital (2 LMGs)
  3 Ambulance Companies (2 LMGs ea)

Other
  1 (mot) Military Police Company
  1 (mot) Field Post 1 (mot) SS "KB" Platoon

On 6/27/42 the 5th SS Panzer Battalion was organized and equipped as follows:

1 Panzer Staff Company
1 Medium Panzer Company
2 Light Panzer Companies

Mk II	12
Mk III (50 kz)	12
Mk III (50 lg)	24
Mk IV (kz)	4
Cmd	1

5th SS Panzer Division "Wiking"

Formed on 11/9/42 by the renaming of the SS Division "Wiking" while it was serving in Southern Russia as the SS Panzergrenadier Division "Wiking." It had:

1/,2/,3/SS Panzergrenadier Regiment "Germania"
1/,2/SS Panzergrenadier Regiment "Nordland"
1/,2/,3/SS Panzergrenadier Regiment "Westland"
SS Panzer Battalion "Wiking"
1/,2/,3/,4/5th SS Artillery Regiment
SS Panzerjäger Battalion "Wiking"
SS Reconnaissance Battalion "Wiking"
SS Flak Battalion "Wiking"
SS Pioneer Battalion "Wiking"
SS Signals Battalion "Wiking"
SS Feldersatz Battalion "Wiking"
SS Division Support (Einheiten) "Wiking"

On 3/29/43 the two panzer grenadier regiments both formed three battalions, and a schützen regiment with two battalions was organized. The Nordland Regiment was detached in the summer of 1943 to join the 11th SS Panzergrenadier Division Nordland.

When the Finnisches Freiwilligen-Bataillon der Waffen-SS was stood down in March of 1943, and disbanded in June and July of the same year, the Estnisches SS-Freiwilligen Bataillon Narwa (Estonian) was used to replace the Finns as the third Battalion of the SS-Panzergrenadier Regiment Nordland. The Estonians stayed with the Wiking Division when the Nordland Regiment was detached to become the nucleus of a new division. The Estonians attached to Wiking were actually one of three battalions then forming up at the Heidelager SS-Truppenubungsplatz (training ground) in Debica, Poland, in early 1943 as the 1.Estnisches SS-Frw.Grenadier Regiment. They lost the 1st (Narwa) Battalion, but later acquired sufficient manpower to constitute the 3rd SS-Freiwilliger Brigade (45th & 46th SS-Freiwilliger Regiments) before being formed into a full SS-Grenadier division in January 1944. In October 1943, the Wiking was reorganized as a panzer division. The Estonians became 3/10th SS-Panzergrenadier Regiment Westland. By April of 1944 the Narwa Battalion would be detached from Wiking and renamed 20th SS-Fusilier-Battalion, part of the Estonian 20.SS Freiwilliger Grenadier Division. During it's time with Wiking Division the Estonian battalion was commanded by the German SS-Sturmbannfuhrer Georg Eberhardt. Reports of the battalion's strength vary, but it may have been as high as 1,280 men when attached to SS Panzergrenadier Regiment Westland. The honorific title Narwa was also reported to have been unofficially continued as part of its new SS Fusilier Battalion designation.

The Panzer Regiment was increased to two battalions and a new sturmgeschütz battalion was raised. On 7/1/43 the divisions panzer battalion and panzer inventory were as follows:

1/5th SS Panzer Regiment
1 Panzer Staff Company
1 Medium Panzer Company
2 Light Panzer Companies

Mk II	4
Mk III (50 kz)	1
Mk III (50 lg)	14
Mk III (75)	8
Mk IV (kz)	1
Mk IV (lg)	16
Cmd	1

On 8/9/43 the OKH ordered twelve Wespe self-propelled 105mm guns sent to the division. In August 1943 the division was organized and equipped as follows:

Division Staff
1 Division Staff (2 LMGs)
1 (mot) Mapping Detachment
1 (mot) "KB" Detachment
1 (mot) Escort Company
  1 Motorcycle Messenger Platoon (6 LMGs)
  1 Infantry Gun Section (2 75mm leIG)
  1 Self Propelled Flak Section (4 20mm guns)
  1 (motZ) Panzerjäger Platoon (3 75mm PAK 40)
  1 Infantry Platoon (2 80mm mortars, 6 LMGs & 4 HMGs)

SS Panzergrenadier Regiment
1 (mot) Regimental Staff
3 (mot) Battalions, each with
  3 Panzergrenadier Companies (4 HMGs, 18 LMGs, 2 80mm mortars & 2 flamethrowers)
  1 Heavy Company
    1 Mortar Platoon (6 80mm mortars)
    1 Panzerjäger Platoon (3 75mm PAK 40)
    1 Infantry Gun Section (4 75mm leIG)
    1 Anti-Tank Rifle Platoon (3 heavy anti-tank rifles)
1 (motZ) Infantry Gun Section (4 150mm sIG)
1 Self Propelled Flak Company (12 20mm guns)
1 Motorcycle Company (3 75mm PAK 40, 4 HMGs, 18 LMGs & 2 80mm mortars)
1 (mot) Pioneer Company (18 LMGs & 6 flamethrowers)

SS Panzergrenadier Regiment
1 (mot) Regimental Staff
1 (mot) Regimental Staff Company
  1 Motorcycle Messenger Platoon
  1 Panzerjäger Platoon (3 75mm PAK 40)
  1 Signals Platoon
2 (mot) Battalions, each with
  3 Panzergrenadier Companies (4 HMGs, 18 LMGs, 2 80mm mortars & 2 flamethrowers)
  1 Heavy Company
    1 Mortar Platoon (6 80mm mortars)
    1 Panzerjäger Platoon (3 75mm PAK 40)
    1 Infantry Gun Section (4 75mm leIG)
    1 Anti-Tank Rifle Platoon (3 heavy anti-tank rifles)
1 (half track) Battalion
  3 Panzergrenadier Companies (4 HMGs, 34 LMGs, 2 80mm mortars & 2 flamethrowers)
  1 Heavy Company
    1 Infantry Gun Section (4 75mm leIG)
    1 Panzerjäger Platoon (3 75mm PAK 40)
    1 Anti-Tank Rifle Platoon (3 heavy anti-tank rifles)

1 (motZ) Infantry Gun Section (4 150mm sIG)
1 Self Propelled Flak Company (12 20mm guns)
1 Motorcycle Company (3 75mm PAK 40, 4 HMGs, 18 LMGs & 2 80mm mortars)
1 (mot) Pioneer Company (18 LMGs & 6 flamethrowers)

SS Panzer Battalion "Wiking"
1 Panzer Staff (1 LMG)
1 Panzer Staff Company (2 LMGs)
3 Sturmgeschütz Companies (7 StuGs ea)

SS Reconnaissance Regiment "Wiking"
1 (mot) Staff Company
  1 Signals Platoon
  1 Panzerjäger Platoon (3 75mm PAK 40 & 3 LMGs)
  1 Motorcycle Platoon (6 LMGs)
  1 Self Propelled Flak Platoon (4 20mm guns)
1 Armored Car Copany (18 20mm & 24 LMGs)
1 (mot) Light Reconnaissance Suply Column
2 **Reconnaissance Battalions**, each with
  2 (mot) Reconnaissance Companies (2 80mm mortars, 4 HMGs, 18 LMGs & 3 heavy anti-tank rifles)
  1 (mot) Support Company
    1 Pioneer Platoon (4 LMGs)
    1 Panzerjäger Platoon (3 75mm PAK 40 & 3 LMGs)
    1 Infantry Gun Platoon (4 75mm leIG)

SS Flak Battalion "Wiking"
1 (mot) Staff Company (1 LMG)
1 Self Propelled Medium Flak Company (9 37mm guns)
3 (motZ) Heavy Flak Batteries (4 88mm, 3 20mm & 2 LMGs)
1 (mot) Light Flak Supply Column

5th SS Artillery Regiment
1 Regimental Staff
1 Regimental Staff Battery

1st Battalion
1 Battalion Staff
1 Battalion Staff Battery (6 LMGs)
3 Self Propelled leFH Batteries (6 105mm leFH SdKfz 124 Wespe ea)

2nd & 3rd Battalion
Staff & Staff Battery (6 LMGs)
2 (motZ) Batteries (6 105mm leFH & 2 LMGs ea)

4th Battalion
Staff & Staff Battery (6 LMGs)
2 (motZ) Batteries (6 150mm sFH & 2 LMGs ea)
1 (motZ) Battery (6 105mm sK 18/40 guns & 2 LMGs ea)

SS Panzerjäger Battalion "Wiking"
1 Self Propelled Panzerjäger Company (9 75mm PAK 40 & 9 LMGs)

2 (motZ) Panzerjäger Companies (9 75mm PAK 40 & 9 LMGs)

SS Pioneer Battalion "Wiking"
1 (mot) Reconnaissance Company (6 HMGs & 9 LMGs)
1 (halftrack) Pioneer Company (40 LMGs & 6 flamethrowers)
2 (mot) Pioneer Companies (18 LMGs & 6 flame-throwers)
1 (mot) Brüko B (4 LMGs)
1 (mot) Light Pioneer Supply Column (2 LMGs)

SS Signals Battalion "Wiking"
1 Panzer Radio Company (25 LMGs)
1 (mot) Telephone Company (6 LMGs)
1 (mot) Light Signals Supply Column (2 LMGs)

SS Division Support (Einheiten) "Wiking"
4 (mot) (120 ton) Transportation Companies (8 LMGs ea)
1 (mot) (60 ton) Heavy Supply Column (4 LMGs)
4 (mot) Heavy Fuel Columns (4 LMGs ea)
1 (mot) Supply Company (8 LMGs)
1 (mot) Maintenance Company (4 LMGs)

SS Maintenance Battalion "Wiking"
3 (mot) Maintenance Companies (4 LMGs ea)
1 (mot) Heavy Replacement Company (4 LMGs)

SS Commissariat Battalion "Wiking"
1 (mot) Field Bakery (4 LMGs)
1 (mot) Butcher Company (4 LMGs)
1 (mot) Divisional Administration (4 LMGs)
1 (mot) Field Post Office (2 LMGs)
1 (mot) Maintenance Company (2 LMGs)

SS Medical Battalion "Wiking"
2 (mot) Medical Companies (4 LMGs)
1 (mot) Field Hospital (2 LMGs)
3 (mot) Ambulances (1 LMG ea)

Other
SS Military Police Company "Wiking" (6 LMGs)

On 10/22/43 the division was renamed the 5th SS Panzer Division "Wiking" and the panzer grenadier regiments were renamed as follows:

9th SS Panzergrenadier Regiment "Germania"
10th SS Panzergrenadier Regiment "Westland"

The remainder of the units were renumbered "5th." The Narwa Panzergrenadier Battalion became the 3/10th SS Panzergrenadier Regiment, then it became the 20th Fusilier Battalion, was detached, and became part of the 20th Estonian Freiwilligen Division. The division suffered extremely heavy losses in the battle of the Korsun-Shevchnekovskii Pocket, which ended 2/17/44. In April 1944 the division's panzer battalion and panzer inventory were as follows:

1/5th Panzer Regiment
1 Panzer Staff Company
4 Panzer Companies
MkV   79

On 16 June 1944 the division was reorganized by Army Group Center. The 5th SS Panzer Reconnaissance Battalion and the 3/10th Panzergrenadier Regiment "Westland" were newly formed at this time. The bulk of the division passed into American captivity near Rastadt in May 1945. In May 1944 OKII records show the division organized and equipped as follows:

Division
Division Staff
Divisional Escort Company
Motorcycle Platoon (6 LMGs)
Self Propelled Flak Battery (4 20mm guns)
Self Propelled Anti-Tank Platoon (3 LMGs & 3 75mm PAK 40)
Infantry Gun Platoon (2 75mm leIG)
Mixed Panzergrenadier Platoon (4 HMGs, 6 LMGs, & 2 80mm mortars)

5th SS Panzer Regiment
Regimental Staff
1st Panzer Battalion
(1–4th Companies) (MkV Panthers)
1 Panzer Maintenance Platoon
2nd Panzer Battalion
(5–8th Companies) (Mk IV Panzers)
1 Panzer Maintenance Company

9th "Germania" SS Panzergrenadier Regiment
Regimental Staff
1st Battalion
1–3rd Companies (4 HMGs, 18 LMGs, 2 80mm mortars & 2 flamethrowers)
4th Company
1 Mortar Platoon (2 LMGs & 4 120mm mortars)
1 Panzerjäger Platoon (3 LMGs & 3 75mm PAK 40)
2 Infantry Gun Sections (1 LMG & 2 75mm leIG ea)
2nd Battalion (6–10th Companies) (same as 1st Battalion)
3rd (halftrack) Battalion (11–15th Companies)
1–3rd (halftrack) Companies (4 HMGs, 40 LMGs, 2 80mm mortars, 2 flamethrowers, 7 20mm guns & 2 75mm guns)
4th Company
1 Pioneer Platoon (13LMGs & 6 flamethrowers)
1 Infantry Gun Section (1 LMG & 2 75mm leIG)
1 Panzerjäger Platoon (8 LMGs & 3 75mm PAK 40)
1 Gun Platoon (8 LMGs & 6 75mm guns)

16th (self-propelled flak) Company (12 20mm & 4 LMGs)

17th (self-propelled infantry gun) Company (6 150mm sIG & 8 LMGs)

18th (mot) Pioneer Company (2 HMGs, 12 LMGs, 6 flamethrowers & 2 80mm mortars)

10th "Westland" SS Panzergrenadier Regiment
same as 9th SS Panzergrenadier Regiment

5th SS Reconnaissance Battalion
Battalion Staff

Heavy Platoon (6 SdKfz 234/3 with 75mm KwK & 6 LMGs)

1 Armored Car Company (18 20mm & 24 LMGs)

1 (halftrack) Armored Car Company (16 20mm & 25 LMGs)

2 (halftrack) Companies (49 LMGs, 2 80mm mortars & 3 75mm guns)

1 (halftrack) Company
1 Pioneer Platoon (13 LMGs & 6 flamethrowers)
1 Panzerjäger Platoon (8 LMGs & 3 75mm PAK 40)
1 Infantry Gun Section (2 75mm leIG & 4 LMGs)
1 Gun Section (8 LMGs & 6 75mm guns)
1 (mot) Reconnaissance Supply Column (3 LMGs)

5th SS Panzerjäger Battalion
Battalion Staff

3 Self Propelled Panzerjäger Companies (14 75mm PAK 40 & 14 LMGs ea)

5th SS Panzer Artillery Regiment
1 Regimental Staff & Staff Battery (2 LMGs)
1 Self Propelled Flak Battery (4 quad 20mm guns & 2 LMGs)

1st (Self Propelled) Battalion
Staff & (self-propelled) Staff Battery (3 LMGs & 3 20mm guns)

2 Self Propelled leFH Batteries (6 105mm leFH SdKfz 124 Wespe ea)

1 Self Propelled sFH Battery (6 150mm sFH SdKfz 165 Hummel)

2nd Battalion
Staff & Staff Battery (3 LMGs & 3 20mm guns)
2 (motZ) Batteries (6 105mm leFH & 2 LMGs ea)

3rd Battalion
same as 2nd Battalion

4th Battalion
Staff & Staff Battery (3 LMGs & 3 20mm guns)
2 (motZ) Batteries (6 150mm sFH & 2 LMGs ea)
1 (motZ) Battery (6 105mm sK 18/40 guns & 2 LMGs ea)

5th SS Flak Battalion
Staff & Staff Battery
3 (motZ) heavy Flak Batteries (4 88mm, 3 20mm & 2 LMGs ea)

1 (motZ) Medium Flak Batteries (9 37mm & 4 LMGs ea)

1 (motZ) Searchlight Platoon (4 600mm searchlights)

5th SS Panzer Pioneer Battalion
Staff (2 LMGs)
1 (halftrack) Pioneer Company (2 HMGs, 46 LMGs, 3 heavy anti-tank rifles, 2 80mm mortars & 6 flamethrowers)

2 (mot) Pioneer Companies (2 HMGs, 18 LMGs, 2 80mm mortars & 6 flamethrowers)

1 (mot) Heavy Panzer Bridging Train (5 LMGs)
1 (mot) Light Panzer Bridging Train (3 LMGs)

5th SS Panzer Signals Battalion
1 Panzer Telephone Company (14 LMGs)
1 Panzer Radio Company (20 LMGs)
1 (mot) Signals Supply Column (1 LMG)

5th SS Feldersatz Battalion
5 Companies

5th SS Supply Troop
1–7th/5th SS (mot) 120 ton Transportation Companies (8 LMGs ea)
5/5th SS (mot) 20 ton Light Flak Supply Column
5th SS (mot) Workshop Company (4 LMGs)
5th SS (mot) Supply Company (8 LMGs)

5th SS Truck Park
1/,2/,3/5th SS (mot) Maintenance Companies (4 LMGs)
5th SS (mot) 75 ton Heavy Maintenance Supply Column

Medical
1/,2/5th SS (mot) Medical Companies (2 LMGs ea)
1/,2/,3/5th SS Ambulances

Administration
5th SS (mot) Bakery Company (6 LMGs)
5th SS (mot) Butcher Company (6 LMGs)
5th SS (mot) Divisional Administration Platoon (2 LMGs)
5th SS (mot) Military Police Troop (5 platoons) (15 LMGs)
5th SS (mot) Field Post Office (2 LMGs)

5th SS Freiwilligen Sturmbrigade "Wallonien"

Formed on 6/1/43 as the SS Sturmbrigade Wallonien using the 373th Wallon Infantry Battalion and new recruits. It was organized with a staff, a staff company, three panzer grenadier companies, a machine-gun company, an infantry support gun company, a heavy panzerjäger company, a sturmgeschütz battery, a light flak company, and a heavy flak battery. It was entirely motorized. In July 1943 the brigade was organized as follows:

Battalion Staff
  1 Battalion Staff
  1 (mot) Staff Company
    1 Motorcycle Platoon (3 LMGs)
    1 Pioneer Platoon (4 LMGs & 6 flamethrowers)
    1 Signals Platoon
1 (mot) Battalion
  3 (mot) Companies (18 LMGs, 2 HMGs, & 2 80mm mortars)
  1 (mot) Company (8 HMGs & 6 80mm mortars)

1 (motZ) Infantry Gun Company (2 150mm sIG & 4 leIGs)
1 (motZ) Panzerjäger Company (9 75mm PAK 40 & 9 LMGs)
1 Sturmgeschütz Battery (10 Stugs)
1 Self Propelled Light Flak Battery (12 20mm guns)
1 (motZ) Heavy Flak Battery (4 88mm, 3 20mm, & 2 LMGs)
1 (mot) Heavy Supply Column

On 10/22/43 it was renumbered the 5th SS Freiwilligen Sturmbrigade "Wallonien." The brigade suffered extremely heavy losses in the battle of the Korsun-Shevchnekovskii Pocket, which ended 2/17/44. On 28 April 1944 it was reorganized after heavy combat and on 6/28/44 it formed a second battalion and the sturmgeschütz battery became a battalion, but had only ten sturmgeschützen. On 18 October 1944 it was enlarged into the 28th SS Freiwilligen Grenadier Division Wallonien.

SS Mountain Kampfgruppe Nord (North)

The kampfgruppe was formed on 2/28/41. The SS Flak Battalion Nord was raised on 4/21/41 and was still forming when the brigade entered Russia. The 20mm flak battery arrived in Norway on 7/15/41. The flak battalion headquarters and remaining batteries arrived on 7/22/41. On 22 April 1941 the Kampfgruppe Nord contained:

6th SS Infantry Regiment
  1st–3rd Battalions
  13th Company
  14th Company
7th SS Infantry Regiment
  1st–3rd Battalions
  13th Company
  14th Company

Reconnaissance Battalion
Artillery Regiment
  1st (light) Battalion
  2nd (light) Battalion
  3rd (light) Battalion
2 Pioneer Companies
Signals Battalion
Supply Troop
Divisional Administration
Medical Service
Military Police Detachment
Field Post Office

On 22 June 1941 the brigade was organized as follows:

Headquarters
  Brigade Headquarters
  1 (mot) Mapping Detachment

6th & 7th SS Infantry Regiments
  1 (mot) Infantry Regiment Staff
  1 (mot) Headquarters Company
    Company Headquarters
    Signals Platoon

Motorcycle Platoon
Pioneer Platoon (3 LMGs)
13th (mot) Infantry Gun Company
Company Headquarters
3 Light Infantry Gun Platoons (6 75mm leIG)
1 Heavy Infantry Gun Platoon (2 150mm sIG)
14th Light (mot) Panzerjäger Company (12 37mm PAK 36 & 4 LMGs)
Motorcycle Platoon (3 LMGs)
3 (mot) Infantry Battalions, each with
1 (mot) Battalion Headquarters
3 (mot) Infantry Companies (12 LMGs & 3 50mm mortars)
1 (mot) Machine Gun Company (12 LMGs & 80mm mortars)

9th SS (mot) Infantry Regiment
1 (mot) Headquarters Company
Company Headquarters
Signals Platoon
Motorcycle Platoon
13th (mot) Infantry Gun Company
Company Headquarters
3 Light Infantry Gun Platoons (6 75mm leIG)
1 Heavy Infantry Gun Platoon (2 150mm sIG)
14th Light (mot) Panzerjäger Company (12 37mm PAK 36 & 4 LMGs)
Motorcycle Platoon (3 LMGs)
15th (mot) Pioneer Company (9 LMGs)
3 (mot) Infantry Battalions
1 (mot) Battalion Headquarters
3 (mot) Infantry Companies (12 LMGs & 3 50mm mortars)
1 (mot) Machine Gun Company (12 LMGs & 80mm mortars)

SS Nord Artillery Regiment
Regimental Headquarters
(mot) Signals Platoon
(mot) Artillery Calibration Battery
1st & 2nd (mot) Battalions
Battalion Headquarters
(mot) Signals Platoon
1 (mot) Calibration Section
3 (motZ) Batteries (105mm mountain howitzers & 2 LMGs each)
3rd (mot) Battalion
Battalion Headquarters
(mot) Signals Platoon
1 (mot) Calibration Section
2 (motZ) Batteries (4 150mm sFH & 2 LMGs ea)
1 (motZ) Battery (4 100mm K18 & 2 LMGs ea)

SS Nord Flak Battalion
Battalion Headquarters
1 Self Propelled Light Flak Battery (12 20mm guns)
1 (motZ) Heavy Flak Battery (4 88mm flak guns & 2 20mm guns)
1 (motZ) Light Flak Battery (12 20mm flak guns)

SS Nord Reconnaissance Battalion
Battalion Staff
1 (mot) Signals Platoon
1 Motorcycle Company (18 LMGs, 4 HMGs & 3 50mm mortars)
1 (mot) Heavy Reconnaissance Company
Panzerjäger Platoon (1 LMG & 3 37mm PAK 36)
Pioneer Platoon (3 LMGs)

SS Nord Pioneer Battalion
2 (mot) Pioneer Companies (9 LmGs ea)

SS Nord Signals Battalion
Battalion Headquarters
1 (mot) Telephone Company (2 LMGs)
1 (mot) Radio Company (2 LMGs)

Nord (North) SS Mountain Division

Formed on 2/28/41 as the SS Kampfgruppe Nord, by September 1941 it had expanded into a division with:

6th SS (mot) Infantry Regiment (former SS Totenkopf Standarte 6)
1st Battalion (1–4th Companies)
2nd Battalion (5–8th Companies)
3rd Battalion (5–14th Companies)
Light Infantry Column
1/,2/,3/7th SS (mot) Infantry Regiment (earlier SS Totenkopf Standarte 7) (same as 6th SS (mot) Infantry Regiment)

1/,2/,3/8th SS (mot) Infantry Regiment (earlier SS Totenkopf Standarte K) (same as 6th SS (mot) Infantry Regiment)
SS Kampfgruppe/Division Nord Reconnaissance Battalion
(with 1 motorcycle and 1 heavy company, later 2 motorcycle companies & 1 heavy company)
1/,2/,3/SS Kampfgruppe/Division Nord Artillery Regiment
1st Battalion
1–2nd Light Batteries
3rd Heavy Battery

2nd Battalion
    4–5th Light Batteries
3rd Battalion
    6–7th Light Batteries
    1–3rd Artillery Columns
SS Kampfgruppe/Division Nord Pioneer Battalion (2 companies)
SS Kampfgruppe/Division Nord Reconnaissance Battalion
    Staff and Signals Platoon
    Motorcycle Company
    Heavy Company
SS Kampfgruppe/Division Nord Flak Battalion
    1st (20mm) Battery
    2nd (37mm) Battery
    3rd (88mm) Battery
    Flak Column
SS Kampfgruppe/Division Nord Signals Battalion
    Staff
    1st (Telephone) Company
    2nd (Radio) Company
SS Nord Supply Service
    Divisional Supply Command
    Maintenance Company
    1–2nd Heavy Transport Companies
    1–4th Light Transport Companies Supply Company
SS Nord Commissary Service
    Administration Bureau
    Bakery Company
    Butcher Company
Medical Service
    Medical Company
    1–2nd Ambulance Companies
Other
    Field Post Office
    Military Police Detachment

In December 1941 the 9th SS Infantry Regiment was detached from the division and serving on the Wolchow front. On 1/15/42 the SS Division Nord was converted into a mountain division. The division was able to form only one motorized schützen battalion, two mountain jäger battalions, and a light and a heavy artillery battalion. The missing portions were re-formed in Germany. In September 1942 the SS Division Nord became the SS Mountain Division Nord.

6th SS Mountain Division "Nord"

Ordered formed in Ticino, Finland, on 1/15/42. Because of troop shortages in Finland, the missing units were organized at the Wildflecken training camp in Germany. Here the SS Assault Brigade "Wallonien" and "Carlemagne" (Karl der Grosse), the Mountain Jäger Battalions I and IV, two mountain artillery units, were organized and shipped to Finland during the summer. The division re-formed and became operational upon their arrival. The 6th "Nord" Division underwent almost constant organizational change. On 6/20/42 it was organized as follows:

Division
    1 Mountain Division Staff (2 LMGs)
    1 (mot) Mapping Detachment
6th SS Gebirgsjäger Regiment
    1 Regimental Staff
    1 Regimental Staff Company
    1 Signals Platoon
    1 Bicycle Platoon (2 LMGs)
  1st Mountain Battalion
    1 Battalion Staff
    3 Mountain Companies (9 LMGs, 2 HMGs, 2 80mm mortars 4 lePzB 39 anti-tank rifles)
    1 Heavy Mountain Company (8 HMGs & 6 80mm mortars)
    1 Mountain Support Company
    1 Signals Platoon
    1 Pioneer Platoon (4 LMGs)
  2nd Mountain Battalion
    same as 1st Battalion
(mot) Mountain Panzerjäger Company (13 37mm PAK 36 & 4 LMGs)
Infantry Gun Company (4 75mm sIG)
SS Schützen (mot) Battalion (Gebirgs-Division Nord)
    1 Battalion Staff
    3 (mot) Companies (18 LMGs, 4 HMGs, 3 lePzB 39 anti-tank rifles & 2 80mm mortars)
    1 (mot) Heavy Company (8 HMGs & 6 80mm mortars)
    1 (mot) Support Company
    1 Signals Platoon
    1 Panzerjäger Platoon (3 37mm PAK 36)
    1 Pioneer Platoon (4 LMGs)
(mot) Artillery Regiment
    1 Regimental Staff
    1 (mot) Regimental Staff Battery
    1 (mot) Calibration Detachment
  1st Battalion
    1 Battalion Staff

1 (mot) Battalion Staff Battery
3 (motZ) Batteries (4 105mm leFH & 2 LMGs ea)
2nd Battalion
same as 1st Battalion
Independent
1 (motZ) Battery (4 150mm sFH 18 & 2 LMGs)
Flak Battalion
1 Flak Battalion Staff
1 (mot) Flak Battalion Staff Battery
1 (mot) Signals Platoon
1 (motZ) Battery (4 88mm, 4 20mm & 3 LMGs)
1 (motZ) Battery (9 37mm guns)
1 (motZ) Battery (12 20mm & 3 LMGs ea)
2 (motZ) Battery (12 15mm & 3 LMGs ea)
1 (mot) Light Flak Supply Column
Reconnaissance Battalion
2 Motorcycle Companies (2 80mm mortars, 4 HMGs, 18 LMGs & 3 anti-tank rifles)
1 (mot) Reconnaissance Company
1 Pioneer Platoon (3 LMGs)
1 Panzerjäger Platoon (4 50mm PAK 38 & 1 LMG)
1 Infantry Gun Section (2 75mm leIG)
Signals Battalion
1 (tmot) Mountain Radio Company (2 LMGs)
2 (tmot) Mountain Telephone Companies (2 LMGs ea)
1 (mot) Light Supply Column
Pioneer Battalion
2 Pioneer Companies (9 LMGs, 2 HMGs, & 2 flamethrowers each)
Divisional Supply Troops
1st–14th (mot) Light Supply Columns
Administration
1 (mot) Butcher Company (2 LMGs)
1 (mot) Bakery Company (2 LMGs)
1 (mot) Administration Company (2 LMGs)
Medical
1 (mot) Mountain Medical Company (2 LMGs)
1 (tmot) Mountain Medical Company (2 LMGs)
3 Ambulances (2 LMGs ea)
Other
1 (mot) Ordnance Platoon (3 LMGs)
1 (mot) Field Post Office
1 (mot) Military Intelligence Platoon

The division had a theoretical total of 48 lePzB 39, 2 sPzB 41, 343 LMGs, 60 HMGs, 32 80mm mortars, 24 37mm PAK 36, 4 50mm PAK 38, 4 leIG, 10 100mm nebelwerfers, 13 20mm flak, 9 37mm flak, 4 88mm flak, 12 105mm leFH 18 and 4 150mm sFH 18.

On 8/4/42 there were further changes. The two mountain support companies of the mountain regiment added a section of three nebelwerfers. The regimental panzerjäger company was reorganized and now had 2 50mm guns, 9 37mm guns, 4 LMGs and a nebelwerfer battery of three launchers. A separate light infantry gun force was added that consisted of two gun sections, each with two 75mm leIG. The divisional panzerjäger company was reequipped with 2 50mm and 9 37mm PAK. The artillery was reorganized as follows:

(mot) Artillery Regiment
1 Regimental Staff
1 (mot) Regimental Staff Battery
1 (mot) Calibration Detachment
1st Battalion
1 Battalion Staff
1 (mot) Battalion Staff Battery
3 (motZ) Batteries (4 105mm leFH & 2 LMGs ea)
2nd Battalion
1 Battalion Staff
1 (mot) Battalion Staff Battery
2 (motZ) Batteries (4 150mm sFH 18 & 2 LMGs)
Attached
3 (motZ) Batteries (4 105mm leFH & 2 LMGs ea)
3rd Btry/520th (motZ) Artillery Battalion (4 105mm leFH & 2 LMGS)

The pioneer battalion added a (mot) pioneer company equipped the same as the other two, a (mot) light pioneer supply column, and a (mot) bridging train. The supply troop was radically upgraded, now having seven heavy (mot) supply columns (2 LMGs ea), two light (mot) supply columns (2 LMGs ea), two (mot) maintenance companies (2 LMGs ea), and a (mot) supply company (2 LMGs). The flak battalion, reconnaissance battalion, signals battalion, administration, medical ordnance, etc. remained unchanged.

When Reinhard Heydrich was killed in Czechoslovakia on 6/4/42, his name was given to the 6th Gebrigs Jäger Regiment. On 8/22/42 the division was radically altered. The infantry strength rose to seven battalions, the artillery radically increased, the panzerjäger battalion was built up and the supply troops were reorganized yet again. Equipment wise, the lePzB 39 and sPzB 41 were eliminated from the division. The division was organized as follows:

Division
1 Mountain Division Staff (2 LMGs)
1 (mot) Mapping Detachment
SS Mountain Infantry Regiment "Reinhard Heydrich" (formed from Staff/,1/6th SS Gebirgs Infantry Regiment, SS 4th Gebirgs-Jäger Battalion, and 3/7th SS Gebirgs Infanterie Regiment)
1 Regimental Staff
1 Regimental Staff Company

1 Signals Platoon
1 Bicycle Platoon (2 LMGs & 2 anti-tank rifles)
1st & 2nd Mountain Battalions, each with
1 Battalion Staff
3 Mountain Companies (9 LMGs, 2 HMGs, 2 80mm mortars & 2 flamethrowers)
1 Heavy Mountain Company (8 HMGs & 6 80mm mortars)
1 Mountain Support Company
1 Signals Platoon
1 Pioneer Platoon (4 LMGs)
1 Nebelwerfer Platoon (3 launchers)
(mot) Mountain Panzerjäger Company (2 50mm PAK 38, 9 37mm PAK 36 & 4 LMGs)
Nebelwerfer Battery (6 launchers)
(mot) Light Supply Column (2 LMGs)
(horse drawn) Mountain Supply Column
7th SS Mountain Regiment (from 1st, 2nd, & 3rd SS Gebirgs-Jäger Battalions)
same as SS Mountain Infantry Regiment Reinhard Heydrich
SS Schützen (mot) Battalion (Gebirgs-Division Nord)
(from 1/7th SS Gebirgs Infanterie Regiment)
1 Battalion Staff
3 (mot) Companies (18 LMGs, 4 HMGs, & 2 80mm mortars)
1 (mot) Heavy Company (8 HMGs & 6 80mm mortars)
1 (mot) Support Company
1 Signals Platoon
1 Panzerjäger Platoon (3 37mm PAK 36)
1 Pioneer Platoon (3 LMGs)
446th Sturmgeschütz Battery (7 StuGs)
SS "Nord" Panzerjäger Battalion
1 Panzerjäger Battalion Staff (1 LMG)
2 (mot) Panzerjäger Companies (9 50mm PAK 38 & 9 LMGs)
1 Self Propelled Panzerjäger Company (9 76.2mm PAK & 9 LMGs)
SS Gebirgs-Artillerie Regiment
1 Artillery Regimental Staff
1 (mot) Artillery Regimental Staff Battery
1st Battalion
1 Mountain Artillery Battalion Staff
1 Mountain Artillery Battalion Staff Battery
3 Mountain Batteries (4 75mm & 2 LMGs ea)
2nd Battalion
same as 1st Battalion
3rd Battalion
1 (mot) Artillery Battalion Staff
1 (mot) Artillery Battalion Staff Battery
3 (motZ) Batteries (4 105mm leFH & 2 LMGs ea)

4th Battalion
1 (mot) Artillery Battalion Staff
1 (mot) Artillery Battalion Staff Battery
2 (motZ) Batteries (4 150mm sFH & 2 LMGs ea)
1 (motZ) Battery (4 100mm K18 & 2 LMGs)
SS "Nord" Reconnaissance Battalion
1 Battalion Staff
1 (mot) Signals Platoon
2 Motorcycle Companies (2 80mm mortars, 4 HMGs, 18 LMGs)
1 (mot) Reconnaissance Company
1 Pioneer Platoon (3 LMGs)
1 Panzerjäger Platoon (3 50mm PAK 38 & 1 LMG)
1 Infantry Gun Section (2 75mm leIG)
SS "Nord" Flak Battalion
1 Flak Battalion Staff
1 (mot) Flak Battalion Staff Battery
1 (mot) Signals Platoon
1 (motZ) Battery (4 88mm, 4 20mm & 3 LMGs)
1 (motZ) Battery (9 37mm guns)
1 (motZ) Battery (12 20mm & 3 LMGs)
2 (motZ) Battery (12 15mm & 3 LMGs ea)
1 (mot) Light Flak Supply Column
Signals Battalion
1 Mountain Radio Company (2 LMGs)
2 Mountain Telephone Companies (2 LMGs ea)
1 (mot) Light Supply Column
SS "Nord" Pioneer Battalion
1 (mot) Mountain Pioneer Battalion Staff
1 (tmot) Mountain Signals Platoon (2 LMGs)
1 (mot) Pioneer Company (9 LMGs & 2 flame-throwers)
1 (mot) "B" Bridging Column (2 LMGs)
1 (mot) Light Supply Column
SS "Nord" Divisional Support Units
1st–2nd (mot) Light Supply Columns (2 LMGs ea)
1st–5th (mot) Heavy Supply Columns (2 LMGs ea)
1st–2nd (mot) Fuel Columns (2 LMGs ea)
1 (mot) Maintenance Company (2 LMGs)
1 (mot) Supply Company (2 LMGs)
2 (mot) Ordnance Companies (2 LMGs ea)
Administration
1 (mot) Butcher Company (2 LMGs)
1 (mot) Bakery Company (2 LMGs)
1 (mot) Administration Company (2 LMGs)
Medical
1 (mot) Mountain Medical Company (6 LMGs)
1 (tmot) Mountain Medical Company (2 LMGs)
3 Ambulances (2 LMGs ea)
Other
1 (mot) Ordnance Company (3 LMGs)
2 (mot) Vehicle Maintenance Companies (3 LMGs)
1 (mot) Field Post Office
1 (mot) Military Intelligence Platoon

The organization underwent some unit transfers on 9/2/42. The 2/Reinhard Heydrich and 3/7th SS Mountain Regiment were detached, as was the 446th Sturmgeschütz Battalion. The infantry regiments lost their train elements. The lePzB 39 and sPzB 41 anti-tank rifles were restored to the infantry companies. The 1/,2/Nord Artillery Regiment were detached. The divisional support units were revised to four light and three heavy (mot) supply columns, two (mot) heavy fuel columns, two maintenance companies, and a supply company. The division was theoretically equipped with 644 submachine guns, 286 LMG 34s, 88 HMGs 34, 64 80mm mortars, 36 flamethrowers, 18 100mm nebelwerfers, 4 sPzB 41, 60 lePzB 39, 24 37mm PAK 36, 22 50mm PAK 38, 4 75mm leIG, 12 105mm leFH 18, 8 150mm sFH, 15 20mm flak guns, 9 37mm flak guns, 4 88mm flak guns, and 12 15mm MG 38s.

The next change occurred on 10/3/42. The 446th Sturmgeschütz Battalion was reassigned. The infantry regained its light (mot) supply columns and mountain supply columns as it had on 8/22/42. The independent (mot) light mountain supply column was replaced by a horse drawn supply column. The panzerjäger battalion appears to have lost its self-propelled battery, but later notes dating from 12/25/42 indicate that the guns had not yet been shipped to Finland. The only other change was a major reorganization of the artillery. The artillery was now organized as follows:

SS Gebirgs-Artillerie Regiment
1 Artillery Regimental Staff
1 (mot) Artillery Regimental Staff Battery
1st Battalion
1 Mountain Artillery Battalion Staff
1 Mountain Artillery Battalion Staff Battery
3 Mountain Batteries (4 75mm & 2 LMGs ea)
2nd Battalion
same as 1st Battalion
3rd Battalion
1 (mot) Artillery Battalion Staff
1 (mot) Artillery Battalion Staff Battery
3 (motZ) Batteries (4 105mm leFH & 2 LMGs ea)
4th Battalion
1 (mot) Artillery Battalion Staff
1 (mot) Artillery Battalion Staff Battery
2 (motZ) Batteries (4 150mm sFH & 2 LMGs ea)
1 (motZ) Battery (4 100mm K18 & 2 LMGs)
2 (motZ) Batteries (4 105mm leFH & 2 LMGs ea)

The division theoretically had 644 submachine guns, 386 LMG 34, 88 HMG 34, 64 80mm mortars, 36 flamethrowers 4 sPzB 41, 60 lePzB 39, 24 37mm PAK 226, 22 50mm PAK 38, 7 sturmgeschütz, 4 75mm leIG, 20 105mm leFH 18, 8 150mm sFH, 15 20mm flak guns, 9 37mm flak guns, 4 88mm flak guns, and 12 15mm MG 38s.

On 12/25/42 the 100mm nebelwerfer launchers in the infantry regiments were ordered increased from three to six in number. However, this does not appear to have happened. The 4th Artillery Battalion detached its two 105mm leFH batteries. The motorcycle companies of the reconnaissance regiment were issued three anti-tank rifles. The panzerjäger battalion appears to have added part of the third assigned battery. The constitution of what arrived is unclear. Certainly the self-propelled anti-tank guns are shown as not being present, but some sort of an infantry detachment was present, as the battery is shown as being present and equipped with 6 80mm mortars, 4 HMGs and 9 LMGs.

The supply troops were reorganized again, now having six (mot) heavy supply columns, two (mot) heavy fuel columns, and a (mot) supply company. All were equipped with two LMGs each. A veterinary company (1 LMG), a (mot) military police company (3 LMGs), and an SS (mot) construction company (10 LMGS) were added to the division.

On 2/1/43 the three infantry companies in each battalion added two flamethrowers each. The presence of this incredible number of flamethrowers and the very high number of submachine guns gave the division a tremendous firepower. Though numerically smaller than a regular infantry division, the Nord Division was most certainly their equal or superior in combat power.

On 2/1/43 the two 105mm batteries were restored to the 4th Artillery Battalion, but they now contained six 105mm leFH and 3 LMGs each. The self-propelled 76.2mm panzerjägers (probably Marder I) still appear to have not arrived. The motorcycle companies of the reconnaissance battalion changed their equipment and how had 2 80mm mortars, 4 HMGs, 18 LMGs, and 3 anti-tank rifles. The battalion staff also added a motorized section with two sPzB 41 anti-tank rifles. The (mot) light pioneer supply column was now armed with 2 LMGs and 2 flamethrowers. The supply troops raised the number of (mot) heavy supply columns to seven.

The question of the self-propelled 76.2mm panzerjägers (probably Marder I) resolved on 4/25/43, when documentation indicates the arrival of nine of the scheduled self-propelled anti-tank vehicles. However, on 5/1/43 the self-propelled guns appear to have been detached and replaced by the assignment, but non-arrival, of towed 75mm PAK guns. On 6/1/43 the division was organized as follows:

Division
1 Mountain Division Staff (2 LMGs)
1 (mot) Mapping Detachment

SS Mountain Infantry Regiment "Reinhard Heydrich"
- 1 Regimental Staff
- 1 Regimental Staff Company
  - 1 Signals Platoon
  - 1 Bicycle Platoon (2 LMGs & 2 anti-tank rifles)

1st, 2nd, & 3rd Mountain Battalions, each with
- 1 Battalion Staff
- 3 Mountain Companies (2 LMGs, 2 HMGs, 3 PzBu, 2 80mm mortars & 2 flamethrowers)
- 1 Heavy Mountain Company (8 HMGs & 6 80mm mortars)
- 1 Mountain Support Company
  - 1 Signals Platoon
  - 1 Pioneer Platoon (4 LMGs)
  - 1 Nebelwerfer Platoon (3 launchers)
- **(mot) Mountain Panzerjäger Company** (2 50mm PAK 38, 9 37mm PAK 36 & 4 LMGs)
- **Nebelwerfer Battery** (6 launchers)
- **(mot) Light Supply Column** (2 LMGs)
- **(horse drawn) Mountain Supply Column**

7th SS Mountain Regiment
- same as SS Mountain Infantry Regiment Reinhard Heydrich

SS Schützen (mot) Battalion (Gebirgs-Division Nord)
- 1 Battalion Staff
- 1 (mot) Signals Platoon
- 1 Motorcycle Messenger Detachment
- 3 (mot) Companies (18 LMGs, 4 HMGs, 3 PzBu & 2 80mm mortars)
- 1 (mot) Heavy Company (8 HMGs & 6 80mm mortars)
- 1 (mot) Support Company
  - 1 Signals Platoon
  - 1 Panzerjäger Platoon (3 37mm PAK 36)
  - 1 Pioneer Platoon (3 LMGs)

SS "Nord" Panzerjäger Battalion
- 1 Panzerjäger Battalion Staff (1 LMG)
- 2 (mot) Panzerjäger Companies (9 50mm PAK 38 & 9 LMGs)
- 1 Self Propelled Panzerjäger Company (9 76.2mm PAK, 6 120mm mortars, 4 HMGs & 8 LMGs)

SS Gebirgs-Artillerie Regiment
- 1 Artillery Regimental Staff
- 1 (mot) Artillery Regimental Staff Battery (2 LMGs)
- 1 (mot) Survey Battery (16 LMGs)

1st Battalion
- 1 Mountain Artillery Battalion Staff
- 1 Mountain Artillery Battalion Staff Battery
- 1st–3rd Mountain Batteries (4 75mm & 2 LMGs ea)

2nd Battalion
- same as 1st Battalion, 4th–6th Batteries

3rd Battalion
- 1 (mot) Artillery Battalion Staff
- 1 (mot) Artillery Battalion Staff Battery
- 7th–9th (motZ) Batteries (4 105mm leFH & 2 LMGs ea)

4th Battalion
- 1 (mot) Artillery Battalion Staff
- 1 (mot) Artillery Battalion Staff Battery
- 10th–11th (motZ) Batteries (4 150mm sFH & 2 LMGs ea)
- 12th (motZ) Battery (4 100mm K18 & 2 LMGs)

Attached
- 1 (mot) Battery (6 76.2mm & 2 LMGs)
- 1 (mot) Battery (6 unk light howitzers & 2 LMGs)

SS "Nord" Reconnaissance Battalion
- 1 Battalion Staff
- 1 (mot) Signals Platoon (8 LMGs)
- 1 (mot) Machine Gun Company (8 HMGs)
- 2 Motorcycle Companies (2 80mm mortars, 4 HMGs, 18 LMGs)
- 1 (mot) Reconnaissance Company
  - 1 Pioneer Platoon (4 LMGs)
  - 1 Panzerjäger Platoon (3 50mm PAK 38, 37mm PAK 36 & 1 LMG)
  - 1 Infantry Gun Section (2 75mm leIG)

SS "Nord" Flak Battalion
- 1 (mot) Flak Battalion Staff Battery
- 1 (mot) Signals Platoon
- 1 (motZ) Battery (4 88mm, 4 20mm & 3 LMGs)
- 1 (motZ) Battery (12 37mm guns)
- 1 (motZ) Battery (12 20mm, 2 quad 20mm & 4 LMGs)
- 2 (motZ) Battery (12 15mm & 3 LMGs ea)
- 1 (mot) Light Flak Supply Column

Signals Battalion
- 1 (tmot) Mountain Radio Company (2 LMGs)
- 2 (tmot) Mountain Telephone Companies (2 LMGs ea)
- 1 (mot) Signals Light Supply Column

SS "Nord" Pioneer Battalion
- 1 (mot) Mountain Pioneer Battalion Staff
- 1 (mot) Mountain Signals Platoon (18 LMGs, 3 PzBu & 6 flamethrowers)
- 2 Pioneer Companies (9 LMGs, 3 PzBu & 6 flamethrowers ea)
- 1 (mot) "B" Bridging Column (2 LMGs)
- 1 (mot) Light Supply Column (2 LMGs & 2 flamethrowers)

SS "Nord" Divisional Support Units
- Staff (3 LMGs)
- 1st–4th (mot) Transportation Column (4 LMGs ea)
- 1 (mot) Maintenance Company (2 LMGs)
- 1 (mot) Fuel Column (2 LMGs)
- 1 (mot) Supply Company (2 LMGs)

1 (mot) Ordnance Company (2 LMGs)
SS Nord Maintenance Battalion
  2 (mot) Maintenance Companies (2 LMGs ea)
Administration
  1 (mot) Butcher Company (2 LMGs)
  1 (mot) Bakery Company (2 LMGs)
  1 (mot) Administration Company (2 LMGs)
Medical
  1 (mot) Mountain Medical Company (6 LMGs)
  1 (tmot) Mountain Medical Company (2 LMGs) 3
  Ambulances (2 LMGs ea)
Other
  1 (mot) Ordnance Company (3 LMGs)
  2 (mot) Vehicle Maintenance Companies (3 LMGs)
  1 (mot) Field Post Office
  1 (mot) Military Intelligence Platoon (10 LMGs)

The regiments were renumbered and on 10/22/43 named the 11th SS Gebirgs-Jäger Regiment "Reinhard Heydrich" and the 12th SS Gebirgs-Jäger Regiment. All other units received the number 6. At the same time the division was renamed the 6th SS Mountain Division "Nord."

The Norwegian Ski-Jäger Battalion (SS Ski-Jäger-Battalion Norge) (three companies) and the Norwegian Polizei Ski Company were assigned to the division in 1943. When the division was sent to the western front in 1944 the Norwegian Ski-Jäger Battalion remained in Norway and in February 1944 its was renamed the 506th SS Ski Battalion. OKH records dated 4/27/44 show the division organized and equipped as follows:

Division Staff
  1 (mot) Divisional Mapping Detachment
  Divisional Band
11th "R. Heydrich" SS Gebirgsjäger Division
  1 Regimental Staff
  1 Regimental Staff Company
    1 Signals Platoon
    1 Mountain Biccyle Platoon (3 LMGs)
    1 Anti-Tank Platoon (2 heavy anti-tank rifles)
  1st (Mountain) Battalion
    3 Companies (2 HMGs, 9 LMGs, 3 light anti-tank rifles, 2 80mm mortars, & 2 flamethrowers)
    1 Machine Gun Company (12 HMGs, 6 80mm mortars)
    1 Heavy Company
      1 Pioneer Platoon (4 LMGs)
      1 Signals Platoon
      1 Anti-Tank Platoon (3 light rocket launchers)
  2nd & 3rd Battalions
    same as 1st Battalion
  Mountain Nebelwerfer Battery (6 100mm nebelwerfers & 2 LMGs)

(motZ) Mountain Panzerjäger Company (2 50mm PAK 38, 9 37mm PAK 36 & 4 LMGs)
(mot) Light Supply Column
12th SS Gebirgsjäger Battalion
  same as 11th SS Gebirgsjäger Battalion
6th (mot) Battalion
  3 Companies (4 HMGs, 18 LMGs, 3 light anti-tank rifles, 2 80mm mortars, & 2 flamethrowers)
  1 Machine Gun Company (12 HMGs, 6 80mm mortars)
  1 Heavy Company
    1 Pioneer Platoon (4 LMGs)
    1 Infantry Gun Section (2 75mm leIG)
    1 Anti-Tank Platoon (3 50mm PAK 38)
SS "Norge" Jäger Ski Battalion
  3 Ski Companies (10 LMGs & 2 80mm mortars)
  1 Ski Machine Gun Company (6 HMGs, 2 75mm leIG & 4 self-propelled 20mm flak guns)
6th SS Reconnaissance Battalion
  2 Motorcycle Companies (4 HMGs, 18 LMGs, 3 light anti-tank rifles & 2 80mm mortars ea)
  1 (mot) Reconnaissance Company (4 HMGs, 18 LMGs, 3 light anti-tank rifles, & 2 80mm mortars ea)
  1 (mot) Reconnaissance Company
    1 Pioneer Platoon (4 LMGs)
    1 Panzerjäger Platoon (3 LMGs, 2 50mm PAK 38 & 2 37mm PAK 35)
    1 Infantry Gun Section (2 75mm leIG)
6th SS Panzerjäger Battalion
  1 Battalion Staff (1 LMG)
  2 (motZ) Panzerjäger Companies (9 50mm PAK 50 & 9 LMGs)
  1 Self Propelled Heavy Panzerjäger Company (75mm PAK 40 & 9 LMGs)
  1 Mortar Company (4 HMGs & 6 80mm mortars)
6th SS Gebirgs-Artillerie Regiment
  1 Artillery Regimental Staff
  1 (mot) Artillery Regimental Staff Battery
  1st & 2nd Battalions, each with
    1 Mountain Artillery Battalion Staff
    1 Mountain Artillery Battalion Staff Battery
    3 Mountain Batteries (4 75mm & 2 LMGs ea)
  3rd Battalion
    1 (mot) Artillery Battalion Staff
    1 (mot) Artillery Battalion Staff Battery
    3 (motZ) Batteries (4 105mm leFH & 2 LMGs ea)
  4th Battalion
    1 (mot) Artillery Battalion Staff
    1 (mot) Artillery Battalion Staff Battery
    2 (motZ) Batteries (4 150mm sFH & 2 LMGs ea)
    1 (motZ) Battery (4 100mm K18 & 2 LMGs)
  Attached by Army
    2 (motZ) Batteries (4 105mm leFH & 2 LMGs ea)

6th SS "Nord" Flak Battalion
1 Flak Battalion Staff
1 (mot) Flak Battalion Staff Battery
1 (mot) Signals Platoon
3 (motZ) Batteries (4 88mm, 4 20mm & 3 LMGs ea)
1 (motZ) Battery (9 37mm guns & 4 LMGs)
1 (motZ) Battery (2 quad 20mm & 4 LMGs)
2 Self Propelled Light Batteries (12 20mm & 4 LMGs ea)
1 (mot) Light Flak Supply Column (2 LMGs)

6th SS "Nord" Signals Battalion
1 (tmot) Mountain Radio Company (5 LMGs)
1 (tmot) Mountain Telephone Company (5 LMGs)
1 (mot) Light Supply Column

6th SS "Nord" Pioneer Battalion
1 (mot) Mountain Pioneer Battalion Staff
1 (tmot) Mountain Signals Platoon (2 LMGs)
1 (mot) Pioneer Company (9 LMGs, 3 light anti-tank rifles & 2 flamethrowers)
1 (mot) "B" Bridging Column (2 LMGs)
1 (mot) Light Supply Column (2 LMGs & 2 flamethrowers)

6th SS "Nord" Divisional Support Units
1 (mot) 120 ton Transportation Column

1 (mot) Heavy Supply Column (4 LMGs)
2 (mot) Heavy Fuel Columns (4 LMGs ea)
3 Mountain Light Supply Columns (2 LMGs ea)
6th SS (mot) Workshop Company (2 LMGs)
6th SS (mot) Supply Company (2 LMGs ea)

Truck Park
2 Truck Parks
6th SS (mot) Maintenance Company (2 LMGs)

Administration
6th SS (mot) Butcher Company (2 LMGs)
6th SS (mot) Bakery Company (2 LMGs)
6th SS (mot) Administration Company (2 LMGs)

Medical
1/,2/6th SS (tmot) Mountain Medical Companies (2 LMGs ea)
1/,2/,3/6th SS Ambulances (2 LMGs ea)

Other
1 (tmot) Veterinary Company (2 LMGs)
6th SS (mot) Field Post Office
6th SS (mot) Military Police Troop (3 LMGs)

On 6/21/44 the 12th SS Gebirgs-Jäger Regiment was named "Michael Gaismair." The division was captured in Bavaria and Thuringia by the Americans in May 1945.

6th SS Freiwilligen Sturmbrigade "Langemarck"

Formed on 5/31/43 as the SS Sturmbrigade "Langemarck," from the Flanders Volunteer Legion. This legion had consisted of the 1st Panzergrenadier Battalion (four companies), an infantry support gun company, a heavy anti-tank company, a sturmgeschütz battery, a light flak battery, and a heavy flak battery. All the units were motorized. In June 1943 the brigade organized and equipped as follows:

Brigade Staff
1 Brigade Staff
1 (mot) Brigade Staff Company
1 Signals Platoon
1 Pioneer Platoon (4 LMGs & 6 flamethrowers)
1 Motorcycle Platoon (6 LMGs)
1 War Correspondent Platoon
1st (mot) Battalion, each with
3 (mot) Grenadier Companies (2 HMGs, 18 LMGs, 2 80mm mortars)
1 (mot) Machine Gun Company (8 HMGs & 6 80mm mortars)
5th (motZ) Infantry Gun Company (2 150mm sIG & 4 75mm leIG)

6th (motZ) Panzerjäger Company (9 75mm PAK 40 & 9 LMGs)
7th Sturmgeschütz Company (10 StuGs)
8th Self Propelled Light Flak Company (12 20mm guns)
9th (motZ) Heavy Flak Company (4 88mm, 3 20mm & 2 LMGs)
10th (mot) ("Marsch") Reserve Column

In May 1944 OKH records show the brigade organized and equipped as follows:

Brigade Staff
1 Brigade Staff
1 (mot) Brigade Staff Company
1 Signals Platoon
1 Pioneer Platoon (4 LMGs)
1 Motorcycle Platoon (6 LMGs)
1st (mot) Battalions, each with
1st–3rd (mot) Grenadier Companies (2 HMGs, 18 LMGs, 2 80mm mortars)
4th (mot) Machine Gun Company (8 HMGs & 6 80mm mortars)

5th (motZ) Panzerjäger Company (9 75mm PAK 40 & 9 LMGs)

2nd (mot) Battalions, each with

6th–8th (mot) Grenadier Companies (2 HMGs, 18 LMGs, 2 80mm mortars)

9th (mot) Machine Gun Company (8 HMGs & 6 80mm mortars)

10th (motZ) Panzerjäger Company (9 75mm PAK 40 & 9 LMGs)

11th (motZ) Infantry Gun Company (2 150mm sIG & 4 75mm leIG)

12th Sturmgeschütz Company (10 StuGs)

13th Self Propelled Light Flak Company (12 20mm guns)

14th (motZ) Heavy Flak Company (4 88mm, 3 20mm & 2 LMGs)

1 Feldersatz Company

1 (mot) Heavy Supply Column

On 10/22/43 it was redesignated as the 6th SS Freiwilligen Sturmbrigade. On 4/29/44 it was brought into Bohemia and rebuilt. On 6/28/44 it raised a second panzer grenadier battalion. The sturmgeschütz battery became a battalion, but did not increase its strength. The order of 10/18/44 redesignated it as the 27th SS Freiwilligen Grenadier Division "Langemarck."

7th SS Freiwilligen-Gebirgs (Mountain) Division "Prinz Eugen"

The division was ordered formed in early 1942 but was not fully formed until October. After March it was known as the 7th SS Division. It was renamed the SS Freiwilligen Division "Prinz Eugen" on 4/1/42. In 1943 it would be renamed the SS Freiwilligen-Gebirgs Division "Prinz Eugen" and was renamed on 10/22/43 as the 7th SS Freiwilligen-Gebirgs Division "Prinz Eugen." The division was formed in the Serbian Banat from 15,000 drafted ethnic Germans. When organized, it consisted of:

1/,2/,3/,4/1st SS Mountain Jäger Regiment "Prinz Eugen"

1/,2/,3/,4/2nd SS Mountain Jäger Regiment "Prinz Eugen"

SS Bicycle Battalion "Prinz Eugen" (3 companies)

SS Cavalry Battalion "Prinz Eugen" (2 sqns, no staff)

SS Panzer Battalion "Prinz Eugen" (1 co)

1/,2/,3/,4/SS Mountain Artillery Regiment "Prinz Eugen" (4th (heavy) Battalion formed in the winter 1942)

SS Signals Battalion "Prinz Eugen" (2 cos) (3 in 1943)

SS Pioneer Battalion "Prinz Eugen" (2 cos) (3 in 1943)

SS Mountain Jäger Battalion "Prinz Eugen" (4 companies, later 5)

Support Troops "Prinz Eugen"

On 4 April 1942 it was organized as follows:

Division Staff
Mapping Detachment
Music Platoon (band)
Military Police Detachment
War Correspondent Platoon

Division Staff Defense Company

1st SS Mountain Jäger Regiment "Prinz Eugen"
  1st Battalion: 1st–6th Companies
  2nd Battalion: 7th–12th Companies
  3rd Battailon: 13th–18th Companies
  4th Battailon: 19th–23rd Companies

2nd SS Mountain Jäger Regiment "Prinz Eugen"
  1st Battalion: 1st–6th Companies
  2nd Battalion: 7th–12th Companies
  3rd Battailon: 13th–18th Companies
  4th Battailon: 19th–23rd Companies

Artillery Regiment "Prinz Eugen"
  1st Battalion: 1st & 2nd Batteries
  2nd Battalion: 3rd & 4th Batteries
  3rd Battalion: 5th, 6th & 7th Batteries
  4th Battalion: 8th, 9th & 10th Batteries

Bicycle Battalion "Prinz Eugen"

Cavalry Reconnaissance Squadron "Prinz Eugen"

SS Panzer Battalion "Prinz Eugen"
  German Armored Company
  Captured Armor Company (Renault M-18 tanks)

Pioneer Battalion "Prinz Eugen"

Signals Battalion "Prinz Eugen"

Division Supply Detachment "Prinz Eugen"

Flak Battalion "Prinz Eugen"

Administration Battalion "Prinz Eugen"

Maintenance Company "Prinz Eugen"

Medical Battalion "Prinz Eugen"

Veterinary Detachment "Prinz Eugen"

During the winter of 1942/43 the following were raised:

SS Reconnaissance Battalion "Prinz Eugen" (4 sqns)

SS Panzerjäger Battalion "Prinz Eugen" (3 companies)

SS Motorcycle Battalion "Prinz Eugen" (3 companies)
SS Flak Battalion "Prinz Eugen" (3 companies)

In March 1943 the division contained:

Division Staff
1 Divisional Staff (2 LMGs)
1 (mot) Mapping Detachment
1 (mot) Escort Company (9 LMGs, 3 50mm mortars & 2 37mm PAK 36)

13th Waffen SS Gebirgsjäger Regiment
1 Mountain Regimental Staff & Staff Company
    1 Mountain Signals Platoon
    1 Mountain Bicycle Platoon
1 Mountain Support Company (9 LMGs, 3 50mm mortars & 2 37mm PAK 36)

1st Battalion
1 Battalion Staff
1 Mountain Signals Platoon
3 Gebirgsjäger Companies (9 LMGs, 3 50mm mortars & 2 anti-tank rifles)
1 Gebirgsjäger Machine Gun Company (8 HMGs,)
1 Gebirgsjäger Heavy Company
    1 Pioneer Platoon (4 LMGs & 2 flamethrowers)
    1 Infantry Gun Platoon (2 75mm leIG)
    1 Panzerjäger Platoon (2 37mm PAK 36)
    1 Mortar Platoon (6 80mm mortars)
1 Streif (alpin) Company (8 LMGs, 3 50mm mortars)

2nd Battalion
same as 1st Battalion

3rd Battalion
same as 1st Battalion

4th Battalion
1 Battalion Staff
1 Mountain Signals Platoon
1 Mountain Reconnaissance Company (2 HMGs, 9 LMGs, 6 light armored cars)
1 Mountain Pioneer Company
    1 Pioneer Platoon (12 LMGs)
    1 Bridging Platoon
    1 Pack Mule Platoon
    1 Flamethrower Platoon (6 flamethrowers)
1 Mountain Heavy Company (2 LMGs & 6 100mm nebelwerfers)
1 (mot) Light Supply Column

14th Waffen SS Gebirgsjäger Regiment
same as 13th Waffen SS Gebirgsjäger Regiment

Panzerjäger Battalion
1 Battalion Staff & Staff Platoon (1 LMG)
3 (motZ) Medium Panzerjäger Company (9 50mm PAK & 9 LMGs)

Mountain Bicycle Battalion
3 Mountain Bicycle Companies

Cavalry Battalion
2 Cavalry Squadrons (12 LMGs ea)

7th SS Mountain Artillery Regiment
1 Regimental Staff & Staff Battery

1st Battalion
1 Battalion Staff & Staff Battery (2 LMGs)
2 Batteries (4 75mm mountain guns & 2 LMGs ea)
1 Light Mountain Supply Train

2nd Battalion
1 Battalion Staff & Staff Battery (2 LMGs)
2 (motZ) Batteries (4 100mm K18 & 2 LMGs ea)

3rd Battalion
1 Battalion Staff & Staff Battery (2 LMGs)
3 Batteries (4 88mm & 2 LMGs)
1 Light Mountain Supply Train

4th Battalion
1 Battalion Staff & Staff Battery (2 LMGs)
2 (motZ) Batteries (4 150mm sFH & 2 LMGs ea)
1 (motZ) Battery (4 105mm mountain guns & 2 LMGs ea)
1 (mot) Light Supply Train

1171st Light Panzer Reconnaissance Company

7th Reconnaissance Battalion
1 (mot) Signals Platoon
2 Motorcycle Squadrons (2 HMGs & 9 LMgs)
1 (mot) Reconnaissance Company
    1 Panzerjäger Platoon (3 37mm PAK 36 & 3 LMGs)
    1 leIG Platoon (2 75mm leIG)
    1 Pioneer Platoon (4 LMGs)

7th SS Flak Battalion
1 Staff & (mot) Staff Battery
1 (motZ) Light Flak Battery (12 20mm & 2 LMGs)
1 (motZ) Medium Flak Battery (9 37mm & 4 LMGs)
1 (motZ) Heavy Flak Battery (4 88mm & 2 LMGs)

7th SS Pioneer Battalion
1 Battalion Staff
1 (tmot) Mountain Pioneer Company (4 LMGs & 6 flamethrowers)
1 Mountain Pioneer Company (4 LMGs & 6 flamethrowers)
1 (mot) Pioneer Brüko B Bridging Train
1 (mot) Light Pioneer Supply Column
1 (mot) Pioneer Maintenance Column

7th SS Signals Battalion
1 (tmot) Telephone Company (2 LMGs)
1 (tmot) Radio Company (2 LMGs)
1 (tmot) Supply Column (2 LMGs)

Supply Troop
3 Light (mot) Supply Columns (2 LMGs ea)
3 Light (tmot) Supply Columns (2 LMGs ea)
6 Light (horse drawn) Mountain Supply Columns (2 LMGs ea)

1 (mot) Fuel Column (2 LMGs)
1 (mot) Supply Company (6 LMGs)
2 (mot) Maintenance Companies (2 LMGs ea)
Other
1 (mot) Butcher Company (2 LMGs)
1 (mot) Bakery Company (2 LMGs)
1 (mot) Divisional Administration (2 LMGs)
3 (tmot) Mountain Medical Companies (2 LMGs)
1 (tmot) Mountain Ambulance (2 LMGs)
1 (mot) Ambulance (2 LMGs)
1 Mountain Veterinary Company (2 LMGs)
1 (tmot) Veterinary Company (2 LMGs)
1 (mot) Military Police Det (2 LMGs)
1 (horse mounted) Military Police Det (2 LMGs)
1 (mot) Field Post Office (2 LMGs)
1 (mot) Military Police Detachment (2 LMGs)

During the summer of 1943 the motorcycle battalion was disbanded and the 1st SS Mountain Jäger Regiment was reinforced by the addition of a 22nd and 23rd Company. A feldersatz battalion with five companies was organized. On 10/22/43 the division was renamed the 7th SS Freiwilligen Gebirgs Division and on 11/13/44 the two mountain jäger regiments were renamed the 13th SS Freiwilligen Gebirgsjäger Regiment "Artur Phleps" and the 14th SS Freiwilligen Gebirgsjäger Regiment. The remaining formations were all numbered as the 7th Battalion, etc, except for the Reconnaissance Battalion which became the 105th Reconnaissances Battalion of the V SS Corps. In July 1944 the division had:

Division Staff
1 Divisional Staff (2 LMGs)
1 (mot) Mapping Detachment
1 (mot) Escort Company (2 HMGs, 12 LMGs, 2 80mm mortars & 3 150mm sIG)
1 (half track) Reconnaissance Platoon (10 LMGs & 5 halftracks)
1 Panzer Reconnaissance Platoon (5 Mk II Tanks & 5 LMGs)
13th Waffen SS Gebirgsjäger Regiment
1 Mountain Regimental Staff & Staff Company
1 Mountain Signals Platoon
1 Mountain Bicycle Platoon
1 Mountain Support Company (2 HMGs, 12 LMGs, 3 50mm mortars & 2 75mm leIG)
1 Mountain Flak Battery (3 20mm & 1 LMG)
1st Battalion
1 Battalion Staff
1 Mountain Signals Platoon
3 Gebirgsjäger Companies (2 HMGs, 12 LMGs, & 3 50mm mortars)
1 Gebirgsjäger Machine Gun Company (8 HMGs)
1 Gebirgsjäger Heavy Company

1 Pioneer Platoon (4 LMGs & 2 flamethrowers)
1 leIG Platoon (2 75mm leIG)
1 Panzerjäger Platoon (2 37mm PAK 36)
1 Mortar Platoon (6 80mm mortars)
1 Streif (alpin) Company (2 HMGs, 12 LMGs, & 3 50mm mortars)
2nd Battalion
same as 1st Battalion
3rd Battalion
same as 1st Battalion
4th Battalion
1 Battalion Staff
1 Mountain Signals Platoon
1 Mountain Reconnaissance Company (2 HMGs, 9 LMGs, 6 light armored cars)
1 Mountain Pioneer Company
1 Pioneer Platoon (12 LMGs)
1 Bridging Platoon
1 Pack Mule Platoon
1 Flamethrower Platoon (6 flamethrowers)
1 Mountain Heavy Company (2 LMGs & 6 100mm nebelwerfers)
1 Streif (alpin) Company (2 HMGs, 12 LMGs, & 3 50mm mortars)
1 (mot) Light Supply Column
14th Waffen SS Gebirgsjäger Regiment
same as 13th Waffen SS Gebirgsjäger Regiment
Panzerjäger Battalion
1 Battalion Staff & Staff Platoon (1 LMG)
1 (motZ) Heavy Panzerjäger Company (9 75mm PAK & 9 LMGs)
1 (motZ) Medium Panzerjäger Company (9 50mm PAK & 9 LMGs)
1 Self Propelled Flak Company (10 20mm flak & 10 LMGs)
7th Reconnaissance Battalion
1 Mountain Bicycle Squadrons (2 HMGs, 12 LMGs & 3 50mm mortars)
1 (mot) Reconnaissance Company
1 Armored Car Platoon (6 light armored cars)
1 Mortar Platoon (6 80mm mortars)
1 leIG Platoon (3 75mm leIG & 3 LMGs)
1 Pioneer Platoon (4 LMGs)
Cavalry Battalion
2 Cavalry Squadrons (2 HMGs, 9 LMGs & 2 80mm mortars ea)
7th SS Mountain Artillery Regiment
1 Regimental Staff & Staff Battery (4 self-propelled quad 20mm)
1st Battalion
1 Battalion Staff & Staff Battery (2 LMGs)
2 Batteries (4 75mm mountain guns & 2 LMGs ea)
1 Light Mountain Supply Train

2nd Battalion
  same as 1st Battalion
3rd Battalion
  1 Battalion Staff & Staff Battery (2 LMGs)
  2 Batteries (4 105mm mountain howitzers & 2
    LMGs ea)
  1 Light Mountain Supply Train
4th Battalion
  1 Battalion Staff & Staff Battery (2 LMGs)
  2 (motZ) Batteries (4 150mm sFH & 2 LMGs ea)
  1 (motZ) Battery (4 105mm mountain guns & 2
    LMGs ea)
  1 (mot) Light Supply Train
7th SS Flak Battalion
  1 Staff & (mot) Staff Battery
  1 (motZ) Light Flak Battery (12 20mm & 2 LMGs)
  1 (motZ) Medium Flak Battery (9 37mm & 4
    LMGs)
  1 (motZ) Heavy Flak Battery (4 88mm, 3 20mm &
    2 LMGs)
  1 (mot) Light Supply Column
7th SS Pioneer Battalion
  1 Battalion Staff
  1 (mot) Mountain Pioneer Company (2 HMGs,
    18 LMGs, 4 flamethrowers, & 2 80mm mortars)
  2 Mountain Pioneer Companies (2 HMGs, 9
    LMGs, 6 flamethrowers, & 2 80mm mortars ea)
  1 Pioneer Supply Column
  1 (mot) Pioneer Brüko B Bridging Train
  1 (mot) Light Pioneer Supply Column
  1 (mot) Pioneer Maintenance Column
7th SS Signals Battalion
  2 (tmot) Telephone Companies (5 LMGs ea)
  1 (mot) Radio Company (5 LMGs)
  1 (tmot) Supply Column (2 LMGs)
Feldersatz Battalion
  2–5 Companies
Supply Troop
  4 Light (mot) Supply Columns (2 LMGs ea)
  3 Light (horse drawn) Supply Columns (4 LMGs ea)
  6 Light (horse drawn) Mountain Supply Columns
    (3 LMGs ea)
  2 (mot) Fuel Columns (2 LMGs ea)
  1 (mot) Supply Company (6 LMGs)
  2 (mot) Maintenance Companies (2 LMGs ea)
Other
  1 (mot) Butcher Company (9 LMGs)
  1 (mot) Bakery Company (4 LMGs)
  1 (mot) Divisional Administration Platoon (7
    LMGs)
  1 (tmot) Mountain Medical Company (4 LMGs)
  1 (mot) Medical Company (4 LMGs)
  1 (tmot) Mountain Ambulance (2 LMGs)
  1 (mot) Ambulance (2 LMGs)

  1 Mountain Stretcher Bear Company (4 LMGs)
  1 (mot) Medical Supply Company (4 LMGs)
  2 Veterinary Companies (2 LMGs ea)
  1 (mot) Field Post Office (2 LMGs)
  1 (mot) Military Police Detachment (2 LMGs)

By 1 August 1944 the division had undergone some
rather radical reorganization and reequipping. Field
returns for that date indicate it had the following organization and equipment:

Staff
  1 Divisional Band
  1 (mot) Mapping Detachment
  1 (tmot) Military Police Detachment (4 LMGs)
13th Waffen SS Gebirgsjäger Regiment
  1 Mountain Regimental Staff & Staff Company
    1 Mountain Signals Platoon
    1 Cavalry Platoon
    1 Mountain Bicycle Platoon
    1 Mortar Section (? - 120mm mortars & 7 LMGs)
1st Battalion
  1 Battalion Staff
  1 Battalion Staff Company
    1 Mountain Signals Platoon
    1 Mountain Pioneer Platoon (3 LMGs)
  3 Gebirgsjäger Companies (2 HMGs, 10 LMGs, &
    2 80mm mortars)
  1 Gebirgsjäger Machine Gun Company (7 HMGs,
    2 LMGs, 3 37mm PAK & ? - 120mm mortars &
    2 LMGs)
2nd Battalion
  same as 1st Battalion
3rd Battalion
  same as 1st Battalion
  1 Infantry Gun Company (6 75mm leIG)
  1 Panzerzerstörer Company
    1 Staff Platoon (3 LMGs)
    1 (motZ) Panzerjäger Platoon (3 75mm PAK 40 &
      3 LMGs)
    1 Panzerschrecke Platoon (3 LMGs & ? Panzer-
      schrecke)
  1 Alpine Sturm Company (1 HMG, 10 LMGs, 1
    80mm mortar)
  1 Light Mountain Supply Column (3 LMGS)
14th Waffen SS Gebirgsjäger Regiment
  same as 13th Waffen SS Gebirgsjäger Regiment
7th Reconnaissance Battalion
  1 (mot) Staff Company
    1 Signals Platoon
    1 Pioneer Platoon (3 LMGs)
    1 Half Track Platoon (4 halftracks & 5 LMGs)
  2 Mountain Bicycle Squadrons (2 HMGs, 10
    LMGs ea)

1 Cavalry Squadron (2 HMGs & 12 LMGs)
1 (mot) Reconnaissance Company
  1 Mortar Platoon (6 80mm mortars)
  1 leIG Platoon (2 75mm leIG & 1 LMG)
  1 Panzerjäger Platoon (? - 75m PAK & 2 LMGs)

Panzerjäger Battalion
1 (mot) Battalion Staff & Staff Platoon (1 LMG)
1 (motZ) Heavy Panzerjäger Company (12 75mm PAK & 12 LMGs)
1 Sturmgeschütz Company (12 StuGs)
1 (motZ) Flak Company (12 20mm Mountain guns & 2 LMGs)

7th SS Mountain Artillery Regiment
1 Regimental Staff & (tmot) Staff Battery (4 self-propelled quad 20mm)

1st Battalion
1 Battalion Staff & Staff Battery (2 LMGs)
3 Batteries (4 75mm mountain guns & 2 LMGs ea)
1 Light Mountain Supply Train

2nd Battalion
same as 1st Battalion

3rd Battalion
1 Battalion Staff & Staff Battery (2 LMGs)
3 Batteries (4 105mm mountain howitzers & 2 LMGs ea)
1 Light Mountain Supply Train

4th Battalion
1 Battalion Staff & Staff Battery (2 LMGs)
1 (mot) Calibration Detachment
2 (motZ) Batteries (4 150mm sFH & 2 LMGs ea)
1 (motZ) Battery (4 105mm mountain guns & 2 LMGs ea)
1 (mot) Light Supply Train

7th SS Pioneer Battalion
1 Battalion Staff (3 LMGs)
1 (tmot) Battalion Staff Company (3 LMGs)
1 (mot) Mountain Pioneer Company (1 HMG, 16 LMGs, 6 flamethrowers, & 1 80mm mortar)
2 Mountain Pioneer Companies (2 HMGs, 9 LMGs, 6 flamethrowers, & 1 80mm mortar ea)

1 (mot) Pioneer Brüko B Bridging Train (8 LMGs)

7th SS Signals Battalion
1 (tmot) Telephone Companies (6 LMGs)
1 (tmot) Mountain Telephone Companies (5 LMGs)
1 (tmot) Radio Company (5 LMGs)
1 (mot) Supply Column (1 LMG)

Feldersatz Battalion
1 Company (1 HMG & 5 LMGs)
1 Company (6 LMGs & 1 75mm leIG)
1 Mountain Company (6 LMGs & 1 37mm PAK 36)
1 Company (6 LMGs & 1 80mm mortar)
1 Company (5 LMGs & 2 flamethrowers)

Supply Troop
1 (mot) 120 Transportation Company (5 LMGs)
1 Light (horse drawn) Mountain Supply Column (3 LMGs)
2 Light (horse drawn) Mountain Supply Columns (4 LMGs ea)
3 Light (horse drawn) Supply Columns (4 LMGs ea)
1 Mountain Supply Company (1 LMG)
1 (mot) Maintenance Company (6 LMGs)

Other
1 (mot) Butcher Company (6 LMGs)
1 (mot) Bakery Company (4 LMGs)
1 (mot) Divisional Administration Company (4 LMGs)
2 (tmot) Mountain Medical Company (4 LMGs ea)
1 (tmot) Mountain Ambulance (4 LMGs)
1 (mot) Ambulance (4 LMGs)
1 Mountain Stretcher Bear Company (4 LMGs)
1 (mot) Decontamination Company (4 LMGs)
1 Veterinary Company (16 LMGs)
1 (mot) Field Post Office (2 LMGs)

After heavy losses near Nisch in October 1944 the division was rebuilt. It was taken captive near Cilli by the Yugoslavians in 1945.

8th SS Cavalry Division "Florian Geyer"

The SS began raising cavalry formations in the pre-war period, with the first apparently being formed on 15 January 1934. The initial combat formation was the SS-Totenkopf-Reiterstandarte, which was formed as a mounted detachment in Berlin during the second week of September 1939 and intended for operational deployment in Poland. It consisted of a staff and four squadrons. At the end of its first week of formation, it had 27 officers, 424 men, and 399 horses. In November 1939 it underwent a reorganization and expansion, growing to 12 squadrons. The first eight were standard cavalry squadrons, the 9th was a replacement squadron, the 10th was a heavy squadron, the 11th a technical squadron, and the 12th was a horse battery. Its duties consisted of garrison duties and the escorting of prisoners of war. It was organized as follows:

Regimental Staff
Regimental Band
(mot) Signals Platoon
Medical Detachment
1st Battalion
  1st Squadron (2 platoons ea)
  2nd Squadron
  3rd Squadron
  4th Squadron
  5th (Machine Gun) Squadron
2nd Battalion
  1 (mot) Panzerabwehr Platoon
  1 (tmot) Cavalry Pioneer Platoon
3rd Battalion
  6th Squadron
  7th Squadron
  8th Squadron

9th Squadron
10th (Machine Gun) Squadron
4th Battalion
  1 (mot) Panzerabwehr Platoon
  1 (tmot) Cavalry Pioneer Platoon
Attached
  2 Horse Batteries (75mm guns)
  2 Cavalry Support Batteries (probably 75mm leIG)
  2 Bicycle Squadrons
  2 (mot) Light Cavalry Supply Columns

In May 1940 the 13th and 14th squadrons were formed. The Reiterstandarte was increased to 1,809 officers and men, which had become unwieldly, so it was decided to form it into two units on 5/15/40. At this time it contained:

1st SS-Reiterstandarte
  Staff
  1–4 Squadrons
  5–6th (Heavy) Squadrons
  7th bicycle Squadron
  Horse Battery

2nd SS-Reiterstandarte
  Staff
  1–4 Squadrons
  5–6th (Heavy) Squadrons
  7th bicycle Squadron
  Horse Battery

In the autumn of 1940 there was yet another reorganization. It was unofficially redesignated SS-Totenkopf-Kavallerie Regiment 1 and this would become its formal name in January 1941. The regiment then contained:

1st Half Regiment
  1st Abteilung (Detachment)
    1st Squadron
    2nd Squadron
    3rd Squadron
    4th Squadron
    5th (Machine Gun) Squadron
  2nd Detachment
    6th (technical) Squadron
    7th (horse artillery) Squadron
    8th (bicycle reconnaissance) Squadron
    9th (cavalry gun) Squadron
    Light Cavalry Column
2nd Half Regiment
  3rd Detachment
    1st Squadron
    2nd Squadron
    3rd Squadron
    4th Squadron
    5th (Machine Gun) Squadron
  4th Detachment
    6th (technical) Squadron
    7th (horse artillery) Squadron

    8th (bicycle reconnaissance) Squadron
    9th (cavalry gun) Squadron
    Light Cavalry Column

In March 1941 it underwent yet another reorganization and now had:

SS-Kavallerie-Regiment 1
  Signals Platoon
  Motorcycle Dispatch Platoon
  1st Squadron
  2nd Squadron
  3rd Squadron
  4th (Machine Gun) Squadron
  5th (mortar/infantry gun) Squadron
  6th (technical) Squadron
  7th (bicycle reconnaissance) Squadron
  8th (horse artillery) Squadron
  Light Cavalry Column
SS-Kavallerie-Regiment 2
  Signals Platoon
  Motorcycle Dispatch Platoon
  1st Squadron
  2nd Squadron
  3rd Squadron
  4th (Machine Gun) Squadron
  5th (mortar/infantry gun) Squadron
  6th (technical) Squadron

7th (bicycle reconnaissance) Squadron
8th (horse artillery) Squadron
Light Cavalry Column
SS-Kavallerie Ersatzabteilung (replacement detachment)
  1st Replacement Squadron
   1 Armored Car Platoon
   1st Platoon
   2nd Platoon
   Machine Gun Platoon
  2nd Replacement Squadron
   1st Platoon
   2nd Platoon
   3rd Platoon
  3rd Replacement Squadron
   1st Platoon
   2nd Platoon
   3rd Platoon

On 6/21/41 in the invasion of Russia both regiments were attached to the Headquarters Staff "Reichsführer-SS." By the end of July these two formations were recognized as separate regiments, as on 7/30/41 they appear officially as two separate regiments in OKH documents. At this time they were organized as follows:

SS-Kavallerie-Regiment 1
  Signals Platoon
  Motorcycle Dispatch Platoon
  Regimental Band
  1st Squadron
   Armored Car Platoon
   1st Platoon
   2nd Platoon
   3rd Platoon
  2nd Squadron
   same as 1st Squadron
  3rd Squadron
   same as 1st Squadron
  4th (Machine Gun) Squadron
   3 Platoons

5th (heavy) gun) Squadron
  3 Platoons
6th (technical) Squadron
  Anti-Tank Platoon
  Pioneer Platoon
7th (bicycle reconnaissance) Squadron
  Armored Car Platoon
  1st Platoon
  2nd Platoon
  3rd Platoon
8th (horse artillery) Squadron
  Weapons Section
  Ammunition Section
Light Cavalry Column
SS-Kavallerie-Regiment 2
  Signals Platoon
  Motorcycle Dispatch Platoon
  1st Squadron
  2nd Squadron
  3rd Squadron
  4th (Machine Gun) Squadron
  5th (heavy) Squadron
  6th (technical) Squadron
  7th (bicycle reconnaissance) Squadron
   Armored Car Platoon (not a component of the regiment)
   1st Platoon
   2nd Platoon
   3rd Platoon
  8th (horse artillery) Squadron
  Light Cavalry Column

In October 1941 the SS Cavalry Brigade served as part of the Kommandostab "Reichsführer-SS" with the 1st and 2nd SS (mot) Infantry Brigades, the "Reichsführer-SS" Escort Battalion, the SS Flak Detachment "Ost," the Flak Detachment Kommandostab "Reichsführer-SS," a signals detachment, an administrative detachment, and a supply troop. On 12/20/41 the brigade was organized as follows:

Brigade Staff
  Motorcycle Messenger Platoon
  Postal Unit
  Brigade Music Staff
SS-Kavallerie-Regiment 1
  Signals Platoon
  1st Squadron
   Armored Car Platoon
   1st Platoon
   2nd Platoon
   3rd Platoon

  2nd Squadron
   same as 1st Squadron
  3rd Squadron
   same as 1st Squadron
  4th (Machine Gun) Squadron
   3 Platoons
  5th (heavy gun) Squadron
   4 Platoons
  Light Cavalry Column

SS-Kavallerie-Regiment 2
  Signals Platoon
  Motorcycle Dispatch Platoon
  1st Squadron
  2nd Squadron
  3rd Squadron
  4th (Machine Gun) Squadron
  5th (heavy) Squadron
  Light Cavalry Column
  Bicycle Reconnaissance Detachment
    1st Squadron
      3 Platoons
    2nd Squadron

1 Armored Cart Platoon
  3 Platoons
  3rd Squadron
  3 Platoons
Artillery Battalion
  2 Batteries
Flak Battery
  2 Platoons
Pioneer Company
  2 Platoons
Veterinary Company
Signals Company
Medical Company

The organization of the brigade was not static and on 2/23/42 it consisted of:

Brigade Staff
  1 (mot) Mapping Detachment
1st Regiment
  1 Bicycle Platoon (3 LMGs)
  1 (tmot) Signals Platoon
  1 Motorcycle Messenger Platoon (3 LMGs)
  4 Squadrons (12 LMGs & 3 50mm mortars ea)
  1 Heavy Squadron (4 80mm mortars & 8 HMGs)
  1 Support Squadron
    1 (mot) Pioneer Platoon (3 LMGs)
    1 Self Propelled Panzerjäger Platoon (4 guns)
    1 Infantry Gun Battery (4 75mm leIG & 2 LMGs)
2nd Regiment
  same as 1st
Horse Artillery Regiment
  1 (tmot) Staff Battery
  1 (mot) Munitions Column
  1st & 2nd Battalions, each with
    2 Batteries (4 75mm field guns & 2 LMGs ea)
  1 (mot) Battery (4 150mm sFH 18 & 2 LMGs)
(mot) Flak Battalion
  1 (mot) Staff Battery
  1 Self Propelled Battery (12 20mm guns)
  1 Self Propelled Battery (9 37mm guns)
  1 (motZ) Heavy Battery (4 88mm guns)
  1 Self Propelled Flak Platoon (3 20mm guns)
  1 (mot) Munitions Column
(mot) Panzerjäger Company
  (9 50mm PAK 38 & 6 LMGs)
Bicycle Reconnaissance Battalion
  1 (mot) Signals Platoon
  2 Bicycle Squadrons (9 LMGs, 2 HMGS & 3 50mm mortars ea)
  1 (mot) Panzerjäger Platoon (4 50mm PAK 38 & 2 LMGs)

  1 (mot) Infantry Gun Section (2 75mm leIG)
  1 (mot) Pioneer Platoon (3 LMGs)
(mot) Pioneer Battalion
  2 (mot) Pioneer Companies (2 flamethrowers & 12 LMGs ea)
  1 (mot) Brüko B (2 LMGs)
  1 (mot) Light Pioneer Column (2 LMGs)
(tmot) Signals Battalion
  2 (tmot) Signals Companies (4 LMGS ea)
Supply Troop
  6 (mot) Light Supply Columns (2 LMGs ea)
  1 (mot) Light Fuel Column (2 LMGs)
  1 (mot) Maintenance Company (2 LMGs)
  1 (mot) Supply Platoon (2 LMGs)
Administrative & Support Units
  1 (mot) Field Bakery (2 LMGs)
  1 (mot) Butcher Company (2 LMGs)
  1 (mot) Administrative Detachment (2 LMGs)
  1 (mot) Medical Company (2 LMGs)
  2 Ambulance Companies (2 LMGs ea)
  1 (mot) Military Police Troop (2 LMGs)
  1 (mot) Field Post Office (2 LMGs)

The division began forming in early 1942. On 20 April 1942 the division contained:

1st SS Cavalry Regiment (staff squadron & 5 squadrons)
2nd SS Cavalry Regiment (staff squadron & 5 squadrons)
SS Artillery Regiment (2 batteries)
SS Bicycle Reconnaissance Battalion (staff, 1 heavy squadron and 3 squadrons)
SS Pioneer Company
SS Flak Company SS Signals Company
SS Veterinary Company
SS Medical Company

The formation continued and in September 1942 the SS Cavalry Brigade by the formation of a third regiment, the artillery, and support troops became a full division. The division was entitled the SS Cavalry Division and, between 16 May 1941 and 15 October 1942, it was organized and equipped as follows:

Divisional Staff
Divisional Staff (4 HMGs)
1 (mot) Mapping Detachment
1st, 2nd & 3rd SS Cavalry Regiments
Regimental Staff Company
1 (tmot) Signals Platoon
1 Bicycle Platoon (3 LMGs)
1 Motorcycle Platoon (6 LMGs)
4 Cavalry Squadrons (12 LMGs & 3 50mm mortars ea)
1 Heavy Cavalry Squadron (8 HMGs & 4 80mm mortars)
1 Support Company, with
1 (mot) Engineer Platoon (3 LMGs)
1 Self Propelled Panzerjäger Company (4 50mm PAK 38 & 2 LMGs)
1 Infantry Support Gun Platoon (4 75mm leIG)
1 Infantry Gun Battery, with
7 self-propelled sIG 150mm
1 Panzerjäger Battalion
1 Self Propelled Panzerjäger Co (Marder) (9 75mm PAK 40 & 6 LMGs)
1 (mot) Panzerjäger Co (9 50mm PAK 38 & 6 LMGs)
1 Bicycle Battalion
2 Bicycle Companies (3 50mm mortars, 2 HMGs & 9 LMGs ea)
1 (mot) Support Company, with
1 (mot) Engineer Platoon (3 LMGs)
1 Self Propelled Panzerjäger Company (4 50mm PAK 38 & 2 LMGs)
1 Infantry Support Gun Platoon (2 75mm leIG)
1 Flak Battalion
1 (mot) Battalion Staff Battery
1 Self Propelled Flak Battery (12 20mm guns)
1 Self Propelled Flak Battery (9 37mm guns)
1 (motZ) Flak Battery (4 88mm guns & 3 Self Propelled 20mm guns)
1 Artillery Regiment, with
1 Horse Artillery Battalion, with
Battalion Staff
3 Horse Batteries (4 75mm lFK 18 guns & 2 LMGs)
1 Light (mot) Supply Column
1 (mot) Battalion
Battalion Staff
2 (motZ) Batteries (4 105mm leFH 18 & 2 LMGs ea)
1 (motZ) Battery (4 150mm sFH 18 & 2 LMGs)
1 (mot) Light Supply Column

1 Signals Battalion
2 (tmot) Signals Companies
1 Light (mot) Signals Supply Column (2 LMGs)
1 (mot) Pioneer Battalion
2 (mot) Pioneer Companies (18 LMGs & 2 flamethrowers ea)
1 (mot) Light "B" Bridging Train (2 LMGs)
1 (mot) Light Engineering Supply Column (2 LMGs)
Supply Train
8 (mot) Light Supply Columns (2 LMGs ea)
1 (mot) Light Fuel Supply Column (2 LMGs)
1 (mot) Maintenance Company (2 LMGs)
1 (mot) Light Supply Company (2 LMGs)
Medical
1 (mot) Medical Company (2 LMGs)
3 Ambulance Companies (2 LMGs ea)
Other
1 (mot) Divisional Administration Platoon
1 (mot) Butcher Company
1 (mot) Bakery Company
1 (mot) Military Police Company
1 (mot) Field Post
1 Veterinary Company
1 (mot) SS "KB" Platoon

On 10/22/43 the SS Cavalry Division changed its name to the 8th SS Kavallerie Division.

15th SS Cavalry Regiment (6 squadrons)
16th SS Cavalry Regiment (6 squadrons)
17th SS Cavalry Regiment (6 squadrons)
8th SS Bicycle Reconnaissance Battalion (3 squadrons)
8th SS Panzerjäger Battalion (2 companies)
8th SS Sturmgeschütz Battery
1/,2/8th SS Artillery Regiment
8th SS Pioneer Battalion (2 companies)
8th SS Flak Battalion (3 batteries)
8th SS Signals Battalion (2 companies)
8th SS Feldersatz Battalion (4 companies)

The 18th SS Cavalry Regiment was formed November 1943 and around the same time a 4th (heavy) Company was added to the Bicycle Reconnaissance Battalion. On 3/17/44 the artillery regiment raised a new second battalion and the old 2nd Battalion became the new 3rd Battalion. The reconnaissance battalion was restructured into a panzer reconnaissance battalion (five companies) and the sturmgeschütz battery was raised to the strength of a battalion with three batteries. It was at this time that the division was renamed the 8th SS Kavallerie Division "Florian Geyer." In June the 8th SS Sturmgeschütz Battalion was absorbed into the 8th Panzerjäger Battalion. In July 1944 the division was organized as follows:

WAFFEN SS DIVISIONS AND BRIGADES

Division Staff
  1 Divisional Staff (2 LMGs)
  1 (mot) Mapping Detachment
  8th (mot) Military Police Detachment (2 LMGs)
  1 (mot) "Kb" Platoon
15th Waffen SS Cavalry Regiment
  1 Regimental Staff & (mot) Staff Squadron
    1 Signals Platoon (3 LMGs)
    1 Pioneer Platoon (8 LMGs)
  4 Cavalry Squadrons (2 HMGs, 18 LMGs, & 2 80mm mortars)
  1 Machine Gun Squadron (8 HMGs & 6 80mm mortars)
  1 Heavy Squadron
    1 Pioneer Platoon (4 LMGs)
    1 Panzerjäger Platoon (3 75mm pAK & 3 LMGs)
    1 Support Platoon (1 LMG, 4 75mm leIG, & 4 20mm flak guns)
16th Waffen SS Cavalry Regiment
  same as 15th Regiment
17th Waffen SS Cavalry Regiment
  same as 15th Regiment
18th Waffen SS Cavalry Regiment
  same as 15th Regiment
8th SS Panzerjäger Battalion
  3 (motZ) Panzerjäger Companies (9 75mm PAK & 9 LMGs)
8th SS Sturmgeschütz Battalion
  1 Battalion Staff & Staff Platoon (3 LMGs)
  3 Sturmgeschütz Companies (10 StuG & 2 LMGs ea)
8th Panzer Reconnaissance Battalion
  1 Battalion Staff (12 LMGs)
  1 Armored Car Company (18 20mm & 24 LMGs)
  1 (mot) Reconnaissance Companies (4 HMGs, 18 LMGS & 2 80mm mortars)
  1 Heavy Company
    1 Pioneer Platoon (4 LMGs & 6 flamethrowers)
    1 Panzerjäger Platoon (3 75mm PAK & 3 LMGs)
    1 leIG Platoon (1 LMG & 2 75mm leIG)
    1 Flak Battery (1 LMG & 4 20mm flak guns)
  1 Supply Company (2 LMGs)
8th Artillery Regiment
  1 Regimental Staff & (mot) Staff Battery (6 LMGs)
  1st, 2nd & 3rd Battalions, each with
    1 Battalion Staff & Staff Battery (2 LMGs)

  3 Batteries (4 105mm leFH & 4 LMGs ea)
8th SS Flak Battalion
  1 Battalion Staff & Staff Battery (1 LMG)
  1 (motZ) Heavy Battery (4 88mm, 3 20mm & 4 LMGs)
  1 (motZ) Medium Battery (9 37mm & 4 LMGs)
  1 (motZ) Light Battery (12 20mm & 2 LMGs)
Pioneer Battalion
  1 Battalion Staff (6 LMGs)
  3 (mot) Pioneer Companies (2 HMGs, 18 LMGs, 6 flamethrowers, & 2 80mm mortars ea)
Signals Battalion
  1 (mot) Telephone Company (6 LMGs)
  1 (mot) Radio Company (7 LMGs)
  1 (mot) Supply Column (1 LMG)
Feldersatz Battalion
  2–5 Companies
Supply Troop
  1 (tmot) Supply Battalion Staff (2 LMGs)
  3 (mot) 120 ton Transportation Companies (8 LMGs ea)
  2 (mot) Light Artillery Supply Columns
  1 (mot) Light Flak Supply Columns
  1 (mot) Light Supply Column (2 LMGs)
  4 (horse drawn) Supply Columns (4 LMGs)
  1 (mot) Supply Company (2 LMGs)
  1 (mot) Maintenance Company (4 LMGs)
Other
  8th SS 8th (mot) Butcher Company (2 LMGs)
  8th SS (mot) Bakery Company (2 LMGs)
  8th SS (mot) Divisional Administration Company (2 LMGs)
  1/,2/8th SS (mot) Medical Companies (4 LMGs ea)
  8th SS (mot) Decontamination Company
  1/,2/,3/8th SS Ambulances
  8th SS (mot) Medical Supply Company (4 LMGs)
  1/,2/8th SS Veterinary Company (6 LMGs)
  8th SS (mot) Field Post Office

The 17th SS Cavalry Regiment was detached and used to assist in the formation of the 22nd Freiwilligen Cavalry Division. The division then retained only the 15th, 16th, and 18th Cavalry Regiments. The division was destroyed in Budapest on 2/12/45. Only 170 men escaped.

9th SS Panzer Division "Hohenstaufen"

Formed on 2/1/43 as the 9th SS Panzergrenadier Division. On 3/1/43 it was given the name "Hohenstaufen." The division was formed with one battalion of Panther Mk V tanks and one of Mk IV tanks. On 8/9/43 the OKH ordered 12 Wespe self-propelled 105mm guns sent to the division.

In October 1943 the panzer battalion was expanded into a regiment with the assignment of a sturmgeschütz battalion. On 10/3/43 it was renamed SS Panzer Division "Hohenstaufen." The assigned Motorcycle Regiment was reorganized into the 9th SS Panzer Reconnaissance Battalion. On 10/22/43 the division was again renamed and became the 9th SS Panzer Division "Hohenstaufen." The 1st and 2nd Panzergrenadier Regiments (Hohenstaufen) were redesignated as the 19th and 20th SS Panzergrenadier Regiments. The division then had:

19th SS Panzergrenadier Regiment
  1st Battalion (1–4th Companies)
  2nd Battalion (5–8th Companies)
  3rd Battalion (9–12th Companies)
  13th (infantry gun) Company
  14th (flak) Company
  15th (motorcycle) Company
  16th (pioneer) Company
20th SS Panzergrenadier Regiment
  same as 19th SS Panzergrenadier Regiment
9th SS Panzer Regiment
  1st (Sturmgeschütz) Battalion
  2nd (Panther) Battalion
9th SS Artillery Regiment
  1st Battalion (3 self-propelled batteries)
  2nd Battalion (3 batteries)
  3rd Battalion (3 batteries)
  4th Battalion (3 batteries)
9th SS Reconnaissance Battalion (5 companies)
  9th SS Panzerjäger Battalion (originally 9th SS Sturmgeschütz Battalion with 3 batteries. Became panzerjäger battalion in February 1944)
9th SS Flak Battalion
9th SS Pioneer Battalion (3 companies)
9th SS Armored Signal Battalion (2 companies)
9th SS Divisional (Einheiten) Support Units

In April 1944 the panzer inventory and organization of the panzer element of the 9th SS Panzer Division was as follows:

2/9th SS Panzer Regiment
  1 Regimental Staff Company
  1 Self Propelled 20mm Flak Platoon
  1 Battalion with
    1 Battalion Staff Company
    2 Medium Panzer Companies
    2 Sturmgeschütz Companies
    Mk IV (lg)   49
    StuG   44
    Flak 38 (t)   12
    Cmd   3

Immediately before the Allied invasion of Normandy the 9th SS Panzer Regiment was as follows:

1/,2/9th SS Panzer Regiment
  1 Battalion
    1 Panzer Staff Company
    4 Medium Panzer Companies (Mk V)
  1 Battalion
    1 Panzer Staff Company
    2 Medium Panzer Companies (Mk IV)
    2 Sturmgeschütz Companies (StuG)
    Mk IV (lg)   46
    Mk V   79
    StuG   40

The division fought at Normandy, Arnhem, and in the Ardennes Offensive. In the summer of 1944 the 10th SS Panzer Division Frundsberg detached the 4/21st SS Panzergrenadier Regiment, which was used to form the new 2/19th SS Panzergrenadier Regiment. During the summer of 1944 the division was ordered reorganized and reequipped as follows:

Division Staff
  1 Divisional Staff (2 LMGs)
  1 Divisional Band
  9th SS (mot) Mapping Detachment
  9th SS (mot) Military Police Detachment (15 LMGs)
  9th SS (mot) Escort Company
    1 Self Propelled Flak Battery (4 20mm flak, 4 HMGs & 6 LMGs)
    1 Motorcycle Platoon (6 LMGs)
9th SS Panzer Regiment
  1 Regimental Staff & (mot) Staff Company
    1 Panzer Signals Platoon
    1 Panzer Platoon
    1 Panzer Flak Battery (8 37mm flak guns)
    1 Panzer Maintenance Company (4 LMGs)
1st Panzer Battalion
  1 Battalion Staff (1 LMG)
  1 Battalion Staff Company (11 LMGs)
  4 Panzer Companies (22 Mk V Panther Tanks ea)
  1 (mot) Supply Company (4 LMGs)
2nd Panzer Battalion
  1 Battalion Staff (1 LMG)
  1 Battalion Staff Company (11 LMGs)
  4 Panzer Companies (22 Mk IV Tanks ea)
  1 (mot) Supply Company (4 LMGs)
19th SS Panzergrenadier Regiment
  1 Regimental Staff & (mot) Staff Company
    1 Staff Platoon
    1 Signals Platoon
    1 Motorcycle Platoon (4 LMGs)
1st Battalion
  1 Battalion Staff
  1 (mot) Supply Company (4 LMGs)

3 (mot) Panzergrenadier Companies (4 HMGs, 18 LMGs & 2 80mm mortars)
1 (mot) Heavy Panzergrenadier Company
1 Mortar Platoon (2 LMGs & 4 120mm mortars)
1 Panzerjäger Platoon (3 75mm & 4 LMGs)

2nd & 3rd Battalions, each with
same as 2nd Battalion

1 Self Propelled Heavy Infantry Gun Company
(6 150mm sIG & 8 LMGs)

1 Self Propelled Flak Company
(12 20mm & 2 LMGs)

1 (mot) Pioneer Company
(2 HMGs, 12 LMGS, 2 80mm mortars & 18 flamethrowers)

20th SS Panzergrenadier Regiment
1 Regimental Staff & (mot) Staff Company
1 Staff Platoon (1 LMG)
1 Signals Platoon (7 LMGs)
1 Motorcycle Platoon (4 LMGs)

1st (mot) Battalion
same as 1/19th SS Panzergrenadier Regiment

2nd (mot) Battalion
same as 1st Battalion

3rd (mot) Battalion
1 Battalion Staff (6 LMGs)
1 (mot) Supply Company (4 LMGs)
3 (halftrack) Panzergrenadier Companies (4 HMGs, 29 LMGs, 2 80mm mortars, 6 20mm & 2 75mm leIG)
1 (halftrack) Heavy Panzergrenadier Company
1 Mortar Platoon (2 LMGs & 4 120mm mortars)
1 Panzerjäger Platoon (6 75mm & 4 LMGs)

1 Self Propelled Heavy Infantry Gun Company
(6 150mm sIG & 8 LMGs)

1 Self Propelled Flak Company
(12 20mm & 2 LMGs)

1 (mot) Pioneer Company
1 (mot) Pioneer Staff Platoon (1 LMG)
1 (halftrack) Pioneer Platoon (12 LMGs, 1 20mm & 6 flamethrowers)
1 (mot) Pioneer Platoon (8 LMGs & 12 flamethrowers)
1 (mot) Pioneer Platoon (2 HMGs & 2 80mm mortars)
1 (halftrack) Pioneer Platoon (6 LMGs & 6 flamethrowers)

9th SS Panzerjäger Battalion
1 Battalion Staff & Staff Platoon (1 LMG & 1 Jagdpanzer IV)
2 Jagdpanzer Companies (14 Jagdpanzer IV)
1 (motZ) Panzerjäger Company (12 75mm PAK & 12 LMGs)
1 (mot) Supply Company (3 LMGs)

9th SS Panzer Reconnaissance Battalion
1 Battalion Staff (3 LMGs)

1 Battalion Staff Company
1 Armored Car Platoon (3 75mm, 13 20mm & 16 LMGs)
1 (mot) Signals Platoon (7 LMGs)
1 Armored Car Company (16 20mm & 25 LMGs)
1 (halftrack) Reconnaissance Company (2 75mm, 2 80mm mortars, & 44 LMGs)
1 (halftrack) Reconnaissance Company (4 HMGs, 29 LMGs, 2 80mm mortars, 6 20mm & 2 75mm guns)
1 (halftrack) Reconnaissance Company
1 Staff Platoon (2 LMGs)
1 Panzerjäger Platoon (6 75mm, 2 LMGs)
1 Platoon (2 LMGs & 6 80mm mortars)
1 Pioneer Platoon (13 LMGs)
1 Supply Company (4 LMGs)

9th SS Artillery Regiment
1 Regimental Staff & (mot) Staff Battery (2 LMGs)
1 Self Propelled Flak Battery (4 quad 20mm guns)

1st Self Propelled Battalion
1 Battalion Staff & Staff Battery (2 LMGs)
1 Self Propelled Battery (6 150mm sFH SdKfz 165 Hummels & 4 LMGs)
2 Self Propelled Batteries (6 105mm leFH SdKfz 124 Wespe & 4 LMGs ea)

2nd & 3rd Battalions, each with
1 Battalion Staff & Staff Battery (2 LMGs)
2 (motZ) Batteries (6 105mm leFH & 6 LMGs ea)

4th Battalion
1 Battalion Staff & Staff Battery (2 LMGs)
2 (motZ) Batteries (6 150mm sFH & 6 LMGs ea)
1 (motZ) Battery (6 105mm K & 6 LMGs ea)

9th SS Flak Battalion
1 Battalion Staff & Staff Battery (1 LMG)
3 (motZ) Heavy Batteries (4 88mm, 3 20mm & 4 LMGs)
1 (motZ) Medium Battery (9 37mm & 4 LMGs)
1 (mot) Searchlight Battery (4 600mm searchlights)

9th SS Pioneer Battalion
1 Battalion Staff (2 LMGs)
1 (mot) Battalion Staff Company (6 LMGs)
1 (halftrack) Reconnaissance Platoon (8 LMGs)
1 (halftrack) Pioneer Company (2 HMGs, 46 LMGs, 6 flamethrowers, & 2 80mm mortars)
2 (mot) Pioneer Companies (2 HMGs, 18 LMGs, 6 flamethrowers, & 2 80mm mortars ea)
1 (mot) Light Panzer Bridging Train (3 LMGs)

9th SS Signals Battalion
1 Panzer Telephone Company (14 LMGs)
1 Panzer Radio Company (20 LMGs)
1 (mot) Supply Column (1 LMG)

9th SS Feldersatz Battalion
2–5 Companies

9th SS Supply Troop
- 1 (tmot) Supply Battalion Staff (2 LMGs)
- 6 (mot) 120 ton Transportation Companies (8 LMGs ea)
- 1 (mot) Supply Company (8 LMGs)
- 1 (mot) Ordnance Company (4 LMGs)
- 2 (mot) Maintenance Companies (5 LMGs ea)
- 1 (mot) Maintenance Company (4 LMGs)
- 1 (mot) Maintenance Supply Column (4 LMGs)

Other
- 9th SS (mot) Bakery Company (5 LMGs)
- 9th SS (mot) Butcher Company (4 LMGs)
- 9th SS (mot) Divisional Administration Platoon (2 LMGs)
- 1/,2/9th SS (mot) Medical Companies (4 LMGs ea)
- 9th SS (mot) Decontamination Company
- 1/,2/,3/9th SS Ambulances (1 LMG ea)
- 9th SS (mot) Field Post Office (2 LMGs)

After Normandy the division was reorganized with a panther battalion organized with four companies, each with 14 Mk V Panther tanks. The second battalion was a mixed battalion, having two companies each with 14 Mk IV tanks and two sturmgeschütz companies, each with 14 sturmgeschütz. On 9/12/44 the panzerjager battalion was equipped with 28 Jagdpanzer IV. By 9/25/44 the division had been reduced to the strength of a very weak kampfgruppe. It consisted of:

Kampfgruppe Kraft
Köhnken Battalion
- 1 Battalion Staff
- 2 Panzergrenadier Companies
- 1 Panzerjäger Platoon (2 37mm PAK 36 & 2 English anti-tank guns)
- 1 Flak Battery (3 20mm guns)
- 1 Mortar Platoon (7 80m mortars)
- 1 Heavy Machine Gun Platoon (3 HMGs)
Kaue Battalion
- 1 Battalion Staff
- 2 Panzergrenadier Companies
280th Sturmgeschütz Battalion
- 1 Battalion Staff
- 3 Sturmgeschütz Companies (9 StuGs total)
502nd SS Werfer Battalion
- 1 Companies (6 launchers & 1 50mm PAK 38 ea)
Kampfgruppe Bindmann
SS Panzer Reconnaissance Battalion
- 1 Battalion Staff
- 1 Company (3 75mm KwK & 5 LMGs)
- 1 Company (1 37mm PAK 36, 12 LMGs & 3 80mm mortars)
- 1 Company (11 LMGs & 1 75mm PAK 40)

10th Panzer Regiment
- 1 Company (3 Panther Mk V Tanks)
Flak Battery (8 20mm & 2 37mm flak guns)
37th Fortress Machine Gun Battalion
- 4 Companies (11 LMGS, 32 HMGs & 12 80mm mortars total)
Kampfgruppe Gerhard
Staff/School Regiment
Schoerken Battalion
Ship Cadre Battalion
Ladew Flak Kampfgruppe (8 20mm & 12 Russian 88mm guns)
Flak Battery Krüge (5 20mm & 4 88mm guns)
4th Luftwaffe Werft Abtielung 119/XI
191st Artillery Regiment
- 7 Batteries (3 105mm leFH ea)
- 1 Battery (2 105mm leFH)

The division was extensively rebuilt and by 12/8/44 its panzer inventory and the organization of the panzer regiment were as follows:

1/,2/9th SS Panzer Regiment
- 1 Battalion
  - 1 Panzer Staff Company
  - 4 Medium Panzer Companies (Mk V)
- 1 Battalion
  - 1 Panzer Staff Company
  - 2 Medium Panzer Companies (Mk IV)
  - 2 Sturmgeschütz Companies (StuG)

StuG	28
Mk IV (lg)	32
Mk V	33 (+25 enroute)
FlakpzIV (37)	8

On 2/1/45 the panzer inventory and organization of the 9th SS Panzer Regiment were as follows:

1/,2/9th SS Panzer Regiment
- 1 Panzer Staff Company
- 1 Battalion
  - 1 Panzer Staff Company
  - 4 Medium Panzer Companies (Mk V)
- 1 Battalion
  - 1 Panzer Staff Company
  - 2 Medium Panzer Companies (Mk IV)
  - 2 Sturmgescütz Companies (StuG)

StuG	25
Mk IV (lg)	26
Mk V	31
FlakpzIV	4

The division was taken prisoner by the Americans at Steyer.

10th SS Panzer Division "Frundsberg"

Formed on 2/1/43 in southwest France as the 10th SS Panzer Division. The division was formed with one battalion of Panther Mk V tanks and one of Mk IV tanks. On 6/1/43 it was given the title "Karl der Gross." The division had:

1st SS Panzergrenadier Regiment "Frundsberg"
  1st Battalion
    1–4th Companies
  2nd Battalion
    5–8th Companies
  3rd Battalion
    9–12th Companies
  13th (infantry gun) Company
  14th (flak) Company
  15th (motorcycle) Company
  16th (pioneer) Company
1/,2/,3/2nd SS Panzergrenadier Regiment "Frundsberg"
  same as 1st SS Panzergrenadier Regiment
1/,2/10th SS Panzer Regiment (2 battalions plus pioneer company)
10th SS Motorcycle Regiment
  Staff & Staff Company
  Armored Car Platoon
  1st & 2nd Battalions
SS Sturmgeschütz Battalion (3 batteries)
1/,2/,3/,4/SS Artillery Regiment (each battalion had 3 batteries)
SS Panzerjäger Battalion (3 companies)
SS Flak Battalion (4 batteries)
SS Pioneer Battalion (3 companies)
SS Armored Signal Battalion (2 companies)
SS Divisional (Einheiten) Support Units

During the summer of 1943 the 10th SS Motorcycle Regiment was disbanded and converted into the 10th SS Panzer Reconnaissance Battalion. Shortly later the the 10th SS Feldersatz Battalion with a staff and five companies was organized and organization of the 10th SS Panzerjäger Battalion was abandoned.

On 8/9/43 the OKH ordered 12 Wespe self-propelled 105mm guns sent to the division.

On 10/3/43 it was redesignated as the SS Panzer Division Frundsberg. On 10/22/43 the division was designated as the "10th" and the two panzer grenadier regiments were renumbered the 21st and 22nd SS Panzergrenadier Regiments. The division had:

1/,2/,3/21st SS Panzergrenadier Regiment

1/,2/,3/22nd SS Panzergrenadier Regiment
1/,2/10th SS Panzer Regiment (1st bn had panther tanks)
1/,2/,3/,4/10th SS Panzer Artillery Regiment
10th SS Reconnaissance Battalion (5 companies)
10th SS Panzerjäger Battalion (3 companies)
10th SS Flak Battalion
10th SS Pioneer Battalion (3 companies)
10th SS Armored Signal Battalion (2 companies)
10th SS Divisional (Einheiten) Support Units

In April 1944 the panzer inventory and organization of the armored element of the division were as follows:

2/10th SS Panzer Regiment
  1 Regimental Staff Company
  1 Battalion with
    1 Battalion Staff Company
    2 Medium Panzer Companies
    2 Sturmgeschütz Companies
    Mk IV (lg)   49
    StuG   44
    Cmd   3

OKH records dated 5/11/44 show the division organized and equipped as follows:

Division
  Division Staff (2 LMGs)
  (mot) Mapping Detachment
  Divisional Escort Company
    Motorcycle Platoon (6 LMGs)
    Self Propelled Flak Battery (4 20mm guns)
    Self Propelled Anti-Tank Platoon (3 LMGs & 3 75mm PAK 40)
    Infantry Gun Platoon (2 75mm leIG)
    Mixed Panzergrenadier Platoon (4 HMGs, 6 LMGs, & 2 80mm mortars)
2nd SS Panzer Regiment
  Regimental Staff
  1st Panzer Battalion
    Staff Panzer Company
    (1–4th Companies) (Mk V Panthers)
    1 Panzer Maintenance Platoon
  2nd Panzer Battalion
    Staff Panzer Company
    Panzer Flak Battery (37mm Flak 43)
    (5–6th Companies) (Mk IV Panzers)
    (7–8th Companies) (Sturmgeschütz)
    1 Panzer Maintenance Company

1 Halftrack Pioneer Company (40 LMGs & 6 flame-throwers)

1 (mot) Panzer Supply Column

21st SS Panzergrenadier Regiment
Regimental Staff
1st (halftrack) Battalion
1–3rd Companies (4 HMGs, 40 LMGs, 2 80mm mortars, 2 flamethrowers, 7 20mm guns & 2 75mm guns)
4th Company
1 Pioneer Platoon (13 LMG & 6 flamethrowers)
1 Panzerjäger Platoon (8 LMGs & 3 75mm PAK 40)
1 Infantry Gun Section (4 LMG & 2 75mm leIG ea)
1 Gun Platoon (8 LMGs & 6 75mm guns)
2nd (mot) Battalion (6–10th Companies)
1–3rd Companies (4 HMGs, 18 LMGs, 2 80mm mortars & 2 flamethrowers)
4th Company
1 Mortar Platoon (2 LMGs & 4 120mm mortars)
1 Panzerjäger Platoon (3 LMGs & 3 75mm PAK 40)
2 Infantry Gun Sections (1 LMG & 2 75mm leIG ea)
3rd (mot) Battalion (11–15th Companies) (same as 2nd Battalion)
16th (self-propelled flak) Company (12 20mm & 4 LMGs)
17th (self-propelled infantry gun) Company (6 150mm sIG & 8 LMGs)
18th (mot) Pioneer Company (2 HMGs, 12 LMGs, 6 flamethrowers & 2 80mm mortars)
22nd SS Panzergrenadier Regiment
Staff same as 21st Panzergrenadier Regiment
Three battalions like 2/21st Panzergrenadier Regiment
10th SS Reconnaissance Battalion
Battalion Staff
Heavy Platoon (6 SdKfz 234/3 with 75mm KwK & 6 LMGs)
1 Armored Car Company (18 20mm & 24 LMGs)
1 (halftrack) Armored Car Company (16 20mm & 25 LMGs)
2 (halftrack) Companies (49 LMGs, 2 80mm mortars & 3 75mm guns)
1 (halftrack) Company
1 Pioneer Platoon (13 LMGs & 6 flamethrowers)
1 Panzerjäger Platoon (8 LMGs & 3 75mm PAK 40)
1 Infantry Gun Section (2 75mm leIG & 4 LMGs)
1 Gun Section (8 LMGs & 6 75mm guns)
1 (mot) Reconnaissance Supply Column (3 LMGs)

10th SS Panzerjäger Battalion
Battalion Staff
3 Self Propelled Panzerjäger Companies (14 75mm PAK 40 & 14 LMGs ea)
10th SS Panzer Artillery Regiment
1 Regimental Staff & (mot) Staff Battery (2 LMGs)
1 Self Propelled Flak Battery (4 quad 20mm & 2 LMGs)
1st (Self Propelled) Battalion
Staff & (self-propelled) Staff Battery (2 LMGs & 3 20mm guns)
2 Self Propelled leFH Batteries (6 105mm leFH SdKfz 124 Wespe & 4 LMGs ea)
1 Self Propelled sFH Battery (6 150mm sFH SdKfz 165 Hummel & 4 LMGs)
2nd Battalion
Staff & Staff Battery (2 LMGs & 3 20mm guns)
2 (motZ) Batteries (6 105mm leFH & 2 LMGs ea)
3rd Battalion
same as 2nd Battalion
4th Battalion
Staff & Staff Battery (2 LMGs & 3 20mm guns)
2 (motZ) Batteries (6 150mm sFH & 2 LMGs ea)
1 (motZ) Battery (6 105mm sK 18/40 guns & 2 LMGs ea)
10th SS Flak Battalion
Staff & Staff Battery
3 (motZ) heavy Flak Batteries (4 88mm, 3 20mm & 2 LMGs ea)
1 (motZ) Medium Flak Batteries (9 37mm & 4 LMGs ea)
1 (motZ) Searchlight Platoon (4 600mm searchlights)
10th SS Panzer Pioneer Battalion
Staff (14 LMGs & 1 50mm PAK 38)
1 (halftrack) Pioneer Company (2 HMGs, 43 LMGs, 3 heavy anti-tank rifles, 2 80mm mortars & 6 flamethrowers)
2 (mot) Pioneer Companies (2 HMGs, 18 LMGs, 2 80mm mortars & 6 flamethrowers)
1 (mot) Heavy Panzer Bridging Train (5 LMGs)
1 (mot) Light Pioneer Supply Column (3 LMGs)
10th SS Panzer Signals Battalion
1 Panzer Telephone Company (14 LMGs)
1 Panzer Radio Company (20 LMGs)
1 (mot) Signals Supply Column (1 LMG)
10th SS Feldersatz Battalion
5 Companies
10th SS Supply Troop
1–7th/10th SS (mot) 120 ton Transportation Companies (8 LMGs ea)
10th SS (mot) 20 ton Light Flak Supply Column
10th SS (mot) Workshop Company (4 LMGs)
10th SS (mot) Supply Company (8 LMGs)

10th SS Truck Park
1/,2/,3/10th SS (mot) Maintenance Companies (4 LMGs)
10th SS (mot) 75 ton Heavy Maintenance Supply Column

Medical
1/,2/10th SS (mot) Medical Companies (2 LMGs ea)
1/,2/,3/10th SS Ambulances

Administration
10th SS (mot) Bakery Company (6 LMGs)
10th SS (mot) Butcher Company (6 LMGs)
10th SS (mot) Divisional Administration Platoon (2 LMGs)
10th SS (mot) Military Police Troop (5 platoons) (15 LMGs)
10th SS (mot) Field Post Office (2 LMGs)

The 10th SS Panzerjäger Battalion was re-formed in June 1944. After Normandy the division was reorganized with a single panzer battalion organized with two companies, each with 14 Mk V Panther tanks and two companies with 14 Mk IV tanks. In the autumn of 1944 the 2/19th SS Panzergrenadier Regiment became the 4/21st SS Panzergrenadier Regiment. On 9/12/44 the panzerjager battalion was equipped with 28 Jagdpanzer IV. In June 1944 the panzer inventory and organization of the division were as follows:

    2/10th SS Panzer Regiment
      1 Battalion
        1 Panzer Staff Company
        2 Medium Panzer Companies (Mk IV)
        2 Sturmgeschütz Companies (StuG)
        Mk IV (lg)   39
        StuG   38
        PzBef III   3

On 12/10/44 it stood as follows:

    1/10th Panzer Regiment
      1 Battalion
        1 Panzer Staff Company
        2 Medium Panzer Companies (Mk V)
        2 Medium Panzer Companies (Mk IV)
        Mk V   10 (+ 25 enroute)
        Mk IV (lg)   2 (+ 34 enroute)

On 1/3/45 orders were issued to build the 10th SS Panzer Regiment to full strength, that is a Panther Battalion with 60 tanks and a Mk IV Battalion with 45 tanks. Twenty-five Panthers were delivered between 6–10 January and eight Mk IV were delivered on 15 January. By 2/8/45 the panzer inventory and organization stood as follows:

    1/,2/10th SS Panzer Regiment
      1 Panzer Staff Company
      1st Battalion
        1 Panzer Staff Company
        4 Medium Panzer Companies (Mk V)
      2nd Battalion
        1 Panzer Staff Company
        3 Medium Panzer Companies (Mk IV)
        Mk IV (lg)   38
        Mk V   53
        FlakpzIV (37)   8

On 5/1/45 the division re-formed the 10th SS Panzergrenadier Ausbildungs und Ersatz Battalion. Though the war ended on 5/8/45, the division did not immediately surrender. It was in the Sudeten region of Czechoslovakia, around Teplitz. On 5/9/45 it was engaged by Russian tanks by Bruex and continued its withdrawal westwards in small groups. Many of its soldiers were taken prisoner by the Soviets and Czechs, however the 10th Reconnaissance Battalion surrendered to the U.S. 102nd Infantry Division in Tangermünde on the Elbe.

11th SS Freiwilligen Panzergrenadier Division "Nordland"

Formed in July 1943, it began its history as the SS Panzergrenadier Division 11 (German). It was formed from the SS Freiwilligen Legion Norwegen, SS Panzergrenadier Regiment Nordland, and the Danish Freikorps. The 11th SS Panzer Regiment was to be formed with two battalions with six companies, a heavy company and a pioneer company, however, this was changed to a single battalion with four companies and a pioneer company. The organization was not completed and only a single battalion was formed. This panzer battalion was given the name "Hermann von Salza" in December 1943. The other battalion became the 103rd SS Panzer Battalion, later the 503rd Panzer Battalion. The division had:

    SS Panzergrenadier Regiment "Norge"
      1st Battalion (from SS Freiwilligen Legion Norwegen)

2nd Battalion (from SS Panzergrenadier Regiment Nordland)

3rd Battalion (from SS Panzergrenadier Regiment Nordland)

13th (infantry gun) Company

14th (flak) Company

1/,2/,3/SS Panzergrenadier Regiment "Danmark" (from SS Freikorps Danemark) organized the same as SS Panzergrenadier Regiment "Norge"

SS Panzer Battalion (4 companies)

1/,2/,4/11th SS Artillery Regiment (3rd battalion never formed, 4th Battalion was heavy) (had a flak platoon attached)

1/,2/11th SS Motorcycle Regiment (total 6 companies) (in Aug 1943 became the 11th SS Panzer Reconnaissance Battalion—5 companies)

SS Panzerjäger Battalion (3 companies) (never completed)

SS Sturmgeschütz Battalion (3 batteries)

SS Flak Battalion (4 batteries)

SS Pioneer Battalion (3 companies)

SS Armored Signal Battalion (2 companies)

SS Divisional (Einheiten) Support Units

On 10/22/43 the division was renamed the 11th SS Freiwilligen Panzergrenadier Division "Nordland" and the panzer grenadier regiments became the 23rd Panzergrenadier Regiment "Norge" and the 24th Panzergrenadier Regiment "Danmark." The division's flak battalion was detached on 1 December 1943. On 5/10/44 OKH records show the division organized and equipped as follows:

Division
  Division Staff
  Divisional Escort Company
    Motorcycle Platoon (6 LMGs)
    Self Propelled Flak Battery (4 20mm guns)
    Self Propelled Anti-Tank Platoon (3 LMGs & 3 75mm PAK 40)
    Infantry Gun Platoon (2 75mm leIG)
    Mixed Panzergrenadier Platoon (4 HMGs, 6 LMGs, & 2 80mm mortars)
23rd "Norge" SS Panzergrenadier Regiment
  Regimental Staff
  1st Battalion
    1–3rd Companies (4 HMGs, 18 LMGs, 2 80mm mortars & 2 flamethrowers)
    4th Company
      1 Mortar Platoon (2 LMGs & 4 120mm mortars)
      1 Panzerjäger Platoon (3 LMGs & 3 75mm PAK 40)
      2 Infantry Gun Sections (1 LMG & 2 75mm leIG ea)

2nd Battalion (6–10th Companies) (same as 1st Battalion)

3rd Battalion (11–15th Companies) (same as 1st Battalion)

16th (self-propelled flak) Company (12 20mm & 4 LMGs)

17th (self-propelled infantry gun) Company (6 150mm sIG)

18th (mot) Pioneer Company (2 HMGs, 12 LMGs, 6 flamethrowers & 2 80mm mortars)

24th "Danmark" SS Panzergrenadier Regiment
same as 23rd "Norge" SS Panzergrenadier Regiment

11th SS Panzerjäger Battalion
  1 Staff & Staff Battery (7 LMGS)
  1 Self Propelled Flak Company (12 20mm guns & 2 LMGs)
  1 Self Propelled Panzerjäger Company (12 75mm PAK 40 & 12 LMGs)
  1 (motZ) Panzerjäger Company (12 75mm PAK 40 & 12 LMGs)

11th SS Sturmgeschütz Battalion
  1 Staff & Staff Battery (2 LMGs)
  1 Panzer Maintenance Platoon (2 LMGs)
  3 Sturmgeschütz Batteries (10 StuGs & 2 LMGs)

11th SS Reconnaissance Battalion
  1 Light Armored Car Company (24 LMGs & 18 20mm guns)
  3 (mot) Reconnaissance Companies (4 HMGs, 18 LMGs, & 2 80mm mortars)
  1 (mot) Reconnaissance Company
    1 Pioneer Platoon (4 LMGs & 6 flamethrowers)
    1 Panzerjäger Platoon (3 LMGs & 3 75mm PAK 40)
    1 Infantry Gun Section (1 LMG & 2 75mm leIG)

11th SS Artillery Regiment
  1 Regimental Staff & (mot) Staff Battery (2 LMGs)
  1 Self Propelled Flak Battery (4 quad 20mm & 2 LMGs)
  1st, 2nd & 3rd (motZ) Battalion, each with
    Staff & Staff Battery (2 LMGs)
    2 (motZ) Batteries (6 105mm leFH & 2 LMGs ea)
  4th Battalion
    Staff & Staff Battery (2 LMGs)
    2 (motZ) Batteries (6 150mm sFH & 2 LMGs ea)
    1 (motZ) Battery (6 105mm sK 18/40 guns & LMGs ea)

11th SS Flak Battalion
  Staff & Staff Battery
  3 (motZ) heavy Flak Batteries (4 88mm, 3 20mm & 2 LMGs ea)
  1 (motZ) Medium Flak Batteries (9 37mm & LMGs ea)
  1 (motZ) Searchlight Platoon (4 600mm searchlight

11th SS Panzer Pioneer Battalion
  Staff (2 LMGs)
  3 (mot) Pioneer Companies (2 HMGs, 18 LMGs, 2 80mm mortars & 6 flamethrowers)
  1 (mot) Light Panzer Bridging Train (3 LMGs)

11th SS Panzer Signals Battalion
  1 (mot) Telephone Company (6 LMGs)
  1 (mot) Radio Company (7 LMGs)
  1 (mot) Signals Supply Column (1 LMG)

11th SS Feldersatz Battalion
  5 Companies

11th SS Supply Troop
  1–3th/11th SS (mot) 120 ton Transportation Companies (8 LMGs ea)
  4–6th/11th SS (mot) 90 ton Transportation Companies (6 LMGs ea)
  11th SS Light 20 ton Light Flak Supply Column
  11th SS (mot) Workshop Company (4 LMGs)
  11th SS (mot) Supply Company (8 LMGs)

11th SS Truck Park
  1/,2/,3/11th SS (mot) Maintenance Companies (4 LMGs)
  11th SS (mot) 75 ton Heavy Maintenance Supply Column

Medical
  1/,2/11th SS (mot) Medical Companies (2 LMGs ea)
  1/,2/,3/11th SS Ambulances

Administration
  11th SS (mot) Bakery Company (6 LMGs)
  11th SS (mot) Butcher Company (6 LMGs)
  11th SS (mot) Divisional Administration Platoon (2 LMGs)
  11th SS (mot) Military Police Troop (5 platoons) (15 LMGs)
  11th SS (mot) Field Post Office (2 LMGs)

Documents indicate that the 3/Danmark Panzergrenadier Regiment was later equipped with halftracks, but the date of this equipment conversion is not known. Those same documents indicate that the division was to have formed a two battalion panzer regiment in addition to the strumgeschütz battalion. In this conversion the reconnaissance battalion had two armored car companies, two halftrack companies, and one heavy halftrack reconnaissance company. The artillery regiment was to reequip the first battalion with two six-gun batteries of 105mm Wespe and one six-gun battery of 150mm Hummels. In addition, a self-propelled panzerjäger battalion with three ten-gun companies was to be formed. With the fall of Berlin the division passed into Russian captivity.

12th SS Panzer Division "Hitlerjugend"

Formed in July 1943, the division was operational and in action by April 1944. When formed, it was organized and equipped as follows:

Division Staff
  Division Staff (2 LMGs)
  1 (mot) Mapping Detachment
  1 (mot) "KB" Detachment
  Divisional Escort Company
    Motorcycle Platoon (6 LMGs)
    Infantry Gun Platoon (2 75mm leIG)
    Self Propelled Flak Battery (4 20mm guns)
    Self Propelled Anti-Tank Platoon (3 LMGs & 3 75mm PAK 40)
    Mixed Panzergrenadier Platoon (4 HMGs, 6 LMGs, & 2 80mm mortars)

12th SS Panzer Regiment
  Regimental Staff
  1st & 2nd Panzer Battalions, each with
    1 Panzer Battalion Staff
    1 Self Propelled Light Flak Platoon (6 20mm guns)
    4 Medium Panzer Companies
    1 (halftrack) Pioneer Company (40 LMGs & 6 flamethrowers)
    1 Panzer Maintenance Company

1st SS Panzergrenadier Regiment Hitlerjugend
  1 Regimental Staff
  1 Regimental Staff Company 1 (mot) Signals Platoon
    1 (mot) Panzerjäger Platoon (3 75mm PAK 40)
    1 Motorcycle Platoon
  3 (mot) Infantry Battalions, each with
  3 Companies (4 HMGs, 18 LMGs, 2 80mm mortars & 2 flamethrowers)
    1 Heavy Company (6 80mm mortars, 3 75mm PAK 40 & 4 75mm leIG)
    1 (motZ) Infantry Gun Company (4 150mm sIG)
  1 Self Propelled Flak Company (12 20mm guns)
  1 Motorcycle Company (2 80mm mortars, 4 HMGs, 18 LMGs, & 3 75mm PAK 40)
  1 (mot) Pioneer Company (18 LMGs & 6 flamethrowers)

2nd SS Panzergrenadier Regiment Hitlerjugend
same as 1st SS Panzergrenadier Regiment Hitlerjugend, except
3rd (halftrack) Battalion
1–3rd (halftrack) Companies (4 HMGs, 34 LMGs, 2 80mm mortars, & 2 flamethrowers)
4th (halftrack) Company
1 Infantry Gun Section (6 75mm guns)
1 Panzerjäger Platoon (3 75mm PAK 40)
1 Infantry Gun Platoon (2 75mm leIG)
12th SS Reconnaissance Battalion
2 Light Armored Companies (25 LMGS & 18 20mm guns)
2 (halftrack) Reconnaissance Companies (4 HMGs, 36 LMGs, 2 80mm mortars, & 6 75mm leIG)
1 (halftrack) Heavy Reconnaissance Company
1 Panzerjäger Platoon (3 75mm PAK 40)
1 (halftrack) Gun Platoon (6 75mm guns)
1 Infantry Gun Platoon (2 75mm leIG)
1 Pioneer Platoon (18 LMGs & 1 75mm leIG)
12th SS Artillery Regiment
1 Regimental Staff & (mot) Staff Battery (2 LMGs)
1 Self Propelled Flak Battery (4 quad 20mm & 2 LMGs)
1st (Self Propelled) Battalion
Staff & (self-propelled) Staff Battery (2 LMGs & 3 20mm guns)
2 Self Propelled leFH Batteries (6 105mm leFH SdKfz 124 Wespe & 6 LMGs ea)
1 Self Propelled sFH Battery (6 150mm sFH SdKfz 165 Hummel & 6 LMGs)
2nd Battalion
Staff & Staff Battery (2 LMGs)
2 (motZ) Batteries (6 105mm leFH & 6 LMGs ea)
3rd Battalion
Staff & Staff Battery (2 LMGs)
3 (motZ) Batteries (4 150mm sFH & 6 LMGs ea)
1 (motZ) Battery (4 100mm K 18 guns & 6 LMGs ea)
12th SS Panzerjäger Battalion
3 Self Propelled Panzerjäger Companies (10 75mm PAK 40 & 10 LMGs ea)
12th SS Flak Battalion
Staff & Staff Battery
3 (motZ) heavy Flak Batteries (4 88mm, 3 20mm & 2 LMGs ea)
1 (motZ) Medium Flak Batteries (9 37mm & 4 LMGs ea)
1 (mot) Light Flak Supply Column
12th SS Pioneer Battalion
Staff (2 LMGs)
1 (halftrack) Reconnaissance Platoon (6 75mm guns & 8 LMGs)

1 (halftrack) Pioneer Company (40 LMGs & 6 flamethrowers)
2 (mot) Pioneer Companies (18 LMGs & 6 flamethrowers)
1 (mot) Brüko B (4 LMGs)
1 (mot) Light Pioneer Supply Column (2 LMGs)
12th SS Armored Signal Battalion
1 (mot) Telephone Company (5 LMGs)
1 Panzer Radio Company (35 LMGs)
1 (mot) Signals Supply Column (4 LMGs)
12th SS Divisional Supply Troop
1–4th/12th SS (mot) 120 ton Transportation Companies (8 LMGs ea)
12th SS (mot) Heavy Supply Column
1/,2/,3/,4/12th SS (mot) Heavy Fuel Column (4 LMGs ea)
12th SS (mot) Workshop Company (4 LMGs)
12th SS (mot) Supply Company (8 LMGs)
12th SS Truck Park
1/,2/,3/12th SS (mot) Maintenance Companies (4 LMGs ea)
12th SS (mot) 75 ton Heavy Maintenance Supply Column
Medical
1/,2/12th SS (mot) Medical Companies (2 LMGs ea)
1/,2/,3/12th SS Ambulances (1 LMG ea)
Administration
12th SS (mot) Bakery Company (4 LMGs)
12th SS (mot) Butcher Company (4 LMGs)
12th SS (mot) Division Administration (4 LMGs)
12th SS (mot) Military Police Troop (6 LMGs)
12th SS (mot) Field Post Office (2 LMGs)

The division was formed with one battalion of Panther Mk V tanks and one of Mk IV tanks. On 10/22/43, with the renumbering of the SS, the panzer grenadier regiments were numbered 25th and 26th, while the rest of the division was numbered 12th. The division had:

25th (mot) SS Panzergrenadier Regiment "Hitlerjugend"
1st Battalion (1–4th Companies)
2nd Battalion (5–8th Companies)
3rd Battalion (9–12th Companies)
13th Company (sIG)
14th Company (Flak)
15th Company (Reconnaissance)
16th Company (Pioneer)
26th (half track) SS Panzergrenadier Regiment "Hitlerjugend"
1st Battalion (1–4th Companies)
2nd Battalion (5–8th Companies)
3rd Battalion (9–12th Companies)
13th Company (sIG)

14th Company (Flak)
15th Company (Reconnaissance)
16th Company (Pioneer)
12th SS Panzer Regiment
1st Panzer Battalion (Panther)
2nd Panzer Battalion (Mk IV)
3rd Pioneer Company
12th SS Reconnaissance Battalion (2 Arm.Car companies, 2 panzer reconnaissance companies, & 1 heavy panzer reconnaissance company)
1/,2/,3/12th SS Artillery Regiment
1st Battalion self-propelled
1/,2/12th SS Motorcycle Regiment
12th SS Panzerjäger Battalion (3 self-propelled companies)
12th SS Werfer Battalion (4 batteries) (formed March 1944)
12th SS Flak Battalion (4 batteries)
12th SS Pioneer Battalion (3 companies)
12th SS Armored Signal Battalion (2 companies)
12th SS Divisional (Einheiten) Support Units

The sturmgeschütz battalion was never formed and was dropped in March 1944. Indications are that the 1st SS Panzerjäger Battalion, from the SS Leibstandarte Adolf Hitler Division, was assigned to the Hitlerjugend. However its number was changed. Also formed in March and April 1944 were the SS 12th Werfer Battalion (four batteries—each with 6 150mm launchers, 1 50mm PAK 38, & 1 LMG) and the SS 12th Feldersatz Battalion (staff & nine companies). In June 1944, before the Allied landings at Normandy, the panzer inventory and organization of the armored element of the division was as follows:

1/,2/12th SS Panzer Regiment
1 Panzer Flak Platoon
1 Battalion
1 Panzer Staff Company
4 Medium Panzer Companies (Mk V)
1 Battalion
1 Panzer Staff Company
4 Panzer Companies (Mk IV)
Mk IV (lg)   96
Mk V   66
Flakpz38   12

During the Normandy battles the 12th SS Division was heavily engaged with the allies, most particularly against the Canadians. It formed a number of temporary kampfgruppen during those operations and the organization of a few of those kampfgruppen has been

identified. Kampfgruppe Wünsche was formed on 16 July 1944 and consisted of:

Kampfgruppe Wünsche
Staff/SS-Panzerregiment 12
Mixed Panzer Detachment (18 Pzkw IV, 13 Pzkw V)
1/,3/SS-Panzergrenadier Regiment 26
1 Battery 1/SS-Pz.Artillerieregiment 12

On 23 July 1944 the kampfgruppe was reconstituted as follows:

Kampfgruppe Wünsche
1/SS-Panzerregiment 12
1/SS-Panzerregiment 1
101st Heavy SS-Panzer Battalion
3/SS-Panzergrenadierregiment 26

On 6 August 1944 the kampfgruppe was reconstituted as follows:

Kampfgruppe Wünsche
Staff 1/SS-Panzerregiment 12
3rd Co, 1/SS-Panzerregiment 12
8th Co, 2/SS-Panzerregiment 12
2nd Co, 101st SS Heavy Panzer Battalion
1/,3/SS-Panzergrenadier Regiment 26

Reconnaissance Group Olboeter was organized during the Normandy battles and consisted of:

Reconnaissance Group Olboeter
2nd Co, 1/SS-Panzerregiment 12
9th Co, 3/SS-Panzergrenadierregiment 26
1 Co/SS-Aufkldrungsabeitlung 1
1st Btry, 1/SS-Artillerieregiment 12

Kampfgruppe Waldmüller was organized on 8 August 1944 and contained:

Kampfgruppe Waldmüller
1/SS-Panzergrenadierregiment 25
Division Escort Company, SS-Panzerdivision "Hitlerjugend"
Corps Escort Company, I.SS-Panzerkorps
2/SS-Panzerregiment 12
1 Company, 101st SS Heavy Panzer Battalion
1st Co/SS-Panzerjdgerabeitlung 12

After Normandy the division was reorganized with a single panzer battalion organized with two companies, each with 14 Mk V Panther tanks and two companies with 14 Mk IV tanks. The division was reorganized on 10/6/44. On 11/7/44 the 12th SS Panzer Division "Hitlerjugend" was organized and equipped as follows:

Division Staff
1 Divisional Staff
1 (mot) Mapping Detachment
1 (mot) Escort Company
  1 Machine Gun Platoon (4 HMGs & 6 LMGs)
  1 Motorcycle Platoon (6 LMGS)
  1 Self Propelled Flak Battery (4 20mm flak guns)
1 (mot) Military Police Detachment (15 LMGs)

12th SS Panzer Regiment
1 Panzer Regimental Staff & Staff Company
  1 Panzer Signals Platoon
  1 Panzer Platoon
  1 Panzer Flak Battery (4 37mm & 4 20mm flak guns)
1 (halftrack) Panzer Pioneer Company (2 HMGs, 43 LMGs, 2 80mm mortars & 6 flamethrowers)
1 Panzer Maintenance Company (4 LMGs)

1st Battalion
1 Panzer Battalion Staff (1 LMG)
1 Panzer Battalion Staff Company (5 LMGs & 3 20mm Flak guns)
4 Panzer Companies (22 Panther Mk V Tanks ea)
1 (mot) Supply Company (4 LMGs)

2nd Battalion
1 Panzer Battalion Staff (1 LMG)
1 Panzer Battalion Staff Company (5 LMGs & 3 20mm Flak guns)
4 Panzer Companies (22 Mk IV Tanks ea)
1 (mot) Supply Company (4 LMGs)

25th Panzergrenadier Regiment
1 Panzergrenadier Regimental Staff (2 LMGs)
1 (halftrack) Panzergrenadier Regimental Staff Company
  1 Staff Platoon (1 LMG)
  1 Signals Platoon (7 LMGs)
  1 Motorcycle Platoon (4 LMGS)

1st Battalion
1 Battalion Staff
1 (mot) Supply Company (4 LMGs)
3 (mot) Panzergrenadier Companies (4 HMGs, 18 LMGs & 2 80mm mortars)
1 Heavy Panzergrenadier Company
  1 Panzerjäger Platoon (3 75mm PAK & 3 LMGs)
  2 Heavy Mortar Platoons (2 120mm mortars ea)

2nd Battalion
same as 1st Battalion

3rd Battalion
1 Battalion Staff (6 LMGs)
1 (mot) Supply Company (4 LMGs)
3 (halftrack) Panzergrenadier Companies (3 HMGs, 30 LMGs 2 80mm mortars, 7 20mm & 2 75mm guns)
1 (halftrack) Panzergrenadier Mortar Company
  2 Infantry Gun Platoons (2 LMGs & 6 75mm guns)

2 Heavy Mortar Platoons (2 120mm mortars ea)
1 (mot) Supply Company (4 LMGs)
1 Self Propelled Infantry Gun Company
(6 150mm sIG & 8 LMGS)
1 Self Propelled Flak Company
(12 20mm & 2 LMGs)
1 (mot) Pioneer Company
1 (mot) Staff Platoon (1 LMG)
1 (mot) Platoon (12 LMGs, 1 20mm & 6 flamethrowers)
1 (mot) Platoon (8 LMGs & 12 flamethrowers)
1 (mot) Platoon (2 HMGs & 2 80mm mortars)
1 (mot) Platoon (6 LMGs & 6 flamethrowers)

26th SS Panzergrenadier Regiment
same as 1st SS Panzergrenadier division

12th SS Panzerjäger Battalion
1 Battalion Staff & Staff Platoon (3 jagdpanzers)
2 Jagdpanzer Companies (14 Jagdpanzer IV ea)
1 (motZ) Panzerjäger Company (12 75mm PAK & 12 LMGs)
1 (mot) Supply Company (4 LMGs)

12th Panzer Reconnaissance Battalion
1 Panzer Reconnaissance Battalion Staff (2 LMGs)
1 (mot) Reconnaissance Battalion Staff Company
  1 (mot) Signals Platoon (3 LMGS)
1 Armored Car Company (16 20mm & 25 LMGs)
1 Half Track Reconnaissance Company (2 75mm, 44 LMGs & 2 80mm mortars)
1 Half Track Reconnaissance Company (2 75mm, 7 20mm, 2 80mm mortars, 3 HMGs & 30 LMGs)
1 Half Track Reconnaissance Company
1 Staff Platoon (1 LMG)
1 Panzerjäger Platoon (6 75mm & 2 LMGs)
1 Mortar Platoon (2 LMGs & 6 80mm Mortars)
1 Pioneer Platoon (13 LMG)
1 (mot) Supply Company (4 LMGs)

12th (mot) Flak Battalion
1 Staff & (mot) Staff Battery (2 LMGs)
2 (motZ) Heavy Flak Companies (6 88mm, 3 20mm or 37mm, & 3 LMGs ea)
1 (motZ) Medium Flak Companies (9 37mm & 4 LMGs ea)
1 Self Propelled Flak Battery (3 quad 20mm guns)

12th SS (mot) Nebelwerfer Battalion
1 Staff & (mot) Staff Battery (1 LMG)
3 (mot) Nebelwerfer Batteries (6 150mm launchers & 2 LMGs ea)
1 (mot) Nebelwerfer Battery (6 210mm launcher & 2 LMGs)
1 (mot) Supply Company (3 LMGs)

12th Panzer Artillery Regiment
1 Regimental Staff & (mot) Staff Battery (2 LMGs)
1 Self Propelled Flak Battery (4 quad 20mm guns)

1st Battalion
  1 Battalion Staff & (mot) Staff Battery (2 LMGs)
  1 Flak Battery (2 mountain 20mm flak guns)
  1 Self Propelled Battery (6 150mm sFH Hummels SdKfz 165 & 4 LMGS)
  2 Self Propelled Batteries (6 105mm leFH Wespe SdKfz 124 & 4 LMGS)
2nd Battalion
  1 Battalion Staff & (mot) Staff Battery (2 LMGs)
  1 Flak Battery (2 mountain 20mm flak guns)
  2 (motZ) Batteries (6 105mm leFH & 4 LMGs ea)
3rd Battalion
  1 Battalion Staff & (mot) Staff Battery (2 LMGs)
  1 Flak Battery (2 mountain 20mm flak guns)
  2 (motZ) Batteries (6 105mm keFH & 4 LMGs ea)
4th Battalion
  1 Battalion Staff & (mot) Staff Battery (2 LMGs)
  1 Flak Battery (2 mountain 20mm flak guns)
  1 (motZ) Battery (4 100mm K18 & 4 LMGs)
  2 (motZ) Batteries (4 150mm sFH & 4 LMGs ea)
12th SS Panzer Pioneer Battalion
  1 Battalion Staff
  1 (halftrack) Battalion Staff Company (9 LMGs)
  1 (halftrack) Reconnaissance Platoon (8 LMGs)
  2 (halftrack) Pioneer Platoons (2 HMGs, 43 LMGs, 2 80mm mortars, & 6 flamethrowers)
  2 (mot) Pioneer Companies (2 HMGs, 18 LMGs, 2 80mm mortars & 6 flamethrowers ea)
  1 (mot Light Panzer Bridging Train (3 LMGs)
12th Panzer Signals Troop
  1 Panzer Telephone Company (11 LMGs)
  1 Panzer Radio Company (19 LMGs)
  1 (mot) Supply Platoon (2 LMGs)
12th Feldersatz Battalion
  5 Companies
12th SS Supply Troop
  1 (mot) Supply Battalion Staff
  1 (mot) Supply Battalion Staff Company
  6 (mot) 120 ton Transportation Companies (8 LMGs ea)
  1 (mot) Maintenance Company (4 LMGs)

  1 (mot) Supply Company (8 LMGs)
12th SS Maintenance Troops
  2 (mot) Maintenance Companies (5 LMGs ea)
  1 (mot) Maintenance Company (4 LMGs)
  1 (mot) Heavy Maintenance Supply Column
Other
  12th SS (mot) Butcher Company (4 LMGs)
  12th SS (mot) Bakery Company (5 LMGs)
  12th SS (mot) Divisional Administration Company (4 LMGs)
  1/,2/12th SS (mot) Medical Company (4 LMGs ea)
  12th SS (mot) Medical Supply Company (4 LMGs)
  12th SS (mot) Field Post Office

On 12/8/44 the panzer inventory and the organization of the panzer element of the division were as follows:

1/12th SS Panzer Regiment
  1 Panzer Staff Company
  1 Battalion
    1 Panzer Staff Company
    2 Medium Panzer Companies (Mk V)
    2 Panzer Companies (Mk IV)
    Mk IV (lg)   37
    Mk V   41

On 2/1/45 the panzer inventory and organization was as follows:

1/12th SS Panzer Regiment
  1 Panzer Staff Company
  1 Battalion
    1 Panzer Staff Company
    2 Medium Panzer Companies (Mk V)
    2 Medium Panzer Companies (Mk IV)
    Mk IV (lg)   19
    Mk V   36

The division passed into American captivity near Linz in 1945.

13th Waffen SS Gebirgs Division "Handschar" (1st Croatian)

Himmler first suggested to Hitler the formation of a "Bosnian" on 6 December 1942. Recruiting began in May–June 1942. This division was formed from Croatian, Muslim, and *Volkdetusch* (ethnic Germans living in Croatia) volunteers from Bosnia. It also absorbed the Croatian SS Freiwilligen Division and the Hadziefendic Legion, plus new recruits. The idea was very popular and the Croatian units had problems keeping their troops from deserting to enlist in the division. This popularity apparently had its limits, as in July 1942 the Germans were obliged to use conscription to fill out the division. The division was actually formed on 3/1/43 in France. When formed the division contained:

1/,/2/,3/,4/1st SS Gebirgsjäger Regiment
1/,/2/,3/,4/2nd SS Gebirgsjäger Regiment
1/,/2/,3/,4/13th SS Mountain Artillery Regiment
13th SS Mountain Pioneer Battalion
13th SS Flak Battalion
13th SS Panzerjäger Battalion
13th SS Mountain Signals Battalion
13th SS Reconnaissance Battalion
13th SS Medical Battalion
13th SS Division Supply Troops
13th SS Maintenance Battalion
1/,2/13th SS Mountain Veterinary Companies
1/,2/13th SS Reiter Squadrons

Tensions arose between the Croatian and Muslim elements in the division. The Muslims were particularly upset that the name of the division referenced Croatia, but not Bosnia-Herzegovina. Eventually, the division's name was changed to *"13. SS-Freiwilligen b.h. Division (Kroatian)"* (13th SS Volunteer Boznian-Herzegovinian Division (Croatia).

On 4/30/43 the division was reorganized as a mountain division. In May 1943 the division was organized and equipped as follows:

Division Staff
1 Staff (2 LMGS)
1 (mot) Mapping Detachment
1 Divisional Staff Company (9 LMGS, 3 50mm mortars, 3 HMGs & 2 75mm leIG)
1 (Mot) "KB" Company

SS Freiwilligen Mountain Jäger Regiment
Regimental Staff
Regimental Staff Company
1 Signals Platoon
1 Bicycle Platoon
Regimental Support Company (9 LMGs, 3 50mm mortars, 3 HMGs & 2 75mm leIG)
1 (motZ) Flak Section (3 20mm & 1 LMG)
1st, 2nd, & 3rd Mountain Battalions, each with
1 Battalion Staff
1 Mountain Signals Platoon
3 Mountain Companies (9 LMGs, 3 50mm mortars & 2 HMGs ea)
1 Mountain Machine Gun Company (8 HMGs)
1 Mountain Heavy Support Company
1 Mortar Platoon (6 80mm mortars)
1 Infantry Gun Section (2 75mm leIG)
1 Pioneer Platoon (2 flamethrowers & 6 LMGs)
1 Mountain Assault Company (9 LMGs, 3 50mm mortars)

Mountain Assault Battalion
1 Mountain Reconnaissance Company (9 LMGs & 6 light armored cars)

1 Mountain Support Company
1 Pioneer Platoon (3 LMGs)
1 Bridging Platoon
1 Pioneer Platoon (6 flamethrowers)
1 Mountain Company (9 LMGs & 3 50mm mortars)
1 (mot) Light Supply Column

SS Freiwilligen Mountain Jäger Regiment
same as 1st Battalion

SS Bicycle Battalion
1 Battalion Staff
3 Mountain Bicycle Companies (3 50mm mortars, 2 HMGs & 12 LMGs ea)

SS Reconnaissance Battalion
1 Battalion Staff
2 Motorcycle Companies (2 80mm mortars, 4 HMGs & 18 LMGs ea)
1 (mot) Reconnaissance Company
1 Pioneer Platoon (4 LMGs)
1 Anti-Tank Platoon (3 50mm PAK 38 & 3 LMGs)
1 Infantry Gun Platoon (2 75mm leIG)

SS Cavalry Battalion
2 Cavalry Squadrons (12 LMGs & 1 heavy anti-tank rifle)

SS Panzerjäger Battalion
3 (motZ) Anti-Tank Companies (9 50mm PAK 38 & 9 LMGs ea)

SS Panzer Battalion
1 Light Armored Company

SS Flak Battalion
1 Battalion Staff
1 (mot) Battalion Staff Battery
1 (motZ) Light Flak Battery (2 quad 20mm guns & 1 LMG)
1 (motZ) Light Flak Battery (12 20mm flak guns & 2 LMGs)
1 (motZ) Medium Battery (9 37mm flak & 4 LMGs)
1 (motZ) Heavy Battery (4 88mm guns, 3 20mm guns & 2 LMGs)

SS Mountain Artillery Regiment
1 Regimental Staff & Staff Battery
1st & 2nd Mountain Battalions, each with
1 Battalion Staff & Staff Battery
1 Mountain Ammunition Column
2 Light Mountain Gun Batteries (4 75mm guns & 2 LMGs ea)
3rd Mountain Battalion
1 Battalion Staff & Staff Battery
1 Mountain Ammunition Column
2 Light Mountain Howitzer Batteries (4 75mm howitzers & 2 LMGs ea)
4th Battalion
1 Battalion Staff & (mot) Staff Battery

1 (mot) Calibration Detachment
1 (mot) Heavy Gun Battery (4 100mm guns & 2 LMGs)
2 (mot) Howitzer Batteries (4 150mm sFH & 2 LMGs ea)
1 (mot) Light Supply Column

SS Pioneer Battalion
1 Mountain Pioneer Battalion Staff
1 (tmot) Mountain Pioneer Company (9 LMGs & 4 flamethrowers)
1 Mountain Pioneer Company (9 LMGs & 1 flamethrowers)
1 (mot) Pioneer Maintenance Platoon
1 (mot) Bridging Train (2 LMGs)
1 (mot) Mountain Pioneer Supply Column
1 (mot) Maintenance Platoon (2 LMGs)

SS Signals Battalion
1 (tmot) Mountain Telephone Company (2 LMGs)
1 (mot) Mountain Radio Company (2 LMGs)
1 (mot) Light Signals Supply Column (2 LMGs)

SS Support Troops
1 (mot) 90 ton Transportation Column (6 LMGs)
3 (horse drawn) Light Supply Columns (4 LMGs ea)
6 (horse drawn) Light Mountain Columns (3 LMGs ea)
2 (mot) Light Fuel Columns (2 LMGs)
1 Pack Mule Platoon (2 LMGs)
1 "FW" Squadron (2 LMGs)
1 Maintenance Platoon (2 LMGs)
2 (mot) Maintenance Companies (2 LMGs ea)
1 (mot Supply Company (6 LMGs)
1 (mot) Bakery Company (4 LMGs)
1 (mot) Butcher Company (9 LMGs)
1 (mot) Administration Platoon (7 LMGs)
1 (mot) Medical Company (4 LMGs)
1 (tmot) Medical Company (4 LMGs)
1 (tmot) Mountain Ambulance (2 LMGs)
1 (mot) Ambulance (2 LMGs)
2 unknown Medical Detachments (2 LMGs)
1 Mountain Veterinary Company (2 LMGs)
1 Veterinary Park (2 LMGs)
1 Field Park (2 LMGs)
1 (mot) Military Police Platoon (2 LMGs)
1 (mounted) Military Police Platoon (2 LMGs)

On 7/2/43 it was renamed the Croatian SS Freiwilligen Gebirgs (Mountain) Division. There were a few slight changes in the division's organization and the names of the various units were changed to the following:

1st Croatian SS Freiwilligen Mountain Jäger Regiment
Regimental Staff

Regimental Staff Company
1 Signals Platoon
1 Bicycle Platoon
Regimental Support Company (9 LMGs, 3 50mm mortars, 3 HMGs & 2 75mm leIG)
1 (motZ) Flak Section (3 20mm & 1 LMG)

1st, 2nd, & 3rd Mountain Battalions, each with
1 Battalion Staff
1 Mountain Signals Platoon
3 Mountain Companies (9 LMGs, 3 50mm mortars & 2 HMGs ea)
1 Mountain Machine Gun Company (8 HMGs)
1 Mountain Heavy Support Company
1 Mortar Platoon (6 80mm mortars)
1 Anti-Tank Platoon (3 37mm PAK)
1 Infantry Gun Section (2 75mm leIG)
1 Pioneer Platoon (2 flamethrowers & 6 LMGs)
1 Mountain Assault Company (9 LMGs, 3 50mm mortars)

Mountain Assault Battalion
1 Mountain Reconnaissance Company (9 LMGs & 6 light armored cars)
1 Mountain Support Company
1 Pioneer Platoon (3 LMGs)
1 Bridging Platoon
1 Pioneer Platoon (6 flamethrowers)
1 Mountain Company (9 LMGs & 3 50mm mortars)
1 (mot) Light Supply Column

2nd Croatian SS Freiwilligen Mountain Jäger Regiment
same as 1st Battalion

Croatian SS Reconnaissance Battalion, 13th Division
same as May 1943

Croatian SS Cavalry Battalion, 13th Division
same as May 1943

Croatian SS Panzerjäger Battalion, 13th Division
same as May 1943

Croatian SS Panzer Battalion, 13th Division
same as May 1943

Croatian SS Flak Battalion, 13th Division
same as May 1943

Croatian SS Mountain Artillery Regiment, 13th Division
same as May 1943

Croatian SS Pioneer Battalion, 13th Division
same as May 1943

Croatian SS Signals Battalion, 13th Division
same as May 1943

SS Support Troops, 13th Division
1 (mot) 120 ton Transportation Column (6 LMGs)
3 (horse drawn) Light Supply Columns (4 LMGs ea)
6 (horse drawn) Light Mountain Columns (3 LMGs ea)
2 (mot) Medium Fuel Columns (2 LMGs)

1 Pack Mule Platoon (2 LMGs)
1 "FW" Squadron (2 LMGs)
1 Maintenance Platoon (2 LMGs)
2 (mot) Maintenance Companies (2 LMGs ea)
1 (mot) Supply Company
1 (mot) Bakery Company (4 LMGs)
1 (mot) Butcher Company (9 LMGs)
1 (mot) Administration Platoon (7 LMGs)
1 (mot) Field Post Office
1 (mot) Medical Company (4 LMGs)
1 (tmot) Medical Company (4 LMGs)
1 (tmot) Mountain Ambulance (2 LMGs)
1 (mot) Ambulance (2 LMGs)
2 unknown Medical Detachments (2 LMGs)
1 Mountain Veterinary Company (2 LMGs)
1 Veterinary Park (2 LMGs)
1 Field Park (2 LMGs)
1 (mot) Military Police Platoon (2 LMGs)
1 (mounted) Military Police Platoon (2 LMGs)

During the summer of 1943 tensions between the Bosnians and Croatians provoked a Muslim mutiny. On 17 September the mutiny erupted and the mutineers planned to murder their officers. Several officers were murdered but the plans for escape by the mutineers were not particularly well developed and the mutiny was quickly suppressed. The mutineers were executed with little formality, though the division was required to witness the punishment as an example for all.

On 10/22/43 the division was renamed the 13th SS Freiwilligen Bosnisch-Herzegowinisch Gebirgs Division (1st Croatian). The two infantry regiments were renamed the 27th SS Freiwilligen Mountain Jäger Regiment (1st Croatian) and the 28th SS Freiwilligen Mountain Jäger Regiment (2nd Croatian).

In June 1943 it was renamed the 13.Waffen-Gebirgs-Division der SS "Handschar" (13th Waffen SS Mountain Division "Handschar"). Early in 1944 the division contained:

1/,2/,3/27th SS Freiwilligen Mountain Jäger Regiment (4 companies per battalion)
1/,2/,3/28th SS Freiwilligen Mountain Jäger Regiment (4 companies per battalion)
13th SS Reconnaissance Battalion
13th SS Panzerjäger Battalion
1/,2/,3/,4/13th SS Mountain Artillery Regiment
13th SS Flak Battalion (4 batteries)
13th SS Pioneer Battalion (3 companies)
13th SS Signals Battalion (staff & 3 companies)
13th Gebirgs-Jäger-Ausbildungs und Ersatz Battalion
13th SS Support Troops

OKH records dated 3/12/44 show the division organized and equipped as follows:

Divisional Staff
1 Divisional Staff (2 LMGs)
1 (mot) Mapping Detachment
Staff & mapping det (39/50/156)[1]
1 Propaganda Platoon (3/22/15)
1 Escort Company (5/35/222) (2 HMGs, 12 LMGs, 2 80mm mortars & 3 75mm PAK 40)
27th & 28th SS Gebirgsjäger Regiments, each with (117/673/4,395)
1 Regimental Staff
1 Regimental Staff Company
1 Mountain Signals Platoon
1 Mountain Bicycle Platoon
1 Regimental Staff Company (2 HMGs, 12 LMGs & 3 50mm mortars)
1 Mountain Flak Battery (3 20mm guns & 1 LMG)
1st Battalion (31/199/1,394)
1 Mountain Battalion Staff
1 Mountain Signals Platoon
2 Companies (2 HMGs, 12 LMGs, 3 50mm mortars)
1 Machine Gun Company (8 HMGs)
1 Heavy Company
1 Mountain Pioneer Platoon (4 LMGs & 2 flamethrowers)
1 Panzerjäger Platoon (3 37mm PAK 36)
1 Infantry Section (2 75mm leIG)
1 Mortar Platoon (6 80mm mortars)
1 Alpine Streif Company (2 HMGs, 12 LMGs & 3 50mm mortars)
2nd Battalion
same as 1st Battalion
3rd Battalion
1 Mountain Battalion Staff
1 Mountain Signals Platoon
1 Alpine Streif Company (2 HMGs, 12 LMGs & 3 50mm mortars)
1 Company (2 HMGs & 9 LMGs)
1 Nebelwerfer Company (6 100mm launchers & 2 LMGs)
1 Pioneer Company
1 Mountain Pioneer Platoon (12 LMGs)
1 Mountain Pioneer Platoon (6 flamethrowers)
1 Bridging Platoon
13th SS Mountain Artillery Regiment, 13th Division (124/445/2,988)
1 Regimental Staff & Staff Battery (4 quad 20mm self-propelled guns)

[1]Numbers are authorized numbers of officers, NCOs and men as of 2/15/44.

1st & 2nd Battalions, each with
1 Battalion Staff & Staff Battery
2 Mountain Batteries (4 75mm mountian guns &
    2 LMGs ea)
1 Mountain Supply Column

3rd Battalion
1 Battalion Staff & Staff Battery
2 Mountain Batteries (4 105mm mountian how-
    itzers & 2 LMGs ea)
1 Mountain Supply Column

4th Battalion
Staff & Staff Battery (2 LMGs)
1 Calibration Detachment
2 (motZ) Batteries (6 150mm sFH & 2 LMGs ea)
1 (motZ) Battery (6 105mm sK 18/40 guns & 2
    LMGs ea)

13th SS Cavalry Battalion, 13th Division
2 Cavalry Squadrons (5/32/208 per squadron) (2
    HMGs, 9 LMGs & 2 80mm mortars)

13th SS Panzerjäger Battalion, 13th Division
(24/94/382)
1 Battalion Staff
1 Self Propelled Panzerjäger Company (10 75mm
    PAK 40 & 10 LMGs)
1 (motZ) Panzerjäger Company (9 75mm PAK 40
    & 9 LMGs)
1 (motZ) Panzerjäger Company (9 50mm PAK 38
    & 9 LMGs)

13th SS Flak Battalion, 13th Division (29/108/540)
1 (motZ) Heavy Flak Battery (4 88mm, 3 20mm &
    2 LMGs)
1 (motZ) Medium Flak Battery (9 37mm & 4
    LMGs)
1 (motZ) Light Flak Battery (12 20mm & 2 LMGs)

**13th SS Mountain Pioneer Battalion, 13th Divi-
sion** (32/140/962)
1 (tmot) Mountain Pioneer Company (9 LMGs &
    4 flamethrowers)
2 Mountain Pioneer Companies (9 LMGs & 4
    flamethrowers ea)
1 (mot) Light Mountain Pioneer Supply Column
    (2 LMGs)
1 (mot) "B" Bridging Train (2 LMGs)

13th SS Mountain Signals Battalion, 13th Division
(26/138/630)
2 (tmot) Mountain Telephone Companies (5
    LMGs ea)
1 (mot) Mountain Radio Company (5 LMGs)
1 (mot) Mountain Signals Supply Column (2
    LMGs)

13th SS Bicycle Battalion, 13th Division (25/113/629)
2 Mountain Bicycle Companies (2 HMGs, 12
    LMGs & 3 50mm mortars)
1 Heavy Company

1 Armored Car Platoon (6 armored cars with 4
    LMGs)
1 Mortar Platoon (6 80mm mortars)
1 Panzerjäger Platoon (3 LMGs & 3 50mm PAK
    38)
1 Pioneer Platoon (4 LMGs)

13th SS Supply Troop, 13th Division (44/206/1,438)
4 (mot) Light Supply Columns (2 LMGs ea)
3 Light Supply Columns (4 LMGs ea)
4 Light Mountain Supply Columns (3 LMGs ea)
1 (mot) Light Fuel Column (2 LMGs)
1 (mot) Supply Company (6 LMGs)
1 (mot) Ordnance Company (2 LMGs)

13th SS Truck Park
1/12th (mot) Maintenance Company (7/13/73) (2
    LMGs)
2/12th (mot) Maintenance Company (3/13/47) (2
    LMGs)

Medical (36/123/774)
1/13th SS (tmot) Mountain Medical Company (4
    LMGs)
2/13th SS (mot) Medical Company (2 LMGs)
13th SS (mot) Decontamination Company (2 LMGs)
13th SS (tmot) Ambulance Platoon (2 LMGs)
13th SS (mot) Ambulance Platoon (2 LMGs)
13th SS Mountain Stretcher Bearer Company (2
    LMGs)

Administration (13/63/298)
13th SS (mot) Bakery Company (4 LMGs)
13th SS (mot) Butcher Company (9 LMGs)
13th SS (mot) Divisional Administration Platoon (7
    LMGs)
13th SS (mot) Field Post Office

Other
13th SS (mot) Military Police Troop (2 LMGs)
    (3/59/4)
1/,2/13th SS Veterinary Companies (14/47/333) (2
    LMGs ea)

Field returns from 1 August 1944 show the division
was, in fact, organized and equipped slightly differently.
It apparently was organized as follows:

Divisional Staff
1 Divisional Staff (2 LMGs)
1 Divisional Band
1 (mot) Mapping Detachment
1 (tmot) Military Police Troop (3 LMGs)

27th SS Gebirgsjäger Regiment
1 Regimental Staff
1 Regimental Staff Company
    1 Mountain Signals Platoon
    1 Mountain Bicycle Platoon
    1 Cavalry Platoon
    1 Mortar Platoon (4 120mm mortars & 7 LMGs)

1st Battalion
  1 Mountain Battalion Staff
  1 Mountain Battalion Staff Company
    1 Mountain Signals Platoon
    1 Mountain Pioneer Platoon (3 LMGs)
  3 Companies (2 HMGs, 11 LMGs, 2 50mm mortars)
  1 Heavy Company
    1 Machine Gun Platoon (8 HMGs & 2 LMGs)
    1 Mortar Platoon (4 120mm mortars & 2 LMGs)
2nd Battalion
  same as 1st Battalion
3rd Battalion
  same as 1st Battalion
1 Infantry Gun Company (6 75mm leIG)
1 Panzerzerstörer Company
  1 Staff Platoon (1 LMG)
  1 (motZ) Panzerjäger Platoon (3 75mm PAK 40 & 5 LMGs)
  1 Panzerschrecke Platoon (30 Panzerschrecke & 2 LMGs)
1 Alpine Streif Company (2 HMGs, 11 LMGs & 2 80mm mortars)
1 Light Mountain Supply Column
28th SS Gebirgsjäger Regiment
  same as 27th SS Gebirgsjäger Regiment
13th SS Panzerjäger Battalion, 13th Division
  1 (mot) Battalion Staff & Staff Company (1 LMG)
  1 Sturmgeschütz Company (10 StuGs)
  1 (motZ) Panzerjäger Company (12 75mm PAK 40 & 12 LMGs)
  1 (motZ) Falk Company (12 20mm mountain flak guns & 2 LMGs)
13th SS Reconnaissance Battalion, 13th Division
  2 Mountain Bicycle Companies (4 HMGs & 10 LMGs ea)
  1 Cavalry Squadron (2 HMGs & 9 LMGs)
  1 Heavy Company
    1 Staff Platoon (1 LMG)
    1 Mortar Platoon (6 80mm mortars)
    1 Panzerjäger Platoon (3 LMGs & 3 75mm PAK 40)
    1 Infantry Gun Platoon (4 75mm leIG & 2 LMGs)
13th SS Mountain Artillery Regiment, 13th Division
  1 Regimental Staff (1 LMG)
  1 Regimental Staff Battery (2 LMGs & 4 quad 20mm self-propelled guns)
1st Battalion
  1 Battalion Staff & Staff Battery (2 LMGs)
  3 Mountain Batteries (4 75mm mountain guns & 2 LMGs ea)
2nd Battalion
  same as 1st Battalion

3rd Battalion
  1 Battalion Staff & Staff Battery
  3 Mountain Batteries (4 105mm mountian howitzers & 2 LMGs ea)
4th Battalion
  Staff & Staff Battery (2 LMGs)
  1 Calibration Detachment
  2 (motZ) Batteries (4 150mm sFH & 2 LMGs ea)
  1 (motZ) Battery (4 100mm sK 18/40 guns & 2 LMGs ea)
13th SS Feldersatz Battalion, 13th Division
  5 Companies
13th SS Mountain Pioneer Battalion, 13th Division
  1 Mountain Staff (2 LMGs)
  1 (tmot) Mountain Staff Company (2 LMGs)
  1 (mot) Mountain Pioneer Company (2 HMGs, 9 LMGs, 6 flamethrowers, & 2 80mm mortars)
  2 Mountain Pioneer Companies (2 HMGs, 9 LMGs, 6 flamethrowers, & 2 80mm mortars)
  1 (mot) "G" Bridging Train (2 LMGs)
13th SS Mountain Signals Battalion, 13th Division
  2 (tmot) Mountain Telephone Companies (5 LMGs ea)
  1 (tmot) Mountain Radio Company (5 LMGs)
  1 (mot) Mountain Signals Supply Column (2 LMGs)
13th SS Supply Troop, 13th Division
  3 Mountain Light Supply Columns (4 LMGs ea)
  3 Light Supply Columns (4 LMGs ea)
  1 (mot) 120 ton Transportation Company
  1 Mountain Supply Company (6 LMGs)
13th SS Truck Park
  12th (mot) Maintenance Company (2 LMGs)
Medical
  1/2/13th SS (tmot) Mountain Medical Company (4 LMGs ea)
  13th SS (mot) Decontamination Company (2 LMGs)
  13th SS Mountain Stretcher Bearer Company (2 LMGs)
  13th SS (mot) Ambulance Platoon (2 LMGs)
  13th SS (tmot) Mountain Ambulance Platoon (2 LMGs)
Administration
  13th SS Veterinary Company (2 LMGs)
  13th SS (mot) Bakery Company (6 LMGs)
  13th SS (mot) Butcher Company (4 LMGs)
  13th SS (mot) Divisional Administration Company (2 LMGs)

On 24 September 1944 the reconnaissance, panzerjäger, and pioneer battalions and the artillery were separated from the division and declared "Special Troops of the Reichsführer SS." They were to serve with neither the Handschar or Kama Divisions, but under the direct tactical control of the IX SS Mountain Corps. They were redesignated as follows:

13th SS Reconnaissance Battalion	—	509th SS Reconnaissance Battalion
13th SS Panzerjäger Battalion	—	509th SS Panzerjäger Battalion
13th SS Pioneer Battalion	—	509th SS Pioneer Battalion
13th SS Artillery Regiment	—	509th SS Artillery Regiment

In August 1944 the division began suffering heavily from desertion, resulting from the defeats and rumors of defeats of the Germans. In response to this, the division was reduced, by the order of 9/26/44, to two infantry regiments, each with two battalions, a pioneer company, a signals company and a feldersatz battalion. The reconnaissance battalion, the panzerjäger battalion, the mountain artillery regiment, and the mountain pioneer battalion were permanently detached as Special Troops Reichsführer SS and renumbered with the number 509th. It appears that the flak battalion had already been transferred by June 1944. Beginning 25 October and lasting into November 1944 unreliable parts of the division were disarmed. One disarming was ordered by the commander of the 118th Jäger Division who took it upon himself to order the disarmament the 1st Company/13th Panzerjäger Battalion, but this order was later countermanded. About 900 to 1,000 Bosnians, who were disarmed, were organized into two labor battalions and the rest were turned over to the 1st Mountain Division to serve as non-combatant auxiliaries. In 1945 what remained of the division was taken prisoner by the English near Villach.

14th Waffen SS Grenadier Division (1st Galician)

On 7/5/43 Himmler ordered the call-up of volunteers to form a Ukranian division. The division was ordered formed on 8/1/43 as the 14th Galizische SS Freiwilligen Division. It was formed from ethnic Germans and Ukrainians. The division was to be organized as a Type 44 n.A. Division, with three infantry regiments, each with two battalions. The three 3rd Battalions were detached from the division and reorganized into the 14th SS Fusilier Battalion (four companies) and the 14th SS Feldersatz Battalion (five companies). On 10/22/43 the division was renamed the 14th Galizische SS Freiwilligen Infanterie Division and the infantry regiments were renamed and renumbered the 29th, 30th, and 31st SS Freiwilligen Grenadier Regiments. Each had only two battalions. The artillery regiments and other units were numbered the "14th." The division was organized and equipped as follows:

Division Staff
  1 Divisional Staff (2 LMGs)
  1 (mot) Mapping Detachment
  1 (mot) "KB" Detachment
SS 1st Freiwilligen Regiment (Galizische)
  1 Regimental Staff
  1 Regimental Staff Company
    1 Bicycle Platoon
    1 Signals Platoon
    1 Pioneer Platoon (3 LMGs)

3 **Battalions**, each with
  3 Companies (12 LMGs & 2 80mm mortars)
  1 Machine Gun Company (12 HMGs & 4 120mm mortars)
  1 Infantry Gun Company (2 150mm sIG & 6 75mm leIG)
  1 Panzerjäger Company (9 75mm PAK 40 & 9 LMGs)
SS 2nd Freiwilligen Regiment (Galizische)
same as SS 1st Freiwilligen Regiment (Galizische)
SS 3rd Freiwilligen Regiment (Galizische)
same as SS 1st Freiwilligen Regiment (Galizische)
SS Bicycle Battalion (Galizische)
  2 Bicycle Companies (2 HMGs, 12 LMGs, & 2 80mm mortars)
SS Panzerjäger Battalion (Galizische)
  1 Battalion Staff
  1 Self Propelled Panzerjäger Company (10 75mm PAK 40 & 10 LMGs)
  2 (motZ) Panzerjäger Companies (9 75mm PAK 40 & 9 LMGs)
SS Artillery Regiment (Galizische)
  1 Regimental Staff
  1 Regimental Staff Battery
1st, 2nd 7 3rd 2nd Battalions, each with
  1 Battalion Staff & Staff Battery
  3 Batteries (4 105mm leFH 18 & 2 LMGs ea)
3rd Battalion
  1 Battalion Staff & Staff Battery
  3 Mountain Batteries (4 150mm sFH & 2 LMGs ea)

SS Flak Battalion (Galizische)
  1 (mot) Battalion Staff Company (1 LMG)
  1 (motZ) Heavy Flak Battery (4 88mm, 3 20mm & 2 LMGs)
  1 (motZ) Medium Flak Battery (9 37mm & 4 LMGs)
  1 (motZ) Light Flak Battery (12 20mm & 2 LMGs)
  1 (mot) Light Flak Supply Column
SS Pioneer Battalion (Galizische)
  3 Pioneer Companies (9 LMGs, 2 80mm mortars & 4 flamethrowers ea)
  1 Light Mountain Pioneer Supply Column (2 LMGs)
SS Signals Battalion (Galizische)
  1 (tmot) Telephone Companies (6 LMGs ea)
  1 (mot) Radio Company (4 LMGs)
  1 (mot) Signals Supply Column (2 LMGs)
SS Divisional Supply Troops (Galizische)
  2 Heavy Supply Columns (6 LMGs ea)
  1 (mot) (120 ton) Transportation Company (8 LMGs)
  1 (mot) Light Fuel Column (2 LMGs)
  1 (tmot) Supply Company (6 LMGs)
  1 (mot) Maintenance Company (4 LMGs)
Medical
  1 Medical Company (2 LMGs)
  1 (mot) Medical Company (2 LMGs)
  2 (mot) Ambulance Companies (1 LMG ea)
Other
  1 Veterinary Company (4 LMGs)
  1 (mot) Bakery Company (4 LMGs)
  1 (mot) Butcher Company (9 LMGs)
  1 (mot) Division Administration (4 LMGs)
  1 (mot) Military Police Troop (2 LMGs)
  1 Military Police Troop (1 LMG)
  1 (mot) Field Post Office

From the three infantry regiments volunteers were drawn off to form the 4th–7th Galizische SS Freiwilligen Regiments (Police). The 6th and 7th Regiments were disbanded by 1/31/44 and the 4th and 5th Regiments were disbanded on 6/9/44. Their manpower was returned to the parent division. In May 1944 OKH records show the division organized and equipped as follows:

Staff
  14th SS Divisional Staff (2 LMGs)
  14th SS (mot) Mapping Detachment
  14th SS (mot) Military Police Detachment (1 LMG)
29th SS Grenadier Regiment
  1 Regimental Staff
  1 Regimental Staff Company
    1 Staff Platoon (1 LMG)
    1 Signals Platoon
    1 Pioneer Platoon (6 LMGs)

    1 Cavalry Platoon (3 LMGs)
  1st Battalion
    3 Companies (16 LMGs & 2 80mm mortars)
    1 Machine Gun Company (12 HMGs, 3 LMGs, & 6 80mm mortars)
  2nd Battalion
    same as 1st Battalion
  Infantry Gun Company (2 150mm sIG, 6 75mm leIG & 4 LMGs)
  1 (motZ) Panzerjäger Company (12 75mm PAK 40 & 13 LMGs)
30th SS Grenadier Regiment
  same as 29th SS Grenadier Regiment
31st SS Grenadier Regiment
  same as 29th SS Grenadier Regiment
14th SS Divisional Fusilier Battalion
  1 Battalion Staff (1 LMG)
  3 Fusilier Companies (16 LMGs & 2 80mm mortars) (one on bicycles)
  1 Machine Gun Company (12 HMGs, 3 LMGs, & 6 80mm mortars)
14th SS Panzerjäger Battalion
  1 (motZ) Panzerjäger Company (12 75mm PAK 40 & 13 LMGs)
14th SS Artillery Regiment
  1 Regimental Staff & Staff Battery (1 LMG)
  1st, 2nd, & 3rd Battalions, each with
    1 Battalion Staff & Staff Battery (1 LMG)
    3 Batteries (4 105mm leFH & 5 LMGs)
  4th Battalion
    1 Battalion Staff & Staff Battery (1 LMG)
    3 Batteries (4 150mm sFH & 5 LMGs)
14th SS Pioneer Battalion
  1 Staff (4 LMGs)
  3 Pioneer Companies (2 HMGs, 9 LMGs, 6 flamethrowers, & 2 80mm mortars) (one on bicycles)
14th SS Signals Battalion
  1 Battalion Staff & Staff Pack Company
  1 (tmot) Telephone Company (6 LMGs)
  1 (mot) Radio Company (5 LMGs)
  1 (tmot) Signals Supply Column (1 LMG)
14th SS Feldersatz Battalion
  5 Companies
14th SS Supply Troop
  1/14th SS (mot) 90 ton Transportation Company (6 LMGs)
  2/,3/14th SS 60 ton Transportation Company (8 LMGs)
  1 (mot) Light Flak Supply Column
  1 Supply Company (6 LMGs)
Truck Park
  14th SS (mot) Maintenance Company (6 LMGs)
Medical
  14th SS Medical Companies (4 LMGs)
  14th SS (mot) Medical Companies (4 LMGs)
  1/14th SS Medical Supply Company (4 LMGs)

Administration

  14th SS (tmot) Bakery Company (6 LMGs)
  14th SS (tmot) Butcher Company (4 LMGs)
  14th SS (tmot) Divisional Administration Platoon
    (2 LMGs)
  14th SS (mot) Veterinary Company (6 LMGs)
  14th SS (mot) Field Post Office (1 LMG)

The panzerjäger battalion was scheduled to raise a self-propelled panzerjäger company (14 75mm PAK 40 & 15 LMGs). If and when it was raised is not known. In August 1944 the division became the 14th Waffen SS Grenadier Division (1st Galizische) and the infantry regiments became the 29th–31st Freiwilligen Grenadier Regiments. The order of 6/1/44 directed the formation of 3rd Battalions in the grenadier regiments. The bicycle battalion appears to have been disbanded in June 1944. On 8/7/44 the division had:

  1/,2/,3/29th Waffen Grenadier Regiment (1st Gal.)
  1/,2/,3/30th Waffen Grenadier Regiment (2nd Gal.)

  1/,2/,3/31st Waffen Grenadier Regiment (3rd Gal.)
  1/,2/,3/,4/14th SS Artillery Regiment (Galizische)
    (12 batteries)
  Fusilier Battalion/14th Waffen SS Grenadier Division (4 companies)
  SS 14th Panzerjäger Battalion (Galizische) (3 companies)
  SS 14th Flak Battalion (Galizische) (3 batteries)
  SS 14th Pioneer Battalion (Galizische) (3 companies)
  SS 14th Signals Battalion (Galizische) (2 companies)
  SS 14th Division Supply Troops (Galizische)

On 9/28/44 the division was rebuilt in Slovakia. On 1/15/45 it was renamed the 14th Waffen Grenadier Division Der SS (Ukrain Nr. 1). On 4/25/45 it ceased being part of the Waffen SS and was reassigned to the Ukranian National Army, a fiction ordered formed on 3/15/45. In May 1945 the division passed into American and British captivity after a rush westwards to escape Soviet captivity.

15th Waffen SS Grenadier Division (1st Lettish)

When the Germans captured Latvia in 1941 they organized several police regiments. They were used to form the Lettish SS Freiwilligen Legion on 10 February 1943. In September 1943 the Lettish SS Freiwilligen Legion became the Lettisch-SS-Freiwilligen Division and this would become the 15th Waffen SS Grenadier Division shortly thereafter. By November 1943 the division was in action against the Russians.

In May 1943 the Lettish SS Freiwilligen Legion was organized and equipped as follows:

Division Staff
  1 Legion Staff (2 LMGs)
  1 (mot) Mapping Detachment
  1 (mot) "KB" Detachment
3 Regiments, each with
  1 Regimental Staff
  1 Regimental Company
    1 Signals Platoon
    1 Pioneer Platoon (3 LMGs)
    1 Bicycle Platoon
  1st, 2nd & 3rd Battalion, each with
    3 Companies (12 LMGs, 3 light anti-tank rifles & 2 80mm mortars)
    1 Machine Gun Company (12 HMGs & 4 120mm mortars)

  1 Infantry Gun Company (2 150mm sIG & 6 75mm leIG)
  1 (mot) Panzerjäger Battery (9 75mm PAK 40 & 6 LMGs)
SS Bicycle Battalion (Lettish Legion)
  2 Bicycle Companies (3 50mm mortars, 2 HMGs, 12 LMGs & 1 heavy anti-tank rifle)
SS Panzerjäger Battalion (Lettish Legion)
  2 (motZ) Panzerjäger Companies (12 75mm PAK 40 & 8 LMGs)
  1 Self Propelled Flak Company (12 20mm flak guns)
SS Artillery Regiment (Lettish Legion)
  1 Regimental Staff & Staff Battery
  1 Self Propelled Flak Battery (2 quad 20mm guns)
1st, 2nd, & 3rd Battalions, each with
  1 Battalion Staff & Staff Battery
  3 Batteries (4 105mm leFH & 2 LMGs ea)
4th Battalion
  1 Battalion Staff & Staff Battery
  3 Batteries (4 150mm sFH & 2 LMGs ea)
SS Pioneer Battalion (Lettish Legion)
  3 Pioneer Companies (9 LMGs, 2 80mm mortars & 6 flamethrowers ea)
  1 Light Pioneer Supply Column (2 LMGs)
SS Signals Battalion (Lettish Legion)
  1 (tmot) Telephone Company (6 LMGs)

1 (mot) Radio Company (4 LMGs)
1 (mot) Light Signals Supply Column (2 LMGs)

SS Support Troops (Lettish Legion)
1 (mot) 120 ton Transportation Company (8 LMGs)
2 (horse drawn) Heavy Supply Columns (6 LMGs)
1 (mot) Light Fuel Column (2 LMGs)
1 (tmot) Supply Column (6 LMGs)
1 (mot) Maintenance Company
1 (mot) Bakery Company
1 (mot) Butcher Company
1 (mot) Administration Platoon
1 (horse drawn) Medical Company
1 (mot) Medical Company
2 (mot) Ambulances
1 Veterinary Company
1 (mot) Military Police Troop (1 LMG)
1 (mot) Field Post Office

The Legion had, by this time, detached the 4th and 5th Regiments to the Lettish SS Freiwilligen Brigade (later 2nd Brigade). On 10/22/43 the regiments were renumbered and the division renamed the 15th Lettish SS Freiwilligen Division. The regiments were renumbered as follows:

32nd SS Freiwilligen Grenadier Regiment (1st Lettish)
33rd SS Freiwilligen Grenadier Regiment (2nd Lettish)
34th SS Freiwilligen Grenadier Regiment (3rd Lettish)
15th SS Freiwilligen Artillery regiment (1st Lettish)

The other units were numbered "15th." The division was reorganized into a Type 44 Infantry Division and the bicycle battalion became the 15th SS Fusilier Battalion with four companies. The three grenadier regiments retained their third battalions. In June 1944 the division was renamed the 15th Waffen SS Grenadier Division (1st Lettish) and the Freiwilligen Grenadier Regiments became Waffen Grenadier Regiments. In May 1944 the division had:

32nd SS Freiwilligen Regiment (Lettische Nr. 3)
1st Battalion
1–3rd Companies (16 LMGs & 2 80mm mortars)
4th Company (12 HMGs, 3 LMGs & 6 80mm mortars)
2nd Battalion (5–8th Companies) (same as 1st Battalion)
3rd Battalion (9–12th Companies) (same as 1st Battalion)
13th (IG) Company (2 150mm sIG, 6 75mm leIG, & 4 LMGs)
14th (panzerjäger) Company (12 75mm PAK 40 & 13 LMGs)

33rd SS Freiwilligen Regiment (Lettische Nr. 4)
same as 32nd SS Regiment
34th SS Freiwilligen Regiment (Lettische Nr. 5)
same as 32nd SS Regiment
15th SS Fusilier Battalion
1 Bicycle Fusilier Company (16 LMGs & 2 80mm mortars)
2 Fusilier Companies (16 LMGs & 2 80mm mortars ea)
1 Machine Gun Company (12 HMGs, 3 LMGs, & 6 80mm mortars)
15th SS Panzerjäger Battalion
1 (motZ) Panzerjäger Company (12 75mm PAK 40 & 13 LMGs)
1 Self Propelled Panzerjäger Company (14 75mm PAK 40 & 15 LMGs) (projected, not raised at this time)
15th SS Artillery Regiment (Lettische Nr. 1)
1 Regimental Staff & Staff Battery (1 LMG)
1st Battalion
1 Battalion Staff & Staff Battery (1 LMG)
3 Batteries (4 105mm leFH & 5 LMGs)
2nd Battalion
same as 1st Battalion
3rd Battalion
same as 1st Battalion
4th Battalion
1 Battalion Staff & Staff Battery (1 LMG)
3 Batteries (4 150mm sFH & 5 LMGs)
15th SS Flak Battalion
1 Staff & Staff Battery (1 LMG)
1 (motZ) Heavy Flak Battery (4 88mm, 3 20mm & 2 LMGs)
1 (motZ) Medium Flak Battery (9 37mm & 4 LMGS)
1 (motZ) Light Flak Battery (12 20mm & 4 LMGs)
15th SS Pioneer Battalion
1 Staff (4 LMGs)
3 Pioneer Companies (2 HMGs, 9 LMGs, 6 flamethrowers, & 2 80mm mortars) (one on bicycles)
14th SS Signals Battalion
1 Battalion Staff & Staff Pack Company
1 (tmot) Telephone Company (6 LMGs)
1 (mot) Radio Company (5 LMGs)
1 (tmot) Signals Supply Column (1 LMG)
14th SS Feldersatz Battalion
5 Companies
15th SS Supply Troops
1 (mot) 90 ton Transportation Company (6 LMGs)
1 60 ton Transportation Companies (8 LMGs ea)
1 (mot) Light Supply Columns
15th SS Supply Company (6 LMGs)
15th SS Truck Park
15th SS (mot) Maintenance Companies (6 LMGs)

Medical
 15th SS Medical Company (4 LMGs)
 15th SS (mot) Medical Company (4 LMGs)
 15th SS (mot) Supply Medical Company (4 LMGs)
Administration
 15th SS (tmot) Bakery Company (6 LMGs)
 15th SS (tmot) Butcher Company (6 LMGs)
 15th SS (tmot) Divisional Administration Platoon
  (2 LMGs)
 15th SS Veterinary Company (6 LMGs)
 15th SS (mot) Field Post Office (2 LMGs)

On 7/16/44 the division was destroyed and the survivors were united with the 19th (2nd Lettish) Division. In August the cadre of the division was taken to West Prussia, with the exception of the artillery regiment, which remained in combat. In December three "Bau" Regiments were formed:

1/,2/,3/1st Bau-Regiment (15th SS Division)
1/,2/,3/2nd Bau-Regiment (15th SS Division)
1/,2/,3/3rd Bau-Regiment (15th SS Division)

The division was reorganized by the order of 9/8/44 in West Prussia and raised to:

1/,2/,3/32nd Waffen SS Grenadier Regiment (3rd
 Lettish)
1/,2/,3/33rd Waffen SS Grenadier Regiment (4th
 Lettish)
1/,2/,3/34th Waffen SS Grenadier Regiment (5th
 Lettish)

1/,2/,3/,15th Waffen SS Artillery Regiment (2nd Lettish Artillery Regiment)
Fusilier Battalion/15th Waffen SS Grenadier Division

After being destroyed in Pommerania, the division was re-formed in Neubrandenburg. It was taken into Russian captivity near Neuruppin in 1945. Most of its men were executed by the Soviets as traitors.

Sturmbrigade "Reichsführer SS"

On 1 February 1943 the Escort Battalion Reichsführer SS was expanded into the SS Sturmbrigade Reichsführer SS. It served Himmler as an escort brigade. The Sturmbrigade Reichsführer SS contained:

3 Schützen Companies
1 Machine Gun Company
1 Panzerjäger Company
1 Infantry Gun Company
1 Staff Company

1 Sturmgeschütz Battery
1 88mm Flak Battery
1 20mm Flak Battery
1 Light (mot) Transportation Company

This formation lasted only until 10/3/43. At that point it appears to have been reorganized as follows:

Staff
Grenadier Battalion (8 cos)
Panzerjäger Battalion (3 cos)

Sturmgeschütz Battalion
Flak Battalion

In the middle of February 1943 the brigade was serving in France. On 16 June 1943 it absorbed a grenadier battalion from the 356th Infantry Division. With the invasion of Italy it was sent south, joined by the 505th Self Propelled Artillery Battalion. The brigade was sent to Corsica were it served as part of the island's garrison. The brigade was removed from Corsica on 15 September 1943 and sent to Italy where it was reorganized into the 16th Reichsführer SS Panzergrenadier Division on 10/2/43.

16th Panzergrenadier Division "Reichsführer SS"

On 10/3/43 the Sturmbrigade Reichsführer SS was expanded into the 16th SS Panzergrenadier Division Reichsführer SS. The division was initially organized with a single panzer battalion with four companies and a sturmgeschütz battalion with three batteries.

In November the two panzer grenadier regiments were numbered 33rd and 34th. On 11/12/43 they were renumbered 35th and 36th. The Reichsführer Escort Battalion was re-formed in September 1943 and exchanged with the 2/35th SS Panzergrenadier Regiment in June 1944. In 1945 an SS Escort Battalion z.b.V. appears on the army rolls. The division had:

35th SS Panzergrenadier Regiment
  1st Battalion (1–4th Companies)
  2nd Battalion (5–8th Companies)
  3rd Battalion (9–12th Companies)
  13th Company
  14th Company
  15th Company
36th SS Panzergrenadier Regiment
  1st Battalion (1–4th Companies)
  2nd Battalion (5–8th Companies)
  3rd Battalion (9–12th Companies)
  13th Company
  14th Company
  15th Company
16th SS Panzer Battalion (4 companies)
16th SS Panzer Reconnaissance Battalion (5 companies)
1/,2/,3/16th SS Artillery Regiment
16th SS Flak Battalion (4 batteries)
16th SS Sturmgeschütz Battalion (3 batteries)[2]
16th SS Pioneer Battalion (3 companies)
16th SS Signals Battalion (2 companies)
16th SS Feldersatz Battalion
16th SS Support Troops

In May 1944 OKH records show the division organized and equipped as follows:

Division
Division Staff
(mot) Mapping Detachment
Divisional Escort Company
  Motorcycle Platoon (6 LMGs)
  Self Propelled Flak Battery (4 20mm guns)

  Self Propelled Anti-Tank Platoon (3 LMGs & 3 75mm PAK 40)
  Infantry Gun Platoon (2 75mm leIG)
  Mixed Panzergrenadier Platoon (4 HMGs, 6 LMGs, & 2 80mm mortars)

16th SS Panzer Battalion
Battalion Staff (17 LMGs)
Battalion Staff Panzer Platoon (8 tanks)
1–4th Companies (17 Mk IV tanks ea)
1 Panzer Maintenance Company

35th (mot) SS Panzergrenadier Regiment
Regimental Staff
1st Battalion
  1–3rd Companies (4 HMGs, 18 LMGs, 2 80mm mortars & 2 flamethrowers)
  4th Company
    1 Mortar Platoon (2 LMGs & 4 120mm mortars)
    1 Panzerjäger Platoon (3 LMGs & 3 75mm PAK 40)
    2 Infantry Gun Sections (2 75mm leIG ea)
2nd Battalion (6–10th Companies) (same as 1st Battalion)
3rd Battalion (11–15th Companies) (same as 1st Battalion)
16th (self-propelled flak) Company (12 20mm & 4 LMGs)
17th (motZ infantry gun) Company (6 150mm sIG & 7 LMGs)
18th (mot) Pioneer Company (2 HMGs, 12 LMGs, 6 flamethrowers & 2 80mm mortars)

36th (mot) SS Panzergrenadier Regiment
same as 35th SS Panzergrenadier Regiment

16th SS Reconnaissance Battalion
Battalion Staff
1 Armored Car Company (18 20mm & 24 LMGs)
3 (halftrack) Companies (4 HMGs, 18 LMGs, & 2 80mm mortars)
1 (halftrack) Company
  1 Pioneer Platoon (4 LMGs & 6 flamethrowers)
  1 Panzerjäger Platoon (3 LMGs & 3 75mm PAK 40)
  1 Infantry Gun Section (2 75mm leIG & 4 LMGs)
1 (mot) Reconnaissance Supply Column (3 LMGs)

16th SS Panzerjäger Battalion
Battalion Staff
1 Self Propelled Panzerjäger Company (14 75mm PAK 40 & 14 LMGs)
1 (motZ) Panzerjäger Company (12 75mm PAK 40 & 12 LMGs)
1 Self Propelled Flak Company (12 20mm & 4 LMGs)

---

[2] Renamed the 16th SS Panzerjäger Battalion in June 1944.

16th SS Panzer Artillery Regiment

1 Regimental Staff & (mot) Staff Battery (2 LMGs)

1 Self Propelled Flak Battery (4 quad 20mm & 2 LMGs)

1st, 2nd & 3rd (Self Propelled) Battalions, each with

Staff & Staff Battery (6 LMGs)

2 (motZ) Batteries (6 105mm leFH & 2 LMGs ea)

4th Battalion

Staff & Staff Battery (2 LMGs)

2 (motZ) Batteries (6 150mm sFH & 2 LMGs ea)

1 (motZ) Battery (6 105mm sK 18/40 guns & 2 LMGs ea)

16th SS Flak Battalion

Staff & Staff Battery

3 (motZ) heavy Flak Batteries (4 88mm, 3 20mm & 2 LMGs ea)

1 (motZ) Medium Flak Batteries (9 37mm & 4 LMGs ea)

1 (motZ) Searchlight Platoon (4 600mm searchlights)

16th SS Panzer Pioneer Battalion

Staff (2 LMGs)

3 (mot) Pioneer Companies (2 HMGs, 18 LMGs, 2 80mm mortars & 6 flamethrowers)

1 (mot) "K" Bridging Train (3 LMGs)

16th SS Panzer Signals Battalion

1 (mot) Telephone Company (6 LMGs)

1 (mot) Radio Company (7 LMGs)

1 (mot) Signals Supply Column (1 LMG)

16th SS Feldersatz Battalion

5 Companies

16th SS Supply Troop

1–3rd/16th SS (mot) 120 ton Transportation Companies (8 LMGs ea)

4–6th/16th SS (mot) 90 ton Transportation Companies (6 LMGs ea)

16th SS (mot) 20 ton Light Flak Supply Column

16th SS (mot) Workshop Company (2 LMGs)

16th SS (mot) Supply Company (8 LMGs)

16th SS Truck Park

1/16th SS (mot) Maintenance Companies (4 LMGs)

2/16th SS (mot) Maintenance Companies (5 LMGs)

16th SS (mot) 75 ton Heavy Maintenance Supply Column

Medical

1/,2/16th SS (mot) Medical Companies (2 LMGs ea)

1/,2/,3/16th SS Ambulances

Administration

16th SS (mot) Bakery Company (6 LMGs)

16th SS (mot) Butcher Company (4 LMGs)

16th SS (mot) Divisional Administration Platoon (2 LMGs)

16th SS (mot) Military Police Troop (5 platoons) (15 LMGs)

16th SS (mot) Field Post Office (2 LMGs)

By June 1944 the 16th SS Panzer Battalion had been reorganized with a Sturmgeschütz Staff Company and three Sturmgeschütz Companies. In June 1944 the 2/35th Panzergrenadier Regiment and the Reichsführer SS Escort Battalion exchanged places. The order of 9/26/44 detached the reconnaissance battalion, the panzerjäger battalion, the mountain artillery regiment, and the mountain pioneer battalion from the 13th SS Mountain Division Hanschar, renumbered them as the 509th, and assigned them to the 16th SS Panzergrenadier Reichsführer SS Division.

In December 1944 the artillery regiment formed a new 3rd Battalion and the old 3rd Battalion was redesignated as the 4th Battalion. In February 1945 the panzerjäger battalion was transferred to the newly forming 32nd SS Division. In April 1945 it was renamed the 32nd Panzerjäger Battalion.

17th SS Panzergrenadier Division "Götz von Berlichingen"

Established on 10/3/43, it was formed in France on 11/15/43 with detachments from the 10th SS Panzer Division. The division was initially organized with a single panzer battalion with four companies and a sturmgeschütz battalion with three batteries. In May 1944 OKH records show the division organized and equipped as follows:

Division

Division Staff

(mot) Mapping Detachment

Divisional Escort Company

Motorcycle Platoon (6 LMGs)

Self Propelled Flak Battery (4 20mm guns)

Self Propelled Anti-Tank Platoon (3 LMGs & 3 75mm PAK 40)

Infantry Gun Platoon (2 75mm leIG)

Mixed Panzergrenadier Platoon (4 HMGs, 6 LMGs, & 2 80mm mortars)

17th SS Panzer Battalion

Battalion Staff (17 LMGs)

Battalion Staff Panzer Platoon (8 tanks)

Self Propelled Flak Battery (3 quad 20mm guns)
1–4th Companies (17 Mk IV tanks ea)
1 Panzer Maintenance Company

37th (mot) SS Panzergrenadier Regiment
Regimental Staff
1st Battalion
  1–3rd Companies (4 HMGs, 18 LMGs, 2 80mm mortars & 2 flamethrowers)
  4th Company
    1 Mortar Platoon (2 LMGs & 4 120mm mortars)
    1 Panzerjäger Platoon (3 LMGs & 3 75mm PAK 40)
    2 Infantry Gun Sections (2 75mm leIG ea)
2nd Battalion (6–10th Companies) (same as 1st Battalion)
3rd Battalion (11–15th Companies) (same as 1st Battalion)
16th (self-propelled flak) Company (12 20mm & 4 LMGs)
17th (motZ infantry gun) Company (6 150mm sIG & 7 LMGs)
18th (mot) Pioneer Company (2 HMGs, 12 LMGs, 6 flamethrowers & 2 80mm mortars)

38th (mot) SS Panzergrenadier Regiment
same as 35th SS Panzergrenadier Regiment

17th SS Reconnaissance Battalion
Battalion Staff
1 Armored Car Company (18 20mm & 24 LMGs)
3 (halftrack) Companies (4 HMGs, 18 LMGs, & 2 80mm mortars)
1 (halftrack) Company
  1 Pioneer Platoon (4 LMGs & 6 flamethrowers)
  1 Panzerjäger Platoon (3 LMGs & 3 75mm PAK 40)
  1 Infantry Gun Section (2 75mm leIG & 4 LMGs)
1 (mot) Reconnaissance Supply Column (3 LMGs)

17th SS Panzerjäger Battalion
Battalion Staff (7 LMGs)
1 Self Propelled Panzerjäger Company (14 75mm PAK 40 & 14 LMGs)
1 (motZ) Panzerjäger Company (12 75mm PAK 40 & 12 LMGs)
1 Self Propelled Flak Company (12 20mm & 4 LMGs)

17th SS Panzer Artillery Regiment
1 Regimental Staff & (mot) Staff Battery (2 LMGs)
1 Self Propelled Flak Battery (4 quad 20mm & 2 LMGs)
1st, 2nd, & 3rd (Self Propelled) Battalion, each with
Staff & Staff Battery (6 LMGs)
2 (motZ) Batteries (6 105mm leFH & 2 LMGs ea)
4th Battalion
Staff & Staff Battery (2 LMGs)

2 (motZ) Batteries (6 150mm sFH & 2 LMGs ea)
1 (motZ) Battery (6 105mm sK 18/40 guns & 2 LMGs ea)

17th SS Flak Battalion
Staff & Staff Battery
3 (motZ) heavy Flak Batteries (4 88mm, 3 20mm & 2 LMGs ea)
1 (motZ) Medium Flak Batteries (9 37mm & 4 LMGs ea)
1 (motZ) Searchlight Platoon (4 600mm searchlights)

17th SS Panzer Pioneer Battalion
Staff (2 LMGs)
3 (mot) Pioneer Companies (2 HMGs, 18 LMGs, 2 80mm mortars & 6 flamethrowers)
1 Self Propelled Medium Flak Battery (9 37mm guns & 4 LMGs)
1 (mot) Light Armored Bridging Train (3 LMGs)

17th SS Panzer Signals Battalion
1 (mot) Telephone Company (6 LMGs)
1 (mot) Radio Company (7 LMGs)
1 (mot) Signals Supply Column (1 LMG)

17th SS Feldersatz Battalion
5 Companies

17th SS Supply Troop
1–3rd/17th SS (mot) 120 ton Transportation Companies (8 LMGs ea)
4–6th/17th SS (mot) 90 ton Transportation Companies (6 LMGs ea)
17th SS (mot) 20 ton Light Flak Supply Column
17th SS (mot) Workshop Company (2 LMGs)
17th SS (mot) Supply Company (8 LMGs)

17th SS Truck Park
1/17th SS (mot) Maintenance Companies (4 LMGs)
2/17th SS (mot) Maintenance Companies (5 LMGs)
17th SS (mot) 75 ton Heavy Maintenance Supply Column

Medical
1/,2/17th SS (mot) Medical Companies (2 LMGs ea)
1/,2/,3/17th SS Ambulances

Administration
17th SS (mot) Bakery Company (6 LMGs)
17th SS (mot) Butcher Company (4 LMGs)
17th SS (mot) Divisional Administration Platoon (2 LMGs)
17th SS (mot) Military Police Troop (6 LMGs)
17th SS (mot) Field Post Office (2 LMGs)

By June 1944 the 17th SS Panzer Battalion was converted over to sturmgeschütz and its panzer inventory and organization were as follows:

17th SS Panzer Battalion
1 Sturmgeschütz Staff & Staff Company
1 Panzer Flak Platoon
3 Sturmgeschütz Companies

StuG	42
Cmd	3
Flakpz38	12

During June 1944 the Sturmgeschütz Battalion was renamed the 17th SS Panzerjäger Battalion. It had two (motZ) companies and one self-propelled company. On 7/29/44 the division was heavily engaged by St. Lo and nearly totally destroyed. The division was re-formed by Paris and in the Compiègne by the absorption of the 49th and 51st SS Panzergrenadier Brigades. The newly re-formed 38th SS Panzergrenadier Regiment was destroyed again on 11/22/44 near Metz. On 1/1/45 the 38th SS Panzergrenadier Regiment was re-formed by renaming the 1/,2/,3/SS Panzergrenadier Ausbildung (Training) Regiment, the Heavy Panzerjäger Company, the Flak Company, and the Pioneer Company. On 12/10/44 the panzer inventory and organization of the

17th SS Panzer Battalion were as follows:

17th SS Panzer Battalion
1 Sturmgeschütz Staff & Staff Company
3 Sturmgeschütz Companies

StuG	17 (+17 enroute)
Cmd	3
Flakpz38	6
FlakpzIV (2V)	4 (enroute)

In March 1945 the artillery regiment raised a new third battalion from the 2nd Artillery Battalion of the 32nd SS Freiwilligen Grenadier Battalion and the old 3rd Battalion became the new 4th Battalion. It appears that the new 3rd Battalion never reached the division.

The division fought in the Saarpfalz and Franken during the last months of the war. It withdrew through Niederbayern and finally surrendered to the U.S. 101st Airborne Division south of Kufstein, now in Austrian territory, on 5/6/45.

18th SS Freiwilligen Panzergrenadier Division "Horst Wessel"

Formed on 1/25/44 from the 1st SS (mot) Brigade. In May 1944 OKH records show the division organized and equipped as follows:

Division
  Division Staff
  (mot) Mapping Detachment
  Divisional Escort Company
    Motorcycle Platoon (6 LMGs)
    Self Propelled Flak Battery (4 20mm guns)
    Self Propelled Anti-Tank Platoon (3 LMGs & 3 75mm PAK 40)
    Infantry Gun Platoon (2 75mm leIG)
    Mixed Panzergrenadier Platoon (4 HMGs, 6 LMGs, & 2 80mm mortars)
18th SS Sturmgeschütz Battalion
  Battalion Staff (17 LMGs)
  Battalion Staff Sturmgeschütz Platoon
  Flak Battery (3 quad 20mm guns)
  3 Sturmgeschütz Companies (10 StuGs & 2 LMGs ea)
  1 Panzer Maintenance Platoon (2 LMGs)
39th (mot) SS Panzergrenadier Regiment
  Regimental Staff
  1st Battalion

1–3rd Companies (4 HMGs, 18 LMGs, 2 80mm mortars & 2 flamethrowers)
    4th Company
      1 Mortar Platoon (2 LMGs & 4 120mm mortars)
      1 Panzerjäger Platoon (3 LMGs & 3 75mm PAK 40)
      2 Infantry Gun Sections (2 75mm leIG ea)
  2nd Battalion (6–10th Companies) (same as 1st Battalion)
  3rd Battalion (11–15th Companies) (same as 1st Battalion)
  16th (self-propelled flak) Company (12 20mm & 4 LMGs)
  17th (motZ infantry gun) Company (6 150mm sIG & 7 LMGs)
  18th (mot) Pioneer Company (2 HMGs, 12 LMGs, 6 flamethrowers & 2 80mm mortars)
40th (mot) SS Panzergrenadier Regiment
  same as 35th SS Panzergrenadier Regiment
18th SS Reconnaissance Battalion
  Battalion Staff
  1 Armored Car Company (18 20mm & 24 LMGs)
  3 (halftrack) Companies (4 HMGs, 18 LMGs, & 2 80mm mortars)

1 (halftrack) Company
  1 Pioneer Platoon (4 LMGs & 6 flamethrowers)
  1 Panzerjäger Platoon (3 LMGs & 3 75mm PAK 40)
  1 Infantry Gun Section (2 75mm leIG & 4 LMGs)
  1 (mot) Reconnaissance Supply Column (3 LMGs)

18th SS Panzerjäger Battalion
Battalion Staff
1 Self Propelled Panzerjäger Company (14 75mm
PAK 40 & 14 LMGs)
1 (motZ) Panzerjäger Company (12 75mm PAK 40
& 12 LMGs)
1 Self Propelled Flak Company (12 20mm & 4 LMGs)

18th SS Panzer Artillery Regiment
  1 Regimental Staff & (mot) Staff Battery (2 LMGs)
  1 Self Propelled Flak Battery (4 quad 20mm & 2
  LMGs)
1st, 2nd, & 3rd (Self Propelled) Battalions, each
with
  Staff & Staff Battery (6 LMGs)
  2 (motZ) Batteries (6 105mm leFH & 2 LMGs ea)
4th Battalion
  Staff & Staff Battery (2 LMGs)
  2 (motZ) Batteries (6 150mm sFH & 2 LMGs ea)
  1 (motZ) Battery (6 105mm sK 18/40 guns & 2
  LMGs ea)

18th SS Flak Battalion
Staff & Staff Battery
3 (motZ) heavy Flak Batteries (4 88mm, 3 20mm &
2 LMGs ea)
1 (motZ) Medium Flak Batteries (9 37mm & 4
LMGs ea)
1 (motZ) Searchlight Platoon (4 600mm searchlights)

18th SS Pioneer Battalion
Staff (2 LMGs)
3 (mot) Pioneer Companies (2 HMGs, 18 LMGs, 2
80mm mortars & 6 flamethrowers)
1 (mot) "K" Bridging Train (3 LMGs)

18th SS Signals Battalion
1 (mot) Telephone Company (6 LMGs)

1 (mot) Radio Company (7 LMGs)
1 (mot) Signals Supply Column (1 LMG)
18th SS Feldersatz Battalion
5 Companies
18th SS Supply Troop
1–3rd/18th SS (mot) 120 ton Transportation Companies (8 LMGs ea)
4–6th/18th SS (mot) 90 ton Transportation Companies (6 LMGs ea)
18th SS (mot) 20 ton Light Flak Supply Column
18th SS (mot) Workshop Company (2 LMGs)
18th SS (mot) Supply Company (8 LMGs)
18th SS Truck Park
1/18th SS (mot) Maintenance Companies (4 LMGs)
2/18th SS (mot) Maintenance Companies (5 LMGs)
18th SS (mot) 75 ton Heavy Maintenance Supply
Column
Medical
1/2/18th SS (mot) Medical Companies (2 LMGs ea)
1/,2/,3/18th SS Ambulances
Administration
18th SS (mot) Bakery Company (6 LMGs)
18th SS (mot) Butcher Company (4 LMGs)
18th SS (mot) Divisional Administration Platoon (2
LMGs)
18th SS (mot) Military Police Troop (6 LMGs)
18th SS (mot) Field Post Office (2 LMGs)

Sometime after the division was organized, the pioneer companies were converged into a pioneer battalion
and the flak companies were converged into the flak
battalion. In addition the four company 18th SS Panzerjäger Battalion and the 18th SS Feldersatz Battalion
were organized.

The division was renamed the 18th SS Freiwilligen
Panzergrenadier Division "Horst Wessel" prior to
October 1944. In February 1945 the division formed
the panzerjäger battalion, which it had lacked prior to
that date.

19th Waffen SS Grenadier Division (2nd Lettish)

Formed on 1/7/44 from the 2nd Lettish SS Freiwilligen
Brigade, it was originally named the 19th Lettish SS
Freiwilligen Division. During July 1944 the division
was organized and equipped as follows:

Division Staff
1 Divisional Staff (2 LMGs)
1 Divisional Band

52nd (mot) Mapping Detachment
52nd (mot) Military Police Detachment (3
LMGs)
42nd Waffen Grenadier SS Regiment (lettische Nr 1)
1 Grenadier Regimental Staff & Staff Company
  1 Staff Platoon (1 LMG)
  1 Signals Platoon
  1 Pioneer Platoon (6 LMGs)

1 Bicycle Platoon (3 LMGs)
1st Battalion
1 Battalion Staff (1 LMG)
3 Grenadier Companies (2 HMGs & 13 LMGs)
1 Machine Gun Company (6 HMGs, 3 LMGs 4 120mm mortars & 6 80mm mortars)
2nd Battalion
same as 1st Battalion
3rd Battalion
same as 1st Battalion
1 Infantry Gun Company (2 150mm sIG, 6 75mm leIG, & 5 LMGS)
1 Panzerjäger Company
1 Headquarters Platoon (1 LMG)
1 Panzerzerstörer Platoon (36 panzerschrecke & 2 LMGs)
1 (motZ) Panzerjäger Platoon (3 75mm PAK & 3 LMGs)
43rd Waffen Grenadier SS Regiment (lettische Nr 2)
same as 42nd Waffen SS Grenadier Regiment
44th Waffen Grenadier SS Regiment (lettische Nr 6)
same as 42nd Waffen SS Grenadier Regiment
52nd SS Panzerjäger Battalion
1 Battalion Staff & (mot) Staff Platoon (1 LMG)
1 Sturmgeschütz Company (10 StuG & 12 LMGs)
1 (motZ) Panzerjäger Company (12 75mm PAK & 12 LMGs)
1 (motZ) Flak Company (12 20mm flak & 2 LMGs)
52nd SS Fusilier Battalion
1 Battalion Staff (1 LMG)
1 (bicycle) Fusilier Company (2 HMGs & 13 LMGs)
2 Fusilier Companies (2 HMGs & 13 LMGs ea)
1 Heavy Company (6 HMGs, 3 LMGs, 4 120mm mortars & 6 80mm mortars)
19th SS Artillery Regiment (Lettisch Artillerie Regiment Nr. 2)
1 Regimental Staff & Staff Battery (1 LMG)
1st Battalion
1 Battalion Staff & Staff Battery (2 LMGs)
3 Batteries (4 105mm leFH & 5 LMGs ea)
2nd Battalion
same as 1st Battalion
3rd Battalion
same as 1st Battalion
4th Battalion
1 Battalion Staff & Staff Battery (2 LMGs)
3 Batteries (4 150mm sFH & 5 LMGs ea)
52nd SS Pioneer Battalion
1 Battalion Staff (4 LMGs & 2 flamethrowers)
1 (bicycle) Pioneer Company (2 HMGs, 9 LMGs, 6 flamethrowers, & 2 80mm mortars)
2 Pioneer Companies (2 HMGs, 9 LMGs, 6 flamethrowers, & 2 80mm mortars ea)

52nd SS Signals Battalion
1 (tmot) Telephone Company (5 LMGs)
1 (mot) Radio Company (4 LMGs)
1 (tmot) Supply Column (2 LMGs)
52nd SS Feldersatz Battalion
2–5 Companies
52nd SS Supply Troop
1 (tmot) Supply Battalion Staff (2 LMGs)
2 (mot) 90 ton Transportation Companies (6 LMGs ea)
2 (horse drawn) 60 ton Transportation Company (8 LMGs ea)
1 Supply Company (8 LMGs)
52nd SS Maintenance Troops
1 (mot) Maintenance Company (4 LMGs)
Other
52nd SS (mot) Butcher Company (2 LMGs)
52nd SS (mot) Bakery Company (4 LMGs)
52nd SS (mot) Divisional Administration Company (2 LMGs)
1/52nd SS (horse drawn) Medical Company (4 LMGs)
2/52nd SS (mot) Medical Company (2 LMGs)
52nd SS (mot) Medical Supply Company (4 LMGs)
52nd SS Veterinary Company (6 LMGs)
52nd SS (mot) Field Post Office

The 52nd SS Flak Battalion was not incorporated into the division and retained its number until it was disbanded in September 1944. The formation of a 3rd Battalion in the three grenadier regiments was completed from the 1st and 2nd SS Training Regiments of the 2nd Lettish SS Freiwilligen Brigade, but they were later disbanded. In June the division was renamed the 19th Waffen SS Grenadier Division (2nd Lettish). The 42nd, 43rd, and 44th Freiwilligen Grenadier Regiments became Waffen SS Grenadier Regiments. When the 15th Waffen SS Grenadier Division (1st Lettish) was destroyed in July 1944 its survivors were united with the 19th Waffen SS Grenadier Division. The 42nd and 43rd Regiments were then renamed "1st Lettish" and "2nd Lettish," no later than 10/11/44. On 2/15/45 the division had:

42nd Waffen SS Grenadier Regiment "Valdemars Veiss" (1st Lettish)
43rd Waffen SS Grenadier Regiment "Hinrich Schuldt" (2nd Lettish)
44th Waffen SS Grenadier Regiment (6th Lettish)
19th Waffen SS Artillery Regiment (2nd Lettish Artillery Regiment)
19th SS Fusilier Battalion
19th SS Flak Battalion (3 batteries) (probably lost in September 1944)

19th SS Panzerjäger Battalion (2 companies)
19th SS Freiwilliger Pioneer Battalion (3 companies)
19th SS Signals Battalion (2 companies)
19th SS Divisional (Einheiten) Support Units

On 15 January 1945 the 42nd Waffen SS Regiment was given the name "Valdemars Veiss" and the 43rd was given the name "Hinrich Schuldt." On 8 May 1945 the division passed into Russian captivity in Courland. Most of its soldiers were apparently executed by the Soviets as traitors.

20th Waffen SS Grenadier Division

The division began life as the Estonian Legion. As such it had:

Staff & Staff Company
1st Battalion (1–4th Companies)
2nd Battalion (5–8th Companies)
3rd Battalion (9–12th Companies)
Heavy Mortar Company
Infantry Panzerjäger Company

On 2/22/43 the Legion formed a replacement and training battalion. On 3/23/43 the 1st Battalion was detached and became a (mot) SS Grenadier Battalion in the 5th SS Division "Wiking."

On 23 March 1943, the legion was redesignated the 1st Estonisches SS Freiwilligen Grenadier Regiment and contained:

Staff
1st Battalion (1–4th Companies)
2nd Battalion (5–8th Companies)
3rd Battalion (9–12th Companies)
13th (Heavy Mortar) Company
14th (Panzerjäger) Company
15th (Pioneer) Company

On 4/4/43, 800 Estonians from the 1st Battalion were detached from the Estonian Legion and incorporated for active duty with the 5th SS Panzer-Grenadier Division Wiking. This Estonian battalion replaced the Finnish Volunteer Battalion that was attached to the Wiking Division from 12/2/41 to June 1943. The Estonian Battalion was referred to as the "Estnische Freiwilligen Bataillon Narwa." Later the battalion was renamed "SS Panzer-grenadier Battalion Narwa." By April 1944, the Narwa Battalion was pulled out of the Wiking Division and added to the formation of the 20th SS Estonian Division as part of "SS Fusilier Battalion Nr. 20."

During the summer of 1943 the regiment expanded into two regiments and became the Estonian 53rd Frei-willigen Brigade. In October 1943 the brigade had 6,069 men, including 183 officers, 987 NCOs, 4,086 soldiers and 813 hiwis. It was organized and equipped as follows:

Brigade Staff
1 Brigade Staff
1 Motorcycle Messenger Platoon (6 LMGs)
1 (motZ) Panzerjäger Platoon (3 75mm PAK 40 and 3 LMGs)
1 (mot) "KB" Troop
2 (mot) Infantry Regiments, each with
2 Battalions
3 Companies (16 LMGs & 2 80mm mortars)
1 Machine Gun Company (12 HMGs, 1 LMG, 4 120m mortars)
1 Infantry Gun Company (150mm sIG & 6 75mm leIG)
1 (tmot) Panzerjäger Company (12 75mm PAK 40 & 13 LMGs)
1 Pioneer Company (2 HMGs, 9 LMGs, 2 80mm mortars & 6 flamethrowers)
(mot) Flak Battalion
1 (mot) Staff Company (1 LMG)
1 (mot) Heavy Flak Company (4 88mm, 3 20mm & 2 LMGs)
1 Self Propelled Light Flak Company (12 20mm & 4 LMGs)
1 Self Propelled Medium Flak Company (9 37mm & 4 LMGs)
1 (mot) Light Flak Supply column
Artillery Battalion
1 Battalion Staff Battery (2 LMgs)
3 Batteries (4 105mm leFH 18 & 5 LMGs ea)
1 (mot) Signals Company (3 LMGs)

On 10/22/43 the brigade was renamed the 3rd Estonian SS Freiwilligen Brigade. The regiments were renumbered on 11/12/43. The brigade had:

Brigade Staff
1st SS Freiwilligen Grenadier Regiment (later 45th Regiment)

1st Battalion (1–4th Companies)
2nd Battalion (4–8th Companies)
3rd Battalion (9–12th Companies)
13th (Heavy Mortar) Company
14th (Panzerjäger) Company
15th (Pioneer) Company (added later)
2nd SS Freiwilligen Grenadier Regiment (later 46th Regiment)
1st Battalion (1–4th Companies)
2nd Battalion (5–8th Companies)
3rd Battalion (9–12th Companies)
13th (Heavy Mortar) Company
14th (Panzerjäger) Company
15th (Pioneer) Company (added later)
53rd SS Panzerjäger Battalion
53rd SS Artillery Battalion
53rd SS Flak Battalion
53rd SS Signals Company
53rd SS Feldersatz Battalion

On 1/24/44 the 20th Estonian SS Freiwilligen Division began forming from the 3rd Estonian SS Freiwilligen Brigade. In May 1944 OKH records show the division organized and equipped as follows:

Division
Division Staff
(mot) Mapping Detachment
(mot) Military Police Detachment (1 LMG)
45th SS Grenadier Regiment
Regimental Staff
1st Battalion
1–3rd Companies (16 LMGs & 2 80mm mortars)
4th Machine Gun Company (12HMGs, 3 LMGs & 6 80mm mortars)
2nd Battalion (6–10th Companies) (same as 1st Battalion)
3rd Battalion (11–15th Companies) (same as 1st Battalion)
1 (motZ) Infantry Gun Company (2 150mm sIG, 6 75mm leIG, & 4 LMGs)
1 (tmot) Panzerjäger Company (3 75mm PAK 40, 3 50mm PAK 38, & 13 LMGs)
46th SS Panzergrenadier Regiment
same as 45th Grenadier Regiment
47th SS Panzergrenadier Regiment
same as 45th Grenadier Regiment
54rd SS Fusilier Battalion
Battalion Staff
1 (bicycle) Fusilier Companies (16 LMGs & 2 80mm mortars)
2 Fusilier Companies (16 LMGs & 2 80mm mortars)
1 Machine Gun Company (12 HMGs, 3 LMGs, & 6 80mm mortars)

20th SS Panzerjäger Battalion
Battalion Staff
1 (motZ) Panzerjäger Company (12 75mm PAK 40 & 12 LMGs)
1 Self Propelled Panzerjäger Company (14 75mm PAK 40 & 15 LMGs) (not yet raised)
53rd SS Flak Battalion
1 (motZ) Heavy Flak Battery (4 88mm, 3 20mm & 2 LMGs)
1 (motZ) Medium Flak Battery (9 37mm & 4 LMGs)
1 (motZ) Light Flak Battery (12 20mm & 4 LMGs)
20th SS Panzer Artillery Regiment
1 Regimental Staff & (mot) Staff Battery (1 LMG)
1st (Self Propelled) Battalion
Staff & Staff Battery (6 LMGs)
3 (motZ) Batteries (4 105mm leFH & 2 LMGs ea)
2nd Battalion
same as 1st Battalion
3rd Battalion
same as 1st Battalion
4th Battalion
Staff & Staff Battery (2 LMGs)
3 (motZ) Batteries (4 150mm sFH & 2 LMGs ea)
53rd SS Pioneer Battalion
Staff (2 LMGs)
3 Pioneer Companies (2 HMGs, 18 LMGs, 2 80mm mortars & 6 flamethrowers) (one on bicycles)
53rd SS Signals Battalion
1 (tmot) Telephone Company (6 LMGs)
1 (mot) Radio Company (5 LMGs)
1 (tmot) Signals Supply Column (1 LMG)
53rd SS Feldersatz Battalion
5 Companies
53rd SS Supply Troop
1/53rd SS (mot) 90 ton Transportation Companies (6 LMGs)
2/,3/53rd SS 60 ton Transportation Companies (8 LMGs ea)
53rd SS (mot) 20 ton Light Flak Supply Column
53rd SS (mot) Supply Company (6 LMGs)
53rd SS Truck Park
53rd SS (mot) Maintenance Companies (6 LMGs)
Medical
1/,2/53rd SS (mot) Medical Companies (2 LMGs ea)
53rd SS Decontamination Company
53rd SS (mot) Medical Supply Company (2 LMGs)
Administration
53rd SS Veterinary Company (6 LMGs)
53rd SS (mot) Bakery Company (6 LMGs)
53rd SS (mot) Butcher Company (4 LMGs)
53rd SS (mot) Divisional Administration Platoon (2 LMGs)
53rd SS (mot) Military Police Troop (6 LMGs)
53rd SS (mot) Field Post Office (2 LMGs)

In June 1944 the division was renamed as the 20th Waffen SS Grenadier Division (1st Estonian) and the word "Freiwilligen" was replaced by "Waffen." During the retreat through Estonia the division was heavily mauled and the 1/45th SS Grenadier Regiment was nearly destroyed. The order of 10/6/44 reorganized the division with:

1/,2/,3/45th Waffen SS Grenadier Regiment (1st Estonian)

1/,2/,3/46th Waffen SS Grenadier Regiment (2nd Estonian)

1/,2/,3/47th Waffen SS Grenadier Regiment (3rd Estonian)

1/,2/,3/,4/20th Waffen SS Artillery Regiment (1st Estonian Artillery Regiment)

20th Divisional (Einheiten) Support Troops

The 20th SS Flak Battalion was not re-formed. Upon the German capitulation the division passed into Russian captivity north of Prague.

21st Waffen SS Mountain Division "Skanderbeg" (1st Albanian)

Formed on 5/1/44 in northern Albania from Islamic Albanians. In May 1944 OKH records show the division was to be organized and equipped as follows:

Division Staff
1 Divisional Staff
1 (mot) Mapping Detachment
2 Mountain Regiments, each with
1 Regimental Staff
1 Regimental Band
1 Staff Company
1 Signals Platoon
1 Bicycle Platoon
1 Cavalry Platoon (3 LMGs)
1 Infantry Gun Section (1 LMG & 2 75mm leIG)
1 Mountain Flak Battery (4 20mm guns)
3 **Battalions**, each with
3 Companies (12 LMGs & 2 80mm mortars)
1 Machine Gun Company (4 HMGs, 2 75mm leIG, & 6 80mm mortars)
1 Heavy Company
1 Pioneer Platoon (4 LMGs)
1 Mountain Signals Platoon
Infantry Gun Company (6 75mm leIG & 4 LMGs)
(motZ) Panzerjäger Company (6 75mm PAK 40 & 9 LMGs)
1 Mountain Supply Column (3 LMGs)
21st SS Panzerjäger Battalion
2 (motZ) Panzerjäger Companies (9 75mm PAK 40 & 9 LMGs)
1 (motZ) Mountain Flak Company (12 20mm & 2 LMGs)
21st SS Reconnaissance Battalion
1 (mot) Staff Company
1 Staff Platoon (1 LMG)
1 Signals Platoon
1 Pioneer Platoon (4 LMGs)

2 Bicycle Companies (4 HMGs, 12 LMGs, 2 80mm mortars ea)
1 Cavalry Squadron (2 HMGs & 9 LMGs)
1 (mot) Company
1 Pioneer Platoon (4 LMGs)
1 Panzerjäger Platoon (3 LMGs & 3 37mm PAK 36)
1 Infantry Gun Section (2 75mm leIG)
21st SS Mountain Artillery Regiment
1 Regimental Staff & (tmot) Staff Battery
1st Battalion
1 Battalion Staff & Staff Battery
3 Mountain Batteries (4 75mm mountian guns & 2 LMGs ea)
1 Mountain Supply Column
2nd Battalion
same as 1st Battalion
3rd Battalion
same as 1st Battalion
4th Battalion
Staff & Staff Battery (2 LMGs)
1 Calibration Detachment
3 (motZ) Batteries (6 150mm sFH & 2 LMGs ea)
21st SS Freiwilligen Pioneer Battalion
2 Mountain Pioneer Companies (9 LMGs & 6 flamethrowers)
1 (mot) Mountain Pioneer Company (2 HMGs, 18 LMGs, 2 80mm mortars, & 6 flamethrowers)
1 (mot) "G" Bridging Train (2 LMGs)
1 (mot) Pioneer Supply Column (2 LMGs)
21st SS Feldersatz Battalion
4 Companies
21st SS Freiwilligen Signals Battalion
2 (tmot) Mountain Telephone Companies (5 LMGs ea)
1 (tmot) Mountain Radio Company (5 LMGs)
1 (mot) Signals Supply Column (1 LMG)

WAFFEN SS DIVISIONS AND BRIGADES

21st SS Mountain Supply Troops
    1 (mot) 120 ton Transportation Company (8 LMGs)
    1 (mot) 90 ton Transportation Company (6 LMGs)
    2 Light Mountain Supply Columns (4 LMGs)
    2 Light Supply Columns (4 LMGs)
    1 (tmot) Mountain Supply Company (6 LMGs)
    1 (mot) Maintenance Company (4 LMGs)
Administration
    1 (mot) Butcher Company
    1 (mot) Bakery Company
    1 (mot) Divisional Administration Platoon
Medical
    2 (tmot) Mountain Medical Companies (4 LMGs)
    2 Ambulance Platoons
Other
    1 Mountain Veterinary Company
    1 (mot) Military Police Troop (3 LMGs)
    1 (mot) Field Post Office

On 10/11/44 the division had:

1/,2/,3/50th SS Gebirgs-Jäger Regiment (1st Albanian)
1/,2/,3/51st SS Gebirgs-Jäger Regiment (2nd Albanian)
21st SS Reconnaissance Battalion (4 companies)
SS Freiwilligen Panzerjäger Battalion, 21st SS Division (3 companies)
1/,2/,3/,4/21st SS Mountain Artillery Regiment (from 1st Albanian Artillery Regiment)
SS Freiwilligen Pioneer Battalion, 21st SS Division (3 companies)
SS Feldersatz Battalion, 21st SS Division
SS Freiwilligen Signals Battalion, 21st SS Division (3 companies)
SS Mountain Supply Troop, 21st SS Division

However, despite the theoretical organization, manpower was lacking. On 1 October 1944 the division had only 3,504 recruits. The division was disbanded at the end of 1944. Its German staff was absorbed into the SS Gebirgsjäger Regiment 14, of the Prinz Eugen Division.

22nd SS Freiwilligen Cavalry Division

Formed on 4/29/44 from Hungarian volunteers in the 8th SS Cavalry Division, which stood in Hungary at that time. At the end of 1944 the division was given the title "Maria Theresia." The division had:

17th SS Freiwilligen Cavalry Regiment (from 8th SS Cavalry Division)
52nd SS Freiwilligen Cavalry Regiment
53rd SS Freiwilligen Cavalry Regiment
22nd SS Artillery Regiment
22nd Divisional (Einheiten) Support Units, including

22nd SS Panzerjäger Battalion (3 companies)
22nd SS Reconnaissance Battalion (5 companies)
22nd SS Flak Battalion
22nd SS Pioneer Battalion (3 companies)
22nd SS Signals Battalion (2 companies)
22nd SS Feldersatz Battalion

Originally the three cavalry regiments were numbered 52nd, 53rd, and 54th, but the numbering changed to what is shown above in September 1944. The division was destroyed in Budapest in February 1945.

23rd Waffen SS Mountain Division "Kama" (2nd Croatian)

Hitler ordered the division organized on 28 May 1944. The 23rd Waffen-Gebirg Division der SS "Kama" (kroatische Nr. 2) was envisioned as a second Croatian Waffen SS division, and sister unit to the 13th Waffen-Gebirg Division der SS "Handschar." As with "Handschar," it was to have a mostly Croatian Muslim composition (at that point the Croatian province of Bosnia), but insufficient reliable Muslims were available, so Croatian Catholics were also accepted into its ranks. The approval for the formation of this unit was given on 17 June 1944. It was trained in the Bachska Region of the former Yugoslavia, lasting until October

1944, when the approach of the Red Army forced the SS to disband it. The division was fully formed on 6/10/44 and contained:

Divisional Staff (2 LMGs)
    1 (mot) Mapping Detachment
    1 (tmot) Military Police Detachment (2 LMGs)
    1 Mountain Staff Escort Company (11 LMGs, 6 120mm mortars)
1/,2/,3/,4/55th Waffen Gebirgs-Jäger Regiment (3rd Croatian)
Regimental Staff

Regimental Staff Company
  1 Signals Platoon
  1 Mounted Reconnaissance Platoon
  1 Mountain Bicycle Platoon (3 LMGs)
Each battalion
  1 Battalion Staff Company
  1 Signals Platoon
  1 Pioneer Platoon (3 LMGs)
  3 Gebirgs-Jäger Companies (9 LMGs ea)
  3 Gebirgs-Jäger Machine Gun Company (6 HMGs & 6 80mm mortars)
Heavy Company
  Panzerzerstörer Platoon (1 LMG, 54 88mm Panzerschrecke)
  1 (mot) Panzerjäger Platoon (6 50mm PAK 38 & 3 LMGs)
  1 Infantry Gun Section (2 75mm leIG & 1 LMG)
  1 Mountain Supply Column
1/,2/,3/,4/56th Waffen Gebirgs-Jäger Regiment (4th Croatian)
  same as 44th Waffen Gebirgs-Jäger Regiment
1/,2/,3/,4/24th Waffen Gebirgs-Artillerie Regiment (2nd Croatian)
23rd SS Panzerjäger Battalion (3 companies)
23rd SS Reconnaissance Battalion (4 squadrons)
23rd SS Flak Battalion
23rd SS Pioneer Battalion (3 companies)
23rd SS Mountain Signals Battalion
23rd SS Feldersatz Battalion
23rd Divisional (Einheiten) Troops

When the 23th SS Mountain Division "Kama" was formed, each battalion of the 13th SS Artillery Regiment detached the personnel from one battery to assist in the formation of the new division. In addition, 1,000 Moslems were detached by the order of 9/24/44 to form the SS Generalkommando IX in Croatia, eventually to also be incorporated into the 13th SS Mountain Division "Handschar." On that same date, the remaining German cadre personnel and equipment were sent to Hungary and organized into a SS Grenadier Division that later became the 31st SS Freiwilligen Grenadier Division. All of the numbers were changed accordingly and the 23rd SS Division disappeared. In the fall of 1944, shortly after the division was formed, the two mountain regiments were numbered 55th and 56th. In late 1944 the division was engaged in Hungary, fighting the Russians. It was ordered moved back to Bosnia and on 17 October 1944 the division mutinied. The reliable elements were taken from the division and sent to the 13th "Handschar" Division and the division itself was formally dissolved on 31 October 1944. The designation "23rd Waffen SS Division" was then given to the Dutch Panzer-Grenadier being formed.

23rd SS Freiwilligen Panzergrenadier Division "Nederland" (1st Dutch)

A division was ordered formed 2/10/45 from the 4th SS Freiwilligen Panzergrenadier Brigade "Nederland." The division was to be organized and equipped as follows:

Division Headquarters
1 Divisional Staff (2 LMGs)
1 (mot) Mapping Detachment
1 Divisional Escort Company
  1 Motorcycle Platoon (6 LMGs)
  1 Infantry Gun Platoon (2 75mm leIG)
  1 Self Propelled Flak Battery (4 20mm guns)
  1 Panzerjäger Platoon (3 LMGs & 3 75mm PAK 40)
  1 Mixed Panzergrenadier Platoon (4 HMGs, 6 LMGs, & 2 80mm mortars)
48th SS Freiwilligen Panzergrenadier Regiment "General Seyffard" (1st Dutch)
1 Regimental Staff
1 (mot) Regimental Staff Company
  1 Motorcycle Messenger Platoon (6 LMGs)
  1 Signals Platoon
  1 Panzerjäger Platoon (3 LMGs & 3 75mm PAK 40)
1st (mot) Battalion (1–4th Companies)
  3 Panzergrenadier Companies (4 HMGs, 18 LMGs, 2 80mm mortars & 2 flamethrowers)
  1 Heavy Company (6 80mm mortars, 3 75mm PAK 40, & 4 75mm leIG)
2nd (mot) Battalion (5–8th Companies)
  same as 1st Battalion
3rd (mot) Battalion (9–12th Companies)
  same as 1st Battalion
13th (motZ) Infantry Gun Company (4 150mm sIG)
14th Self Propelled Flak Company (12 20mm guns)
15th Motorcycle Company (2 80mm mortars, 4 HMGs, 18 LMGs & 3 75mm PAK 40)
16th (mot) Pioneer Company (18 LMGs & 6 flamethrowers)
49th SS Freiwilligen Panzergrenadier Regiment "de Ruyter" (2nd Dutch)
1st (mot) Battalion (1–4th Companies)
  same as 1st Battalion/48th SS Panzergrenadier Regiment

2nd (mot) Battalion (5–8th Companies)
same as 1st Battalion/48th SS Panzergrenadier Regiment
3rd (half-track) Battalion (9–12th Companies)
   3 Panzergrenadier Companies (4 HMGs, 34 LMGs 2 80mm mortars & 2 flamethrowers)
   1 Heavy Company (6 80mm mortars, 3 75mm PAK 40, & 6 75mm guns)
13th (motZ) Infantry Gun Company (4 150mm sIG)
14th Self Propelled Flak Company (12 20mm guns)
15th Motorcycle Company (2 80mm Mortars, 4 HMGs, 18 LMGs & 3 75mm PAK 40)
16th (mot) Pioneer Company (18 LMGs & 6 flamethrowers)

23rd SS Panzer Regiment
Regimental Staff
1st & 2nd Panzer Battalions, each with
   1 Panzer Battalion Staff
   1 Self Propelled Light Flak Platoon (6 20mm guns)
   4 Medium Panzer Companies
   1 (half-track) Pioneer Company (40 LMGs & 6 flamethrowers)
   1 Panzer Maintenance Company
23rd SS Artillery Regiment (formerly the 54th Artillery Regiment)
   1 Regimental Staff & (mot) Staff Battery (2 LMGs)
   1 Self Propelled Flak Battery (4 quad 20mm guns)
   1st Battalion
   1 Battalion Staff & (mot) Staff Battery (2 LMGs)
   1 Self Propelled Battery (6 150mm sFH Hummels SdKfz 165 & 6 LMGS)
   2 Self Propelled Batteries (6 105mm leFH Wespe SdKfz 124 & 6 LMGS ea)
   2nd Battalion
   1 Battalion Staff & (mot) Staff Battery (2 LMGs)
   3 (motZ) Batteries (4 105mm leFH & 6 LMGs ea)
   3rd Battalion
   1 Battalion Staff & (mot) Staff Battery (2 LMGs)
   1 Flak Battery (2 mountain 20mm flak guns)
   3 (motZ) Batteries (4 150mm sFH & 6 LMGs ea)
   1 (motZ) Battery (4 100mm K18 & 6 LMGs)
23rd SS Panzerjäger Battalion
   1 Sturmgeschütz Battalion Staff (1 LMG)
   1 Sturmgeschütz Battalion Staff Company (2 LMGs)
   3 Sturmgeschütz Companies (10 Stugs ea)
23rd SS Reconnaissance Battalion
   1 Battalion Staff
   2 Armored Car Companies (25 LMGs & 16 20mm guns)
   2 (half-track) Reconnaissance Platoons (2 HMGs, 54 LMGs, 2 80mm mortars, & 2 75mm leIG)
   1 (half-track) Heavy Reconnaissance Company
   1 Panzerjäger Platoon (3 75mm PAK 40)
   1 Gun Platoon (6 75mm guns)

1 Infantry Gun Platoon (2 75mm leIG)
1 Pioneer Platoon (16 LMGs & 1 75mm leIG)
1 (mot) Light Reconnaissance Supply Column
23rd SS Flak Battalion
   1 (mot) Flak Battalion Staff Company (1 LMG)
   3 (motZ) Heavy Flak Battery (4 88mm, 3 20mm & 2 LMGs)
   1 Self Propelled Medium Flak Battery (9 37mm & 4 LMGs)
   1 (motZ) Light Flak Supply Column
23rd SS Pioneer Battalion
   Staff (2 LMGs)
   1 (half-track) Reconnaissance Platoon (6 75mm guns & 8 LMGs)
   1 (half-track) Pioneer Company (40 LMGs & 6 flamethrowers)
   2 (mot) Pioneer Companies (18 LMGs & 6 flamethrowers)
   1 (mot) Brüko B (4 LMGs)
   1 (mot) Light Pioneer Supply Column (2 LMGs)
23rd SS Signals Company
   1 (mot) Telephone Company (5 LMGs)
   1 Panzer Radio Company (35 LMGs)
   1 (mot) Signals Supply Column (4 LMGs)
23rd SS Divisional Supply Troop
   1–4th/23rd SS (mot) 120 ton Transportation Companies (8 LMGs ea)
   23rd SS (mot) Heavy Supply Column
   1/,2/,3/,4/23rd SS (mot) Heavy Fuel Column (4 LMGs ea)
   23rd SS (mot) Workshop Company (4 LMGs)
   23rd SS (mot) Supply Company (8 LMGs)
23rd SS Truck Park
   1/,2/,3/23rd SS (mot) Maintenance Companies (4 LMGs ea)
   23rd SS (mot) 75 ton Heavy Maintenance Supply Column
Medical
   1/,2/23rd SS (mot) Medical Companies (2 LMGs ea)
   1/,2/,3/23rd SS Ambulances (1 LMG ea)
Administration
   23rd SS (mot) Bakery Company (4 LMGs)
   23rd SS (mot) Butcher Company (4 LMGs)
   23rd SS (mot) Division Administration (4 LMGs)
   23rd SS (mot) Military Police Troop (6 LMGs)
   23rd SS (mot) Field Post Office (2 LMGs)

It is probable that the 23rd SS Panzer Regiment was never raised. Indications are that the 15th and 16th Companies of the Panzergrenadier Regiments were never raised either. At the end of the war the division had:

1/,2/,3/48th SS Freiwilligen Panzergrenadier Regiment "General Seyffard" (1st Dutch)

1/,2/,3/49th SS Freiwilligen Panzergrenadier Regiment "de Ruyter" (2nd Dutch)
23rd SS Reconnaissance Battalion
1/,2/23rd Artillery Regiment (formerly the 54th Artillery Regiment)
23rd SS Panzerjäger Battalion
23rd SS Pioneer Battalion
23rd SS Signals Battalion

23rd SS Feldersatz Battalion
23rd Divisional (Einheiten) Troops

The 48th Regiment was incorporated into the 15th Waffen SS Grenadier Division. It was then replaced by being re-formed from a panzer grenadier school as the SS Regiment Klotz. The division was captured by the Russians in the Halbe Pocket.

24th Waffen SS Gebirgs Division "Karstjäger"

On 10 July 1942 the SS-Karstwehr Company was established at the Dachau SS Training Camp. On 15 November 1942 it was authorized to be expanded into a full battalion and by the summer of 1943 the battalion was fully formed. The division was ordered into existence on 7/18/44 and formation began on 8/1/44. In the late summer of 1944 the division staff was operational and one full mountain infantry regiment (59th SS Gebirgsjäger Regiment) and part of an artillery regiment were organized (SS 24th Gebirgs-Artillerie Regiment). The 60th SS Gebirgsjäger Regiment was only partially formed. In theory the division had:

Divisional Staff
  Staff (2 LMGs)
  Divisional Band
  1 (mot) Mapping Detachment
  1 (tmot) Military Police Detachment (3 LMGs)
59th SS Gebirgsjäger Regiment
  1 Regimental Staff
  1 Regimental Staff Company
    1 Signals Platoon
    1 Mounted Reconnaissance Platoon
    1 Bicycle Platoon
    1 Mortar Platoon (4 120mm mortars & 2 LMGs)
  3 Battalions, each with
    3 Gebirgsjäger Companies (2 HMGs, 11 LMGs, & 2 80mm mortars ea)
    1 Gebirgsjäger Machine Gun Company
      1 Machine Gun Platoon (6 HMGs & 2 LMGs)
      1 Mortar Platoon (4 120mm mortars & 2 LMGs)
    1 Infantry Gun Company (6 75mm leIG & 4 LMGs)
    1 Panzerjäger Company
      1 Panzerzerstörer Platoon (54 88mm Panzerschreck & 3 LMGs)
      1 Panzerjäger Platoon (3 75mm PAK 40 & 3 LMGs)
    1 Gebirgsjäger Company (2 HMGs, 11 LMGs, & 2 80mm mortars)
60th SS Gebirgsjäger Regiment
  same as 59th SS Gebirgsjäger Regiment

24th SS Gebirgs Artillery Regiment
  1st, 2nd & 3rd Battalions, each with
    1 Staff Battery
    3 Batteries (4 75mm mountain guns & 2 LMGS ea)
  4th Battalion
    1 Staff Battery
    1 Calibration Detachment
    2 (motZ) Batteries (4 150mm sFH & 5 LMGs)
    1 (motZ) Battery (4 100mm K18 & 6 LMGs)
24th SS Gebirgs Reconnaissance Battalion
  1 (mot) Battalion Staff Company
    1 Signals Detachment
    1 Pioneer Platoon (3 LMGs)
    2 Bicycle Companies (18 LMGs & 4 HMGs)
    1 Mounted Company (2 HMGs & 9 LMGs)
    1 (mot) Heavy Reconnaissance Company
      Infantry Gun Platoon (4 75mm leIG & 2 LMGs)
      Panzerjäger Section 3 75mm PAK 40 & 2 LMGs)
      Mortar Platoon (6 120mm mortars & 3 LMGs)
24th SS Gebirgs Panzerjäger Battalion
    1 (motZ) Panzerjäger Company (12 75mm PAK 40 & 12 LMGs)
    1 (motZ) Mountain Flak Company (12 20mm & 2 LMGs)
    1 Sturmgeschütz Battery (10 StugS & 12 LMGs)
24th SS Gebirgs Signals Battalion
    2 (tmot) Mountain Telephone Companies (3 LMGs ea)
    1 (tmot) Mountain Radio Company (3 LMGs)
    1 (mot) Mountain Signals Supply Column (1 LMG)
24th SS Divisional Supply
    1 Staff (2 LMGs)
    1 (mot) (120-ton) Transportation Company (6 LMGS)
    3 Mountain Supply Column (2 LMGs ea)
    3 Light Supply Columns (2 LMGs ea)
    1 Mountain Supply Company (2 LMGs)
24th SS Divisional Administration
    1 (mot) Field Bakery (6 LMGs)
    1 (mot) Butcher Company (4 LMGs)

1 (mot) Divisional Administration (2 LMGs)
1 (mot) Field Post Officer (1 LMG)
24th SS (mot) Maintenance Company (4 LMGs)
24th SS Mountain Veterinary Company (2 LMGs)
24th SS Medical Battalion
2 (tmot) Mountain Medical Companies (4 LMGs ea)
1 (mot) Medical Platoon
1 Mountain Medical Pack Company (4 LMGs)
1 (mot) Ambulance (2 LMGs)
1 Mountain Ambulance (2 LMGs)

However, the division probably never exceeded the following organization:

Staff
Staff/59th SS Gebirgsjäger Regiment
1/59th SS Gebirgsjäger Regiment
2/59th SS Gebirgsjäger Regiment
3/59th SS Gebirgsjäger Regiment
60th SS Gebirgsjäger Regiment (only partially formed)
1/24th SS Gebirgs Artillery Regiment (3 batteries 4 75mm mountain guns each)
24th SS Gebirgs Signals Battalion (1 mixed signals company)
24th SS Divisional Supply

1 (mot) (120-ton) Transportation Company
1 Mountain Supply Column

Constant fighting prevented it from ever becoming a full division, so on 5 December 1944 it was ordered reorganized as a Mountain Brigade. The internal regimental structure was scrapped. The SS Karstjäger Brigade had:

Brigade Staff
Staff Company
1st Battalion (1–4th Companies)
2nd Battalion (5–8th Companies)
Armored Assault Company (formed from the former panzerjäger company)
Mountain Artillery Battery (formed from the nucleus of the 24th SS Gebirgs Artillery Regiment)

In February 1945 it was again named the 24th Waffen SS Gebirgs (Kartsjäger) Division, but it only contained the 59th SS Gebirgsjäger Regiment. At the end of April 1945 the remains of the brigade were merged with the replacement troops of the 7th SS Gebirgs Division "Prinz Eugen." On 1 May 1945 they surrendered to the British 6th Armored Division.

25th Waffen SS Grenadier Division "Hunyadi" (1st Hungarian)

Formed on 11/2/44 in Hungary by the merging of Hungarian recruit depots and volunteers. The division had:

1/,2/61st Waffen SS Grenadier Division (1st Hungarian)
1/,2/62nd Waffen SS Grenadier Division (2nd Hungarian)
1/,2/63rd Waffen SS Grenadier Division (3rd Hungarian)
1/,2/,3/,4/25th Waffen SS Artillery Regiment (1st Hungarian Artillery Regiment)
1st (light) Battalion (1–3rd Companies) (75mm PAK)
2nd (light) Battalion (4–6th Companies) (105mm leFH)

3rd (light) Battalion (8–9th Companies) (105mm leFH)
4th (heavy) Battalion (10–11th Companies) (150mm sFH)
25th SS Panzerjäger Battalion (3 companies)
25th SS Pioneer Battalion (2, later 3 companies)
25th SS Signals Battalion (2 companies)
25th SS Feldersatz Battalion

In December 1944 the division organized a 25th SS Ski Battalion. The 1/61st Grenadier Regiment was equipped with bicycles. In May 1945 the division passed into American captivity. The Hungarian nationals were returned to Hungary.

26th SS Panzer Division

Formed on 8/10/44 by the renaming of the 49th SS Panzergrenadier Brigade. It was to have had the 66th and 67th Panzergrenadier Regiments. The division was disbanded on 8 September 1944, and used to re-form the 37th Panzergrenadier Regiment of the 17th Panzergrenadier Division "Götz von Berlichingen."

26th Waffen SS Grenadier Division (2nd Hungarian)

Formed on 1/29/45. In March it had:

1/,2/,3/64th Waffen SS Grenadier Regiment (4th Hungarian)
1/,2/,3/65th Waffen SS Grenadier Regiment (5th Hungarian)
1/,2/,3/85th Waffen SS Grenadier Regiment (6th Hungarian)
1/,2/,3/,4/26th Waffen SS Artillery Regiment (2nd Hungarian Artillery Regiment)
26th Waffen SS Pioneer Battalion (2 companies)
26th Waffen SS Panzerjäger Battalion (3 companies)
26th Waffen SS Fusilier Battalion
26th Waffen SS Signals Battalion (2 companies)
26th Divisional (Einheiten) Support Units

It was still forming as the war ended.

27th SS Panzer Division

Formed on 8/10/44 by the renaming of the 51st SS Panzergrenadier Brigade. It was to have had the 68th and 69th Panzergrenadier Regiments. It was disbanded on 9/8/44 and used to re-form the 38th Panzergrenadier Regiment 17th SS Panzergrenadier Division "Gotz von Berlichingen."

27th SS Freiwilligen Grenadier Division "Langemarck"

This division began its history as the SS Freiwilligen Sturmbrigade "Langemarck" on 5/31/43, which was renamed the 6th SS Freiwilligen-Sturmbrigade "Langemarck" on 10/22/43. It consisted of:

Brigade Staff
1st Battalion (3 companies & 1 heavy co)
2nd Battalion (4 heavy companies)
Infantry Gun Company
Sturmgeschütz Battery
Flak Battery
Panzerjäger Company
Light Supply Column

Its depot was the SS Grenadier Ersatz Battalion "Ost," which was in Breslau. The division was formed on 10/19/44 from the 6th SS Freiwilligen Sturmbrigade "Langemarck." It had:

1/,2/66th SS Grenadier Regiment
1/,2/67th SS Grenadier Regiment
1/,2/68th SS Grenadier Regiment
1/,2/,3/,4/27th SS Artillery Regiment
27th SS Panzerjäger Battalion (3 cos)
27th SS Fusilier Battalion
27th SS Pioneer Battalion
27th SS Signals Battalion
27th SS Feldersatz Battalion
27th Divisional Support Units

In May 1945 the division withdrew through Mecklenburg and was taken prisoner around Neustrelitz.

28th SS Panzer Division

Formed on 8/10/44 the division was formed with the 70th and 71st Panzergrenadier Regiments. A reinforced brigade (SS Panzer Brigade Gross) was eventually formed with two infantry battalions, a panzerjäger battalion (four companies), a panzer reconnaissance battalion (three companies), and a supply unit. The unit was to have been fully organized in September, but that never happened.

28th SS Freiwilligen Grenadier Division "Wallonien"

This division began its history as the SS Freiwilligen Brigade Wallonien, formed on 6/1/43. On 7/3/43 it was renamed the SS Sturmbrigade "Wallonien" and contained a brigade staff, five rifle companies, and a feldersatz company. By the end of 1943 it organized a sturmgeschütz battery. The brigade continued to expand and in early 1944 it contained:

Brigade Staff
Staff Company
1st Battalion (1–4th Companies)
2nd Battalion (5–8th Companies)
Infantry Gun Company
Panzerjäger Company
1st & 2nd Flak Companies
Feldersatz Company

In May 1944 OKH records show the brigade organized and equipped as follows:

Brigade Staff
  Brigade Staff
  (mot) Brigade Staff Company
1st & 2nd (mot) Battalion
  3 (mot) Grenadier Companies (2 HMGs, 18 LMGs, & 2 80mm mortars)
  1 (mot) Machine Gun Company (8 HMGs & 6 80mm mortars)
1 (motZ) Infantry Gun Company (2 150mm sIG & 4 75mm leIG)
(motZ) Panzerjäger Company (9 75mm PAK 40 & 9 LMGs)
(motZ) Flak Company (4 80mm, 3 20m & 2 LMGs)
Sturmgeschütz Company (10 StuGs)
Feldersatz Company
1 (mot) Heavy Supply Column

The division was formed on 10/19/44 from the 5th SS Freiwilligen Sturmbrigade Wallonien, which had only two battalions. The division had:

1/,2/69th SS Freiwilligen Grenadier Regiment
1/,2/70th SS Freiwilligen Grenadier Regiment
1/,2/71st SS Freiwilligen Grenadier Regiment
1/,2/,3/,4/28th SS Artillery Regiment
28th SS Feldersatz Battalion (5 companies)
28th SS Panzerjäger Battalion (3 companies)
28th SS Pioneer Battalion (2 companies)
28th SS Signals Battalion (2 companies)
28th SS Divisional (Einheiten) Support Units

In May 1945 the division was taken prisoner by the Soviets in Schwerin.

29th Waffen SS Grenadier Division (1st Russian)

The history of the 29th Waffen SS Grenadier Division begins in the town of Lokot on the edge of the Bryansk Forest, about halfway between Orec and Kursk. Because of the forest, which held large numbers of partisans and fugitives from the Red Army, the mayor of Lokot, K. Voskoboinkov, was permitted by the Wehrmacht to establish a self-defense force of about 500 men to protect themselves and the German lines of communications. The mayor had undertaken to provide food and materials to the 2nd Panzer Army.

Voskoboinkov was killed in battle and his place was taken by Kaminski. Kaminski had tried to form a Russian Nazi party, but had failed. However, he was otherwise a very successful man. Under his guidance this original self-defense force was expanded into a small army of around 10,000 men, organized in five infantry regiments, supported by an artillery force of 36 guns, an armored battalion with 24 T-34 Russian tanks, plus medical, signals and engineer units. This force was given the name *Russkaya Osvoboditelnaya Narodnaya Armiya* (Russian Liberation Peoples' Army or R.O.N.A.)

By the fall of 1943, as the Germans were falling back from Russia, the R.O.N.A., now consisting of 15,000 men, followed by 10,500 civilians and 1,500 cows,

withdrew to the Polish-Czech border region. In March 1944 the R.O.N.A. was renamed the *Volksheer Brigade* (People's Army Brigade). In July it was taken into the SS as the Sturmbrigade R.O.N.A.

This force was formally organized into a division on 8/1/44 with the 72nd, 73rd, and 74th SS Regiments. The division was formed in Warsaw with the 6,000–7,000 men of the Kaminski Brigade. The organization, etc., of the division is unknown.

Shortly thereafter Kaminski was executed by a SS firing squad. The accusations of looting were probably justified, based on later revelations of his lavish lifestyle. Though his death was blamed on Polish partisans, the morale of the R.O.N.A. began to collapse. The division's organization stopped and its men were distributed to other SS formations.

29th Waffen SS Grenadier Division (1st Italian)

Formed on 3/9/45 by the reorganization of the Waffen SS Grenadier Brigade (1st Italian). The formation of the three regiments and the artillery was not completed. The division was to be organized and equipped as follows:

Division Staff
1 Medical Company
1 (mot) Vehicle Park
1st Transportation Company
2nd Transportation Company
Propaganda Company
81st Waffen-Grenadier Regiment (1st Italian)
1st Battalion
1–5th Companies
2nd Battalion
6–10th Companies
82nd Waffen-Grenadier Regiment (2nd Italian)
1st Battalion
1–5th Companies
2nd Battalion
6–10th Companies

3rd Battalion
11–15th Companies
Italian Waffen-SS Training Battalion
29th SS Artillery Regiment (1st Italian)
1st Battalion
3 Batteries
2nd Battalion
3 Batteries
29th SS Panzerjäger Abteilung
1 Staff
1st Battery (20mm guns)
2nd Battery (47mm/32 guns)
3rd Battery (75mm/18 guns)
4th Battery (75mm/42 guns) 4th Battery (75mm/48 guns)
29th SS Fusilier Battalion "Debica"
1–4th Companies
09th SS Pioneer Company
29th SS Signals Company
29th SS Feldersatz Battalion
5 Companies

30th Waffen SS Grenadier Division (2nd Russian)

Formed on 8/1/44 with four regiments (Osterreich, Grautz, Mocha & Schmidt), which had been organized as the Siegling Schutzmannschaft (Schuma) Brigade. It was formed from White Ruthenian, Ukrainian and

Russian volunteers. The division had:

1/,2/75th Waffen SS Grenadier Regiment (4th Russian
1/,2/76th Waffen SS Grenadier Regiment (5th Russian

1/,2/77th Waffen SS Grenadier Regiment (6th Russian)
1/,2/30th Waffen SS Artillery Regiment (2nd Russian
Artillery Regiment) (each battalion had 3 batteries
of Russian guns)
30th SS Reconnaissance Battalion (staff, staff squadron
& 3 cavalry squadrons)
30th SS Pioneer (bicycle) Company
30th SS Signals Company
30th SS Reconnaissance Battalion (3 cavalry squadrons
& 1 bicycle company)
30th SS Feldersatz Battalion (staff, 3 infantry companies, 1 heavy co, & 1 pioneer company)
30th SS Supply Regiment

In August the Siegling Brigade, then in Warsaw,
was transferred to the Belfort area and all three regiments
were raised to a strength of three battalions by the order
of 10/18/44. The division supply commander was
reduced to a supply troop. In August 1944, 2,300 mutineers were assigned to the 1st and 2nd Entrenchment
Regiments. As an Einsatz Battalion, on 9/12/44 the
Murawjew Battalion was formed. In September the
artillery consisted solely of a staff and staff battery, two
batteries of captured 122mm Russian guns, and a nebelwerfer battery.

On 10/24/44 the 75th Regiment was formed from
the 1/1st and 2/2nd; the 76th was formed from the
1/,2/4th; the 77th was formed from the Murawjew Battalion and the 654th Ost (Eastern Volunteer) Battalion.
This resulted in the division coming to full strength.

On 11/2/44 the 77th was disbanded, the 2/77th
became the 2/76th, the old 2/76th became the new
1/76th and the old 1/76th was disbanded. On 1/11/45 the
30th Waffen SS Grenadier Division (2nd Russian) was
disbanded. On 1/15/45 the Russians were sent to the
newly forming 600th Infantry Division (Vlassov) and the
Germans and Ruthanians were used to form the Waffen
SS Grenadier Brigade (1st White Ruthenian). It had only
a single regiment (three battalions), a panzerjäger battalion, an artillery battalion, a cavalry reconnaissance
squadron and a feldersatz battalion. On 3/9/45 the
brigade was redesignated again as the 30th Waffen SS
Grenadier Division (1st White Ruthenian) with only one
regiment, the 75th Waffen SS Grenadier Regiment (1st
White Ruthenian). The division was formally disbanded
in April 1945 and the German cadre was sent to form the
38th Waffen SS Grenadier Division "Niebelungen."

31st SS Freiwilligen Grenadier Division

Formed on 10/1/44 in Hungary from the German cadre
of the 23rd SS Division. It had:

78th SS Freiwilligen Grenadier Regiment
  1st Battalion (1–4th Companies)
  2nd Battalion (5–8th Companies)
  3rd Battalion (9–12th Companies)
  13th Company
  14th Company
79th SS Freiwilligen Grenadier Regiment
  1st Battalion (1–4th Companies)
  2nd Battalion (5–8th Companies)
  3rd Battalion (9–12th Companies)
  13th Company
  14th Company
80th SS Freiwilligen Grenadier Regiment
  1st Battalion (1–4th Companies)
  2nd Battalion (5–8th Companies)
  3rd Battalion (9–12th Companies)
  13th Company
  14th Company

31st SS Freiwilligen Fusilier Battalion
31st SS Freiwilligen Panzerjäger Battalion
1/,2/,3/,4/31st SS Freiwilligen Artillery Regiment
31st SS Freiwilligen Flak Battalion
31st SS Freiwilligen Pioneer Battalion
31st SS Freiwilligen Signals Battalion
31st SS Freiwilligen Feldersatz Battalion
31st Commander SS Division Supply Troop

The division was organized of native Germans and
ethnic Germans drawn from the Reich. It absorbed the
Police Regiment Brixen. On 1/18/45 it was organized as
a "Type 45" Division. It was taken prisoner by the Russians at Königgrätz.

32nd SS Freiwilligen Grenadier Division "30 Januar"

Formed starting on 1/30/45, and in the space of five days, with the 86th and 87th SS Regiments, by using Kampfgruppe Schill and the men drawn from the disbanded recruit depots in Kurmark. The artillery regiment came from the SS Artillery Training and Replacement Regiment in Prague. The pioneer battalion was formed from the Hradischko Pioneer School. The Kampfgruppe Schill became Panzergrenadier Regiment Schill in October 1944. It became the 86th SS Regiment. The Kurmark Recruit Depot and other sources formed the 87th Regiment. The 88th Regiment was to have been formed, but insufficient troops were found. The division had:

1/,2/86th SS Freiwilligen Grenadier Regiment
1/,2/87th SS Freiwilligen Grenadier Regiment
1/,2/,3/32nd SS Freiwilligen Artillery Regiment
32nd SS Panzerjäger Battalion (former 16th SS Panzerjäger Bn) (2 companies & a flak company)
32nd SS Fusilier Battalion
32nd SS Flak Battalion (3 batteries)
32nd SS Pioneer Battalion (2 companies)
32nd SS Signals Battalion (2 companies)
32nd SS Feldersatz Battalion
32nd SS Supply Regiment

33rd Waffen SS Grenadier Division "Charlemagne" (1st French)

The French SS Freiwilligen Grenadier Regiment was formed in August 1943. In July 1944 it became the French SS Freiwilligen Sturmbrigade only to change its name in September to the Französische Brigade der bzw. SS Waffen Brigade der SS "Charlemagne" (Französische Nr. 1). At that time it had:

Brigade Staff
German Command Staff
1/,2/1st Grenadier Regiment
1/,2/2nd Grenadier Regiment
SS Panzerjäger Battalion
SS Artillery Battalion
SS Pioneer Company
SS Signals Company
Feldersatz Company
Französische Ausbildungs und Ersatz Bataillon der SS

On 10/11/44 the Grenadier Regiments were numbered 57 and 58 and the brigade units received the number 57. The division was formed on 2/10/45 in West Prussia from the SS Waffen Grenadier Brigade "Charlemagne" (1st French) with:

57th SS Waffen Grenadier Regiment (1st French)
1st Battalion (1–4th Companies)
2nd Battalion (5–8th Companies)
58th SS Waffen Grenadier Regiment (2nd French)
1st Battalion (1–4th Companies)
2nd Battalion (5–8th Companies)
33rd SS Artillery Battalion (3 batteries)
33rd SS Panzerjäger Battalion
33rd SS Pioneer Company
33rd SS Signals Company
33rd SS Feldersatz Company

By April 1945 the division consisted of a grenadier regiment with two grenadier battalions and one heavy battalion (panzerjäger company, jagdpanzer company, flak company), signal section and armored section. The division was destroyed detraining at Hammerstein. The remains were organized into the "Sturmbatallion Franzosische nr. 1" which was destroyed south of Berlin in late April 1945.

34th SS Freiwilligen Grenadier Division "Landstorm Nederland"

Formed in February 1943 from the SS Freiwilligen Brigade "Landstorm Nederland." In May 1944 OKH records show the SS Freiwilligen Brigade "Landstorm Nederland" organized and equipped as follows:

Brigade Staff
- 1 Brigade Staff
- 1 (mot) Signals Platoon
- 1 Motorcycle Platoon (3 LMGs)
- 1 Brigade Band

3 Bicycle Battalions, each with
- 3 Bicycle Companies (12 LMGs, 2 80mm & 3 50mm mortars)
- 1 (mot) Machine Gun Company (12 HMGs, 2 LMGs & 6 37mm PAK 36)
- 1 (motZ) Panzerjäger Company (12 37mm PAK 36 & 4 LMGs)
- 2 (motZ) Infantry Gun Companies (6 75mm leIG ea)
- 1 (mot) Medical Company (2 LMGs)

When formed the 34th SS Freiwilliger Division had:

- 1/,2/83rd SS Freiwilligen Regiment (3rd Dutch)
- 1/,2/84th SS Freiwilligen Regiment (4th Dutch)
- 34th SS Artillery Regiment
- 34th SS Panzerjäger Battalion (former 1st & 2nd SS Panzerjäger Companies "Nordwest")
- 34th Waffen SS Flak Battalion (former "Clingendaal" flak battery)
- 34th SS Feldersatz Battalion
- 34th SS Pioneer Company
- 34th SS Signals Company
- 34th SS Support Troops

On 8 May 1945 the division capitulated in the Rhine-Waal region.

35th SS Polizei Grenadier Division

Formed about 15 February 1945 on the Oder front with the 1st and 2nd Polizei Regiments z.b.V.[3] (formerly the SS Polizei Brigade Wirth). These regiments were renumbered 29th and 30th SS Polizei Regiments on 3/16/45. They were, at that time, joined by the old 14th SS Polizei Regiment, and renumbered 89th, 90th, and 91st. The division was formed with:

- 1/,2/,3/89th SS und Polizei Grenadier Regiment (3rd Bn later disbanded)
- 1/,2/90th SS und Polizei Grenadier Regiment
- 1/,2/91st SS und Polizei Grenadier Regiment
- 1/,2/,3/35th SS Polizei Artillery Regiment
- 35th SS Polizei Panzerjäger Battalion
- 35th SS Polizei Fusilier Battalion (4 companies)
- 35th SS Polizei Pioneer Battalion (3 companies)
- 35th SS Polizei Signals Battalion (2 companies)
- 35th SS Division Supply Regiment

The division was destroyed in the Halbe Pocket and taken prisoner by the Russians on 7 May 1945.

36th Waffen SS Grenadier Division

The division's history began with the forming of the Wilddieb-Kommand Oranienburg on 6/15/40. On 9/1/40 it was known as the SS-Sonderbataillon Dirlewanger. By September 1943 the Sonderkommando Dirlewanger was renamed the Dirlewanger Regiment. It had three battalions, each with four companies, and an ersatz company.

During June 1944 it was reduced to a battalion strength and was again known as the Dirlewanger Battalion. In the fall of 1944 it was reinforced and became the SS Sturmbrigade Dirlewanger. The brigade had a staff, the 1/,2/,3/1st Regiment, the 1/,2/,3/2nd Regiment, and a fusilier company.

The division was formed on 2/20/45 on the Oder from the SS Sturmbrigade Dirlewanger. On 12/19/44 the Dirlewanger SS Sturmbrigade consisted of two regiments (each of three battalions), an artillery battalion, a division fusilier company, a pioneer company, and a signals company. The regiments were numbered the 72nd Waffen SS Grenadier Regiment and the 73rd Waffen SS Grenadier Regiment.

The Dirlewanger SS Sturmbrigade had a reputation as being little more than a band of criminals in black uniforms. Its reputation was by far the worst of all the SS units.

The 36th Waffen SS Grenadier Division appears to have had a panzer battalion consisting of a staff and two sturmgeschütz batteries, two companies of the 681st

---

z.b.V. is the abbreviation of a German phrase meaning on "special assignment, duty, or employment."

Heavy Panzerjäger Battalion (each with eight 88mm guns), 687th Army Pioneer Brigade, and 1244th Grenadier Regiment. In April 1945 the division was fighting to the south of Berlin and on 29 April it was taken prisoner by the Soviets in the Halbe Pocket.

37th SS Freiwilligen Cavalry Division

Formed on 2/20/45 near Pressburg with part of the 8th and 22nd Cavalry Divisions. It had:

1/,2/92nd SS Freiwilligen Cavalry Regiment
1/,2/93rd SS Freiwilligen Cavalry Regiment
37th SS Artillery Battalion (3 batteries)
37th SS Pioneer Battalion (2 companies)
37th SS Feldersatz Battalion (staff & 4 companies)

Though never formed, the number 94th was set aside for the third regiment designated to be raised for this division. The division appears to have also received the name "Lützow," but this is not certain. It served in Hungary and surrendered there.

38th SS Grenadier Division "Nibelungen"

Formed in April 1945 from the SS Junker School at Bad Tölz with the 95th SS Grenadier Regiment, the 96th SS Grenadier Regiment, and the 97th SS Grenadier Regiment.

The division was assigned to the upper Rhine and on 4/7/45 it consisted of only the SS Brigade "Nibelungen," which included 1/,2/95th Regiment, 1/,2/96th Regiment and 1/97th Regiment. These seven battalions had a total field strength of 2,719 men. On 8 May 1945 the division was taken prisoner by the Americans.

49th SS Panzergrenadier Brigade

Formed in March 1944 in Denmark as the SS-Kampfgruppe 1. On 6/18/44 it was renamed the 49th Panzergrenadier Brigade. It was initially organized from troops drawn from the Troop Training Station in Königsbruck. It had a staff, a staff company, two battalions (each with four companies), and a pioneer company. It was sent to defend the coast of Denmark in June 1944. In June 1944 the Artillery Battalion and the 3/2nd SS Kampfgruppe joined the brigade. The brigade now had:

Brigade Staff
Brigade Staff Company
1st, 2nd & 3rd Battalions
13th Infantry Gun Company (may not have existed)
14th Flak Company
15th Pioneer Company
16th Transportation Company
49th Artillery Battalion

However, by August 1944 it was in north central France, around Compiègne. On 8/10/44 it was renamed the 26th SS Panzer Division.

51st SS Panzergrenadier Brigade

Formed in March 1944 as the SS Kampfgruppe 3, it was renamed the 51st SS Panzergrenadier Brigade on 6/18/44. Like the 49th SS Panzergrenadier Brigade, it was initially sent to Denmark. It consisted of:

Staff & Staff Company
1st Battalion (4 companies)
2nd Battalion (4 companies)
9th Pioneer Company

10th Flak Company
11th Transportation Company
51st Artillery Battalion (3 batteries)

On 10 August 1944 it was renamed and became the 27th SS Panzer Division.

SS Panzer Brigade Gross

Formed in August 1944 in Courland as an "Alarmverband" (alarm unit or formation) using troops from the SS Panzer Troop Training Center at Seelager. The brigade had:

1st Infantry Battalion (1st–4th Companies)
2nd Infantry Battalion (5th–8th Companies)
Mixed Panzer Battalion (4 companies)
Panzer Reconnaissance Battalion (3 companies)

In August the brigade was considered for enlargement into the 28th SS Panzer or Panzergrenadier Division, but by September the idea was dropped. In November 1944 it was sent to Westphalia and used to rebuild the shattered SS Panzer Divisions. The unit was stricken from the records in April 1945.

SS Brigade "Böhmen und Mären"

Formed in April 1945 as SS-Kampfgruppe "Trabandt" it had three grenadier battalions, a pioneer battalion, and a mixed artillery battalion. It was taken prisoner by the Soviets near Pregarten.

SS-Freiwilligen-Legion Flandern

Formed on 7/15/41 in Radom, it was also known as the SS-Freiwilligen Verband Flandern and as the Flandern Bataillon. It later became a full regiment known as the SS Freiwilligen Verband Nordwest, which, in turn, became two battalions of the Freiwilligen Standarte Nordwest. On 9/24/41 it became the independent SS Freiwilligen Legion Flandern, standing as a reinforced infantry battalion with five motorized companies. On 5/31/43 it was formed into the SS Sturmbrigade Langemarck.

THE GERMAN ORDER OF BATTLE

Französische (French) SS Freiwilligen Sturmbrigade

Ordered organized on 3/3/43, its organization was slowed by competition from the Légion Volontaire Francaise and the 638th (French) Infantry Regiment, which was part of the army. Despite these difficulties, on 10/22/43 a Französisch SS Freiwilligen Grenadier Regiment was formed and on 11/12/43 it was designated the Französische SS Freiwilligen Regiment 57. In July 1944 it was renamed the Französische Freiwilligen Sturmbrigade and apparently had two battalions. On 8/28/44 it became the 1st Regiment of the Französische SS Brigade and on 10/11/44 the Waffen Grenadier Regiment der SS 57 (französische) Nr. 1.

SS Brigade Schuldt

Formed on 21 December 1943 it contained:

7th Battalion, Leibstandarte SS Adolf Hitler
1st Battalion, SS Polizei Regiment 1 (mot)
Luftwaffe Führer Flak Battalion

It served on the Eastern Front, but its fate is unknown.

Latvian SS Freiwilligen Legion

Formed on 2/26/43 in Latvia. On 5/18/43 it was divided into the Latvian SS Volunteer Division (15th Latvia SS Volunteer Division after 10/22/43) and the Latvian SS Volunteer Brigade (after 10/22/43 the 2nd Latvian SS Volunteer Brigade). It had:

1/,2/,3/1st SS Volunteer Regiment, Latvian SS Volunteer Legion
1/,2/,3/2nd SS Volunteer Regiment, Latvian SS Volunteer Legion
1/,2/,3/3rd SS Volunteer Regiment, Latvian SS Volunteer Legion
1/,2/,3/4th SS Volunteer Regiment, Latvian SS Volunteer Legion
1/,2/,3/5th SS Volunteer Regiment, Latvian SS Volunteer Legion
SS Bicycle Battalion, Latvian SS Volunteer Legion (later 15th SS Bicycle Battalion)
SS Panzerjäger Battalion, Latvian SS Volunteer Legion (later 15th SS Panzerjäger Battalion)
Latvian SS Volunteer Legion Artillery Regiment (later 15th SS)
Latvian SS Volunteer Legion Pioneer Battalion (later 15th SS)
Latvian SS Volunteer Legion Signals Battalion (later 15th SS)
Latvian SS Volunteer Legion Medical Battalion (later 15th SS)
Latvian SS Volunteer Legion Administrative Troops (later 15th SS)

The 1st through 5th Regiments became the 32nd, 33rd, 34th, 42nd, and 43rd SS Freiwilligen Grenadier Regiments respectively.

Lettische SS Freiwilligen Legion

The Legion was formed on 2/26/43 by absorbing all the Lettish SS Volunteer units. On 5/18/43 it was divided up and distributed between the Lettish SS Freiwilligen Division and the Lettish SS Freiwilligen Brigade. It contained:

1st SS Volunteer Regiment, Lettish SS Volunteer Legion
2nd SS Volunteer Regiment, Lettish SS Volunteer Legion
3rd SS Volunteer Regiment, Lettish SS Volunteer Legion
4th SS Volunteer Regiment, Lettish SS Volunteer Legion

5th SS Volunteer Regiment, Lettish SS Freiwilligen Legion
SS Bicycle Battalion, Lettish SS Freiwilligen Legion
SS Panzerjäger Battalion, Lettish SS Freiwilligen Legion
Artillery Regiment, Lettish SS Freiwilligen Legion
Signals Battalion, Lettish SS Freiwilligen Legion
Medical Battalion, Lettish SS Volunteer Legion
Supply Troops, Lettish SS Volunteer Legion

Kaukasischer (Caucasian) Waffenverband der SS

This formation was organized in February 1945 as a "reiter" or cavalry detachment. It consisted of:

1/,2/SS Waffengruppe Armenien (Armenia)
1/,2/SS Waffengruppe Aserbeidschan (Azerbaijan)

1/,2/SS Waffengruppe Georgien (Georgia)
1/,2/SS Waffengruppe Nordkaukasus (North Caucasus)

SS Waffengruppe Krim (Crimea)

Formed in February 1945 with the East Turkistanies remaining after the organization of the Waffen Gebergsjäger Regiment der SS (tartar Nr. 1).

SS Freiwilligen Legion Nederlande

Formed on 7/12/41 as the SS Freiwilligen Verband Niederlande Nordwest, as a regiment-sized formation, in Cracow. On 7/26/41 it was reduced to the strength of a single battalion. On 9/24/41 the formation of the SS Freiwilligen Verband Nordwest was abandoned, and for that reason the SS Freiwilligen Legion Niederlande was organized as a motorized infantry regiment with three battalions alongside the SS Freiwilligen Legion Flandern. On 2/9/43 the 1st Company was entitled, "General Seyffardt." On 10/23/43 the Legion became the first regiment of the 4th SS Freiwilligen Grenadier Brigade Nederland and received the number 48.

Landstorm Niederland

Organized in 1943 in regimental strength, on 11/2/44 it became:

SS Freiwilligen Grenadier Brigade Landstorm Nederland, with
  83rd SS Freiwilligen Grenadier Regiment (from 2nd & 3rd Bns, Landstorm Nederlande)
  84th SS Freiwilligen Grenadier Regiment (from 1st Bn, Landstorm Nederlande and SS Wach Battalion 3 Amersfoort)

60th SS Panzerjäger Battalion
1/,2/60th SS Artillery Regiment
60th SS Feldersatz Battalion
60th SS Brigade Support Troops

In February 1945 the brigade was used to form the 34th SS Freiwilligen Grenadier Division Landstorm Nederland.

Osttürkischer Waffenverband der SS

Organized in February 1945, it was to be formed with:

1/,2/SS Waffengruppe Idel-Ural
1/,2/SS Waffengruppe Turkestan
1/,2/SS Waffengruppe Krim (Crimea)

1st Ostmuselmanisches (East Muslim) SS Regiment

Formed in March 1944, in March 1945 its 1st and 2nd Battalions were absorbed into the Waffengruppe SS Turkestan Nr. 1 and its 3rd Battalion was absorbed into the Waffengruppe SS Idel-Ural of the Osttürkischer Waffenverband der SS.

SS Sturm Brigade Wallonien

Formed on 6/1/43 in Wildflecken from the Walloon Legion (373rd Walloon Infantry Battalion) of the German Army.

3 Grenadier Companies
1 Machine Gun Company
1 Infantry Support Gun Company
1 Heavy Flak Company

1 Heavy Panzerjäger Company
1 Sturmgeschütz Battery
1 Light Flak Company

On 10/22/43 it was reorganized into the 5th SS Freiwilligen Sturmbrigade Wallonien.

SS Waffen Grenadier Brigade (White Ruthenia)

Formed on 1/15/45 from the non-Russians of the 30th
SS Waffen Grenadier Division (2nd Russian). It had:

1/,2/,3/1st Grenadier Regiment
Panzerjäger Battalion
Artillery Battalion
Feldersatz Battalion

Reiter Squadron
Pioneer Company
Signals Company
Supply Troops

On 3/9/45 the brigade was again renamed the 30th Waffen Grenadier Division (White Ruthenian No. 1) and the infantry regiment was renamed the 75th SS Waffen Grenadier Regiment (White Ruthenian No. 1).

Serbian SS Freiwilligen Corps

Formed in March 1945, but the organization was not completed. It was to be formed as follows:

Corps Staff
  Staff Company
  Signals Company
  Musical Corps
I Regiment
  1st Battalion (1–3rd Companies)
  2nd Battalion (4–6th Companies)
  3rd Battalion (7–9th Companies)
  1st Heavy Company

2nd Heavy Company
3rd Heavy Company
II Regiment
  same as I Regiment
III Regiment
  same as I Regiment
IV Regiment
  same as I Regiment
V Regiment
  same as I Regiment
Training Battalions, 1–3 companies & school company

2
German Luftwaffe Divisions, Airlanding, and Fallschirmjäger Forces 1939–1945

The airborne troops of the Third Reich entered into WWII as two formations. The first was the Luftwaffe's 7th Flieger Division, which had the only true paratroopers in Hitler's arsenal, and the second was the 22nd Air Landing Division, which was part of the Army. As with the Waffen-SS, the airborne forces of Germany were a highly political organization, not because of any inherent political nature of the forces, but because Hermann Göring, commander of the Luftwaffe, was a political creature fighting for power and a place of favor in the Führer's eyes.

The origins of the German paratroops began in September 1935 when the order was issued to Major Bruno Bräuer of the Luftwaffe to organize a paratroop battalion. The Army also formed a battalion, but not until 1937. In July 1938 these two forces, Bräuer's Air Corps Paratroopers and Major Heidrich's Army Paratroopers, were merged to form the 7th Flieger Division, the first such force in western Europe. It was placed under the command of Generalmajor Kurt Student. By the beginning of World War II, this force had grown to a total strength of 4,000 men.

The 1st Fallschirmjäger Regiment was organized before World War II began. In the fall of 1939 the 1/,2/2nd Fallschirmjäger Regiment were organized. The Staff/,3/2nd Fallschirmjäger Regiment were not formed until the summer of 1940. The 3rd Fallschirmjäger Regiment was organized in the summer of 1940 as was the 1st Luftland-Sturm-Regiment. These three regiments were brought together and joined with a Fallschirmjäger panzerjäger battalion, an artillery battalion, a flak battalion, a machine-gun battalion, and a pioneer battalion to form the 7th Flieger Division in late 1939.

The German paratroopers began their military career with the invasion of Belgium. In one of the most daring exploits in military history, a small band of German paratroopers, 80 in all, landed on top of the impregnable fortress of Eben-Emael and within a few minutes defeated its 1,200-man garrison. Further drops occurred in Belgium and Holland, with the paratroopers proving their worth. Their career had begun

showered with glory.

The organization of the German paratroops continued and during the winter of 1940/41 the Generalkommando XI Fliegerkorps was organized with a Lehr Battalion and a Pioneer Battalion.

Their second major operation began in May 1941, when the target was the island of Crete. The XI and VIII Fliegerkorps, with a total of 500 Ju-52 transports, 280 bombers, 180 fighters and 40 reconnaissance planes, supported and moved 15,750 airborne infantry into what was the first divisional-sized paratroop operation in military history. Unfortunately for the German fallschirmjäger, the British defenders of Crete were able to inflict tremendous losses on them before finally capitulating. The British navy took a further toll by totally destroying the seaborne portion of the invasion. The losses were so great that the airborne portion of the German army effectively ceased to exist and Hitler was so appalled by the losses that he never again contemplated any major airborne operations.

During the winter of 1941 the German army in Russia suffered massive losses. Rushing to curry favor, Göring plunged in with an offer to raise an infantry formation of loyal Nazi youth, untainted by the stench of the Prussian General Staff, from his Luftwaffe personnel. As a result, 22 Luftwaffe Felddivisionen (Field Divisions) were formed. These units were under-armed, under-organized, and poorly led excuses for infantry that, by 1943, were absorbed into the Army or disbanded. Their organizations were inconsistent and they were generally unsuited for warfare in the East.

During the winter of 1941/42 the Luftwaffe Schützen Brigade z.b.V was organized. In the summer of 1942 the 4th and 5th Fallschirmjäger Regiments were organized, the latter with two battalions of the 1st Luftlande-Sturm Regiment. During 1942 the Ramcke Fallschirmjäger Brigade was organized and dispatched to Africa where it fought with Rommel.

Having failed with the Luftwaffe Field Divisions, Göring turned once again to his paratroopers. In May 1943 the 7th Flieger Division was reorganized into the 1st Fallschirmjäger Division. It would soon be joined by the 2nd through 10th, 20th, 21st, and Erdmann Fallschirmjäger Divisions. In addition, Göring's personal regiment, the Hermann Göring Regiment, was to begin a steady expansion into the *"General Commando Parachute-Panzer Corps Hermann Göring."*

The use of the term *"Fallschirmjäger"* had almost ceased to mean anything relating to airborne operations. It had become an honorary title much as "Guard" was in many other armies of the world.

The last German combat jump of note occurred in Sicily when they were rushed to plug the holes in the German lines and dropped almost directly onto the toes of the advancing British. Their timely intervention, however costly, was what it took to hold the German line together and give them time to organize their orderly and successful withdrawal from Sicily.

The Fallschirmjäger were soon equipped with every type of infantry equipment, including assault guns and heavy artillery. Indeed, their equipment varied considerably and could, under no circumstances, be described as consistent. Their baggy pants and unique helmets made them stand apart from the rest of the German armed forces and they never let the Army forget that they were different.

The Fallschirmjäger fought extensively in Normandy and in Italy, opposing the Allied landings in Normandy and holding the fortress of Monte Cassino.

Their operational integration into the German Army became complete soon after the first Fallschirmjäger Army was organized. The 1st Fallschirmjäger Army was formed on 1 February 1944. Organized with the I and II Fallschirmjäger Corps and five fallschirmjäger divisions, Göring finally had his own personal army. This, however, did not last long. On 16 September 1944 it contained only one fallschirmjäger division and six army infantry divisions.

Before the war was over the 1st Fallschirmjäger Army would contain SS divisions, panzer brigades and panzer divisions, but seldom more than one fallschirmjäger division. The original army with five fallschirmjäger divisions was never re-established.

The fallschirmjägers developed a reputation as pugnacious and aggressive fighters who grudgingly yielded any ground to the enemies of the Reich.

7th Flieger Division

The origins of this division extend back before the outbreak of the war. It was the first operational parachute formation in the German armed forces and was part of the Luftwaffe. Initially formed of small groups of elite commandos, by 10 May 1940 the division was formed and consisted of:

Divisional Staff
Reconnaissance Staffel
Transportation Staffel
7th Artillery Battery
7th Signals Company
7th Transportation Company
7th Medical Company
106th Light Flak Battery
Anti-tank Battery
Motorcycle Platoon
1/,2/,3/1st Fallschirmjäger Regiment (4 companies per battalion)
1/,2/2nd Fallschirmjäger Regiment (4 companies per battalion)

By the time of the Crete operation, 20 May 1941, the division was reinforced and consisted of:

Divisional Staff
Transportation Staffel
7th Pioneer Battalion
7th Artillery Battalion
7th Machine Gun Battalion
7th Anti-tank Battalion
Motorcycle Platoon
1/,2/,1/1st Fallschirmjäger Regiment (4 companies per bn)
1/,2/,1/2nd Fallschirmjäger Regiment (4 companies per bn)
1/,2/,1/3rd Fallschirmjäger Regiment (4 companies per bn)

After heavy casualties in Crete the division began the slow process of rebuilding. In October 1941 it was serving in Russia with Army Group North and contained:

1 Signals Company
1st Fallschirmjäger Regiment
　1 Signals Platoon
　1 Pioneer Platoon
　3 Battalions, each with
　　1 Signals Platoon
　　4 Fallschirmjäger Companies

13th (Infantry Gun) Company
14th (Panzerjäger) Company
2nd Company, Fallschirmjäger Panzerjäger Battalion
3rd Fallschirmjäger Regiment
1 Signals Platoon
1 Pioneer Platoon
3 Battalions, each with
1 Signals Platoon
4 Fallschirmjäger Companies
13th (Infantry Gun) Company
14th (Panzerjäger) Company

2nd Company, Fallschirmjäger Flak Battalion (20mm guns)
Fallschirmjäger Pioneer Battalion
1 Signals Platoon
3 Fallschirmjäger Pioneer Companies
Fallschirmjäger Artillery Battalion
1 Signals Platoon
2 Artillery Batteries (6 75mm mountain guns)
2nd Co/Fallschirmjäger Medical Battalion

In May 1943 it was re-formed into the 1st Fallschirmjäger (Parachute) Division.

22nd Luftlandung (Airlanding) Division

Mobilized on 8/18/39 with:

22nd Infantry Division
22nd (mot) Mapping Detachment
22nd Motorcycle Messenger Platoon
1/,2/,3/47th Infantry Regiment
1 Signals Platoon
1 Regimental Band
3 Battalions, each with
3 Infantry Companies (9 LMGs, 2 HMGs & 3 50mm mortars ea)
1 Heavy Company (8 HMGs & 6 80mm mortars)
1 Pioneer Company (9 LMGs)
1 Infantry Gun Company (2 150mm sIG & 6 75mm leIG)
1 (mot) Anti-Tank Company (12 37mm PAK 36 & 4 LMGs)
1 Light Infantry Supply Column
1/,2/,3/16th Infantry Regiment
same as 47th Infantry Regiment
1/,2/,3/85th Infantry Regiment
same as 47th Infantry Regiment
22nd Panzer Abwehr Battalion
1 (mot) Signals Platoon
3 (mot) Anti-Tank Companies (12 37mm PAK36 & 4 LMGs ea)
46th (mot) Heavy Machine Gun Company (12 20mm)
22nd Reconnaissance Battalion
2 Bicycle Squadrons (9 LMGs & 2 LMGs ea)
1 Anti-Tank Platoon (3 37mm PAK 36 & 1 LMG)
1 (mot) Infantry Gun Section (2 75mm leIG)
22nd Artillery Regiment
1 Signals Platoon
1 (mot) Weather Detachment
1st, 2nd & 3rd Battalions, each with
3 Batteries (4 105mm leFH & 2 LMGs ea)
4/22nd Artillery Regiment
3 Batteries (4 150mm sFH & 2 LMGs ea)
22nd Pioneer Battalion
1 Pioneer Company (9 LMGS ea)
1 (mot) Pioneer Company (9 LMGS ea)
1 (mot) Bridging Column
1 (mot) Light Pioneer Supply Column
22nd Signals Battalion
1 (tmot) Telephone Company
1 (mot) Radio Company
1 (mot) Light Signals Supply Column
22nd Feldersatz Battalion
3 Companies (9 LMGs, 2 HMGs & 3 50mm mortars)
22nd Divisional Supply troop
1–2/22nd Light (mot) Supply Columns
3–8/22nd Light (mot) Supply Columns
9/22nd (mot) Light Fuel Column
22nd (mot) Maintenance Platoon
22nd (mot) Supply Company
Other
22nd (mot) Field Bakery
22nd (mot) Field Butcher Company
22nd Divisional Administration
22nd (mot) Field Hospital
22nd Medical Company
1/,2/22nd (mot) Ambulances
22nd Veterinary Company
22nd (mot) Military Police Detachment
22nd (mot) Field Post Office

In the winter of 1940/41 the 22nd Flak Battalion was assigned to the division. Each regiment re-formed its 13th, 14th, and Staff Companies into 4th Battalions. From 10 February through the summer of 1941 the division was organized and equipped as follows:

Divisional Staff
Division HQ Company (2 LMGs)
1st (mot) Mapping Platoon

16th Infantry Regiment
Regimental Staff Company
Signals Platoon
Engineer Platoon (3 LMGs)
Regimental Band
3 Battalions
3 Infantry Companies (12 LMGs, 3 50 Mortars)
1 Heavy Support Company (12 HMGs & 6 80mm Mortars)
1 Machine Gun Company (8 HMGs, 6 80mm mortars)
1 Cavalry Platoon
1 Infantry Support Gun Company (2 150mm sIG & 6 75mm leIG)
Panzerjäger (motorized) Company (6 LMGs, 2 50mm PAK 38, 9 37mm PAK 36 & 4 LMGs)

47th Infantry Regiment
Regimental Staff Company
Signals Platoon
Engineer Platoon (3 LMGs)
Regimental Band
3 Battalions
3 Infantry Companies (12 LMGs, 3 50 Mortars)
1 Heavy Support Company (12 HMGs & 6 80mm Mortars)
1 Machine Gun Company (8 HMGs, 6 80mm mortars)
1 Cavalry Platoon
1 Infantry Support Gun Company (2 150mm sIG & 6 75mm leIG)
Panzerjäger (motorized) Company (6 LMGs, 2 50mm PAK 38, 9 37mm PAK 36 & 4 LMGs)

65th Infantry Regiment
Regimental Staff Company
Signals Platoon
Engineer Platoon (3 LMGs)
Regimental Band
3 Battalions
3 Infantry Companies (12 LMGs, 3 50 Mortars)
1 Heavy Support Company (12 HMGs & 6 80mm Mortars)
1 Machine Gun Company (8 HMGs, 6 80mm mortars)
1 Cavalry Platoon
1 Infantry Support Gun Company (2 150mm sIG & 6 75mm leIG)
Panzerjäger (motorized) Company (6 LMGs, 2 50mm PAK 38, 9 37mm PAK 36 & 4 LMGs)

22nd Reconnaissance Battalion
1 Mounted (tmot) Staff Signals Platoon
1 Bicycle Company (2 HMGs, 9 LMGs & 3 50mm mortars)
1 Bicycle Company (3 50mm mortars, 2 HMGs, & 9 LMGs)
1 (mot) Support Company
Panzerjäger Platoon (1 LMG & 3 37mm PAK 36)
Armored Car Section (2 LMGs)
Infantry Support Gun Platoon (2 75mm leIG)

22nd Panzerjäger Battalion
3 (mot) Panzerjäger Companies (12 37mm PAK 36 & 6 LMGs)

22nd Artillery Regiment
Regimental Staff
Regimental Band
Meteorology Section
3 Artillery Battalions, each with
1 Staff Battery
Calibration Section
3 Batteries (3 105mm leFH & 2 LMGs)

22nd Signals Battalion
1 (tmot) Telephone Company
1 (mot) Radio Company
1 Light (mot) Signals Supply Column

22nd Pioneer Battalion
2 Pioneer Companies (9 LMGs)
1 (mot) Pioneer Company (9 LMGs)
1 Light (mot) Engineer Supply Column

22nd Feldersatz (Replacement) Battalion
3 Rifle Companies

22nd Commissary Service
1 (mot) Bakery Section
1 (mot) Butcher Section
1 (mot) Quartermaster Section

22nd Supply Troops
1st & 3rd Companies., Light Motorized Supply Columns
4–6th Companies., Horse Drawn Supply Columns
8–10th Companies., Light Horse Drawn Supply Columns
2 Light (mot) Fuel Supply Columns
1 Maintenance (mot) Company
1 Light (mot) Supply Company

Other
1st & 2nd Medical Companies (1 motorized, one foot)
1 (mot) Field Hospital
2 Ambulance Columns
1 Veterinary Company
1 (mot) Military Police Platoon
1 (mot) Field Post Office

On 7/29/42 the division was reorganized and renamed "Air Landing Motorized Tropical". The 1/58th Artillery Regiment was detached and the 4/207th Artillery Regiment temporarily became the 4/22nd Artillery Regiment. The heavy machine-gun and anti-tank battalions were broken into four equal strength companies and distributed by platoons to the battalions. The 2/22nd Artillery Regiment and 47th Grenadier Regiment became Kampfgruppe Buhse and were sent to Africa, where they were destroyed in 1943. The 22nd Reconnaissance Battalion became the 122nd Panzer Reconnaissance Battalion. The 716th Heavy Artillery Battalion became the 4/22nd Artillery Regiment.

In 1943 the 2/22nd Artillery Regiment and the 1/47th Grenadier Regiment (formed from the 22nd Feldersatz Battalion) were rebuilt. In March 1943 the Sturmbrigade Rhodos was formed in the division and it contained a single reinforced battalion. In February 1943 a battalion was reorganized as the "Rhodos" Fusilier Bataillon.

During 1942 and early 1943 the infantry regiments contained a staff company, three battalions, and a motorized infantry gun company. There was no panzerjäger company. The reconnaissance battalion was the 122nd Panzer Reconnaissance Battalion. It contained an armored car company, three motorcycle companies, and a heavy panzer reconnaissance company. The panzerjäger battalion contained a (motZ) and two self-propelled companies. The 22nd Flak Battalion, with three self-propelled 20mm batteries was added to the division. The artillery regiment was reorganized with three battalion staffs, two mountain gun batteries, five (mot) 105mm leFH batteries, and three horse-drawn 150mm sFH batteries. The pioneer and signals battalions were fully motorized. The division was reduced to a single medical company and there was no feldersatz battalion. In September 1943 the division was organized and equipped as follows:

22nd Infantry Division
 Divisional Staff (2 LMGs)
 1st (mot) Mapping Detachment
16th Grenadier Regiment
 1 Regimental Staff
 1 Regimental Band
 1 Regimental Staff Company
  1 Signals Platoon
  1 Pioneer Platoon (3 LMGs)
  1 Bicycle Reconnaissance Platoon
  1 Panzerjäger Platoon (3 75m PAK & 3 LMGs)
 1st & 2nd (tmot) Infantry Battalions, each with
  4 Grenadier Companies (2 HMGs, 18 LMGs, 2 75mm PAK 40 & 3 80mm mortars)
 3rd (mot) Infantry Battalions
  4 Grenadier Companies (2 HMGs, 18 LMGs, 2 75mm PAK 40 & 3 80mm mortars)
 Infantry Gun Company
  (2 150mm sIG & 4 75mm leIG)

65th Grenadier Regiment
 same as 16th Regiment, except all (tmot)
122nd Reconnaissance Battalion
 1 Armored Car Company (24 LMGs & 18 20mm)
 3 Motorcycle Companies (2 80mm mortars, 3 light anti-tank rifles 4 HMGS & 18 LMGs)
 1 (mot) Reconnaissance Company
  1 Pioneer Platoon (4 LMGs)
  1 Panzerjäger Platoon (3 LMGs & 3 75mm PAK 40)
  1 Infantry Gun Platoon (2 75mm leIG)
22nd Panzerjäger Battalion
 2 Self Propelled Panzerjäger Companies (9 76.2mm PAK & 6 LMGs)
 1 (motZ) Panzerjäger Company (9 50mm PAK & 9 LMGs)
22nd Artillery Regiment
 1 Regimental Staff, Staff Battery, & Regimental Band
 1 (mot) Light Supply Column
 1st Battalion
  1 Battalion Staff & Staff Battery
  2 (motZ) Batteries (4 105mm leFH & 2 LMGs ea)
  1 (motZ) Battery (4 100mm K & 2 LMGs)
 2nd Battalions
  same as 1st Battalion
 3rd Battalion
  1 Battalion Staff & Staff Battery
  3 Batteries (4 155mm French howitzers & 2 LMGs)
22nd Flak Battalion
 1 Battalion Staff (1 LMG)
 3 (motZ) Flak Batteries (12 20mm & 7 LMGS ea)
22nd Pioneer Battalion
 1 Battalion Staff (2 LMGs)
 3 (mot) Pioneer Companies (9 LMGS, 3 heavy anti-tank rifles)
 1 Light Pioneer Supply Column (2 LMGs)
22nd Signals Battalion
 1 (mot) Telephone Company (6 LMGs)
 1 (mot) Radio Company (4 LMGs)
 1 (mot) Signals Supply Column (1 LMG)
1st Supply Troop
 1 Supply Troop Staff (2 LMGs)
 22nd (mot) 120 ton Transportation Company (4 LMGs)
 22nd (tmot) Supply Company (6 LMGs)
 22nd (mot) Maintenance Company
Administration
 22nd (mot) Bakery Company
 22nd (mot) Butcher Company
 22nd (mot) Administration Platoon
Medical
 2/22nd Medical Company (2 LMGs)
 1/,2/22nd Ambulance Companies

Other
22nd (mot) Military Police Detachment (1 LMG)
22nd (mot) Field Post Office

In May 1944 the division appears to have been fully re-formed. On 15 July 1944 it was organized and equipped as follows:

22nd Infantry Division
Divisional Staff (2 LMGs)
1st (mot) Mapping Detachment
1 Divisional Band
16th Grenadier Regiment
1 Regimental Staff
1 Regimental Band
1 Regimental Staff Company
1 Signals Platoon
1 Pioneer Platoon (6 LMGs)
1 Motorcycle Messenger Platoon (6 LMGs)
1 Panzerjäger Platoon (3 75m PAK & 4 LMGs)
1st & 2nd (tmot) Infantry Battalions, each with
4 Grenadier Companies (2 HMGs, 14 LMGs, 1 75mm PAK 40 & 2 80mm mortars)
3rd (mot) Infantry Battalions
4 Grenadier Companies (2 HMGs, 14 LMGs, 1 75mm PAK 40 & 2 80mm mortars)
Infantry Gun Company
(2 150mm sIG & 4 75mm leIG)
47th Grenadier Regiment
same as 16th Regiment, except all no 3rd Battalion
65th Grenadier Regiment
same as 16th Regiment
122nd Reconnaissance Battalion
1 (mot) Signals Platoon (2 LMGs)
1 Armored Car Company (24 LMGs & 18 20mm)
1 Motorcycle Company (2 80mm mortars, 4 HMGS & 18 LMGs)
2 (mot) Reconnaissance Companies (2 80mm mortars, 4 HMGS & 18 LMGs ea)
1 (mot) Reconnaissance Company
1 Pioneer Platoon (4 LMGs)
1 Panzerjäger Platoon (3 LMGs & 3 75mm PAK 40)
1 Infantry Gun Platoon (2 75mm leIG)
1 (mot) Supply Company (3 LMGs)
22nd Panzerjäger Battalion
1 (mot) Staff Company (2 LMGs)
1st (motZ) Panzerjäger Company (9 75mm PAK 40 & 10 LMGs)
2nd & 3rd Self Propelled Panzerjäger Companies (9 76.2mm PAK & 13 LMGs ea)
22nd Artillery Regiment
1 Regimental Battery

1st Battalion
1 Battalion Staff & Staff Battery
3 (motZ) Batteries (4 105mm leFH & 2 LMGs ea)
2nd Battalion
1 Battalion Staff & Staff Battery
3 Batteries (4 75mm mountain guns & 2 LMGs)
3rd Battalions
same as 1st Battalion
4th Battalion
1 Battalion Staff & Staff Battery
3 (motZ) Batteries (4 155mm (f) howitzers & 2 LMGs ea)
22nd Flak Battalion
1 Battalion Staff (1 LMG)
2 Self Propelled Flak Batteries (11 20mm & 7 LMGS ea)
1 (motZ) 20mm Flak gun)
1 (motZ) Flak Battery (7 20mm)
22nd Pioneer Battalion
1 Battalion Staff (2 LMGs)
3 (mot) Pioneer Companies (2 HMGs, 9 LMGS, & 1 80mm mortar)
1 Light Pioneer Supply Column (2 LMGs)
22nd Signals Battalion
1 (mot) Telephone Company (3 LMGs)
1 (mot) Radio Company (2 LMGs)
1 (mot) Signals Supply Column (1 LMG)
Feldersatz Battalion
2 Companies
1st Supply Troop
1 Supply Troop Staff (2 LMGs)
1/,2/22nd (mot) (120 ton) Transportation Company
22nd (mot) Supply Company
Administration
22nd (tmot) Bakery Company
22nd (tmot) Butcher Company
22nd (tmot) Administration Platoon
Medical
2/22nd Medical Company (2 LMGs)
1/,2/22nd Ambulance Companies
Other
22nd (mot) Maintenance Company
22nd (mot) Military Police Detachment (1 LMG)
22nd (mot) Field Post Office (1 LMG)

1st Luftlande-Sturm-Regiment

This is an unusual formation that deserves special consideration, even though the thrust of this work is at the divisional/brigade level. The 1st Luftlande-Sturm-Regiment was an independent Luftwaffe formation that generally operated with the 7th Flieger Division or under the XI Fliegerkorps as a glider-borne infantry formation. It was formed in 1940 with three battalions, though a fourth was later organized. In 1942 the staff became the staff of the Meindl Luftwaffe Division, the 2nd and 3rd Battalions were assigned to the 5th Fallschirmjäger Regiment, and the 1st and 4th Battalions remained independent. In early 1943 the 4th Battalion became the 2/6th Fallschirmjäger Regiment and at the end of January 1944 the 1st Battalion became the 1/12th Fallschirmjäger Regiment.

In 1940 each battalion had three companies, with a 13th and 14th Independent Company being assigned to the regiment. In the winter of 1940/41 the regiment was reorganized and each battalion had four companies. There were no further independent companies. In 1942, with only two battalions remaining, each battalion still had four companies.

1st Luftwaffe Feld (Field) Division

Formed summer 1942 in Königsberg:

1st–4th Battalions (16 companies)
Panzerjäger (AT) Battalion (3 companies)
Artillery Battalion (3 batteries)
Flak Battalion (3 batteries)
Radfahr (bicycle) Company
Pioneer Company
Luftnachrichten (Communications & Signal) Company

During 1943 the 1st Luftwaffe Artillery Regiment was formed by building the 1st and 2nd Battalions from scratch and using the existing artillery battalion as the 3rd Battalion, the Flak Battalion as the 4th Battalion, and the Panzerjäger (AT) Battalion as the 5th Battalion. On 11/1/43 it was transferred to the army and was renamed as the 1st Field Division (L). The 4th (Flak) Battalion became the 1/40th Flak Regiment.

1st Feld (Field) Division (L)

Formed 11/1/43 when the 1st Luftwaffe Field Division was absorbed into the Army. It had:

1/,2/,3/,4/1st Jäger Regiment (L)
1/,2/,3/1st Artillery Regiment (L)
1st Division Support Units (L)

In January 1944 it was destroyed by Novgorod and the survivors incorporated into the 28th Jäger Division.

2nd Luftwaffe Field Division

Formed in September 1942 in Luftgau III at the Gross-Born Training Camp with:

1/,2/,3/,4th Battalions (16 companies & no staff)
Panzerjäger Battalion (3 companies)
Artillery Battalion (3 batteries)
Flak Battalion (3 batteries)
Pioneer Company
Luftwaffe Signals Company

In 1943 the 2nd Luftwaffe Artillery Regiment was formed by building the 1st and 2nd Battalions from scratch and using the existing battalion as the 3rd Battalion, the Flak Battalion became the 4th Battalion, and the Panzerjäger Battalion became the 5th Battalion. The 5th Battalion, however, was soon reestablished as a panzerjäger battalion. On 10/15/43 Army Group Center demanded that the division be disbanded because it had sustained exceptionally high material losses and lost almost its entire complement of heavy weapons. The 4th (Flak) Battalion/2nd Artillery Regiment became the 1/50th Flak Regiment. The remainder were transferred to the 6th Luftwaffe Field Division.

The 2nd Infantry Battalion became the 2/53rd Luftwaffe Jäger Regiment, and the 3/2nd Artillery Regiment became the 4/6th Artillery Regiment. The division was destroyed near Lake Yeserishche in Russia on 10/6/43.

3rd Luftwaffe Field Division

Formed summer 1942 at the Gross-Born Training Camp with:

1/,2/,3/,4th Battalions (no regimental staff) (16 companies)
Panzerjäger Battalion
Artillery Battalion
Flak Battalion
Pioneer Company
Luftwaffe Signals Company
Division Support Units

In 1943 the division formed the 3rd Luftwaffe Artillery Regiment with the existing battalion becoming the 3rd Battalion, the flak battalion as the 4th Battalion and the panzerjäger battalion as the 5th Battalion. On 1/22/44 the division was transferred to the army, but on 12/2/44, after heavy losses near Vitebsk, it was disbanded and its troops distributed between the 4th and 6th Luftwaffe Field Divisions. The division staff, and 1/,2nd Battalions were used to form the 51st Jäger Regiment (L) (4th Luftwaffe Field Division(L). The 3rd and 4th Battalions formed the 52nd Jäger Regiment (L) in the 6th Field Division (L). The 1/3rd Artillery Regiment became the new 3/6th, and the 2/3rd became the 3/4th. The 4th (Flak) Battalion was returned to the Luftwaffe and became the 1/43rd Flak Regiment.

4th Luftwaffe Field Division

Formed summer 1942 at the Gross-Born training camp with:

1/,2/,3/,4th Battalions (no regimental staff, 16 companies)
Panzerjäger Battalion (3 companies)
Artillery Battalion (3 batteries)
Flak Battalion (3 batteries)
Bicycle Company
Pioneer Company
Luftwaffe Signals Company
Division Support Units

In 1943 the 4th Luftwaffe Artillery Regiment was formed, the 3rd Battalion from the existing artillery battalion. The 4th Battalion was formed from the flak battalion and the panzerjäger battalion became the 5th Battalion. On 11/1/43 it was assigned to the army and became the 4th Field Division (L).

4th Field Division (L)

Formed 11/1/43 by Vitebsk by the absorption of the 4th and part of the 3rd Luftwaffe Field Division into the Army. The division had:

- 1/,2/49th Jäger Regiment (L) (from Staff 486th Grenadier Regiment & 1/4th and 2/4th Luftwaffe Jäger Battalions)
- 1/,2/50th Jäger Regiment (L) (from Staff 268th Grenadier Regiment & 3/4th and 4/4th Luftwaffe Jäger Battalions)
- 1/,2/51st Jäger Regiment (L) (from a newly formed staff & 1/3rd and 2/3rd Luftwaffe Jäger Battalions)
- 4th Füsilier Battalion (L) (from the Bicycle Company, 3rd Luftwaffe Field Division)
- 1/,2/,3/,4/4th Artillery Regiment (L) (1/,2/44th from 4th Luftwaffe Regiment, 3/4th from 3/3rd Artillery Regiment (L), & 4/4th newly formed).

On 4/24/44 OKH records show the division organized and equipped as follows:

Staff
- 1 Divisional Staff (2 LMGs)
- 4th (mot) Mapping Detachment (L)
- 1104th (tmot) Military Police Detachment

49th Jäger Regiment (L)
- 1 Regimental Staff Company (1 LMG)
    - 1 Signals Platoon
    - 1 Pioneer Platoon (6 LMGs)
    - 1 Cavalry Platoon (3 LMGs)
- **2 Battalions**, each with
    - 3 Jäger Companies (2 HMGS & 13 LMGs)
    - 1 Machine Gun Company (6 HMGs, 3 LMGs, 4 120mm mortars & 6 80mm mortars)
- **1 Infantry Gun Company**
    - (2 150mm sIG, 6 75mm leIG, & 5 LMGs)
- **1 (tmot) Panzerjäger Company**
    - (12 75mm PAK 40 & 13 LMGs)

50th Jäger Regiment (L)
- same as 49th Jäger Regiment (L)

51st Jäger Regiment (L)
- same as 49th Jäger Regiment (L)

4th Panzerjäger Battalion (L)
- 1 (motZ) Panzerjäger Company (12 75mm PAK 40 & 13 LMGs)
- 1 (motZ) Light Flak Company (12 20mm flak guns & 2 LMGs)
- 1104th Sturmgeschütz Battery (L) (10 StuGs & 12 LMGs)

4th Artillery Regiment (L)
- 1 Regimental & Regimental Staff Battery (1 LMG)
- **1st Battalion**
    - 1 Battalion & Battalion Staff Battery (2 LMGs)
    - 3 Batteries (4 105mm leFH & 5 LMGs ea)
- **2nd Battalion**
    - 1 Battalion & Battalion Staff Battery (2 LMGs)
    - 3 Batteries (4 75mm French guns & 5 LMGs ea)
- **3rd Battalion**
    - same as 2nd Battalion
- **4th Battalion**
    - 1 Battalion & Battalion Staff Battery (2 LMGs)
    - 3 Batteries (4 155mm French howitzers & 5 LMGs ea)

4th Fusilier Battalion (L)
- 2 Fusilier Companies (2 HMGS & 13 LMGs)
- 1 Bicycle Fusilier Company (2 HMGS & 13 LMGs)
- 1 Machine Gun Company (6 HMGs, 3 LMGs, 4 120mm mortars & 6 80mm mortars)

4th Pioneer Battalion (L)
- Battalion Staff (4 LMG)
- 1 Bicycle Pioneer Company (2 HMGs, 9 LMGs, 6 flamethrowers & 2 80mm mortars)
- 2 Pioneer Companies (2 HMGs, 9 LMGs, 6 flamethrowers & 2 80mm mortars)

4th Signals Battalion (L)
- 1 (tmot) Telephone Company (6 LMGs)
- 1 (mot) Radio Company (5 LMGs)
- 1 (tmot) Signals Supply Column (1 LMG)

4th Feldersatz Battalion (L)
- 2 Companies

4th Divisional Supply Troops (L)
- 4th (mot) 90 ton Transportation Company (L) (6 LMGs)
- 1/,2/4th 60 ton Transportation Company (L) (6 LMGs)
- 4th Supply Company (L) (6 LMGs)
- 4th Maintenance Company (L) (4 LMGs)

Administration
- 4th (mot) Butcher Company (L) (2 LMGs)
- 4th (mot) Bakery Company (L) (4 LMGs)
- 4th (mot) Administration Company (L) (4 LMGs)

Medical Battalion
- 1/4th (mot) Medical Company (L)
- 2/4th Medical Company (L)
- 4th Medical Supply Company (L)

Other
- 4th Veterinary Troop (L)
- 904th (mot) Field Post Office

The division was destroyed on 6/25/44 while part of Army Group Center near Vitebsk. It was disbanded on 8/3/44. The remnants went to the Corps Detachment H.

5th Luftwaffe Field Division

Formed in October 1942 in the troop training center at Gross-Born with:

1/,2/,3/,4th Battalions (no regimental staff, 16 companies)
Panzerjäger Battalion (3 companies)
Artillery Battalion (3 batteries)
Flak Battalion (3 batteries)
Bicycle Company
Pioneer Company
Luftwaffe Signals Company
Division Support Units

It served in the Crimea and Kuban bridgehead. During the summer the division formed an artillery regiment. In the summer of 1943 it was intended to provide the division with an artillery regiment. The former artillery battalion became the 3rd Battalion, the flak battalion became the 4th Battalion, and the panzerjäger battalion became the 5th Battalion. However, the Staff, 1st and 2nd Battalions were never organized. The infantry then formed two regimental staffs and two new battalions. The division had:

1/,2/,3/9th Luftwaffejäger Regiment
1/,2/,3/10th Luftwaffejäger Regiment
1/Artillery Regiment (2 artillery batteries)
3/Artillery Regiment (former flak battalion—4 batteries)
Panzerjäger Battalion (3 towed companies & a sturmgeschütz battery)
Pioneer Company
Luftwaffe Signals Company
Division Support Units

On 11/1/43 the division was passed to the army and became the 5th Field Division (L). The staff and 3/9th Luftwaffe Jäger Regiment and the 10th Luftwaffe Jäger Regiment were disbanded. The flak battalion remained with the Luftwaffe as the 1/17th (motorized) Flak Regiment.

5th Field Division (L)

Formed 11/1/43 by the absorption of the 5th Luftwaffe Field Division into the Army. The division had only a kampfgruppe with:

1/,2/9th Jäger Regiment (L)
5th Artillery Battalion (L)
5th Divisional (Einheiten) Support Units (L)

In May 1944, while in Bessarabia, it was disbanded and the Jäger Regiment was absorbed into the 76th Infantry Division. The rest was distributed to the 320th and 335th Infantry Divisions.

6th Luftwaffe Field Division

Formed September 1942 at the Gross-Born Training Area with:

1st, 2nd, 3rd, 4th Battalions (no regt'l staff) (16 companies)
Panzerjäger Battalion (3 companies)
Artillery Battalion (3 batteries)
Flak Battalion (3 batteries)
Pioneer Company
Signals Company
Divisional Support Units

In 1943 an artillery regiment was formed with the existing artillery battalion becoming the 3rd Battalion, the flak battalion becoming the 4th Battalion, and the panzerjäger battalion becoming the 5th Battalion. The staff, 1st and 2nd Battalions were newly raised. The panzerjäger battalion was later made independent. On 4/24/44 OKH records show the division organized and equipped like the 4th Field Division (L). The artillery regiment was organized slightly differently, with the 1/,2/,3/6th Artillery Regiment (L) each having three light howitzer batteries (four 105mm leFH & 5 LMGs ea). The 4/6th Artillery Regiment (L) had two batteries with four 155mm French howitzers each and one battery of four 150mm sFH and two LMGs. The feldersatz battalion had four companies.

On 11/1/43 the Division was transferred to the army as the 6th Field Division (L). During the course of the winter it was reinforced with part of the disbanded 2nd and 3rd Luftwaffe Field Divisions. The 4th (Flak) Battalion of the artillery regiment remained with the Luftwaffe and became the 1/34th Flak Regiment.

6th Field Division (L)

Formed 11/1/43 by the transfer of the 6th Luftwaffe Field Division to the army.

1/,2/52nd Jäger Regiment (L) (from Staff 471st Grenadier Regiment & 3/3rd & 4/3rd Luftwaffe Jäger Regiments)

1/,2/53rd Jäger Regiment (L) (from 1/6th & 2/2nd Luftwaffe Jäger Regiments and new staff)

1/,2/54th Jäger Regiment (L) (from 3/6th and 4/6th Luftwaffe Jäger Regiments and staff/459th Grenadier Regiment

6th Fusilier Battalion (L) (newly raised)

1/,2/,3/,4/6th Artillery Regiment (L) (from Staff/,3/2nd Luftwaffe Artillery Regiment, & 1/,3/6th & 1/3rd Luftwaffe Artillery Regiment

On 1/8/44 the division was reduced to a strength of 436 men by fighting on the Russian front. It was destroyed and disbanded on 8/3/44.

7th Luftwaffe Field Division

Formed in the fall of 1942 with:

1st, 2nd & 3rd Battalion (no regimental staff)
Panzerjäger Battalion (3 companies)
Artillery Battalion (3 batteries)
Flak Battalion (3 batteries)
Bicycle Company
Pioneer Company
Signals Company

On 12 December 1942 the division contained:

1st, 2nd, 3rd & 4th Battalions, each had
  3 Companies (18 LMGs, 6 HMGs, 2 80mm mortars each)
  1 Heavy Company (2 20mm Flak guns, 4 80mm mortars & 8 HMGs)
Artillery Battalion
  2 (mot) Mountain Batteries (4 105mm howitzers each)
  1 Assault Gun Battery (4 75mm assault guns)

Flak Battalion
  1 Heavy (mot) Flak Battery (4 88mm Flak guns)
  2 Light (mot) Flak Battery (12 20mm Flak guns)
Panzerjäger Battalion
  1 (tmot) Company (3 75mm PAK 41 & 3 50mm PAK 38 guns)
  1 (tmot) Company (4 75mm PAK 41 & 3 50mm PAK 38 guns)
  1 (tmot) Company (9 50mm PAK 38 guns)
(mot) Pioneer Company (25 LMGs)
Mounted Reconnaissance Platoon (some vehicles) (6 LMGs)
Luftwaffe Signals Company
  1 (mot) Signals Detachment
  1 (mot) Radio Detachment
  1 (mot) Telephone Detachment
Supply Units
  1 Medical Company
  1 Field Hospital
  1 30 ton Light (mot) Supply Column
  1 60 ton Heavy (mot) Supply Column

1 (mot) Supply Company
1 (mot) Maintenance Company
1 (mot) Butcher Detachment
1 (mot) Field Bakery
1 (mot) Post Office

After heavy losses in Russia its remains were incorporated into the 15th Luftwaffe Field Division. The panzerjäger battalion became the panzerjäger battalion of the 15th Luftwaffe Field Division.

8th Luftwaffe Field Division

Formed 10/29/42 from the 42nd Flieger Regiment and contained:

1st, 2nd, 3rd, 4th Battalion (no regimental staff, soon reduced to 1st & 2nd Battalion)
Panzerjäger Battalion (3 companies)
Artillery Battalion (3 batteries)
Flak Battalion (3 batteries)
Pioneer Company

Signals Company
Support Troops

In December 1942 the division was sent into the Don Bend to support Stalingrad and was destroyed. The survivors were incorporated into the 15th Luftwaffe Field Division.

9th Luftwaffe Field Division

Formed in October 1942 from the 62nd Flieger Regiment and other forces into:

1/,2/,3/17th Luftwaffejäger Regiment
1/,2/,3/18th Luftwaffejäger Regiment
1/,2/,3/,4/9th Luftwaffe Artillery Regiment
9th Panzerjäger Battalion Luftwaffe Field Division
Pioneer company
Signals Company
Support Troops

On 11/1/43 standing before Leningrad, the division was taken into the army, except for the 4th (Flak) Artillery

Battalion, which became the 1/2nd Flak Regiment and remained with the Luftwaffe.

9th Field Division (L)

Formed on 11/1/43 from the 9th Luftwaffe Field Division when it was incorporated into the Army. It consisted of:

1/,2/,3/17th Jäger Regiment (L)
1/,2/,3/18th Jäger Regiment (L)
9th Fusilier Battalion (L)
1/,2/,3/9th Artillery Regiment (L)
9th Divisional (Einheiten) Support Units (L)

The division was destroyed in the Oranienbaum pocket and disbanded on 2/12/44. The survivors were distributed to the 61st, 225th, and 227th Infantry Divisions.

10th Luftwaffe Field Division

Formed in October 1942 with:

1/,2/,3/19th Luftwaffe Jäger Regiment
1/,2/,3/20th Luftwaffe Jäger Regiment
1/,2/,3/,4/10th Luftwaffe Artillery Regiment
10th Luftwaffe Field Division Panzerjäger Battalion
Pioneer Company

Signals Company
Support Troops

On 11/1/43 the division was transferred to the army. Only the 4/10th Luftwaffe Artillery Regiment (the flak battalion) remained with the Luftwaffe and was redesignated the 2/32nd Flak Regiment.

10th Field Division (L)

Formed on 1 November 1943 by the transfer of the 10th Luftwaffe Field Division into the army. It contained:

1/,2/,3/19th Jäger Regiment (L)
1/,2/,3/20th Jäger Regiment (L)
1/,2/,3/10th Artillery Regiment (L)
10th Divisional (Einheiten) Support Units (L)

On 2/3/44 the division was disbanded by the 18th Army. The staff of the artillery regiment became the staff of the 931st Artillery Special Employment Staff. Its 1st and 2nd Battalions became the 1003rd and 1004th Army Coastal Artillery Battalions. The remainder of the division was absorbed into the 170th Infantry Division.

11th Luftwaffe Field Division

Formed in October 1942 from the 21st Flieger Regiment.

1/,2/,3/21st Luftwaffe Jäger Regiment
1/,2/,3/22nd Luftwaffe Jäger Regiment
1/,2/,3/,4/11th Luftwaffe Artillery Regiment
11th Luftwaffe Field Division Panzerjäger Battalion
Bicycle Company
2nd Luftwaffe Pioneer Battalion
Signals Company
Support Troops

On 8/30/43 the division was organized and equipped as follows:

Divisional Staff
1 Division Staff
1 Bicycle Company (2 HMGs & 18 LMGs)
1 (mot) Mapping Detachment
21st Luftwaffe Jäger Regiment
1 Signals Platoon
1 Pioneer Platoon (4 LMGs)

3 (tmot) Battalions, each with
3 Companies (18 LMGs, 6 HMGs & 2 80mm mortars) (each company had 25 machine pistols)
1 Machine Gun Company (4 LMGs, 8 HMGs, 4 80mm mortars & 4 20mm flak guns)
22nd Luftwaffe Jäger Regiment
same as 21st Luftwaffe Jäger Regiment
11th Panzerjäger Battalion (L)
3 (mot)Panzerjäger Companies (5 75mm PAK 40, 9 50mm PAK 38 & 6 LMGs)
1 Sturmgeschütz Company (4 75mm PAK 40)
11th Artillery Regiment (L)
1 (tmot) Regimental Staff Battery
1 (mot) Signals Platoon
4 (mot) Light Supply Columns (2 LMGs ea)
1st Battalion
1 (tmot) Battalion Staff Battery
1 (tmot) Signals Platoon
3 Batteries (4 75mm (h) guns & 2 LMGs)
2nd Battalion
1 (tmot) Battalion Staff Battery

1 (tmot) Signals Platoon
3 Batteries (4 75mm guns (f) & 2 LMGs)
3rd Battalion
1 (tmot) Battalion Staff Battery
1 (tmot) Signals Platoon
2 Batteries (4 75mm (f) guns & 2 LMGs)
4th Battalion
1 Signals Platoon
2 Batteries (12 20mm guns & 2 LMGs ea)
2 Batteries (4 88mm guns, 3 20mm guns & 6 LMGs ea)

11th Pioneer Battalion (L)
1 (tmot) Signals Platoon
1 (mot) Pioneer Company (9 LMGs)
2 (tmot) Pioneer Companies (9 LMGs ea)
Signals
1 (mot) Signals Company
Other
1 (mot) Heavy Supply Column (2 LMGs)
2 (mot) Light Supply Columns (2 LMGs ea)
11th (tmot) Supply Company
11th Butcher Company
11th Field Bakery
11th Divisional Administration
11th (tmot) Medical Company
11th (mot) Ambulance Company
9/III (mot) Luftwaffe Field Hospital
11th Veterinary Company
11th (tmot) Maintenance Company
11th (tmot) Military Police Detachment (2 LMGs)
11th (tmot) Field Post Office

As the division was stationed in Greece as part of the occupational garrison forces, it had the following units assigned to it from the Army level:

Harbor Command Melos
1 Flak Section (3 20mm flak guns)
1 Flak Section (2 20mm flak guns)
2 Flak Section (1 20mm flak gun)
1 Coastal Battery (3 75mm guns)
1 Construction Company
837th Coastal Artillery Battalion
Battalion Staff (3 LMGs)
3 Batteries (6 155mm (f) guns ea)
3 Panzerjäger Batteries (2 47mm (t) & 2 20mm flak guns ea)
Pioneers
6th Construction Battalion (3 cos)
1 (mot) Construction Supply Column
2/6th Pioneer Battalion

On 11/1/43, in Greece, the division became the 11th Field Division (L). Only the 4 (Flak)/11th Luftwaffe

Artillery Regiment remained with the Luftwaffe and it became the 1/28th Flak Regiment. On 7/15/44 the division was organized and equipped as follows:

Divisional Staff
1 Division Staff
1 (mot) Mapping Detachment
21st (L) Jäger Regiment
1 Regimental Staff Company
1 Signals Platoon
1 Bicycle Platoon
1 Pioneer Platoon (10 LMGs)
3 Battalions, each with
3 Companies (13 LMGs, 1 HMG & 2 80mm mortars) (each company had 25 machine pistols)
1 Machine Gun Company (1 LMGs, 8 HMGs, 4 80mm mortars & 4 20mm flak guns)
1 Mountain Gun Battery (6 75mm guns & 5 LMGs)
1 Panzerjäger Company (12 75mm PAK 40 & 13 LMGs)
22nd (L) Jäger Regiment
same as 21st Luftwaffe Jäger Regiment
11th (L) Panzerjäger Battalion
1st (mot) Panzerjäger Company (12 75mm PAK 40 & 12 LMGs)
1 Sturmgeschütz Company (4 75mm StuGs)
11th (L) (mot) Fusilier Battalion
1 Fusilier Battalion Staff (1 LMG)
3 (mot) Fusilier Companies (13 LMGs & 2 80mm mortars)
1 (mot) Fusilier Company (12 HMGs, 1 LMG & 2 80mm mortars)
11th (L) Artillery Regiment
1 (tmot) Regimental Staff Battery
1 (mot) Signals Platoon
4 (mot) Light Supply Columns (2 LMGs ea)
1st & 2nd Battalions, each with
1 (mot) Battalion Staff Battery
1 (mot) Signals Platoon
3 (motZ) Batteries (4 105mm leFH guns & 2 LMGs)
3rd Battalion
1 (mot) Battalion Staff Battery
1 (mot) Signals Platoon
1 (motZ) Battery (4 152mm (r) howitzers & 2 LMGs)
2 (motZ) Batteries (4 105mm (j) guns & 2 LMGs)
11th (L) Pioneer Battalion
1 (tmot) Signals Platoon
3 (mot) Pioneer Company (2 HMGs, 9 LMGs, 2 80mm mortars, & 3 flamethrowers)
11th (L) Signal Battalion
1 (mot) Radio Company (6 LMGs)
1 (mot) Telephone Company (6 LMGs)
1 (mot) Signals Supply Column

11th (L) Feldersatz Battalion
  5 Companies
11th (L) Divisional Supply Troop
  1/11th (L) (mot) (90 ton) Transportation Company
    (6 LMGs)
  2/11th (L) (mot) (120 ton) Transportation Company
    (6 LMGs)
  11th (L) (mot) Supply Company (6 LMGs)
Other
  11th (L) (mot) Butcher Company
  11th (L) (mot) Field Bakery

11th (L) (mot) Divisional Administration
1/,2/11th (L) (mot) Medical Company
11th (mot) Ambulance Company
11th (L) Veterinary Company
11th (L) (tmot) Maintenance Company
**11th (L) (tmot) Military Police Detachment (1
  LMG)**
11th (L) (tmot) Field Post Office (1 LMG)

11th Field Division (L)

Formed on 11/1/43 with the transfer to the army of the 11th Luftwaffe Field Division. On 4/24/44 OKH records show the division organized and equipped as follows:

Staff
  1 Divisional Staff (2 LMGs)
  11th (mot) Mapping Detachment (L)
  1111th (tmot) Military Police Detachment
21st Jäger Regiment (L)
  1 Regimental Staff Company (1 LMG)
    1 Signals Platoon
    1 Pioneer Platoon (6 LMGs)
    1 Bicycle Platoon (3 LMGs)
  3 Battalions, each with
    3 Jäger Companies (2 HMGS & 13 LMGs)
    1 Machine Gun Company (6 HMGs, 3 LMGs, 4
      120mm mortars & 6 80mm mortars)
  1 Infantry Gun Company
    (2 150mm sIG, 6 75mm leIG, & 5 LMGs)
  1 (tmot) Panzerjäger Company
    (equipment unknown)
22nd Jäger Regiment (L)
  same as 21st (L) Jäger Regiment
11th (mot) Fusilier Battalion (L)
  3 (mot) Fusilier Companies (2 HMGS & 13
    LMGs)
  1 (mot) Machine Gun Company (6 HMGs, 3
    LMGs, 4 120mm mortars & 6 80mm mortars)
11th Panzerjäger Battalion (L)
  1/11th (motZ) Panzerjäger Company (12 75mm
    PAK 40 & 13 LMGs)
  1011th Sturmgeschütz Battery (10 StuGs & 12
    LMGs)
11th Artillery Regiment (L)
  1 Regimental & Regimental Staff Battery (1 LMG)
  1st Battalion
    1 Battalion & Battalion Staff Battery (2 LMGs)

  3 Batteries (4 105mm leFH & 5 LMGs ea)
  2nd Battalion
    same as 1st Battalion
  3rd Battalion
    1 Battalion & Battalion Staff Battery (2 LMGs)
    2 Batteries (105mm Yugoslav howitzers & 5 LMGs
      ea)
    1 Battery (152mm Russian howitzers & 5 LMGs)
11th Pioneer Battalion (L)
  Battalion Staff (4 LMG)
  3 (mot) Pioneer Companies (2 HMGs, 9 LMGs, 6
    flamethrowers & 2 80mm mortars)
11th Signals Battalion (L)
  1 (tmot) Telephone Company (6 LMGs)
  1 (mot) Radio Company (5 LMGs)
  1 (tmot) Signals Supply Column (1 LMG)
11th Feldersatz Battalion (L)
  2 Companies
11th Divisional Supply Troops (L)
  1/11th (mot) (90 ton) Transportation Company
    (L) (6 LMGs)
  2/11th (mot) (120 ton) Transportation Company
    (L) (8 LMGs)
  11th (tmot) Supply Company (L) (6 LMGs)
Administration
  11th (mot) Butcher Company (L) (2 LMGs)
  11th (mot) Bakery Company (L) (4 LMGs)
  11th (mot) Administration Company (L) (4
    LMGs)
Medical Battalion
  1/11th (mot) Medical Company (L)
  2/11th Medical Company (L)
  11th Medical Supply Company (L)
Other
  11th Maintenance Company (L) (4 LMGs)
  11th Veterinary Troop (L)
  911th (mot) Field Post Office (1 LMG)

The division served in Greece in 1944 and on 15 August 1944 it was organized and equipped as follows:

Staff
11th (mot) Mapping Detachment (L)
1111th (tmot) Military Police Detachment

21st & 22nd Jäger Regiments (L), each with
1 Regimental Staff Company (1 LMG)
1 Signals Platoon
1 Pioneer Platoon (6 LMGs)
1 Bicycle Platoon (4 LMGs)
3 Battalions, each with
3 Jäger Companies (13 LMGs & 2 80mm mortars ea)
1 Machine Gun Company (8 HMGs, 1 LMG, 4 20mm flak guns & 4 80mm mortars)
1 Infantry Gun Company
(6 75mm Mountain guns, 3 105mm leFH & 5 LMGs)
1 (tmot) Panzerjäger Company
(12 75mm PAK 40 & 13 LMGs)

11th (mot) Fusilier Battalion (L)
3 (mot) Fusilier Companies (13 LMGs & 2 80mm mortars)
1 (mot) Machine Gun Company (12 HMGs, 1 LMGs, & 2 80mm mortars)

11th Panzerjäger Battalion (L)
1/11th (motZ) Panzerjäger Company (12 75mm PAK 40 & 13 LMGs)
1011th Sturmgeschütz Battery (L) (4 StuGs, 3 HMGs & 6 LMGs)

11th Artillery Regiment (L)
1 Regimental & Regimental Staff Battery (2 LMGs)
1st Battalion
1 (motZ) Battalion & Battalion Staff Battery (2 LMGs)
3 (motZ) Batteries (4 105mm leFH & 5 LMGs ea)
2nd Battalion
same as 1st Battalion
3rd Battalion
1 (motZ) Battalion & Battalion Staff Battery (2 LMGs)
2 (motZ) Batteries (105mm Yugoslav howitzers & 5 LMGs ea)
1 (motZ) Battery (152mm Russian howitzers & 5 LMGs)

11th Pioneer Battalion (L)
Battalion Staff (4 LMG)
3 (mot) Pioneer Companies (2 HMGs, 9 LMGs, 6 flamethrowers & 2 80mm mortars)

11th Signals Battalion (L)
1 (mot) Telephone Company (6 LMGs)
1 (mot) Radio Company (5 LMGs)

1 (mot) Signals Supply Column

11th Feldersatz Battalion (L)
1 Company (13 LMGs & 2 80mm mortars)
1 Company (14 LMGs & 2 80mm mortars)
1 Company (6 LMGs)
1 Company (8 HMGs, 280mm mortars, 2 50mm mortars)
1 Company (4 HMGs & 11 LMGs)
1 Panzerjäger Section (3 75mm PAK 40)

11th Supply Troops (L)
1/11th (mot) (90 ton) Transportation Company (L) (6 LMGs)
2/11th (mot) (120 ton) Transportation Company (L) (8 LMGs)
11th (tmot) Supply Company (L) (6 LMGs)

Administration
11th (mot) Butcher Company (L) (6 LMGs)
11th (mot) Bakery Company (L)
11th (mot) Administration Company (L)

Medical Battalion
1/11th (mot) Medical Company (L) (2 LMGs)
2/11th Medical Company (L) (2 LMGs)
11th Medical Supply Company (L) (2 LMGs)

Other
11th Maintenance Company (L) (4 LMGs)
11th Veterinary Troop (L) (6 LMGs)
911th (mot) Field Post Office (1 LMG)

On 2/2/45 the 3rd Luftwaffe Jäger Regiment was redesignated the 111(L) Luftwaffe Jäger Division. In 1945 the division added the Staff/111th Jäger Regiment, but no new battalions. The 3/21st and 3/22nd Jäger Regiments were probably placed under it as the 1/,2/111th Jäger Regiment.

12th Luftwaffe Field Division

Formed at the end of 1942 from the 12th Flieger Regiment. It had:

1/,2/,3/23rd Luftwaffe Jäger Regiment
1/,2/,3/24th Luftwaffe Jäger Regiment
1/,2/,3/12th Luftwaffe Artillery Regiment
Panzerjäger Battalion, 12th Luftwaffe Field Division
12th Luftwaffe Pioneer Battalion
Bicycle Company
Signals Company
Support Troops

On 11/1/43 the division was converted to the 12th Field Division (L). However, the 4th (Flak) Battalion/12th Luftwaffe Artillery Regiment became the 2/6th Flak Regiment and remained with the Luftwaffe.

12th Field Division (L)

Formed on 11/1/43 in northern Russia near Ladoga. On 4/24/44 OKH records show the division organized and equipped as follows:

Staff
1 Divisional Staff (2 LMGs)
12th (mot) Mapping Detachment (L)
1112th (tmot) Military Police Detachment

23rd & 24th Jäger Regiment (L), each with
1 Regimental Staff Company (1 LMG)
1 Signals Platoon
1 Pioneer Platoon (6 LMGs)
1 Cavalry Platoon (3 LMGs)
3 Battalions, each with
3 Jäger Companies (2 HMGS & 13 LMGs)
1 Machine Gun Company (6 HMGs, 3 LMGs, 4 120mm mortars & 6 80mm mortars)
1 Heavy Mortar Company
(unknown number of 120mm mortars)
1 (tmot) Panzerjäger Company
(unknown number of 75mm PAK 40)

12th Fusilier Battalion (L)
2 Fusilier Companies (2 HMGS & 13 LMGs)
1 Bicycle Fusilier Company (2 HMGS & 13 LMGs)
1 Machine Gun Company (6 HMGs, 3 LMGs, 4 120mm mortars & 6 80mm mortars)
12th Artillery Regiment (L)
1 Regimental & Regimental Staff Battery (1 LMG)
1st & 2nd Battalions, each with
1 Battalion & Battalion Staff Battery (2 LMGs)
3 Batteries (4 75mm guns & 5 LMGs ea)
3rd Battalion
1 Battalion & Battalion Staff Battery (2 LMGs)

3 Batteries (4 105mm leFH & 5 LMGs ea)
4th Battalion
1 Battalion & Battalion Staff Battery (2 LMGs)
3 Batteries (4 155mm French howitzers & 5 LMGs ea)
12th Panzerjäger Battalion (L)
1 (motZ) Panzerjäger Company (12 75mm PAK 40 & 13 LMGs)
1 (motZ) Light Flak Company (12 20mm flak guns & 2 LMGs)
1112th Sturmgeschütz Battery (L) (10 StuGs & 12 LMGs)
12th Pioneer Battalion (L)
Battalion Staff (4 LMG)
3 Pioneer Companies (2 HMGs, 9 LMGs, 6 flamethrowers & 2 80mm mortars)
12th Signals Battalion (L)
1 (tmot) Telephone Company (6 LMGs)
1 (mot) Radio Company (5 LMGs)
1 (tmot) Signals Supply Column (1 LMG)
12th Feldersatz Battalion (L)
1 Company
12th Supply Troops (L)
12th (mot) 90 ton Transportation Company (L) (6 LMGs)
1/,2/12th 60 ton Transportation Company (L) (6 LMGs)
12th Supply Company (L) (6 LMGs)
12th Maintenance Company (L) (4 LMGs)
Administration
12th (mot) Butcher Company (L) (2 LMGs)
12th (mot) Bakery Company (L) (4 LMGs)
12th (mot) Administration Company (L) (4 LMGs)

Medical Battalion
1/12th (mot) Medical Company (L)
2/12th Medical Company (L)
12th Medical Supply Company (L)
Other
12th Veterinary Troop (L)
912th (mot) Field Post Office

In April 1944 it was re-formed and merged with the 13th Field Division (L). It then had:

1/,2/23rd Jäger Regiment (L)
1/,2/24th Jäger Regiment (L)

1/,2/25th Jäger Regiment (L) (from the 1/25th and 1/26th of the 13th Field Division (L).)
12th Fusilier Battalion (L) (from 1/374th Grenadier Regiment of the 207th Security Division)
1/,2/,3/11th Artillery Regiment (L)
12th Divisional (Einheiten) Support Units (L)

In December 1944 the 1/23rd, 2/24th, and 2/25th Infantry Regiments were disbanded. The Lettland Infantry Security Battalion became the 2/23rd Infantry Regiment. Including the 12th Fusilier Battalion (L), the division had only five battalions.

13th Luftwaffe Field Division

Formed on 11/15/42 from the 13th Flieger Regiment:

1/,2/,3/25th Jäger Regiment
1/,2/,3/26th Jäger Regiment
1/,2/,3/,4/13th Artillery Regiment
Panzerjäger Battalion, 13th Luftwaffe Field Division
13th Luftwaffe Pioneer Battalion
Bicycle Company

Signals Company
13th Divisional (Einheiten) Support Units

On 11/1/43 the division was transferred to the army as the 13th Field Division (L). However, the 4/13th Artillery Regiment, the flak battalion, remained part of the Luftwaffe as the 1/54th Flak Regiment.

13th Field Division (L)

Formed in northern Russia (Ladoga) from the 13th Luftwaffe Field Division. The division had:

1/,2/25th Jäger Regiment (L)
1/,2/26th Jäger Regiment (L)
1/,2/,3/13th Artillery Regiment (L)
13th Divisional (Einheiten) Support Units (L)

In April 1944 it was merged with the 12th Field Division (L) to form a Type 44 Division. The 1/25th and 1/26th Jäger Regiments were merged to form a new 25th Jäger Regiment.

14th Luftwaffe Field Division

Formed at the end of 1942 from the 61st Flieger Regiment. It contained:

1/,2/,3/27th Jäger Regiment
1/,2/,3/28th Jäger Regiment
1/,2/,3/14th Artillery Regiment
Panzerjäger Battalion, 14th Luftwaffe Field Division
14th Luftwaffe Pioneer Battalion

Bicycle Company
Signals Company
14th Divisional (Einheiten) Support Units

On 1/11/43, while in Norway, it was transferred to the army, except for the 3/14th Artillery Regiment (the Flak Battalion), which was retained in the Luftwaffe as the 1/15th Flak Regiment.

14th Field Division (L)

Formed on 11/1/43 in Norway by the absorption of the 14th Luftwaffe Field Division into the army. The division had:

    1/,2/,3/27th Jäger Regiment (L)
    1/,2/,3/28th Jäger Regiment (L)
    14th Fusilier Battalion (L)
    1/,2/14th Artillery Regiment (L)
    14th Divisional (Einheiten) Support Units (L)

On 4/24/44 OKH records show the division organized and equipped as follows:

Staff
    1 Divisional Staff (2 LMGs)
    14th (mot) Mapping Detachment (L)
    1114th (tmot) Military Police Detachment

27th Jäger Regiment (L)
    1 Regimental Staff Company (1 LMG)
        1 Signals Platoon
        1 Pioneer Platoon (6 LMGs)
        1 Cavalry Platoon (3 LMGs)
    2 Battalions, each with
        3 Jäger Companies (2 HMGS & 13 LMGs)
        1 Machine Gun Company (6 HMGs, 3 LMGs, 4 120mm mortars & 6 80mm mortars)
    1 (mot) Panzerjäger Company
        (equipment unknown)

28th Jäger Regiment (L)
    same as 27th Jäger Regiment (L)

14th Fusilier Battalion (L)
    2 Fusilier Companies (2 HMGS & 13 LMGs)
    1 Bicycle Fusilier Company (2 HMGS & 13 LMGs)
    1 Machine Gun Company (6 HMGs, 3 LMGs, 4 120mm mortars & 6 80mm mortars)

14th Panzerjäger Battalion (L)
    1/,2/14th (motZ) Panzerjäger Companies (L) (12 75mm PAK 40 & 13 LMGs ea)
    1114th Sturmgeschütz Battery (L) (4 StuGs)

4th Artillery Regiment (L)
    1 Regimental & Regimental Staff Battery (1 LMG)
    1st Battalion
        1 Battalion & Battalion Staff Battery (2 LMGs)
        3 Batteries (4 105m 334(h) guns & 5 LMGs ea)
    2nd Battalion
        1 Battalion & Battalion Staff Battery (2 LMGs)
        2 Batteries (4 155mm French howitzers & 5 LMGs ea)
        1 Battery (4 88mm guns & 5 LMGs)

14th Pioneer Battalion (L)
    Battalion Staff (4 LMG)
    1 Bicycle Pioneer Company (2 HMGs, 9 LMGs, 6 flamethrowers & 2 80mm mortars)
    2 Pioneer Companies (2 HMGs, 9 LMGs, 6 flamethrowers & 2 80mm mortars)

14th Signals Battalion (L)
    1 (tmot) Telephone Company (6 LMGs)
    1 (mot) Radio Company (5 LMGs)
    1 (tmot) Signals Supply Column (1 LMG)

14th Feldersatz Battalion (L)
    2 Companies

4th Divisional Supply Troops (L)
    14th (mot) 90 ton Transportation Company (L) (6 LMGs)
    1/,2/14th 60 ton Transportation Company (L) (6 LMGs)
    14th Supply Company (L) (6 LMGs)
    14th Maintenance Company (L) (4 LMGs)

Administration
    14th (mot) Butcher Company (L) (2 LMGs)
    14th (mot) Bakery Company (L) (4 LMGs)
    14th (mot) Administration Company (L) (4 LMGs)

Medical Battalion
    1/14th (mot) Medical Company (L)
    2/14th Medical Company (L)
    14th Medical Supply Company (L)

Other
    14th Veterinary Troop (L)
    914th (mot) Field Post Office

In 1945 the division was part of the XXXIII Army Corps and serving in Norway. OKH records show that the division was heavily equipped, far beyond its authorized compliment. The jäger battalions were designated as bicycle compliments. The jäger companies averaged 4 HMGs and 16 LMGs each. The machine-gun companies averaged 8 HMGS, 3 LMGs, 10 80mm mortars and 4 20mm guns each. Each jäger battalion had, in addition, a very mixed and inconsistent collection of French 25mm and 37mm guns, Norwegian 75mm guns, French HMGs, flamethrowers, searchlights and light fortress guns.

The fusilier battalion's three fusilier companies each had two HMGs and 13 LMGs. It also had 6 HMGs, 3 LMGS, 10 80mm mortars, and 4 37mm leIG. It also had a collection of French 50mm mortars, French HMGS, and Yugoslav 75mm guns beyond its authorized equipment. The panzerjäger battalion had a very mixed collection of equipment. The first (motZ) panzerjäger company had 9 50mm PAK 38 and 9 LMGs. The second (motZ) panzerjäger company had 6 75 PAK 40, 3 50mm PAK 38, and 4 LMGs. The 1014th Sturmgeschütz (L) apparently had 10 StuGs and the battalion had, as unauthorized additional equipment, 5 37mm French guns, 6 French LMGs, and 1 French 47mm gun. Similarly, ever other unit had a variety of French, Norwegian, and some Dutch equipment assigned to it beyond its authorized compliment.

In 1945 the division formed the 55th Jäger Regiment (L), but it had no staff. The 3/27th and 3/28th Jäger Regiments were used to form this new regiment.

15th Luftwaffe Field Division

Formed at the end of 1942 with:

1/,2/,3/29th Jäger Regiment
1/,2/,3/30th Jäger Regiment
1/,2/,3/,4/15th Artillery Regiment
Panzerjäger Battalion, 15th Luftwaffe Field Division
15th Luftwaffe Pioneer Battalion
Bicycle Company
Signals Company
15th Divisional (Einheiten) Support Units

In March 1943 the division absorbed the remains of the 7th and 8th Luftwaffe Field Divisions. On 11/1/43, after suffering heavy casualties, the division was absorbed into the 336th Infantry Division. The 4/15th Artillery Regiment, the flak battalion, became the Luftwaffe's 1/46th Flak Regiment.

16th Luftwaffe Field Division

Formed on 12/1/42 with:

1/,2/,3/31st Luftwaffe Jäger Regiment
1/,2/,3/32nd Luftwaffe Jäger Regiment
1/,2/,3/16th Luftwaffe Artillery Regiment
Panzerjäger Battalion, 16th Luftwaffe Field Division
16th Luftwaffe Pioneer Battalion
Reconnaissance Platoon
Signals Company
Support Troops, 16th Luftwaffe Field Division

On 11/1/43 the division was transferred to the Army. The 3/16th Artillery Regiment remained with the Luftwaffe and became the 1/53rd Flak Regiment.

16th Field Division (L)

Formed in November 1943 in Holland from the 16th Luftwaffe Field Division:

1/,2/31st Jäger Regiment (L)
1/,2/32nd Jäger Regiment (L)
1/,2/46th Jäger Regiment (L)
16th Fusilier Battalion (L)
1/,2/,3/16th Artillery Regiment (L) (3rd Battalion not formed until June 1944)

16th Divisional (Einheiten) Support Troops

On 4/24/44 OKH records show the division organized and equipped as follows:

Staff
1 Divisional Staff (2 LMGs)
16th (mot) Mapping Detachment (L)
1116th (tmot) Military Police Detachment

31st Jäger Regiment (L)
  1 Regimental Staff Company (1 LMG)
    1 Signals Platoon
    1 Pioneer Platoon (6 LMGs)
    1 Cavalry Platoon (3 LMGs)
  2 Battalions, each with
    3 Jäger Companies (2 HMGS & 13 LMGs)
    1 Machine Gun Company (6 HMGs, 3 LMGs, 4 120mm mortars & 6 80mm mortars)
  1 Infantry Gun Company
    (2 150mm sIG, 6 75mm leIG, & 5 LMGs)
  1 Panzerzerstörer Company
    (3 LMGs, 3 75mm PAK 40, & 36 panzerschreck)
32nd Jäger Regiment (L)
same as 31st Jäger Regiment (L)
46th Jäger Regiment (L)
same as 31st Jäger Regiment (L)
16th Fusilier Battalion (L)
  2 Fusilier Companies (2 HMGS & 13 LMGs)
  1 Bicycle Fusilier Company (2 HMGS & 13 LMGs)
  1 Machine Gun Company (6 HMGs, 3 LMGs, 4 120mm mortars & 6 80mm mortars)
16th Panzerjäger Battalion (L)
  1/16th (motZ) Panzerjäger Company (L) (12 75mm PAK 40 & 13 LMGs)
  3/14th Self Propelled Light Flak Company (12 20mm flak guns & 2 LMGs)
  1114th Sturmgeschütz Battery (L) (10 StuGs & 12 LMGs)
16th Artillery Regiment (L)
  1 Regimental & Regimental Staff Battery (1 LMG)
  1st Battalion
    1 Battalion & Battalion Staff Battery (2 LMGs)
    4 Batteries (4 76.2mm Russian guns, 2 20mm & 2 LMGs ea)
  2nd Battalion
    1 Battalion & Battalion Staff Battery (2 LMGs)

    3 Batteries (4 122mm Russian howitzers, 2 20mm guns & 2 LMGs ea)
16th Pioneer Battalion (L)
  Battalion Staff (4 LMG)
  1 Bicycle Pioneer Company (2 HMGs, 9 LMGs, 6 flamethrowers & 2 80mm mortars)
  2 Pioneer Companies (2 HMGs, 9 LMGs, 6 flamethrowers & 2 80mm mortars)
16th Signals Battalion (L)
  1 (tmot) Telephone Company (6 LMGs)
  1 (mot) Radio Company (5 LMGs)
  1 (tmot) Signals Supply Column (1 LMG)
16th Feldersatz Battalion (L)
  2 Companies
16th Divisional Supply Troops (L)
  16th (mot) 90 ton Transportation Company (L) (6 LMGs)
  16th 60 ton Transportation Company (L) (6 LMGs)
  16th Supply Company (L) (6 LMGs)
  16th Maintenance Company (L) (4 LMGs)
Administration
  16th (mot) Butcher Company (L) (2 LMGs)
  16th (mot) Bakery Company (L) (4 LMGs)
  16th (mot) Administration Company (L) (4 LMGs)
Medical Battalion
  1/16th (mot) Medical Company (L)
  2/16th Medical Company (L)
  16th Medical Supply Company (L)
Other
  16th Veterinary Troop (L)
  916th (mot) Field Post Office

In July 1944 the division was destroyed in Normandy. It was officially disbanded on 8/4/44, with its infantry going to the 21st Panzer Division and the remainder going to the 16th Infantry Division (30th Wave).

17th Luftwaffe Field Division

Formed at the end of 1942 with:

1/,2/,3/33rd Luftwaffe Jäger Regiment
1/,2/,3/34th Luftwaffe Jäger Regiment
1/,2/,3/17th Luftwaffe Artillery Regiment
Panzerjäger Battalion, 17th Luftwaffe Field Division
17th Luftwaffe Pioneer Battalion
Reconnaissance Company, 17th Luftwaffe Field Division
Signals Company, 17th Luftwaffe Field Division

Support Troops, 17th Luftwaffe Field Division

On 11/1/43 it was transferred to the Army. The 3/17th Luftwaffe Artillery Regiment was retained by the Luftwaffe as the 1/20th Flak Regiment.

17th Field Division (L)

Formed on 11/1/43 at Le Havre when the 17th Luftwaffe Field Division was transferred to the Army. During the winter the 47th Jäger Regiment was newly built. The 1/33rd Luftwaffe Jäger Regiment became the 1/47th and the 1/34th became the 2/47th Luftwaffe Jäger Regiment. The third battalions of the 33rd and 34th Luftwaffe Jäger Regiments were then renumbered as the first battalions. The division had:

    1/,2/33rd Jäger Regiment (L)
    1/,2/34th Jäger Regiment (L)
    1/,2/47th Jäger Regiment (L)
    17th Fusilier Battalion (L)
    1/,2/17th Artillery Regiment (L)
    17th Divisional (Einheiten) Support Troops (L)

On 3/20/44 the 835th North Caucasus Battalion became the 3(Nordkauk)/34th Luftwaffe Jäger Regiment. On 4/24/44 OKH records show the division was a garrison or static division and that it was organized and equipped as follows:

Staff
    1 Divisional Staff (2 LMGs)
    17th (mot) Mapping Detachment (L)
    1117th (tmot) Military Police Detachment (1 LMG)
33rd Jäger Regiment (L)
    1 Regimental Staff Company (1 LMG)
    1 Signals Platoon
    1 Pioneer Platoon (6 LMGs)
    2 Battalions, each with
    3 Jäger Companies (2 HMGS, 1 flamethrower & 13 LMGs)
    1 Machine Gun Company (2 HMGs, 12 LMGs, 1 flamethrower, & 2 80mm mortars)
    14th (tmot) Panzerjäger Company (12 75mm PAK 40 & 13 LMGs)
34th Jäger Regiment (L)
    Staff like 33rd Jäger Regiment (L)
    three battalions, like 1/33rd Jäger Regiment (L)
47th Jäger Regiment (L)
    same as 33rd Jäger Regiment (L)
17th Fusilier Battalion (L)
    2 Fusilier Companies (2 HMGS & 13 LMGs)
    1 Bicycle Fusilier Company (2 HMGS & 13 LMGs)
    1 Machine Gun Company (6 HMGs, 3 LMGs, 4 120mm mortars & 6 80mm mortars)
17th Artillery Regiment (L)
    1 Regimental & Regimental Staff Battery (1 LMG)

1st Battalion
    1 Battalion & Battalion Staff Battery (2 LMGs)
    3 Batteries (4 105mm French howitzers, 1 20mm gun, & 2 LMGs ea)
2nd Battalion
    1 Battalion & Battalion Staff Battery (2 LMGs)
    3 Batteries (4 155mm Czech howitzers & 5 LMGs ea)
17th Panzerjäger Battalion (L)
    1 (motZ) Panzerjäger Company (12 75mm PAK 40 & 13 LMGs)
    1 (motZ) Light Flak Company (12 20mm flak guns & 2 LMGs)
    1117th Sturmgeschütz Battery (L) (10 StuGs & 12 LMGs)
17th Pioneer Battalion (L)
    Battalion Staff (4 LMG)
    3 Pioneer Companies (9 LMGs, 6 flamethrowers)
17th Signals Battalion (L)
    1 (tmot) Telephone Company (6 LMGs)
    1 (tmot) Radio Company (5 LMGs)
17th Feldersatz Battalion (L)
    2 Companies
17th Supply Troops (L)
    17th (mot) Heavy Supply Column (L) (4 LMGs)
    17th 60 ton Transportation Company (L) (6 LMGs)
    17th Supply Company (L) (6 LMGs)
    17th Maintenance Company (L) (4 LMGs)
Administration
    17th Butcher Company (L) (2 LMGs)
    17th Bakery Company (L) (4 LMGs)
    17th Administration Company (L) (4 LMGs)
Medical Battalion
    1/17th (mot) Medical Company (L)
    17th Medical Supply Company (L)
Other
    17th Veterinary Troop (L)
    917th (mot) Field Post Office

On 5/27/44 orders were sent out for the divisional anti-tank artillery equipment to be upgraded. The 1st Company of the panzerjäger battalion had 6 75mm PAK 40 and 6 50mm PAK 38. The 50mm guns were replaced by 75mm PAK 40s. The 14th Company of the 33rd Jäger Regiment (L) had 6 75mm PAK 97/38 and to these were added 36 88mm Panzerschreck. Later three of the PAK 97/38 would be replaced by 75mm PAK 40. The 14th Companies of the 34th and 47th

Jäger Regiments (L) had 6 50mm PAK 38, three of which were ordered replaced by 3 75mm PAK 40. They also each received 36 88mm Panzerschrecks.

By June 1944 the 17th Artillery Regiment (L) had reequipped its batteries and rebuilt itself. The equipment and unit designation changes were as follows:

Old Unit	Equipment	New Designation	New Equipment
1st Battery	105mm leFH 325 (f)	1st Battery	105mm leFH 325 (f)
2nd Battery	105mm leFH 325 (f)	2nd Battery	105mm leFH 325 (f)
3rd Battery	105mm leFH 325 (f)	3rd Battery	105mm leFH 325 (f)
4th Battery	155mm sFH 414 (f)	4th Battery	150mm sFH 25 (t)
5th Battery	155mm sFH 414 (f)	5th Battery	150mm sFH 25 (t)
6th Battery	155mm sFH 414 (f)	6th Battery	150mm sFH 25 (t)

Other units assigned to the 17th Field Division (L) were reassigned to the 1149th Army Artillery Battalion as follows:

Old Unit	Equipment	New Designation	New Equipment
Nord Battalion			
A/Le Havre Ger.Btry	155mm sFH 414 (f)	1st Battery	155mm sFH 414 (f)
266th St. Btry	150mm sFH 25 (t)	2nd Battery	150mm sFH 25 (t)
350th St. Btry	155mm sFH 414 (f)	3rd Battery	150mm sFH 25 (t)
Ost Battalion			
351st St. Btry	155mm sFH 414 (f)	1st Battery	155mm sFH 414 (f)
313th St. Btry	75mm FK16 n.A.	3rd Battery	155mm sFH 414 (f)
420th St. Btry	155mm sFH 414 (f)	3rd Battery	155mm sFH 414 (f)

In May 1944 the 3/34th Jäger Regiment (L) was formed from the 835th Battalion of the North Caucasus Legion. In June 1944 the 3rd (flak) Battery of the panzerjäger battalion was reequipped with 37mm guns. In September 1944 the division was crushed in battles in France and was disbanded on 9/27/44. Its survivors were transferred to the 167th Volks Grenadier Division in Slovakia.

18th Luftwaffe Field Division

Formed at the end of 1942 from the 52nd Flieger Regiment. It had:

1/,2/,3/35th Luftwaffe Jäger Regiment (1st–13th Companies)

1/,2/,3/36th Luftwaffe Jäger Regiment (1st–13th Companies

1/,2/,3/18th Luftwaffe Artillery Regiment (1st–10th Batteries)

Panzerjäger Battalion, 17th Luftwaffe Field Division (3 cos)

18th Luftwaffe Pioneer Battalion (3 coys)

Reconnaissance Company, 18th Luftwaffe Field Division

Signals Company, 18th Luftwaffe Field Division

Supply Troops, 18th Luftwaffe Field Division
  1st Heavy Truck Column
  2nd Light Truck Column
  4th Light Truck Column
  6th Light Horse Drawn Column
  7th Small Truck Column
  8th Light Truck Column
  9th Light Truck Column
  10th Light Truck Column

11th Light Truck Column
Supply Company
Maintenance Company
Ordnance Troops, 18th Luftwaffe Field Division
Divisional Administration Detachment
Bakery Company
Butcher Company
Field Post Office
Military Police Troop
Medical & Veterinary Service, 18th Luftwaffe Field Division

(mot) Luftwaffe Medical Company
(mot) Luftwaffe Medical Platoon
(mot) Luftwaffe Veterinary Company
Luftwaffe Horse Depot

On 11/1/43 it was transferred to the Army and redesignated as the 18th Field Division (L). The 3/18th Luftwaffe Artillery Regiment became the 2/52nd Flak Regiment.

18th Field Division (L)

Formed on 11/1/43. The 1/36th Luftwaffe Jäger Regiment and the 3/35th became the 1/,2/48th Luftwaffe Jäger Regiment, respectively. The third battalions of the 35th and 36th regiments were then renumbered as the first battalions.

1/,2/35th Jäger Regiment (L)
1/,2/36th Jäger Regiment (L)
1/,2/48th Jäger Regiment (L)
18th Fusilier Battalion (L)
1/,2/18th Artillery Regiment (L) (3rd Battalion formed 9/44)
18th Divisional (Einheiten) Troops (L)

On 4/24/44 OKH records show the division was a garrison or static division and that it was organized and equipped as follows:

Staff
1 Divisional Staff (2 LMGs)
18th (mot) Mapping Detachment (L)
1118th (tmot) Military Police Detachment (1 LMG)
35th Jäger Regiment (L)
1 Regimental Staff Company (1 LMG)
1 Signals Platoon
1 Pioneer Platoon (6 LMGs)
2 **Battalions**, each with
3 Jäger Companies (2 HMGS, 1 flamethrower & 12 LMGs)
1 (bicycle) Jäger Company (2 HMGS, 1 flamethrower & 12 LMGs)
1 (tmot) Panzerjäger Company (12 75mm PAK 40 & 13 LMGs)
1 Infantry Gun Company (6 75mm leIG)
36th Jäger Regiment (L)
same as 35th Jäger Regiment (L)

48th Jäger Regiment (L)
same as 35th Jäger Regiment
18th Fusilier Battalion (L)
3 Fusilier Companies (2 HMGS & 13 LMGs)
1 Bicycle Fusilier Company (2 HMGS & 13 LMGs)
18th Artillery Regiment (L)
1 Regimental & Regimental Staff Battery (1 LMG)
1st Battalion
1 Battalion & Battalion Staff Battery (2 LMGs)
3 Batteries (4 76.2mm Russian guns, 1 20mm gun & 3 LMGs ea)
2nd Battalion
1 Battalion & Battalion Staff Battery (2 LMGs)
3 Batteries (4 155mm French howitzers, 1 20mm gun& 3 LMGs ea)
3rd Battalion
same as 2nd Battalion
18th Panzerjäger Battalion (L)
1 (motZ) Panzerjäger Company (12 75mm PAK 40 & 13 LMGs)
1118th Sturmgeschütz Battery (L) (4 StuGs)
18th Pioneer Battalion (L)
Battalion Staff (4 LMG)
3 Pioneer Companies (9 LMGs, 6 flamethrowers)
18th Signals Battalion (L)
1 (tmot) Telephone Company (6 LMGs)
1 (tmot) Radio Company (5 LMGs)
18th Divisional Supply Troops (L)
18th (mot) Heavy Supply Column (L) (4 LMGs)
18th 60 ton Transportation Company (L) (6 LMGs)
18th Supply Company (L) (6 LMGs)
18th Maintenance Company (L) (4 LMGs)
Administration
18th Butcher Company (L) (2 LMGs)
18th Bakery Company (L) (4 LMGs)
18th Administration Company (L) (4 LMGs)

Medical Battalion
    1/18th (mot) Medical Company (L)
    18th Medical Supply Company (L)
Other
    18th Veterinary Troop (L)
    918th (mot) Field Post Office

On 5/27/44 orders were sent out for the divisional anti-tank artillery equipment to be replaced. The panzerjäger battalion's (motZ) companies were changed from 6 75mm PAK 40 and 6 75mm PAK 97/38 guns to 12 75mm PAK 40 guns. The grenadier regiment's anti-tank companies were reequipped from 3 50mm PAK 38 to 3 75mm PAK 40, 3 75mm PAK 97/38, and 36 88mm Panzerschreck.

By June 1944 the 18th Artillery Regiment (L) had reequipped its batteries and rebuilt itself. The equipment and unit designation changes were as follows:

Old Unit	Equipment	New Designation	New Equipment
1st Battery	150mm sFH (t).	1st Battery	75mm FK 39
2nd Battery	150mm sFH (t).	2nd Battery	75mm FK 39
3rd Battery	105mm leFH 14/19 (t)	3rd Battery	75mm FK 39
4th Battery	155mm sFH 414 (f)	4th Battery	155mm sFH 414 (f)
5th Battery	155mm sFH 414 (f)	5th Battery	155mm sFH 414 (f)
696th G. Btry	155mm sFH 414 (f)	6th Battery	155mm sFH 414 (f)
417th St. Btry	155mm sFH 414 (f)	7th Battery	155mm sFH 414 (f)
344th St. Btry	155mm sFH 414 (f)	8th Battery	155mm sFH 414 (f)
309th St. Btry	105mm lFH 14/19 (t)	9th Battery	155mm sFH 414 (f)

In June 1944 the 3rd (flak) Battery of the panzerjäger battalion was reequipped with 37mm guns. In September 1944 the division was destroyed in the Mons (Belgium) Pocket and the remainder was incorporated into the 18th Volks Grenadier Division. It was officially disbanded on 9/14/44.

19th Luftwaffe Field Division

Formed on 3/1/43 and consisted of:

1/,2/,3/37th Luftwaffe Jäger Regiment
1/,2/,3/38th Luftwaffe Jäger Regiment
1/,2/,3/,4/19th Luftwaffe Artillery Regiment
Panzerjäger Battalion, 19th Luftwaffe Field Division
Luftwaffe 19th Pioneer Battalion
Bicycle Company, 19th Luftwaffe Field Division

Signals Company, 19th Luftwaffe Field Division
Support Troops, 19th Luftwaffe Field Division

On 11/1/43 it was transferred to the army and became the 19th Field Division (L). However, the 4/19th Luftwaffe Artillery Regiment remained with the Luftwaffe and became the 1/35th Flak Regiment.

19th Field Division (L)

Formed on 11/1/43 in the Netherlands from the 19th Luftwaffe Field Division. During the winter of 1943/44 the 45th Jäger Regiment (L) was formed. On 4/24/44

OKH records show the division organized and equipped as follows:

Staff
1 Divisional Staff (2 LMGs)
19th (mot) Mapping Detachment (L)
1119th (tmot) Military Police Detachment
37th, 38th, & 45th Jäger Regiments (L), each with
1 Regimental Staff Company (1 LMG)
1 Signals Platoon
1 Pioneer Platoon (6 LMGs)
1 Cavalry Platoon (3 LMGs)
2 Battalions, each with
3 Jäger Companies (2 HMGS & 13 LMGs)
1 Machine Gun Company (6 HMGs, 3 LMGs, 4 120mm mortars & 6 80mm mortars)
1 (tmot) Panzerjäger Company (12 75mm PAK 40 & 13 LMGs)
19th Fusilier Battalion (L)
2 Fusilier Companies (2 HMGS & 13 LMGs)
1 Bicycle Fusilier Company (2 HMGS & 13 LMGs)
1 Machine Gun Company (6 HMGs, 3 LMGs, 4 120mm mortars & 6 80mm mortars)
19th Artillery Regiment (L)
1 Regimental & Regimental Staff Battery (1 LMG)
1st Battalion
1 Battalion & Battalion Staff Battery (2 LMGs)
3 (motZ) Batteries (4 75.2mm Russian howitzers & 5 LMGs ea)
2nd Battalion
1 Battalion & Battalion Staff Battery (2 LMGs)
3 Batteries (4 75.2mm Russian guns & 5 LMGs ea)
3rd Battalion
1 Battalion & Battalion Staff Battery (2 LMGs)
3 (motZ) Batteries (4 122mm Russian howitzers & 5 LMGs)
Attached
1 (motZ) Battery (4 105mm Polish guns & 2 LMGs)
19th Panzerjäger Battalion (L)
1/19th (motZ) Panzerjäger Company (L) (12 75mm PAK 40 & 13 LMGs)
2/19th (motZ) Light Flak Company (L) (12 20mm flak guns & 2 LMGs)
1019th Sturmgeschütz Battery (L) (10 StuGs & 12 LMGs)

19th Pioneer Battalion (L)
Battalion Staff (4 LMG)
1 (mot) Pioneer Company (2 HMGs, 9 LMGs, 6 flamethrowers & 2 80mm mortars)
2 Pioneer Companies (2 HMGs, 9 LMGs, 6 flamethrowers & 2 80mm mortars)
19th Signals Battalion (L)
1 (tmot) Telephone Company (6 LMGs)
1 (mot) Radio Company (5 LMGs)
1 (tmot) Signals Supply Column (1 LMG)
19th Feldersatz Battalion (L)
4 Companies
194th Divisional Supply Troops (L)
19th (mot) 120 ton Transportation Company (L) (8 LMGs)
2/19th (mot) Heavy Supply Column (L) (4 LMGs)
19th Supply Company (L) (6 LMGs)
19th Maintenance Company (L) (4 LMGs)
Administration
19th (mot) Butcher Company (L) (2 LMGs)
19th (mot) Bakery Company (L) (4 LMGs)
19th (mot) Administration Company (L) (4 LMGs)
Other
1/19th Medical Company (L)
2/19th (mot) Medical Company (L)
19th Medical Supply Company (L)
19th Veterinary Troop (L)
919th (mot) Field Post Office

In fact, apparently it was not until 5/1/44 that the 1019th Sturmgeschütz Battalion was assigned to the division. By June 1944 the 19th Artillery Regiment (L) had reequipped its batteries. The 1st–3rd Batteries (1st Battalion) retained their 76.2mm lKH 290(4) and the 4th–6th Batteries (2nd Battalion) retained their 75mm FK39, but the 7th and 8th Batteries (3rd Battalion) replaced their sFH 25 (t) heavy howitzers with Russian 122mm sFH 396 (r) howitzers. The Lehr Battery (3rd Battalion) replaced its 155mm sFH 414 (f) with 122mm sFH 396 (r) howitzers and a 10th Battery was organized equipped with 105mm K29 (p) guns.

19th Luftwaffe Sturm Division

Formed on 6/1/44 by renaming the 19th Field Division (L). It was destroyed in Italy. The infantry cadre was sent to Denmark on 8/15/44 where it was used to re-form the 19th Grenadier Division. The artillery remained in Italy with the staff/,2/19th Artillery Regiment (L) becoming the 719th Artillery Regiment (19th Grenadier Division then in Denmark), the 1/19th Artillery Regiment (L) was assigned to the 20th Field Division (L) and the 3/19th became the 1154th Army Artillery Battalion. The fusilier battalion became the 20th Fusilier Battalion (L).

20th Luftwaffe Field Division

Formed on 3/8/43 with the 23rd Flieger Regiment.

1/,2/,3/39th Luftwaffe Jäger Regiment
1/,2/,3/40th Luftwaffe Jäger Regiment
1/,2/,3/,4/20th Luftwaffe Artillery Regiment
Panzerjäger Battalion, 20th Luftwaffe Field Division
20th Luftwaffe Pioneer Battalion
Bicycle Company, 20th Luftwaffe Field Division

Signals Company, 20th Luftwaffe Field Division
Divisional (Einheiten) Support Troops, 20th Luftwaffe Field Division

On 11/1/43 the division was transferred to the Army. The 4/20th Luftwaffe Artillery Regiment became the 1/48th Flak Regiment and remained with the Luftwaffe.

20th Field Division (L)

Formed on 11/1/43 with the transfer of the 20th Luftwaffe Field Division to the Army. On 11/17/43 it became a bicycle formation. It had:

1/,2/39th Jäger Regiment (L) (Bicycle Regiment)
1/,2/40th Jäger Regiment (L) (Bicycle Regiment)
1/,2/,3/20th Artillery Regiment (L) (3/20th from 995th Artillery Bn)
20th Divisional (Einheiten) Support Units (L)

On 4/24/44 OKH records show the division organized and equipped as follows:

Staff
1 Divisional Staff (2 LMGs)
20th (mot) Mapping Detachment (L)
1120th (tmot) Military Police Detachment
1 Motorcycle Platoon (3 LMGs)
39th Jäger Regiment (L)
1 (mot) Regimental Staff Company (1 LMG)
  1 Signals Platoon
  1 Pioneer Platoon (3 LMGs)
  1 Motorcycle Platoon (6 LMGs)
2 **Battalions,** each with
  3 Bicycle Jäger Companies (16 LMGs)
  1 (mot) Mortar Company (12 80mm mortars)
  1 (mot) Machine Gun Company (12 HMGs)
1 **(motZ) Panzerjäger Company**
  (6 37mm PAK 36 & 5 LMGs)
1 **(motZ) Panzerjäger Company**
  (6 50mm PAK 38 & 6 LMGs)
1 **(motZ) Flak Company**
  (12 20mm flak guns & 4 LMGs)
40th Jäger Regiment (L)
  same as 39th Jäger Regiment (L)

20th Artillery Regiment (L)
  1 Regimental & Regimental Staff Battery (1 LMG)
1st Battalion
  1 Battalion & (mot) Battalion Staff Battery (2 LMGs)
  2 Batteries (4 76.2mm guns & 5 LMGs)
2nd Battalion
  same as 1st Battalion
3rd Battalion
  1 Battalion & Battalion Staff Battery (2 LMGs)
  3 Batteries (4 122mm Russian howitzers & 5 LMGs ea)
20th Panzerjäger Battalion (L)
  1 (motZ) Panzerjäger Company (12 75mm PAK 40 & 12 LMGs)
  1120th Sturmgeschütz Battery (L) (10 StuGs & 12 LMGs)
20th Pioneer Battalion (L)
  1 Bicycle Pioneer Company (2 HMGs, 9 LMGs, 6 flamethrowers & 2 80mm mortars)
  1 (mot) Pioneer Company (2 HMGs, 9 LMGs, 6 flamethrowers & 2 80mm mortars)
20th Signals Company (L)
  (6 LMGs)
20th Feldersatz Battalion (L)
  3 Bicycle Companies
20th Divisional Supply Troops (L)
  1/20th (mot) 120 ton Transportation Company (L) (8 LMGs)
  2/20th 60 ton Transportation Company (L)
  20th (mot) Supply Company (L) (12 LMGs)
  20th Maintenance Company (L) (4 LMGs)
Administration
  20th (mot) Bakery Company (L) (6 LMGs)
  20th (mot) Butcher Company (L) (4 LMGs)
  20th (mot) Administration Company (L) (2 LMGs)

Medical Battalion

1/20th (mot) Medical Company (L)

2/20th Medical Company (L)

20th Medical Supply Company (L)

Other

20th Veterinary Troop (L)

920th (mot) Field Post Office (1 LMG)

On 6/1/44 it became the 20th Luftwaffe Sturm Division.

20th Luftwaffe Sturm Division

The division was formed on 6/1/44. In July 1944 it was joined by the remains of the disbanded 19th Luftwaffe Sturm Division (Feldersatz Battalion, Fusilier Battalion, Panzerjäger Battalion, Pioneer Battalion, Signal Battalion, and support troops) and the 1/19th Artillery Regiment (L) became the 1/20th Artillery Regiment (L). On 11/28/44 the division was ordered disbanded and its infantry sent to the 26th Panzer Division. On 1/3/45 the 39th and 40th Luftwaffe Jäger Regiments became the 1228th and 1229th Feldausbildung Grenadier Regiments; the 20th Feldersatz Battalion became the 1/227th Feldausbildung Grenadier Regiment, the 1/20th Artillery Regiment became the 155th Feldausbildung Artillery Battalion, the 20th Pioneer Battalion became the 155th Feldausbildung Pioneer Battalion. The 20th Support Units became the 155th Support Regiment (155th Feldausbildung Division); the Staff/,3/20th Artillery Regiment became the Staff/,3/650th Artillery Regiment (710th Infantry Division); the 2/20th Artillery Regiment became the 4/661st Artillery Regiment (114th Jäger Division); the 20th Fusilier Battalion became the 1057th Mountain Reconnaissance Battalion (157th Mountain Division); the 20th Panzerjäger Battalion became the 1048th Panzerjäger Battalion (148th Infantry Division); two batteries (2nd & 3rd Btrys/20th Artillery Regiment) were transferred to the 142nd Artillery Regiment (42nd Jäger Division) and the signal battalion was placed at the disposal of OB West.

21st Luftwaffe Field Division

Formed in December 1942 by Army Group North from the Meindel Luftwaffe Division (1st–5th Field Regiments) and on 12/12/42 took the place of the General Odebrecht Group (Luftwaffe Field). The division had:

1/,2/,3/41st Luftwaffe Jäger Regiment

1/,2/,3/42nd Luftwaffe Jäger Regiment

1/,2/,3/,4/21st Luftwaffe Artillery Regiment

Panzerjäger Battalion, 21st Luftwaffe Field Division

21st Luftwaffe Pioneer Battalion

Reconnaissance Company, 21st Luftwaffe Field Division

Signals Company, 21st Luftwaffe Field Division

Supply Units, 21st Luftwaffe Field Division

Later the 1/,2/,3/43rd Luftwaffe Jäger Regiment from the 22nd Luftwaffe Division was added to the division. On 11/1/43 the division was transferred to the Army.

21st Field Division (L)

Formed on 11/1/43 by the transfer of the 21st Luftwaffe Field Division into the Army. The division had:

1/,2/41st Jäger Regiment (L)

1/,2/42nd Jäger Regiment (L)

1/,2/43rd Jäger Regiment (L)

21st Fusilier Battalion (L)

1/,2/,3/,4/21st Artillery Regiment (L)

21st Divisional (Einheiten) Troops (L)

On 4/24/44 OKH records show the division organized and equipped as follows:

Staff
1 Divisional Staff (2 LMGs)
21st (L) (mot) Mapping Detachment
1121st (tmot) Military Police Detachment
41st, 42nd, & 43rd (L) Jäger Regiments, each with
1 Regimental Staff Company (1 LMG)
1 Signals Platoon
1 Pioneer Platoon (6 LMGs)
1 Bicycle Platoon (3 LMGs)
2 Battalions, each with
3 Jäger Companies (2 HMGS & 13 LMGs)
1 Machine Gun Company (6 HMGs, 3 LMGs, 4 120mm mortars & 6 80mm mortars)
1 Infantry Gun Company
(2 150mm sIG, 6 75mm leIG, & 5 LMGs)
1 (tmot) Panzerjäger Company
(12 75mm PAK 40 & 13 LMGs)
21st Fusilier Battalion (L)
2 Fusilier Companies (2 HMGS & 13 LMGs)
1 Bicycle Fusilier Company (2 HMGS & 13 LMGs)
1 Machine Gun Company (6 HMGs, 3 LMGs, 4 120mm mortars & 6 80mm mortars)
21st Panzerjäger Battalion (L)
1 (motZ) Panzerjäger Company (12 75mm PAK 40 & 13 LMGs)
1121st (L) Sturmgeschütz Battery (10 StuGs & 12 LMGs)
21st Artillery Regiment (L)
1 Regimental & Regimental Staff Battery (1 LMG)
1st, 2nd & 3rd Battalions, each with
1 Battalion & Battalion Staff Battery (2 LMGs)
3 (motZ) Batteries (4 75mm French guns & 5 LMGs)
4th Battalion
1 Battalion & Battalion Staff Battery (2 LMGs)
3 Batteries (4 155mm French howitzers & 5 LMGs ea)
21st Pioneer Battalion (L)
Battalion Staff (4 LMG)
1 Bicycle Pioneer Company (2 HMGs, 9 LMGs, 6 flamethrowers & 2 80mm mortars)

2 Pioneer Companies (2 HMGs, 9 LMGs, 6 flame-throwers & 2 80mm mortars)
21st Signals Battalion (L)
1 (tmot) Telephone Company (6 LMGs)
1 (mot) Radio Company (5 LMGs)
1 (tmot) Signals Supply Column (1 LMG)
21st Feldersatz Battalion (L)
3 Companies
21st Divisional Supply Troops (L)
21st (L) (mot) 90 ton Transportation Company (6 LMGs)
1/,2/21st (L) 60 ton Transportation Company (6 LMGs)
21st (L) Supply Company (6 LMGs)
21st (L) Maintenance Company (4 LMGs)
Administration
21st (L) (mot) Butcher Company (2 LMGs)
21st (L) (mot) Bakery Company (4 LMGs)
21st (L) (mot) Administration Company (4 LMGs)
Medical Battalion
1/21st (L) (mot) Medical Company (4 LMGs)
2/21st (L) Medical Company (4 LMGs)
21st (L) Medical Supply Company (4 LMGs)
21st (L) (mot) Field Hospital Company (4 LMGs)
Other
21st (L) Veterinary Troop
21st (mot) Field Post Office

In November 1944 the division was disbanded. The 1/41st, 1/42nd, and 1/43rd became the 21st Luftwaffe Regimental Group and, along with the 1/,2/21st Artillery Regiment (L), was assigned to the 329th Infantry Division. The 2/41st, 2/42nd, 2/43rd Jäger Regiments (L) and the 3/21st Artillery Regiment (L) were disbanded. By mid-November only the staff of the division continued to exist. The bulk of the division had been destroyed in combat in early November 1944. On 8 May 1945 what remained of the division passed into Russian captivity in Courland.

22nd Luftwaffe Field Division

This division was to be formed in 1943 by Army Group North from the Meindl Luftwaffe Division. It was to have:

1/,2/,3/43rd Luftwaffe Jäger Regiment
1/,2/,3/44th Luftwaffe Jäger Regiment
1/,2/,3/,4/22nd Luftwaffe Artillery Regiment

Panzerjäger Battalion, 22nd Luftwaffe Field Division
Luftwaffe Pioneer Battalion
Reconnaissance Company, 22nd Luftwaffe Field Division
Signals Company, 22nd Luftwaffe Field Division
Supply Troops, 22nd Luftwaffe Field Division

The division was not formed. The 43rd Luftwaffe Jäger Regiment was sent to the 21st Luftwaffe Field Division, the panzerjäger battalion was converted into the 88th (mot) Light Flak Battalion, and the pioneer battalion became army troops. The staff became, in December 1943, the staff of the 23rd Flak Division, the signals company became the 140th Signal Operations Company in the 20th Flak Division. The remainder of the division was disbanded in November 1943.

Meindl Luftwaffe Division

Formed in early 1942 by Army Group North from the Staff/1st Luftwaffe Sturm Regiment. On 3/6/42 the division had:

1/,2/,3/,4/1st Luftwaffe Field Regiment
1/,2/,3/,4/2nd Luftwaffe Field Regiment
1/,2/,3/,4/3rd Luftwaffe Field Regiment
1/,2/,3/,4/4th Luftwaffe Field Regiment

1/,2/,3/,4/5th Luftwaffe Field Regiment
Staff/14th Luftwaffe Field Regiment
Luftwaffe Signals Battalion
1st Luftwaffe Ski Battalion (attached)

In December 1942 the division was broken into the 21st and 22nd Luftwaffe Field Divisions and three Luftwaffe Field Battalions.

Luftwaffenjäger Brigade

Formed from the Ramcke Parachute Brigade in August 1942 in North Africa. It contained:

1/3rd Fallschirmjäger Regiment
2/,3/1st Luftlande-Sturm Regiment (5th Fallschirmjäger and later Hermann Göring Jäger Regiment)
Barenthin Luftwaffe Regiment.

The brigade was destroyed in Tunis on 1 May 1943.

1st Fallschirm-Armee

Formed in March 1944 from the XI Fliegerkorps. The army troops assigned to it consisted of the:

Senior ARKO 1st Fallschirmjäger Army Corps
1st Luftwaffe Fallschirm Signals Regiment (later 21st)
1st Luftwaffe Fallschirm Armee Supply Troops
  1st Supply Battalion (late 21st Fallschirm)
  Transport Battalion, 1st Fallschirm Armee (later 21st)
  Ambulance Battalion, 1st Fallschirm Armee (later 21st)
Feldersatz Battalion, Fallschirmjäger Armee
Sturm Battalion, Fallschirmjäger Armee
1st Fallschirm Bicycle Battalion
1st Fallschirm Werfer Battalion

Convalescence Battalion, Fallschirmjäger Army
21st Fallschirmjäger Lehr Regiment
21st Sturmgeschütz Brigade
21st Transportation Battalion

The "Senior ARKO" or "*Höherer Artilleriekommandeur der Fallschirm-Armee 1*" was formed in January 1944 in France as army troops for the 1st Fallschirm Army. The 1/,2/,3/21st Fallschirmjäger-Lehr-Regiment was formed in February 1944 from the 1/7th Fallschirmjäger Regiment and was designated as the Fallschirmjäger Lehr Regiment. In June 1944, while in Nantes, it was renamed the 21st Fallschirmjäger Lehr. It was rebuilt 2/11/45, after heavy losses, and was renamed 210th on 3/28//45. The regiment saw action at Arnhem in October 1944 and Roermund in February 1945. I contained three battalions and the 13th–16th Companies.

The 1st Fallschirm Panzer Regiment began formation in January 1944 as an army troop (attached to 1st Fallschirm Army, with two battalions—each four companies (1st Battalion 1st–4th Companies & 2nd Battalion 5th–8th Companies). It was renamed the 21st Fallschirm Panzer Regiment in June 1944. Formation was never completed and it never saw any combat. It was officially disbanded August 1944.

The 1st Fallschirm Bicycle Battalion began formation in January 1944 as an army troop for the 1st Fallschirm Army, with five companies. It was renamed the 21st Fallschirm Bicycle Battalion in June 1944. Its formation was never completed and it never saw any combat. It was officially disbanded in August 1944.

The 21st Fallschirm Sturmgeschütz Brigade was formed in January 1944 with four batteries. It was renamed the 1st Luftwaffe Sturmgeschütz Brigade in April 1944 and renamed the 11th Fallschirm Sturmgeschütz Brigade in June 1944. It fought mainly in Italy, but moved to western Europe in 1945 and operated independently. On 3/12/45 it was attached to the 5th Fallschirmjäger Division at Nieder-Breisig. On 3/28/45 it was renamed the 111th Fallschirm Sturmgeschütz Brigade.

The 1st Heavy Werfer Battalion (schwere Werfer-Abteilung der Fallschirm-Armee 1) was formed in January 1944 with four batteries. It was renamed the 21st Fallschirm Werfer Battalion in June 1944. On 3/28/45 it was renamed the 210st Fallschirm Werfer Battalion.

The 1st Fallschirm Pioneer Regiment was formed in January 1944 with three battalions, and was renamed the 21st Fallschirm Pioneer Regiment in June 1944. The regiment was disbanded in June or July 1944. The 2nd Battalion was renamed 2nd Fallschirm Pioneer Ersatz und Ausbildungs Battalion. A new 1st Battalion (1st—4th companys) was formed in July 1944 from XI Fliegerkorps Corps Pioneer Battalion. The staff was re-formed in December 1944, but was disbanded in January 1945. The 2nd Battalion (5th–8th coys) was re-formed January 1945, but was attached to the 8th Fallschirmjäger Division. On 3/15/45 the 1st Battalion was renamed Fallschirm Pioneer Battalion z.b.V. Hermann Göring. Each battalion theoretically contained 520 men and had of three pioneer companies and a 4th heavy machine-gun company.

The 1st Fallschirm Army Signals Regiment was organized with three battalions. In theory, each battalion had 379 men and consisted of two companies (1st radio and 2nd telephone) and a light supply column. It was formed on 11/30/43, with the Staff/,1/,2/3rd Battalion being formed the 41st Luftwaffe Signals Battalion (1st from 4/41 and 2nd from 3/41). In June 1944 it was redesignated the 21st Fallschirm Army Signals Regiment and on 3/28/45 it was renamed the 210th Fallschirm Army Signals Regiment.

The 1st Fallschirm Supply Battalion was formed in June 1944 from the XI Fliegerkorps Supply Battalion and the XI Fliegerkorps' Schützen Company z.b.V. (as 3rd Coy). When it was renumbered the 21st Battalion is not known, but on 3/28/45 it was redesignated the 210th Fallschirm Supply Battalion.

The Ambulance Battalion of the 1st Fallschirm Army was formed in January 1944 in France with four companies. In June 1944 it was renumbered the 21st Fallschirm Medical Training Battalion and raised to a strength of six companies. On 3/28/45 it was renumbered the 210th Fallschirm Medical Training Battalion.

The 21st Fallschirm Army Weapons School was formed on 2/11/45 with sixteen companies. However, its formation was canceled on 3/7/45. An order was issued on 3/28/45 redesignating it the 210th, but it had long since ceased to exist.

The Sturm-Bataillon was formed in November 1944 with five companies. Little is known about its history or organization. The *Genesenden-Bataillon der Fallschirm-Armee 1.* was formed in August 1944 with five companies using 4/3rd Fallschirmjäger Ersatz und Ausbildung Regiment in Gardelegen.

In May 1944 OKH records show the Army troops were theoretically organized and equipped as follows:

21st Fallschirmjäger Panzer Regiment
1 Regimental Staff (10 LMGs) & Staff Company (6 tanks)
1 Panzer Maintenance Company (8 LMGs)
1st & 2nd Panzer Battalions
1 Battalion Staff (27 LMGs) & Staff Company (12 tanks)
4 Panzer Companies (5 Mk II & 14 Mk IV tanks ea)
1 (mot) Panzer Supply Column
21st Fallschirmjäger Pioneer Regiment
1 Pioneer Regimental Staff
1 (mot) Fallschirmjäger Radio Platoon (2 LMGs)
3 (mot) Battalions, each with
1 (mot) Fallschirmjäger Radio Platoon (2 LMGs)
4 Fallschirmjäger Pioneer Companies (2 HMGS, 11 LMGs & 2 80mm mortars ea)
1 (mot) Pioneer Light Supply Column
21st Fallschirmjäger Signals Regiment
3 Battalions, each with
3 Various Companies
1 (mot) Light Supply Column
1 Air Liaison Signals Detachment
Fallschirmjäger (mot) Lehr Battalion
1 Fallschirmjäger Battalion Staff (2 LMGs)
1 (mot) Fallschirmjäger Radio Platoon (2 LMGs)

3 (mot) Companies (20 LMGs & 3 80mm mortars)

1 (mot) Machine Gun Company (8 HMGs, 2 LMGs, 2 75mm leIG, & 4 80mm mortars)

21st Heavy Nebelwerfer Battalion

1 Battalion Staff & Staff Battery (3 LMGs)

4 (motZ) Batteries (6 300mm launchers, 1 unknown PAK & 7 LMGs)

21st Fallschirmjäger Bicycle Battalion

3 Fallschirmjäger Bicycle Companies (2 HMGs & 13 LMGs ea)

2 Fallschirmjäger Motorcycle Companies (4 HMGS, 19 LMGs, & 2 80mm mortars ea)

21st Military Police Battalion

3 (mot) Companies (9 LMGs ea)

21st Fallschirmjäger Army Supply Troops

21st Fallschirmjäger Supply Battalion

4 (mot) Supply Companies (10 LMGs ea)

21st Transportation Battalion

4 (mot) 240 ton Transportation Companies (9 LMGs ea)

21st Administration Troops

10 various companies

21st Medical Evacuation Detachment

9 various companies

In November 1944, after the subordination of the 15th Army, it was temporarily renamed Army Group Student. On 3/28/45 all of the army troops were renumbered as the 210th.

Generalkommando I Fallschirm-Korps

Formed in January 1944 from the Generalkommando II Luftwaffen-Feldkorps, it contained:

122nd ARKO (Army)

Luftwaffe Signals Battalion of the I Fallschirm-Korps

I Luftwaffe Corps Reconnaissance Battalion (became 11th Fallschirm Reconnaissance Battalion)

I Luftwaffe Corps Artillery Regiment (became the 11th Fallschirm Artillery Regiment)

1st Luftwaffe Sturmgeschütz Battalion (became the 11th Fallschirm Sturmgeschütz Brigade)

1st Fallschirm Flak Regiment (June 1944) (became 11th Fallschirm Flak Regiment

1st Fallschirm Machine Gun Battalion

11th Fallschirm Supply Detachment

In May 1944 OKH records show the corps forces organized and equipped as follows:

Corps Staff

1 Corps Staff

1 Air Liaison Detachment

676th (mot) Military Police Troop (5 LMGs)

1 (mot) Mapping Detachment

11th Fallschirmjäger Reconnaissance Battalion

1st Armored Car Company (25 LMGs, 18 20mm & 6 StuGs)

1 Half Track Reconnaissance Battalion

2 Companies (47 LMGs & 2 80mm mortars ea)

1 Company

1 Staff Platoon (3 LMGs)

1 Pioneer Platoon (13 LMGs)

1 Infantry Gun Section (4 LMGs & 2 75mm leIG)

1 Flak Platoon (2 LMGs & 4 20mm guns)

1 Panzerjäger Platoon (3 LMGs & 3 75mm PAK 40)

1 Panzerjäger Platoon (7 LMGs & 6 75mm PAK 40)

1 (mot) Supply Company

11th Sturmgeschütz Brigade

1 Brigade Staff (1 LMG) & Staff Battery (2 LMGs)

3 Sturmgeschütz Batteries (10 StuGs & 12 LMGs ea)

11th Fallschirmjäger Flak Regiment

1 Regimental Staff (4 LMGs)

3 Battalions, each with

1 Battalion Staff (4 LMGs)

3 (motZ) Heavy Flak Batteries (4 88mm, 3 20mm & 4 LMGs)

1 Self Propelled Medium Flak Battery (12 37mm & 6 LMGs)

1 Self Propelled Light Fallschirmjäger Battery (12 20mm guns)

1 (mot) Heavy (60 ton) Flak Supply Column

11th Fallschirmjäger Artillery Regiment

1 Regimental Staff & (mot) Staff Battery (2 LMGs)

1 Observation Battery (2 LMGs)

1st & 2nd Battalions, each with
  1 Battalion Staff & (mot) Staff Battery (2 LMGs)
  4 Heavy Howitzer Batteries (4 150mm sFH & 5 LMGs ea)
  1 (mot) Light Artillery Supply Column
3rd Battalion
  1 Battalion Staff & (mot) Staff Battery (2 LMGs)
  1 Heavy Gun Batteries (4 100mm K 18 guns & 5 LMGs ea)
  1 (mot) Light Artillery Supply Column
11th Fallschirmjäger Signals Battalion
  1 (mot) Fallschirmjäger Radio Company

1 (mot) Fallschirmjäger Telephone Company
1 (mot) Fallschirmjäger Intercept Company
1 (mot) Signals Supply Column
11th Fallschirmjäger Supply Troop Command
  10th (120 ton) (mot) Transportation Column (9 LMGs)
  11th (mot) Supply Company (10 LMGs)
  11th (mot) Maintenance Company (5 LMGs)
  941st (mot) Field Post Office

Generalkommando II Fallschirm-Korps

Formed in January 1944 from the Generalkommando Fliegerkorps XIII. It was destroyed in August 1944 in the Falaise Pocket. However, it was re-formed. It contained:

12th Fallschirm Artillery Kommandeur (ARKO)
Luftwaffe Signals Battalion of the II Fallschirm Corps
2nd Luftwaffe Corps Reconnaissance Battalion (June 1944) (became the 12th Fallschirm Reconnaissance Battalion)
2nd Luftwaffe Corps Artillery Regiment (June 1944) (became the 12th Fallschirm Artillery Regiment)
2nd Luftwaffe Sturmgeschütz Battalion (became 12th Fallschirm Sturmgeschütz Brigade)
2nd Fallschirm Flak Regiment (became 12th Fallschirm Flak Regiment)
2nd Fallschirm Machine Gun Battalion
12th Fallschirm Supply Detachment

In May 1944 OKH records show the corps forces organized and equipped as follows:

Corps Staff
  1 Corps Staff
  1 Air Liaison Detachment
  675th (mot) Military Police Troop (5 LMGs)
  1 (mot) Mapping Detachment
12th Fallschirm Reconnaissance Battalion
  1st Armored Car Company (25 LMGs, 18 20mm & 6 StuGs)
  1 Half Track Reconnaissance Battalion
    2 Companies (47 LMGs & 2 80mm mortars ea)
    1 Company
      1 Staff Platoon (3 LMGs)
      1 Pioneer Platoon (13 LMGs)
      1 Infantry Gun Section (4 LMGs & 2 75mm leIG)

    1 Flak Platoon (2 LMGs & 4 20mm guns)
    1 Panzerjäger Platoon (3 LMGs & 3 75mm PAK 40)
    1 Panzerjäger Platoon (7 LMGs & 6 75mm PAK 40)
  1 (mot) Supply Company
12th Sturmgeschütz Brigade
  1 Brigade Staff (1 LMG) & Staff Battery (2 LMGs)
  3 Sturmgeschütz Batteries (10 StuGs & 12 LMGs ea)
12th Fallschirm Artillery Regiment
  1 Regimental Staff & (mot) Staff Battery (2 LMGs)
  1 Observation Battery (2 LMGs)
1st & 2nd Battalions each with
  1 Battalion Staff & (mot) Staff Battery (2 LMGs)
  4 Heavy Howitzer Batteries (4 150mm sFH & 5 LMGs ea)
  1 (mot) Light Artillery Supply Column
3rd Battalion
  1 Battalion Staff & (mot) Staff Battery (2 LMGs)
  1 Heavy Gun Batteries (4 100mm K 18 guns & 5 LMGs ea)
  1 (mot) Light Artillery Supply Column
12th Fallschirm Flak Regiment
  1 Regimental Staff (4 LMGs)
  3 Battalions, each with
    1 Battalion Staff (4 LMGs)
    3 (motZ) Heavy Flak Batteries (4 88mm, 3 20mm & 4 LMGs)
    1 Self Propelled Medium Flak Battery (12 37mm & 6 LMGs)
    1 Self Propelled Light Fallschirmjäger Battery (12 20mm guns)
    1 (mot) Heavy (60 ton) Flak Supply Column
12th Fallschirm Signals Battalion
  1 (mot) Fallschirmjäger Radio Company

1 (mot) Fallschirmjäger Telephone Company
1 (mot) Fallschirmjäger Intercept Company
1 (mot) Signals Supply Column
12th Fallschirm Supply Troop Command
    20th (120 ton) (mot) Transportation Column (9 LMGs)

12th (mot) Supply Company (10 LMGs)
12th (mot) Maintenance Company (5 LMGs)
942nd (mot) Field Post Office

1st Fallschirmjäger (Parachute) Division

Formed on 5/1/43 in southern France by renaming the 7th Flieger Division:

    1/,2/,3/1st Fallschirmjäger (Parachute) Regiment
    2/,3/,4/3rd Fallschirmjäger Regiment
    1/,2/,3/4th Fallschirmjäger Regiment
    1st Fallschirm Panzerjäger Battalion (6 companies, reduced to 3 in 1943)
    1/,3/1st Fallschirm Artillery Regiment
    1/,4/1st Fallschirm Flak Battalion
    1st Fallschirm Pioneer Battalion (4 companies)
    Luftnachrichten (Communications & Signal) Battalion
        Fallschirmjäger Division (2 companies)
    1st Fallschirm Divisional (Einheiten) Support Units

The 1/1st Fallschirmjäger Regiment was formed at Stendal 4/1/38, from the 4/Regiment General Göring (Landespolizei). The 2/1st Fallschirmjäger Regiment was formed 1/1/39 from the Army Fallschirm Battalion in Braunschweig, together with an all new 3/1st Fallschirmjäger Regiment in Gardelegen. The regiment did not receive a staff until 6/1/39, when a staff was formed in Stendal. The regiment began the war with three battalions, each with four companies.

In February 1944 the division detached the 3/1st Fallschirmjäger Regiment to the 3rd Fallschirmjäger Division. In March 1944 a new 3/1st Fallschirmjäger Regiment had to be formed when the old 3/1st Fallschirmjäger Regiment was detached and used to create the 3rd Fallschirmjäger Division.

Organization 1939
    1st Battalion (1st–4th companies)
    2nd Battalion (5th–8th companies)
    3rd Battalion (9th–12th companies)
Organization 1940
    1st Battalion (1st–4th companies)
    2nd Battalion (5th–8th companies)
    3rd Battalion (9th–12th companies)
    13th (Panzerjäger) Company
    13th (120mm mortar) Company

Organization 1944
    1st Battalion (1st–4th companies)
    2nd Battalion (5th–8th companies)
    3rd Battalion (9th–12th companies)
    13th (Panzerjäger) Company
    14th (120mm mortar) Company
    15th (Pioneer) Company

The 3rd Fallschirmjäger Regiment was formed on 6/1/40 with 3 battalions (3rd formed 8/1/40), from cadres of the 1st Fallschirmjäger Regiment. The 4/3rd Fallschirmjäger Regiment was formed in the summer 1943. 1/3rd Fallschirmjäger Regiment was transferred to Africa in June 1942, joining Brigade Ramcke, and was destroyed in Tunisia May 1943. The new 4/3rd Fallschirmjäger Regiment was soon redesignated 1/3rd Fallschirmjäger Regiment. In March 1944 the 3/3rd Fallschirmjäger Regiment was used to form the 5th Fallschirmjäger Division, by becoming the 1/13th Fallschirmjäger Regiment. A new 3/3rd Fallschirmjäger Regiment was formed in May 1944.

Organization 1940
    1st Battalion (1st–4th companies)
    2nd Battalion (5th–8th companies)
    3rd Battalion (9th–12th companies)
    13th (Panzerjäger) Company
    14th (120mm mortar) Company
Organization 1944
    1st Battalion (1st–4th companies)
    2nd Battalion (5th–8th companies)
    3rd Battalion (9th–12th companies)
    4th Battalion (15th–18th companies)
    13th (Panzerjäger) Company
    14th (120mm mortar) Company
Organization 1944
    1st Battalion (1st–4th companies)
    2nd Battalion (5th–8th companies)
    3rd Battalion (9lh–12th companies)
    13th (Panzerjäger) Company
    14th (120mm mortar) Company
    15th (Pioneer) Company

The 3rd Fallschirmjäger Regiment saw action independently under 7th Flieger Division, but from May 1943 served with the 1st Fallschirmjäger Division. It served in Crete, Russia, and the 1st Battalion served as part of the Ramcke Brigade in Africa.

The 4th Fallschirmjäger Regiment was formed in September 1942 with three battalions (3rd Bn from 3/2nd Fallschirmjäger Regiment). In April 1944 the 3/4th Fallschirmjäger Regiment was used to form the 5th Fallschirmjäger Division, and was used to form the 1/14th Fallschirmjäger Regiment. A replacement battalion was raised in the original 4th Regiment.

Organization 1944
    1st Battalion (1st–4th companies)
    2nd Battalion (5th–8th companies)
    3rd Battalion (9th–12th companies)
    4th Battalion (15th–18th companies)
    13th (Panzerjäger) Company
    14th (120mm mortar) Company

The 4th Fallschirmjäger Regiment saw action independently under the 7th Flieger Division, but from May 1943 served with the 1st Fallschirmjäger Division.

The 1st Fallschirm Panzerjäger Battalion was formed in 1939 as 7th Anti-Tank Company for the 7th Flieger Division, and in 1940 was renamed the Fallschirm Panzerjäger Battalion. Its equipment seems to have varied considerably. In 1943 it is known to have had 50mm PAK 38, 42mm PAK 41 and Marder II with 75mm PAK 40. At Monte Cassino Gefreiter Fries, from the 2nd Company, commanded the dug-in Panther tank turret. He received the Knight's Cross on 9/5/44 for knocking out 17 Allied tanks between 21 and 22 May 1944.

The 1st Fallschirm Flak Battalion was formed in 1940 as the Fallschirm Flak Battalion. It contained four batteries and was assigned to the 7th Flieger Division. In May 1943 it was renamed 1st Fallschirm Flak Battalion (containing only the 1st and 4th Companies), was attached to 1st Fallschirmjäger Division. During the winter of 1943/44 the flak battalion was raised from four to five batteries.

The 1st Fallschirm Artillery Regiment had been formed in summer 1938 as 7th Gun Battery. In the summer of 1940 it was expanded and became the Fallschirm Artillery Battalion. In the winter of 1941/1942 it was enlarged and became the 1st Fallschirm Artillery Regiment with two battalions. The 3/1st Fallschirm Artillery Regiment was formed a year later. During the winter of 1943/44 the artillery regiment was raised to a full regiment with three battalions (nine batteries). In February 1943 2/1st Fallschirm Artillery Regiment was redesignated 1/2nd Fallschirm Artillery Regiment. In May 1943 the 1st Fallschirm Artillery Regiment was assigned to the division. At the same time Fallschirm Panzerjäger Battalion was renamed 1st Fallschirm Panzerjäger Battalion, established with six companies and assigned to the division.

In January 1944 the 1st Fallschirm Flak Battalion was reinforced to five batteries. In theory the battalion contained 824 men and contained a total of 18 88mm AA guns and 18 20mm AA guns. In 1944, probably about the same time, the 1st Fallschirm Panzerjäger Battalion was reduced to five companies, and later to four companies. Replacement troops were provided by Fallschirm-Ersatz Battalion1 in Aschersleben.

In June 1944 the 1st Fallschirm Artillery Regiment was reorganized, with 3/1st Fallschirm Artillery Regiment becoming 2/1st Fallschirm Artillery Regiment and a new 3/1st Fallschirm Artillery Regiment was formed from scratch.

Organization 1941
    1st Battalion (1st–4th Batteries)
    2nd Battalion (5–8th Batteries)
Organization 1942
    1st Battalion (1st–3rd Batteries)
    2nd Battalion (4–6 Batteries)
    3rd Battalion (7–9 Batteries)
    4th Battalion (13–16th Batteries)
Organization 1943
    1st Battalion (1st–3rd Batteries)
    2nd Battalion (4–6 Batteries)
    4th Battalion (13–16th Batteries)
Organization 1944
    1st Battalion (1st–3rd Batteries)
    2nd Battalion (4–6 Batteries)
    3rd Battalion (7–9 Batteries)

After the invasion of Crete the remains of the division were reorganized and attached to Army Group North. In October it was organized and equipped as follows:

7th Flieger Division
    1 Signals Company
    1st Fallschirmjäger Regiment
        1 Signals Platoon
        1 Pioneer Platoon
        3 Battalions, each with
            1 Signals Platoon
            4 Fallschirmjäger Companies
        13th (Infantry Gun) Company
        14th (Panzerjäger) Company
        2nd Company, Fallschirmjäger Panzerjäger Battalion
    3rd Fallschirmjäger Regiment
        1 Signals Platoon

1 Pioneer Platoon
3 Battalions, each with
  1 Signals Platoon
  4 Fallschirmjäger Companies
13th (Infantry Gun) Company
14th (Panzerjäger) Company
2nd Company, Fallschirmjäger Flak Battalion (20mm guns)
Fallschirmjäger Pioneer Battalion
  1 Signals Platoon
  3 Fallschirmjäger Pioneer Companies
Fallschirmjäger Artillery Battalion
  1 Signals Platoon
  2 Artillery Batteries (6 75mm mountain guns)
2nd Co/Fallschirmjäger Medical Battalion

On 1 February 1944 the division was organized and equipped as follows:

Division Headquarters
1 Division Staff
1 Fallschirmjäger Motorcycle Platoon
1 (mot Military Police Detachment (3 LMGs)

1st Fallschirmjäger Regiment
1 Fallschirmjäger Regimental Staff
1 Fallschirm Signals Platoon
1 Fallschirmjäger Bicycle Platoon
1 Fallschirm Pioneer Platoon

1st Fallschirmjäger Battalion
1 Fallschirmjäger Battalion Staff
1 Fallschirm Signals Platoon
3 Fallschirmjäger Companies (20 LMGs & 2 120mm mortars)
1 Heavy Fallschirmjäger Company (8 HMGs, 3 LMGs, 4 120mm mortars & 2 75mm leIG guns)

2nd Fallschirmjäger Battalion
1 Fallschirmjäger Battalion Staff
1 Fallschirm Signals Platoon
3 Fallschirmjäger Companies (20 LMGs & 2 120mm mortars)
1 Heavy Fallschirmjäger Company (8 HMGs, 3 LMGs, 4 120mm mortars & 2 75mm leIG guns)

3rd Fallschirmjäger Battalion
1 Fallschirmjäger Battalion Staff
1 Fallschirm Signals Platoon
3 Fallschirmjäger Companies (20 LMGs & 2 120mm mortars)
1 Heavy Fallschirmjäger Company (8 HMGs, 3 LMGs, 4 120mm mortars & 2 75mm leIG guns)

13th Fallschirmjäger Nebelwerfer Company (9 150mm launchers)

14th Fallschirm Panzerjäger Company (12 75mm PAK)

1 (mot) Fallschirmjäger Supply Column
3rd Fallschirmjäger Regiment
same as 1st Fallschirmjäger Regiment
4th Fallschirmjäger Regiment
same as 1st Fallschirmjäger Regiment
1/1st Fallschirm Artillery Regiment
1 Fallschirm Artillery Battalion Staff & Staff Battery
1 Fallschirm Signals Platoon
3 Fallschirmjäger Light Howitzer Batteries (4 105mm light guns each)
1 (mot) Artillery Supply Column
1st Fallschirm Panzerjäger Battalion
1 Fallschirm Panzerjäger Battalion Staff
1 Signals Platoon
3 Fallschirm Panzerjäger Batteries (12 75mm PAK each)
1st Fallschirm Pioneer Battalion
1 Fallschirm Pioneer Battalion Staff
1 Fallschirm Signals Platoon
4 Fallschirm Pioneer Companies (2 HMGs, 9 LMGs & 2 120mm mortars ea)
1st Fallschirm Flak Battalion
1 Fallschirm Flak Battalion Staff
1 (mot) Signals Platoon
3 (motZ) Heavy Flak Batteries (4 88mm guns)
1 Self Propelled Medium Flak Battery (12 37mm guns)
1 Fallschirmjäger Self Propelled Light Flak Battery (12 20mm guns)
1 (mot) Flak Supply Column
1st Fallschirm Signals Battalion
1 Fallschirm Signals Battalion Staff
1 (mot) Fallschirm Radio Company
1 (mot) Fallschirmjäger Telephone Intercept Company
1 (mot) Signals Supply Column
1st Fallschirm Medical Battalion
1/,2/1st (mot) Fallschirm Medical Companies
1st Fallschirmjäger Field Hospital
3 (mot) Ambulance Companies
Division Support Units
1 (mot) Supply Staff
1 (mot) Supply Company
1 (mot) Heavy Fuel Column
1 (mot) Heavy Supply Column
4 (mot) Light Supply Columns
2 (mot) Maintenance Companies
1 (mot) Divisional Administration Detachment
1 (mot) Bakery Company
1 (mot) Butcher Company
1 (mot) Field Post Office

By March 1944 the artillery regiment stood as follows:

1/1st Fallschirm Artillery Regiment
1 Fallschirm Artillery Battalion Staff & Staff Battery
1 Fallschirm Signals Platoon
1st–3rd Fallschirmjäger Light Gun Batteries (4 75mm Mountain guns)
1 (mot) Artillery Supply Column

3/1st Fallschirm Artillery Regiment
1 Fallschirm Artillery Battalion Staff & Staff Battery
1 Fallschirm Signals Platoon
7–9th Fallschirmjäger Medium Gun Batteries (4 100mm mountain guns)
1 (mot) Artillery Supply Column

In July 1944 the division was organized and equipped as follows:

Divisional Staff
1 Divisional Staff (6 LMGs)
1 Fallschirmjäger Motorcycle Platoon (12 LMGs)
1 (mot) Military Police Detachment

1st, 3rd & 4th Fallschirmjäger Regiments, each with
1 Fallschirmjäger Regimental Staff (3 LMGs)
1 (mot) Fallschirmjäger Signals Platoon (2 LMGs)
1 Fallschirmjäger Bicycle Platoon (3 LMGs)
3 Fallschirmjäger Battalions, each with
1 Fallschirmjäger Battalion Staff (2 LMGs)
1 (mot) Fallschirmjäger Signals Platoon (2 LMGs)
3 Fallschirmjäger Companies (20 LMGs & 3 80mm mortars)
1 Fallschirmjäger Heavy Company (8 HMGs, 2 LMGs, 2 75mm leIG & 4 80mm mortars)
13th (mot) Fallschirmjäger Mortar Company (9 120mm mortars & 6 LMGs)
14th (motZ) Fallschirmjäger Panzerjäger Company (12 75mm PAK & 12 LMGs)
15th (mot) Fallschirmjäger Pioneer Company (2 HMGs, 11 LMGs & 2 80mm mortars)
(mot) Fallschirmjäger Supply Column

1st (mot) Fallschirm Mortar Battalion
1 (mot) Fallschirm Mortar Battalion Staff
1 (mot) Fallschirm Mortar Battalion Staff Battery (4 LMGs)
3 (mot) Fallschirm Mortar Companies (12 120mm mortars & 14 LMGs ea)

1st Fallschirmjäger Artillery Regiment
1 Fallschirmjäger Artillery Regimental Staff
1 (mot) Fallschirmjäger Artillery Regimental Staff Battery (2 LMGs)
1st & 2nd Battalions, each with
1 Battalion Staff & (mot) Staff Battery (2 LMGs)
3 Batteries (4 105mm leFH & 5 LMGs ea)
1 (mot) Supply Column
3rd Battalion
1 Battalion Staff & (mot) Staff Battery (2 LMGs)

3 Batteries (4 150mm sFH & 5 LMGs ea)
1 (mot) Supply Column

1st (mot) Fallschirm Panzerjäger Battalion
1 (mot) Fallschirmjäger Signals Platoon (2 LMGs)
3 (motZ) Fallschirmjäger Panzerjäger Companies (12 75mm PAK & 12 LMGs)

1st Fallschirm Flak Battalion
1 (mot) Flak Battalion Staff
3 (motZ) Heavy Flak Batteries (6 88mm, 3 20mm & 4 LMGs)
1 Self Propelled Medium Flak Battery (12 37mm & 6 LMGs)
1 Self Propelled Fallschirmjäger Light Flak Battery (12 20mm & 6 LMGs)
1 (mot) Heavy Flak Supply Column

1st Fallschirm Pioneer Battalion
1 (mot) Fallschirmjäger Battalion Staff
1 (mot) Fallschirmjäger Signals Platoon (2 LMGs)
4 (mot) Fallschirmjäger Pioneer Companies (2 HMGS, 11 LMGs, 2 80mm mortars)
1 (mot) Pioneer Supply Column

1st Fallschirm Signals Battalion
1 (mot) Fallschirmjäger Signals Company
1 (mot) Fallschirmjäger Radio Company (5 LMGs)
1 (mot) Fallschirmjäger Signals Supply Column

1st Fallschirm Supply Troop
1 (mot) Supply Troop Staff (2 LMGs)
2 (mot) 120ton Transportation Companies (9 LMGs)
1 (mot) Supply Company (10 LMGs)
1 (mot) Maintenance Company (5 LMGs)
1 (mot) Maintenance Platoon (2 LMGs)

1st Fallschirm Medical Battalion
11th & 12th (mot) Fallschirmjäger Medical Companies (9 LMGs ea)
11th & 12th Fallschirmjäger Ambulances (attached)
1 (mot) Field Hospital (6 LMGs) (1 Ambulance (attached)

Other
1 (mot) Bakery Company (3 LMGs)
1 (mot) Butcher Company (1 LMG)
1 (mot) Divisional Administration Platoon (2 LMGs)
927th (mot) Field Post Office (2 LMGs)

In December 1944 the 1st Fallschirmjäger Feldersatz (replacement) Battalion was raised. On 2/16/45 a generic Fallschirmjäger organization was established.

In late May 1943 the division was stationed in Flers (near Avignon), in reserve, under the XI Fliegerkorps/ Heeresgruppe D. The first parts of the division arrived in Sicily on 8/12/43, directly under XIV Corps, and immediately went into combat defending the island. Was the last unit to leave Sicily on 9/17/43. The division rested in Calabria during the remainder of August and

early September and remained in Italy for the remainder of the war.

2nd Fallschirmjäger Division

The division was formed in February 1943 in Western France (Vannes/Bretagne area) under the 7th Army. The division was formed using the 2nd Fallschirmjäger Regiment and the 2/1st Fallschirm Artillery Regiment. The two new regiments, 6th and 7th Fallschirmjäger Regiments, were formed from various other units: 100th Luftwaffe Feld Battalion, 4/1st Luftlande-Sturm-Regiment and the Lehr-Bataillon/XI Fliegerkorps. The division initially consisted of the following units:

1/,2/,3/2nd Fallschirmjäger Regiment
1/,2/,3/6th Fallschirmjäger Regiment
1/,2/,3/7th Fallschirmjäger Regiment
2nd Fallschirm Panzerjäger Battalion (5 companies)
1/2nd Fallschirm Artillery Regiment (4 batteries)
2nd Fallschirm Pioneer Battalion (4 companies)
2nd Fallschirm Medical Battalion (2 coys)
Luftnachrichten (Communications & Signal) Battalion
2nd Fallschirmjäger Division (2 companies)
2nd Fallschirm Divisional (Einheiten) Support Units

During 1944 the following units were raised in Italy:

2nd Fallschirm Flak Battalion (5 batteries) (raised in early 1944)
2nd Fallschirm Machine Gun Battalion (3 companies) (formed from the 3/Barenthin Luftwaffe Regiment)

The 2nd Fallschirmjäger Regiment was formed on 8/26/39 with 1/,2/2nd Fallschirmjäger Regiment (1st at Gardelegen, 2nd at Tangermünde) from cadres of 1st Fallschirmjäger Regiment. The Stab and 3/2nd 1st Fallschirmjäger Regiment was formed 7/1/40. In September 1942 3/2nd Fallschirmjäger Regiment was redesignated 3/4th Fallschirmjäger Regiment, and was replaced in 1943. The 1/2nd Fallschirmjäger Regiment remained in Italy when the 2nd Fallschirmjäger-Division moved to Russia in December 1943, and was redesignated 1/10th 1st Fallschirmjäger Regiment. A new 1st Battalion was formed later, but it never joined the rest of the regiment and operated independently on the Western front. It was used to re-form the new 2nd Fallschirmjäger Regiment in Amersfoort, Holland.

The main part of the regiment was destroyed when Brest fell on 9/19/44. It was re-formed December 1944 in Amersfoort, and finally surrendered in the Ruhr pocket.

Prior to February 1943 it fought as an independent unit under the 7th Flieger-Division.

Organization 1939
1st Battalion (1st–4th companies)
2nd Battalion (5th–8th companies)
3rd Battalion (9th–12th companies)
1st Anti-Tank Battery
2nd Anti-Tank Battery
Infantry Gun Battery
Organization 1940
1st Battalion (1st–4th companies)
2nd Battalion (5th–8th companies)
3rd Battalion (9th–12th companies)
13th (Panzerjäger) Company
14th (120mm mortar) Company
Organization 1942
1st Battalion (1st–4th companies)
2nd Battalion (5th–8th companies)
13th (Panzerjäger) Company
14th (120mm mortar) Company
Organization 1943
1st Battalion (1st–4th companies)
2nd Battalion (5th–8th companies)
3rd Battalion (9th–12th companies)
13th (Panzerjäger) Company
14th (120mm mortar) Company
Organization 1944
1st Battalion (1st–4th companies)
2nd Battalion (5th–8th companies)
3rd Battalion (9th–12th companies)
13th (Panzerjäger) Company
14th (120mm mortar) Company
15th (Pioneer) Company

The 6th Fallschirmjäger Regiment was formed in February 1943 in the Vannes/Bretagne area, 1/6th 1st Fallschirmjäger Regiment from 100th Luftwaffe-Feld-Bataillon, 2/6th from 4/1st Luftlande-Sturm-Regiment, and the Staff/,3/6th 1st Fallschirmjäger Regiment were newly raised. When the division left Italy for Russia, the

2/6th Fallschirmjäger Regiment remained behind and became the 1/11th 1st Fallschirmjäger Regiment. The rest of the regiment was disbanded. The 1/6th 1st Fallschirmjäger Regiment became the 1/7th 1st Fallschirmjäger Regiment while the remainder of the regiment was divided between the 2nd and 7th Fallschirmjäger Regiments. In October 1943 the 3/6th Fallschirmjäger Regiment was detached when the division left Italy and used to form the cadre of the 8th Fallschirmjäger Regiment.

The 6th Fallschirmjäger Regiment was re-formed in Köln-Wahn in January 1944. In April 1944 the 6th Fallschirmjäger Regiment moved to Normandy (Lessay/Mont Castre/Carentan area) and was attached to the 91st Luftlande-Division, under LXXXIV Corps/7th AOK. Before 6/6/44 the 1st Fallschirmjäger Regiment was briefly attached to the 2nd Fallschirmjäger Division. The 6th Fallschirmjäger Regiment operated independently for the remainder of the war.

The 7th Fallschirmjäger Regiment was formed in February 1943 in the Vannes/Bretagne area, the 2/7th 7th Fallschirmjäger Regiment was formed from Lehr-Bataillon/XI Fliegerkorps, the rest of the regiment was newly raised. When the division left Italy for Russia, 1/7th Fallschirmjäger Regiment remained behind and became 1/21st Fallschirmjäger-Lehr Regiment. A new 1/7th Fallschirmjäger Regiment was formed from 1/6th Fallschirmjäger Regiment. It surrendered in Brest on 9/19/44. After heavy casualties the 7th Fallschirmjäger Regiment was re-formed in December 1944, in Amersfoort, Holland. It surrendered in April 1945.

Both the 6th and 7th Fallschirmjäger Regiments were organized as follows in 1943 and 1944:

Organization 1943
    1st Battalion (1st–4th companies)
    2nd Battalion (5th–8th companies)
    3rd Battalion (9th–12th companies)
    13th (Panzerjäger) Company
    14th (120mm mortar) Company
Organization 1944
    1st Battalion (1st–4th companies)
    2nd Battalion (5th–8th companies)
    3rd Battalion (9th–12th companies)
    13th (Panzerjäger) Company
    14th (120mm mortar) Company
    15th (Pioneer) Company

The 2nd Fallschirm Artillery Regiment was formed in February 1943 with only 1/2nd Fallschirm Artillery Regiment, which was formed from 2/1st Fallschirm Artillery Regiment. The Staff/,2/,3/2nd Fallschirm Artillery Regiment were formed in May 1944, near Luneville, when the 2nd Fallschirmjäger Division was recovering in Germany.

The 2nd Fallschirm Panzerjäger Battalion was formed in February 1943 with six companies, but by July 1944 it was reduced to three companies. Replacement troops were provided by the 2nd Fallschirm-Ersatz Battalion in Stendal. It is known to have used captured Italian 75/18 M40 assault guns during the early parts of the Italian campaign.

In late May 1943 the division moved to Ales and Nimes, and became subordinated to Fliegerkorps XI/Heeresgruppe D as a strategic reserve, together with the 1st Fallschirmjäger Division. A month later the division was ordered to Italy, and took up station guarding the coast between the Tiber estuary and Tarquinia, now directly under Oberbefehlshaber Süd. On 9/9/43 the unit moved into Rome, to disarm its garrison. The only major resistance was encountered at Monterotondo, which was dealt with by the 2/6th Fallschirmjäger Regiment. Three days later, the 1st Company of 7th Fallschirmjäger Regiment, participated in the rescue of Mussolini at Gran Sasso d'Italia. In the next two months, the division remained stationed near Rome, but part of the division participated in two major actions: 9/17/43 2/7th Fallschirmjäger Regiment at Elba and 11/12/43 1/2nd Fallschirmjäger Regiment at Leros. The rest of the division remained in reserve, subordinated directly to OB Süd. During its stay in Italy the division was joined by the 2nd Fallschirm Machine-Gun and 2nd Fallschirm Flak Battalion.

The Feldersatz Battalion and the 2nd Fallschirm Flak Battalion were formed in December 1943. In theory the flak battalion contained 824 men and consisted of five batteries with a total of 18 88mm AA guns and 18 20mm AA guns.

In place of the 2nd Fallschirmjäger Machine-Gun Battalion, the Fallschirmjäger Granatwerfer (Mortar) Battalion was raised in early 1944. The 6th Fallschirmjäger Regiment was disbanded during the winter and re-formed again in January 1944. The 2nd and 7th Regiment were sent in May to the Wahn Training Camp for refitting and were then joined by the newly reorganized 6th Fallschirmjäger Regiment.

In late November 1943 the division transferred to Shitomir in Russia, now under XXXXII Corps/4th Panzer AOK. Part of the division remained in Italy however, and was used to form the 4th Fallschirmjäger Division. The units were 1/2nd, 2/6th and 1/7th Fallschirmjäger Regiment. At this time the 6th Fallschirmjäger Regiment was disbanded. The 1/6th Fallschirmjäger Regiment became the new 1/7th Fallschirmjäger Regiment. Thus the division arrived in Russia with only two regiments. Until April 1944 the division fought in Russia. On 6/5/44 the division was organized and equipped as follows:

Division Staff
1 Division Staff
1 Division Staff Company (12 LMGs)
1 Bicycle Reconnaissance Company (3 LMGs)
1 (mot) Military Police Troop

2nd Fallschirmjäger Regiment
1 Regimental Staff (2 LMGs & 2 anti-tank rifles)
1 Signals Platoon (2 LMGs & 2 anti-tank rifles)
1 Bicycle Reconnaissance Company (3 LMGs & 2 anti-tank rifles)

1st Battalion
Staff Company (equipment unknown)
1 Signals Platoon
4 Companies (equipment unknown)

2nd Battalion
Staff Company (1 anti-tank rifle & 3 LMGs)
1 Signals Platoon
3 Companies (13 LMGs, 2 80mm mortars, & 3 anti-tank rifles ea)
1 Heavy Company (6 HMGs, 1 recoiless rifle, 3 anti-tank rifles)

3rd Battalion
Staff Company (1 anti-tank rifle, 2 80mm mortars & 3 LMGs)
1 Signals Platoon
3 Companies (16 LMGs, 2 80mm mortars, & 3 anti-tank rifles ea)
1 Heavy Company (6 HMGs, 1 recoiless rifle, 3 anti-tank rifles)

Mortar Company (? 120mm mortars, 4 anti-tank rifles & 8 LMGs)
Infantry Gun Company (6 75mm leIG, 2 150mm sIG, 12 anti-tank rifles & 24 LMGs)
Pioneer Company (4 LMGs & 4 anti-tank rifles)

6th Fallschirmjäger Regiment
Assigned, but not present

7th Fallschirmjäger Regiment
1 Regimental Staff (2 LMGs)
1 Signals Platoon (no weapons indicated
1 Bicycle Reconnaissance Company (6 LMGs)

1st Battalion
Staff Company (1 LMG)
1 Signals Platoon
3 Companies (10 LMGs & 3 anti-tank rifles ea)
1 Heavy Company (2 HMGs, 2 LMGs, 3 80mm mortars)

2nd Battalion
Staff Company (2 anti-tank rifles & 2 LMGs)
1 Signals Platoon
3 Companies (9 LMGs, 2 80mm mortars, & 2 anti-tank rifles)
1 Heavy Company (4 HMGs, 2 LMGs, 3 80mm mortars)

3rd Battalion
Staff Company (2 LMGs)
1 Signals Platoon
3 Companies (9 LMGs, 2 80mm mortars, & 3 anti-tank rifles)
1 Heavy Company (2 HMGs, 2 LMGs, 3 anti-tank rifles, 4 80mm mortars)

Mortar Company (? 120mm mortars, 10 anti-tank rifles & 10 LMGs)
Infantry Gun Company (? leIG & sIG, 24 anti-tank rifles & 17 LMGs)
Pioneer Company (4 LMGs & 4 anti-tank rifles)

I/2nd Artillery Regiment
1 Staff Battery (4 LMGs)
1 Radio Platoon
3 Batteries (4 105mm recoiless rifles & 8 LMGs ea)
1 (mot) Light Supply Column

Flak Battalion (not present)
1st–3rd (motZ) Heavy Flak Batteries (4 88mm & 3 20mm guns)
4th (Self Propelled) Flak Company (9 37mm flak guns)
5th (Self Propelled) Flak Company (12 20mm flak guns)
(Self Propelled) Flak Platoon (3 quad 20mm flak guns)
(motZ/self-propelled) Platoon (? 78mm guns)

2nd Fallschirmjäger Panzerjäger Battalion
1 Battalion Staff (4 LMGs)
1 Radio Platoon
4th, 5th & 6th Batteries (4 75mm PAK, 12 LMGs & 12 anti-tank rifles)

2nd Fallschirmjäger Pioneer Battalion
4 Pioneer Companies (14 LMGs ea)

2nd Fallschirmjäger Signals Battalion
1st (mot) Signals Company (7 LMGs)
2nd (mot) Radio Company (7 LMGs)
1 (mot) Light Supply Column (2 LMGs)

Medical Troops
1 (mot) Medical Company (10 LMGs)
1 (mot) Medical Company (no weapons indicated)
1 Field Hospital (8 LMGs)

Administration Troops
1 (mot) Field Post Office
1 (mot) Bakery Company
1 (mot) Butcher Company
1 (mot) Administrative Platoon

Supply Troops
1 (mot) Ordnance Platoon
1 (mot) Maintenance Platoon
2 (mot) Transportation Companies
4 (mot) Light Supply Companies
1 (mot) Heavy Supply Company

1 (mot) Heavy Fuel Column
1 (mot) Supply Company

The Schirmer Fallschirmjäger Battalion was detached in January 1944 to form the cadre of the 16th Fallschirmjäger Regiment. By the invasion of Normandy the re-formed 6th Fallschirmjäger Regiment was assigned to the 91st Luftlande Division in Normandy. At the time of the invasion the division contained:

Division Staff
1/,2/,3/2nd Fallschirmjäger Regiment
1/,2/,3/6th Fallschirmjäger Regiment
1/,2/,3/7th Fallschirmjäger Regiment
1/,2/,3/2nd Fallschirm Artillery Regiment (3 btrys per bn)
2nd Fallschirm Panzerjäger Battalion
2nd Fallschirm Flak Battalion (5 coys)
2nd Fallschirm Mortar Battalion (3 coys)
2nd Fallschirm Pioneer Battalion (4 coys)
2nd Fallschirm Signals Battalion
2nd Fallschirm Medical Battalion
2nd Fallschirm Feldersatz Battalion
Feldersatz Battalion, 2nd Fallschirmjäger Division (5 companies)
2nd Fallschirm Divisional Supply Troop

In May 1944 the depleted division moved to Köln-Wahn for a period of rest and rebuilding. In less than a month the division was on the move again, this time to Normandy, now under XXV Corps/7th AOK. There it was joined by the new 6th Fallschirmjäger Regiment, however this was to be shortlived, on D-Day the regiment again became independent. The division saw only little combat in June 1944, and in July was in reserve, under 7th AOK, in the Quimper-Landerneau area. In August and September the division participated in the defense of Brest (XXV Corps, directly under Heeresgruppe D). When Brest fell on 9/19/44, the division surrendered, except for the 6th and 1/2nd Fallschirmjäger Regiment which escaped encirclement at Brest, and, the 2nd Fallschirm Flak Battalion. The flak battalion operated in Luftgau II in 1945, and ended the war in Danzig, with the 4th battery attached to 9th Fallschirmjäger Division.

The order to re-form the division was issued on 9/24/44 (to be completed 11/1/44), and all remnants of the old division were reunited in Amersfoort, Holland. On 12/6/44 it was filled out with troops from the Oldenburg, Halle, and Berlin areas. The 6th Fallschirmjäger Regiment and the 1/2nd Fallschirm Artillery Regiment were replaced by the 23rd Fallschirmjäger Regiment and the newly raised 3/6th Fallschirm Artillery Regiment. The 2nd Fallschirm Panzerjäger Battalion was rebuilt with three companies. The feldersatz battalion was rebuilt from scratch. The 1/2nd Fallschirm Artillery Regiment was destroyed in Brest 9/19/44, but the remainder of the artillery regiment escaped, and joined the newly formed 2nd Fallschirmjäger division in December 1944.

The 23rd Fallschirmjäger Regiment had been formed in December 1944 in Amersfoort (Holland) from replacement troops from home. Originally intended for the new 8th Fallschirmjäger Division it was reassigned to the 2nd Fallschirmjäger Division to replace the missing 6th Fallschirmjäger Regiment. The 23rd Fallschirmjäger Regiment surrendered in the Ruhr pocket 1945.

Organization 1944
 1st Battalion (1st–4th companies)
 2nd Battalion (5th–8th companies)
 3rd Battalion (9th–12th companies)
 13th (Panzerjäger) Company
 14th (120mm mortar) Company
 15th (Pioneer) Company

The new division was combat ready in early December 1944, with three new regiments: 2nd, 7th and 23rd Fallschirmjäger Regiment. The new troops were provided from Oldenburg, Halle and the Berlin area. The division went into combat in January 1945 in Holland without its artillery regiment.

The artillery regiment was reorganized on 2/8/45. Its new staff was formed from the Staff/12th Fallschirm Artillery Regiment, the new 1/2nd Fallschirm Artillery Regiment from 3/6th Fallschirm Artillery Regiment and a new 3/2nd Fallschirm Artillery Regiment from 2/12th.

Organization 1943
 1st Battalion (1st–4th Batteries)
Organization 1944
 1st Battalion (1st–3rd Batteries)
 2nd Battalion (4–6 Batteries)
 3rd Battalion (7–9 Batteries)

On 3/22/45 the Staff/3rd Fallschirmjäger Regiment was used to rebuild the 9th Fallschirmjäger Division. The division had:

1/,2/,3/2nd Fallschirmjäger Regiment
1/,2/,3/7th Fallschirmjäger Regiment
1/,2/,3/23rd Fallschirmjäger Regiment
1/,2/,3/2nd Fallschirm Artillery Regiment (3 btrys per bn)
2nd Fallschirm Panzerjäger Battalion (3 companies)
2nd Fallschirm Flak Battalion (5 batteries)

Feldersatz Battalion, 2nd Fallschirmjäger Division
(5 companies)
2nd Fallschirm Feldersatz Battalion (5 companies)
2nd Fallschirm Mortar Battalion (3 companies)
2nd Fallschirm Pioneer Battalion (4 companies)

2nd Fallschirm Medical Battalion (2 companies)
2nd Fallschirm Signals Battalion (3 companies)

It was destroyed in the Ruhr Pocket in 1945.

3rd Fallschirmjäger (Parachute) Division

The division was ordered formed on 11/1/43 and was to be completed on 2/1/44. It was organized in France. The 3rd Fallschirm Panzerjäger Battalion was formed in January 1944 at Reims. In March 1944 the 3/1st Fallschirmjäger Regiment joined it from Italy. The division contained:

1/,2/,3/5th Fallschirmjäger (Parachute Rifle) Regiment
1/,2/,3/8th Fallschirmjäger Regiment
1/,2/,3/9th Fallschirmjäger Regiment
3rd Fallschirmjäger Granatwerfer (Mortar) Battalion (3 companies) (formed early June 1944)
3rd Fallschirm Panzerjäger Battalion
3rd Fallschirm Artillery Regiment (only 1 battalion until June 1944, when 2nd & 3rd Battalions were formed)
3rd Fallschirm Pioneer Battalion (4 companies)
3rd Luftnachrichten (Communications & Signal) Battalion
3rd Fallschirmjäger Division (2 companies)
3rd Fallschirmjäger Versorgenheiten (Support Units)

The 5th Fallschirmjäger Regiment was formed in May 1942, Staff/,1/5th Fallschirmjäger Regiment were newly raised, the 2/,3/5th were formed from 2/,3/1st Luftlande-Sturm-Regiment. In June 1942 2/5th Fallschirmjäger Regiment was sent to Africa and joined Brigade Ramcke, while the rest of the regiment transferred to Reims (training for Operation Hercules, the attack on Malta). Stab, 1/,3/5th Fallschirmjäger Regiment were transferred to Tunisia in November 1942, joining Brigade Ramcke. 2/5th 1st Fallschirmjäger Regiment was apparently disbanded shortly afterwards. In February 1943 the 5th Fallschirmjäger Regiment was redesignated Jäger Regiment Hermann Göring, now part of Division General Göring. The 5th Fallschirmjäger Regiment was destroyed in May 1943.

The 2/5th Fallschirmjäger Regiment was re-formed in October 1943 and saw action in South Russia together with 2nd Fallschirmjäger Division, but was destroyed at Kirovograd. Only the Staff/5th Fallschirmjäger Regiment survived and in June 1944 it became Staff/16th Fallschirmjäger Regiment.

An entire new regiment began forming in January 1944 in Reims, later Brest. When 3/1st Fallschirmjäger Regiment arrived in Brest in March 1944, it became the basis of the new 5th Fallschirmjäger Regiment. The regiment was almost totally destroyed in Normandy, and had to be re-formed in Oldenzaal, October 1944.

The 8th Fallschirmjäger Regiment was formed in January 1944 at Reims with new recruits. The regiment was decimated in Normandy, and had to be rebuilt in Oldenzaal, in October 1944.

The 9th Fallschirmjäger Regiment was formed in January 1944 at Reims with new recruits. The regiment was almost totally destroyed at Falaise, and had to be rebuilt in October 1944, at Oldenzaal. The 9th Fallschirmjäger Regiment was again destroyed in March 1945, and was replaced by the 6th Fallschirmjäger Regiment in the division.

In 1944 the 5th, 8th and 9th Fallschirmjäger Regiments were organized as follows:

1st Battalion (1st–4th companies)
2nd Battalion (5th–8th companies)
3rd Battalion (9th–12th companies)
13th (Panzerjäger) Company
14th (120mm mortar) Company
15th (Pioneer) Company

The 3rd Fallschirm Flak Battalion was formed in January 1944 in France. In about February 1944, the division moved to the Brest area, under II Fallschirm Corps/Heeresgruppe D. The division was not ready for combat until May 1944, now under 2nd Fallschirm Corps/7th AOK. Replacement troops were provided by the Fallschirm-Ersatz Bataillon 2 in Stendal.

On 3/3/44 the division was organized and equipped as follows:

Division Staff
1 Division Staff (10 LMGs)
1 Division Staff Company (10 LMGs & 2 80mm mortars)
1 Bicycle Reconnaissance Company (no LMGs)

5th Fallschirmjäger Regiment
1 Regimental Staff (2 LMGs & 2 anti-tank rifles)
1 Signals Platoon (2 LMGs & 2 anti-tank rifles)
1 Bicycle Reconnaissance Company (3 LMGs)
1st (mot) Battalion
Staff Company (1 LMG)
1 Signals Platoon
3 Companies (13 LMGs, & 3 80mm mortars)
1 Heavy Company (9 LMGs, 8 HMGs, & 2 75mm leIG)
2nd (mot) Battalion
Staff Company (1 LMG)
1 Signals Platoon
3 Companies (13 LMGs 3 80mm mortars)
1 Heavy Company (9 LMGs, 8 HMGs, & 2 75mm leIG)
3rd (mot) Battalion
Staff Company (1 LMG)
1 Signals Platoon
3 Companies (13 LMGs, & 3 80mm mortars)
1 Heavy Company (9 LMGs, 8 HMGs, & 2 75mm leIG)
(mot) Infantry Gun Company (2 75mm leIG & 5 LMGs) (guns might be Russian)
(mot) Panzerjäger Company (3 panzerschrecke & 3 LMGs)
(mot) Pioneer Company (4 LMGs & 6 flamethrowers)
8th Fallschirmjäger Regiment
same as 5th Fallschirmjäger Regiment
9th Fallschirmjäger Regiment
same as 5th Fallschirmjäger Regiment
3rd Fallschirmjäger Artillery Battalion
1 Fallschirmjäger Battalion Staff
1 (mot) Fallschirmjäger Battalion Staff Battery (3 LMGs)
1 (mot) Fallschirmjäger Signals Platoon (3 LMGs)
3 Fallschirmjäger Batteries (4 105mm leFH, 4 LMGs & 3 20mm guns)
3rd Fallschirmjäger Flak Battalion
1 Fallschirmjäger Flak Battalion Staff
1 Fallschirmjäger (mot) Signals Platoon
1 (mot) Light Supply Column
3 (motZ) Heavy Flak Batteries (4 88mm, 2 20mm guns & ? LMGs)
1 Self Propelled Flak Battery (9 37mm flak guns)
1 Fallschirmjäger Self Propelled Flak Battery (12 20mm guns)
3rd Fallschirmjäger Panzerjäger Battalion
1 Fallschirmjäger Panzerjäger Battalion Staff
1 Fallschirmjäger (mot) Signals Platoon
3 Fallschirmjäger Panzerjäger Companies (4 75mm PAK 40 & 3 LMGs ea)

3rd Fallschirmjäger Pioneer Battalion
1 Fallschirmjäger Pioneer Battalion Staff (3 LMGs)
1 Fallschirmjäger (mot) Signals Platoon (1 LMG)
4 Fallschirmjäger (mot) Pioneer Companies (6 LMGs, 1 HMG & 6 flamethrowers)
1 Fallschirmjäger (mot) Light Supply Column (1 LMG & 2 flamethrowers)
3rd Fallschirmjäger Signals Battalion
1 Fallschirmjäger (mot) Signals Company (1 LMG)
1 Fallschirmjäger (mot) Radio Company (1 LMG)
1 Fallschirmjäger (mot) Supply Column
3rd Fallschirmjäger Supply Troops
1 (mot) Transportation Column (3 light supply columns)
1 (mot) Transportation Column (1 light, 1 heavy supply column & 1 fuel supply column)
1 (mot) Supply Company
1 (mot) Maintenance Platoon
1 (mot) Maintenance Company
Other
1 (mot) Butcher Company
1 (mot) Baker Company
1 (mot) Administrative Platoon
1/3rd (mot) Medical Company
2/3rd (mot) Medical Company
3 Ambulances
1 (mot) Fallschirmjäger Field Hospital
1 (mot) Military Police Troop (1 LMG)
1 (mot) Field Post Office

On 6/6/44 the division was stationed about midway between Quimper and Brest, and went into combat under 2nd Fallschirm Corps/7th AOK. The division saw heavy combat in Normandy, which severely depleted the division. It was partly destroyed in the Falaise pocket. The 3rd Fallschirm Panzerjäger Battalion was destroyed at Falaise, and rebuilt at Oldenzaal in October. On 6/2/44 the division was organized and equipped as follows:

Division Staff
1 Fallschirmjäger Division Staff (6 LMGs)
1 Fallschirmjäger Motorcycle Company (12 LMGs)
648th (mot) Military Police Troop (3 LMGs)
5th Fallschirmjäger Regiment
1 Regimental Staff (3 LMGs)
1 Signals Platoon (2 LMGs)
1 Bicycle Reconnaissance Company (3 LMGs)
1st (mot) Battalion
Staff Company (2 LMGs)
1 Signals Platoon (2 LMGs)
3 Companies (20 LMGs & 3 80mm mortars)

1 Heavy Company (8 HMGs, 2 LMGs, 4 80mm mortars, & 2 75mm leIG)

2nd (mot) Battalion

same as 1st Battalion

3rd (mot) Battalion

same as 1st Battalion

13th (mot) Mortar Company

(9 120mm mortars & 6 LMGs)

14th (mot) Panzerjäger Company

(12 75mm PAK 40 & 12 LMGs)

15th (mot) Pioneer Company

(2 HMGS, 11 LMGs & 2 80mm Mortars)

8th Fallschirmjäger Regiment

same as 5th Fallschirmjäger Regiment

9th Fallschirmjäger Regiment

same as 5th Fallschirmjäger Regiment

3rd Fallschirmjäger Mortar Battalion

1 Fallschirmjäger Battalion Staff & (mot) Staff Company (4 LMGs)

3 (mot) Fallschirmjäger Mortar Companies (12 120mm mortars & 14 LMGS ea)

3rd Fallschirmjäger Panzerjäger Battalion

1 Fallschirmjäger Battalion Staff

1 Fallschirmjäger Signals Platoon (2 LMGS)

3 (motZ) Fallschirmjäger Panzerjäger Companies (12 75mm PAK 40 & 12 LMGs ea)

3rd Fallschirmjäger Artillery Regiment

1 Fallschirmjäger Regimental Staff & (mot) Staff Battery (2 LMGs)

1st Battalion

1 Fallschirmjäger Battalion Staff & (mot) Staff Battery (2 LMGs)

3 Fallschirmjäger Batteries (4 105mm leFH & 5 LMGs ea)

2nd Battalion

same as 1st Battalion

3rd Battalion

1 Fallschirmjäger Battalion Staff & (mot) Staff Battery (2 LMGs)

3 Fallschirmjäger Batteries (4 150mm sFH & 5 LMGs ea)

3rd Fallschirmjäger Flak Battalion

1 Fallschirmjäger Flak Battalion Staff (4 LMGs)

1 (mot) Heavy (60 ton) Supply Column

3 (motZ) Heavy Flak Batteries (4 88mm, 2 20mm guns & 4 LMGs)

1 Self Propelled Flak Battery (9 37mm flak guns)

1 Fallschirmjäger Self Propelled Flak Battery (12 20mm guns)

3rd Fallschirmjäger Pioneer Battalion

1 Fallschirmjäger Pioneer Battalion Staff (3 LMGs)

1 Fallschirmjäger (mot) Signals Platoon (1 LMG)

4 Fallschirmjäger (mot) Pioneer Companies (2 HMGS, 11 LMGs & 2 80mm mortars)

3rd Fallschirmjäger Signals Battalion

1 Fallschirmjäger (mot) Signals Company

1 Fallschirmjäger (mot) Radio Company (5 LMGs)

1 Fallschirmjäger (mot) Supply Column

3rd Fallschirmjäger Supply Troops

31st & 32nd (mot) Transportation Columns (9 LMGs ea)

3rd (mot) Supply Company (10 LMGs)

1 (mot) Maintenance Platoon (2 LMGs)

1 (mot) Maintenance Company (5 LMGs)

Other

3rd (mot) Butcher Company (1 LMG)

3rd (mot) Baker Company (3 LMGs)

3rd (mot) Administrative Platoon (2 LMGs)

943rd (mot) Field Post Office

31st (mot) Medical Company

32nd (mot) Medical Company

31st & 32nd Ambulances

1 (mot) Fallschirmjäger Field Hospital

During August and September 1944 the division fought on, while withdrawing to the German border, ending up in Aachen in September 1944. From 9/24/44 to 10/5/44 the division was rebuilt in Oldenzaal, Belgium. The division was rebuilt with the following units:

XXVI Luftwaffe Fortress Battalion
XXX Luftwaffe Fortress Battalion
XXXII Luftwaffe Fortress Battalion
XXXIII Luftwaffe Fortress Battalion
XXXIV Luftwaffe Fortress Battalion
XXXV Luftwaffe Fortress Battalion
XXXVII Luftwaffe Fortress Battalion
Det/22nd Flieger Regiment
Det/51st Flieger Regiment
Det/53rd Flieger Regiment

The division first saw combat at Arnhem as part of Kampfgruppe Becker. The division participated in the Battle of the Bulge, and was decimated in the defensive battles in Germany in 1945. The division was ordered to Niederbreisig on 3/15/45 by OB West, to be rebuilt yet again. The 9th Fallschirmjäger Regiment was totally destroyed and was replaced by the independent 6th Fallschirmjäger Regiment. The division surrendered in the Ruhr-pocket.

The 3rd Fallschirm Flak Battalion had been detached in late 1944 or early 1945 and operated independently in Bohemia during 1945. Apparently in 1945 the flak battalion was renamed 2/20th Flak Regiment, and was reformed from the 1/12th Fallschirm Flak Regiment.

On 2/8/45 the artillery was reorganized. The Staff/,1/,3/3rd Fallschirm Artillery Regiment was rebuilt using the Staff/,2/,3/4th Fallschirm Artillery Regiment. The 2/3rd Fallschirm Artillery Regiment was rebuilt by renaming the 1/3rd Fallschirm Artillery Regiment. Later the 9th Fallschirmjäger Regiment was destroyed and replaced by the 6th. It was again destroyed in the Ruhr pocket in 1945, the survivors passing into American captivity.

4th Fallschirmjäger (Parachute) Division

Formation begun 11/5/43 (to be completed 2/1/44) in Venice, Italy, using the following units from the 2nd Fallschirmjäger division:

1/2nd Fallschirmjäger Regiment
2/6th Fallschirmjäger Regiment
1/1st Luftlande-Sturm-Regiment

A large number of Italian paratroopers from the Nembo and Folgore Divisions also joined the new division. The division contained the following units:

1/,2/,3/10th Fallschirmjäger (Parachute) Regiment
1/,2/,3/11th Fallschirmjäger Regiment
1/,2/,3/12th Fallschirmjäger Regiment
4h Fallschirm Panzerjäger Battalion (3 companies)
1/4th Fallschirm Artillery Regiment (2nd & 3rd Battalions were raised later)
4th Fallschirm Flak Battalion (5 batteries)
4th Fallschirm Pioneer Battalion (4 companies)
4th Luftnachrichten (Communications & Signal) Battalion
4th Fallschirmjäger Division (2 companies)
4th Fallschirmjäger Versorgenheiten (Support Units)

The 10th Fallschirmjäger Regiment was formed in January 1944 in Italy with many Italian volunteers, with the 1/10th Fallschirmjäger Regiment being formed from the 1/2nd Fallschirmjäger Regiment. The 11th Fallschirmjäger Regiment was formed at the same time, with the 1/11th being formed from the 2/6th Fallschirmjäger Regiment. The 1/12th Fallschirmjäger Regiment formed from the 1/1st Luftlande-Sturm-Regiment. The remainder of the three regiments were organized from new drafts. The organization of these regiments was as follows:

Organization 1944
1st Battalion (1st–4th companies)
2nd Battalion (5th–8th companies)
3rd Battalion (9th–12th companies)
13th (Panzerjäger) Company
14th (120mm mortar) Company

The 4th Fallschirm Panzerjäger Battalion was formed in January 1944. Theoretically it contained 484 men and consisted of three companies, the 1st company with 16 75mm towed AT guns (later only 12 guns), the 2nd company with 4 StuG III (later increased to 14 StuG III), and the 3rd company with 12 20mm AA guns (self-propelled).

The 4th Fallschirm Flak Battalion was formed in December 1943 in Italy. In theory the battalion contained 824 men and consisted of five batteries with a total of 18 88mm AA guns and 18 20mm AA guns. Replacement troops were provided by 1st Fallschirm Ersatz Bataillon, located in Aschersleben. Formation of the division was completed February 1944, and the division went into combat at Anzio, under 1st Fallschirm Corps/14th AOK.

In June 1944 the division detached the existing 1/4th Fallschirm Artillery to the newly forming 6th Fallschirmjäger Division. In exchange it received the 1/6th Fallschirmjäger Artillery Regiment as its 1st Battalion and new 2nd and 3rd battalions were raised. The 4th Fallschirmjäger Granatwerfer Battalion was raised with three companies. The newly restructured artillery regiment never joined the division, leaving it with no artillery. On 11/25/44 a Feldersatz Battalion was organized. On 6/2/44 the division was organized and equipped as follows:

Division Staff
1 Fallschirmjäger Division Staff (6 LMGs)
1 Fallschirmjäger Motorcycle Company (12 LMGs)
650th (mot) Military Police Troop (3 LMGs)
10th Fallschirmjäger Regiment
1 Regimental Staff (3 LMGs)
1 Signals Platoon (2 LMGs)
1 Bicycle Reconnaissance Company (3 LMGs)
  1st (mot) Battalion
  Staff Company (2 LMGs)
  1 Signals Platoon (2 LMGs)
  3 Companies (20 LMGs & 3 80mm mortars)
  1 Heavy Company (8 HMGs, 2 LMGs, 4 80mm mortars, & 2 75mm leIG)
  2nd (mot) Battalion
  same as 1st Battalion

3rd (mot) Battalion
same as 1st Battalion
13th (mot) Mortar Company
(9 120mm mortars & 6 LMGs)
14th (mot) Panzerjäger Company
(12 75mm PAK 40 & 12 LMGs)
15th (mot) Pioneer Company
(2 HMGS, 11 LMGs & 2 80mm Mortars)
11th Fallschirmjäger Regiment
same as 5th Fallschirmjäger Regiment
12th Fallschirmjäger Regiment
same as 5th Fallschirmjäger Regiment
4th Fallschirmjäger Mortar Battalion
1 Fallschirmjäger Battalion Staff & (mot) Staff Company (4 LMGs)
3 (mot) Fallschirmjäger Mortar Companies (12 120mm mortars & 14 LMGS ea)
4th Fallschirmjäger Panzerjäger Battalion
1 Fallschirmjäger Battalion Staff
1 Fallschirmjäger Signals Platoon (2 LMGS)
3 (motZ) Fallschirmjäger Panzerjäger Companies (12 75mm PAK 40 & 12 LMGs ea)
4th Fallschirmjäger Artillery Regiment
1 Fallschirmjäger Regimental Staff & (mot) Staff Battery (2 LMGs)
1st Battalion
1 Fallschirmjäger Battalion Staff & (mot) Staff Battery (2 LMGs)
3 Fallschirmjäger Batteries (4 105mm leFH & 5 LMGs ea)
2nd Battalion
same as 1st Battalion
3rd Battalion
1 Fallschirmjäger Battalion Staff & (mot) Staff Battery (2 LMGs)
3 Fallschirmjäger Batteries (4 150mm sFH & 5 LMGs ea)
4th Fallschirmjäger Flak Battalion
1 Fallschirmjäger Flak Battalion Staff (4 LMGs)
1 (mot) Heavy (60 ton) Supply Column
3 (motZ) Heavy Flak Batteries (4 88mm, 2 20mm guns & 4 LMGs)
1 Self Propelled Flak Battery (9 37mm flak guns)
1 Fallschirmjäger Self Propelled Flak Battery (12 20mm guns)

4th Fallschirmjäger Pioneer Battalion
1 Fallschirmjäger Pioneer Battalion Staff (3 LMGs)
1 Fallschirmjäger (mot) Signals Platoon (1 LMG)
4 Fallschirmjäger (mot) Pioneer Companies (2 HMGS, 11 LMGs & 2 80mm mortars)
4th Fallschirmjäger Signals Battalion
1 Fallschirmjäger (mot) Signals Company
1 Fallschirmjäger (mot) Radio Company (5 LMGs)
1 Fallschirmjäger (mot) Supply Column
4th Fallschirmjäger Supply Troops
41st & 42nd (mot) Transportation Columns (9 LMGs ea)
4th (mot) Supply Company (10 LMGs)
4th (mot) Maintenance Platoon (2 LMGs)
4th (mot) Maintenance Company (5 LMGs)
Other
4th (mot) Butcher Company (1 LMG)
4th (mot) Baker Company (3 LMGs)
4th (mot) Administrative Platoon (2 LMGs)
944th (mot) Field Post Office
41st (mot) Medical Company
42nd (mot) Medical Company
41st & 42nd Ambulances
4th (mot) Fallschirmjäger Field Hospital

On 2/8/45 the Staff/,2/,3/,4th Fallschirm Artillery Regiment detached to the 3rd Fallschirmjäger Division to become the Staff/1,/,3/3rd Fallschirm Artillery Regiment. The 1/4th became the Fallschirm Artillery Battalion z.b.V. Hermann Göring with the Ersatz Brigade "HG." The division had no artillery until a new 4th Fallschirm Artillery Regiment, with three battalions, was formed on 3/13/45.

The division remained in Italy until the end of the war, surrendering between Vicenza and Bolzano in May 1945.

5th Fallschirmjäger (Parachute) Division

Formed 3/2/44 in Reims (ordered 11/5/43). The division was formed from the Fallschirmjäger Lehr Battalion, 3/3rd Fallschirmjäger Regiment and 3/4th Fallschirmjäger Regiment, and a large number of new recruits. The division consisted of the following units:

1/,2/,3/13th Fallschirmjäger (Parachute) Regiment
1/,2/,3/14th Fallschirmjäger Regiment
1/,2/,3/15th Fallschirmjäger Regiment
5th Fallschirm Panzerjäger Battalion (3 companies)
1/5th Fallschirm Artillery Regiment (2nd & 3rd Battalions formed by June 1944)
5th Fallschirm Flak Battalion (5 batteries)
5th Fallschirm Pioneer Battalion (4 companies)
5th Luftnachrichten (Communications & Signal) Battalion
5th Fallschirmjäger Division (2 companies)
5th Fallschirm Divisional (Einheiten) Support Units

The division's three fallschirmjäger regiments were formed in March 1944 in Reims. The 1/13th Fallschirmjäger Regiment was formed from the 3/3rd Regiment. In May 1944 the 1/13th 13th Fallschirmjäger Regiment was renamed 1/115th, and a new 1/13th was formed. The 13th Fallschirmjäger Regiment was attached to the 77th Infantry Division during the fighting in Normandy and was destroyed in June 1944 at St. Lo. The 13th Fallschirmjäger Regiment was re-formed in November 1944 in the Hague-Amsterdam area.

The 1/14th Fallschirmjäger Regiment formed from the 3/4th Fallschirmjäger Regiment. In May 1944 the 1/14th Fallschirmjäger Regiment was renamed the 3/15th and a new 1/14th was raised. The 14th Fallschirmjäger Regiment was attached to the Panzer Lehr Division during the fighting in Normandy, and was destroyed there. The 14th Fallschirmjäger Regiment was re-formed in November 1944 in the Hague-Amsterdam area.

In June 1944 as the 15th Fallschirmjäger Regiment was forming the forming 1/,3/15th were replaced by 1/13th and 1/14th Fallschirmjäger Regiments, so that the regiment became combat ready before the rest of the division. The regiment was attached to the 17th SS Panzer Grenadier Division in Normandy, and was destroyed there. The 15th Fallschirmjäger Regiment was re-formed in October 1944 in the Hague-Amsterdam area. On 6/1/44 the division was organized and equipped as follows:

Division Staff
1 Divisional Staff (2 LMGs)
1 Fallschirmjäger Bicycle Company
1 (mot) Military Police Detachment
15th Fallschirmjäger Regiment
1 Regimental Staff (4 LMGs)
1 Signals Platoon (2 LMGs)
1 Fallschirmjäger Bicycle Company (3 LMGs)
1 (mot) (30 ton) Fallschirmjäger Light Supply Column
1st Battalion
1 Battalion Staff (4 LMGs)

1 Signals Platoon
3 Fallschirmjäger Companies (11 LMGs ea)
1 Heavy Fallschirmjäger Company (8 HMGs & 1 80mm mortar)
2nd Battalion
same as 1st Battalion
3rd Battalion
same as 1st Battalion
Pioneer Company (7 LMGs)
Fallschirmjäger Panzerjäger Company (1 75mm PAK & 1 LMG)
Fallschirmjäger Heavy Company (8 Rocket launchers & 7 LMGS)
14th Fallschirmjäger Regiment
1 Regimental Staff (4 LMGs)
1 Signals Platoon (2 LMGs)
1 Fallschirmjäger Bicycle Company (3 LMGs)
1 (mot) (30 ton) Fallschirmjäger Light Supply Column
1st Battalion
1 Battalion Staff (2 LMGs)
1 Signals Platoon
3 Fallschirmjäger Companies (13 LMGs ea)
1 Heavy Fallschirmjäger Company (8 HMGs, 2 75mm leIG & 2 80mm mortars)
2nd Battalion
same as 1/14th
3rd Battalion
same as 1/14th
Pioneer Company (2 HMGs & 7 LMGs)
Fallschirmjäger Panzerjäger Company (1 75mm PAK & 1 LMG)
Fallschirmjäger Heavy Company (unknown)
13th Fallschirmjäger Regiment
1 Regimental Staff (4 LMGs)
1 Signals Platoon (2 LMGs)
1 Fallschirmjäger Bicycle Company (3 LMGs)
1 (mot) (30 ton) Fallschirmjäger Light Supply Column
1st Battalion
1 Battalion Staff (1 LMG)
1 Signals Platoon
3 Fallschirmjäger Companies (13 LMGs ea)
1 Heavy Fallschirmjäger Company (8 HMGs & 2 75mm leIG)
2nd Battalion
same as 1/13th
3rd Battalion
same as 1/13th
Pioneer Company (9 LMGs)
Fallschirmjäger Panzerjäger Company (1 75mm PAK & 1 LMG)
Fallschirmjäger Heavy Company (9 rocket launchers & 9 LMGs)

5th Fallschirm Artillery Regiment

Fallschirm Artillery Regimental Staff
Signals Platoon

1st Battalion

Fallschirm Artillery Battalion Staff (4 LMGs)
Signals Platoon
3 Fallschirmjäger Batteries (4 75mm & 12 LMGs ea)

5th Fallschirm Flak Battalion

Fallschirm Artillery Battalion Staff (4 LMGs)
Signals Platoon
3 (motZ) Heavy Flak Batteries (4 88mm, 3 20mm & 3 LMGs ea)
1 Self Propelled Medium Flak Company (9 37mm guns & 3 LMGs)
1 Self Propelled Light Flak Company (12 20mm guns & 3 LMGs)

5th Fallschirm Pioneer Battalion

Fallschirm Pioneer Battalion Staff
4 Pioneer Companies (2 HMGs, 5 LMGs & 6 flamethrowers)

5th Luftnachrichten (Communications & Signal) Battalion

1 Fallschirm Radio Company
1 Fallschirm Signals Company
1 (mot) Fallschirmjäger Light Supply Column

5th Fallschirm Medical Battalion

3 Ambulances
2 Fallschirm Medical Companies

5th Fallschirm Divisional (Einheiten) Support Units

5 (mot) Light Supply Columns
1 (mot) Fuel Column
1 (mot) Feldzug Platoon (4 LMGs)
3 (mot) Maintenance Companies
1 (mot) Bakery Company
1 (mot) Butcher Company
1 (mot) Administration Company
1 (mot) Field Post Office

All three of the division's regiments were organized and equipped as follows:

Organization 1944
1st Battalion (1st–4th companies)
2nd Battalion (5th–8th companies)
3rd Battalion (9th–12th companies)
13th (Panzerjäger) Company
14th (120mm mortar) Company
15th (Pioneer) Company

The 5th Fallschirm Panzerjäger Battalion was formed in March 1944 in Reims. It contained 484 men in three companies, 1st company with 16 75mm towed AT guns (later only 12 guns), 2nd company with 4 StuG III (later increased to 14 StuG III) and the 3rd company with 12 20mm AA guns (self-propelled).

The 5th Fallschirm Flak Battalion was formed in January 1944 at Reims. In theory the battalion contained 824 men and consisted of five batteries with a total of 18 88mm AA guns and 18 20mm AA guns. Replacement troops were provided by the 3rd Fallschirm Ersatz Battalion in Nürnberg-Buchenbühl.

In May 1944 the division moved to Rennes (6/6/44 HQ at Rennes, reserve under 7th AOK). The division was not ready for combat on D-Day, and only the 15th Fallschirmjäger Regiment was transferred to the front line. As the regiment only had its 2nd Battalion ready, a new 1/15th Fallschirmjäger Regiment was formed from the 1/13th Fallschirmjäger Regiment (ex. 3/3rd Fallschirmjäger Regiment) and a new 3/15th Fallschirmjäger Regiment from 1/14th Fallschirmjäger Regiment (ex. 3/4th Fallschirmjäger Regiment). The 15th Fallschirmjäger Regiment operated together with the 17th SS Panzer Grenadier Division. Most of the division was severely decimated in the fighting in Normandy during July 1944. The remnants fought on during August 1944. The Division received new recruits in September 1944 and was partly re-formed from parts of the 22nd, 51st and 53rd Flieger Regiments. The 5th Fallschirm Mortar Battalion and Staff/, 1/5th Fallschirmjäger Regiment was transferred to the 7th Fallschirmjäger Division.

In May 1944 the division added the 5th Fallschirm Mortar Battalion (three companies).

The 5th Fallschirm Panzerjäger Battalion was destroyed July 1944 in Normandy and rebuilt with three companies in November 1944 in Holland. The 15th Regiment absorbed the 1/13th and 1/14th Fallschirmjäger Regiments to re-form its 1st and 3rd Battalions as the regiment was rebuilt. The 5th Fallschirm Flak Battalion was re-formed in November 1944 as well.

In October 1944 the division was rebuilt in the Hague-Amsterdam area (ordered 9/24/44 to 11/1/44). A new 5th Fallschirm Mortar Battalion was added in November 1944, together with a new 5th Fallschirmjäger Regiment. The XXV Luftwaffe Fortress Battalion was absorbed on 2/20/45 and the division was ordered to refit 3/15/45 by OB West.

In 1945 the 5th Fallschirm Flak Battalion seems to have become the 2/6th Flak Regiment, and was re-formed from 3/12th Fallschirm Flak Regiment.

Most of the division surrendered at Nürnberg in March 1945, while the rest surrendered in the Ruhr pocket and at Harz.

6th Fallschirmjäger (Parachute) Division

The division was formed in June 1944 in Amiens (15th AOK), with the following units:

1/,2/,3/16th Fallschirmjäger Regiment
1/,2/,3/17th Fallschirmjäger Regiment
1/,2/,3/18th Fallschirmjäger Regiment
6th Fallschirm Panzerjäger Battalion (3 companies)
6th Fallschirmjäger Granatwerfer Battalion (3 companies)
1/,2/,3/6th Fallschirm Artillery Regiment
6th Fallschirm Flak Battalion (5 batteries)
6th Fallschirm Pioneer Battalion (4 companies)
6th Fallschirm Signals Battalion (2 companies)
6th Fallschirm Divisional (Einheiten) Support Units

The three Fallschirmjäger regiments of the division were formed in June 1944 at Amiens. While the 16th Fallschirmjäger Regiment was forming, it was (with a new staff from Staff of the 1/5th Fallschirmjäger Regiment) flown to Stendal, and in June 1944 it was flown to Vilna in Lithuania, where it operated as part of Kampfgruppe Oberst Schirmer. On 6/2/44 the division was organized and equipped as follows:

Division Staff
1 Fallschirmjäger Division Staff (6 LMGs)
1 Fallschirmjäger Motorcycle Company (12 LMGs)
650th (mot) Military Police Troop (3 LMGs)
16th Fallschirmjäger Regiment
1 Regimental Staff (3 LMGs)
1 Signals Platoon (2 LMGs)
1 Bicycle Reconnaissance Company (3 LMGs)
1st (mot) Battalion
Staff Company (2 LMGs)
1 Signals Platoon (2 LMGs)
3 Companies (20 LMGs & 3 80mm mortars)
1 Heavy Company (8 HMGs, 2 LMGs, 4 80mm mortars, & 2 75mm leIG)
2nd (mot) Battalion
same as 1st Battalion
3rd (mot) Battalion
same as 1st Battalion
13th (mot) Mortar Company
(9 120mm mortars & 6 LMGs)
14th (mot) Panzerjäger Company
(12 75mm PAK 40 & 12 LMGs)
15th (mot) Pioneer Company
(2 HMGS, 11 LMGs & 2 80mm Mortars)
17th Fallschirmjäger Regiment
same as 5th Fallschirmjäger Regiment

18th Fallschirmjäger Regiment
same as 5th Fallschirmjäger Regiment
6th Fallschirmjäger Mortar Battalion
1 Fallschirmjäger Battalion Staff & (mot) Staff Battery (4 LMGs)
3 (mot) Fallschirmjäger Mortar Companies (12 120mm mortars & 14 LMGS ea)
6th Fallschirmjäger Panzerjäger Battalion
1 Fallschirmjäger Battalion Staff
1 Fallschirmjäger Signals Platoon (2 LMGS)
3 (motZ) Fallschirmjäger Panzerjäger Companies (12 75mm PAK 40 & 12 LMGs ea)
6th Fallschirmjäger Artillery Regiment
1 Fallschirmjäger Regimental Staff & (mot) Staff Battery (2 LMGs)
1st Battalion
1 Fallschirmjäger Battalion Staff & (mot) Staff Battery (2 LMGs)
3 Fallschirmjäger Batteries (4 105mm leFH & 5 LMGs ea)
2nd Battalion
same as 1st Battalion
3rd Battalion
1 Fallschirmjäger Battalion Staff & (mot) Staff Battery (2 LMGs)
3 Fallschirmjäger Batteries (4 150mm sFH & 5 LMGs ea)
6th Fallschirmjäger Flak Battalion
1 Fallschirmjäger Flak Battalion Staff (4 LMGs)
1 (mot) Heavy (60 ton) Supply Column
3 (motZ) Heavy Flak Batteries (4 88mm, 2 20mm guns & 4 LMGs)
1 Self Propelled Flak Battery (9 37mm flak guns)
1 Fallschirmjäger Self Propelled Flak Battery (12 20mm guns)
6th Fallschirmjäger Pioneer Battalion
1 Fallschirmjäger Pioneer Battalion Staff (3 LMGs)
1 Fallschirmjäger (mot) Signals Platoon (1 LMG)
4 Fallschirmjäger (mot) Pioneer Companies (2 HMGS, 11 LMGs & 2 80mm mortars)
6th Fallschirmjäger Signals Battalion
1 Fallschirmjäger (mot) Signals Company
1 Fallschirmjäger (mot) Radio Company (5 LMGs)
1 Fallschirmjäger (mot) Supply Column
6th Fallschirmjäger Supply Troops
61st & 62nd (mot) Transportation Columns (9 LMGs ea)
6th (mot) Supply Company (10 LMGs)

6th (mot) Maintenance Platoon (2 LMGs)
6th (mot) Maintenance Company (5 LMGs)
Other
6th (mot) Butcher Company (1 LMG)
6th (mot) Baker Company (3 LMGs)
6th (mot) Administrative Platoon (2 LMGs)
946th (mot) Field Post Office
61st (mot) Medical Company
62nd (mot) Medical Company
61st & 62nd Ambulances
6th (mot) Fallschirmjäger Field Hospital

When the division was formed the 16th Fallschirmjäger Regiment was sent to Wilna (Russia) where, on 9/24/44, the 16th Fallschirmjäger Regiment became the 3rd Fallschirm Panzer Grenadier Regiment "HG", of the Fallschirmjäger Panzer Corps Hermann Göring. The 16th Fallschirmjäger Regiment was re-formed 10/15/44 in Holland.

While the 17th and 18th Fallschirmjägers were forming, they became involved in the fighting in France, and formation was never completed. Both regiments were re-formed in October 1944 in Meppel. The organization of all three regiments was as follows:

Organization 1944
1st Battalion (1st–4th companies)
2nd Battalion (5th–8th companies)
3rd Battalion (9th–12th companies)
13th (Panzerjäger) Company
14th (120mm mortar) Company
15th (Pioneer) Company

The 6th Fallschirm Panzerjäger Battalion was formed in June 1944 in France. In theory it contained 484 men and three companies, 1st company with 16 75mm towed AT guns (later only 12 guns), 2nd company with 4 StuG III (later increased to 14 StuG III) and the 3rd company with 12 20mm AA guns (self-propelled).

The 6th Fallschirm Flak Battalion was formed in June 1944 in France. In theory the battalion contained 824 men and consisted of five batteries with a total of 18 88mm AA guns and 18 20mm AA guns. Replacement troops were provided by the Fallschirm-Ersatz Battalion 3 in Nürnberg-Buchenbühl.

The remainder of the division (at kampfgruppe strength only) went into action immediately in Normandy, and was mostly destroyed. Its remnants were to be used to form the Hübner, Grossmehl, Laytved-Hardegg, and Greve Regiments, later the 7th Fallschirmjäger Division (Erdmann). However, it could not be pulled out of the front line in time. The 6th Fallschirm Panzerjäger Battalion was rebuilt in October 1944. The 6th Fallschirm Flak Battalion saw no action in Normandy and did not serve with the 6th Fallschirmjäger division.

The division was ordered re-formed on 10/15/44 in Meppel, Holland. The division was formed from the few remaining remnants of the old division and from the XXIX, XXXI, XXXVIII, and XL Luftwaffe Fortress Battalions.

On 15 October 1944 the division was re-formed and the 6th Fallschirm Flak Battalion was redesignated 7th Fallschirm Flak Battalion. On 11/15/44 a feldersatz battalion was organized. On 2/8/45 it became the 1/6th Fallschirm Artillery Regiment and was replaced by the 3/11th Fallschirmjäger Regiment.

In 1945 the new 7th Fallschirm Flak Battalion operated independently on the Eastern front (Upper Schlesia). In 1945 the 7th Fallschirm Flak Battalion apparently was renamed the 190th Flak Battalion, and was re-formed from the 2/12th Fallschirm Flak Regiment. The division surrendered to the British in May 1945 at Zutphen in Fortress Holland.

7th Fallschirmjäger Division

Formed on 10/9/44 from the Erdmann Fallschirmjäger Division. The Erdmann Division had been formed from part of the 6th Fallschirmjäger Division and Fallschirmjäger School forces in Germany, the Menzel Regiment, Grossmehl Regiment, Laytved-Hardegg Regiment, the Greve Regiment, and the Schäger and Schluckebier Battalions, and the Grunwald Panzerjäger Battalion near Bitsch. On 9 September 1944 it was sent to Arnhem where it was to fight the Allied landings. It had:

1/,2/,3/19th Fallschirmjäger Regiment (from Menzel Regiment)
1/,2/,3/20th Fallschirmjäger Regiment (from Grossmehl Regiment)

1/,2/,3/21st Fallschirmjäger Regiment (from Laytved-Hardegg & Greve Regiments)
7th Fallschirm Panzerjäger Battalion (3 companies) (from Grunwald Battalion)
1/,2/,3/7th Fallschirm Artillery Regiment (from Staff/l,1/6th Fallschirm Artillery Regiment
7th Fallschirm Flak Battalion (5 batteries)
7th Fallschirm Granatwerfer Battalion (3 companies)
7th Fallschirm Pioneer Battalion (4 companies)
7th Fallschirm Signals Battalion (2 companies)
7th Fallschirmjäger Supply Troops

The 19th Fallschirmjäger Regiment was formed on 11/25/44 from the Menzel Fallschirmjäger Regiment. The Staff/,1/,2/19th Fallschirmjäger Regiment were formed from the Staff/,1/,2/Menzel Fallschirmjäger Regiment. The 3/19th Fallschirmjäger Regiment was formed from scratch.

The 20th Fallschirmjäger Regiment was formed on 11/25/44 from the Grossmehl Fallschirmjäger Regiment. The Staff/,1/,2/20th Fallschirmjäger Regiment were formed using the Staff/,1/,2/Grossmehl Fallschirmjäger Regiment. The 3/20th Fallschirmjäger Regiment was newly raised.

The 21st Fallschirmjäger Regiment was formed on 11/25/44 from the Laytved-Hardegg and Greve Fallschirmjäger Regiments. The Staff/,1/,2/21st were formed from the Staff/,1/,2/Laytved-Hardegg and the 3/21st was formed from the 1/Greve Fallschirmjäger-Ersatz- und Ausbildungs-Regiment. All three regiments were organized as follows:

Organization 1944
1st Battalion (1st–4th companies)
2nd Battalion (5th–8th companies)
3rd Battalion (9th–12th companies)
13th (Panzerjäger) Company
14th (120mm mortar) Company
15th (Pioneer) Company

The 7th Fallschirm Panzerjäger Battalion was formed in November 1944 from the Grunwald Fallschirm Panzerjäger Battalion. In theory it contained 484 men and 3 companies, 1st company with 16 75mm towed AT guns (later only 12 guns), 2nd company with 4 StuG III (later increased to 14 StuG III) and the 3rd company with 12 20mm AA guns (self-propelled).

The 7th Fallschirm Flak Battalion was formed in November 1944 in Holland from the 6th Fallschirm Flak Battalion. In theory the battalion contained 824 men and consisted of five batteries with a total of 18 88mm AA guns and 18 20mm AA guns. Replacement troops were provided by 3rd Fallschirmjäger Ersatz Battalion.

Between 11/30/44 and 2/20/45 it absorbed the XXIV and XXVIII Luftwaffe Fortress Battalions. On 2/8/45 the artillery was formed with the 1st Battalion formed from the 1/6th Artillery Regiment, the 2nd Battalion from the 2/3rd Artillery Regiment, and the 3rd Battalion coming from the 1/7th Artillery Regiment. The division was captured near Oldenburg and went into British captivity.

8th Fallschirmjäger Division:

The division was ordered formed on 9/24/44 (with the 22nd, 23rd and 24th Fallschirmjäger Regiment), but formation was canceled on 10/15/44. The 23rd Fallschirmjäger Regiment went to the 2nd Fallschirmjäger division, and the Fallschirm Signals Battalion was transferred to the army on 1/2/45. The division was re-formed in January 1945, at Köln-Wahn from various ad-hoc units. By February 1945 its organization was complete and it contained:

1/,2/,3/22nd Fallschirmjäger Regiment (formed in March 1945) (from Schellman Fallschirmjäger Regiment)
1/,2/,3/32nd Fallschirmjäger Regiment (sent to 2nd Fallschirmjäger Division) (from Jungwirth, Gramse and Rahs Fallschirmjäger Battalions plus new drafts)

1/,2/,3/24th Fallschirmjäger Regiment (formed in March 1945) (from Hübner Fallschirmjäger Regiment)
8th Fallschirm Signals Battalion (2 companies)
8th Fallschirmjäger Feldersatz Battalion (5 companies)
8th Fallschirmjäger Supply Troops

The three fallschirmjäger regiment were formed in February 1945 at Köln-Wahn. The 22nd Fallschirmjäger Regiment was formed from the Schellmann Fallschirmjäger Regiment. The 24th Fallschirmjäger Regiment was formed from the Hübner Fallschirmjäger Regiment. The 32nd Fallschirmjäger Regiment was formed as follows: Staff/32nd from the Jungwirth Fallschirmjäger Battalion, 1/32nd from the Gramse Battalion, the 2/32nd from the Rahs Battalion and 3/32nd was raised from new drafts.

The 23rd Fallschirmjäger Regiment, originally assigned to the division, was sent to the 2nd Fallschirmjäger Division. The organization of these three regiments was as follows:

Organization 1944
  1st Battalion (1st–4th companies)
  2nd Battalion (5th–8th companies)
  3rd Battalion (9th–12th companies)
  13th (Panzerjäger) Company
  14th (120mm mortar) Company

Formation of other subordinated units were planned. Replacement troops were provided by 4th Fallschirmjäger Ersatz Battalion. On 2/20/45 XXVII Luftwaffe Fortress Battalion was absorbed by the division. The division was refreshed 3/15/45 at Wesel, by order of Oberbefehlshaber West. The division surrendered in the Ruhr pocket.

9th Fallschirmjäger Division

The division was ordered formed on 9/24/44, but formation was delayed until 10/25/44. The newly formed fallschirm signals battalion was transferred to the army (85th Infantry Division) on 1/2/45. The division was formed between December 1944 and February 1945 in the Stettin area, from various regular and ad-hoc units. The actual formation took place in early February 1945 in the Stettin area. On 3/17/45 the division had:

1/,2/,3/25th Fallschirmjäger Regiment
1/,2/,3/26th Fallschirmjäger Regiment
1/,2/,3/27th Fallschirmjäger Regiment
1/,2/,3/9th Fallschirm Artillery Regiment
9th Fallschirm Panzerjäger Battalion (3 companies)
9th Fallschirm Flak Battalion
9th Fallschirm Signals Battalion
9th Fallschirm Pioneer Battalion
9th Fallschirm Feldersatz Battalion
9th Fallschirm Supply Troops
9th Fallschirm Medical battalion

The 25th, 26th, and 27th Fallschirmjäger Regiments were formed in February 1945 in the Stettin area. The 25th Fallschirmjäger Regiment was formed as follows: Staff/,1/25th were formed from Staff/,3/Fallschirmjäger Regiment z.b.V., the 2/25th from the Brandenburg Fallschirmjäger Battalion, and 3/25th from Hermann Fallschirmjäger Battalion. In late February 1945 the 2/25th was flown into Breslau, renamed the 67th Fallschirmjäger Battalion, and replaced.

The 26th Fallschirmjäger Regiment was formed as follows: 1/,2/26th were formed from 1/,2/Fallschirmjäger Regiment z.b.V., and 3/26th from 52nd Fallschirm Panzerjagd Battalion. In late February 1945 the 3/26th Fallschirmjäger Regiment was flown into Breslau, renamed the 68th Fallschirmjäger Battalion, and replaced. The 1/,2/,3/27th Fallschirmjäger Regiment was

formed from the 51st, 53rd, and 54th Fallschirm Panzerjagd Battalions. All three regiments were organized as follows:

Organization 1944
  1st Battalion (1st–4th companies)
  2nd Battalion (5th–8th companies)
  3rd Battalion (9th–12th companies)
  13th (Panzerjäger) Company
  14th (120mm mortar) Company
  15th (Pioneer) Company

The 9th Fallschirm Artillery was formed from the 2/,3/2nd and 3/12th Fallschirm Artillery Regiments. The Feldersatz Battalion was formed from the 56th Fallschirmjäger Battalion. The 9th Fallschirm Panzerjäger (Zerstörer) Battalion was formed in February 1945. In theory it contained 484 men and three companies, 1st company with 16 75mm towed AT guns (later only 12 guns), 2nd company with 4 StuG III (later increased to 14 StuG III) and the 3rd company with 12 20mm AA guns (self-propelled).

The 9th Fallschirm Flak Battalion was formed in February 1945 from the 3/12th Fallschirm Flak Regiment. In theory the battalion contained 824 men and consisted of five batteries with a total of 18 88mm AA guns and 18 20mm AA guns.

The division was rebuilt on 2/3/45 using parts of the 8th Fallschirmjäger Division. Its organization was slightly different from the standard organization in that it had no mortar battalion and its panzerjäger battalion was less heavily equipped than normal.

In late February 1945 2/25th Fallschirmjäger Regiment and 3/26th Fallschirmjäger Regiment were flown into Fortress Breslau and left the division. The division saw combat in the Stargard-Dramburg area, and was refreshed in the Prenzlau area (March 1945). It was to have absorbed elements of the 2nd Fallschirmjäger Division by 3/23/45, but this was apparently canceled. On 2/6/45 the division was organized and equipped as follows:

Division Staff
- 1 Division Staff (6 LMGs)
- 1 (mot) Reconnaissance Company (7 LMGs)
- 1 Fallschirmjäger Motorcycle Platoon (12 LMGs)
- 1 Motorcycle Platoon (2 LMGs)
- 1 (mot) Military Police Detachment (3 LMGs)
- 1 (mot) Mapping Platoon

25th Fallschirmjäger Regiment
- 1 Fallschirmjäger Regimental Staff (3 LMGs)
- 1 (mot) Fallschirmjäger Signals Platoon (2 LMGs)
- 1 (mot) Fallschirmjäger Bicycle Platoon (3 LMGs)
- **3 Fallschirmjäger Battalions**, each with
  - 1 Fallschirmjäger Battalion Staff (2 LMGs)
  - 1 (mot) Fallschirmjäger Radio Platoon (2 LMGs)
  - 1 Self Propelled Flak Platoon (4 20mm flak guns)
  - 3 (mot) Companies (20 LMGs & 3 80mm mortars)
  - 1 (mot) Heavy Company (8 HMGs, 2 LMGS, 2 75mm leIG & 4 80mm mortars)
- **13th (mot) Fallschirmjäger Mortar Company** (9 120mm mortars & 6 LMGs)
- **14th (mot) Fallschirmjäger Panzerjäger Company** (12 75mm PAK & 12 LMGs)
- **15th (mot) Fallschirmjäger Pioneer Company** (2 HMGs, 1 LMGs, 2 80mm mortars)
- **Other**
  - 1 (mot) Fallschirmjäger Supply Column
  - 1 Self Propelled Flak Platoon (3 27mm guns)

26th Fallschirmjäger Regiment
same as 25th Fallschirmjäger Regiment

27th Fallschirmjäger Regiment
same as 25th Fallschirmjäger Regiment

9th Fallschirmjäger Flak Regiment
- Fallschirmjäger Flak Regimental Staff
- Fallschirmjäger Flak Regimental Staff Battery

1st Flak Battalion
- 1 Fallschirmjäger Staff (4 LMGS)
- 1 Fallschirmjäger Signals Company
- 1 Self Propelled Flak Battery (3 20mm flak guns)
- 3 (motZ) Heavy Flak Batteries (6 88mm, 3 20mm & 4 LMGS ea)
- 1 Self Propelled Medium Flak Battery (12 37mm & 6 LMGs)
- 1 Self Propelled Fallschirmjäger Light Flak Battery (12 20mm & 6 LMGs)
- 1 (mot) 60 ton Flak Supply Column

2nd Battalion
same as 1st Battalion

9th Fallschirmjäger Artillery Regiment
- 1 Fallschirmjäger Artillery Regimental Staff
- 1 Fallschirmjäger Artillery Regimental Staff Battery (2 LMGs)

1st Fallschirmjäger Artillery Battalion
- 1 Fallschirmjäger Artillery Battalion Staff
- 1 (mot) Fallschirmjäger Artillery Battalion Staff Battery (2 LMGs)
- 3 (motZ) Fallschirmjäger Batteries (4 105mm leFH 18 & 5 LMGS)
- 1 (mot) Supply Column

2nd Fallschirmjäger Artillery Battalion
same as 1st Battalion

3rd Fallschirmjäger Artillery Battalion
- 1 Fallschirmjäger Artillery Battalion Staff
- 1 (mot) Fallschirmjäger Artillery Battalion Staff Battery (2 LMGs)
- 3 (motZ) Fallschirmjäger Batteries (4 150mm sFH 18 & 5 LMGS)
- 1 (mot) Supply Column

Fallschirmjäger Panzerjäger Battalion
- 1 Fallschirmjäger Panzerjäger Battalion Staff
- 1 Fallschirmjäger Radio Platoon (2 LMGs)
- 3 (mot) Fallschirmjäger Panzerzerstörer Companies (equipped only with panzerschrecke)

Fallschirmjäger Pioneer Battalion
- 1 Fallschirmjäger Pioneer Battalion Staff
- 1 (mot) Fallschirmjäger Signals Platoon (2 LMGs)
- 1 Self Propelled Flak Platoon (3 20mm guns)
- 3 (mot) Fallschirmjäger Pioneer Companies (2 HMGs, 11 LMGs & 2 80mm mortars)
- 1 (mot) Light Supply Column

Fallschirmjäger Signals Battalion
- 1 Fallschirmjäger Signals Battalion Staff
- 1 Self Propelled Flak Platoon (3 20mm guns)
- 1 (mot) Signals Company
- 1 (mot) Radio Company (5 LMGs)

Fallschirmjäger Supply Troop
- 1 Fallschirmjäger Supply Troop Staff
- 2 (mot) Transportation Companies (9 LMGs & 3 self-propelled 20mm)
- 1 (mot) Supply Company (10 LMGs & 3 self-propelled 20mm)
- 1 (mot) Maintenance Company (5 LMGs & 3 self-propelled 20mm)
- 1 (mot) Maintenance Platoon (2 LMGs & 3 self-propelled 20mm)
- 1 (mot) Bakery Company (3 LMGs & 3 self-propelled 20mm)
- 1 (mot) Butcher Company (1 LMG & 3 self-propelled 20mm)
- 1 (mot) Administration Platoon
- 1 (mot) Field Post Office

Fallschirmjäger Medical Battalion
2 (mot) Medical Companies (9 LMGs ea)
1 (mot) Field Hospital (6 LMGs)
3 Ambulances

On 4/8/45 the division still had 11,600 men in the Berlin area. It surrendered to the Russians in May 1945.

10th Fallschirmjäger Division

The division was ordered formed on 9/24/44, but formation was postponed on 10/15/44. The new fallschirm signals battalion was transferred to the army on 1/2/45.

Organization of the division began again in the Graz area on 3/1/45. The division was formed from many various units. Each fallschirmjäger regiment and artillery regiment of the 1st and 4th Fallschirmjäger Division in Italy, gave up a battalion for the new division. These had all arrived in Graz by 8/4/45 (nine train loads).

The new 10th and 11th Fallschirmjäger Divisions were formed using 4,000 men from four Air War Schools (Luftkriegsschulen), 1,200 from five flight leader schools (Flugzeugführerschulen), and 2,400 men from JG101.

4th Luftkriegsschulen
7th Luftkriegsschulen (7 remained at Tullny)
10th Luftkriegsschulen
11th Luftkriegsschulen
A5 Flugzeugführerschulen
A14 Flugzeugführerschulen
A23 Flugzeugführerschulen
A25 Flugzeugführerschulen
A115 Flugzeugführerschulen
JG101 (2,400 men)
715th Infantry Division (heavy weapons)

A further 4,000 men were to have been taken over from 14th SS Grenadier Division, but this was canceled. On 4/17/45 the division had a strength of 10,700 men. The division consisted of the following units:

1/,2/,3/28th Fallschirmjäger Regiment
1/,2/,3/29th Fallschirmjäger Regiment
1/,2/,3/30th Fallschirmjäger Regiment
10th Fallschirm Panzerjäger Battalion (5 companies)
1/,2/,3/10th Fallschirm Artillery Regiment
20th Fallschirm Signals Battalion (2 companies)

The 28th, 29th, and 30th Fallschirmjäger Regiments were formed in March 1945 in Graz. The 28th saw action at St. Pölten and Brünn, the 29th saw action at Gratwin, Graz and Iglau, and the 30th saw action at St. Pölten, Ried and Graz.

The 10th Fallschirm Panzerjäger Battalion was formed with five companies in April 1945. It did not join the division, but remained in Luftgau XI.

The units were divided between Graz and Luftgau XI. They served under XXIV Corps/1st Panzer AOK in May 1945, with parts in reserve under 6th Panzer AOK. The main parts surrendered to the Russians in Iglau.

11th Fallschirmjäger Division

Formed on 3/1/45 in Linz area. Formation was to have been completed by 5/1/45, but was canceled 4/8/45. Collection of troops in the Linz area apparently continued, despite the cancellation. By 4/20/45, 1,100 men had arrived in Linz, with a further 2,700 in Gardelegen, and 650 in Hörsching.

The new 10th and 11th Fallschirmjäger divisions were formed using 4,000 men from four Luftkriegsschulen, 1,200 from five Flugzeugführerschulen, and 2,400 men from JG101.

4th Luftkriegsschulen
7th Luftkriegsschulen (7 remained at Tullny)
10th Luftkriegsschulen
11th Luftkriegsschulen
A5 Flugzeugführerschulen
A14 Flugzeugführerschulen
A23 Flugzeugführerschulen
A25 Flugzeugführerschulen
A115 Flugzeugführerschulen
JG101 (2,400 men)
715th Infantry Division (heavy weapons)

A further 4,000 men were to have been taken over from 14th SS Grenadier Division, but this was canceled. The division was to have consisted of the following units:

1/,2/,3/37th Fallschirmjäger Regiment
1/,2/,3/38th Fallschirmjäger Regiment
1/,2/,3/39th Fallschirmjäger Regiment
1/,2/,3/Fallschirm Artillery Regiment
11th Fallschirm Panzerjäger Battalion
11th Fallschirm Pioneer Battalion
11th Fallschirm Signals Battalion
11th Signals Troop

The formation of the 37th, 38th, and 39th Fallschirmjäger Regiments began in March 1945 and was never completed. The 11th Fallschirm Panzerjäger Battalion was formed in Luftgau III in March 1945. In theory it contained 484 men and three companies, 1st company with 16 75mm towed AT guns (later only 12 guns), 2nd company with 4 StuG III (later increased to 14 StuG III) and the 3rd company with 12 20mm AA guns (self-propelled). It operated independently. The division is not known to have ever contained more than 2,700 men and its fate is not known.

20th Fallschirmjäger Division

Formed on 3/20/45 in northern Holland as a Field Ausbildungs Division. The division had:

1/,2/,3/58th Fallschirmjäger Regiment
1/,2/,3/59th Fallschirmjäger Regiment
1/,2/,3/60th Fallschirmjäger Regiment
20th Fallschirm Artillery Battalion (6 batteries) (2 went to the 21st Division)
20th Fallschirm Panzerjäger Battalion (3 companies) (1 went to 21st Division)
20th Fallschirm Flak Battalion (3 batteries) (all sent to 21st Division)

20th Fallschirm—Granatwerfer Battalion (4 companies) (1 to 21st Division)
1/,2/20th Fallschirm Pioneer Regiment
20th Fallschirmjäger Kraftfahr Battalion (4 companies)
20th Fallschirm Medical Battalion (2 companies)

21st Fallschirmjäger Division

Formation ordered on 5/5/45 in northern Holland, as a field training division, using parts of the Fallschirmjäger Ersatz und Ausbildungs Division and the Gericke Sturm-Brigade. It was organized as follows:

1/,2/61st Fallschirmjäger Regiment
1/,2/62nd Fallschirmjäger Regiment
1/,2/63rd Fallschirmjäger Regiment
21st Fallschirmjäger Battalion (2 batteries) (from 20th Division)
21st Fallschirm Pioneer Battalion (3 companies)
Panzerjäger Company (from 20th Fallschirmjäger Division)
Granatwerfer Company (from 20th Fallschirmjäger Division)
Signals Company (from 20th Fallschirmjäger Division)

The 61st Fallschirmjäger Regiment was formed on 4/5/45 from the Schaller Fallschirmjäger Regiment. In April 1945 it operated together with the 8th Fallschirmjäger Division.

The 62nd Fallschirmjäger Regiment was formed on 4/5/45 from the Henner Fallschirmjäger Cadre Regiment and Luftwaffe ground personnel. It operated with the 9th Fallschirmjäger Division around Stettin during April 1945. It was also known as the 62nd Fallschirmjäger Battalion and had four companies.

The 63rd Fallschirmjäger Regiment was formed on 4/5/45 from Heute Fallschirmjäger Regiment. It operated with the 9th Fallschirmjäger Division around Stettin during April 1945. It was also known as the 63rd Fallschirmjäger Battalion and had 4 four companies. In theory, all three regiments were organized as follows:

Organization 1944
  1st Battalion (1st–5th companies)
  2nd Battalion (6th–10th companies)

The 20th Fallschirm Flak Battalion was formed on 4/5/45 with three companies. Despite its number, it was not used by the 20th Fallschirmjäger Division, but was instead attached to the 21st Fallschirmjäger Division.

Erdmann Fallschirmjäger Division

Formed in September 1944 in the Bitsch area from Alarm units. On 9/9/44 it went to Holland to defend against the British landings at Arnhem. It contained:

1/,2/Menzel Fallschirmjäger Regiment
1/,2/Grossmehl Fallschirmjäger Regiment
1/,2/Laytved-Hardegg Fallschirmjäger Regiment

1/,2/Greve Fallschirmjäger Regiment
1/,2/Hübner Fallschirmjäger Regiment
Grunwald Fallschirm Panzerjäger Battalion

On 10/9/44 the division was re-formed into the 7th Fallschirmjäger Division.

Hermann Göring Parachute (Fallschirmjäger) Brigade

Formed in March 1942, the brigade contained:

Brigade Staff
Brigade Staff Company
1/Schützen Regiment Hermann Göring
  1–4th Schützen Companies
2/Schützen Regiment Hermann Göring
  5–8th Schützen Companies
  9th Heavy Infantry Gun Company
3/Schützen Regiment Hermann Göring
  10th Motorcycle Company
  11th Panzer Pioneer Company
  12th Panzerjäger Company
  13th Panzer Company
  Panzer Repair Platoon
1/Flak Regiment Hermann Göring
  1–3rd (heavy) Flak Battery
  4–5th (light) Flak Battery
  14th (light) Flak Battery
2/Flak Regiment Hermann Göring
  5–8th (heavy) Flak Battery
  9–10th (light) Flak Battery
  11th Howitzer Battery
3/Flak Regiment Hermann Göring
  (formation not complete)
  11–13th Light Howitzer Battery
  (105mm leFH)
4/Flak Regiment Hermann Göring
  15–17th Batteries
Wachbataillon Hermann Göring
  1–3 Wachkompagnien

A battle report for the 3/Herman Göring Fallschirmjäger Regiment dated 3/3/43 shows the battalion as having lost, among other weapons 19 MP 40, 9 LMGs, 1 HMG, 2 50mm mortars, 3 80mm mortars, 2 28mm PzBu41, 3 50mm PAK 38, 1 75mm PAK 40, 1 light gun of undetermined caliber, 10 bicycles, 10 trucks, 1 armored car, and 8 PzMk III tanks! That same report shows the 2/Flak Regiment Herman Göring lost 5 LMGs, 4 88mm guns, and 6 20mm guns.

Fallschirmjäger Ausbildungs (Training) und Ersatz (Replacement) Division

On 3/13/45 it had:

1st Fallschirmjäger Ausbildungs Regiment
2nd Fallschirmjäger Ausbildungs Regiment
3rd Fallschirmjäger Ausbildungs Regiment
4th Fallschirmjäger Ausbildungs Regiment
1st, 2nd, 3rd, & 4th Fallschirmjäger Ersatz Battalions
1st Fallschirm Pioneer Ausbildungs und Ersatz Battalion
2nd Fallschirm Pioneer Ausbildungs und Ersatz Battalion
Fallschirm Panzer Zerstörer Ausbildungs Battalion
Fallschirm Panzerjäger Ausbildungs und Ersatz Battalion

Fallschirm Artillery Ausbildungs und Ersatz Battalion
Fallschirm Granatwerfer Lehr Battalion
Fallschirm Signals Ausbildungs und Ersatz Battalion

The division was used to form the 20th Fallschirmjäger Division on 4/5/45.

Luftwaffe Signals Ersatz (Replacement) Division

Formed on 5/27/44 with:

1st Luftwaffe Signals Ersatz Regiment
2nd Luftwaffe Signals Ersatz Regiment
3rd Luftwaffe Signals Ersatz Regiment

On 9/20/44 it was combined with the Luftwaffe Signals Ausbildungs Division to form the Luftwaffe Signals Ausbildungs and Ersatz Division.

Luftwaffe Signals Ausbildungs (Training) Division

Formed in 1942 with:

301st Luftwaffe Signals Ausbildungs Regiment
302nd Luftwaffe Signals Ausbildungs Regiment
303rd Luftwaffe Signals Ausbildungs Regiment
305th Luftwaffe Signals Ausbildungs Regiment

On 9/20/44 it was combined with the Luftwaffe Signals Ersatz Division to form the Luftwaffe Ausbildungs and Ersatz Division.

Luftwaffe Signals Ausbildungs (Training) und Ersatz (Replacement) Division

Formed on 9/20/44 with:

1st Luftwaffe Signals Ausbildungs und Ersatz Regiment
2nd Luftwaffe Signals Ausbildungs und Ersatz Regiment
3rd Luftwaffe Signals Ausbildungs und Ersatz Regiment
4th Luftwaffe Signals Ausbildungs Regiment
5th Luftwaffe Signals Ausbildungs Regiment

Ramcke Parachute Brigade

Formed in early 1942 for the planned invasion of Malta, it consisted of:

1/2nd Fallschirmjäger Regiment—Major Kroh
1/3rd Fallschirmjäger Regiment—Major von der Heydte
2/5th Fallschirmjäger Regiment—Major Hubner
Fallschirmjäger Lehr Battalion XI Fliegerkorps—Major Burckhardt
2/Fallschirmjäger Artillery Regiment (12 75mm Mountain Guns)[1]

Panzerjäger Artillery Company (12 37mm PAK 36 guns)
Tietjen Engineer Company

During 1942 it dispatched to Africa where it fought with Rommel. Its headquarters arrived by air in Tobruk on 15 June 1942. The 1/2nd arrived 4 August 1943, the 1/3rd arrived 10 August 1942, and the 2/5th arrived 17 August 1942. They were assigned to the Panzerarmee Afrika on 15 August 1943 as the Luftwaffenjäger Brigade. The brigade went into captivity on 13 May 1943.

31st Fallschirmjäger Regiment

The 30th Fallschirmjäger Regiment was formed on 8/2/45 in Holland from parts of the Fallschirmjäger-Ersatz-und Ausbildungs-Regiment Hermann Göring. It operated in Holland as Heerestruppe.

Organization 1944
1st Battalion (1st–4th companies)
2nd Battalion (5th–8th companies)

3rd Battalion (9th–12th companies)
13th (Panzerjäger) Company
14th (120mm mortar) Company
15th (Pioneer) Company

The regiment was not assigned to any of the divisions and fought as an independent unit.

58th Fallschirmjäger Regiment

The 58th Fallschirmjäger Regiment was formed on 4/5/45 in the Oldenburg area from the 2nd Fallschirmjäger-Ausbildungs-Regiment.

Organization 1944
1st Battalion (1st–5th companies)

2nd Battalion (6th–10th companies)
3rd Battalion (11th–15th companies)

The regiment was not assigned to any of the divisions and fought as an independent unit.

59th Fallschirmjäger Regiment

The 59th Fallschirmjäger Regiment was formed on 4/5/45 in the Oldenburg area from the 3rd Fallschirmjäger-Ausbildungs-Regiment.

Organization 1944
1st Battalion (1st–5th companies)

2nd Battalion (6th–10th companies)
3rd Battalion (11th–15th companies)

The regiment was not assigned to any of the divisions and fought as an independent unit.

[1] There is some evidence that some of these might have been 76.2mm guns.

60th Fallschirmjäger Regiment

The 60th Fallschirmjäger Regiment was formed on 4/5/45 in the Oldenburg area from the 4th Fallschirmjäger-Ausbildungs-Regiment.

The regiment was not assigned to any of the divisions and fought as an independent unit.

Organization 1944
  1st Battalion (1st–5th companies)
  2nd Battalion (6th–10th companies)
  3rd Battalion (11th–15th companies)

Fallschirmjäger Regiment z.b.V.

The Fallschirmjäger Regiment z.b.V. was formed 11/25/44 (Staff only) to command the Schäfer and Schluckebier Fallschirmjäger Battalions. On 12/31/44 these two battalions became 1/,2/Fallschirmjäger Regiment z.b.V. In January 1945 the 3/Fallschirmjäger Regiment z.b.V. was formed in Dramburg from personnel of 1/,2/KG200 in Wittstock. The regiment was disbanded on 3/17/45. The Staff/,3/Fallschirmjäger Regiment z.b.V. became Staff/,1/25 Fallschirmjäger Regiment and the 1/,2/Fallschirmjäger Regiment z.b.V. became 1/,2/26th Fallschirmjäger Regiment.

Organization 1944
  1st Battalion (1st–4th companies)
  2nd Battalion (5th–8th companies)
  3rd Battalion (9th–12th companies)
  13th (Panzerjäger) Company
  14th (120mm mortar) Company
  15th (Pioneer) Company

Menzel Fallschirmjäger Regiment

The Menzel Fallschirmjäger Regiment was formed on 8/20/44 in Bitsch as an alarm-unit, Staff/,1/,2/Menzel were formed from Staff, Training Staff and Jäger Battalion/Fallschirm-Waffenschule. On 11/25/44 it was renamed the 19th Fallschirmjäger Regiment and assigned to the 17th Fallschirmjäger Division.

Organization 1944
  1st Battalion (1st–4th companies)
  2nd Battalion (5th–8th companies)

Grossmehl Fallschirmjäger Regiment

The Grossmehl Fallschirmjäger Regiment was formed on 8/20/44 in Bitsch as an alarm-unit, with, apparently, some portions of the 6th Fallschirmjäger Division. On 11/25/44 it was renamed the 20th Fallschirmjäger Regiment and reassigned to the 7th Fallschirmjäger Division.

Organization 1944
  1st Battalion (1st–5th companies)
  2nd Battalion (6th–10th companies)

Laytved-Hardegg Fallschirmjäger Regiment

The Laytved-Hardegg Fallschirmjäger Regiment was formed on 8/20/44 in Bitsch as an alarm-unit. On 11/25/44 it was renamed the 21st Fallschirmjäger Regiment and reassigned to the 7th Fallschirmjäger Division.

Organization 1944
- 1st Battalion (1st–5th companies)
- 2nd Battalion (6th–10th companies)

Greve Fallschirmjäger-Ersatz- und Ausbildungs-Regiment

The Greve Fallschirmjäger-Ersatz- und Ausbildungs-Regiment was formed in September 1944 as an alarm-unit, from the 1st Fallschirmschule. On 11/25/44 it was redesignated the 3/21st Fallschirmjäger Regiment and reassigned to the 7th Fallschirmjäger Division.

Organization 1944
- 1st Battalion (1st–5th companies)
- 2nd Battalion (6th–10th companies)

Hübner Fallschirmjäger Regiment

The Hübner Fallschirmjäger Regiment was formed on 8/20/44 in Bitsch as an alarm-unit. It operated as an independent unit after November 1944. On 3/15/44 it was redesignated as the 24th Fallschirmjäger Regiment and reassigned to the 8th Fallschirmjäger Division.

Organization 1944
- 1st Battalion (1st–5th companies)
- 2nd Battalion (6th–10th companies)

Schellmann Fallschirmjäger Regiment

The Schellmann Fallschirmjäger Regiment was formed in February 1945 as an alarm-unit. On 3/15/45 it was redesignated as the 22nd Fallschirmjäger Regiment and reassigned to the 8th Fallschirmjäger Division.

Jungwirth Fallschirmjäger Regiment

The Jungwirth Fallschirmjäger Regiment was formed in February 1945 to control the Gramse and Rahs Fallschirmjäger Battalions. On 3/15/45 it was redesignated as the 32nd Fallschirmjäger Regiment and reassigned to the 8th Fallschirmjäger Division.

11th Fallschirm-Artillerie-Kommandeur (ARKO)

The ARKO was formed 2/24/45 as a corps troop 1st Fallschirm Corps and was renamed the 111th ARKO on 3/28/45.

2nd Luftwaffe Sturmgeschütz Battalion

The battalion was formed in January 1944 with four batteries. It was renamed the 2nd Luftwaffe Sturmgeschütz Brigade in March 1944. Two months later it was renamed the 12th Fallschirm Sturmgeschütz Brigade and it became the 121st Fallschirm Sturmgeschütz Brigade on 3/28/45. It fought in Normandy, Holland and in 1945 at Kleve (Lower Rhein) as a corps troop under the 2nd Fallschirm Corps.

21st Fallschirm Sturmgeschütz Brigade

The brigade was formed 1/19/45 from Fallschirm Sturmgeschütz Brigade Schmitz, with four batteries. On 3/28/45 it was redesignated the 210th Fallschirm Sturmgeschütz Brigade. It served under the 1st Fallschirm Army as an army troop.

Schmitz Fallschirm-Sturmgeschütz-Brigade

The Schmitz Fallschirm Sturmgeschütz Brigade was formed in June 1944 from 2/2nd Fallschirm Panzerjäger Battalion with four companies. It served under the 1st Fallschirm Army.

20th Fallschirm-Pionier-Regiment

Formed 4/5/45 from the 1st and 2nd Fallschirm-Pionier-Ausbildungs-und Ersatz Battailons. The 1st Battalion contained the 1st–5th Companies and the 2nd Battalion contained the 6th–10th Companies.

1st Luftwaffe Corps Signals Battalion

The battalion was formed in January 1944. It was renamed the 11th Luftwaffe Corps Signals Battalion in June 1944 and the 111th Luftwaffe Corps Signals Battalion on 3/28/45.

2nd Luftwaffe Corps Signals Battalion

The battalion was formed in February 1944. It was renamed the 12th Luftwaffe Corps Signals Battalion in June 1944 and the 121th Luftwaffe Corps Signals Battalion on 3/28/45.

21st Transportation Battalion

The battalion was formed in January 1944 as 1st Fallschirm Army Transport Battalion. It became the 21st Fallschirm Transport Battalion in June 1944 and the 210th on 3/28/45. It served as an army troop under the 1st Fallschirm Army.

Kommandeur der Fallschirmjäger-Schulen

The Commander of the Fallschirmjäger Schools was formed in January 1945 in Berlin-Tempelhof, subordinated to Kommandeur General der Ausbildungs- und Ersatztruppen der Fallschirm-Armee, with:

Offizierschule Goslar
Oberjägerschule Salzwedel

21st Fallschirm Army Weapons School

The school was formed 2/11/45 with 16 companies, but was canceled on 3/7/45. The order of 3/28/45 redesignated it the 210th, but it did not exist at that time.

1st Fallschirm School

The school was formed in 1936 in Stendal as 1st Fallschirm School. In 1942 it moved to Wittstock a. d. Dosse, arriving in December, and was renamed 2nd Fallschirm School in 1943. It was re-formed in 1943/44 in Dreux from 4th Fallschirm School. On 8/20/44 it was redesignated Greve Fallschirmjäger Regiment and was subordinated to Erdmann Fallschirmjäger Division.

2nd Fallschirm School

The school was formed in Stendal. In 1942 and moved to Braunschweig-Broitzen. It was apparently disbanded 1943 and re-formed later that year at Wittstock a. d. Drosse, from the 1st Fallschirm School.

3rd Fallschirm School

The school was formed in Braunschweig-Broitzen and was operational in December 1942. In 1943 it moved to Kraljewo. It was disbanded in the summer of 1944.

4th Fallschirm School

The school was formed 1942/43 in Dreux. In 1943/44 it was redesignated Fallschirmschule 1. Re-formed in Freiburg in 1944 to Salzwedel, Luftgau III.

2nd Fallschirm Army Feldersatz Regiment

Formed in December 1944 from Flieger-Regiment 93, with a 1st and 2nd Battalion and a total of 13 companies. In February 1945 the 2nd Battalion was redesignated 8th Fallschirm Feldersatz Bataillon.

20th Fallschirm Panzerjäger Battalion

The 20th Fallschirm Panzerjäger Battalion was formed on 4/5/45 from the Hildesheim Fallschirm Panzerjäger Ausbildungs und Ersatz Battalion. In theory it contained 484 men and three companies, 1st company with 16 75mm towed AT guns (later only 12 guns), 2nd company with 4 StuG III (later increased to 14 StuG III) and the 3rd company with 12 20mm AA guns (self-propelled). One company was detached to the 21st Fallschirm-Jäger-Division.

Grunwald Fallschirm Panzerjäger Battalion

The Grunwald Fallschirm Panzerjäger Battalion was formed on 8/20/44 in Bitsch as an alarm-unit. In October 1944 it absorbed the remnants of 6th Fallschirm Mortar Battalion. In November 1944 it was redesignated as the 7th Fallschirm Panzerjäger Battalion.

1st Fallschirm-Flak-Regiment

The 1st Fallschirm Flak Regiment was formed in January 1944. In June 1944 it was renamed the 11th Fallschirm Flak Regiment. In late 1944 its battalions operated independently. The staff was in Rosenheim (Luftgau VII) in November 1944, and in 1945 moved to Stettin (I Flak Corps). In 1945 the 1st Battalion was in the Middle Reine area (Luftgau XIV), the 2nd Battalion was attached to the 5th Panzer Army, and the 3rd Battalion was in the Upper Reine area (Luftgau V), but would later move to Berlin, to support the 9th Fallschirm Jäger Division.

On 3/28/45 the 1st Fallschirm Flak Regiment was renamed the 11th Fallschirm Flak Regiment.

One source claims that the regiment was disbanded in 1945, 1st Battalion becoming 2/16th Flak Regiment, 2nd Battalion becoming the 11th Fallschirm Flak Battalion, and 3rd Battalion becoming the 12th Fallschirm Flak Battalion. This is however uncertain. After this, only the 11th Fallschirm Flak Battalion was attached to 1st Fallschirm Corps.

Organization
  1st Battalion (1st–5th Batteries)
  2nd Battalion (6th–10th Batteries)
  3rd Battalion (11th–15th Batteries)

2nd Fallschirm-Flak-Regiment

The 2nd Fallschirm Flak Regiment was formed in January 1944. In June 1944 it was renamed 12th Fallschirm Flak Regiment. The battalions fought individually in 1945. The staff was sent to the Eastern front in 1945, to control various flak units under II Flak Corps. In April 1945, the staff was attached to the 15th Flak Brigade at Templin, while the 1st and 2nd Battalions were in Luftgau VI on the lower Reine, and 3rd Battalion was in the Middle Rhine area (Luftgau XIV). The 3rd Battalion was renamed 9th Fallschirm Flak Battalion on 3/17/45. The 2nd Fallschirm Flak Regiment became 121st Fallschirm Flak Regiment 3/28/45.

One source claims that the regiment was disbanded in 1945, 1st Battalion becoming 3rd Fallschirm Flak Battalion, 2nd Battalion becoming 6th Fallschirm Flak Battalion, and 3rd Battalion becoming 5th Fallschirm Flak Battalion. This is however uncertain. By this time only the 12th Fallschirm Flak Battalion (ex. 3/11th Fallschirm Flak Regiment) was now attached to 2nd Fallschirm Corps.

Organization
   1st Battalion (1st–5th Batteries)
   2nd Battalion (6th–10th Batteries)
   3rd Battalion (11th–15th Batteries)

9th Fallschirm-Flak-Regiment

The 9th Fallschirm Flak Regiment was planned to be formed in December 1944, but was canceled. It was to have consisted of two battalions each with three heavy and two light batteries, for service under 9th Fallschirmjäger Division.

Organization of the Fallschirmjäger Divisional Units

Each fallschirmjäger regiment had, theoretically, 3,206 men. They had three battalions, each of which had four companies (1st Battalion: 1st–4th companies, 2nd Battalion: 5th–8th companies, 3rd Battalion: 9th–12th companies), a 13th (anti-tank) company, a 14th (mortar) company. On 5/6/44 a 15th company (Pioneer) was ordered formed in all regiments.

Each battalion had a theoretical strength of 853 men organized into three rifle companies (1st–3rd, 5th–7th, 9th–11th companies) and one machine-gun company (4th, 8th and 12th companies). Each rifle company had 170 men and 20 LMGs. The machine-gun company had 205 men, 8 HMGs, 4 80mm mortars and 2 75mm recoilless guns. The battalions had a total of 853 men, 66 LMGs, 8 HMGs, 12 80mm mortars and 2 75mm recoilless guns.

The 13th Company: 186 men, 3 75mm PAK 40 (towed) and a number of panzerschrecke. The 14th Company: 163 men, 9 or 12 120mm mortars. The 15th Company had around 100 men.

The artillery regiments theoretically had 1,571 men organized in three battalions. Each battalion had three batteries (1st Bn: 1st–3rd Btrys; 2nd Bn: 4th–6th Btrys; 3rd Bns: 7th–9th Btrys). The 1st and 2nd Battalions each had 12 105mm leFH, while the 3rd Battalion had 12 150mm howitzers.

In theory, the fallschirmjäger panzerjäger battalions contained 484 men and consisted of three companies, 1st company with 16 75mm towed AT guns (later only 12 guns), 2nd company with 4 StuG III (later increased to 14 StuG III) and the 3rd company with 12 20mm AA guns (self-propelled).

The fallschirm flak battalion were to contain 824 men and consisted of five batteries equipped with a total of 18 88mm AA guns and 18 20mm AA guns.

3

Organizational History of German Naval Divisions 1945

The history of naval infantry in the German army starts before WWI. The German naval infantry consisted of three "Seebataillonen" or Sea Battalions, which were designed for service in Germany's overseas colonies. During WWI their numbers were expanded and they grew to a force of three Naval Regiments and a Sailor Regiment that were organized into the Naval Division. However, with the signing of the Treaty of Versailles the German Naval Infantry ceased to exist.

When WWII started the Germans had not reorganized any naval infantry. The first units were organized in 1940 near Narvik with the crews of the destroyers sunk by the British in Narvik Harbor. Thus the Kothe, Erdmenger, and Freytag "Marine-Bataillonen" and the Berger "Marine-Regiment" were formed. In November 1943 the Klüver Marine-Infanterie-Bataillon was organized in southern Russia and in early 1944 the Hossfeld and Klemm Marine-Battaillonen were formed in the Crimea for the defense of Sebastopol.

With the collapse of the German army in France many naval bases were cut off. In Bordeaux the crew of the sunken destroyer Z37, the 12th U-Boat Flotilla and the 8th Minesweeping Flotilla were used to organize the Weber Marine Brigade. The sailors in St. Nazaire formed the Josephi, Emminga, Lieser, Haackert, and Wurffel Naval Grenadier Battalions (Marine-Grenadier-Bataillonen) from the various arsenals, 6th Picket Flotilla, and the 2nd Mind Sweeper Flotilla. In La Rochelle the John and Zapp Marine Regiments were formed from the crews of the 3rd U-Boat Flotilla and

the 8th and 44th Mine Sweeper Flotillas. In the Gironde-Süd Fortress the Tirpitz and Narvik Naval Battalions were formed from the 2nd Mine Sweeper Flotilla and the 8th Destroyer Flotilla.

The first large scale formations were organized in 1944 when the North Naval Rifle Brigade (Marine-Schützen-Brigade Nord) was organized from the 1st, 2nd, 3rd, and 4th Marine Infantry Regiments, which contained the 301st through 316th Marine Schützen Battalions. In February 1945 the 1st Naval Division was organized on the Vistula. After that a number of other naval divisions were organized.

With the exception of the Weber Naval Brigade and the Nord Naval Brigade the major naval formations were all formed in 1945. All of them were a desperation response to the pending destruction of the Third Reich. By the time that they were organized, if they were ever truly organized at all, the infrastructure of the Third Reich had collapsed. Supplies of new materials were almost unobtainable. As a result, their organization was very unique. Necessity and the absence of regular supplies forced them to be equipped with what was available and organized with whatever sailors and officers could be found.

Their histories were brief and, because of when and how they were formed, very little is known about them. They tended to serve as garrisons of cities and were probably never deployed into the field. They vanished when their garrisons were occupied by the Allies at the end of the war.

1st Naval Infantry Division

Formed February 1945 in Stettin from the Marine Schützen Brigade Nord, which contained:

1st Marine Schützen Regiment
    301st–304th Marine Schützen Battalion
2nd Marine Schützen Regiment
    305th–308th Marine Schützen Battalion

3rd Marine Schützen Regiment
    309th–312th Marine Schützen Battalion
4th Marine Schützen Regiment
    313th–316th Marine Schützen Battalion

The 3rd Marine Schützen Regiment was sent to the Vistula in January–February 1945. The other regiments were used to form the division. It was later reorganized and redesignated as the 1st Naval Infantry Division. It was organized as a Type 45 Division and contained:

1/,2/1st Marine (Naval) Infantry Regiment
1/,2/2nd Marine (Naval) Infantry Regiment
1/,2/4th Marine (Naval) Infantry Regiment
Division Füsilier company (became Battalion with 4 Companies in April)
Naval Artillery Regiment, 1st Naval Division (only 1 bn, with 4? batteries)
Panzerjäger Battalion, 1st Naval Division (4 Companies, 5 in April 1945)

Naval Feldersatz (Reserve) Battalion, 1st Naval Division (6 Companies)

According to official sources, on 4/15/45 it added:

Pioneer Battalion (4 Companies)
Nachrichten Battalion (4 Companies)

On 4/26/45 the division received the 787th Artillery Regimental Staff z.b.V. It also received two army artillery units, the 2nd Battery/37th Artillery Regiment and the 2nd Battery/41st Artillery Regiment.

2nd Naval Infantry Division

Formed March 1945 in Schleswig-Holstein.

5th Marine (Naval) Grenadier Regiment
6th Marine (Naval) Grenadier Regiment
7th Marine (Naval) Grenadier Regiment
2nd Marine (Naval) Fusilier Battalion
2nd Marine (Naval) Artillery Regiment

2nd Marine (Naval) Panzerjäger Battalion
2nd Marine (Naval) Pioneer Battalion
2nd Marine (Naval) Signals Battalion
2nd Marine (Naval) Feldersatz (Replacement) Battalion
200th Marine (Naval) Supply Regiment

3rd Naval Infantry Division

Formed 4/1/45 in Pomerania from the 163rd Infantry Division. The 163rd Infantry Division had been formed on 11/10/39 as a 7th Wave Division and had served in Finland until 1944. In March 1945 it was destroyed while part of the 3rd Panzer Army in Pomerania. On 4/1/45 it passed to the Navy. It was organized with:

8th Marine (Naval) Grenadier Regiment
(formerly 307th Grenadier Regiment?)
9th Marine (Naval) Grenadier Regiment
(formerly 310th Grenadier Regiment?)

10th Marine (Naval) Grenadier Regiment
(formerly 324th Grenadier Regiment?)
Marine (Naval) Artillery Regiment
(formerly 234th Artillery Regiment)
3rd Marine (Naval) Division Einheiten (Support) Troop
(formerly 234th Division Einheiten)

The 126th and 128th Marine (Naval) Schützen Battalions were also assigned to the division.

11th Naval Division

Formed in March 1945 in Holland with:

Staff (from 2nd Ship's Cadre Regiment)
111th Naval Schützen Regiment (from 14th Ship's Cadre Battalion)

112th Naval Schützen Regiment (from 16th Ship's Cadre Battalion)
113th Naval Schützen Regiment (from 20th Ship's Cadre Battalion)

16th Naval Infantry Division

Formed in March 1945 in Holland with:

Staff (from 4th Schiff Stamm (Ship's Cadre) Regiment)
161st Marine Schützen Regiment (from 6th Schiff Stamm (Ship's Cadre) Regiment)
162nd Marine Schützen Regiment (from 10th Schiff Stamm (Ship's Cadre) Regiment)
163rd Marine Schützen Regiment (from 24th Schiff Stamm (Ship's Cadre) Regiment)

On 4/12/45 the division was renamed the "Tarn" Division and appears to have been organized with:

604th Grenadier Regiment (from 219th ID)
219th Fusilier Grenadier Battalion
191th Grenadier Battalion
219th Grenadier Regiment (from 730rd ID)
703rd Fusilier Battalion
579th Grenadier Regiment

Weber Naval Brigade

Formed in August 1944 in Bordeaux by the Commander of the Naval Arsenal. It contained:

von Pflugk-Harttung Naval Regiment
Badermann Naval Regiment
Kühnemann Naval Regiment

It was disbanded in September 1944, during the withdrawal from France.

4

Russian Formations in German Service

The Cossacks

The Cossacks have always held a romantic and exciting position in the literature and mind of the world. The Germans were no less susceptible to this and during the campaign in Russia not only were the Cossacks desirable because of their military virtues, but by some miracle the researchers at Alfred Rosenberg's Eastern Ministry claimed to have discovered that the Cossack was not a Slav, but a Germanic being descended of the Ostrogoths.

Irrespective of this official blessing by the Ostministerium, the Cossacks had, in fact, been operating as volunteers with the German Army almost from the start of the campaign. During the summer of 1942 the XXX Panzer Corps had captured so many prisoners that providing escorts to take them to the rear had become a problem. Almost on a whim, someone at Corps headquarters suggested that the pro-German Don and Kuban Cossacks should be separated from the rest of the prisoners, armed and equipped, and used to escort the prisoners. Thus was born the Cossack Squadron under Captain Zagorodnyy. As they departed with their long column of prisoners, no one ever expected to see them again, but in September Captain Zagorodnyy reappeared, saluted, and requested his next assignment. Recognizing a good thing when they saw one, Zagorodnyy and his men were given four weeks training and converted into the 1/82nd Cossack Squadron of the German Army. The 1/82nd should be read 1st Squadron, 82nd Grenadier Regiment.

In a similar manner, dozens of other units acquired Cossack auxiliaries. They were most welcome because of their knowledge of the terrain and the enemy. As a result of the Soviet destruction of the nascent Cossack Republic in 1921, these men were more than willing to join any enemy of the Soviets and came in tremendous numbers.

In October 1942 the Germans established a semi-autonomous "Cossack District" in the Kuban with a population of about 160,000 persons. A Nazi party was founded under Vasili Galzkov and its members recognized Adolf Hitler as the supreme defender of the Cossack nation. The Cossacks then began forming hundertschaft or *sotni* of 100 men, one of which was to

be assigned to each of the German Security Divisions in the region. The doors swung open even further and all volunteers who came forward, be they residents of the "liberated" areas, prisoners of war, or defectors, were gladly taken into the Wehrmacht.

Cossack volunteers came from three sources, 1.) the liberated Cossack territories, 2.) the prisoner of war camps, and 3.) defectors from the Soviet Army. This latter category could be significant, as in one instance on 22 August 1941, when the entire 436th Infantry Regiment, with all its officers and men, deserted to the Germans. Major I.N. Kononov, commander of the 436th Infantry Regiment was later given command of the 102nd Cossack Battalion, which later became the 600th Cossack Battalion. This unit was classified as a Cossack unit although only about 60 percent of its strength were ethnic Cossacks.

In Army Group South, Oberstleutnant Jungschulz and Lehman raised and commanded the cossack regiments which bore their names. A third regiment was raised in Army Group Center, but it was named in honor of General Platov, the commander of Cossacks during the Napoleonic wars. All three of these regiments had about 2,000 men formed around a German cadre of about 150 men. The Army Group Center also had the Boeselager Mounted Detachment, which was a security formation with about 650 men.

Yet another formation existed that was known as the Plastun (dismounted) Cossack (Infantry) Regiment. This began life as Oberstleutnant von Renteln's 6th Cossack Regiment and was later reorganized into the 622nd and 623rd Cossack Battalions, plus the 638th Independent Cossack Company. This force was later reorganized into the 630th Grenadier Regiment, taking the number of a disbanded German regiment.

The German officer most closely associated with the Cossacks was Generalmajor Helmuth von Pannwitz. Pannwitz had served as a cavalry officer in the First World War and was serving on the Russian front. He formed a close friendship with Nikolai Kulakov, the Ataman, or clan chief, of the Terek Cossacks. Kulakov promised a close and active cooperation with the

Germans against the Soviets. He was also an ardent anti-communist and between the two of them decided to form a Cossack regiment. Pannwitz took this promise to his commanding officer, General Zeitzler, and Zeitzler accepted this offer of assistance, promising Pannwitz that he would command any regiment formed. In one of those interesting stories that often comes from war, Pannwitz asked where he was to find this troop he was to command. Zeitzler responded that "You'll have to find them for yourself." Being a highly motivated individual, Pannwitz toured the front in a Fieseler "Storch" reconnaissance/liaison plane and soon managed to corral a force of 1,000 men and six captured tanks. This mass of men was to become the "*Reiterverband von Pannwitz.*"

Not stopping there, Pannwitz was soon advocating the formation of a Cossack Division. In early 1943 he was given approval and soon over 12,000 men were assembled in Kherson. This included the various existing Cossack formations that were then organized and serving in the German Army.

Six full cavalry regiments were organized as were a number of support units. Only the 55th Motorcycle Reconnaissance Section was comprised entirely of Germans. Eventually two full divisions were formed.

Unfortunately, just as their formation was completed, the Russians had pushed the Germans back on the defensive, overrunning the Cossack homelands. The Cossacks were sent westward with their families fleeing with them. Their march stopped in Tolmezzo, Northern Italy, in October 1944. The Cossacks operated in Yugoslavia against Tito.

It was about this time that Himmler began moving to absorb the Cossacks into the SS. He even envisioned the formation of a 3rd Cossack Division. This division, however, was never to be formed.

A 3rd and 4th Cavalry Division were formed late in the war, but their formation was never completed and what little was organized quickly fell into Allied hands.

1st Cossack Division

Formed on 8/4/43 with the Pannwitz Reiterverband, which provided the staff, the Platov Cossack Cavalry Regiment, and the von Jungschulz Cossack Cavalry Regiment. The division had:

1st Don Cossack Reiter (Cavalry) Brigade
1/,2/1st Don Cossack Reiter Regiment
1/,2/2nd Siberian Cossack Regiment
1/,2/3rd Sswodno Cossack Reiter Regiment
Don Cossack Artillery Battalion
2nd Kaukasus Cossack Reiter Brigade
1/,2/4th Kuban Cossack Reiter Regiment
1/,2/5th (Don) Cossack Reiter Regiment
1/,2/6th Terek Cossack Reiter Regiment
Kuban Cossack Artillery Battalion
55th Division Support Troops

Over 12,000 men were assembled when the division was forming. They were sent to Mlawa, north of Warsaw, to what had been the largest pre-war depot for the Polish cavalry. Though most of the men had been recruited from the Cossack areas of Russia, a very large percentage came from the prisoner of war camps and from the *ostarbeiter* (east workers) throughout Germany. The only German component of the division was, reputedly, the all-German 55th Motorcycle Platoon. However, none of the organizations located in OKH

records indicates the existence of this unit. In the summer of 1943 the division was organized as follows:

1st Cossack Division
1 Division Staff & Divisional Band
Don Cossack Brigade
Signals Platoon
1st Don Cossack Regiment
Signals Platoon
2 Cossack Battalions, each with
4 Cossack Squadrons (9 LMGs & 2 50mm mortars)
1 Support Squadron (8 80mm mortars & 6 50mm PAK 38)
2nd Cossack Regiment
Signals Platoon
1 Cossack Bicycle Battalion
4 Cossack Squadrons (9 LMGs & 2 50mm mortars)
1 Battalion
4 Cossack Squadrons (9 LMGs & 2 50mm mortars)
1 Support Squadron (8 80mm mortars & 6 50mm PAK 38)
3rd (Sswodno) Cossack Regiment
same as 1st (Don) Cossack Regiment
Kaukasus Cossack Brigade

4th (Kuban) Cossack Regiment
    same as 1st (Don) Cossack Regiment
5th Cossack Regiment
    same as 2nd Cossack Regiment
6th Cossack Regiment
    same as 1st (Don) Cossack Regiment
Cossack Artillery Regiment
  Don Cossack Artillery Battalion
    1 Battalion Staff
    1 Battalion Staff Battery
    3 Horse Batteries (4 75mm K18 & 2 LMGs ea)
  Kuban Cossack Artillery Battalion
    same as Don Cossack Artillery Battalion
Cossack (tmot) Pioneer Battalion
    2 Cossack Pioneer Companies
    1 Cossack Pioneer Company (forming)
    1 Cossack Pioneer Construction Company (forming)
    1 "C" Bridging Train
    1 (horse drawn) Pioneer Supply Train
Cossack (tmot) Signals Battalion
    1/,2/Cossack (tmot) Signals Company
    3/Cossack (tmot) Radio Company
    1 (tmot) Signals Supply Column
Supply Troops
    1 (mot) 90 ton Transportation Company (3 LMGs)
    1 60 ton Transportation Company (8 LMGs)
    2 Heavy Supply Columns
    1 Supply Company (6 LMGs)
Maintenance Troops
    3/88th (mot) Maintenance Company
Administration
    1 Bakery Company
    1 Butcher Company
    1 (mot) Divisional Administration Platoon
Medical
    1/,2/(tmot) Cossack Medical Companies
    1/,2/(tmot) Cossack Ambulance Companies
Veterinary Troops
    1 Veterinary Company
    1 (mot) Veterinary Supply Column
Other
    1 (mot) Military Police Detachment

The 1st, 2nd & 4th Squadrons of the 600th Cossack Battalion, formerly with the 145th Grenadier Regiment (65th Infantry Division) was brought into the division on 7/10/43. The 3rd and 5th Squadrons arrived on 7/15/43 and all five squadrons were then incorporated into the Platov Cossack Regiment. This organization for the Cossack regiments proved inadequate and by November one squadron was converted into a machine gun squadron. A few other changes were implemented

as well and in November 1943 the division was organized and equipped as follows:

1st Cossack Division
    1 Division Staff & Divisional Band
Don Cossack Brigade
  1st Don Cossack Regiment
    2 Cossack Battalions, each with
      3 Cossack Squadrons (9 LMGs & 2 50mm mortars)
      1 Machine Gun Squadron (8 HMGs & 4 80mm mortars)
      1 Support Squadron (8 80mm mortars & 6 50mm PAK 38)
  2nd Cossack Regiment
    1 Cossack Bicycle Battalion
      3 Cossack Squadrons (9 LMGs & 2 50mm mortars)
      1 Machine Gun Squadron (8 HMGs & 4 80mm mortars)
    1 Battalions
      3 Cossack Squadrons (9 LMGs & 2 50mm mortars)
      1 Machine Gun Squadron (8 HMGs & 4 80mm mortars)
    1 Support Squadron (8 80mm mortars & 6 50mm PAK 38)
  3rd (Sswodno) Cossack Regiment
    same as 1st (Don) Cossack Regiment
Kaukasus Cossack Brigade
  4th (Kuban) Cossack Regiment
    same as 1st (Don) Cossack Regiment
  5th Cossack Regiment
    same as 2nd Cossack Regiment
  6th Cossack Regiment
    same as 1st (Don) Cossack Regiment
Cossack Artillery Regiment
  Don Cossack Artillery Battalion
    unchanged
  Kuban Cossack Artillery Battalion
    unchanged
Cossack Pioneer Battalion
    3 Cossack Pioneer Companies
    1 Cossack Pioneer Construction Company
    1 "C" Bridging Train
    1 Pioneer Supply Train
Cossack Signals Battalion
    unchanged
Supply Troops
    1 (mot) 90 ton Transportation Company (3 LMGs)
    3 60 ton Transportation Companies (8 LMGs ea)
    1 Supply Company (6 LMGs)
Maintenance Troops
    3/88th (mot) Maintenance Company

Administration
   unchanged
Medical
   unchanged
Veterinary Troops
   unchanged
Other
   1 (mot) Military Police Detachment

As the Germans withdrew from the Crimea and Kuban, thousands of Cossack families fled with them. A Cossack settlement was established in Novogrudok, in Belorussia. While there, the Cossacks organized their own self-defense force, without waiting for German authorization to do so. However, as the Soviet Army got closer, the Cossacks were withdrawn to Tolmezzo, in northern Italy. At that time, the settlement reportedly contained 15,590 men, women, and children.

The division was sent, not to Russia, but to Yugoslavia, where they participated in the famous Operation *"Rösselsprung"* (knight's move), which was designed to capture Tito.

During the summer of 1944 the second brigade was separated from the division and both were expanded into full divisional strength.

In November 1944 the SS announced that it intended to take over both divisions. Pannwitz chose not to resist and realized that it would permit the two divisions to maintain a regular supply of modern arms and equipment. Shortly thereafter both divisions joined the Waffen SS and became part of the SS Cossack Cavalry Corps, which consisted of the 1st and 2nd Cossack Cavalry Divisions.

Himmler projected the formation of a third Cossack division to be based on Renteln's Cossack Regiment, then designated 360th Fortress Grenadier Regiment, and that it would include the Kalmuck Cavalry Corps. This proposed organization was never ordered mobilized.

On 17 March 1945 the division is shown, in German OKH records, as having the following strength:

1st Cossack Division: Oberst Wagner (commanding)
   1 strong infantry battalion (not from division)[1]
   7 medium infantry battalions (one battalion not from division)
   4 light artillery batteries
   5 heavy anti-tank guns

The two cossack divisions fought in Yugoslavia and when the war ended fought their way north into Austria and Northern Italy. They were interned by the British 8th Army outside Volkermarkt. Efforts to negotiate an escape to the west failed. The Yalta Agreements required the surrendering of all Soviet citizens to the Russian authorities. The British 6th Armored Division felt obliged to conform to this agreement and throughout May the bulk of the Cossacks were handed over. Though many escaped and disappeared into the countryside, the British sent 22,502 Cossacks back to the Soviet Union and to their deaths or years of internment in the notorious Soviet Gulag system. The leadership of the Cossack Corps, both German and Cossack, were executed by the NKVD. This included General Helmuth von Pannwitz, General Peter Krasnov, and General Andrei Shkuro, who were hung in 1947.

2nd Cossack Division

Formed November 1944 from the 2nd Cossack Cavalry Brigade. It contained the:

   3rd Kuban Cossack Reiter Regiment
   5th Don Cossack Reiter Regiment
   6th Terek Cossack Reiter Regiment
   2nd Divisional Service Units

On 17 March 1945 the division is shown, in German OKH records, as having the following strength:

2nd Cossack Division: commanding officer unknown
   5 strong infantry battalions (1 battalion not from the division)
   4 medium infantry battalions (1 battalion not from the division)
   1 cut up infantry battalion (1 battalion not from the division)
   5 light artillery batteries
   11 heavy anti-tank guns

[1] The strengths of the battalions are defined as follows:
   Strong Battalion: 400+ men
   Medium Battalion: 300–400 men
   Cut up battalion: 200–300 men
   Weak Battalion: 100–200 men
   Wrecked Battalion: 1–100 men

Cossack Plastun Brigade

In late February 1945 the 5th Cossack Regiment was expanded into a brigade-sized formation. The 5th Regiment was renumbered as the 7th Regiment and a new 8th Regiment was formed. It was slated to be organized into a full division, but the war ended before this could be done. This brigade was called the *Plastun* brigade, because it was "dismounted."

XV Cossack Corps

The XV Cossack Corps was organized on 25 February 1945, with the 1st and 2nd Cossack Divisions and the 1st and 2nd Cavalry Brigades. The 1st Division was commanded by Oberst Constantine Wagner and the second by Oberst Joachim von Schülz. The final formation in the division was a third brigade, built around Kononov's 5th Cossack Regiment. The corps was organized and commanded as follows:

Commanding General:	Helmut von Pannwitz
Chief of Staff:	Oberstleutnant von Steinsdorf
Operations:	Captain Graf von Schweinitz
Quartermaster:	Major Schneider
Intelligence:	Major Graf zu Eltz
Adjudant's Section:	Major Hemminghoffen
Legal:	Dr. Müller
General Staff	
Administrative Section:	Senior Official Hecht
Senior Staff Doctor:	Doctor d.R.Grass
Senior Staff Veterinarian:	Dr. Schwerdtfeger
Corps Engineer Officer:	Major Jans
Liaison to Ataman Staff:	Oberst von Renteln
Corps Signal Officer:	Major Schmidt
Corps Recon Section:	Major Weil
1st Cossack Division:	
Commanding Officer:	Oberst von Baath
Operations Officer:	Major Schlie
Quartermaster:	Major Gundel
1st Don Cossack Regt:	Oberst Wagner
2nd Siberian Cossack Regt:	Oberst Freiherr von Nolcken
4th Kuban Regiment:	Oberstleutnant von Klein
1st Cossack Artillery Regt:	Major von Eisenharte Rothe
2nd Cossack Division:	
Commanding Officer:	Oberst von Schültz
Operations Officer:	Major Rojhan
Quartermaster:	Captain Graf von Schmettow
3rd Kuban Cossack Regt:	Oberstleutnant Lehmann
5th Don Cossack Regiment:	Oberstleutnant Graf zu Eltz
6th Terek Cossack Regt:	Oberstleutnant Prinz zu Salm-Horstmar
2nd Cossack Artillery Regt:	Major Graf von Kottulinsky
Platsun Brigade:	
Commanding Officer:	Oberst Ivan Kononov
German Liaison Officer:	Major Graf von Rittberg

7th Platsun Regiment:	Oberstleutnant Borrisov
8th Platsun Regiment:	Major Scharow
Reconnaissance Section:	Hauptman Bondarenko

Other Cossack Formations

Not all the Cossack units were absorbed into Pannwitz's two Cossack divisions. In the Ukraine the 68th, 72nd, 73rd and 74th Schuma Battalions were formed in early 1944 and were classified as Cossack Mounted Front line Companies (*Kossacken-Reiter-Front-Abteilungen*) In northern Italy, during November 1944, there were four Platsun Regiments, one Terek, one Kuban, and two Don, as well as a cavalry formation of 962 men, a 376 man Reserve Regiment, and a 386 escort squadron (*Begleit Eskadron*).

The Cossack units were subject to changing their names periodically. A review of OKH records turned up several orders directing such name changes, but the reasons were not provided. A listing of those Cossack unit name changes that were gleaned from the limited selection of orders found follows.

An OKH order issued on 11/8/42 to Army Group Center directed the changing of the names of Cossack units assigned to it as follows:

Old Name	New Name
102nd Cossack Battalion	600th Cossack Battalion
1/6th Cossack Regiment	622nd Cossack Battalion
2/6th Cossack Regiment	623rd Cossack Battalion
1/7th Cossack Regiment	624th Cossack Battalion
2/7th Cossack Regiment	625th Cossack Battalion
559th Cossack Squadron	627th Ost Battalion
Cossack Unit, 137th Infantry Division	1st & 2nd Cossack Companies, 137th

The same order directed that the Cossack Battalion of the Chevallerie Group/LIX Corps, be renamed the 631st Cossack Battalion. An order issued on 10/23/42 directed the Cossack Hundertschaft (16th Corps) be renamed the 655th Cossack Squadron. It was serving in Army Group North. On 11/30/42 another order was issued for Army Group B and directed the following name changes:

Old Name	New Names
318th Reiter Battalion	213th Cossack Battalion
213th Reiter Battalion	3rd (Cossack) Battalion/57th Security Regt
Russian Battery	553rd Cossack Battery
580th Cossack Battalion	580th Ost Reiter Battalion
Sec. Hundertschaft 1/580th (2 cos)	
Sec. Hundertschaft 2/580th (2 cos)	4–7th (Ost) Companies, 581st Military Police Bn
Sec. Hundertschaft 3/580th (2 cos)	
Sec. Hundertschaft 4/580th (3 cos)	
Sec. Hundertschaft 5/580th (2 cos)	4–10th (Ost) Companies/552nd Wach Battalion
Sec. Hundertschaft 6/580th (2 cos)	
Sec. Hundertschaft 7/580th (3 cos)	
Sec. Hundertschaft 8/580th (2 cos)	4–10th (Ost) Companies/581st Wach Battalion
Sec. Hundertschaft 9/580th (2 cos)	
407th Cossack Hundertschaft	407th Ost Company
455th Cossack Hundertschaft	455th Ost Company
45th Cossack Hundertschaft	45th Ost Company

1st Co/75th Cossack Hundertschaft	1/75th Ost Company
2nd Co/75th Cossack Hundertschaft	2/75th Ost Company
82nd Cossack Hundertschaft	182nd Ost Company
323rd Cossack Hundertschaft	323nd Ost Company
340th Cossack Hundertschaft	340th Ost Company
377th Cossack Hundertschaft	377th Ost Company
383rd Cossack Hundertschaft	383rd Ost Company
387th Cossack Hundertschaft	387th Ost Company
68th Cossack Squadron	168th Ost Reiter Squadron
1/299th Cossack Squadron	1/299th Ost Reiter Squadron
2/299th Cossack Squadron	2/299th Ost Reiter Squadron
385th Cossack Squadron	385th Ost Reiter Squadron
403rd Reiter Battalion	403rd Cossack Battalion
Cossack Squadron, 113th Infantry Division	113th Cossack Squadron
Cossack Hundertschaft, IV Corps	404th Cossack Company

Yet another order, dated 1/15/43, directed that the 590th Korück Cossack Company z.b.V. become the 638th Cossack Company and that the 443rd Cossack Squadron be expanded to 443rd Cossack Battalion consisting of a staff, one squadron and two companies.

It is not possible to list all the Cossack formations raised, but OKH records have provided a partial listing of them, their equipment when known, and the units to which they were assigned. That listing follows:

Army Group South: As of 11/15/42.

Jungschultz Cossack Regiment
3 Battalions, each with 4 companies (21 LMGs, 8 HMGs, 2 50mm mortars & 7 anti-tank rifles. (organization as of 4/30/43)
3rd (Cossack) Battalion/57th Security Regiment
4 Squadrons (6 LMGs ea)
213th Cossack Battalion
4 Squadrons (no heavy weapons)
299th Cossack Battalion
2 Squadrons (3 LMGs & 3 50mm mortars ea)
403rd Cossack Battalion
3 Companies (3 LMGs & 5 50mm mortars ea)
1 Company (8 HMGs & 4 82mm mortars)
581st Cossack Battalion
2 Squadrons (5 LMGs & 2 50mm mortars ea)
1 Squadron (9 LMGs & 8 50mm mortars)
1 Squadron (9 LMGs & 1 50mm mortar)
1/444th Cossack Regiment
(organization unknown)
2/444th Cossack Regiment
(organization unknown)
1/454th Cossack Regiment
(organization unknown)
2/454th Cossack Regiment
(organization unknown)

113th Cossack Squadron
(5 LMGs)
1st Cossack Ausbildungs Battalion, Army Group B/South
3 Companies (2 LMGs & 1 50mm mortar ea)
2nd Cossack Ausbildungs Battalion, Army Group B/South
3 Companies (2 LMGs & 1 50mm mortar ea)
3rd Cossack Ausbildungs Battalion, Army Group B/South
3 Companies (2 LMGs & 1 50mm mortar ea)
(mot) Cossack Company, 3rd Panzer Corps
(weapons unknown)
404th Cossack Company
(6 LMGs)
553rd Cossack Battery
(4 122mm Russian guns)

Army Group Center: As of 11/15/42

443rd Cossack Battalion
1 Cossack Squadron (no heavy weapons)
2 Cossack Companies (no heavy weapons)
600th Cossack Battalion
2 Cavalry Squadrons (7 LMGs, 4 HMGs, 1 50mm & 3 82mm mortars)
2 Bicycle Squadrons (2 50mm mortars, 3 HMGs & 6 LMGs)
1 Gun Company (2 anti-tank guns & 2 infantry guns)
622nd Cossack Battalion
5 cos, LMGs & 50mm mortars
623rd Cossack Battalion
5 cos, LMGs & 50mm mortars
624th Cossack Battalion
5 cos, LMGs & 50mm mortars
625th Cossack Battalion
5 cos, LMGs & 50mm mortars

631st Cossack Battalion
1 Staff Company
1 Pioneer Platoon (3 LMGs)
1 Signals Platoon
1 Anti-Tank Platoon (3 PAK)
1 Mortar Platoon (6 82mm mortars)
3 Rifle Companies (12 LMGs & 3 50mm mortars)
1 Machine Gun Company (12 HMGs)
1st Cossack Company, 137th Brigade
(6 LMGs, 2 50mm mortars, 1 heavy anti-tank rifle & 2 82mm mortars)
2nd Cossack Company, 137th Brigade
(6 LMGs, 2 50mm mortars, 1 heavy anti-tank rifle & 2 82mm mortars)
638th Cossack Company
(LMGs & 50mm mortars)

Army Group North: As of 11/15/42

655th Cossack Squadron
(no heavy weapons)

Army Group A: As of 3/25/43

Platov Cossack Regiment
Kuban Cossack Regiment
1st & 2nd Cossack Companies, 97th Jäger Division

Formations with Army Group South on 4/30/43

Cossacks
Cossack Ausbildungs Company
213th Cossack Battalion
4 squadrons & 1 machine gun squadron
5th Kuban Cossack Battalion
4 squadrons
161st Cossack Battalion
4 squadrons
126th Cossack Battalion
4 squadrons
1st Cossack Squadron (6th Panzer Division)
Cossack Hundertschaft (57th Infantry Division)
1/82nd Cossack Squadron (XXX Panzer Corps)
Corps Cossack Squadron (III Panzer Corps)
Dr Doll Kalmuck Verband
3 Battalions (5 sqns ea)
1 Battalion (4 sqns)
Ost Ausbildungs Squadron Kranz (Cossack)
(3 sqns)
1/,2/454th Cossack Regiment
3 squadrons in each battalion
3/,4/454th Cossack Regiment
4 squadrons in each battalion

244th Cossack Squadron
403rd Ost Ritter (Cossack) Battalion
1 Squadron
1 Company
1 Machine Gun Company
(27 LMGs, 4 HMGs 15 50mm mortars, 3 82mm mortars & 3 anti-tank rifles total)

Cossack Units in Service in OB West: As of 1/15/44.

1st Army
LXXX Corps
von Renteln Ost Staff z.b.V.
623rd Cossack Battalion, 708th Grenadier Division
622nd Cossack Battalion, 708th Grenadier Division
LXXXVI Corps
625th Cossack Battalion, 344th Grenadier Division
624th Cossack Battalion, 344th Grenadier Division
638th Cossack Company, 344th Grenadier Division

Cossack Formations in German Service: As of 3/27/45.

6th Panzer Army
Cossack Squadron (6th Panzer Division)
Army Group Center
4th Cossack Construction Company, 9th Grenadier Regiment
1st Panzer Army
574th Cossack Battalion
4th Panzer Army
57th Cossack Battalion
213th Cossack Battalion
443rd Cossack Battalion
4th Army Group
6th Cossack Construction Company, 46th Grenadier Regiment
4th Cossack Construction Company, 97th Grenadier Regiment

The Kalmucks

The Kalmucks are a mongolic people who inhabit a region northwest of the Caspian Sea and west of the Volga. They are a nomadic people and are Tibetan Buddhists. An autonomous Kalmuck Republic was established in this region in 1935 by Stalin, but abolished immediately after WWII because of the Kalmuck's active cooperation with the Germans during the war.

The Kalmucks have a military history and served with the Russian army from shortly before the Napoleonic wars. There is a famous story of a French general mocking the wild looking Kalmucks, armed with bows and arrows, who suggested that they were militarily worthless in an era of muskets and cannons. His leg was shortly thereafter pinioned to his saddle by a Kalmuck arrow. No doubt his attitude changed considerably and immediately.

When the Germans reached the Kalmuck regions, their attitude towards the Kalmucks was conciliatory, no doubt because they realized that they did not need to stir up another people along their already horribly overextended lines of communications. On the staff of the 16th (mot) Infantry Division were a number of officers familiar with the Kalmuck language, most notably a Russian born Sudeten German officer named Otmar Werva, who had adopted the name Otto Doll. He had served as a cavalry officer in the Russian White Army during the Russian Civil War. Later he joined Admiral Canaris' *Abwehr* and served, for a time, in Odessa.

In August 1943 Doll was ordered to establish contact with the leaders of the Kalmuck people and sent into a most inhospitable region. He apparently made an excellent impression, no doubt enhanced by his promises of the establishment of an independent Kalmuck state after the war.

The Kalmucks responded positively, abolishing the hated collective farming system, and returning to the traditional nomadic pastoralism. A national committee was established to act as a provisional government, but was probably little more than part of the German military administration. However, the Kalmucks policed their own region, established a regional militia and security units much like the *Schuma* units in other regions. In addition to these defensive troops, a number of independent mounted squadrons patrolled the region without German garrisons.

The first regular Kalmuck military unit formed was the 103rd Defense Troop (*Abwehrtrupp 103*). It was raised in August 1941 and served to prevent Soviet Partisan harassment of the German rear areas. In September 1942 the 16th (mot) Infantry Division raised and equipped two squadrons of Kalmuck cavalry, equipping them with German and captured Russian equipment. On 10/17/41 they were officially incorporated into the German army and on 11/30/41 they were given the names *1st and 2nd Kalmückenschwadron 66*. They were lightly armed, having as heavy weapons only nine light machine guns each.

Dr. Doll's unit was "offically" formed on 10/17/42, and was initially known as the Kalmücken-Legion. Sonderführer Werba was the only known officer who could actually translate the unique language of the Kalmuck people, so he was chosen to lead the unit. It was for security reasons that the formation was given the name Dr. Doll. Werba led the formation until his death in July of 1944. The formation itself was renamed as the Kalmücken-Verband Dr. Doll in February 1943. It consisted of four battalions, each of five squadrons and a "Jagdschwadron." It had a total strength of around 3,400 men in August of 1943. The formation was later expanded to two brigades each of two regiments, and given the name "Kalmücken Kavalerie Korps," but this may only be an unofficial title, as the records do not indicate if this name was ever official. It may well have contineud to be officially known as Kalmücken-Verband Dr. Doll. It continued to fight well into 1945 in both Poland and the Balkans. It was taken captive by the partisan forces of Tito when the war finally ended.

When the formation of the Cossack Cavalry Division was being considered in 1943, Colonel Nazorov's Kalmuck Regiment was sent to Kherson in the Ukraine to join it, but the German authorities decided that they were not suitable because of their very different ethnic background.

When Stalingrad fell in January 1943 the Red Army moved to reconquer the Kalmuck steppes. Fearing reprisals, the populace evacuated during the summer of 1943 and fled westwards. The Germans actively recruited among the evacuees, further increasing their Kalmuck forces. On 4/30/43 OKH records show that Dr. Doll's Kalmuck Verband had a strength of three battalions, each with five squadrons, and a 4th Battalion with only four squadrons. By July 1943 several Kalmuck cavalry squadrons were formed and by August the formation of the Kalmuck Cavalry Corps (*Kalmückische Kavallerie Korps*, or KKK) had occurred. The corps consisted of a headquarters staff and four detachments, each with six squadrons. Each squadron had three, instead of the former two, troops apiece. One squadron in each detachment was classified as the *Jagdschwadron* and served as an elite troop.

217

In June 1944 the KKK contained four battalions, each of which had six squadrons, but the 9th, 10th, 11th, 15th and 16th were left behind in the Kalmuck steps to perform guerilla war behind the Soviet lines. Though it is not known which parts of it were so equipped, it is known that parts of the KKK were mounted on bactrian camels.

In July 1944 Dr. Doll was killed in action by the Soviets. After his death the KKK was reorganized into two brigades, each with two regiments. It had a strength of 174 officers, 374 NCOs, and 2,917 rank and file. It was equipped with German, Dutch, and Russian equipment. Initially the Germans provided only a small number of "advisors," but after July all the senior officer positions were filled by Germans.

The KKK retreated through the Ukraine into Poland, where it fought at Radom in January 1945 and was virtually wiped out. The small remainder withdrew into Bavaria and was organized into a dismounted cavalry regiment, which was sent to join the XV Cossack Cavalry Corps in Croatia.

The Ostvolk (Eastern People)

Russia was far from a monolithic structure. It contained numerous diverse ethic groups, many of which had long histories of resenting Russian suzerainty and domination. Combined with the longstanding hatred of Russia, the new Soviet regime was often even more hated, even by the Russians, so when the Germans invaded, their initial reception was often one of liberator rather than one of conqueror. Deserters appeared in the hundreds before German units offering their services in any capacity and they were taken in gladly. They were given the names "*Hilfsfreiwilliger*" (Volunteer Helpers) or *Hiwis* for short. Initially, their functions were the various menial tasks such as cooking, digging latrines, officers' batmen, etc., but more than once they jumped into combat roles when the opportunity arose. Hundreds of the Hiwis were gradually sucked into the role of combatant, despite the lack of orders and the German ethnic attitudes of the period. The 134th Infantry Division began openly enlisting Russians in July 1941. Other divisions refrained from such overt violation of Hitler's orders, but more than willingly took the Russians on an unofficial basis.

During the winter of 1941/42 the first *Osttruppen* or Eastern Troops were formed. By early 1942 six battalions of Osttruppen were formed in Army Group Center under Oberst von Tresckow. These units were given territorial designations, like Volga, Berezina, and Pripet. Initially they were used in the rear on antipartisan operations with the security divisions, but slowly they were brought forward into the front lines.

In early 1942 racist elements of the German hierarchy brought this to Hitler's attention. He responded to the movement by prohibiting the use of Russian "sub humans" as soldiers and on 2/10/42 issued a Führer Order that limited the use of those existent units to rear area operations only. Despite his obvious displeasure, the Osttruppen continued to expand. The OKH was to authorize the use of Hiwis up to 10 to 15 percent of divisional strength and by August 1942 official regulations were issued governing uniforms, pay, decoration, and insignia. By early 1943 an estimated 80,000 Russians were serving the Wehrmacht in *Ostbataillonen*.

The formation of Russian units in the German Army would have been quite limited had not Soviet General Vlassov been captured in July 1942. He had been a prominent general after the war erupted, but in March 1942 he was ordered to liberate Leningrad with the 2nd Soviet Assault Army. His attack failed and his army of nine infantry divisions, six infantry brigades, and an armored brigade were surrounded, abandoned by Stalin, and crushed, leaving the Germans with 32,000 prisoners.

Among the German High Command there had always been some hope of forming a Russian army to assist them in the conquest of Soviet Russia. As time progressed, it became apparent that Vlassov was the ideal man to form this army. As the war progressed and the German effort in Russia began failing, Hitler was eventually persuaded to permit the formation of the army.

The first steps occurred in August 1942 when General Köstring formed an Inspectorate which was to organize Caucasian troops. Köstring, however, ignored this limitation and took all volunteers possible. When Köstring retired in January 1943 the post of *General der Ostruppen* was created and given to General Hellmich, who had no previous experience with the Russians. Fortunately, Hellmich and Köstring's service overlapped and the two men agreed on Köstring's earlier decisions. The Osttruppen was absorbing not only Caucasians, but Ukrainians, Russians, Azerbaijanis, and Turkistanis. In January 1944 Köstring, now apparently out of retirement, took over from Hellmich with the new title *General der Freiwilligen Verbände* (General of Volunteer Units).

In the meantime, Hitler had authorized the formation of a Russian army under Vlassov. In November 1942 a Russian National Committee was established in Berlin with Vlassov serving as chairman. It then issued the Smolensk Manifesto, calling for the destruction of Stalinism, the conclusion of an honorable peace with Germany, and Russian participation in the "New Europe." The German Army intelligence them proceeded to drop copies of leaflets over the Russian lines, as well as a carefully planned accident which resulted in their being dropped over German lines as well. It appears that Hitler had forbidden any release of this in the German press.

During the winter of 1942/43, faced with the destruction of the 6th Army in Stalingrad and Rommel's expulsion from North Africa, Hitler began to reconsider the role he had allocated to Vlassov's *Russkaia Osvoboditelnaia Armiia* or ROA. The desertion rate from the Soviet army rose to 6,500 in July 1943, compared to 2,500 the previous year, as a result of ROA propaganda and the future looked bright. However, in September 1943 Hitler announced that the ROA was to be dissolved. The German generals pleaded with him, pointing out that the Russian front would collapse, as there were currently 78 Ost battalions, 122 companies, one regiment and innumerable supply, security, and other units then serving with the German Army, not to mention the thousands of Hiwis in the German units. Certainly there were 750,000 Russians then serving in the German Army and some estimates go so far as to suggest that 25 percent of the German Army on the Russian front was made up of ethnic Russians.

A screaming and raging Hitler was eventually brought to compromise and only those units whose loyalty was suspect were to be disbanded and the rest would be transferred to the West. This being left in Wehrmacht hands, the disbandings were limited to 5,000 men and serious procrastination prevented many transfers westwards. However, by October 1943 large numbers of Ostruppen did begin moving west. This was accomplished by exchanging Ost battalions for German battalions in the west. These Ost battalions were then formally incorporated into the German divisions where they were assigned. The morale of the Osttruppen began to collapse. Vlassov was persuaded to write them an open letter announcing these transfers were only a temporary expediency and hinted at bigger and better things. When the Allies invaded Normandy they were startled to find that many of their German prisoners were, in fact, Russians and they soon had 20,000 ROA prisoners in custody. Though Himmler refused to believe Köstring's reports, at that time there were 100,000 Eastern volunteers in the Luftwaffe and Navy and another 800,000 in the German Army.

The continuing reversal of German military hopes was slowly bringing even the SS around to reconsidering the desirability of Russian troops. In the east the SS was, by late 1943, regularly rounding up 15–20-year olds to serve as Flak helpers. There was discussion of the creation of an Eastern Moslem SS Division and several Slavic legions were forming in the SS. Himmler soon began considering himself as the leader of the "Army of Europe" and began taking any non-German human material he could find into his hands. It was not long before he saw Vlassov's ROA as another force that could be added. Himmler approached Vlassov and proposed the formation of a Committee for the Liberation of the Peoples of Russia (*Komitet Osvobozhdeniia Narodov Rossi* or K.O.N.R.) It was to be allowed to raise an army of five divisions, two of which were to be raised immediately. The personnel would be drawn from the existing ROA units and from among the Ostarbeiter then in Germany.

The first two units formed were placed under Vlassov's command on 1/28/45, the 600th and 650th Russian Divisions. In Neuren an air force or air division was organized that consisted of an air transport squadron, a reconnaissance squadron, a flak regiment, a paratrooper battalion, and a flying training unit. This force of some 4,000 men was assigned to General V.I. Maltsev. On 2/1/45 Göring formally handed this division over to Vlassov's command. By March 1945 the KONR numbered some 50,000 men. The Cossack Cavalry Corps was promised to Vlassov by Himmler, as was the Russian Guard Corps in Serbia, but in fact neither was ever placed under his command.

The KONR fought its first battle in February 1945 when a force of the 600th Division attacked in Pomerania and its engagement was a complete success. Hundreds of Soviet soldiers changed sides and joined it. In March it moved to the Oder front and was ordered to attack the Soviet Army near Frankfurt. However, it was so pounded by the Soviets that it withdrew to the south and back into Czechoslovakia. On 5/5/45 the Czech communists began a revolt in Prague and Buniachenko ordered the 600th Division to assist them. Their assistance was refused by the Czechs and, as the war ended the next day, the division was taken prisoner by the Americans.

The 650th Division, except for one regiment, were captured by the Russians and either executed or sent into the Russian Gulag. Vlassov was snatched from American hands by the Russians, suffered through a short show trial, and was quickly executed along with the major leaders of the KONR.

599th Russian Brigade

Formed in April 1945 in Aalborg, Denmark, as part of the Russian Liberation Army under Vlassov. It contained:

1/,2/,3/1604th Grenadier Regiment (from 714th (Russian) Grenadier Regiment)

1/,2/,3/1605th Grenadier Regiment
1/,2/,3/1606th Grenadier Regiment

The division was intended to be expanded to form the 3rd Vlassov Division.

600th (Russian) Infantry Division

Formed on 12/1/44 as part of the Russian Liberation Army under Vlassov with what was to have become the 29th Waffen SS Grenadier Division (1st Russian). On 2/28/45 it contained:

1/,2/1601st Grenadier Regiment
1/,2/1602nd Grenadier Regiment
1/,2/1603rd Grenadier Regiment

1/,2/,3/,4/1600th Artillery Regiment
1600th Division Support Units

650th (Russian) Division

Formed in March 1945 as part of Vlassov's Russian Liberation Army. The division was organized with prisoners of war and contained, on 4/5/45:

1/,2/1651st Grenadier Regiment
1/,2/1652nd Grenadier Regiment
1/,2/1653rd Grenadier Regiment

1/,2/,3/,4/1650th Artillery Regiment
1650th Divisional Support Units

The division was not fully formed and remained in Münsingen until overrun. On 17 January 1945 the organization of the 650th Infantry (Russian) Division was established as follows:

Division Staff
  Division Staff (2 LMGs)
  1650th (mot) Mapping Detachment
  1650th (mot) Military Police Detachment (3 LMGs)
1651st Infantry Regiment
  Regimental Staff
  Staff
  Staff Company (3 LMGs)
    1 Signals Platoon
    1 Engineer Platoon (6 LMGs)
    1 Reconnaissance Platoon (3 LMGs)
    1 Signals Platoon

2 Battalions, each with
  3 Infantry Companies (9 LMGs ea)
  1 Heavy Company (8 HMGs, 4 75mm infantry support guns, 1 LMG & 6 80mm mortars)
13th Infantry Support Company
  (2 150mm leIG, 1 LMG, 8 120mm mortars & 4 LMGs)
14th Panzerjäger Company
  (54 Panzerschreck, 18 Reserve Panzerschreck & 4 LMGs)
1652nd Infantry Regiment
  same as 1651st
1653rd Infantry Regiment
  same as 1651st
1650th (mounted) Reconnaissance Battalion
  4 Squadrons, each with (9 LMGs, 2 80mm mortars)

650th Panzerjäger Battalion
1 Staff
1 (mot) Staff Company (1 LMG)
1st Company (12 75mm PAK & 12 LMGs)
2nd (armored) Company
    14 Assault Guns (sturmgeschütz) & 16 LMGs
    Detachment captured Russian tanks
3rd (mot) Flak Company (9 37mm Flak guns & 5 LMGs)

650th Artillery Battalion
1 Staff
1 Staff Battery (1 LMG)
1st, 2nd & 3rd Battalions, each with
1 Staff
1 Staff Battery (1 LMG)
2 105mm leFH Batteries (4 105mm leFH & 4 LMGs ea)
1 75mm Battery (6 75mm guns & 3 LMGs)
4th Battalion
1 Staff
1 Staff Battery (1 LMG)
2 150mm sFH Batteries (6 150mm howitzers & 4 LMGs ea)

650th (bicycle) Pioneer Battalion
2 (bicycle) Pioneer Companies, each with (2 HMGs, 9 LMGs, 6 flamethrowers & 2 80mm mortars)
1 Pioneer Company (2 HMGs, 9 LMGs, 6 flamethrowers & 2 80mm mortars)

650th Signals Battalion
1 (tmot) Telephone Company (4 LMGs)
1 (tmot) Radio Company (2 LMGs)
1 (tmot) Signals Supply Detachment (2 LMGs)

650th Feldersatz Battalion
1 Supply Detachment
5 Replacement Companies, with a total of (50 LMGs, 12 HMGs, 6 80mm mortars, 1 120mm mortar 1 75mm leIG, 1 75mm PAK, 1 20mm/37mm Flak, 2 flamethrowers, 1 105mm leFH 18, 6 Panzerschrecke, & 56 Sturm Gewehr 41)

650th Divisional Support Regiment
Supply Troop
1650th (mot) 120 ton Transportation Company (4 LMGs)
1/,2/1650th Horse Drawn (30 ton) Transportation Companies (2 LMGs ea)
1650th Horse Drawn Supply Platoon
Other
1650th Ordnance Troop
1650th (mot) Vehicle Maintenance Troop
1650th Supply Company (3 LMGs)
1650th (mot) Field Hospital
1650th (mot) Medical Supply Company
1650th Veterinary Company (2 LMGs)

1650th (mot) Field Post Office

In a parallel formation to the ROA and KONR another large force of Russians was formed in March 1942 by German Intelligence. This force was the *Versuchsverband Mitte* (Experimental Formation of Army Group Center).

Though officially known as *Abwehr Abteilung 203* the unit was to have several names—Verband Graukopf, Boyarsky Brigade, Russian Special Duty Battalion, Ostintorf Brigade, and finally the Russian National Peoples Army (*Russkaia Natsionalnaya Narodnaya Armiya* or RNNA).

The unit was started when a Russian emigre, Sergi Ivanov, recruited several prominent Russian prisoners of war and other Russian exiles, to the German cause. Ivanov, acting as a liaison officer for the Abwehr, worked with Igor Sakharov, son of a White Russian General and emigre to Germany, and slowly they organized a force of 3,000 former prisoners of war. By December 1942 they had 7,000 men training.

A brigade was formed consisting of four battalions, an artillery battalion, and an engineer battalion. The organization of the units was based on the Russian model. In August 1942 Colonel Boyarsky took command. In December Feldmarschal von Kluge inspected the brigade, was pleased with what he saw, and expressed his pleasure with its actions in combat in the German rear in May 1942. He then stated that he would issue the unit German uniforms and weapons and split it into a number of infantry battalions, which would be assigned to various German combat divisions.

This offhanded command shattered the brigade's morale and 300 men promptly deserted. It had seen itself as the cadre of a Russian army of liberation. Despite their protests, the brigade was broken into the 633rd, 634th, 635th, 636th, and 637th Ost Battalions and employed in antipartisan operations.

The Ethnic Legions

As mentioned earlier, the invading Germans were often seen as liberators by the various ethnic minorities living under the Soviet yoke. In the fall of 1941, as Hitler visited his East Prussian headquarters, he was approached by General Erkilet of the Turkish General staff, who urged him to intercede on behalf of the Soviet prisoners of war of Turkic nationality. Hitler, hoping to recruit Turkey as an ally, was sympathetic. He granted permission in November 1941 for the formation of a Turkistani Legion. Before the end of the year three more ethnic legions were formed. An OKH order dated 12/30/41 formed the Caucasian Moslem Legion, Georgian Legion, and Armenian Legion. Later the Caucasian Moslem Legion was split into the North Caucasian Legion and the Azerbaijani Legion. In mid-1942 the Crimean Tartar and Volga Tartar Legions were raised.

Despite his approval of the formation of national committees, Hitler was determined that these would never become a threat to German security and limited them to raising units no larger than a battalion and that these units be widely distributed throughout the German army to prevent any massing of them.

In May 1943, however, Hitler permitted the formation of the 162nd (Turkish) Infantry Division, to serve as the parent unit for the various legion battalions.

There was also the *Sonderverband Bergmann*, a Caucasian unit formed by Admiral Canaris in December 1941. It was recruited from Georgian, Armenian, Azerbaijani and other Caucasian prisoners of war built around a cadre of like ethnic pre-war anti-Soviet emigres living in Germany.

The original intention of the Sonderverband Bergmann was one of a fifth column to be parachuted behind the Soviet Army, but so many volunteers appeared that it combat as follows:

was quickly organized into a two-battalion regiment. These two battalions were thrown into the lines in the east and were soon exhausted by casualties.

In August 1942 General Köstring was appointed Inspector General of Turkic and Caucasian Forces. He applied his knowledge of the Russian peoples and his managerial skills such that in September 1944 the following strengths of these peoples in the German Army were reported by the OKH.

In Legions and Replacement Battalions
Armenians	11,600	
Azerbaijanis	13,000	
Georgians	14,000	
North Caucasians	10,000	
Total		48,600

In Pioneer and Transport Units
Armenians	7,000	
Azerbaijanis	4,795	
Georgians	6,800	
North Caucasians	3,000	
Total		21,595

In German Army Battalions	25,000
In the Luftwaffe & Waffen SS	7,000
Grand Total	102,195

This listing does not include the Turkistanis, probably because they were long past being minor legions and had been fully incorporated into a full combat unit the 162nd Infantry Division.

However, some details are known about the establishment of independent Turkistani battalions. The following table shows when a number of independent Turkistani battalions were organized and ready for combat as follows:

Date	10/2/42	11/10/42	12/1/42	1/10/43	1/15/43	1/25/43
Battalions	812th	784th	785th	803rd	797th	799th
		806th		810th	798th	
				797th	803rd	
					810th	
					786th	
					825th	

Date	2/1/43	2/15/43	2/20/43	3/1/43	3/10/43	4/15/43
Battalions	822nd	828th	817th	788th	827th	789th
	818th	790th		835th		
	813th	787th		791st		
		826th				

Various records indicate that the 1/76th (377th Infantry Division) and 1/389th (45th Infantry Division) were Turkish Battalions. On 2/15/43 the 452nd and 781st Turkish Battalions were assigned to Army Group A, the 783rd, 785th, and 787th to Army Group B, and the 450th, 782nd, and 784th to Army Group Don.

German records show that the following Turkish battalions were ready and assigned to German divisions as follows in September 1942:

Turkistani Battalion	1/9th Infantry Division
Turkistani Battalion	1/73rd Infantry Division
Turkistani Battalion	1/76th Infantry Division
Turkistani Battalion	1/94th Infantry Division
Turkistani Battalion	1/98th Infantry Division
Turkistani Battalion	1/111th Infantry Division
Turkistani Battalion	1/125th Infantry Division
Turkistani Battalion	1/295th Infantry Division
Turkistani Battalion	1/298th Infantry Division
Turkistani Battalion	1/370th Infantry Division
Turkistani Battalion	1/371st Infantry Division

German records show that the following Ost battalions were ready and assigned to German divisions as follows on 11/15/42 and 1/1/43:

Georgian Battalion	1/1st Mountain Division
Georgian Battalion	2/198th Infantry Division
Azerbaijani Battalion	1/4th Mountain Division
Azerbaijani Battalion	1/97th Jäger Division
Azerbaijani Battalion	1/101st Jäger Division
Azerbaijani Battalion	2/73rd Infantry Division
Armenian Battalion	2/9th Infantry Division
Turkistani Battalion	1/297th Infantry Division
Turkistani Battalion	1/389th Infantry Division
Turkistani Battalion	1/305th Infantry Division

Turkistani Battalion	1/44th Infantry Division
Turkistani Battalion	1/100th Jäger Division
Turkistani Battalion	1/384th Infantry Division

The Turkistani battalions had German cadres. The battalion staff contained 5 German officers, 2 German warrant officers, 13 German NCOs, and 8 German soldiers. The staff companies contained 1 German officer, 10 German NCOs and 6 German soldiers. The Turkish rifle companies contained 1 German officer, 7 German NCOs, and 4 German soldiers. The Turkish machine gun companies contained 1 German officer, 8 German NCOs, and 5 German soldiers. They were all technical specialists, not combat soldiers, and filled the senior administrative positions in the battalion and companies.

As the war progressed most of the ethnic legions remained under the army. Some, such as the Armenian Legion, were disbanded. When the war ended the 162nd Division was serving in Italy. Fearing the Americans would assume they were Japanese, they chose to surrender to the Italian partisans. When they were repatriated to Russia they were dressed in British battle dress. Their fate, after that, was no doubt the Gulag.

The contribution of the ethnic legions and their support troops was significant, but their loyalty varied. An Armenian unit in Lyons mutinied and the 797th Georgian Battalion simply refused to fight. However, the most serious incidents took place in Albania where a Turkoman battalion murdered its German officers and defected *en masse* and at Texel, on the Dutch coast, where the 1,200 man 822nd Georgian Battalion killed its German cadre and fought against the Germans for a week until they were wiped out.

162nd (Turkish) Infantry Division

Formed on 5/21/43 from the Turkistani, Azerbaijani, and Georgian Legions with the staff of the disbanded 162nd Infantry Division. The division had:

1/,2/,3/303rd Infantry Regiment (from 2nd Turkistani Legion)
1/,2/,3/314th Infantry Regiment (from Azerbaijani Legion)
162nd Division Battalion
1/,2/,3/,4/236th Artillery Regiment (from 1st Turkistani Legion)

936th Pioneer Battalion
936th Divisional Supply Troop
236th Division Support Units

On 8/15/44 the division was expanded by the addition of a third regiment. The 1/,2/329th Infantry Regiment were formed from the 804th and 806th Azerbaijani Battalions and the 162nd Division Battalion. Later the 3/303rd and 2/314th were disbanded. The 3/314th became the 2/314th. The division withdrew to Austria, where it was captured by the English.

Freiwilliger (Volunteer) Stamm Division

Formed in southern France on 2/1/44 with ethnic Slavs and Turks. Its function was to train cadres for all the various groups of ethnic volunteers. The division had:

1st Freiwilliger Stamm Regiment (Turks, Georgians and North Caucasians)
2nd Freiwilliger Stamm Regiment (Armenians and Azerbaijanis)

3rd Freiwilliger Stamm Regiment (Russians and Ukrainians)
4th Freiwilliger Stamm Regiment (Russians and Ukrainians)
5th Freiwilliger Stamm Regiment (Cossacks)

Ost Units Raised and Renamed

On 11/15/42 the 20th Mountain Corps had only one Ost unit. This was the 690th Ost Company. On 11/15/42 Army Group South contained the following Osttruppen. They were organized and armed as shown below:

720th Commander of Ost Troops z.b.V.
(no integral units assigned)
551st Ost Battalion
6 Companies (9 LMGs, 2 HMGs, & 2 50mm mortars ea)
1 Reconnaissance Company (9 LMGs, 2 HMGs, & 2 50mm mortars ea)
1 Bicycle Company (9 LMGs, 2 HMGs, & 2 50mm mortars ea)
555th Ost Wach Battalion
(weapons unknown)
45th Ost Company
(4 LMGs)
1st Ost Company, 75th
(17 LMGs & 4 50mm mortars)
2nd Ost Company, 75th
(9 LMGs & 1 50mm mortar)
113th Ost Company
(no heavy weapons)
179th Ost Company
(no heavy weapons)
182nd Ost Company
(no heavy weapons)
323rd Ost Company
(5 LMGs)
340th Ost Company
(12 LMGs)
377th Ost Company
(no heavy weapons)
383rd Ost Company

(3 LMGs & 2 50mm mortars)
387th Ost Company
(4 LMGs)
407th Ost Company
(10 LMGs & 3 50mm mortars)
448th Ost Company
(12 LMGs, 2 50mm mortars, 2 82m mortars & 47mm guns)
455th Ost Company
(10 LMGs & 3 50mm mortars)
552nd Ost Company
(2 82mm mortars, 2 HMGs, & 6 LMGs)
1st, 2nd & 3rd Ost Companies, 556th
(no heavy weapons)
5th & 6th Ost Companies, 122nd Wach Battalion
(9 LMGs ea)
4–10th Ost Companies, 552nd Wach Battalion
3 Companies (4 LMGs & 3 50mm mortars ea)
1 Company (13 LMGs & 4 50mm mortars)
1 Company (13 LMGs & 5 50mm mortars)
1 Company (9 LMGs & 5 50mm mortars)
1 Company (9 LMGs & 4 50mm mortars)
4th & 5th Ost Companies, 571st Wach Battalion
(9 LMGs ea)
4–10th Ost Companies, 581st
3 Companies (3 LMGs ea)
2 Companies (4 LMGs ea)
2 Companies (3 LMGs & 1 50mm mortar ea)
580th Ost Reiter Battalion
3 Squadrons (11 LMGs & 2 50mm mortars ea)
9th (Ost) Reiter Squadron/4th Bicycle Regiment
(organization unknown)
168th Ost Reiter Squadron
(3 LMGs)
85th Ost Reiter Squadron
(organization unknown)

4th (Ost) Co/370th Pioneer Battalion
(organization unknown)
550th Ost Fz. Battalion
3 Companies (no heavy weapons)
Ost (Ukrainian) Supply Column, 551st Supply Battalion
(equipment unknown)
1–3rd Ost Truck Columns, 128th Supply Troop, 23rd Panzer Division
(equipment unknown)
176th Ost Construction Company
(no heavy weapons)
194th Ost Construction Company
(no heavy weapons)
295th Ost Construction Company
(no heavy weapons)

On 11/15/42 the following units were assigned to Army Group Center.

700th Commander of Ost Troops z.b.V
no integral units
701st Commander of Ost Troops z.b.V
　1st Battalion
　　4 Infantry Companies (12 LMGs & 4 50mm mortars ea)
　2nd Battalion
　　5th Machine Gun Company (12 HMGS & 4 82mm mortars)
　　6th Pioneer Company (4 LMGs)
　　7th Cavalry Squadron (9 LMGs, 2 HMGS & 6 50mm mortars)
　　8th Gun Company (2 122mm howitzers & 2 76.2mm guns)
　　9th Signals Company (no weapons)
702nd Commander of Ost Troops z.b.V
no integral units
703rd Commander of Ost Troops z.b.V
no integral units
704th Commander of Ost Troops z.b.V
no integral units
709th Commander of Ost Troops z.b.V
no integral units
82nd Ost Battalion
organization unknown
134th Ost Battalion
(4 companies—no heavy weapons)
134th Ost Construction Battalion
(4 companies—no heavy weapons)
197th Ost Battalion
3 Companies (12 LMGs, 4 HMGs & 4 50mm mortars)
229th Ost Battalion
(organization unknown)

308th Ost Battalion
1–2nd Companies (9 LMGs)
3rd Cavalry Squadron (no heavy weapons)
4th Company (2 47mm, 4 HMGs, 6 50mm & 2 82mm mortars)
339th Ost Battalion
4 Companies (no heavy weapons)
406th Ost Battalion
2 Companies (3 LMGs & 2 50mm mortars ea)
1 Company (4 HMGs, 12 LMGs & 6 50mm mortars)

412th Ost Battalion
4 Cos—3 LMGs ea)
427th Ost Battalion
2 Companies (12 LMGs & 3 50mm mortars ea)
1439th Ost Battalion
1 Company (12 LMGs & 3 50mm mortars)
441st Ost Battalion
4 Companies (4 HMGs, 6 LMGs, 2 82mm & 2 50mm mortars, & 1 medium AT gun)
1/447th Ost Regiment
5 Companies (no heavy weapons)
1 Squadron (no heavy weapons)
2/447th Ost Regiment
4 Companies (4 HMGs, 5 LMGs, 2 82mm & 2 50mm mortars)
1 Squadron (no heavy weapons)

456th Ost Battalion
3 Companies (no heavy weapons)
601st Ost Battalion
1 Staff Company
　1 Signals Platoon
　1 Bicycle Platoon (3 LMGs)
　1 Pioneer Platoon (2 LMG)
　1 Anti-Tank Platoon (3 medium AT guns)
　1 Infantry Gun Platoon (2 75mm leIG)
3 Companies (12 LMGs, 2 HMGS, 2 50mm & 1 82mm mortar ea)
602nd Ost Battalion
1 Staff Company
　1 Signals Platoon
　1 Bicycle Platoon (3 LMGs)
　1 Pioneer Platoon (2 LMG)
　1 Anti-Tank Platoon (3 medium AT guns)
　1 Infantry Gun Platoon (2 75mm leIG)
3 Companies (12 LMGs, 2 HMGS, 2 50mm & 1 82mm mortar ea)
603rd Ost Battalion
1 Staff Company
　1 Signals Platoon
　1 Bicycle Platoon (3 LMGs)
　1 Pioneer Platoon (2 LMG)
　1 Anti-Tank Platoon (3 medium AT guns)

1 Infantry Gun Platoon (2 75mm leIG)
3 Companies (12 LMGs, 2 HMGS, 2 50mm & 1 82mm mortar ea)

604th Ost Battalion
1 Staff Company
1 Signals Platoon
1 Bicycle Platoon (3 LMGs)
1 Pioneer Platoon (2 LMG)
1 Anti-Tank Platoon (3 medium AT guns)
1 Infantry Gun Platoon (2 75mm leIG)
3 Companies (12 LMGs, 2 HMGS, 2 50mm & 1 82mm mortar ea)

605th Ost Battalion
1 Staff Company
1 Signals Platoon
1 Bicycle Platoon (3 LMGs)
1 Pioneer Platoon (2 LMG)
1 Anti-Tank Platoon (3 medium AT guns)
1 Infantry Gun Platoon (2 75mm leIG)
3 Companies (12 LMGs, 2 HMGS, 2 50mm & 1 82mm mortar ea)

615th Ost Battalion
1 Company (12 LMGs, 4 50mm mortars & 3 82mm mortars)
1 Company (10 LMGs, 4 50mm mortars & 3 82mm mortars)
1 Company (10 LMGs, 4 50mm mortars & 2 82mm mortars)
1 Machine Gun Company (16 HMGs)

616th Ost Battalion
1 Company (12 LMGs, 4 50mm mortars & 3 82mm mortars)
1 Company (10 LMGs, 4 50mm mortars & 3 82mm mortars)
1 Company (10 LMGs, 4 50mm mortars & 2 82mm mortars)
1 Machine Gun Company (16 HMGs)

617th Ost Battalion
1 Company (12 LMGs, 4 50mm mortars & 3 82mm mortars)
1 Company (10 LMGs, 4 50mm mortars & 3 82mm mortars)
1 Company (10 LMGs, 4 50mm mortars & 2 82mm mortars)
1 Machine Gun Company (16 HMGs)

618th Ost Battalion
4 cos, (LMGs & light mortars assigned)

619th Ost Battalion]
3 cos, (LMGs & light mortars assigned)

620th Ost Battalion
3 rifle cos, (LMGs & light mortars assigned)
1 Machine Gun Co. (HMGs only)

627th Ost Battalion
1st Company (10 LMGs & 6 50mm mortars)

2nd Company (11 LMGs, 3 45mm PAK & 5 82mm mortars)
3rd Company (10 LMGs & 6 50mm mortars)
4th Company (weapons unknown)

628th Ost Battalion
Staff Company (2 45mm, 2 HMGs, 5 LMGs, 2 82mm mortars & 1 50mm mortars)
3 Companies (2 45mm, 2 HMGs, 8 LMGs, 2 82mm mortars & 2 50mm mortars)

629th Ost Battalion
Staff Company (2 45mm, 2 HMGs, 5 LMGs, 2 82mm mortars & 1 50mm mortars)
3 Companies (2 45mm, 2 HMGs, 8 LMGs, 2 82mm mortars & 2 50mm mortars)

630th Ost Battalion
Staff Company (2 45mm, 2 HMGs, 5 LMGs, 2 82mm mortars & 1 50mm mortars)
3 Companies (2 45mm, 2 HMGs, 8 LMGs, 2 82mm mortars & 2 50mm mortars)

633rd Ost Battalion
(1 staff company & 3 companies—no heavy weapons)

634th Ost Battalion
(1 staff company & 3 companies—no heavy weapons)

635th Ost Battalion
(1 staff company & 3 companies—no heavy weapons)

636th Ost Battalion
(1 staff company & 3 companies—no heavy weapons)

637th Ost Battalion
(1 staff company & 3 companies—no heavy weapons)

642nd Ost Battalion
4 Cos, no heavy weapons

643rd Ost Battalion
(organization unknown)

10th Ost Company
(3 LMGs)

25th Ost Company
(unknown number of LMGs)

24th Ost Company
(equipment unknown)

34th Ost Company
(6 LMGs & 1 50mm mortar)

37th Ost Company
(12 LMGs & 3 50mm mortars)

1st & 2nd Ost Companies, 84th Battalion
(no heavy weapons)

78th Ost Company
(12 LMGs & 3 50mm mortars)

85th Ost Company
(3 HMGs, 12 LMGs, 1 82mm mortar & 6 50mm mortars)

102nd Ost Company
(12 LMGs & 3 50mm mortars)

110th Ost Company
(2 HMGs, 9 LMGs,1 47mm gun & 2 82mm mortars)

1st & 2nd Ost Companies, 131st Brigade
(no heavy weapons)

152nd Ost Company
(12 LMGs & 3 50mm mortars)

178th Ost Company
(12 LMGs & 3 50mm mortars)

195th Ost Company
(9 LMGs & 4 50mm mortars)

1st Ost Company, 203rd Battalion
(equipment unknown)

205th Ost Company
(4 LMGs & 3 50mm mortars)

1st Ost Company, 221st Battalion
(equipment unknown)

253rd Ost Company
(2 HMGs, 9 LMGs, 2 82mm mortars, 3 50mm mortars & 1 medium PAK)

260th Ost Company
(3 LMGs)

1st Ost Company, 263rd Brigade
(10 LMGs & 3 50mm mortars)

2nd Ost Company, 263rd Brigade
(5 LMGs)

1st Ost Company, 267th Brigade
(15 LMGs & 4 50mm mortars)

2nd Ost Company, 267th Brigade
(7 LMGs & 3 50mm mortars)

268th Ost Company
(3 LMGs)

331st Ost Company
(3 LMGs & 1 50mm mortar)

409th Ost Company
(no heavy weapons)

420th Ost Company
(no heavy weapons)

1st Ost Company, 446th Battalion
(12 LMGs, 2 50mm mortars & 1 82mm mortar)

2nd Ost Company, 446th Battalion
(12 LMGs, 2 50mm mortars & 1 82mm mortar)

453rd Ost Company
(no heavy weapons)

612th Ost Company
(2 HMGs, 5 LMGs & 3 50mm mortars)

613th Ost Company
(LMGs & 50mm mortars)

626th Ost Company
(1 50mm mortar & 2 LMGs)

641st Ost Company, 559th Brigade
(LMGs & 50mm mortars)

5th Ost Company, 555th Security Battalion
(23 LMGs & 3 50mm mortars)

4th Ost Company, 555th Security Battalion
(no heavy weapons)

4th Ost Company, 551st Wach Battalion
(3 LMGs & 2 50mm mortars)

4–6th Ost Companies, 551st Wach Battalion
(equipment unknown)

4th, 5th & 6th Ost Companies, 508th Wach Battalion
(no heavy weapons)

4th Ost Company, 582nd Wach Battalion
(no heavy weapons)

5th Ost Company, 582nd Wach Battalion
(21 LMGs, 4 HMGs & 10 50mm mortars)

5th Ost Company, 722nd Wach Battalion
(equipment unknown)

5th Ost Company, 587th Landesschützen Battalion
(no heavy weapons)

5th Ost Company, 675th Landesschützen Battalion
(no heavy weapons)

5th Ost Company, 826th Landesschützen Battalion
(no heavy weapons)

156th Ost Wach Company, 156th Brigade
(no heavy weapons)

Ost Wach Company, 606th Battalion
(no heavy weapons)

1st, 2nd & 3rd Ost Wach Companies, 607th Battalion
(no heavy weapons)

Ost Wach Company, 608th Battalion
(no heavy weapons)

Ost Wach Company, 609th Battalion
(no heavy weapons)

1st & 3rd Ost Wach Companies, 610th Battalion
(no heavy weapons)

611th Ost Wach Company
(no heavy weapons)

639th Ost Wach Company
(no heavy weapons)

640th Ost Wach Company
(no heavy weapons)

644th Ost Wach Company
(equipment unknown)

645th Ost Wach Company
(equipment unknown)

Reiter Squadron, 201st Brigade
(no heavy weapons)

2nd Ost Reiter Squadron, 203rd Security Brigade
(no heavy weapons)

1st Ost Infantry Company, 203rd Security Brigade
(no heavy weapons)

2nd Ost Reiter Squadron, 221st Security Brigade
(4 LMGs & 6 HMGs)

1st Ost Company, 221st Security Brigade
(2 LMGs & 3 50mm mortars)

Ost Reiter Squadron, 286th Security Brigade
(no heavy weapons)

1st & 2nd Ost Reiter Squadron, 447th Cavalry Battalion
(equipment unknown)
621st Ost Artillery Battalion
2 Batteries (3 76.2mm howitzers ea)
1 Battery (2 122mm howitzers ea)
582nd Ost Battery
(equipment unknown)
614th Ost Battery
(3 76.2mm Russian howitzers)
134th Ost Construction Battalion
(no heavy weapons)
1st & 2nd Ost Radio/Construction Company, 515th
(no heavy weapons)
Ost Supply Company, 221st Supply Troop
(no heavy weapons)
Ost Supply Company, 286th Supply Troop
(no heavy weapons)
4th (Ost) Co/622nd Supply Battalion
(no heavy weapons)
4th (Ost) Co/687th Supply Battalion
(no heavy weapons)
4th (Ost) Co/690th Supply Battalion
(no heavy weapons)
4th & 5th (Ost) Cos/604th Supply Battalion
(equipment unknown)
4th Ost Ersatz Battalion
(equipment unknown)
1/,2/Ost Ersatz Regiment Mitte
(equipment unknown)
582nd Ost Ersatz Company
(equipment unknown)
582nd Ost NCO School

On 11/15/42 those units assigned to Army Group North were organized and equipped as follows:

711th Commander of Ost Troops z.b.V
No integral troops
710th Commander of Ost Troops z.b.V
No integral troops
653rd Ost Battalion
(4 cos—no heavy weapons)
654th Ost Battalion
(4 cos—no heavy weapons)
658th (Estonian) Ost Battalion
2 Cos (8 LMGs, 2 HMGS, 1 50mm & 1 82mm mortar ea)
1 Co (8 LMGs, 2 HMGS, & 1 50mm mortar)
1 Co (8 LMGs & 3 HMGs)
659th (Estonian) Ost Battalion
4 Cos (9 LMGs, 2 HMGs, & 1 50mm mortar ea)
660th (Estonian) Ost Battalion
2 Cos (8 LMGs, 3 HMGS, & 1 50mm mortar ea)

1 Co (8 LMGs, 2 HMGS, & 1 50mm mortar)
1 Co (8 LMGs & 3 HMGs)

661st Ost Battalion
3 Cos (7 LMGs, 2 HMGs, & 2 50mm mortar ea)
1 Co (7 LMGs, 2 HMGs, & 1 50mm mortar)
662nd Ost Battalion
3 Cos (9 LMGs, 1 HMG ea)
1 Co (8 LMGs, 2 HMGS, & 1 50mm mortar)
663rd Ost Battalion
2 Cos (4 LMGs, 1 HMG ea)
2 Cos (5 LMGs, 1 HMG ea)
664th (Finnish) Ost Battalion
3 Cos (10 LMGs, 2 HMGS, & 3 50mm mortars ea)
1 Co (9 LMGs, 2 HMGS, & 3 50mm mortars)
665th Ost Battalion
2 Cos (1 LMG, 3 50mm & 2 82mm mortars ea)
2 Cos (2 LMG, 2 50mm & 2 82mm mortars ea)
1 Co (2 LMGs, 2 50mm & 2 82mm mortars)
667th Ost Battalion
(6 cos, no heavy weapons)
668th Ost Battalion
(6 cos, no heavy weapons)
669th Ost Battalion
(6 cos, no heavy weapons)
59th Ost Company
(equipment unknown)
657th (Estonian) Ost Company
(1 50mm mortar & 4 LMGs)
1st 656th (Turkish) Company
(2 50mm mortars, 3 HMGS, 11 LMGs)
2nd 656th (Turkish) Company
(2 HMGS & 13 LMGs)
650th (Lithuanian) Ost Wach Company
(4 LMGs)
651st (Lithuanian) Ost Wach Company
(4 LMGs)
652nd (Lettish) Ost Wach Company
(equipment unknown)
1st & 2nd Lettish Construction Battalions
(equipment unknown)
1st, 2nd, 3rd, 4th, 5th & 6th Lithuanian Construction Battalions
(equipment unknown)
207th Ost Reiter Battalion
(2 cavalry squadrons—4 LMGs ea & a bicycle squadron—4 LMGs)
281st Ost Reiter Battalion
(2 cavalry squadrons—4 LMGs ea & a bicycle squadron—4 LMGs)
285th Ost Reiter Battalion
(2 cavalry squadrons—4 LMGs ea & a bicycle squadron—4 LMGs)

1st & 2nd Ost Batteries, 670th Artillery Battalion
(4 76.2mm Russian howitzers ea)
666th Ost Pioneer Battalion
4 Companies (6 LMGs ea)
574th Ost Supply Battalion
6 Companies (no heavy equipment)
671st Ost Signals Company
(equipment unknown)

16th Ost Ersatz Battalion
4 Companies (equipment unknown)
Naawa (Estonian) Ost Ersatz Battalion
(equipment unknown)
653rd Ost Ersatz Company
(no heavy weapons)

On 3/25/43, Army Group A was known to contain the following formations:

Ost Battalion, 73rd Infantry Division
Ost Battalion, 198th Infantry Division
4th & 5th Georgian Companies, 71st Pioneer Battalion
4th (Ost) Company, 97th Pioneer Battalion
Ost Construction Company (198th Infantry Division)
15th, 27th, & 43rd Ost Radio & Construction Platoons
51st, 55th, 62nd, & 63rd Ost Radio & Construction Platoons
3rd (Ost) Co/125th Light Transportation Column

On 4/30/43 the following units were serving with Army Group South.

Turkistani Units
6th Co/571st Wach Battalion
7th Co/571st Wach Battalion
4th Co/592nd Supply Battalion
4th Co/575th Supply Battalion
783rd Turkistani Battalion
4 companies
4th Co/591st Wach Battalion
5th Co/507th Wach Battalion
5th Co/619th Supply Battalion
5th Co/600th Supply Battalion
4th Co/606th Supply Battalion
581st Turkistani Battalion
4 Companies
909th Turkistani Battalion
4 Companies
943rd Turkistani Battalion
4 Companies
687th Turkistani Battalion
4 Companies

802nd Turkistani Battalion
1 Staff Company
4 Companies
Sonst. (Special) Ost Volker
4th & 5th (Ukrainian) Ost Co/571st Wach Battalion
1–3rd Ost Cos/556th
559th Ost Mine Clearing
554th Ost Construction Battalion
1 Light Construction Supply Column
5 Companies
51st Ost Signals Company
43rd Ost Signals Company
62nd Ost Signals Company
66th Ost Signals Company
213th Ost Medical Company
448th Ost Company
248th (Ukrainian) Security Hundertschaft
277th Ost Battalion
3 Companies
5th (Ost) Co/122nd Wach Battalion
255th (Ukrainian) Construction Company
109th Ukrainian Construction Battalion
1 (mot) Light Construction Supply Column
4 Companies
454th Ost Construction Battalion
2 Companies
111th Ukrainian Construction Battalion
3 Companies
6th Ukrainian Construction Battalion
8 Companies
Balts
22nd Lettish Battalion
4 Companies
268th Lettish Battalion
3 Companies
117th Ost Battalion
3 Companies
116th Ost Battalion
3 Companies
114th Ost Battalion
3 Companies
17th Lettish Battalion
3 Companies
4th Ost Battalion
3 Companies
119th Ost Wach Battalion
3 Companies
120th Ost Battalion
3 Companies
122nd Ost Battalion
3 Companies
123rd Ost Battalion
3 Companies

130th Ost Battalion (being formed)
3 Companies

The following Ost units were ordered disbanded by OKH on 11/27/43.

Army Group South
3rd Co, 555th Ost Battalion
4th Co, Kranz Ost Battalion
4th (Ukrainian) Co, 571st Supply Battalion
168th (Ukrainian) Construction Battalion

Army Group Center
82nd Ost Battalion
604th Ost Battalion
134th Ost Battalion
2nd Co, 646th Ost Battalion
3rd Co, 629th Ost Battalion
2nd & 3rd Ost Companies, Trubschewsk Reiter
　Detachment
321st Ost Company
340th Ost Company
420th Ost Company
1st & 2nd Ost Companies, 84th Grenadier Regiment
1st & 2nd Ost Companies, 195th Grenadier Regiment
1st Ost Company, 203rd Grenadier Regiment
7th (Ost) Co/581st Military Police Battalion
3rd Co/637th Ost Battalion
3rd (Ost) Co/931st Security Regiment
2nd Platoon/203rd Ost Reiter Squadron
8th & 9th (Ost) Cos/456th Security Regiment
10th Ost Cadre Company, 2nd AOK
389th Turkistani Battalion
1st (Georgian) Battalion
785th Turkistani Company
5th (Volga) Co/80th Construction Pioneer Battalion
Army Group North
668th Ost Battalion
16th Ost Ersatz Battalion
207th Ost Reiter Battalion
1st Co/653rd Ost Battalion
5th Co/666th Ost Pioneer Battalion
V Lithuanian Construction Battalion

On 2/15/44 OKH records show a very large number of Ost battalions in the West. They were moved to the west because Hitler feared their loyalty and because of accusations that they were the cause of a major defeat on the eastern front. In fact, they had rendered valuable service. They had joined because they wanted to fight communism, Soviet fascism, and Stalinism. When they were shipped West their morale fell and their combat effectiveness often collapsed. Those units assigned to OB West were as follows:

W.B.Niederland
826th Volga Battalion
822nd Georgian Battalion
812th Armenian Battalion, 719th Grenadier Division
803rd North Caucasus Battalion, 347th Grenadier Division
787th Turkistani Battalion, 347th Grenadier Division

15th Army
621st Ost Battalion
813th Armenian Battalion, 348th Grenadier Division
835th North Caucasus Battalion, 348th Grenadier Division

LXXXIX Corps
612th Ost Battalion, 712th Grenadier Division
712th Ost Battalion, 712th Grenadier Division
809th Ost Battalion, 171st Grenadier Division

LXXXI Corps
781st Turkistani Battalion, 711th Grenadier Division

7th Army
LXXXIV Corps
439th Ost Battalion, 716th Grenadier Division
642nd Ost Battalion, 716th Grenadier Division
643rd Ost Battalion, 319th Grenadier Division
823rd Georgian Battalion, 319th Grenadier Division
795th Georgian Battalion, 709th Grenadier Division
797th Georgian Battalion, 709th Grenadier Division
281st Ost Cavalry Battalion

LXXIV Corps
630th Ost Battalion, 266th Grenadier Division
629th Ost Battalion, 266th Grenadier Division
627th Ost Battalion, 346th Grenadier Division
602nd Ost Battalion, 346th Grenadier Division
Ost Ausbildungs Regiment, Mitte
285th Ost Battalion
649th Ost Battalion

XXV Corps
752nd Ost Staff, z.b.V.
636th Ost Battalion, 243rd Grenadier Division
798th Georgian Battalion, 243rd Grenadier Division
635th Ost Battalion, 343rd Grenadier Division
633rd Ost Battalion, 343rd Grenadier Division
634th Ost Battalion, 265th Grenadier Division
800th North Caucasus Battalion, 265th Grenadier Division
229th Ost Battalion

19th Army
IV Luftwaffe F.
665th Ost Battalion, 338th Grenadier Division
663rd Ost Battalion, 338th Grenadier Division
666th Ost Battalion, 326th Grenadier Division

681st Ost Battalion, 326th Grenadier Division
807th Azerbaijani Battalion
Kniess Group
1/198th Ost Battalion, 242nd Grenadier Division
2/9th Ost Battalion, 242nd Grenadier Division
661st Ost Battalion
Military Command France
680th Ost Battalion
654th Ost Battalion
615th Ost Battalion
605th Ost Battalion
560th Ost Battalion
555th Ost Battalion
412th Ost Battalion
339th Ost Battalion
263rd Ost Battalion
2/198th Georgian Regiment

The most interesting of all the documents found was an OKH listing dated 3/27/45 of all the Ost units serving in the German Army. This listing is notable for several reasons. Certainly the most significant is the still huge number of Ost units. The second is the almost total absence of battalion-sized formations. What follows is a complete listing of all volunteer units, not just the Ost units, and shows the Army Groups, Corps, Divisions, and Wehrkreise where they were assigned.

Army Group South
1005th North Caucasus Construction Company
3rd & 4th Turkistani Supply Cos, 546th Grenadier Regiment
5th & 6th Turkistani Supply Cos, 151st Grenadier Regiment
South Volunteer Company
15th Russian Signals Company
55th Russian Signals Company
2nd Panzer Army
725th Ukrainian Supply Company
4th Azerbaijani Construction Co, 563rd Division
XXII Mountain Corps
738th Turkistani Pack Supply Column (with 118th Jäger Division)
750th Turkistani Pack Supply Column (with 118th Jäger Division)
118th Armenian Pack Supply Column (with 118th Jäger Division)
II SS Panzer Corps
44th Russian Company (44th Grenadier Regiment)
Army Group Balck
6th AOK Volunteer Ersatz Company
525th Russian Squadron

4th (Turkistani) Construction Company, 506th Grenadier Regiment
4th (Turkistani) Construction Company, 504th Grenadier Regiment
4th (Turkistani) Construction Company, 154th Grenadier Regiment
4th (Ukrainian) Construction Company, 107th Grenadier Regiment
4th (Ukrainian) Construction Company, 64th Grenadier Regiment
796th (Georgian) Supply Battalion
8th Army
4th (Azerbaijani) Construction Co, 597th Grenadier Regiment
4th (Georgian) Construction Co, 507th Grenadier Regiment
4th (North Caucasus) Construction Co, 245th Grenadier Regiment
4th (Armenian) Construction Co, 144th Grenadier Regiment
4th (Turkistani) Construction Co, 135th Grenadier Regiment
4th (Turkistani) Construction Co, 112th Grenadier Regiment
4th (Azerbaijani) Construction Co, 12th Co, 2/107th Grenadier Regiment
4th (Georgian) Construction Co., 8 Co, 2/107th Grenadier Regiment
4th (Turkistani) Construction Co, 52nd Grenadier Regiment
Ukrainian Supply Co, 725th Grenadier Regiment
4th (Armenian) Supply Co, 602nd Grenadier Regiment
6th (Georgian) Supply Co, 602nd Grenadier Regiment
3rd (Georgian) Supply Co, 602nd Grenadier Regiment
4th (Ukrainian) Supply Co, 591st Grenadier Regiment
5th (Armenian) Supply Co, 591st Grenadier Regiment
6th (Ukrainian) Supply Co, 142nd Grenadier Regiment
4th (Uzbeck) Construction Co, 678th Grenadier Regiment
4th (Armenian) Construction Co, 676th Grenadier Regiment
Panzer Corps F
101st Spanish Company, 357th Grenadier Regiment
102nd Spanish Company, 357th Grenadier Regiment
46th Volunteer Ersatz Company
558th Korück
1st Volunteer Ersatz Company, 558th Grenadier Regiment

Army Group Center
200th Volunteer Construction Battalion
2022nd Russian Construction Company
2021st Turkistani Construction Company
2007th Russian Construction Company
2004th Azerbaijani Construction Company
4th Turkistani Construction Company, 1/549th Grenadier Regiment
5th Georgian Construction Company, 404th Grenadier Regiment
5th Armenian Construction Company, 12th Grenadier Regiment
1st Turkistani Worker Brigade
1st Turkistani Worker Battalion
4th Turkistani Worker Battalion
2rd Turkistani Construction Company, 12th Grenadier Regiment
2rd Turkistani Construction Company, 22nd Grenadier Regiment
2rd Turkistani Construction Company, 23rd Grenadier Regiment
5th Turkistani Supply Company, 543rd Grenadier Regiment
3rd Georgian Supply Company, 561st Grenadier Regiment
4th Turkistani Supply Company, 561st Grenadier Regiment
5th Georgian Supply Company, 561st Grenadier Regiment
3rd Georgian Supply Company, 571st Grenadier Regiment
4th Armenian Supply Company, 571st Grenadier Regiment
5th Azerbaijani Supply Company, 571st Grenadier Regiment
6th Turkistani Supply Company, 571st Grenadier Regiment
3rd Volga Supply Company, 592nd Grenadier Regiment
4th Georgian Supply Company, 592nd Grenadier Regiment
5th Turkistani Supply Company, 592nd Grenadier Regiment
3rd Armenian Supply Company, 720th Grenadier Regiment
4th Armenian Supply Company, 720th Grenadier Regiment
5th Ukrainian Supply Company, 720th Grenadier Regiment
1001st Volga Supply Company
Volunteer Ersatz Company

1st Panzer Army
580th Russian Cavalry Battalion
819th Azerbaijani Battalion

551st Ukrainian Supply Battalion
559th Ukrainian Construction Battalion
4 Volga Construction Company, 1/18th Grenadier Regiment
8th Volga Construction Company, 2/18th Grenadier Regiment
12th Armenian Construction Company, 3/18th Grenadier Regiment
4th Turkistani Construction Company, 124th Grenadier Regiment
4th Ukrainian Construction Company, 131st Grenadier Regiment
4th Turkistani Construction Company, 218th Grenadier Regiment
4th Russian Construction Company, 371st Grenadier Regiment
3rd Georgian Supply Company, 607th Grenadier Regiment
1st & 2nd Cos, 553rd Construction Battalion
Volunteer Ersatz Company

XXXXIX Mountain Corps
T 94th (Turkistani) Supply Battalion, 4th Mountain Division

LIX Corps
168th Ukrainian Cavalry Squadron, 68th Grenadier Regiment

XI Corps
5th Russian Construction Co, 97th Jäger Division
4th Ukrainian Construction Co, 97th Jäger Division
7th Russian Company, 97th Jäger Division

Silesian Corps Group
248th Ukrainian Company, 168th Grenadier Regiment

17th Army Group
II Turkistani Worker Battalion
III Turkistani Worker Battalion
420th Russian Company
4th (Turkistani) Construction Company, 120th Grenadier Regiment
4th (Turkistani) Construction Company, 1/153rd Grenadier Regiment
3rd (Volga) Construction Company, 2/153rd Grenadier Regiment
12th (Turkistani) Construction Company, 3/153rd Grenadier Regiment
1st (Russian) Construction Company, 120th Grenadier Regiment
4th (Russian) Construction Company, 508th Grenadier Regiment
3rd (Turkistani) Supply Company, 117th Grenadier Regiment
5th (Turkistani) Supply Company, 349th Grenadier Regiment

4th & 5th Volunteer Construction Cos, 727th Grenadier Regiment

Volunteer Ersatz Company

VIII Corps
182nd Russian Company/254th Infantry Division

XXXXVIII Panzer Corps
448th Russian Supply Company

4th Panzer Army
791st Turkistani Battalion

817th Azerbaijani Battalion

818th Azerbaijani Battalion

7th Eins Regiment

I Russian Construction Battalion

II Russian Construction Battalion

III Russian Construction Battalion

Ukrainian Construction Battalion

Ost Volk Construction Battalion, Fhr Security

Ost Volk Construction Battalion, Dolm Security

Russian Construction Company z.b.V.

4th (Azerbaijani) Construction Company, 1/8th Grenadier Regiment

8th (Armenian) Construction Company, 2/8th Grenadier Regiment

(Ukrainian) Construction Supply Column, 2/8th Grenadier Regiment

4th (Turkistani) Construction Company, 737th Grenadier Regiment

2005th Ukrainian Construction Company

2006th Russian Construction Company

424th Russian Supply Company

5th Turkistani Supply, 606th Grenadier Regiment

6th Turkistani Supply, 619th Grenadier Regiment

Volunteer Ersatz Company

LVII Panzer Corps
457th Turkistani Supply Company

Vistula Army Group
600th Russian Infantry Division

3rd Turkistani Company, 25th Grenadier Regiment

9th Army
553rd Russian Battalion

790th Turkistani Battalion

Turkistani Construction Legion

North Caucasus Construction Legion

4th Azerbaijani Construction Co, 146th Grenadier Regiment

4th Lettish Construction Co, 503rd Grenadier Regiment

4th Lithuanian Construction Co, 738th Grenadier Regiment

3rd Turkistani Supply Co, 533rd Grenadier Regiment

3rd & 4th Turkistani Supply Cos, 551st Grenadier Regiment

3rd Panzer Army
5th Estonian Construction Battalion

644th Ukrainian Company

1st Volga Company, 825th Grenadier Regiment

4th Russian Construction Co, 95th Grenadier Regiment

4th Armenian Construction Co, 254th Grenadier Regiment

4th Georgian Construction Co, 795th Grenadier Regiment

795th Russian Construction Supply Column

3rd Georgian Supply Company, 501st Grenadier Regiment

4th Ukrainian Supply Company, 501st Grenadier Regiment

5th Armenian Supply Company, 501st Grenadier Regiment

6th Turkistani Supply Company, 501st Grenadier Regiment

3rd Turkistani Supply Company, 608th Grenadier Regiment

4th Russian Supply Company, 608th Grenadier Regiment

6th Turkistani Supply Company, 608th Grenadier Regiment

6th Georgian Supply Company, 608th Grenadier Regiment

Oder Corps
1604th Russian Regiment

1/1604th Russian Battalion

2/1604th Russian Battalion

Tettau Corps Group
13th Turkistani Construction Co, 401st Grenadier Regiment

4th White Ruthenian Construction Co, 421st Grenadier Regiment

4th Ukrainian Construction Company, 96th Grenadier Regiment

Army Group North
1002nd Turkistani Construction Company

5th Turkistani Construction Company, 511th Grenadier Regiment

5th Turkistani Construction Company, 2nd Grenadier Regiment

6th Turkistani Supply Company, 102nd Grenadier Regiment

5th Turkistani Supply Company, 102nd Grenadier Regiment

4th Ukrainian Supply Company, 102nd Grenadier Regiment

3rd Turkistani Supply Company, 102nd Grenadier Regiment

5th Turkistani Supply Company, 99th Grenadier Regiment

4th Ukrainian Supply Company, 99th Grenadier Regiment

6th Ukrainian Supply Company, 58th Grenadier Regiment

5th Georgian Supply Company, 23rd Grenadier Regiment

4th Ukrainian Supply Company, 23rd Grenadier Regiment

2nd Army Group
I/111th Azerbaijani Battalion

830th Volga Construction Battalion

4th Turkistani Construction Company, 11th Grenadier Regiment

5th Turkistani Construction Company, 129th Grenadier Regiment

4th Azerbaijani Construction Company, 137th Grenadier Regiment

4th Turkistani Construction Company, 418th Grenadier Regiment

4th Lithuanian Construction Company, 732nd Grenadier Regiment

580th Russian Supply Company

Lithuanian Ersatz Company

XVIII Mountain Corps
7th Russian Battalion, 7th Grenadier Division

Polish Construction Battalion

4th Army Group
9th White Ruthenian Construction Battalion

11th White Ruthenian Construction Battalion

828th Volga Construction Battalion

4th Russian Co, 417th Grenadier Regiment

4th Turkistani Construction Company, 44th Grenadier Regiment

4th Turkistani Construction Company, 46th Grenadier Regiment

4th Turkistani Construction Company, 79th Grenadier Regiment

4th Lithuanian Construction Company, 80th Grenadier Regiment

4th Georgian Construction Company, 91st Grenadier Regiment

4th Ukrainian Construction Company, 134th Grenadier Regiment

4th Turkistani Construction Company, 320th Grenadier Regiment

4th Russian Construction Company, 415th Grenadier Regiment

4th Turkistani Construction Company, 419th Grenadier Regiment

4th Lithuanian Construction Company, 532nd Grenadier Regiment

4th Lithuanian Construction Company, 576th Grenadier Regiment

4th Russian Construction Company, 584th Grenadier Regiment

4th Lithuanian Construction Company, 725th Grenadier Regiment

4th Lithuanian Construction Company, 739th Grenadier Regiment

4th Lithuanian Construction Company, 783rd Grenadier Regiment

4th Lithuanian Construction Company, 796th Grenadier Regiment

2nd Russian Telephone Company, 515th Grenadier Regiment

3rd Turkistani Supply Company, 622nd Grenadier Regiment

3rd Ukrainian Supply Company, 687th Grenadier Regiment

3rd Russian Supply Company, 690th Grenadier Regiment

VI Corps
129th Russian Company, 129th Grenadier Division

XXXXI Corps
Russian Construction Battalion, 129th Grenadier Division

559th Korück
612th Russian Company

640th Ukrainian Company

Samland Army Detachment
639th Ukrainian Company

645th Russian Company

60th Turkistani Construction Company

4th Turkistani Construction Company, 136th Grenadier Regiment

3rd & 4th Russian Supply Companies, 508th Grenadier Regiment

6th Ukrainian Supply Company, 508th Grenadier Regiment

4th Turkistani Supply Company, 687th Grenadier Regiment

Fortress Command Königsberg
169th Lithuanian Construction Company, 69th Grenadier Division

IX Corps
4th Volga Construction Company, 78th Grenadier Regiment

4th Turkistani Construction Company, 128th Grenadier Regiment

Courland Army Group
I Lettish Construction Battalion

315th Lettish Gall Construction Battalion

327th Lettish Gall Construction Battalion

4th Azerbaijani Construction Co, 25th Grenadier Regiment

4th Azerbaijani Construction Co, 121st Grenadier Regiment

4th Georgian Construction Co, 127th Grenadier Regiment

4th Turkistani Construction Co, 132nd Grenadier Regiment

4th Armenian Construction Co, 257th Grenadier Regiment

4th Russian Construction Co, 502nd Grenadier Regiment

4th Ukrainian Construction Co, 505th Grenadier Regiment

4th Lettish Gall Construction Co, 510th Grenadier Regiment

4th Turkistani Construction Co, 562nd Grenadier Regiment

56th Turkistani Construction Company

61st Turkistani Construction Company

4th Armenian Construction Co, 413th Grenadier Regiment

Volga Construction Supply Column, 413th Grenadier Regiment

4th Russian Construction Co, 734th Grenadier Regiment

Russian Construction Supply Column, 734th Grenadier Regiment

1007th Turkistani Construction Company

1008th Turkistani Construction Company

3rd Volga Supply Company, 47th Grenadier Regiment

6th Turkistani Supply Company, 49th Grenadier Regiment

3rd Turkistani Supply Company, 550th Grenadier Regiment

650th Lithuanian Supply Company

652nd Lettish Supply Company

726th Turkistani Supply Company

Lettish Ersatz Company

18th Army

13th Lithuanian Battalion

256th Lithuanian Battalion

21st Volunteer Construction Battalion

326th Lettish Gall Construction Battalion

675th Russian Company, Simson Grenadier Regiment

52nd Turkistani Construction Company

7th Azerbaijani Construction Company, 553rd Grenadier Regiment

3rd Volga Construction Company, 553rd Grenadier Regiment

4th Armenian Construction Company, 55th Grenadier Regiment

4th North Caucasus Construction Company, 101st Grenadier Regiment

4th Russian Construction Company, 141st Grenadier Regiment

4th Armenian Construction Company, 416th Grenadier Regiment

4th Russian Construction Company, 591st Grenadier Regiment

4th Lithuanian Construction Company, 793rd Grenadier Regiment

793rd Lithuanian Construction Supply Column

16th Army

672nd Lettish Pioneer Battalion

4th Turkistani Construction Co, 87th Grenadier Regiment

4th Russian Construction Co, 98th Grenadier Regiment

4th Volga Construction Co, 100th Grenadier Regiment

5th Lettish Construction Co, 100th Grenadier Regiment

4th Volga Construction Co, 108th Grenadier Regiment

4th Georgian Construction Co, 156th Grenadier Regiment

4th Georgian Construction Co, 680th Grenadier Regiment

5th Lettish Construction Co, 680th Grenadier Regiment

4th Volga Construction Co, 786th Grenadier Regiment

786th Volga Construction Supply Column Co, 786th Grenadier Regiment

51st Turkistani Construction Company

54th Turkistani Construction Company

55th Turkistani Construction Company

58th Turkistani Construction Company

59th Turkistani Construction Company

Volunteer Ersatz Company

3rd Turkistani Supply Co, 572nd Grenadier Regiment

4th Azerbaijani Supply Co, 572nd Grenadier Regiment

7th Georgian Supply Co, 572nd Grenadier Regiment

3rd Turkistani Supply Co, 574th Grenadier Regiment

7th Turkistani Supply Co, 574th Grenadier Regiment

W.B.Denmark

599th Russian Brigade (forming)

    1605th Russian Regiment

      662nd Russian Battalion (1/1605th Russian Regiment)

674th Russian Battalion (2/1605th Russian Regiment)
683rd Russian Battalion (3/1605th Russian Regiment)
13th Co/1605th Russian Infantry Gun Company
14th Co/1605th Russian Panzerjäger Company
Kaucausus Regiment
  799th Georgian Battalion
  836th North Caucasus Battalion
  II/Bergman (Azerbaijani) Battalion
1599th Russian Bicycle Battalion
693rd Ukrainian Construction Company
1599th Ukrainian Construction Company

OB West

690th Ukrainian Construction Battalion
4th Russian Construction Company, 19th Grenadier Regiment
4th Russian Construction Company, 59th Grenadier Regiment
4th Russian Construction Company, 801st Grenadier Regiment
4th Armenian Construction Company, 797th Grenadier Regiment
4th Turkistani Panzerjäger Company, 15th Grenadier Regiment
3rd Ukrainian Supply Company, 562nd Grenadier Regiment
4th Turkistani Supply Company, 562nd Grenadier Regiment

Army Group H
25th Army

787th Turkistani Battalion
803rd North Caucasus Battalion
822nd Georgian Battalion
826th Volga Battalion
691st Ukrainian Construction Battalion
812th Armenian Construction Battalion
835th North Caucasus Construction Battalion
1000th Turkistani Supply Battalion

1st Fallschirmjäger Army

651st Ukrainian Supply Battalion

Army Group B

605th Russian Construction Battalion
4th Azerbaijani Construction Co, 544th Grenadier Regiment
4th Volga Construction Co, 677th Grenadier Regiment
4th Russian Construction Co, 799th Grenadier Regiment
4th Russian Construction Co, 803rd Grenadier Regiment

3rd & 4th Turkistani Supply Companies, 522nd Grenadier Regiment
5th & 6th Volga Supply Companies, 522nd Grenadier Regiment
4th Azerbaijani Supply Company, 548th Grenadier Regiment
5th Ukrainian Supply Company, 548th Grenadier Regiment

5th Panzer Army

3rd Volga Supply Company, 562nd Grenadier Regiment
4th Turkistani Supply Company, 562nd Grenadier Regiment

15th Army

4th Russian Regiment
827th Volga Battalion
627th Volga Construction Battalion
905th Russian Construction Company

7th Army

605th Russian Construction Battalion

Army Group G

4th Azerbaijani Supply Company, 593rd Grenadier Regiment

1st Army

5th Turkistani Construction Company, 83rd Grenadier Regiment
3rd Russian Construction Company, 94th Grenadier Regiment
4th Russian Construction Company, 94th Grenadier Regiment
4th Volga Construction Company, 306th Grenadier Regiment
4th Russian Construction Company, 823rd Grenadier Regiment

19th Army

Schmidt Turkistani Construction Battalion
4th Turkistani Construction co, 5th Grenadier Regiment
921st Slovak Construction Battalion

LXIV Corps

4th Ukrainian Construction Co, 785th Grenadier Regiment
785th Ukrainian Construction Supply Column, 785th Grenadier Regiment

XVIII SS Corps

3rd Ukrainian Infantry Regiment, 805th Grenadier Division
601st Russian Construction Battalion

M Oberkommando West
XXV Corps

I/M Russian Battalion, St. Nazaire
634th Russian Battalion, Lorient
636th Russian Battalion, St. Nazaire
643rd Russian Battalion, Jersey

281st Ukrainian Cavalry Battalion, Lorient
285th Ukrainian Bicycle Battalion, Lorient
823rd Georgian Battalion, Guernsey

OB South West
Ligurian Army
4th Italian Construction Co, 432nd Grenadier Regiment
4th Italian Construction Co, 92nd Grenadier Regiment
LXXV Corps
406th Russian Battalion, 5th Mountain Division
617th Russian Battalion, 5th Mountain Division
Lombardy Corps
555th Russian Battalion
14th Army
616th Russian Battalion
412th Russian Battalion
4th Italian Construction Co, 789th Grenadier Regiment
LI Mountain Corps
560th Russian Battalion, 148th Grenadier Division
620th Russian Battalion, 148th Grenadier Division
XIV Panzer Army
412th Russian Battalion
10th Army
4th Italian Construction Co, 430th Grenadier Regiment
4th Italian Construction Co, 488th Grenadier Regiment
4th Italian Construction Co, 482nd Grenadier Regiment
LXXVI Panzer Corps
162nd Turkistani Brigade
556th Russian Battalion
1st & 2nd Russian Companies, 198th Battalion, 98th Grenadier Division
LXXIII z.b.V. Corps
339th Russian Battalion

OB South East
Serbian Russian Brigade
782nd Turkistani Battalion
5th Azerbaijani Construction Company, 106th Grenadier Regiment
422nd Armenian Construction Company
5th Turkistani Construction Company, 515th Grenadier Regiment
4th Italian Panzerjäger Company, 10th Grenadier Regiment
3rd Turkistani Company, 5 Grenadier Regiment
4th Russian Panzerjäger Company, 8th Grenadier Regiment

4th Russian Panzerjäger Company, 43rd Grenadier Regiment
3rd & 4th Azerbaijani Supply Companies, 118th Grenadier Regiment
3rd Turkistani Supply Company, 610th Grenadier Regiment
5th Turkistani Supply Company, 27th Grenadier Regiment

Army Group E
XV Mountain Corps
227th Turkistani Pack Supply Column
XXI Mountain Corps
54th Turkistani Pack Supply Column, 181st Grenadier Division
100th Turkistani Pack Supply Column, 181st Grenadier Division
XXXIV z.b.V. Corps
117th Turkistani Pack Supply Column, 117th Jäger Division
I/Bergman Georgian Battalion
LXXXXI z.b.V. Corps
789th Turkistani Battalion
III/Bergman (North Caucasus) Battalion
842nd North Caucasus Battalion
843rd North Caucasus Battalion
1/125th Armenian Construction Battalion, 297th Grenadier division
1/76th Turkistani Construction Battalion, 297th Grenadier division
845th Arab Battalion, 104th Jäger Division
104th Turkistani Pack Column, 104th Jäger Division
724th Turkistani Pack Column, 104th Jäger Division
734th Turkistani Pack Column, 104th Jäger Division

I Wehrkreis Command
210th Ukrainian Company
13th Turkistani Construction Company, 40th Grenadier Regiment
4th Georgian Construction Company, 107th Grenadier Regiment
3rd Turkistani Company, 26th Grenadier Regiment
2nd Ukrainian Company, 550th Grenadier Regiment

II Wehrkries Command
Armenian Construction Legion
Turkistani and Caucasus Peoples Construction Legion
III Wehrkreis Command
4th Turkistani Construction Battalion (forming)
12th (Caucasus) Panzerjäger Group
13th (Russian) Panzerjäger Unit
14th (Russian) Panzerjäger Unit

IV Wehrkreis Command
  6th Construction Regiment
    1101st Turkistani Construction Battalion
    Georgian Construction Legion
    Volga Construction Legion
    Azerbaijani Construction Legion
  1003rd Volga Supply Company

V Wehrkreis Command
  Volunteer Division
    1st Volunteer Regiment
      Azerbaijani Legion
      North Caucasus Legion
      Turkistani Legion
      Turkistani & Caucasus Battalion
      3rd Ukrainian Battalion
      4th Russian Battalion
    2nd Volunteer Regiment
      Armenian Legion
      Georgian Legion
      Volga Legion
      3 Volunteer Workers Companies (forming)
  Schulen Division
    Ost Volk Battalion
    2 Turkistani Volk Battalions
  650th Division (forming)
    RBA NCO School

851st Russian Construction Battalion
11th Russian Panzerjäger Unit (forming)

IX Wehrkreis Command
  3rd Ukrainian Construction Battalion

XVII Wehrkreis Command
  4th Ukrainian Construction Company, 221st Grenadier Regiment
  6th & 7th Slovakian Construction Companies, 31st Grenadier Regiment
  922nd Slovakian Construction Battalion

XVIII Wehrkreis Command
  4th Lithuanian Construction Company, 730th Grenadier Regiment

German Command, Slovakia
  4th Lithuanian Construction Company, 728th Grenadier Regiment

As with the Cossack units, the various Ost units changed their names on several occasions. A limited number of OKH records were found which list these name changes. Those changes are summarized below:

Army Group North (As of 10/23/42)

Old Name	Became
1st Co., 250th Lithuanian Schutzmanschaft Wacht Battalion	650th Ost (Lith.) Wach Company
2nd Co., 250th Lithuanian Schutzmanschaft Wacht Battalion	651st Ost (Lith.) Wach Company
4th Co., 17th Lettisch Wachmanschaft Wacht Battalion	652nd Ost (Lett.) Wach Company
207th Reiter Battalion 207th Ost Reiter Battalion	
281st Reiter Battalion	281st Ost Reiter Battalion
285th Reiter Battalion	285th Ost Reiter Battalion
410th Russian Security Battalion (16th Corps)	653rd Ost Battalion
510th Russian Security Battalion (16th Corps)	653rd Ost Ersatz Company
410th Russian Ersatz Hundertschaft (16th Corps)	654th Ost Battalion
Erdmann Uzbeck Company	1st Turkistani Co, 656th Battalion
Kiria Usbeck Company	2nd Turkistani Co, 656th Battalion
13th Co./184th Estonian Security Battalion	657th Ost (Est.) Company
181st Estonian Security Battalion (18th AOK)	658th (Est.) Ost Battalion
182nd Estonian Security Battalion (18th AOK)	659th (Est.) Ost Battalion
183rd Estonian Security Battalion (18th AOK)	661st Ost Battalion
184th Estonian Security Battalion (18th AOK)	660th (Est.) Ost Battalion
185th Estonian Security Battalion (18th AOK)	662nd Ost Battalion
186th Estonian Security Battalion (18th AOK)	663rd Ost Battalion
187th Finnish Security Battalion (18th AOK)	664th (Finn.) Ost Battalion
188th Russian Security Battalion (18th AOK)	665th Ost Battalion
189th Russian Security Pioneer Battalion (18th AOK)	666th Ost Battalion
Narwa Estonian Security Ersatz Battalion (18th AOK)	Narwa Ost (Est.) Ersatz Battalion

Army Group Center (As of 11/18/42)

Old Name	Became
447th Volunteer Security Battalion	1/447th Ost Regiment
447th Volunteer Squadron	447th Ost Reiter Squadron
52nd Ukrainian Company	1st Co, 441st Ost Battalion
52nd Jagdkommando	2nd Co, 441st Ost Battalion
339th Volunteer Security Battalion	339th Ost Battalion
84th Security Company	84th Ost Company

Army Group B (As of 11/30/42)

Old Name	Became
1st Ukrainian Company, 571st Wach Battalion	4th (Ost) Company/571st Wach Battalion
2nd Ukrainian Company, 571st Wach Battalion	5th (Ost) Company/571st Wach Battalion
5th Ukrainian Company, 122nd B Wach Battalion	4th (Ost) Company/122nd B Wach Battalion
6th Ukrainian Company, 122nd B Wach Battalion	5th (Ost) Company/122nd B Wach Battalion
6th AOK	
6th Ukrainian Battalion	551st Ost Battalion
Work & Security Co, 48th Panzer Corps	448th Ost Company
Ukrainian Construction Co., 8th Corps	176th Ost Company
Hundertschaft Hilfswachmannschaft, 113th Infantry Division	13th Ost Company
Ukrainian Construction Co, 94th Inf Div	194th Ost Construction Company
Ukrainian Construction Co, 295th Pioneer Bn	295th Ost Construction Company
Hilfswachmannschaft, 79th Infantry Div.	179th Ost Wach Company
4th Panzer AOK	
Volunteer Ukrainian Company, 4th Panzer AOK	552nd Ost Company

Army Group North (As of 12/1/42)

Old Name	Became
16th Freijäger Staff z.b.V.	710th Commander Ost Troops z.b.V.
1/16th Freijäger Regiment	667th Ost Battalion
2/16th Freijäger Regiment	668th Ost Battalion
3/16th Freijäger Regiment	669th Ost Battalion
16th Freijäger Signals Company	671st Ost Signals Company
1st Btry, 16th Freijäger Battalion	1st Btry, 670th Ost Artillery Battalion
2nd Btry, 16th Freijäger Battalion	2nd Btry, 670th Ost Artillery Battalion
653rd Ost Ersatz Company	16th Ost Ersatz Battalion

Army Group Center (As of 11/8/42)

Old Name	Became
1st Experimental Battalion, Center	633rd Ost Battalion
2nd Experimental Battalion, Center	634th Ost Battalion
3rd Experimental Battalion, Center	635th Ost Battalion
4th Experimental Battalion, Center	636th Ost Battalion
5th Experimental Battalion, Center	637th Ost Battalion

Old Name	Became
Brjansk Wach Company	606th Ost Wach Company
1st & 2nd Gomel Wach Companies	1st & 2nd, 607th Ost Wach Companies
Smolensk Wach Company	608th Ost Wach Company
Wjasma Wach Company	609th Ost Wach Company
1st & 2nd Vitebsk Wach Company	1st & 2nd, 610th Ost Wach Companies
Orscha Wach Company	611th Ost Wach Company
Volunteer Ersatz Regiment, Center	Ost Ersatz Regiment, Center
Berezina Kampf Battalion	601st Ost Battalion (Berezina)
Dnjepr Kampf Battalion	602nd Ost Battalion (Dnjepr)
Duna Kampf Battalion	603rd Ost Battalion (Duna)
Pripet Kampf Battalion	604th Ost Battalion (Pripet)
Wolga Kampf Battalion	605th Ost Battalion (Wolga)
201st Reiter Squadron (Russian)	201st Ost Reiter Squadron
339th Wach Company	1st (Ost Company)/203rd
339th Reiter Squadron (Russian)	2nd (Ost Reiter Squadron)/203rd
221st Wach Company	1st (Ost Company)/221st
221st Reiter Squadron (Russian)	2nd (Ost Reiter Squadron)/221st
286th Reiter Squadron (Russian)	286th Ost Reiter Squadron

2nd AOK

1st Volunteer Battalion	615th Ost Battalion
2nd Volunteer Battalion	616th Ost Battalion
3rd Volunteer Battalion	617th Ost Battalion
Volunteer Militia Unit Trubtschewsk	618th Ost Battalion
Volunteer Militia Unit Dimitrovsk	619th Ost Battalion
Volunteer Militia Unit Kromy	620th Ost Battalion
Volunteer Artillery Battalion	621st Ost Artillery Battalion

3rd AOK

Bandenjäger Company XX Corps	420th Ost Company
Bandenjäger Commando Bischler (695th Military Police Battalion)	613th Ost Company

4th AOK

4th Self Defense Ersatz Battalion	4th Ost Ersatz Battalion
Self Defense Company	626th Ost Company
Self Defense Staff Company z.b.V	632nd Ost Staff Company
Self Defense Co/551st Wach Battalion	4th Ost Co/551st Wach Battalion
Self Defense Co/555th Wach Battalion	4th Ost Co/555th Wach Battalion
Don Unit/557th Security Battalion	5th Ost Co/557th Security Battalion
Self Defense Co/582nd Wach Battalion	4th Ost Co/582nd Wach Battalion
Self Defense Co ("Volga")/582nd Wach Bn	5th Ost Co/582nd Wach Battalion
Self defense Battery 302nd Arko	614th Ost Battery
Self Defense Battalion, XII Corps	412th Ost Battalion
456th Self Defense Unit	456th Ost Battalion
34th Self Defense Unit	4th Ost Company
131st Self Defense Unit	121st Ost Company
260th Self Defense Company	260th Ost Company
Self Defense Unit Lt von Schlippe (263rd Infantry Division)	1st (Ost) Company/263rd
Self Defense Unit "Salikow" (263rd Infantry Division)	2nd (Ost) Company/263rd
1st Russian Company, 267th	1st (Ost) Company/267th
2nd Russian Company, 267th	2nd (Ost) Company/267th
268th Self Defense Company	268th Ost Company

Old Name	Became
331st Self Defense Company	331st Ost Company
Russian Self Defense Unit (10th (mot) Infantry Division)	10th Ost Company
Russian Self Defense Hundertschaft Group G.F.P	570612th Ost Company

9th AOK

Old Name	Became
Staff Officer, 582nd Vol. Sec. Troops	582nd Staff Officer of Ost Battalions
Ersatz Company, 582nd Vol. Sec. Troops	582nd Ost Ersatz Company
NCO School	582nd Ost NCO School
582nd Volunteer Battery	582nd Ost Battery
1/582nd Volunteer Regiment	628th Ost Battalion
2/582nd Volunteer Regiment	629th Ost Battalion
3/582nd Volunteer Regiment	630th Ost Battalion
1–3rd Volunteer Platoons, 722nd Wach Bn	5th (Ost) Company/722nd Wach Battalion
VI Volunteer Battalion	406th Ost Battalion
XXIII Volunteer Battalion	308th Ost Battalion
XXVIII Volunteer Battalion	427th Ost Battalion
95th Volunteer Company	195th Ost Company
XXXIX Volunteer Battalion	439th Ost Battalion
78th Volunteer Company	178th Ost Company
102nd Volunteer Company	102nd Ost Company
1st Panzer Volunteer Company	37th Ost Company
5th Panzer Volunteer Company	85th Ost Company
XXXXVI Volunteer Battalion	446th Ost Battalion

Chevallerie Group/LIX Corps

Old Name	Became
Ukrainian Company, 205th Infantry Div.	205th Ost Company

Army Group Center (As of 1/15/43)

Old Name	Became
Newly raised	3rd Ost Wach Company 607
Newly raised	3rd Ost Wach Company 610
1st & 2nd Ost Companies, 441	441st Ost Battalion
447th Ost Battalion	1/447th Ost Battalion
Newly raised	2/447th Ost Battalion
447th Ost Reiter Squadron	1/447th Ost Reiter Squadron
84th Ost Company	1/84th Ost Company
Newly raised	1/84th Ost Company

3rd AOK

Old Name	Became
Bandenjäger Company Zimmeck	1/446th Ost Company
Newly raised	2/446th Ost Company
(Ukrainian) Ost Company (Security) Standortkdtr. Vjasma	639th Ost Wach Company
Ukrainian Security Company	640th Ost Wach Company
446th Ost Battalion	82nd Ost Battalion, 2nd Panzer Division

4th AOK

Old Name	Became
641st Ost Company	Absorbed into 559th Korück
Newly raised	5th (Ost) Company/587th Landesschützen Battalion
Newly raised	4th (Ost) Company/675th Landesschützen Battalion
Newly raised	5th (Ost) Company/826th Landesschützen Battalion
Newly raised	2nd (Ost) Company/131st
131st Ost Company	1st (Ost) Company/131st

Old Name	Became
Newly raised	4th (Ost) Company/622nd Supply Battalion
Newly raised	4th (Ost) Company/687th Supply Battalion
Newly raised	4th (Ost) Company/690th Supply Battalion
5th (Ost) Company/582nd Wach Battalion	Expanded to 642nd Ost Battalion with staff & 3 companies
632nd Ost Staff Company	4th Company, 642nd Ost Battalion
9th AOK	
Newly Raised	110th Ost Company
Newly Raised	253rd Ost Company
Newly Raised	4–6th (Ost) Companies/508th Wach Battalion
Disbanded	37th Ost Company
Newly Raised	152nd Ost Company, 52nd Infantry Division

5

Croatian, Serbian and Montenegrin Formations in German Service

When Yugoslavia was defeated in April 1941, it was divided into a number of smaller states, including Croatia, Serbia, Slovenia, and Montenegro, and a number of portions of its land were absorbed by the victors directly into their states. Among those newly formed or re-formed states, Croatia was probably the most pro-Axis.

The Free State of Croatia was announced on 10 April 1941 by Colonel Slavko Kvaternik. Kvaternik was a follower of Ante Pavelic, who declared himself the *Poglavnik* (leader—Führer) of the Croatian people and Kvaternik was rewarded by being made Commander-in-Chief of the Croatian armed forces. On 17 April it officially joined the Axis by declaring war on England.

Though Croatia was purportedly an independent state, it was little more than a thinly disguised German vassal state. When it established its army, the *Hrvstako Dombranstvo* (Home Defense or Home Army), it did so with the complete blessing and support of Adolf Hitler.

Most of its officers had been officers in the Yugoslavian Army and they retained their ranks or, quite frequently, received greatly elevated ranks. The home army was mostly infantry, but there were some armored formations equipped with German tanks and Hungarian CV 33 and CV 35 tankettes. By November 1941 the *Hrvstako Dombranstvo* was expanded to six divisions and by the end of the war it reached a strength of sixteen divisions. However, it was unreliable at best and desertion was quite high.

An order from the Oberbefhelshaber Südost dated 3 June 1943 shows the Croatian military forces as consisting of:

Staffs
 3 General Commands
 6 Infantry Division Commands
 1 Mountain Division Command
 5 Mountain Brigade Staffs
 4 Independent Infantry Brigade Staffs
Infantry
 12 Infantry Regiments (with 35 battalions)

 18 Mountain Battalions (in the Mountain Brigades)
 1 Bicycle Battalion
Ustaschi
 14 Active Battalions
Militia
 2 Militia Regiments (7 Battalions)
 6 Independent Militia Battalions
 10 Militia Companies
Other Infantry
 14 Railroad Security Battalions
 4 Ustaschi Railroad Security Battalions
Cavalry
 3 Cavalry Battalions
Artillery
 10 Artillery Detachments (with 22 105mm leFH)
 2 Mountain Gun Batteries
 2 Mountain Howitzer Batteries
 4½ Independent Mountain Guns
 4 Position Batteries
Engineers
 4 Pioneer Battalions
 1 Railroad Battalion
Signal Troops
 2 Signals Battalions

Plans had been laid for the formation of four Jäger Battalions, three legion divisions, four mountain brigades and six new railroad security battalions. The planned organization for the Croatian infantry divisions was as follows. (German weapons were planned, but not always available.):

Division Staff
 Staff (2 LMGS)
 1 (mot) Mapping Detachment
 1 Divisional Band
2 Infantry Regiments, each with
 1 Staff Company
  1 Signals Platoon
  1 Pioneer Platoon
  1 Reconnaissance Platoon (either bicycle or mounted)

3 Battalions, each with
  3 Rifle Companies (12 LMGS & 2 80mm mortars)
  1 Machine Gun Company (12 HMGs & 6 80mm mortars)
  1 Mountain Infantry Gun Company (4 75mm guns & 8 80mm mortars)
  1 (tmot) Anti-Tank Battery (9 medium AT guns & 6 LMGs)

Reconnaissance Battalion
  2 Bicycle Companies (4 HMGS, 12 LMGS & 2 80mm mortars ea)
  1 (mot) Company
  Infantry Gun Section (2 75mm leIG)
  1 Anti-Tank Section (3 heavy anti-tank guns & 3 LMGs)
  1 Pioneer Platoon (4 LMGs)

Anti-Tank Battalion
  2 (motZ) Anti-Tank Companies (9 heavy anti-tank guns & 9 LMGs)
  A 20mm Flak Company was planned

Artillery Regiment
  Regimental Staff & Staff Battery (2 LMGs)
  1st Battalion
  Battalion Staff & Staff Battery
  3 Batteries (4 105mm leFH & 2 LMGs ea)
  2nd Battalion
  same as 1st Battalion
  3rd Battalion
  Battalion Staff & Staff Battery
  2 Batteries[1] (4 150mm sFH & 2 LMGs ea)

Signals Battalion
  1 (tmot) Telephone Company (4 LMGs)
  1 (mot) Radio Company (5 LMGs)
  1 (mot) Light Signals Supply Column (1 LMG)

Supply & Support Troops
  1 (mot) Light Supply Column (2 LMGs) (2nd added later)
  2 Heavy Supply Columns (6 LMGs ea)
  1 Light Supply Column (4 LMGs)
  1 Supply Company (6 LMGs)
  1 (mot) Maintenance Company
  1 (mot) Butcher Company
  1 (mot) Bakery Company
  1 (mot) Administration Platoon
  1 (mot) Medical Company
  1 Medical Company
  2 Ambulance Companies
  1 Veterinary Company
  1 (mot) Military Police Troop
  1 (mot) Field Post Office.

The Jäger Brigades were projected to be organized and equipped as follows:

Brigade Staff
  1 Brigade Staff
2 Jäger Regiments, each with
  1 Regimental Staff
  1 Regimental Staff Company
  1 Signals Platoon
  1 Bicycle Platoon
  1 Pioneer Platoon (3 LMGs)
  3 Battalions, each with
  3 Companies (12 LMGs & 3 50mm mortars)
  1 Machine Gun Company (8 HMGs & 6 80mm mortars)
  1 Infantry Gun Company (4 75mm leIG)
  1 Panzerjäger Company (4 37mm PAK 36 & 2 LMGs)
  1 Light Supply Column (2 LMGs)
Panzer Troop
  3 Medium & 2 Light Tanks
2 Artillery Battalions, each with
  1 Battalion Staff
  1 Signals Platoon
  1 Calibration Platoon
  2 Batteries (4 76.2mm Russian guns & 4 LMGs ea)
  1 Light Artillery Supply Column (2 LMGs)
Other
  1 Pioneer Company (9 LMGs, 2 80mm mortars & 3 flamethrowers)
  1 Mixed Signals Company (4 LMGs)
  2 Light (horse drawn) Supply Columns (2 LMGs ea)
  1 (mot) Light Supply Column (2 LMGs)
  1 Butcher Half Company
  1 Bakery Half Company
  1 (mot) Administration Platoon
  1 Medical Company (2 LMGs)
  1 Ambulance
  1 Veterinary Company
  1 (mot) Military Police Detachment (4 LMGs)

The brigades were to be organized in three phases, with the regimental support units, the third artillery batteries, and the second light supply column being added later. The dates for the phases were 1 August, 1 October, and by 31 December 1943 they were to be fully organized.

Field returns from Army Group F for 1 August 1944 show the Croatian Army had four mountain brigades and four jäger brigades. The jäger brigades appear to have vanished by early 1945 and it is probably that they were used as cadres for the formation of the various infantry divisions that were ordered formed, but this is purely speculation.

---

[1] The 150mm batteries appear to have been considered for motorization.

On 1/14/45 the Training Command of the Croatian Army was reorganized into a kampfgruppe and sent to the front. On 2/1/45 the Croatian Army theoretically contained:

Leibgarde Division
1st Sturm Division
1st–6th, 8th, 10th–15th Infantry Divisions
7th & 9th Mountain Divisions
Fast (Mechanized) Brigade
1st–4th Mountain Brigades
7th, 8th, 10th–21st & 23rd Infantry Brigades
I to XX Ustaschi Brigades
Mechanized School Battalion
Armored School Battalion
16th Replacement Division
Agram Cavalry and Driving School
Varasdin Army School
Brod Battle School

There were also the soldiers of the Croatian Legion which consisted of the 369th, 373rd, and 392nd (Croatian) Infantry Divisions and the Croatian Training Brigade in Stockerau, all of which were completely integrated into the Wehrmacht.

When the Soviet Army reached Croatia's borders at the end of the war it had only one division, the 1st Croat Storm Division, which was capable of any significant resistance. It was organized during the winter of 1944/1945 and outfitted with surplus Finnish army uniforms that the Germans had not delivered to Finland before its collapse and surrender to the Soviet Army.

The following listing is how the various mountain and jäger brigades were organized on 1 August 1944.

1st Croatian Jäger Brigade
1 Brigade Staff
4th Croatian Jäger Regiment
1 Regimental Staff
1 Regimental Staff Company
  1 Signals Platoon
  1 Bicycle Platoon
  1 Pioneer Platoon (3 LMGs)
3 Battalions, each with
  3 Companies (12 LMGs & 2 80mm mortars)
  1 Machine Gun Company (8 HMGs & 6 80mm mortars)
1 Infantry Gun Company (4 75mm leIG)
1 Panzerjäger Company (4 37mm PAK 36 & 2 LMGs)
1 Light Supply Column (2 LMGs)
6th Croatian Jäger Regiment
same as 4th Croatian Jäger Regiment

Armored Troop
3 Mk III and 2 Mk II Tanks, plus 2 LMGs
5th Artillery Battalion
1 Battalion Staff
1 Signals Platoon
1 Calibration Platoon
2 Batteries (4 76.2mm Russian guns & 4 LMGs ea) (3rd Battery to be raised later)
1 Light Artillery Supply Column (2 LMGs)
16th Artillery Battalion
same as 5th Artillery Battalion
Other
Pioneer Company (9 LMGs, 2 80mm mortars & 2 flamethrowers)
Signals Company (4 LMGs)
1 Light (horse drawn) Supply Column (2 LMGs) (2nd to be raised later)
1 (mot) Light Supply Column (2 LMGs)
1 Butcher Half Company
1 Bakery Half Company
1 (mot) Administration Platoon
1 Medical Company (2 LMGs)
1 Ambulance
1 Veterinary Company
1 Military Police Detachment (4 LMGs)

2nd Croatian Jäger Brigade
1 Brigade Staff
1st Croatian Jäger Regiment
1 Regimental Staff
1 Regimental Staff Company
  1 Signals Platoon
  1 Bicycle Platoon
  1 Pioneer Platoon (3 LMGs)
3 Battalions, each with (3rd Bn to be formed later)
  3 Companies (12 LMGs & 2 80mm mortars)
  1 Machine Gun Company (8 HMGs & 6 80mm mortars)
1 Infantry Gun Company (4 75mm leIG)
1 Panzerjäger Company (4 37mm PAK 36 & 2 LMGs)
1 Light Supply Column (2 LMGs)
10th Croatian Jäger Regiment
same as 1st Croatian Jäger Regiment
Armored Troop
3 Mk III and 2 Mk II Tanks, plus 2 LMGs
4th Artillery Battalion
1 Battalion Staff
1 Signals Platoon
1 Calibration Platoon
2 Batteries (4 76.2mm Russian guns & 4 LMGs ea) (3rd Battery to be raised later)
1 Light Artillery Supply Column (2 LMGs)

8th Artillery Battalion
  same as 4th Artillery Battalion
Other
  Pioneer Company (9 LMGs, 2 80mm mortars & 2 flamethrowers) Signals Company (4 LMGs)
  1 Light (horse drawn) Supply Column (2 LMGs) (2nd to be raised later)
  1 (mot) Light Supply Column (2 LMGs)
  1 Butcher Half Company
  1 Bakery Half Company
  1 (mot) Administration Platoon
  1 Medical Company (2 LMGs)
  1 Ambulance
  1 Veterinary Company
  1 Military Police Detachment (4 LMGs)

3rd Croatian Jäger Brigade
  1 Brigade Staff
5th Croatian Jäger Regiment
  1 Regimental Staff
  1 Regimental Staff Company
    1 Signals Platoon
    1 Bicycle Platoon
    1 Pioneer Platoon (3 LMGs)
  3 Battalions, each with
    3 Companies (12 LMGs & 2 80mm mortars)
    1 Machine Gun Company (8 HMGs & 6 80mm mortars)
  1 Infantry Gun Company (4 75mm leIG)
  1 Panzerjäger Company (4 37mm PAK 36 & 2 LMGs)
  1 Light Supply Column (2 LMGs)
8th Croatian Jäger Regiment
  same as 5th Croatian Jäger Regiment
Armored Troop
  3 Mk III and 2 Mk II Tanks, plus 2 LMGs
7th Artillery Battalion
  1 Battalion Staff
  1 Signals Platoon
  1 Calibration Platoon
  2 Batteries (4 76.2mm Russian guns & 4 LMGs ea) (3rd Battery to be raised later)
  1 Light Artillery Supply Column (2 LMGs)
18th Artillery Battalion
  same as 7th Artillery Battalion
Other
  Pioneer Company (9 LMGs, 2 80mm mortars & 2 flamethrowers)
  Signals Company (4 LMGs)
  1 Light (horse drawn) Supply Column (2 LMGs) (2nd to be raised later)
  1 (mot) Light Supply Column (2 LMGs)
  1 Butcher Half Company
  1 Bakery Half Company

  1 (mot) Administration Platoon
  1 Medical Company (2 LMGs)
  1 Ambulance
  1 Veterinary Company
  1 Military Police Detachment (4 LMGs)

4th Croatian Jäger Brigade
  1 Brigade Staff
7th Croatian Jäger Regiment
  1 Regimental Staff
  1 Regimental Staff Company
    1 Signals Platoon
    1 Bicycle Platoon
    1 Pioneer Platoon (3 LMGs)
  3 Battalions, each with
    3 Companies (12 LMGs & 2 80mm mortars)
    1 Machine Gun Company (8 HMGs & 6 80mm mortars)
  1 Infantry Gun Company (4 75mm leIG)
  1 Panzerjäger Company (4 37mm PAK 36 & 2 LMGs) (formed later)
  1 Light Supply Column (2 LMGs)
13th Croatian Jäger Regiment
  same as 7th Croatian Jäger Regiment (infantry gun company formed later)
Armored Troop
  3 Mk III and 2 Mk II Tanks, plus 2 LMGs
11th Artillery Battalion
  1 Battalion Staff
  1 Signals Platoon
  1 Calibration Platoon
  2 Batteries (4 76.2mm Russian guns & 4 LMGs ea) (3rd Battery to be raised later)
  1 Light Artillery Supply Column (2 LMGs)
12th Artillery Battalion
  same as 11th Artillery Battalion
Other
  Pioneer Company (9 LMGs, 2 80mm mortars & 2 flamethrowers)
  Signals Company (4 LMGs)
  1 Light (horse drawn) Supply Column (2 LMGs) (2nd to be raised later)
  1 (mot) Light Supply Column (2 LMGs)
  1 Butcher Half Company
  1 Bakery Half Company
  1 (mot) Administration Platoon
  1 Medical Company (2 LMGs)
  1 Ambulance
  1 Veterinary Company
  1 Military Police Detachment (4 LMGs)

1st Croatian Mountain Brigade
  1 Brigade Staff

1st Croatian Mountain Regiment
1 Regimental Staff
1 Regimental Staff Company
1 Signals Platoon
1 Bicycle Platoon
1 Pioneer Platoon (3 LMGs)
3 Battalions, each with
3 Companies (12 LMGs & 2 80mm mortars)
1 Machine Gun Company (8 HMGs & 6 80mm mortars)
1 Infantry Gun Company (4 75mm leIG)
1 Panzerjäger Company (4 37mm PAK 36 & 2 LMGs) (to be formed later)

5th Croatian Mountain Regiment
same as 5th Croatian Mountain Regiment (anti-tank company & 1st Battalion to be formed later)
plus 1 Light Supply Column (2 LMGs)

Armored Troop
3 Mk III and 2 Mk II Tanks, plus 2 LMGs

6th Artillery Battalion
1 Battalion Staff
1 Signals Platoon
1 Calibration Platoon
1st Battery (4 75mm Mountain Guns & 4 LMGs)
2nd Battery (3 100mm Mountain Guns & 4 LMGs)
3rd Battery (4 75mm Mountain Guns & 4 LMGs) (3rd Battery to be raised later)
1 Light Artillery Supply Column (2 LMGs)

3rd Artillery Battalion
same as 6th Artillery Battalion

Other
Pioneer Company (9 LMGs, 2 80mm mortars & 2 flamethrowers)
Mixed Mountain Signals Company (4 LMGs)
1 Light (horse drawn) Supply Column (2 LMGs)
1 Light Pack Horse Mountain Supply Column (to be raised later)
1 (mot) Light 15 ton Supply Column (2 LMGs)
1 Butcher Platoon
1 Bakery Half Company
1 Administration Platoon
1 Mountain Medical Company (3 LMGs)
1 Ambulance
1 Mountain Veterinary Company
1 Military Police Detachment (4 LMGs)

2nd Croatian Mountain Brigade
1 Brigade Staff
2nd Croatian Mountain Regiment
1 Regimental Staff
1 Regimental Staff Company

1 Signals Platoon
1 Bicycle Platoon
1 Pioneer Platoon (3 LMGs)
3 Battalions, each with
3 Companies (12 LMGs & 2 80mm mortars)
1 Machine Gun Company (8 HMGs & 6 80mm mortars)
1 Infantry Gun Company (4 75mm leIG)
1 Panzerjäger Company (4 37mm PAK 36 & 2 LMGs)
1 Light Supply Column (2 LMGs)

9th Croatian Mountain Regiment
same as 2nd Croatian Mountain Regiment

Armored Troop
3 Mk III and 2 Mk II Tanks, plus 2 LMGs

4th Artillery Battalion
1 Battalion Staff
1 Signals Platoon
1 Calibration Platoon
1st Battery (4 75mm Mountain Guns & 4 LMGs)
2nd Battery (3 100mm Mountain Guns & 4 LMGs)
3rd Battery (4 75mm Mountain Guns & 4 LMGs) (3rd Battery to be raised later)
1 Light Artillery Supply Column (2 LMGs)

20th Artillery Battalion
same as 1st Artillery Battalion

Other
Pioneer Company (9 LMGs, 2 80mm mortars & 2 flamethrowers)
Mixed Mountain Signals Company (4 LMGs)
1 Light (horse drawn) Supply Column (2 LMGs)
1 Light Pack Horse Mountain Supply Column (to be raised later)
1 (mot) Light 15 ton Supply Column (2 LMGs)
1 Butcher Platoon
1 Bakery Half Company
1 Administration Platoon
1 Mountain Medical Company (3 LMGs)
1 Ambulance
1 Mountain Veterinary Company
1 Military Police Detachment (4 LMGs)

3rd Croatian Mountain Brigade
1 Brigade Staff
3rd Croatian Mountain Regiment
1 Regimental Staff
1 Regimental Staff Company
1 Signals Platoon
1 Bicycle Platoon
1 Pioneer Platoon (3 LMGs)
1st & 3rd Battalions, each with
3 Companies (12 LMGs & 2 80mm mortars)

1 Machine Gun Company (8 HMGs & 6 80mm mortars)

1 Light Supply Column (2 LMGs)

5th Croatian Mountain Regiment

1 Regimental Staff

1 Regimental Staff Company

1 Signals Platoon

1 Bicycle Platoon

1 Pioneer Platoon (3 LMGs)

3 Battalions, each with

3 Companies (12 LMGs & 2 80mm mortars)

1 Machine Gun Company (8 HMGs & 6 80mm mortars)

1 Infantry Gun Company (4 75mm leIG) (to be formed later)

1 Panzerjäger Company (4 37mm PAK 36 & 2 LMGs)

1 Light Supply Column (2 LMGs)

Armored Troop

3 Mk III and 2 Mk II Tanks, plus 2 LMGs

2nd Artillery Battalion

1 Battalion Staff

1 Signals Platoon

1 Calibration Platoon

1st Battery (4 75mm Mountain Guns & 4 LMGs)

2nd Battery (3 100mm Mountain Guns & 4 LMGs)

3rd Battery (4 75mm Mountain Guns & 4 LMGs) (3rd Battery to be raised later)

1 Light Artillery Supply Column (2 LMGs)

13th Artillery Battalion

same as 6th Artillery Battalion

Other

Pioneer Company (9 LMGs, 2 80mm mortars & 2 flamethrowers)

Mixed Mountain Signals Company (4 LMGs)

1 Light (horse drawn) Supply Column (2 LMGs)

1 Light Pack Horse Mountain Supply Column (to be raised later)

1 (mot) Light 15 ton Supply Column (2 LMGs)

1 Butcher Platoon

1 Bakery Half Company

1 Administration Platoon

1 Mountain Medical Company (3 LMGs)

1 Ambulance

1 Mountain Veterinary Company

1 Military Police Detachment (4 LMGs)

4th Croatian Mountain Brigade

1 Brigade Staff

4th Croatian Mountain Regiment

1 Regimental Staff

1 Regimental Staff Company

1 Signals Platoon

1 Bicycle Platoon

1 Pioneer Platoon (3 LMGs)

3 Battalions, each with (3rd battalion to be formed later)

3 Companies (12 LMGs & 2 80mm mortars)

1 Machine Gun Company (8 HMGs & 6 80mm mortars)

1 Infantry Gun Company (4 75mm leIG)

1 Panzerjäger Company (4 37mm PAK 36 & 2 LMGs) (to be formed later)

1 Light Supply Column (2 LMGs)

8th Croatian Mountain Regiment

same as 4th Croatian Mountain Regiment (infantry gun company & 3rd Battalion to be formed later)

Armored Troop

3 Mk III and 2 Mk II Tanks, plus 2 LMGs

1st Artillery Battalion

1 Battalion Staff

1 Signals Platoon

1 Calibration Platoon

1st Battery (4 75mm Mountain Guns & 4 LMGs)

2nd Battery (3 100mm Mountain Guns & 4 LMGs)

3rd Battery (4 75mm Mountain Guns & 4 LMGs) (3rd Battery to be raised later)

1 Light Artillery Supply Column (2 LMGs)

12th Artillery Battalion

same as 1st Artillery Battalion

Other

Pioneer Company (9 LMGs, 2 80mm mortars & 2 flamethrowers)

Mixed Mountain Signals Company (4 LMGs)

1 Light (horse drawn) Supply Column (2 LMGs)

1 Light Pack Horse Mountain Supply Column (to be raised later)

1 (mot) Light 15 ton Supply Column (2 LMGs)

1 Butcher Platoon

1 Bakery Half Company

1 Administration Platoon

1 Mountain Medical Company (3 LMGs)

1 Ambulance

1 Mountain Veterinary Company

1 Military Police Detachment (4 LMGs)

Croat Volunteers in the Wehrmacht

Almost immediately after the German invasion of Russia, Pavelic called for the Croats to join the German effort to destroy the Soviet state. Large numbers of volunteers appeared immediately and an infantry regiment was raised within weeks. One battalion was formed of Bosnias in Sarajevo and two more were formed in Varazdin. These three battalions were sent to Austria where they were organized into the 369th Reinforced (Croat) Infantry Regiment. The regiment was called "reinforced" because it contained its own artillery, beyond the normal infantry guns. When organized, the regiment contained a regimental staff, a supply company, three battalions, one machine-gun company, one anti-tank company equipped with 37mm PAK 36, and three batteries of 105mm leFH 18 howitzers. Though the majority of the regiment was Croatian, it also contained a sprinkling of German officers and NCOs. This regiment was part of the Wehrmacht, and not a Croat national army formation.

In late August 1941 the regiment was assigned to the 100th Light Division and it marched east. It was involved in the battles for Stalingrad and lost heavily. By February 1943 it was reduced to a strength of a battalion and it was lost when Stalingrad capitulated.

However, in the depot in Stockerau, by December 1942 the Germans raised two new infantry regiments, which were designated the 369th Infantry Division. Further elements were gradually raised until a full division was organized. The soldiers of the division called it the *Vrazja Divizija* or Devil's Division, after the 42nd (Croat) Infantry Division of the WWI Austro-Hungarian Army. The Germans called it the *"Schachbrett Division"* or "checkerboard" division after its distinctive shoulder patch.

The casualities suffered by the division and the problems in Croatia caused the Germans to use this, and the two subsequently raised Croatian divisions, only on counter insurgency operations in Croatia.

When the 373rd Division was raised, it took the title *"Tigar"* or "Tiger" Division and the 392nd was known as the *"Plava Divizija"* or "Blue Division."

Apparently, only the 369th Division was engaged in any serious antipartisan combat.

369th Infantry Division

Formed on 8/21/42 as a German-Croatian Division. It had a German cadre and its manpower was Croatian. The division had:

1/,2/,3/369th Croatian Regiment
1/,2/,3/370th Croatian Regiment
1/,2/,3/,4/369th Croatian Artillery Regiment
369th Division Support Units

On 14 August 1941 the records of the German 17th Army show the reinforced 369th (Croatian) Infantry Regiment was organized as follows:

Reinforced 369th (Croatian) Infantry Regiment
Regimental Staff Company
  1 Signals Platoon
  1 Pioneer Platoon (3 LMGs)
  1 Reconnaissance (mounted) Platoon
  1 Regimental Band
1st, 2nd & 3rd Battalions, each with
  3 Rifle Companies (12 LMGs & 3 50mm mortars)
  1 Machine Company (12 HMGs & 6 80mm mortars)

1 Mortar Company (8 80mm mortars)
1 (horse drawn) Panzerjäger Company (12 37mm PAK 36 & 4 LMGs)
1 Light (horse drawn) Infantry Column
369th Light (Croatian) Artillery Battalion
1 Staff Battery
  1 Signals Platoon
  1 Calibration Detachment
3 (horse drawn) Batteries (4 105mm leFH & 2 LMGs ea)

The grenadier regiments were organized with three infantry battalions and a mortar company replacing the infantry gun companies. The artillery regiment had two light battalions, each with three 105mm leFH batteries, and a heavy battalion with two 150mm sFH batteries. The supply company was horse drawn. The division was missing the (mot) medical company and the feldersatz battalion. In September 1943 the division was organized and equipped as follows:

369th Infantry Division
Divisional Staff (2 LMGs)

369th (mot) Mapping Detachment

369th Grenadier Regiments, each with
- 1 Regimental Staff
- 1 Regimental Staff Company
  - 1 Signals Platoon
  - 1 Pioneer Platoon (3 LMGs)
  - 1 Cavalry Reconnaissance Platoon
- **3 Infantry Battalions**, each with
  - 3 Grenadier Companies (12 LMGs & 3 50mm mortars)
  - 1 Machine Gun Company (12 HMGS & 6 80mm mortars)
- **Infantry Gun Company**
  - (4 47mm Russian guns)
- **(tmot) Panzerjäger Company**
  - (4 LMGs & 12 37mm PAK 36)
- **Mortar Company**
  - (8 80mm mortars)

370th Grenadier Regiments, each with
- 1 Regimental Staff
- 1 Regimental Staff Company
  - 1 Signals Platoon
  - 1 Pioneer Platoon (3 LMGs)
  - 1 Cavalry Reconnaissance Platoon
- **3 Infantry Battalions**, each with
  - 3 Grenadier Companies (9 LMGs & 1 50mm mortar ea)
  - 1 Machine Gun Company (8 HMGS & 6 80mm mortars)
- **Infantry Gun Company**
  - (4 47mm Russian guns)
- **(tmot) Panzerjäger Company**
  - (4 LMGs & 12 37mm PAK 36)
- **Mortar Company**
  - (8 80mm mortars)

369th Reconnaissance Battalion
- 1 (mot) Company
  - 1 Pioneer Platoon (4 LMGs)
  - 1 Panzerjäger Platoon (2 37mm PAK 36)
  - 1 Infantry Gun Sections (2 75mm leIG)
- 2 Bicycle Companies (3 50mm mortars, 2 HMGs, & 12 LMGs)

369th Panzerjäger Battalion
- 2 (motZ) Panzerjäger Companies (equipment unknown)

369th Artillery Regiment
- 1 Regimental Staff & Staff Battery
- **1st Battalion**
  - 1 Battalion Staff & Staff Battery
  - 3 Batteries (3 105mm leFH & 2 LMGs ea)
- **2nd Battalions**
  - same as 1st Battalion
- **3rd Battalion**
  - 1 Battalion Staff & Staff Battery

- 2 Batteries (3 150mm sFH & 2 LMGs ea)

369th Pioneer Battalion
- 1 Battalion Staff (2 LMGs)
- 1 (bicycle) Pioneer Company (9 LMGS & 2 120mm mortars)
- 2 Pioneer Companies (9 LMGS & 2 120mm mortars)
- 1 Light Pioneer Supply Column (2 LMGs)

369th Signals Battalion
- 1 (tmot) Telephone Company (6 LMGs)
- 1 (mot) Radio Company (4 LMGs)
- 1 (tmot) Signals Supply Column (1 LMG)

369th Supply Troop
- 1 Supply Troop Staff (2 LMGs)
- 1/369th (mot) Light Supply Column (2 LMGs)
- 2,3/,4/,5/369th Light Supply Columns (4 LMGs ea)
- 6,7/369th Light Supply Columns
- 369th Supply Company (6 LMGs)
- Maintenance Troops
- 369th (mot) Maintenance Company

Administration
- 369th (mot) Bakery Company
- 369th (mot) Butcher Company
- 369th Administration Platoon

Medical
- 369th Medical Company (2 LMGs)
- 1/,2/369th Ambulance

Other
- 369th Veterinary Company
- 369th (tmot) Military Police Detachment (1 LMG)
- 369th (mot) Field Post Office

The 369th Infantry Division was taken captive by the British in early 1945.

373rd (Croatian) Infantry Division

Formed on 6/1/43 as the second German-Croatian Division with a German cadre and the 7th Croatian Mountain Brigade (four battalions). The division had:

1/,2/,3/383rd (Croatian) Grenadier Regiment (from 1/,2/7th Croatian Mountain Brigade)
1/,2/,3/384th (Croatian) Grenadier Regiment (from 3/,4/7th Croatian Mountain Brigade)
1/,2/,3/373rd Artillery Regiment
373rd Fusilier Battalion
373rd Reconnaissance Battalion
373rd Engineer Battalion
373rd Signals Battalion
373rd Division Support Units

The grenadier regiments were organized with three infantry battalions and a mortar company replacing the infantry gun companies. The artillery regiment had two light battalions, each with three 105mm leFH batteries, and a heavy battalion with two 150mm sFH batteries. The supply company was horse drawn. The division was missing the (mot) medical company and the feldersatz battalion. In September 1943 the division was organized and equipped as follows:

373rd Croatian Infantry Division
Divisional Staff (2 LMGs)
Divisional Band
373rd (mot) Mapping Detachment
383rd & 384th Grenadier Regiments, each with
1 Regimental Staff
1 Regimental Staff Company
1 Signals Platoon
1 Pioneer Platoon (3 LMGs)
1 Cavalry Reconnaissance Platoon
3 Infantry Battalions, each with
3 Grenadier Companies (12 LMGs & 3 50mm mortars)
1 Machine Gun Company (12 HMGS & 6 80mm mortars)
(tmot) Panzerjäger Company
(4 LMGs, 4 50mm PAK 38, & 6 37mm PAK 36)
Support Company
(8 80mm mortars & 4 Russian 47mm guns)
373rd Panzerjäger Battalion
2 (motZ) Panzerjäger Companies (9 50mm PAK 38 & 6 LMGs)
373rd Reconnaissance Battalion
1 (mot) Company
1 Pioneer Platoon (4 LMGs)

1 Armored Car Platoon (2 armored cars)
1 Infantry Gun Sections (2 75mm leIG)
2 Bicycle Companies (3 50mm mortars, 2 HMGs, & 12 LMGs)
373rd Artillery Regiment
1 Regimental Staff & Staff Battery
1st Battalion
1 Battalion Staff & Staff Battery
3 Batteries (4 105mm leFH & 2 LMGs ea)
2nd Battalions
same as 1st Battalion
3rd Battalion
1 Battalion Staff & Staff Battery
2 Batteries (4 150mm sFH & 2 LMGs ea)
373rd Pioneer Battalion
1 Battalion Staff (2 LMGs)
1 (bicycle) Pioneer Company (9 LMGS)
2 Pioneer Companies (9 LMGS ea)
1 Light Pioneer Supply Column (2 LMGs)
373rd Signals Battalion
1 (tmot) Telephone Company (6 LMGs)
1 (mot) Radio Company (4 LMGs)
1 (tmot) Signals Supply Column (1 LMG)
373rd Supply Troop
1 Supply Troop Staff (2 LMGs)
1/373rd (mot) Light Supply Column (2 LMGs)
2/,3/,4/,5/373rd Light Supply Columns (4 LMGs ea)
6/,7/373rd Light Supply Columns
373rd Supply Company (6 LMGs)
Maintenance Troops
373rd (mot) Maintenance Company
Administration
373rd (mot) Bakery Company
373rd (mot) Butcher Company
373rd Administration Platoon
Medical
373rd Medical Company (2 LMGs)
1/,2/373rd Ambulance
Other
373rd Veterinary Company
373rd (tmot) Military Police Detachment (1 LMG)
373rd (mot) Field Post Office

On 1 August 1944 the division was organized as follows:

1/,2/,3/383rd Grenadier Regiment
1/,2/,3/384th Grenadier Regiment
373rd Feldersatz Battalion (4 cos)

THE GERMAN ORDER OF BATTLE

373rd Reconnaissance Battalion
  1 (mot) Staff Company
  2 Bicycle Companies
  1 (mot) Reconnaissance Company
373rd Panzerjäger Battalion
  2 (motZ) Panzerjäger Companies (9 50mm PAK 38)
  1 Panzer Company (4 Italian L6s & 1 Le Tanks)
  1 Panzer Company (5 Italian L6s tanks)
373rd Artillery Regiment
  1st Battalion
    1st–3rd Batteries (4 105mm leFH ea)
  2nd Battalion
    4th–6th Batteries (4 105mm leFH ea)
  3rd Battalion
    7th–9th Batteries (4 105mm leFH ea)
373rd Pioneer Battalion (2 foot & 1 bicycle companies)
373rd Signals Battalion (2 cos)
373rd Supply Troop

1/373rd (mot) Light Supply Column
2/,3/373rd 45 ton Transportation Company
4/373rd 30 ton Transportation Company
1 (mot) Maintenance Company
1 Supply Company
373rd (mot) Butcher Company
373rd (mot) Bakery Company
373rd (mot) Administration Company
373rd Medical Company
373rd "Eg" Medical Company
373rd (mot) Medical Supply Company
373rd Veterinary Company
373rd (tmot) Military Police Troop
373rd (mot) Field Post Office

In the fall of 1944 the division absorbed the 2nd (Croatian) Jäger Brigade as its third regiment (probably the 385th Infantry Regiment). The division was taken captive by the Yugoslavs by Raka, west of Sisak.

392nd (Croatian) Infantry Division

Formed on 8/17/43 with a German cadre and Croatian soldiers as the third Croatian division in the German army. The division had:

1/,2/,3/864th (Croatian) Grenadier Regiment
1/,2/,3/865th (Croatian) Grenadier Regiment
1/,2/392nd Artillery Regiment
392nd Reconnaissance Battalion
392nd Anti-tank Battalion
392nd Engineer Battalion
392nd Signals Battalion
392nd Divisional Support Units

Keilig indicates that in 1943 the 845th Grenadier Regiment may also have been assigned to the division. The grenadier regiments were organized with three infantry battalions and a mortar company replacing the infantry gun companies. The artillery battalions had three light batteries each. The supply company was horse drawn. The division was missing the (mot) medical company and the feldersatz battalion. The division was taken prisoner by the Yugoslavs north of Fiume in 1945. OKH records show that the division was organized and equipped as follows:

392nd Croatian Infantry Division
  Divisional Staff (2 LMGs)
  Divisional Band
  392nd (mot) Mapping Detachment

864th & 865th Grenadier Regiments, each with
  1 Regimental Staff
  1 Regimental Staff Company
    1 Signals Platoon
    1 Pioneer Platoon (3 LMGs)
    1 Cavalry Reconnaissance Platoon
  3 Infantry Battalions, each with
    3 Grenadier Companies (12 LMGs & 3 50mm mortars)
    1 Machine Gun Company (12 HMGS & 6 80mm mortars)
  (tmot) Panzerjäger Company
    (6 LMGs & 9 50mm PAK 38)
  Support Company
    (8 80mm mortars & 4 75mm leIG)
392nd Panzerjäger Battalion
  2 (motZ) Panzerjäger Companies (9 75mm PAK 40 & 6 LMGs ea)
392nd Reconnaissance Battalion
  1 (mot) Company
    1 Pioneer Platoon (4 LMGs)
    1 Panzerjäger Platoon (3 LMGs & 3 75mm PAK 40)
    1 Infantry Gun Sections (2 75mm leIG)
  2 Bicycle Companies (2 80mm mortars, 4 HMGs, & 12 LMGs)
392nd Artillery Regiment
  1 Regimental Staff & Staff Battery

1st Battalion
- 1 Battalion Staff & Staff Battery
- 3 Batteries (4 105mm leFH & 2 LMGs ea)

2nd Battalions
- same as 1st Battalion

392nd Pioneer Battalion
- 1 Battalion Staff (2 LMGs)
- 1 (bicycle) Pioneer Company (9 LMGS)
- 2 Pioneer Companies (9 LMGS ea)
- 1 Light Pioneer Supply Column (2 LMGs)

392nd Signals Battalion
- 1 (tmot) Telephone Company (6 LMGs)
- 1 (mot) Radio Company (4 LMGs)
- 1 (tmot) Signals Supply Column (1 LMG)

392nd Supply Troop
- 1 Supply Troop Staff (2 LMGs)
- 1/392nd Light Supply Column (2 LMGs)
- 4/392nd Light Supply Column (4 LMGs)
- 2/,3/392nd Heavy Supply Columns (6 LMGs ea)
- 392nd Supply Company (6 LMGs)

Maintenance Troops
- 392nd (mot) Maintenance Company

Administration
- 392nd (mot) Bakery Company
- 392nd (mot) Butcher Company
- 392nd Administration Platoon

Medical
- 392nd Medical Company (2 LMGs)
- 1/,2/392nd Ambulance

Other
- 392nd Veterinary Company
- 392nd (tmot) Military Police Detachment (1 LMG)
- 392nd (mot) Field Post Office

Field returns dating from 1 August 1944 indicate that the division was slightly modified in its organization and equipment. According to those records the division was as follows:

392nd Croatian Division
- 1/,2/,3/846th Grenadier Regiment
- 1/,2/,3/847th Grenadier Regiment
- 392nd Reconnaissance Battalion
  - 2 Bicycle Companies
  - 1 (mot) Reconnaissance Company
  - 1 Panzer Company (3 Italian L6 tanks)
  - 1 Panzer Company (7 Italian L6s tanks)
- 392nd Artillery Regiment
  - 1st Battalion
    - 3 Batteries (4 105mm leFH ea)
  - 2nd Battalion
    - 3 Batteries (4 105mm leFH ea)
- 392nd Pioneer Battalion (3 cos)
- 392nd signals Battalion (2 cos)
- 392nd Feldersatz Battalion (5 cos)
- 392nd Supply Troop
  - 1/,4/392nd Light Supply Columns
  - 2/,3//392nd Heavy Supply Columns
  - 392nd Supply Company
- 392nd (mot) Maintenance Company
- 392nd (mot) Bakery Company
- 392nd (mot) Butcher Company
- 392nd (mot) Administration Platoon
- 392nd Medical Company
- 392nd (mot) Medical Supply Company
- 392nd Veterinary Company
- 392nd (mot) Military Police Troop
- 392nd (mot) Field Post Office

Croatian Training Brigade

Formed on 4/20/43 in Stockerau from the 369th Croatian Training Brigade. This is the formation that provided the cadres that were to become the 369th Division and the troops for the other two divisions as they were raised. It contained:

- 1st Battalion (1st–4th Companies)
- 2nd Battalion (5th–8th Companies)
- 3rd Battalion (9th–12th Companies)
- 4th Battalion (13th–16th Companies)
- 17th Company (Officer Training)
- 18th Company (Infantry Signals)
- 19th Company (Pioneers)
- 20th & 21st Companies (Bicycle Reconnaissance)

Artillery Battalion
- 1st & 2nd Companies—light artillery
- 3rd Company—heavy artillery
- 4th Company—motorized artillery
- 5th Company—mixed heavy artillery

Mixed Reconnaissance Battalion
- 1st Company—Infantry Pioneers
- 2nd Company—Pioneers
- 3rd Company—Infantry Panzerjäger
- 4th Company—Panzerjäger
- 5th Company—Vehicle Training
- 6th Company—Administrative Company

In 1944 the brigade stood as follows:

1st–4th Training Battalions
Stockerau Ersatz Regiment (369th, 373rd Ersatz Battalions, 392nd Ersatz Company & XVII Croatian Ersatz Battalion)
Franco-Croatian-Arabian Special Company

The fate of the brigade is unknown.

Serbia Volunteer Corps

Serbia formed three military forces, the Serbian State Guard, which was an armed police force and had a strength of about 2,000 officers and men, the Serbian Frontier Guard, which was a static force, and the Serbian Volunteer Corps. This latter force was the most pro-German of all the Serbian forces. It was formed in September 1941 and originally consisted of 12 companies, each of from 120 to 150 men. In January 1943 its name was officially changed to "Volunteer Command," but the old name seems to have remained in common usage. The Volunteer Command was then reorganized into five battalions, each with three companies. In early 1944 it was expanded into five regiments, each of three battalions. An artillery division was raised, but had the strength of a battalion, about 500 men. Nothing is known about its organization. On 8/15/44 the Volunteer Command was organized and equipped as follows:

Brigade Staff
1 Staff
1 Staff Company (2 LMGs)
1 Telephone Platoon
1 Medical Company

1 Light Supply Column
1 Training Company (2 75mm leIG, 2 120mm mortars, 2 50mm mortars, 4 HMGs, & 12 LMGs)
1 Brigade Band
1st Serbian Infantry Regiment
1 Regimental Staff (2 LMGs)
1 Signals Platoon
1 Regimental Band
1 Replacement Company (2 50mm mortars, 1 HMG & 2 LMGs)
1st, 2nd & 3rd Battalions, each with
3 Companies (1 HMG, 12 LMGs & 2 50mm mortars ea)
1 Heavy Company (4 HMGs, 2 LMGs, 4 80mm mortars & 2 75mm leIG)
2nd Serbian Infantry Regiment
same as 1st Serbian Infantry Regiment
3rd Serbian Infantry Regiment
same as 1st Serbian Infantry Regiment
4th Serbian Infantry Regiment
same as 1st Serbian Infantry Regiment
5th Serbian Infantry Regiment
same as 1st Serbian Infantry Regiment

Russian Schutz (Rifle) Corps

Serbia was not a stable nation. In addition to the official defense forces there was a private army, the Russian Guard Corps, which was free of government control. When the Russian Revolution erupted large numbers of Russians fled Russia and many found asylum in Serbia. Belgrade was a center of anti-Soviet White Russian activity. These émigrés greeted Hitler's 1941 invasion of Russia with great enthusiasm and many thousands rushed forward to join the German "liberation" of Russia. Hitler, however, refused to accept them. Unable to fight in Russia, they still organized and turned to themselves and began forming. On 12 September 1941 Brigadier M. F. Skodumov began organizing the Independent Russian Corps (*Otdel'niy Russkiy Korpus*). Three days later he was arrested by the Germans for acting without orders. Command passed to Major General Boris A. Shteyfon and on 2 October 1941, it was renamed the Russian Guard (or Defense) Corps (*Russkiy Okhranniy Korpus*).

The corps grew slowly and the first three regiments were activated by November 1941. The fourth was raised in April 1942 and the fifth in December 1943. In September 1944 the corps boasted 362 officers, 1,295 NCOs, and 9,540 soldiers. Ethnically, the corps was a mix of Slavs, with the largest group, about 5,000, being Rumanian.

The Guard Corps had no official status until 30 November 1942, when it was absorbed into the German Army as the *Russisches Schutzkorps*. After October 1944 it was renamed the *Russisches Schutzkorps Serbien* (Russian Guard Corps Serbia). When Shteyfon died on 30 April 1945, command passed to A. I. Rogozhin

There was some talk of incorporating the Russian Guard Corps Serbia into Vlassov's Russian Liberation Army, but this came to nothing. It is most probable that the aging White Czarist officers, who made up the bulk of the Russian Schutz Corps' officers and General Vlassov would have found such an arrangement most difficult.

The Schutz Corps was equipped with a mixture of German and surplus Czech equipment. It had practically no mechanical transports and only light weapons. On 8/15/44 the corps consisted of a brigade staff and five regiments. The corps was to be organized and equipped as follows:

Brigade Staff
1 Brigade Staff
2 Half Field Hospitals
1 Supply Company
1 Light Supply Column
1 Signals Platoon
1 Veterinary Company

1st Schutz Regiment
1 Regimental Staff
1 Signals Platoon
1 Pioneer Platoon (3 LMGs)
1 Mounted Infantry Platoon (1 Czech LMG)
1 Support Platoon (1 Czech LMG & 3 37mm Czech Guns)
1 Support Platoon (2 Czech LMGs & 2 75mm leIG)
1 Regimental Band
3 Battalions, each with
3 Companies (12 Czech LMGs ea)

1 Machine Gun Company (4 Czech HMGs & 4 120mm mortars)
2nd Schutz Regiment
same as 1st Schutz Regiment
3rd Schutz Regiment
same as 1st Schutz Regiment
4th Schutz Regiment
same as 1st Schutz Regiment
5th Schutz Regiment
same as 1st Schutz Regiment

In October 1944, now called the Russian Guard Corps Serbia, it was organized and equipped as follows:

1st Schutz Regiment
1 Regimental Staff
1 Signals Platoon
1 Pioneer Platoon
1 Mounted Infantry Platoon
3 Battalions, each with
3 Companies (12 Czech LMGs ea)
1 Machine Gun Company (4 Czech HMGs & 4 80mm mortars)
1 Anti-Tank Platoon (3 37mm & 1 LMG)
1 Anti-Tank Platoon (2 75mm & 2 LMGs)
2nd Schutz Regiment
same as 1st Schutz Regiment
3rd Schutz Regiment
same as 1st Schutz Regiment
Other
1 Ersatz Company
1 Wach Company
1 Supply Company
1 Light Supply Column
1 (tmot) Half Field Hospital

The corps was still an active unit as late as 3/27/45.

Montenegrin Volunteer Corps

Montenegro had also been part of Yugoslavia. Being a tiny portion of that country, its military forces were never large. It did, however, produce one formation of some note. This was the Montenegrin Volunteer Corps. When it was formed is not known, but its history is probably quite similar to that of the Serbian Volunteer Corps. On 8/15/44 it was organized and equipped as follows:

Brigade Staff
1 Brigade Staff
1 Signals Platoon
1 Staff Company (2 50mm mortars & 12 LMGs)
1st Regiment
1 Regimental Staff
1 Replacement Company (2 47mm guns, 1 80mm mortar, 1 50mm mortar, 3 HMGs & 4 LMGs)

2 Battalions, each with
  3 Companies (12 LMGs & 2 50mm mortars)
  1 Machine Gun Company (4 HMGS, 2 LMGs, 4
    80mm mortars & 2 47mm guns)

2nd Regiment
  same as 1st Regiment
3rd Regiment
  same as 1st Regiment

6

Italian Formations in German Service

Italy overthrew Mussolini on 25 July 1943 and quickly surrendered to the Allies, but not all of it surrendered. On 9 October 1943 the remains of the Italian fascist state declared their continuing dedication to the Fascist Victory.

Of the force that remained loyal, two divisions were disbanded in July 1944 and their personnel were used to man German flak units. In July 1944 the Oberkommando der Wehrmacht issued an order directing the formation of an Italian army from the independent Italian battalions and detachments then in German service. By September/December 1944 a newly raised Italian Army had taken form.

A German OKH document dated 11/6/43 indicates that the Germans intended to organize four Italian divisions and ten artillery battalions, possibly mountain artillery, in Germany. It was planned to draw volunteers from among the military internees held by the Germans. They were not to take their oath of allegience to Hitler, but to Mussolini. It was planned to organize the formation staffs of the divisions in early November 1943. The recruit command was to be organized in mid-November, when the officer and NCO cadres were formed. The cadres were to be trained in German schools through mid-January and then the recruits were to be brought to the division training depots.

An order issued in Berlin on 1/18/44 by the Oberkommando des Heeres directed that in the first half of February 1944 the recruits for the 3rd Italian Infantry Division were to be organized in Grafenwöhr. In the beginning of March the cadre and recruits for the 2nd Italian Infantry Division were to be gathered in Senne and the cadre for the 4th Italian Mountain Division were to be gathered in Münsingen. At the end of March the recruits for the 1st Italian Division were to be gathered in Heuberg and those for the 4th Mountain Division were to gather in Münsingen.

That same order states that Mussolini had directed that the divisions be given the following designations:

1st Italian Infantry Division	Bersaglieri Division
2nd Italian Infantry Division	Camice Nere Division
3rd Italian Infantry Division	Granatieri Division
4th Italian Infantry Division	Alpini Division

Initially the divisions were given operational dates as shown in the following chart, but they were apparently revised to the dates shown in the second column:

Division	Initial Operational Date	Revised Operational Date
1st Italian Infantry Division	7/1/44	9/1/44
2nd Italian Infantry Division	8/1/44	10/1/44
3rd Italian Infantry Division	9/1/44	11/1/44
4th Italian Infantry Division	9/1/44	8/1/44

An Italian militia (Guardia Nazionale Repubblicana) was formed in December 1943 from the Blackshirt units (Milizia Volontaria Sicurezza Nazionale) and from the Carabinieri. The Blackshirt brigades were formed by an order of the Secretary of the Fascist Republican Party, issued in June–July, from party members.

On 3/3/44 the following Italian units were operational or in formation and working with the Wehrmacht:

Unit	Location	Status
1st Coastal Fortress Battalion	Alessandria	German cadre
2nd Coastal Fortress Battalion	Alessandria	German cadre
3rd Coastal Fortress Battalion	Tortona	German cadre
4th Coastal Fortress Battalion	Tortona	German cadre

Unit	Location	Status
5th Coastal Fortress Battalion	Modena	German cadre
6th Coastal Fortress Battalion	Modena	German cadre
7th Coastal Fortress Battalion	Ravenna	German cadre
8th Coastal Fortress Battalion	Ravenna	German cadre
9th Coastal Fortress Battalion	Alessandria	German cadre
10th Coastal Fortress Battalion	Padua	German cadre
1/,2/11th Coastal Fortress Battalion	Alessandria	German cadre
1/12th Coastal Fortress Battalion	Verona	Forming
1/13th Coastal Fortress Battalion	Pistoia	Forming
14th Coastal Fortress Battalion	Fiume	German cadre
15th Coastal Fortress Battalion	S.Lucia	German cadre
16th Coastal Fortress Battalion	Gorizia	German cadre
17th Coastal Fortress Battalion	Triest, Pola, Fiume	German cadre
Sardinian Battalion	Triest	German cadre
1–10th/1st Coastal Artillery Bn	Alessandria	German cadre
1–8th/2nd Coastal Artillery Bn	Nov. Liguria, Genoa	German cadre
1–4th/5th Coastal Artillery Bn	Livorno 4th Btry	Forming
1–8th/9th Coastal Artillery Bn	Ravenna, Padua,	6–8th Btrys & Rimini forming
1–10th/13th Coastal Artillery Bn	Fiume & Triest	5–7th & 10th Btrys forming
1–3rd/17th Coastal Artillery Bn	Fiume	German cadre
1st Pioneer Battalion	Alessandria	German cadre
2nd Pioneer Battalion	Nov. Liguria	German cadre
1st Construction Battalion	Voghera	German cadre
2nd Construction Battalion	Cremona	German cadre, forming
3rd Construction Battalion	Cremona	German cadre
1/,2/4th Construction Battalion	Pontepetri	German cadre
5th Construction Battalion	Fiume	German cadre
101st Position Construction Bn	Aquino	Fully Italian
102nd Position Construction Bn	Aquino	Fully Italian
103rd Position Construction Bn	Rome	Fully Italian
104th Position Construction Bn	Florence	Fully Italian
105th Position Construction Bn	Florence	Fully Italian
106th Position Construction Bn	Florence	Fully Italian
107th Position Construction Bn	Aquino	Fully Italian
108th Position Construction Bn	Aquino	Fully Italian
109th Position Construction Bn	Perugia	Forming
110th Position Construction Bn	Pescara	Forming
111th Position Construction Bn	Pescara	Forming
112th Position Construction Bn	Pescara	Forming
113th Position Construction Bn	Asti	Forming
114th Position Construction Bn	Bra	Forming
115th Position Construction Bn	Pavia	Forming
116th Position Construction Bn	Padua	Forming
117th Position Construction Bn	Treviso	Forming
118th Position Construction Bn	Verona	Forming
119th Position Construction Bn	Vicenza	Forming
120th Position Construction Bn	Venice	Forming
121st Position Construction Bn	Rovigo	Forming
130th Position Construction Bn	Reggio	Forming
131st Position Construction Bn	Parma	Forming
132nd Position Construction Bn	Parma	Forming
133rd Position Construction Bn	Saluzzo	Forming
134th Position Construction Bn	Ferrara	Forming
135th Position Construction Bn	S. Giovanni	Forming

Unit	Location	Status
136th Position Construction Bn	Bologna	Forming
137th Position Construction Bn	Bologna	Forming
138th Position Construction Bn	Florence	Forming
Italian Signals Company	Abazzi	German Cadre
1st Transportation Column	Fiume	German Cadre
2nd Transportation Column	Fiume	German Cadre
1st Supply Company	Nice	German Cadre
2nd Supply Company	Sappiane	German Cadre
3rd Supply Company	Varazze	German Cadre, forming
50th Supply Battalion	Milan, Turin	Forming
51st Supply Battalion	Peschiora	Forming
52nd Supply Battalion	Mantua	Forming
53rd Supply Battalion	Northern Italy	Planned
54th Supply Battalion	Northern Italy	Planned
55th Supply Battalion	Northern Italy	Planned
56th Supply Battalion	Northern Italy	Planned
57th Supply Battalion	Northern Italy	Planned
1st Bakery Company	Alessandria	German cadre
2nd Bakery Company	Verona	All Italian, forming
1st Italian Battle School	Alessandria	German Cadre
2nd Italian Battle School	Tortona	German Cadre
3rd Italian Battle School	Ravenna	German Cadre
Münsingen Sturm School	Novara, Vercelli, and mid-Italy	Preparing for transport to Germany

According to OKH documents, on 2/1/45 the Italian Army was organized as follows:

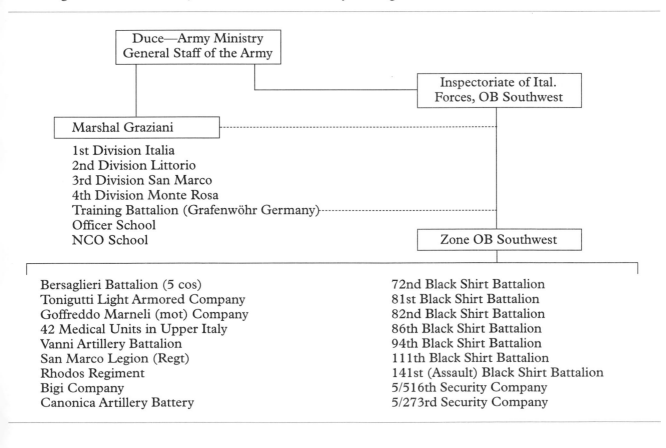

259

In addition, that same document lists the following units as being part of the Italian forces serving with the German army.

Units Assigned to OB South West

Italian Construction Pioneer Battalions
1st, 2nd, 5th, 10th, 117th, 131st, 138th, 142nd, & 147th

Italian Pioneers in German Battalions
3rd Co/1st Pioneer Battalion

Italian Companies in German Construction Battalions
4th Co/430th, 4th Co/432nd, 4th Co/488th, 4th Co/789th, 4th Co/792nd, & 4th Co/820th

Coastal Fortress Battalions
3rd Bn/Luciano Manara
Army Replacement Battalion
1st, 2nd, 3rd, 14th, 15th, 16th, and 17th Coastal Fortress Battalions

Artillery Battalion

2nd Artillery Battalion	2nd, 3rd & 4th Btrys—75mm guns
3rd Artillery Battalion	8th & 9th Btrys—105mm howitzers
	6th & 7th Btrys—75mm guns
4th Artillery Battalion	10th & 13th Btrys—105mm howitzers
	11th Btrys—75mm guns
5th Artillery Battalion	16th Btry—105mm howitzers
	15th Btry French 155mm howitzers
9th Artillery Battalion	29th, 30th & 31st Btrys—French 155mm howitzers
10th Artillery Battalion	32nd, 33rd, & 34th Btrys—French 155mm howitzers
11th Artillery Battalion	35th, 36th, 38th, 39th & 40th Btrys—French 105mm guns
12th Artillery Battalion	37th & 41st Btrys—French 105mm guns
	5th Btry—75mm mountain guns

Supply Troops & Other
54th Supply Troop Command
4th Co/497th Signals Company
50th, 52nd, 57th Supply Companies
1st co/487th Supply Battalion
1st Bakery Company
2nd Co/665th Bakery Battalion
1/,2/1004th Security Battalion
1/,2/1005th Security Battalion
1/1008th Security Battalion
1/,2/1009th Security Battalion
1/,2/1011th Security Battalion
1/,2/113rd Security Battalion
1/115th Security Battalion

Units Assigned to OB South East

Infantry
Kreta Volunteer Legion
Merla Volunteer Battalion
Piazza Volunteer Battalion
3rd Volunteer Battalion
Gabrieli Volunteer Battalion
Fascist Company, 639th Security Regiment
13th (Infantry Gun) Company, 639th Security Regiment
11th Infantry Battalion
422nd Infantry Battalion

Railroad Construction Companies
1–16th Railroad Construction Companies

The most interesting of all the documents found was an OKH listing dated 3/27/45. It shows the following Italian units in the Wehrmacht. These are best described as Hiwis, as that is fundamentally what they were. They were not part of the army under the Italian High Command. Those units found in this listing were:

Ligurian Army
4th Italian Construction Co, 432nd Grenadier Regiment
4th Italian Construction Co, 92nd Grenadier Regiment
14th Army
4th Italian Construction Co, 789th Grenadier Regiment
10th Army
4th Italian Construction Co, 430th Grenadier Regiment

4th Italian Construction Co, 488th Grenadier Regiment
4th Italian Construction Co, 482nd Grenadier Regiment
OB South East
4th Italian Panzerjäger Company, 10th Grenadier Regiment

1st Italian Infantry Division

The division was formed in March 1944. Initially it was organized as the 4th Division and contained the 7th and 8th Infantry Regiments and the 4th Artillery Regiment. However, by August 1944 it was renamed the 1st Division. The division was temporarily disbanded in July 1944 and its personnel were sent to various flak units. However, in August 1944 the division was re-formed and by December it was in combat near Parma, on the right wing of the 14th Army. In January 1945, with the 162nd (Turkistani) Infantry Division, it participated in Operation Totila in the Parma-Fidenza-Salsomaggiore Region. In February 1945 the 1st Regiment, part of an artillery battalion, and the reconnaissance battalion were operating in the Pontremoli-Aulla region. About this time the Replacement Battalion was sent to Germany and used to form the Italian Replacement Brigade. The division was disbanded at the end of April 1945 near Parma. The division was organized and equipped as follows:

Division Staff
1st Bersaglieri Regiment
Regimental Staff
1st Battalion
3 Rifle Companies (10 LMGs ea)
1 Machine Gun Company (12 HMGs & 1 LMG)
1 Support Company
1 Engineer Platoon (4 LMGs)
1 Mortar Platoon (4 120mm, 6 medium & 8 light mortars)
1 Engineer Platoon (4 LMGs)
2nd Battalion
same as 1/1st Regiment
3rd Battalion
same as 1/1st Regiment
1 (mot) Anti-Tank Section[1]
(3 Anti-tank guns)

---
[1] Replaced by a tank destroyer company with panzerschreck platoon with 36 panzerschreck & 2 LMGs, and a gun section with 2–3 (mot) anti-tank guns and 2 LMGs.

1 Mountain Supply Column
2nd Bersaglieri Regiment
same as 1st Bersaglieri Regiment
1st (mot) Anti-Tank Battalion (not formed)
(12 anti-tank guns)

1st Artillery Regiment (formed January 1944)
Regimental Staff
1st Battalion
2 Mountain Batteries (4 75mm howitzers & 5 LMGS ea)
2nd Battalion
2 Mountain Batteries (4 75mm howitzers & 5 LMGS ea)
3rd Battalion
2 Batteries (4 105mm howitzers & 5 LMGS ea)
4th Battalion
(not raised)
2 Batteries (4 150mm howitzers & 5 LMGS ea)
1st Reconnaissance Battalion
2 Bicycle Companies (4 HMGs, 10 LMGs & 2 medium mortars)
1 (mot) Reconnaissance Company (6 LMGs, 4 light infantry guns,
3 anti-tank guns)
1 Engineer Platoon (4 LMGs)
1st Signals Battalion
2 Bicycle Companies (4 HMGs, 10 LMGs & 2 medium mortars)
1 (mot) Reconnaissance Company (6 LMGs, 4 light infantry guns, 3 anti-tank guns)
1 Engineer Platoon (4 LMGs)
1st Engineer Battalion
2 Engineer Companies (2 HMGs, 9 LMGs, 6 flamethrowers & 2 medium mortars ea)
1 (bicycle) Engineer Company (2 HMGs, 9 LMGs, 6 flamethrowers & 2 medium mortars ea)
1 (mot) Engineer Supply Column (2 LMGs)
1st Replacement Battalion
5 Companies

Supply Troops
  1st (mot) 120 ton Transportation Company (8 LMGs)
  3 Mountain Supply Columns (4 LMGs ea)
  1st (partially mot) Supply Company
  1st (mot) Maintenance Company (4 LMGs)
  1st (mot) Bakery Company (6 LMGs)
  1st (mot) Butcher Company (4 LMGs)
  1st (mot) Administration Company (2 LMGs)
  1/,2/1st (mot) Mountain Medical Companies (4 LMGs ea)
  1st (mot) Medical Supply Company

1st Mountain Veterinary Company (6 LMGs)
1st (mot) Field Post Office

The artillery appears to have been expanded as time progressed. Notes indicate that the 1st Battalion raised a third howitzer battery. The 2nd Battalion appears to have converted to 75mm mountain guns and raised a third battery. The 3rd Battery seems to have converted to 75mm guns and raised a third battery. The 4th Battalion appears to have raised a third 150mm battery. This organizational change is indicated as having occurred in all three line divisions.

2nd Italian Infantry Division "Littorio"

The division was formed in April 1944. It was disbanded temporarily in July 1944 and re-formed in August, forming from September through October in Münsingen. The order of 10/14/44 sent the division to Italy. It operated in the region of Pavia-Piacenza-Lodi. In December 1944 the division was in the Alps, operating near Cueno-Monviso-Colle di Maddalena-Cima della Argentera. The division was disbanded in April 1945. Sometime after it was formed the division artillery was expanded and reequipped in the same manner as was that of the 1st Division. The division was organized and equipped as follows:

Division Staff
3rd & 4th Infantry Regiments, each with
  Regimental Staff
  1st Battalion
    3 Rifle Companies (10 LMGs ea)
    1 Machine Gun Company (12 HMGs & 1 LMG)
    1 Support Company
      1 Engineer Platoon (4 LMGs)
      1 Mortar Platoon (4 120mm, 6 medium & 8 light mortars)
      1 Engineer Platoon (4 LMGs)
  2nd Battalion
    same as 1/3rd Regiment
  3rd Battalion
    same as 1/3rd Regiment
  1 (mot) Anti-Tank Section[2]
    (3 Anti-tank guns)
  1 Mountain Supply Column

2nd Artillery Regiment
  Regimental Staff
  1st Battalion
    2 Mountain Batteries (4 75mm howitzers & 5 LMGS ea)
  2nd Battalion
    2 Mountain Batteries (4 75mm howitzers & 5 LMGS ea)
  3rd Battalion
    2 Batteries (4 105mm howitzers & 5 LMGS ea)
  4th Battalion (raised in January 1945)
    2 Batteries (4 150mm howitzers & 5 LMGS ea)
2nd Reconnaissance Battalion
  2 Bicycle Companies (4 HMGs, 10 LMGs & 2 medium mortars)
  1 (mot) Reconnaissance Company (6 LMGs, 4 light infantry guns, 3 anti-tank guns)
  1 Engineer Platoon (4 LMGs)
2nd Reconnaissance Battalion
  2 Bicycle Companies (4 HMGs, 10 LMGs & 2 medium mortars)
  1 (mot) Reconnaissance Company (6 LMGs, 4 light infantry guns, 3 anti-tank guns)
  1 Engineer Platoon (4 LMGs)
2nd Engineer Battalion
  2 Engineer Companies (2 HMGs, 9 LMGs, 6 flamethrowers & 2 medium mortars ea)
  1 (bicycle) Engineer Company (2 HMGs, 9 LMGs, 6 flamethrowers & 2 medium mortars ea)
  1 (mot) Engineer Supply Column (2 LMGs)
2nd Replacement Battalion
  5 Companies
Supply Troops
  2nd (mot) 120 ton Transportation Company (8 LMGs)
  3 Mountain Supply Columns (4 LMGs ea)

---

[2] Replaced by a tank destroyer company with panzerschreck platoon with 36 panzerschreck & 2 LMGs, and a gun section with 2–3 (mot) anti-tank guns and 2 LMGs.

2nd (partially mot) Supply Company
2nd (mot) Maintenance Company (4 LMGs)
2nd (mot) Bakery Company (6 LMGs)
2nd (mot) Butcher Company (4 LMGs)
2nd (mot) Administration Company (2 LMGs)

1/,2/2nd (mot) Mountain Medical Companies (4 LMGs ea)
2nd (mot) Medical Supply Company
2nd Mountain Veterinary Company (6 LMGs)
2nd (mot) Field Post Office

3rd Italian Infantry Division "San Marco"

The division was formed from recruits from the X MAS Flotilla and the Navy. It was organized in mid-1944 and on 7/23/44 it was sent to Italy and the Ligurian coast near Savona. It operated as a coastal security and an anti-partisan formation. In October the 2/6th Infantry Regiment was sent to Serchio Tal and incorporated into the kampfgruppe of the German 4th Mountain Division. In December the 3/5th Infantry Regiment was sent to Passo dell'Abetone. In late March 1945 the division withdrew to Alessandria, across the Po, and then was disbanded. The division was organized and equipped as follows:

Division Staff
5th Naval Infantry Regiment
 Regimental Staff
 1st Battalion
  3 Rifle Companies (10 LMGs ea)
  1 Machine Gun Company (12 HMGs & 1 LMG)
  1 Support Company
   1 Engineer Platoon (4 LMGs)
   1 Mortar Platoon (4 120mm, 6 medium & 8 light mortars)
   1 Engineer Platoon (4 LMGs)
 2nd & 3rd Battalions
  same as 1/5th Naval Regiment
  1 (mot) Anti-Tank Section[3]
   (3 Anti-tank guns)
  1 Mountain Supply Column
6th Naval Infantry Regiment
 same as 5th Naval Regiment
2nd Artillery Regiment
 Regimental Staff
 1st & 2nd Battalions, each with
  2 Mountain Batteries (4 75mm howitzers & 5 LMGS ea)
 3rd Battalion
  2 Batteries (4 105mm howitzers & 5 LMGS ea)
 4th Battalion (raised in October 1944)
  2 Batteries (4 150mm howitzers & 5 LMGS ea)

3rd Reconnaissance Battalion
 2 Bicycle Companies (4 HMGs, 10 LMGs & 2 medium mortars)
 1 (mot) Reconnaissance Company (6 LMGs, 4 light infantry guns, 3 anti-tank guns)
 1 Engineer Platoon (4 LMGs)
3rd Reconnaissance Battalion
 2 Bicycle Companies (4 HMGs, 10 LMGs & 2 medium mortars)
 1 (mot) Reconnaissance Company (6 LMGs, 4 light infantry guns, 3 anti-tank guns)
 1 Engineer Platoon (4 LMGs)
3rd Engineer Battalion
 2 Engineer Companies (2 HMGs, 9 LMGs, 6 flamethrowers & 2 medium mortars ea)
 1 (bicycle) Engineer Company (2 HMGs, 9 LMGs, 6 flamethrowers & 2 medium mortars ea)
 1 (mot) Engineer Supply Column (2 LMGs)
3rd Replacement Battalion
 5 Companies
Supply Troops
 3rd (mot) 120 ton Transportation Company (8 LMGs)
 3 Mountain Supply Columns (4 LMGs ea)
 3rd (partially mot) Supply Company
 3rd (mot) Maintenance Company (4 LMGs)
 3rd (mot) Bakery Company (6 LMGs)
 3rd (mot) Butcher Company (4 LMGs)
 3rd (mot) Administration Company (2 LMGs)
 1/,2/3rd (mot) Mountain Medical Companies (4 LMGs ea)
 3rd (mot) Medical Supply Company
 3rd Mountain Veterinary Company (6 LMGs)
 3rd (mot) Field Post Office

The artillery was expanded and reequipped in the same manner as was that of the 1st Division.

---

[3] Replaced by a tank destroyer company with panzerschreck platoon with 36 panzerschreck & 2 LMGs, and a gun section with 2–3 (mot) anti-tank guns and 2 LMGs.

4th Italian Mountain Division "Monte Rosa"

The division was formed in Münsingen in March/May 1944. The order of 7/7/44 sent it to Italy. Initially the division was known as the 1st Mountain Division, with the 1st Mountain Regiment, but this was changed in August 1944, when it became the 4th Division. The division was sent to the Ligurian Coast between Genoa and La Spezia, where it engaged in antipartisan warfare. In September 1944 the 2/7th and 3/8th Mountain Regiments and 2/4th Artillery Regiment were sent to the Alpine front where they incorporated into the German 5th Mountain Division. In September 1944 the "Saluzzo" Battalion was disbanded as a result of antipartisan actions and casualties. At the end of October the "Vestone" Battalion suffered the same fate. At the end of October part of the division was sent to Garfagnana and organized into two kampfgruppen. The 7th Kampfgruppe was in Garfagnana with the Divisional Staff, Staff/,3/7th and 1/8th Mountain Regiments, the 2/,4/4th Mountain Artillery Regiment, the pioneer and the reconnaissance battalion. Apparently it also included the 2/5th Mountain Regiment "San Marco." The 8th Kampfgruppe was in Liguria with the Staff/,2/8th Mountain Regiment, 1/7th Mountain Regiment, 1/4th Mountain Artillery Regiment, and Replacement Battalion. From 6–30 December 1944 the 7th Kampfgruppe faced the American 92nd Infantry Division in Garfagnana. From January through February the 7th Kampfgruppe was supported by the 1st Italian Bersaglieri Regiment, ("Italia Division").

In March the 8th Kampfgruppe, with the 1/4th Mountain Artillery, and the 1/7th and 1/,2/8th Mountain Infantry Regiments were sent to the Alpine front and incorporated into the German 5th Mountain Division and the 2nd Infantry Division "Littorio." Kampfgruppe 78 remained in Liguria with the replacement battalion, the reconnaissance battalion and the 1/4th Infantry Regiment. The 2/4th Artillery Regiment and the pioneer battalion remained in Garfagnana. The division was disbanded at the end of April 1945. The division was organized and equipped as follows:

Division Staff
7th Mountain Regiment
  Regimental Staff
  1st Battalion "Aosta"
    3 Rifle Companies (2 HMGs, 12 LMGs, 2 light mortars)
    1 Machine Gun Company (6 HMGS & 6 medium mortars)
    1 Support Company

    1 Signals Platoon
    1 Engineer Platoon
    1 Infantry Gun Section (2 light infantry guns)
  2nd Battalion "Bassano"
    same as 1st Battalion
  3rd Battalion "Intra"
    same as 1st Battalion
  1 (mot) Anti-Tank Section[4] (3 Anti-tank guns)
  1 Mountain Supply column
8th Mountain Regiment
  Regimental Staff
  1st Battalion "Brescia"
    same as 1/7th Mountain Regiment
  2nd Battalion "Morbello"
    same as 1/7th Mountain Regiment
  3rd Battalion "Tirano"
    same as 1/7th Mountain Regiment
  1 (mot) Anti-Tank Section[4] (3 Anti-tank guns)
  1 Mountain Supply column
4th Mountain Artillery Regiment
  Regimental Staff
  1st Battalion "Aosta"
    2 Mountain Batteries (4 75mm howitzers & 5 LMGS ea)
  2nd Battalion "Bergamo"
    2 Mountain Batteries (4 75mm howitzers & 5 LMGS ea)
  3rd Battalion "Vicenza"
    2 Mountain Batteries (4 75mm howitzers & 5 LMGS ea)
  4th Battalion "Mantova"
    (raised in January 1945)
    2 Mountain Batteries (4 105mm howitzers & 5 LMGS ea)
Battalion "Saluzzo"
  same as 1/7th Mountain Regiment
Battalion "Vestone"
  same as 1/7th Mountain Regiment
4th Reconnaissance Battalion
  2 Bicycle Companies (4 HMGs, 10 LMGs & 2 medium mortars)
  1 (mot) Reconnaissance Company (6 LMGs, 4 light infantry guns, 3 anti-tank guns)
  1 Engineer Platoon (4 LMGs)

---

[4] Replaced by a tank destroyer company with panzerschreck platoon with 36 panzerschreck & 2 LMGs, and a gun section with 2–3 (mot) anti-tank guns and 2 LMGs.

4th Engineer Battalion
  2 Engineer Companies (2 HMGs, 9 LMGs, 6
  flamethrowers & 2 medium mortars ea)
  1 (bicycle) Engineer Company (2 HMGs, 9 LMGs,
  6 flamethrowers & 2 medium mortars ea)
  1 (mot) Engineer Supply Column (2 LMGs)
4th Signals Battalion
  1 (partially mot) Telephone Company (7 LMGs)
  1 (mot) Radio Company (6 LMGs)
  1 (mot) Signals Supply Column (1 LMG)
4th Replacement Battalion
  5 Companies
Supply Troops
  4th (mot) 120 ton Transportation Company (8
  LMGs)

3 Mountain Supply Columns (4 LMGs ea)
4th (partially mot) Supply Company
4th (mot) Maintenance Company (4 LMGs)
4th (mot) Bakery Company (6 LMGs)
4th (mot) Butcher Company (4 LMGs)
4th (mot) Administration Company (2 LMGs)
1/,2/4th (mot) Mountain Medical Companies (4
  LMGs ea)
4th (mot) Medical Supply Company
4th Mountain Veterinary Company (6 LMGs)
4th (mot) Field Post Office

The artillery was expanded and reequipped in the same manner as was that of the 1st Division.

Centro Addestramento Reparti Specialia

Formed in Parma in April 1944 with three regiments, it was disbanded in June and its personnel were sent to the newly forming divisions. At the end of August the 1st and 2nd Regiments (with four battalions) were sent to Turin and used for antipartisan operations. In August 1944 their strength was 160 officers and 2,000 men. On 9/1/44 the CARS was disbanded again and used to form the 1st Regiment "Cacciatori degli Appeninni." It was organized as follows:

1st Regiment "Cacciatori degli Appeninni"
  1st Battalion "Granatieri"

2nd Battalion "Alpini"
3rd Battalion "Cavalieri di Lombardia" (not formed)
2nd GNR Regiment
  1–3rd Battalions
3rd PFR Regiment "Compagnia della Morte"
  1–2nd Battalions
"Cavalieri di Lombardia" Regiment
  1–2nd Battalions

1st "Cacciatori delgi Appennini" Regiment

Formed as an Appenine Mountain Regiment on 9/1/44 from the CARs in Turin, it was used in antipartisan warfare in Piedmont until November 1944, when it was sent to the Alpine Front (Passo del San Bernardo) and placed under the LXXV Army Corps. It was disbanded in April 1945. It contained:

1st Battalion "Granatieri"
2nd Battalion "Alpini"
3rd Battalion
4th Battalion

R.A.P. (Raggruppamento Anti-Partigiani)

Organized in Bresica in August 1944 for antipartisan actions. By the end of August one battalion was sent to Turin and operated around Aostatal, Pellicetal, and

Turin. On 8/5/44 the force had a strength of 1,515 men. It consisted of the:

1st Battalion "Bersaglieri"
2nd Battalion "Infanterie"
3rd Battalion "Alpini"

4th Battalion (not formed)
10th Special Artillery Battalion

1st Bersaglieri Regiment

Formed in September/October 1943 near Turin, in March 1944 it was incorporated into the 1st Division "Italia" as the 1st Bersaglieri Regiment. It was disbanded as an independent formation on 4/1/44.

3rd Bersaglieri Regiment

Formed in September/October 1943 near Milan, in November it was sent to Alessandria and used in coastal defense. In December it was disbanded and reorganized into Coastal Fortress Battalions. The regiment was formally disbanded at the end of March 1945.

Bersaglieri Battalion		Italian Coastal Fortress Battalion
51st	became	1st
20th	became	2nd
25th	became	3rd
18th	became	4th

8th Bersaglieri Regiment

Formed in August/September 1944 near Verona with three battalions. It was disbanded in April 1945. The 1st Battalion "Benito Mussolini" was formed in October 1943 and in December it was absorbed into the German Army as the 15th Italian Coastal Fortress Battalion. The 2nd Battalion "Goffredo Mameli" was formed in April–May 1944 and placed under the 715th Infantry Division. On 8/1/44 it had 20 officers, 82 NCOs, and 418 rank and file. In December 1944 it was absorbed into the 1st Division "Italia" as the 3/2nd Bersaglieri Regiment. The 3rd Battalion "Enrico Toti" was formed in Verona in September 1944 and remained there until April 1945. In September 1944 it contained 40 officers, 74 NCOs, and 313 rank and file.

"Tagliamento" Mountain Regiment

Formed in September–November 1943 from the 8th Alpini Regiment in Udine. In August–September 1944 it was to have a CCNN (Black Shirt) Battalion assigned to it as a fourth battalion. It apparently had several names: "Tagliamento" Volunteer Regiment, "Tagliamento" Volunteer Police Regiment, and "Tagliamento" Land Defense Alpini Regiment. On 1/30/44 a "Tagliamento" Volunteer Mountain Police Battalion was organized. In March 1945 the regiment had three battalions and a strength of 1,335 men.

1st Italian Coastal Fortress Battalion

Formed from the 51st Bersaglieri Battalion in December 1945 and served in conjunction with the German 356th Infantry Division, LXXXVII Corps, for the defense of the Genoa coastal region. On 8/1/44 it had a total strength of 30 officers, 117 NCOs, and 532 rank and file. It was disbanded in April 1945.

2nd Italian Coastal Fortress Battalion

Formed in December 1943 from the 20th Bersaglieri division and served in conjunction with the German 356th Infantry Division for the defense of the Savona coastal region. On 8/1/44 it had 18 officers, 118 NCOs, and 682 rank and file. It was disbanded in April 1945.

3rd Italian Coastal Fortress Battalion

Formed in December 1943 from the 25th Bersaglieri Battalion in Tortona and served with the German 334th Infantry Division in the coastal defense of the region around Genoa. On 8/1/44 it had a total strength of 21 officers, 115 NCOs, and 573 men. It was disbanded in April 1945.

4th Italian Coastal Fortress Battalion

Formed in December 1943 from the 18th Bersaglieri Regiment, it served under the German 334th Infantry Division in the coast defense of the La Spezia region. On 8/1/44 it had 10 officers, 41 NCOs, and 446 men. It was disbanded at the end of 1944.

5th Italian Coastal Fortress Battalion

Formed in December 1943 and assigned to the LI Mountain Corps, it served as a coast defense formation, working with the German 356th Infantry Division. In May 1944 it was working with the 162nd (Turkistani) Infantry Division. In July 1944 it was disbanded and its troops incorporated into the German Army as Hiwis.

6th Italian Coastal Fortress Battalion

Formed in December 1943 near Modena with the LI Corps. It served on the Island of Elba after January 1944. It was disbanded on 6/18/44 after Elba was overrun by the Allies.

7th Italian Coastal Fortress Battalion

Formed in December 1943 in Ravenna with the Witthöft Corps and then placed under the commander of the Lower Alps. It was disbanded in July 1944 and the remaining personnel were assigned to the Luftwaffe.

8th Italian Coastal Fortress Battalion

Formed in December 1943 in Treviso with the Witthöft Corps. It operated with the 278th Fusilier Battalion. It was disbanded in August 1944 and the remaining personnel were assigned to the 2nd Italian Coastal Fortress Battalion.

9th Italian Coastal Fortress Battalion

Formed in December 1943 in Treviso with the Witthöft Corps it operated with the 933rd Fortress Battalion. It was disbanded in July 1944 and its personnel were absorbed into the Luftwaffe.

10th Italian Coastal Fortress Battalion

Formed in December 1943 in Padua with the Witthöft Corps it operated with the 903rd Fortress Battalion. It was disbanded in July 1944 and its personnel were absorbed into the forces working on the "Green Line."

11th Italian Coastal Fortress Battalion

Formed in December 1943 in Alessandria using the "Bruno Mussolini" Bersaglieri Battalion. It operated with the 356th Infantry Division, LXXXVII Corps.

12th Italian Coastal Fortress Battalion

Formed in December 1943 in Verona under the LXXXVII Corps. In February 1944 it was in La Spezia working with the 356th Feldersatz Battalion. It was incorporated into the 4th Coastal Fortress Battalion in July 1944.

13th Italian Coastal Fortress Battalion

Formed in December 1943 in Pistoia and was assigned to the LI Mountain Corps. After February 1944 it worked with the 451st Military Police Troop. It was disbanded in May–June 1944 and its personnel were sent to the LI Corps as Hiwis.

14th Italian Coastal Fortress Battalion

Formed in December 1943 in Fiume from the Confinaria Militia Battalion. It operated with the German 71st Infantry Division, Kübler Corps. From the end of 1944 it was in Fiume as a security force. On 8/1/44 it had 24 officers, 45 NCOs, and 498 rank and file. It was in Gorizia in 1945 and was disbanded in August 1945.

15th Italian Coastal Fortress Battalion

Formed in December 1943 in Fiume from the "Mussolini" Battalion, 8th Bersaglieri Regiment. It operated with the German 71st Infantry Division and in May it was absorbed by the 188th Reserve Mountain Division. On 8/1/44 it had 31 officers, 69 NCOs, and 609 rank and file. It was disbanded in April 1945.

16th Italian Coastal Fortress Battalion

Formed in December 1943 in Gorizia. It operated with the German Kübler Corps. On 8/1/44 it had 31 officers, 69 NCOs, and 609 rank and file. In August 1944 the 1st Company was disbanded. The remaining three companies were disbanded in April 1945.

17th Italian Coastal Fortress Battalion

Formed in December 1943 and operated with the German 71st Infantry Division. It was disbanded in April 1945.

"Ettore Muti" Battalion

This volunteer battalion was formed in September 1943 in Florence. It served as a security force for Florence until August 1944, when it was sent to Bologna, then to Schio in September. It was disbanded in Verona in April 1945.

"Volontari di Sardegna" Battalion

Formed in December 1943 in Villa Opicinia, north of Triest, and operated with the German 71st Infantry Division. In February 1944 it was determined by the Germans to be unreliable and disarmed.

"Moschettieri delle Alpi" Battalion

Formed in September 1943 in Aosta it served as a local security force. In November 1944 it was absorbed into the "Cacciatori degli Appennini," 2nd Division "Littorio."

"Forli" Assault Battalion

Formed in August 1944 from personnel from the 101st Fighter Squadron as the "Forli" Assault Company and assigned to the German 278th Infantry Division. It fought in the withdrawal from Senio and in January 1945 it was expanded into a battalion.

"Bruno Mussolini" Bersaglieri Battalion

Formed in Santa Lucia d'Isonzo in March 1945 with 625 men.

"San Giusto" (or "Tenegutti") Armored Squadron

Formed in Spoleto in September–October 1943, near Fiume. It never exceeded the strength of a company.

"Leoncello" Armored Squadron

At company strength formed in Desenzano on Lake Garda.

1st Italian Coastal Defense Battalion

Formed in December 1943 in Alessandria, with the 1st–10th Coastal Fortress Batteries. It had ten batteries. The 1st–5th Batteries were stationed in Genoa with the German 356th Infantry Division, the 6th was with the 135th Fortress Brigade in La Spezia, the 7th near Savona, the 8th in Cogoleto with the 356th Infantry Division, and the 9th and 10th batteries were in La Spezia with the 135th Fortress Battalion. In July–August 1944 the 1st–4th Batteries were disbanded, then the battalion was disbanded.

3rd Italian Coastal Defense Battalion

Formed in December 1943 in Genoa from the 11th–8th Italian Fortress Batteries. It had eight batteries. The 1st–6th were in Genoa and the 7th and 8th Batteries were in Imperia with the 356th Infantry Division. In May–June the 17th and 18th Batteries deserted and then the battalion was disbanded.

5th Italian Coastal Defense Battalion

Formed in December 1943 in Livorno from the 19th–22nd Italian Fortress Batteries. It had four batteries. In May–June 1944 the 19th, 21st and 22nd Batteries were disbanded. The remainder of the battalion was disbanded shortly thereafter.

9th Italian Coastal Defense Battalion

Formed in December 1943 by the Witthöft Corps from the 23rd–30th Italian Fortress Batteries. It had eight batteries. The 1st–2nd Batteries were in Ravenna with the 278th Artillery Regiment, the 3rd in Treviso with the 278th

Artillery Regiment, the 4th in Padua with the 903rd Coastal Battalion, and the 5th–8th were in Rimini with the 956th Artillery Regiment. The 23rd–27th Batteries were disbanded in May–June 1944 and quickly followed by the rest of the battalion.

13th Italian Coastal Defense Battalion

Formed in December 1943 near Fiume and Triest from the 31st–39th Italian Fortress Batteries. It was organized with batteries numbered 1st–10th, but no 8th Battery. The 1st–4th Batteries were in Fiume operating with the 236th Artillery Regiment, the 5th–7th were in Padua operating with the 992nd Grenadier Regiment, the 9th–10th were by Triest with the 278th Infantry Division. The staff was disbanded in July 1944.

17th Italian Coastal Defense Battalion

Formed in December 1943 by the Kübler Corps near Fiume with the 40th–42nd Italian Coastal Batteries. It operated with the 278th Infantry Division for the defense of the Fiume coastline and was disbanded in July 1944.

"Noviligure" Italian Coastal Defense Replacement Battalion

Formed in May 1944 in Novi Liguria by the 356th Infantry Division, LXXV Corps. It was disbanded and assigned to the Italian Coastal Fortress Replacement Battalion and the "Novi Liguria" Battery.

1st Italian Artillery Command Unit

Formed in November 1944 with four batteries. It was disbanded in early 1945.

2nd Italian Artillery Command Unit

Formed in November 1944 by the 42nd Jäger Division. In November it had seven batteries numbered 2nd–8th. In January it absorbed the 2nd–4th Batteries of the 1st Artillery Command and established a second battalion with five batteries.

3rd Italian Artillery Command Unit

Formed in November 1944 by the 42nd Jäger Division. In November it contained the 9th and 10th Batteries. In early 1945 the 10th Battery was detached to the 4th Italian Artillery Command Unit and received the 6th–8th Batteries from the 2nd Italian Artillery Command Unit.

4th Italian Artillery Command Unit

Formed in November 1944 with the 11th–13th Batteries. In February 1945 it received the 10th Battery from the 3rd Italian Artillery Command.

6th Italian Artillery Command Unit

Formed in November 1944 by the 148th Infantry Division, LI Mountain Corps, with the 15th and 16th Batteries. It was known to still exist in February 1945.

9th Italian Artillery Command Unit

Formed in November 1944 with the 29th–31st Batteries. In March 1945 it was in Triest with 270 men.

10th Italian Artillery Command Unit

Formed in November 1944 with the 32nd–34th Batteries. It still existed in February 1945.

11th Italian Artillery Command Unit

Formed in November 1944 near Fiume with the 35th, 36th, 38th, 39th, and 40th Batteries. It still existed in March 1945 and had 343 men.

12th Italian Artillery Command Unit "Julia"

Formed in November 1944 with the 37th and 41st Batteries. It still existed in March 1945.

1st Italian Pioneer Battalion

Formed in December 1943 in Alessandria by the 356th Infantry Division, LXXXVII Corps. It was disbanded in July 1944 and the remaining men incorporated as Hiwis into the German Army.

2nd Italian Pioneer

Formed in December 1943 in Novi Liguria by the 334th Infantry Division. After February 1944 it was assigned to the 10th Army in the Nettuno Bridgehead. On 8/1/44 it had 20 officers, 45 NCOs, and 311 rank and file. It was disbanded in March–April 1945.

1st Italian Construction Pioneer Battalion

Formed in December 1943 in Voghera by the 334th Division LI Mountain Corps. On 8/1/44 it had 22 officers, 78 NCOs, and 708 rank and file. It was disbanded in April 1945.

2nd Italian Construction Pioneer Battalion

Formed in December 1943 in Cremona by the Kübler Corps. On 8/1/44 it had 31 officers, 33 NCOs, and 609 rank and file. It was disbanded in April 1944.

3rd Italian Construction Pioneer Battalion

Formed in December 1943 by the LI Mountain Corps. It was apparently disbanded in May 1944 and its troops absorbed into the 3A and 3B Italian Construction Companies, the 57th Railroad Pioneer Company and the 4th Railroad Pioneer Regiment.

4th Italian Construction Pioneer Battalion

Formed in December 1943 in Pesaro by the LI Mountain Corps, it had only two companies. It was disbanded in May–June 1944 and its personnel absorbed by the Wehrmacht as Hiwis.

5th Italian Construction Pioneer Battalion

Formed in December 1943 as the "Covatta" battalion in Fiume by the Kübler Corps. It was assigned to coast defense between Fiume and Pola. On 8/1/44 it had 21 officers, 48 NCOs, and 373 men. It was disbanded in April 1945.

1st Italian Bridge Construction Battalion

Formed in May 1944 in Pavia by the Witthöft Corps. On 8/1/44 it had 26 officers, 83 NCOs, and 385 rank and file. It was disbanded in April 1945.

Italian Light Bridge Construction Battalion

Formed in the winter of 1943/44 with four companies.

147th Italian Technical Battalion

Formed in May 1944 in Bologna by the Witthöft Corps. On 8/1/44 it had 35 officers, 69 NCOs and 197 rank and file.

101st Italian Position Construction Pioneer Battalion

Formed in December 1943 in Florence. In February 1944 it was in the Nettuno Bridgehead with the XIV Panzer Corps. In May–June 1944 it was destroyed. The remains were sent to Bologna where they were disbanded.

102nd Italian Position Construction Pioneer Battalion

Formed in December 1943 in Perugia. It was sent to the Gustav Line and in February 1944 it was in the Nettuno Bridgehead with the XIV Panzer Corps. It was destroyed in May–June 1944. The remains were sent to Bologna and disbanded.

103rd Italian Position Construction Pioneer Battalion

Formed in December 1943 in Florence. In February 1944 it was in the Nettuno Bridgehead with the XIV Panzer Corps. It was destroyed in May–June 1944. The remains were sent to Bologna and disbanded.

104th Italian Position Construction Pioneer Battalion

Formed in December 1943 in Florence. It was sent to the Gustav Line and in February 1944 it was in the Nettuno Bridgehead with the XIV Panzer Corps. It was destroyed in May–June 1944. The remains were sent to Bologna and disbanded.

105th Italian Position Construction Pioneer Battalion

Formed in December 1943 in Florence. It was sent to the Gustav Line and in February 1944 it was in the Nettuno Bridgehead. It was destroyed in May–June 1944. The remains were sent to Bologna and disbanded.

106th Italian Position Construction Pioneer Battalion

Formed in December 1943 in Florence. It was sent to the Gustav Line and in February 1944 it was in the Nettuno Bridgehead with the XIV Panzer Corps. It was destroyed in May–June 1944. The remains were sent to Bologna, then Verona where it was reorganized as the 106th Pioneer Construction Company from the 84th Railroad Pioneer Company.

107th Italian Position Construction Pioneer Battalion

Formed in December 1943 in Florence. It was sent to the Gustav Line and in February 1944 it was in the Nettuno Bridgehead with the XIV Panzer Corps. It was destroyed in May–June 1944. The remains were sent to Bologna and disbanded.

108th Italian Position Construction Pioneer Battalion

Formed in December 1943 in Perugia. It was sent to the Gustav Line. It was destroyed in May–June 1944. The remains were sent to Bologna and disbanded.

109th Italian Position Construction Pioneer Battalion

Formed in December 1943 in Perugia. It was sent to the Gustav Line. It was destroyed in May–June 1944. The remains were sent to Bologna and disbanded.

110th Italian Position Construction Pioneer Battalion

Formed in December 1943 in Pesaro. It was sent to the Gustav Line. It was destroyed in May–June 1944. The remains were sent to Bologna and disbanded.

111th Italian Position Construction Pioneer Battalion

Formed in December 1943 in Pesaro. It was sent to the Gustav Line. It was destroyed in May–June 1944. The remains were sent to Bologna and disbanded in late 1944.

112th Italian Position Construction Pioneer Battalion

Formed in April 1944 in Macerata. It was sent to Bologna and disbanded in October 1944.

113th Italian Position Construction Pioneer Battalion

Formed in Alessandria in January–April 1944. It was sent to the Gustav Line and then to Lugo di Romagna in August to be rebuilt.

114th Italian Position Construction Pioneer Battalion

Formed in Alessandria in January 1944. It was rebuilt in August in Bologna. On 8/1/44 it had 14 officers, 8 NCOs, and 211 men.

115th Italian Position Construction Pioneer Battalion

Formed in Voghera in 1944. It was sent to Pesaro to be rebuilt and then disbanded.

116th Italian Position Construction Pioneer Battalion

Formed in Padua in January 1944. It was sent to the Gustav Line and destroyed in August. The remains were sent to the 116th A and 116th B Italian Companies.

117th Italian Position Construction Pioneer Battalion

Formed in Padua in January 1944. It was sent to the Gustav Line and destroyed in May–June 1944. The remains were incorporated into the 117th Italian Company.

118th Italian Position Construction Pioneer Battalion

Formed in Verona in April 1944. It was disbanded in August 1944 with its remains going into the 135th Italian Position Construction Battalion.

119th Italian Position Construction Pioneer Battalion

Formed in Perugia in April 1944. In August it had 9 officers, 6 NCOs, and 129 men. It was disbanded in November 1944.

120th Italian Position Construction Pioneer Battalion

Formed in Venice in May 1944. It had 6 officers, 9 NCOs, and 47 men in August 1944. It was disbanded shortly later.

121st Italian Position Construction Pioneer Battalion

Formed in Venice in April 1944. It had 24 officers, 38 NCOs, and 301 men in August 1944. It was disbanded in April 1945.

122nd Italian Position Construction Pioneer Battalion

Formed in Faenza in May–August 1944.

123rd Italian Position Construction Pioneer Battalion

Formed in Lugo in May 1944.

124th Italian Position Construction Pioneer Battalion

Formed in Massa Lombarda in May–August 1944. On 8/1/44 it had 36 officers and 97 men.

125th Italian Position Construction Pioneer Battalion

Formed in Casalecchio di Reno in August 1944.

126th Italian Position Construction Pioneer Battalion

Formed in Casalecchio di Reno in August 1944.

127th Italian Position Construction Pioneer Battalion

Formed in July 1944 and disbanded in 1945.

128th Italian Position Construction Pioneer Battalion

Formed from the remains of the 116th and 128th Italian Position Construction Pioneer Battalions. Disbanded September 1944.

129th Italian Position Construction Pioneer Battalion

May not have been raised.

130th Italian Position Construction Pioneer Battalion

Formed in Reggio Emilia in August–December 1944.

131st Italian Position Construction Pioneer Battalion

Formed in April 1944. Destroyed in July and incorporated with the remains of the 121st Position Construction Battalion.

132nd Italian Position Construction Pioneer Battalion

Formed in Parma in May–August 1944.

133rd Italian Position Construction Pioneer Battalion

Formed in Parma in February 1944. In August 1944 it had 16 officers, 26 NCOs, and 178 rank and file.

134th Italian Position Construction Pioneer Battalion

Formed in Ferrara in April 1944. In May–June 1944 it was destroyed, sent to Bologna and then disbanded.

135th Italian Position Construction Pioneer Battalion

Formed in Pesaro. On 8/1/44 it had 9 officers, 13 NCOs, and 134 rank and file.

136th Italian Position Construction Pioneer Battalion

Formed in April 1944 in Ferrara. It was disbanded in late 1944.

137th Italian Position Construction Pioneer Battalion

Formed in January–April 1944. It was apparently disbanded in late August 1944.

138th Italian Position Construction Pioneer Battalion

Formed in Florence in April 1944. It was disbanded in 1945 and incorporated into the remains of another battalion.

139th Italian Position Construction Pioneer Battalion

It was planned to be formed in August 1944 in Voghera, but there is no evidence that it was raised.

140th Italian Position Construction Pioneer Battalion

Formed in May–July 1944 in Tortona with the LXXV Army Corps. It was disbanded shortly thereafter and incorporated into the 142nd Position Construction Battalion.

141st Italian Position Construction Pioneer Battalion

Planned to be formed in August 1944 in Acqui, but may not have been formed.

142nd Italian Position Construction Pioneer Battalion

Formed in May 1944 in Alessandria with the LXXV Corps. In 1945 it absorbed the 140th Position Construction Battalion. On 8/1/44 it had 17 officers, 91 NCOs, and 343 rank and file.

143rd Italian Position Construction Pioneer Battalion

Formed in May–August 1944 in Alessandria with the LXXV Corps and was disbanded shortly thereafter with the remains going to the 142nd Position Construction Battalion.

144th Italian Position Construction Pioneer Battalion

Formed in Voghera and quickly disbanded.

145th Italian Position Construction Pioneer Battalion

Planned to be formed in Cueno, but may not have been raised.

146th Italian Position Construction Pioneer Battalion

Formed in May–August 1944 in Genoa with the LXXV Corps. It was disbanded and its forces given to the 142nd Position Construction Battalion.

10th Italian Mountain Construction Battalion

Raised in late 1944 or early 1945 by the XIV Panzer Corps, it had 18 Officers, 34 NCOs, and 452 rank and file.

65th Italian Construction Battalion

Raised in April 1945 by the German 65th Infantry Division, 14th Army.

142nd Italian Construction Battalion

Raised by the German 42nd Infantry Division and disbanded in 1945.

362nd Worker Battalion

Formed in August 1944 by the German 362nd Infantry Division, 10th Army.

50th "Bomba" Italian Supply Battalion

Formed in Lombardy. On 8/1/44 it had 20 officers, 68 NCOs, 417 rank and file. It was disbanded in late 1944. A few companies were kept after the disbanding and stood as independent companies.

51st "Rose" Italian Supply Battalion

Raised in Reggio Emilia, it was partially disbanded in late 1944. It had, on 8/1/44, 13 officers, 35 NCOs, and 219 rank and file.

52nd "Oneto" Italian Supply Battalion

Raised in Verona and Mantua, it was partially disbanded in late 1944. On 8/1/44, It had 19 officers, 37 NCOs, and 266 rank and file.

53rd Italian Supply Battalion

Deserted en masse in July 1944 and was disbanded. What remained was sent to the 55th Battalion.

54th Italian Supply Battalion

Raised in April 1944 in Bergamo. It was sent to the Gustav Line. On 8/1/44 it had 15 officers, 25 NCOs, and 299 rank and file.

55th Italian Supply Battalion

Raised in Bergamo in February 1944, it served in the 10th and then the 14th Armies in mid-Italy. On 8/1/44 it had 3 officers, 3 NCOs, and 89 rank and file.

56th Italian Supply Battalion

Raised in Bergamo in February 1944. On 8/1/44 it had 10 officers, 16 NCOs, and 152 rank and file.

57th Italian Supply Battalion

Raised in Bergamo in February 1944, it served in the 14th Army. It was disbanded shortly afterward.

NAVAL GROUND UNITS

"Decima" Naval Infantry Division

In January 1944 the formation of a Naval Infantry Brigade was ordered. This expanded and in May 1944 the "Decima" Naval Infantry Division was ordered formed in Piedmont. In June various battalions of the Italian HSSPF were assigned to it. It engaged in anti-partisan combat from May to September 1944 around Torino and Piedmont. In October the "Valanga," "Fulmine," "Barbarigo," and "NP" Battalions were sent to Friaul. From December 1944 to February 1945 the division formed two kampfgruppen. The 1st Kampfgruppe remained around Vicenza and the 2nd Kampfgruppe was sent, in March to the region around Imola-Valli di Comacchio. Shortly thereafter the division was withdrawn to Asiago, then sent to Padua and disbanded.

1st Kampfgruppe, "Decima" Naval Infantry Division

Organized and formed as follows:

"Barbarigo" Battalion: Raised in La Spezia in November 1943. At the end of February 1944 it was in the Nettuno Bridgehead with the German 715th Infantry Division. It was joined with part of the "San Giorgio" Artillery Battalion. It fought in the retreat to Rome, in May in Piedmont, in October in Friaul, and in December 1944–February 1945 in Gorizia.

"Lupo" Battalion: Formed in late 1943, early 1944, in La Spezia. From April to July it was in Tuscany with the "Hermann Göring" Fallschirmjäger Panzer Division. From August to October it was in Piedmont, November in Milan, then in December in the Appenines west of Bologna. In February 1945 it was assigned to the 1st Kampfgruppe and sent to the eastern Appenines.

"NP" Battalion: Formed in La Spezia in October 1943 as a special detachment for the Commander Nuotatori Paracadutisti (Swimmer-Parachutists) of the Army. After May 1944 it was in Turin, after October in Friaul, then to Gorizia. It later became part of the 1st Kampfgruppe.

1st "Colleoni" Artillery Battalion: Formed from the 3rd Artillery Regiment, which was disbanded. It had been raised as part of the original artillery regiment in March 1944. In May it was in Turin, in December in Venetia, and after February 1945 in the 1st Kampfgruppe.

2nd Kampfgruppe, "Decima" Naval Infantry Division

Organized and formed as follows:

"Fulmine" Battalion: Formed in La Spezia in March 1944. It moved to Luccia immediately, then in May to Piedmont. In October it was sent to Friaul and in December to Gorizia. It joined the 2nd Kampfgruppe in February 1945.

"Sagittario" Battalion: Formed in La Spezia in March 1944. It moved, in May, to Piedmont. In December it moved to Gorizia. It joined the 2nd Kampfgruppe in February 1945.

"Freccia" Pioneer Battalion: Formed in February 1944, from May to November 1944 it served in Piedmont, then after January 1945 in Gorizia.

2nd "Da Giussano" Artillery Battalion: Formed initially as part of the 3rd Artillery Regiment in La Spezia in February 1944. From December 1944 to February 1945 it was in Gorizia.

3rd "San Giorgio" Artillery Battalion: Formed initially as part of the 3rd Artillery Regiment in La Spezia in February 1944. In December 1944 it moved to Gorizia.

NAVAL UNITS NOT PART OF THE "DECIMA" NAVAL INFANTRY DIVISION

"Castagnacci" Replacement Battalion

Formed in April 1944 in La Spezia. After May, it served in Piedmont and was disbanded in March 1945.

"San Gusto" Battalion

Formed in Triest in December 1943 and disbanded in April 1945.

"Serenissima" Battalion

Formed in Venice in December 1943 and disbanded in April 1945.

"Adrimento" Battalion

Formed in La Spezia in February 1944. It was later known as the "Giobbe" Battalion.

"Risoluti" Battalion

Formed in Genoa in April 1944.

"Sciré" Battalion

Formed in Arona in May 1944 and disbanded in March 1945.

"Vega" Battalion

Formed in Montorfano in May 1944.

"Pegaso" Battalion

Formed in Montecchio Maggiore in January 1945.

Flak Battalion "Q"

No details known.

ITALIAN AIR FORCE GROUND UNITS

"Folgore" Italian Volunteer Parachute Regiment

Formed in January–February 1944 near Spoleto with the XI Flieger Korps. In February it became the "Nembo" Parachute Battalion and served in the Nettuno bridgehead under the 4th Fallschirmjäger Division. The battalion was sent into Umbria and served under the 65th Division. In May–June it participated in the battle for Rome. In June 1944 the Nembo Battalion was disbanded. What remained was "Nettunia-Nembo" Parachute Company. In early July the Nembo Battalion was re-formed. In September it was sent to Piedmont as part of the Army of Liguria. The battalion was still part of the Air Force. From November 1944 to April 1945 it served in Montinevro, Moncenisio, and Picolo San Bernardo. It was disbanded in April 1945. The regiment contained three battalions and the "Nembo" Parachute Training Battalion.

"D'Abundo" Italian Parachute Battalion

Formed in September 1943 from the XX Parachute Battalion from the Reggio Esercito. It was placed under the 4th Fallschirmjäger Division and provided coastal security for Rome and was then sent to the Gustav Line. In January 1944 it was absorbed into the "Folgore" Regiment.

5th AP Battalion

Formed in September 1944 from aviation personnel for the defense of airfields. It served in the Venegono-Lonate Ceppino Region.

6th Flak Battalion

Formed in September 1944 for airfield defense in the region of Campoformido-Ossoppo.

7th Flak Battalion

Formed in September 1944 for airfield defense in the region of Ghedi.

8th AP Battalion

Formed in September 1944 for airfield defense using aviation personnel. It served in the region of Ponte San Pietro (Bergamo).

9th Airforce Battalion

Formed for security duties and served in the Turin-Milan area.

"Azzurra Aquila" Division

Formed in 1945, the division contained the following battalions. It served until April 1945.

1st Flak Regiment:	Formed in Verona in 1945.
1st Airforce Battalion:	Formed in early 1944.
3rd Airforce Battalion:	Formed in September 1944 in Bassano del Gappa.
4th Airforce Battalion:	Formed the end of 1944 in Vicenza.
5th Flak Regiment:	Formed in 1944 to provide air defense for Lombardy-Piedmont.
2nd Airforce Battalion:	Served in Padua, Turin and Verona.
5th Airforce Battalion:	Served in Brescia, then Verona.
6th Airforce Battalion:	Served in Milan, then Vicenza.
Independent 7th Flak Battalion:	Served in La Spezia, then Turin.
8th Smoke Battalion:	Served in Ferrara
200th Signals Regiment:	Formed in north Italy. From late 1944 through early 1945 it was manned by Italians.

GUARDIA NAZIONALE REPUBLICANA (GNR)

Railroad GNR

1st Legion	In Turin		5th Legion	In Bologna
2nd Legion	In Milan		6th Legion	In Florence
3rd Legion	In Genoa		7th Legion	In l'Aquila
4th Legion	In Verona			
5th Legion	In Triest		**Border Patrol GNR**	
6th Legion	In Bologna		1st Legion	October 1944 in Turin, then Como
7th Legion	In Florence		2nd Legion	In the Como Region
8th Legion	In Ancona		3rd Legion	In the Bolzano-Sondrio region.
9th Legion	In Rome		5th Legion	In Santhià

Forest GNR

Operations Bn	Around Libach, Triest and Gorizia
1st Legion	In Udine
2nd Legion	In Trento
3rd Legion	In Brescia
4th Legion	In Turin

Mail and Telegraph GNR

33 Detachments

Harbor GNR

1st Legion
2nd Legion

MILIZIA DIFESA TERRITORIALE (MDT)
(Territorial Defense Militia)

1st Territorial Militia Regiment

Placed in Triest and had two battalions.

2nd Territorial Militia Regiment

Had four battalions and occupied Capodistria and Pola.

3rd Territorial Militia Regiment

Had two battalions. Formed in October 1943 and stationed in Fiume.

4th Territorial Militia Regiment

Stationed in Gorizia with two battalions.

5th Territorial Militia Regiment

Stationed in Udine with five battalions.

"Tagliamento" Assault Legion

Formed from the 63rd "Tagliamento" Battalion of the Centauro II Armored Division. In September 1943 it was in Rome serving with the 2nd Fallschirmjäger Division. In October 1943 it was serving as a police unit in Abruzzio, then it moved back to Rome. In December 1943 it was placed under the SSPF Upper Italy West. It was stationed in northern Italy. In March 1944 it was given the name "1st Assault Legion". It moved to Pesaro in June and in August was by Vicenza. It was disbanded in Ponte di Legno in April 1945. It contained two battalions.

1st Rome Militia Legion

Formed in Rome between September and November 1943. It was joined with the 1st Sturm Legion in October. It was disbanded in November.

"Etna" Division

This was a security division raised in Brescia in August 1944. It apparently contained the following units:

"Mussolini Assault Legion": Formed in Forli in late September 1943. In October 1944 it was absorbed into the "Tagliamento" Assault Legion.

115th Militia Battalion: Formed in Novara in late 1943. It joined the Etna Division in late 1944.

29th Militia Battalion: Formed in Turin in October 1944 with units returning from Albania. It was incorporated into the Etna Division in October 1944.

"Venezia Giulia" Battalion (2nd Bicycle Battalion): Formed in Padua in November 1943. It joined the Etna Division in October 1944.

"Roma" Battalion (1st Bicycle Battalion): Formed in Brescia in November 1943.

"Mazzarini" Parachute Battalion: Formed in Brescia in September 1943. It joined the Etna Division in October 1943.

"Leonessa" Armored Battalion: Formed in Brescia in October 1944. Joined the Etna Division in late 1944.

"Pontida" Battalion: Formed in Como in between May and October 1944.

"Ruggine" Battalion: Formed in Como in November 1944. Joined the Etna Division in February 1945.

1st "Ruggine" Assault Battalion

Formed in Como in December 1944. In March 1945 it moved to Vercelli.

1st "Ruggine" Tank Destroyer Battalion

Formed in Como in December 1944. In March 1945 it moved to Vercelli. The two Ruggine groups formed the "Ruggine Assault Group."

"9 Settembre" Militia Battalion

Formed in Teramo in October 1943 and operated with the 1st Rome Legion in 1944 on the Island of Elba, the Nettuno Bridgehead, and Ortona. In April 1944 it fought partisans with the 3rd Brandenburg Regiment. From August to November it operated near Piccolo San Bernardo. From November to January 1945 it fought in East Prussia with the Brandenburg Panzer Grenadier Division, then it returned to Vittorio Veneto.

"Carmelo Borg Pisani" Battalion

Formed in Imperia in November 1943. After November 1944 it served in Brescia.

"Ferrara" Battalion

Formed in October 1943 in Sesiatal and served in Ferrara after June 1944.

"Firenze" (also "Toscana") Battalion

Formed in Bologna in December 1944, then served in Schio.

"Marche" Battalion

Formed in Bergamo in April 1944.

"Perugia" Battalion

Formed in Brescia in September–December 1944.

"Romagna" Battalion

Formed in Treviso in November 1944.

"Bologna" Battalion

Formed in Bologna in November 1944.

ITALIAN GROUND UNITS SERVING OUTSIDE OF ITALY

Units Serving in Germany

Italian Replacement and Training Battalion

Formed in Münsingen in 1945.

3/31st Panzer Regiment

Formed in Münsingen in August 1944 from Italians serving in Greece. This unit was an independent army formation that was not assigned to any German division.

1st Naval Smoke Battalion

Formed in March 1944 in Schwinemünde with the 34th and 35th Companies and assigned to the German Navy.

2nd Naval Smoke Battalion

Formed in September 1943 with the 28th, 29th, 32nd, 33rd, and 37th Companies. In the spring of 1944 the 28th and 37th Companies were detached to Gotenhafen.

3rd Naval Smoke Battalion

Formed in 1944 in Wilhelmshaven with the 28th–41st Companies. In the spring of 1944 the 40th and 41st Companies were detached to the 4th Battalion.

4th Naval Smoke Battalion

Formed in the spring of 1944 with the 28th, 37th, 40th, and 52nd Companies drawn from the 2nd and 3rd Battalions. Served in Tulln, then Grossborn. It ended the war with the 40th and 41st Smoke Companies.

5th Naval Smoke Battalion

Formed in Holland in the spring of 1944 with the 50th–52nd Companies.

Units Serving in France

1st "Coniglio" Italian Artillery Battalion

Formed in December 1943 from the 10th Artillery Battalion, XXII Corps. In March 1944 it was in southern France with the 19th Army.

Italian Security Battalion, 19th Army

Formed in October 1943 in Pont Sant-Esprit.

1st Italian Naval Division

Formed in Bordeaux from Italian naval personnel from the submarine forces stationed there. It had a rifle company and two battalions. It was disbanded in May 1945.

Italian Forces in the Southeast

33rd Black Shirt Battalion

Formed in December 1943 and served in Montenegro and Serbia. It was disbanded in early 1944.

72nd Black Shirt Battalion

Formed from the Farini Legion. It was disbanded in 1945.

81st Black Shirt Battalion

It served in Montenegro, Serbia, Croatia, and Agram with the 21st Corps. It was disbanded in 1945.

86th Black Shirt Battalion

Served in Albania, Bosnia, and Croatia with the 21st Army Corps. It was disbanded in 1945.

92nd Black Shirt Battalion

Formed in Albania and served there until July 1944. In October it was assigned to the 92nd Security Regiment in Vrdinik. It returned to Italy in early 1945 and was disbanded in Brescia.

94th Black Shirt Battalion

Formed by the 21st Corps and disbanded in 1945.

111th Black Shirt Battalion

Formed by the 21st Corps and disbanded in 1945.

144th Black Shirt Battalion

Formed in December 1943 in Montenegro, served in Albania, Bosnia, and Croatia with the 21st Corps. It moved to Fiume and in August 1944 it was disbanded, with its troops being assigned to the 82nd Black Shirt Battalion.

"San Marco" Legion

Formed in Croatia by the V SS Mountain Corps with the 40th and 49th Black Shirt Legions. After September 1943 it contained only the 2/40th Black Shirt Battalion. The 40th was disbanded in Slovenia in 1945 and the 49th was disbanded in late 1944.

Italian Crete Volunteer Legion

Formed in Crete in December 1943 from the Siena Infantry Division. It was placed under the Commander of the Fortified Position of Greece. The unit had three battalions:

1st Volunteer Battalion "Merla"
2nd Volunteer Battalion "Piazzi"
3rd Volunteer Battalion "Gabrielli"

Italian Samos Legion

Formed from the 24th "Carroccio" Legion, it had the Samos Infantry Battalion, which was formed from the 25th Militia Assault battalion, and the Samos Artillery Battalion.

Italian Rhodes Regiment

Formed in December 1943 with the various Italian forces in the eastern Aegean. In December it had one rifle battalion, a construction battalion, and an artillery group. In August 1944 it had the Coos Flak Battalion, the Rhodes Rifle Battalion, and the 1st, 2nd, 3rd, and 4th Rhodes Construction Battalions.

Italian Security Battalion, 81st Regiment

Formed in August 1944 in the LXXXXI Corps and in December was assigned to the V SS Corps.

19th Black Shirt Assault Battalion

Nothing is known of this formation.

1st Construction Battalion

Formed October 1943 in the German 369th Infantry Division, 2nd Panzer Army.

1st Construction Battalion

Formed in August 1944 in the LXVIII Corps.

2nd Construction Battalion

Formed in August 1944 in the LXVIII Corps.

2nd Construction Battalion

Formed October 1943 in the German 373rd Infantry Division, 2nd Panzer Army.

3rd Construction Battalion

Formed in October 1943 by the 45th Senior Pioneer Battalion, 2nd Panzer Army.

4th Construction Battalion

Formed in October 1943 by the 501st Road Construction Pioneer Battalion, 2nd Panzer Army.

5th Construction Battalion

Formed in October 1943 by the 664th Brüko "B," 2nd Panzer Army.

8th Construction Battalion

Formed in Croatia by the 2nd Panzer Army.

9th Construction Battalion

Formed by the German 297th Infantry Division in Croatia.

11th Construction Battalion

Formed by the German 181st Infantry Division.

33rd Construction Battalion

Formed by the 15th Panzer Grenadier Division in the Balkans.

36th Construction Battalion

Formed by the German 297th Infantry Division.

37th Construction Battalion

Formed by the German 297th Infantry Division.

42nd Construction Battalion

Formed in June 1944.

54th Construction Battalion

Formed by the German 1st Mountain Division in early 1944 and, in March 1944, assigned to the XXII Mountain Corps.

373rd Construction Battalion

Formed by the German 373rd Infantry Division.

392nd Construction Battalion

Formed by the German 392nd Infantry Division.

422nd Construction Battalion

Formed in August 1944 by the XXII Mountain Corps.

104th Construction Pioneer Battalion

Formed in August 1944 by the XXII Mountain Corps.

7

Slovak Formations in German Service

Slovak Infantry Divisions

In 1939 Hitler availed himself of the existing tensions in Czechoslovakia between the Czechs and the Slovaks to destroy what remained of Czechoslovakia after his theft of the Sudetenland. Slovakia established itself as a German protectorate under Josef Tiso. A one-party state was established and supported by a party militia, the Hlinka Guards, which were modeled on the German storm troopers. Slovakia was allowed to maintain a small army, which was equipped with the Czech equipment that was inside its borders and a small quantity of German equipment. When the Slovak state was formed its army contained the 3rd Mobile Division and the 9th, 10th, 11th, 15th, 16th and 17th Infantry Divisions of the former Czechoslovak state. Shortly after the formation of the Slovak state, the army was downsized and by the order of 2 May 1939, it was reorganized from fifteen infantry regiments and four mountain regiments to five infantry regiments and six independent infantry battalions. Its peacetime strength was planned to be 950 officers, 150 professional non-commissioned officers, 4,800 non-commissioned officers, and 19,100 privates or a total of 25,000 men. In wartime it was to expand to 52,000 men; consisting of 1,700 officers, 300 professional non-commissioned officers, 7,000 non-commissioned and 43,000 privates.

The six independent infantry battalions did not, however, remain long at the battalion strength and were soon converged to form the 6th, 7th and 9th Infantry Regiments.

By 29 August 1939 three infantry divisions were planned. The organization of the three Slovak infantry divisions in 1939 was as follows:

1st Slovak Infantry Division
Division Staff
1/,2/,3/4th Infantry Regiment
1/,2/,3/5th Infantry Regiment
2nd Independent Infantry Battalion
1 Anti-Tank Company
1/,2/, Replacement/1st Cavalry Battalion
1/1st Artillery Regiment (3 btrys, 12 80mm M 17)

2/1st Artillery Regiment (1 btry, 4 75mm Mountain Guns) (2 btrys, 8 100mm M16/19 Howitzers)
3/1st Artillery Regiment (3 btrys, 12 100mm M14/19 Howitzers)
4/1st Artillery Regiment (3 btrys, 12 150mm M25 Howitzers)
1/51st (mot) Artillery Regiment (3 btrys, 12 80mm M30)
2/51st (mot) Artillery Regiment (3 btrys, 12 100mm M30)
2/153rd (Flak) Artillery Regiment (2 btry, 8 83.5mm M22 guns) (1 searchlight battery)
3/153rd (Flak) Artillery Regiment (2 btry, 8 83.5mm M22 guns)
1 Truck Battalion
Pioneers
   Regimental Staff & 2nd Battalion
   Replacement Battalion
3rd Signals Battalion
1st Supply Magazine

2nd Slovak Infantry Division
Division Staff
1/,2/,3/3th Infantry Regiment
Replacement Infantry Battalion
1st Independent Infantry Battalion
3rd Independent Infantry Battalion
4th Independent Infantry Battalion
Bicycle Battalion
Armored Battalion
Reserve Officer Training School
Training Camp
1/,2/, Replacement/2nd Cavalry Battalion
Cavalry Depot
1/2nd Artillery Regiment (3 btrys, 12 80mm M 17)
2/2nd Artillery Regiment (3 btrys, 4 75mm Mountain Guns)
3/2nd Artillery Regiment (3 btrys, 12 100mm M14/19 Howitzers)
4/2nd Artillery Regiment (3 btrys, 12 150mm M25 Howitzers)

1/52nd Artillery Regiment (3 btrys, 12 100mm
M14/19 Howitzers)
2/52nd Artillery Regiment (3 btrys, 12 150mm M25
Howitzers)
3/52nd (mot) Artillery Regiment (3 btrys, 12
105mm guns)
4/52nd (mot) Artillery Regiment (3 btrys, 12
105mm guns)
Verm. Battalion
2nd Truck Battalion
1st Pioneer Battalion
Signals Battalion
2nd Supply Magazine

3rd Slovak Infantry Division
Division Staff
1/,2/,3/1st Infantry Regiment
1/,2/,3/2nd Infantry Regiment
5th Independent Infantry Battalion
6th Independent Infantry Battalion
1/,2/, Replacement/3rd Cavalry Battalion
1/3rd Artillery Regiment (3 btrys, 12 150mm M25
Howitzers)
2/3rd Artillery Regiment (1 btry, 4 75mm Mountain
Guns) (2 btrys, 8 100mm M16/19 Mountain
Howitzers)
3/3rd Artillery Regiment (1 btry, 4 80mm M17
guns) (2 btrys, 8 100mm M14/19 Howitzers)
1/4th Artillery Regiment (1 btry, 4 80mm M17
guns) (2 btrys, 8 100mm M14/19 Howitzers)
2/4th Artillery Regiment (1 btry, 4 75mm M15
Mountain Howitzers) (2 btrys, 8 100mm M14/19
Mountain Howitzers)
3/4th Artillery Regiment (3 btrys, 12 150mm M25
Howitzers)
1/153rd Artillery Regiment (2 btrys, 83.5mm M22
guns) (1 btry, 8 flak guns
Pioneer Company
1 Truck Battalion
Signals Battalion
3rd Supply Magazine

On 1 May 1940 records indicate their structure had
changed slightly. The units assigned to each division on
that date were:

1st Slovak Infantry Division
1/,2/,3/4th Infantry Regiment
1/,2/,3/5th Infantry Regiment
1/,2/,3/7th Infantry Regiment
1/,2/,3/1st Artillery Regiment
1st Cavalry Reconnaissance Group
2nd Cavalry Reconnaissance Group
1/,2/Engineer Regiment

3rd Signals Battalion
1st Group/Automobile Regiment
2nd Slovak Infantry Division
1/,2/,3/6th Infantry Regiment
1/,2/,3/8th Infantry Regiment
1/,2/,3/9th Infantry Regiment
Bicyclist Battalion
1/,2/,3/2nd Artillery Regiment
3rd Cavalry Reconnaissance Group
1st Signals Battalion
2nd Group/Automobile Regiment
3rd Slovak Infantry Division
1/,2/,3/1st Infantry Regiment
1/,2/,3/2nd Infantry Regiment
1/,2/,3/3rd Infantry Regiment
1/,2/,3/3rd Artillery Regiment
3/Engineer Regiment
2nd Signals Battalion
3rd Group/Automobile Regiment

On 1 October 1940 a new army organization was
established and the 2nd Division was disbanded, along
with the 6th, 8th and 9th Infantry Regiments, the
bicycle battalion, the 2nd Cavalry Reconnaissance
Group, the regimental headquarters of the engineer
regiment, the automobile regiment and the 2nd
Armory. The two remaining divisions were reorganized
on a smaller scale and their constituent elements were
renumbered. They were now organized as follows:

1st Slovak Infantry Division
1/,2/1st Infantry Regiment
1/,2/2nd Infantry Regiment
1/,2/3rd Infantry Regiment
1st Cavalry Reconnaissance Group
1/,2/,3/1st Artillery Regiment
1st Engineer Battalion
1st Signals Battalion
1st Automobile Battalion
1st Armory
1st Quartermaster Depot
2nd Slovak Infantry Division
1/,2/4th Infantry Regiment
1/,2/5th Infantry Regiment
1/,2/6th Infantry Regiment
2nd Cavalry Reconnaissance Group
1/,2/,3/2nd Artillery Regiment
2nd Engineer Battalion
2nd Signals Battalion
2nd Automobile Battalion
2nd Armory
2nd Quartermaster Depot

On 22 June 1941 the "Mobile" Group, also known as the
Pilfousek Fast Brigade, was organized. It consisted of:

Headquarters
2nd Cavalry Reconnaissance Squadron
Armored Battalions
   2 Tank Companies
   2 Anti-tank Companies
1/11th Artillery Regiment
2/6th Infantry Regiment
Communications Company
Engineer Platoon
Staff Automobile Unit

The 1st Slovak Division was made operational on 26 June 1941. It was later merged with the Pilfousek Fast Brigade to form the Slovak Fast Division on 11 August 1941. The 2nd Slovak Infantry Division was also made operational on 26 June 1941. It was reorganized on 26 August 1941 into the Slovak Security Division. The 3rd Slovak Division was probably disbanded in order to bring the first two divisions up to strength.

Slovak Fast Division

Also known as the Slovak Schnelle Division, it was formed on 11 August 1941 in the field in Russia. It began its life as the Pilfousek motorized brigade in July 1941. The Pilfousek Fast Brigade was organized using all the motorized units in the Army Group South under the command of the former commanding officer of the 2nd Slovak Division, Rudolf Pilfousek. It consisted of the 1/6th (mot) Infantry Battalion, the 1/11th (mot) Artillery Battalion, the 1st Tank Battalion (containing the 1st & 2nd Tank Companies), the 2nd Reconnaissance Battalion, the 1st Weapons Company, the 2nd Motorcycle Company and I Platoon, 1st Company/3rd (mot) Engineer Battalion.

The Pilfousek Brigade fought in Russia as part of the the 17th Army. It was detached in late July or early August. It was then refitted as a division on 11 August 1941 using parts of the 1st Slovak Division. It returned to the 17th Army by early August 1942. It was with the 1st Panzer Group between October 1941 and August 1942, returned to the 17th Army and remained there until February 1943. In 1943 the division was withdrawn from active fighting because of desertion and loyalty problems. It was disarmed and disbanded at that time. On 21 July 1941 it consisted of:

Headquarters
Motorized Reconnaissance Group
   Headquarters
   1 Armored Car Platoon
   1 Anti-Tank Platoon
   2 Bicycle Companies
   1 Engineer Platoon
2/6th (mot) Infantry Regiment
   Headquarters
   1 Radio Platoon
   1 Anti-Tank Platoon
   1 Mortar Platoon
   1 Infantry Gun Section (75mm guns)

   3 Infantry Companies
   1 Machine Gun Company
Armored Regiment
   Staff Company
   2 Tank Companies
   3 Anti-Tank Companies
1/11th Armored Regiment (later expanded to all three battalions)
   Headquarters
   1 Radio Platoon
   3 Batteries (4 100mm howitzers)
   1 Battery (4 105mm guns)
Engineer Company
Radio Company
15th Anti-aircraft Battery
Automobile Repair Shop
315th Truck Column

As of 1 September 1941, after the battle of Lipovce, the organization and equipment of the Slovak Fast Division was as follows:

Slovak Fast Division
   1 (mot) Staff Company
   1 (mot) Mapping Detachment
   1 Motorcycle Messenger Platoon
   1 (mot) Light Supply Column
20th (mot) Rifle Regiment
   1 (mot) Signals Platoon
   1st & 2nd (mot) Battalions, each with
      3 Rifle Companies (9 LMGs ea)
      1 Heavy Company (12 HMGs & 4 medium mortars)
   1 (mot) Maintenance Company
   1 (mot) Mountain Gun Battery (4 75mm guns)
   1 (mot) Anti-Tank Platoon (12 37mm PAK 36 guns)
21st (mot) Rifle Regiment
   same as 21st Rifle Regiment

11th Reconnaissance Battalion
  1 (mot) Signals Platoon
  1 Bicycle Company
  1 (mot) Heavy Company
    1 (mot) Anti-Tank Platoon (4 37mm PAK 36 guns)
    1 (mot) Pioneer Platoon
    1 (mot) Infantry Gun Platoon (4 leIG)
12th Panzer Battalion
  2 Armored Companies
  1 (mot) Anti-Tank Company (12 37mm PAK 36 guns)
11th Artillery Regiment
  1 (mot) Signals Platoon
  1st & 2nd (mot) Battalions, each with
    1 (mot) Signals Platoon
    1 (mot) Calibration Detachment
    2 (mot) Batteries (4 100mm vz. 30 howitzers ea)
    1 (mot) Battery (4 105mm vz. 35 guns)
8th (mot) Flak Battery (4 20mm guns)
13th (mot) Flak Battery (4 20mm guns)
Luftwaffe Artillery Observation Squadron
11th (mot) Pioneer Battalion
  2 (mot) Pioneer Companies (9 LMGs ea)
  1 (mot) Bridging Column
  1 (mot) Light Pioneer Column
2nd Signals Battalion
  1 (mot) Signals Company
  1 (mot) Radio Company
Supply Troops
  2 (mot) Heavy Supply Columns
  1 (mot) Heavy Fuel Column
  1 (mot) Maintenance Platoon
Administration
  1 (mot) Bakery Company
  1 (mot) Butcher Company
  1 (mot) Park
  1 (mot) Division Administration
Other
  11th (mot) Medical Company
  11th (mot) Ambulance
  6th (mot) Field Post Office
  20th (mot) Military Police Detachment

On 1 November 1942 the Slovak Schnelle Division was
organized and equipped as follows:

Division Staff
  1 (mot) Staff Company
  1 (mot) Light Armored Platoon
20th (mot) Infantry Regiment
  1 (mot) Signals Platoon
  1 (mot) Staff Platoon
  2 (mot) Battalions, each with
    1 (mot) Signals Platoon
    1 (mot) Staff Platoon

    3 (mot) Rifle Companies (9 LMGS ea)
    1 (mot) Heavy Company (12 HMGs & 6 80mm
      mortars)
  1 (mot) Infantry Gun Company (3 150mm guns)
  1 (mot) Anti-Tank Company (12 50mm PAK 38)
5th (mot) Reconnaissance Battalion
  1 (mot) Signals Platoon
  1 (mot) Staff Platoon
  3 Bicycle Companies
  1 (mot) Machine Gun Company (? HMGs)
  1 (mot) Support Company
    1 Mortar Platoon (? 81mm mortars)
    1 Anti-Tank Platoon
    1 Engineer Platoon
(mot) Anti-Tank Company
  (6 50mm PAK 38 anti-tank guns)
(mot) Infantry Gun Section
  (3 150mm sIG)
(mot) Flak Company (probably 4 88mm guns)

(mot) Flak Company (probably 12 20mm flak guns)

11th (mot) Artillery Regiment
  1 (mot) Signals Platoon
  1 (mot) Calibration Detachment
  1 (mot) Battalion
    1 (mot) Signals Platoon
    1 (mot) Calibration Detachment
    3 (mot) Batteries (4 105mm howitzers ea)
  1 (mot) Battalion
    1 (mot) Signals Platoon
    1 (mot) Calibration Detachment
    2 (mot) Batteries (4 105mm howitzers ea)
    1 (mot) Battery (4 100mm K18 guns ea)
31st Artillery Regiment
  1 Signals Platoon
  1 Calibration Detachment
  2 Battalions, each with
    1 Signals Platoon
    1 Calibration Detachment
    3 Batteries (4 Czech 100mm howitzers ea)
Signals Battalion
  1 (mot) Staff Platoon
  1 (mot) Signals Platoon
  1 (mot) Telephone Company
  1 (mot) Radio Company
  1 (mot) Light Signals Supply Column
1 Engineer Company
Support Units
  5 (horse drawn) Light Supply Columns
  1 (mot) Gas Defense Company
  1 (mot) Light Supply Column
  1 (mot) Light Fuel Column
  1 (mot) Supply Company

2 (mot) Maintenance Platoons
1 Motor Park
1 (mot) Bakery Company
1 (mot) Butcher Company
1 (mot) Divisional Administration Detachment

1 (mot) Field Hospital
1 (mot) Medical Company
1 Ambulance
1 (mot) Military Police Detachment
1 (mot) Field Post Office

Slovak Security Division

The Slovak Security Division was formed on 26 August 1941 in Russia using the 2nd Slovak Division. The security divisions were organized in the German Army on the Russian front in the summer of 1942 because of the need to deal with the increased number of Russian partisans and disbanded troops that were behind the main German lines. These divisions were generally stripped of all heavy equipment, i.e. artillery, and expected to deal with Russian guerrillas equipped with nothing but light arms. Formed earlier, the Slovak Security Division was slightly more heavily armed than the German security divisions in that it was equipped with two battalions of Czechoslovakian 100mm light howitzers. Indications are that it was truly an under-equipped infantry division, but that it did not have adequate power to stand in the battle lines with the German infantry divisions, so it was relegated to security functions and given the designation as a security division because it was immediately relegated to rear area duties.

As of 1 September 1941 the organization of the Slovak Security Division was as follows:

Slovak Security Division
1 (mot) Light Supply Column
1 Staff Company
1 Military Police Detachment
101st Infantry Regiment
1st & 2nd Battalions, each with
3 Rifle Companies (9 LMGs ea)
1 Heavy Company (8 HMGS & 2 medium mortars)
1 Anti-Tank Company (12 37mm PAK 36 guns)
1 Staff Company
1 Pioneer Platoon
Replacement Battalion of the Schnelle Division
3 Rifle Companies (9 LMGs ca)
1 Heavy Company (8 HMGS & 2 medium mortars)
1st Cavalry Battalion
2 Squadrons (no heavy weapons)
31st Artillery Regiment,
1 Signals Platoon

1st & 2nd Battalions, each with
1 Signals Platoon
3 Batteries (4 100mm leFH ea)
1st Signals Battalion
1 Radio Company
1 Signals Company
Pioneers
no staff
3rd Pioneer Company
11th Railroad Pioneer Company
Other
2 (mot) Heavy Supply Columns
2nd Bakery Company
2nd Butcher Company
2nd Park
52nd Artisan Company
2nd Medical Park
2nd Medical Company
2nd Field Hospital
2nd Ambulance Company (not mot)
2nd Veterinary Company
8th Field Post Office

As of 1 November 1942 the Slovak Security Division was organized and equipped as follows:

Division Staff
1 Staff Company
1 (mot) Supply Column
1 Military Police Detachment
101st Security Regiment
1 Staff Company
2 Security Battalions, each with
3 Rifle Companies (9 LMGS)
1 Machine Gun Company (8 HMGs & 2 80mm mortars)
1 Anti-Tank Company (12 37mm PAK 36)
1 Infantry Gun Platoon (4 75mm leIG)
1 Reconnaissance Detachment
102nd Security Regiment
1 Staff Company
2 Security Battalions, each with
3 Rifle Companies (9 LMGS)

1 Machine Gun Company (8 HMGs & 2 80mm mortars)
1 Anti-Tank Company (12 37mm PAK 36)
1 Infantry Gun Platoon (4 75mm leIG)
1 Reconnaissance Detachment

Feldersatz Battaliion

101st Security Regiment
3 Rifle Companies (9 LMGS)
1 Machine Gun Company (8 HMGs & 2 80mm mortars)

Reconnaissance Battalion
2 Cavalry Squadrons

31st Artillery Regiment
1 Signals Platoon
1st & 2nd Artillery Battalions, each with
1 Signals Platoon
3 Batteries (4 100mm leFH ea)

Pioneer Battalion
3rd Pioneer Company
11th Railroad Pioneer Company

1st Signals Battalion
1 Telephone Company
1 Radio Company
Support Services
505th (mot) Light Supply Column
506th (mot) Light Supply Column
2nd Bakery Detachment
2nd Butcher Detachment
2nd Infantry Park
2nd Motor Park
52nd Artisan Company
2nd Field Hospital
2nd Medical Company
2nd Ambulance
2nd Veterinary Company
2nd Field Post Office

On 12 August 1943 the division was reorganized into the 2nd Slovak Infantry Division.

1st Slovak Infantry Division

The 1st Slovak Infantry Division was formed on 2 August 1943 from the Slovak Fast Division. The division apparently underwent a reorganization and was then assigned to the German 6th Army in early November 1943 and continued with it until March 1944, when it then joined Army Group Dumitrescu (3rd Rumanian Army) and remained there until mid-May 1944.

Another unit was also organized from parts of the Fast Division in early 1944. This second unit, called the Tartarko Combat Group contained 12 officers and 788 NCOs and men. It consisted of the 2/,3/20th Infantry Regiment, a few 150mm howitzers from the 1/11th Artillery Regiment, a few 37mm antiaircraft guns, the 9th and 13th Light Flak Companies (20mm guns) and the 45th Construction Company.

The 1st Slovak Division was used for security operations behind the lines of Army Group South. In July 1944 the division was pulled from the lines, disarmed, and organized into the 1st Slovak Construction Division.

2nd Slovak Infantry Division

The 2nd Slovak Infantry Division was formed on 1 August 1943 from the Slovak Security Division. Morale was very poor and lack of discipline and desertion became major problems. The division was disarmed on 3 November 1943 and reorganized into a brigade-sized construction unit.

1st Slovak Construction Division

The 1st Slovak Construction Division was organized from the 1st Slovak Infantry Division in July 1944. It was not a successful formation and was dissolved and disarmed on 12 July 1944.

Slovak Construction Units

In 1944 the Germans became increasingly uncomfortable with the reliability of their Slovakian allies. Their existing units were disbanded and used to form construction battalions. The movement of troops from active units to these battalions is not known. Documents suggest that they were numbered the 1st and 2nd Construction Battalions.

The following construction units are known to have been formed and to have existed on 3/27/45. They may,

however, be the remains of the Hlinka Guard, which in February 1945 consisted of an infantry regiment, a flak regiment, and an artillery battery.

921st Slovak Construction Battalion
922nd Slovak Construction Battalion
6th & 7th Slovakian Construction Companies, 31st
    Grenadier Regiment

APPENDIX 1

Standardized Organizations of the Waffen SS Divisions

Theoretical Organization
Waffen SS Mountain Division
9/11/44

Division Staff
  1 Divisional Staff (2 LMGs)
  1 (mot) Mapping Detachment
  1 (tmot) Military Police Detachment (3 LMGs)
2 SS Gebirgsjäger Regiments, each with
  1 Regimental Staff & Staff Company (4 120mm mortars & 7 LMGs)
    1 Staff Platoon
    1 Signals Platoon
    1 Cavalry Platoon
    1 Bicycle Platoon
  1st Battalion
    1 Battalion Staff
    1 Staff Platoon (1 LMG)
    1 Signals Platoon
    1 Pioneer Platoon (4 LMGs)
    3 Gebirgsjäger Companies (2 HMGs, 11 LMGs, & 2 80mm mortars)
    1 Gebirgsjäger Machine Gun Company
      2 Machine Gun Platoons (4 HMGs, 1 LMG ea)
      2 Mortar Platoons (2 120mm mortars & 1 LMG ea)
  2nd Battalion
    same as 1st Battalion
  3rd Battalion
    same as 1st Battalion
  Infantry Gun Company
    (6 75mm leIG & 4 LMGs)
  Panzerjäger Company
    1 Staff Platoon (1 LMG)
    1 Panzerzerstörer Platoon (36 panzerschrecke & 2 LMGs)
    1 Panzerjäger Platoon (3 LMGs & 3 75mm PAK)
  Mountain Heavy Company
    (2 HMGs, 11 LMGs, & 2 80mm mortars)
  Light Mountain Supply Column (3 LMGs)
Panzerjäger Battalion
  1 Battalion Staff & (mot) Staff Platoon (1 LMG)
  1 Sturmgeschütz Company (10 StuG & 12 LMGs)
  1 (motZ) Panzerjäger Company (12 75mm PAK & 12 LMGs)

  1 (motZ) Mountain Flak Company (12 20mm flak & 2 LMGs)
Reconnaissance Battalion
  1 Staff & (mot) Staff Company
    1 Staff Platoon (1 LMG)
    1 Signals Platoon
    1 Pioneer Platoon (4 LMGs)
  2 Bicycle Companies (4 HMGs & 10 LMGs)
  1 Cavalry Company (2 HMGs & 9 LMGs)
  1 (mot) Heavy Company
    1 Staff Platoon (1 LMG)
    1 Infantry Gun Platoon (4 75mm leIG & 4 LMGs)
    1 Panzerjäger Platoon (3 75mm PAK & 3 LMGs)
    1 Mortar Platoon (6 80mm mortars)
Mountain Artillery Regiment
  1 Regimental Staff & (tmot) Staff Battery (2 LMGs & 4 self propelled quad 20mm flak guns)
  1st Battalion
    1 Battalion Staff & Staff Battery (2 LMGs)
    3 Batteries (4 75mm mountain guns & 5 LMGs ea)
  2nd Battalion
    same as 1st Battalion
  3rd Battalion
    1 Battalion Staff & Staff Battery (2 LMGs)
    3 Batteries (4 105mm mountain howitzer 40s & 5 LMGs ea)
  4th (motZ) Battalion
    1 Battalion Staff & (motZ) Staff Battery (2 LMGs)
    1 Calibration Detachment
    2 (motZ) Batteries (4 150mm sFH & 5 LMGs ea)
    1 (motZ) Battery (4 105mm K guns & 5 LMGs)
Pioneer Battalion
  1 Battalion Staff & (tmot) Staff Company (4 LMGs)
  2 Mountain Pioneer Companies (2 HMGs, 9 LMGs, 6 flamethrowers, 2 80mm mortars ea)
  1 (mot) Mountain Pioneer Company (2 HMGs, 9 LMGs, 6 flamethrowers, 2 80mm mortars)
Signals Battalion
  2 (tmot) Mountain Telephone Companies (5 LMGs ea)
  1 (mot) Mountain Radio Company (5 LMGs)

1 (tmot) Mountain Supply Column (2 LMGs)

Feldersatz Battalion
  5 Companies

Supply Troop
  1 (tmot) Supply Battalion Staff (2 LMGs)
  1st (mot) 120 ton Transportation Company (8 LMGs)
  2/,3/,4/Light Mountain Columns (4 LMGs ea)
  5/.,6/,7/Light Columns (4 LMGs ea)
  1 Supply Company (6 LMGs)
  1 (mot) Maintenance Company (4 LMGs)

Other
  1 (mot) Butcher Company (4 LMGs)

1 (mot) Bakery Company (6 LMGs)
1 (mot) Divisional Administration Company (2 LMGs)
1 Veterinary Company (4 LMGs)
1st & 2nd (tmot) Mountain Medical Company (4 LMGs ea)
1 (mot) Decontamination Company
1 Stretcher Bearer Company (4 LMGs)
1 (mot) Medical Supply Company (2 LMGs)
1 (tmot) Medical Supply Company (2 LMGs)
1 (mot) Field Post Office

Theoretical Organization
SS Waffen Grenadier Division
9/15/44

Division Staff
  1 Divisional Staff (2 LMGs)
  1 (mot) Mapping Detachment
  1 (mot) Military Police Detachment (3 LMGs)

3 Waffen SS Grenadier Regiments, each with
  1 Grenadier Regimental Staff & Staff Company
    1 Signals Platoon (1 LMG)
    1 Pioneer Platoon (6 LMGs)
    1 Bicycle Platoon (3 LMGs)

1st Battalion
  1 Battalion Staff (1 LMG)
  3 Grenadier Companies (2 HMGs & 12 LMGs)
  1 Machine Gun Company (6 HMGs, 3 LMGs 4 120mm mortars & 6 80mm mortars)

2nd Battalion
  same as 1st Battalion

3rd Battalion
  same as 1st Battalion

1 Infantry Gun Company
  (2 150mm sIG, 6 75mm leIG, & 5 LMGS)

1 Panzerjäger Company
  1 Headquarters Platoon (1 LMG)
  1 Panzerzerstörer Platoon (36 panzerschrecke & 2 LMGs)
  1 (motZ) Panzerjäger Platoon (3 75mm PAK & 3 LMGs)

Panzerjäger Battalion
  1 Battalion Staff & Staff Platoon (1 LMG)
  1 Sturmgeschütz Company (14 StuG)
  1 (motZ) Panzerjäger Company (12 75mm PAK & 12 LMGs)
  1 (motZ) Flak Company (12 20mm flak & 2 LMGs)

Fusilier Battalion
  1 Battalion Staff (1 LMG)
  1 (bicycle) Fusilier Company (2 HMGs & 13 LMGs)
  2 Fusilier Companies (2 HMGs & 13 LMGs ea)
  1 Heavy Company (6 HMGs, 3 LMGs, 4 120mm mortars & 6 80mm mortars)

Artillery Regiment
  1 Regimental Staff & Staff Battery (1 LMG)

1st Battalion
  1 Battalion Staff & Staff Battery (2 LMGs)
  3 Batteries (4 105mm leFH & 4 LMGs ea)

2nd Battalion
  same as 1st Battalion

3rd Battalion
  same as 1st Battalion

4th Battalion
  1 Battalion Staff & Staff Battery (2 LMGs)
  3 Batteries (4 150mm sFH & 4 LMGs ea)

Pioneer Battalion
  1 Battalion Staff (4 LMGs & 2 flamethrowers)
  1 (bicycle) Pioneer Company (2 HMGs, 9 LMGs, 6 flamethrowers, & 2 80mm mortars)
  2 Pioneer Companies (2 HMGs, 9 LMGs, 6 flamethrowers, & 2 80mm mortars ea)

Signals Battalion
  1 (tmot) Telephone Company (5 LMGs)
  1 (mot) Radio Company (4 LMGs)
  1 (tmot) Supply Column (2 LMGs)

Feldersatz Battalion
  2–5 Companies

Supply Troop
  1 (tmot) Supply Battalion Staff (2 LMGs)

2 (mot) 90 ton Transportation Companies (6
LMGs ea)
2 (horse drawn) 60 ton Transportation Company
(8 LMGs ea)
1 Supply Company (8 LMGs)
Maintenance Troops
1 (mot) Maintenance Company (4 LMGs)
Other
1 (mot) Butcher Company (2 LMGs)

1 (mot) Bakery Company (4 LMGs)
1 (mot) Divisional Administration Company (2
LMGs)
1 (mot) Medical Company (2 LMGs)
1 (horse drawn) Medical Company (4 LMGs)
1 (mot) Medical Supply Company (4 LMGs)
1 Veterinary Company (6 LMGs)
1 (mot) Field Post Office

Theoretical Organization
SS Freiwilliger Grenadier Division 30 January
9/15/44

Division Staff
1 Divisional Staff (2 LMGs)
1 (mot) Mapping Detachment
1 (mot) Military Police Detachment (3 LMGs)
2 Waffen SS Grenadier Regiments, each with
1 Grenadier Regimental Staff & Staff Company
1 Staff Platoon (1 LMG)
1 Signals Platoon
1 Pioneer Platoon (6 LMGs)
1 Bicycle Platoon (3 LMGs)
1st Battalion
1 Battalion Staff (1 LMG)
1 Battalion Supply Platoon (1 LMG)
3 (bicycle) Grenadier Companies (9 LMGs)
1 (bicycle) Machine Gun Company (8 HMGs, 1
LMG, 4 75mm leIG, & 6 80mm mortars)
2nd Battalion
same as 1st Battalion
13th Heavy Support Company
1 sIG Platoon (2 150mm sIG & 1 LMG)
1 Heavy Mortar Platoon (8 120mm mortars & 4
LMGs)
14th Panzerzerstörer Company
(54 + 18 reserve panzerschrecke & 4 LMGs)
Panzerjäger Battalion
1 Battalion Staff & (mot) Staff Platoon (1 LMG)
1 Staff Jagdpanzer Platoon (3 Jagdpanzer IV)
1 Jagdpanzer Company (14 Jagdpanzer IV & 16
LMGs)
1 Escort Platoon
1 StuG Company (14 StuG & 16 LMGs)
1 Escort Platoon
1 (motZ) Panzerjäger Company (12 75mm PAK &
12 LMGs)
1 (mot) Supply Company (3 LMGs)
Artillery Regiment
1 Regimental Staff & Staff Battery (1 LMG)

1st Battalion
1 Battalion Staff & Staff Battery (2 LMGs)
2 Batteries (6 105mm leFH & 4 LMGs ea)
2nd Battalion
same as 1st Battalion
3rd Battalion
same as 1st Battalion
4th (Luftwaffe) Flak Battalion
1 Battalion Staff & Staff Battery
3 Heavy Flak Batteries (4 88mm, 3 20mm, & 2
LMGs ea)
5th (Luftwaffe) Flak Battalion
same as 4th (Luftwaffe) Flak Battalion
Pioneer Battalion
1 Battalion Staff (4 LMGs)
1 (bicycle) Pioneer Company (2 HMGs, 9 LMGs,
6 flamethrowers, & 2 80mm mortars)
1 Pioneer Company (2 HMGs, 9 LMGs, 6 flamethrowers, & 2 80mm mortars ea)
Signals Battalion
1 (tmot) Telephone Company (4 LMGs)
1 (mot) Radio Company (2 LMGs)
1 (tmot) Supply Column (2 LMGs) Feldersatz
Battalion
5 Companies
Supply Troop
1 (mot) 120 ton Transportation Companies (4
LMGs)
2 (horse drawn) 30 ton Transportation Company
(2 LMGs ea)
1 Supply Platoon (2 LMGs)
1 Feldzeug Company
1 (mot) Maintenance Platoon (1 LMG)
Other
1 (mot) Butcher Company
1 (mot) Bakery Company
1 (mot) Divisional Administration Company

1 (mot) Medical Company (2 LMGs)
1 (mot) Medical Supply Company (4 LMGs)

1 Veterinary Company (2 LMGs)
1 (mot) Field Post Office

Theoretical Organization
SS Waffen Grenadier Division
10/30/44

Division Staff
1 Divisional Staff (2 LMGs)
1 (mot) Mapping Detachment
1 (tmot) Military Police Detachment (3 LMGs)
1 Waffen SS Grenadier Regiment
1 Grenadier Regimental Staff & Staff Company
  1 Staff Platoon (1 LMG)
  1 Pioneer Platoon (6 LMGs)
  1 Bicycle Platoon (3 LMGs)
1st Battalion
1 Battalion Staff (1 LMG)
1 Battalion Supply Company (1 LMG)
2 Grenadier Companies (9 LMGs & 2 machine pistol platoons)
1 (bicycle) Grenadier Company (9 LMGs & 2 machine pistol platoons)
1 Machine Gun Company (8 HMGs, 1 LMG, 4 75mm leIG, & 6 80mm mortars)
2nd Battalion
1 Battalion Staff (1 LMG)
1 Battalion Supply Company (1 LMG)
3 Grenadier Companies (9 LMGs & 2 machine pistol platoons)
1 Machine Gun Company (8 HMGs, 1 LMG, 4 75mm leIG, & 6 80mm mortars)
13th Company
1 Heavy Mortar Platoon (8 120mm mortars & 1 LMG)
1 Panzerjäger Platoon (4 PAK & 1 LMG)
14th Panzerzerstörer Company
(72 panzerschreck & 4 LMGs)
2 Waffen SS Grenadier Regiments, each with
1 Grenadier Regimental Staff & Staff Company
  1 Staff Platoon (1 LMG)
  1 Pioneer Platoon (6 LMGs)
  1 Bicycle Platoon (3 LMGs)
1st & 2nd Battalions, each with
1 Battalion Staff (1 LMG)
1 Battalion Supply Company (1 LMG)
3 Grenadier Companies (9 LMGs & 2 machine pistol platoons)
1 Machine Gun Company (8 HMGs, 1 LMG, 4 75mm leIG, & 6 80mm mortars)

13th Company
1 Heavy Mortar Platoon (8 120mm mortars & 1 LMG)
1 Panzerjäger Platoon (4 PAK & 1 LMG)
14th Panzerzerstörer Company
(72 panzerschreck & 4 LMGs)
Panzerjäger Battalion
1 Battalion Staff & Staff Platoon (1 LMG)
1 Sturmgeschütz Company (14 StuG & 16 LMGs)
1 (motZ) Panzerjäger Company (9 75mm PAK & 12 LMGs)
1 (motZ) Flak Company (12 20mm flak & 2 LMGs)
Fusilier Company
(2 HMGs, 9 LMGs, 2 80mm mortars, 2 PAK & 2 machine pistol platoons)
Artillery Regiment
1 Regimental Staff & Staff Battery (1 LMG)
1st Battalion
1 Battalion Staff & Staff Battery (2 LMGs)
3 Batteries (6 75mm FK 40 & 5 LMGs ea)
(each gun 1 RSO or 2nd & 3rd Bn fully horse drawn)
2nd Battalion
1 Battalion Staff & Staff Battery (2 LMGs)
2 Batteries (6 105mm leFH & 5 LMGs ea)
(each gun 1 RSO or 2nd & 3rd Bn fully horse drawn)
3rd Battalion
same as 2nd Battalion
(each gun 1 RSO or 2nd & 3rd Bn fully horse drawn)
4th Battalion (horse drawn)
1 Battalion Staff & Staff Battery (2 LMGs)
2 Batteries (6 150mm sFH & 5 LMGs ea)
(or 75mm FK 40 or 75mm FK 85 if no 150mm sFH)
Pioneer Battalion
1 Battalion Staff (4 LMGs)
2 (bicycle) Pioneer Companies (2 HMGs, 9 LMGs, 6 flamethrowers, 2 80mm mortars & 3 panzerschrecke ea)
Signals Battalion
1 (tmot) Telephone Company (5 LMGs)
1 (mot) Radio Company (5 LMGs)
1 (tmot) Supply Column (2 LMGs)
Feldersatz Battalion
5 Companies (8 LMGs, 2 HMGs, 2 80mm mortars, 1 leIG 37, 1 37mm flak, 1 flamethrower, 2 panzerschreck & 30 MP 44)

Supply Troop
- 1 (tmot) Supply Battalion Staff (2 LMGs)
- 1 (mot) 120 ton Transportation Company (8 LMGs)
- 2 30 ton Transportation Company (4 LMGs ea)
- 1 Supply Platoon (4 LMGs)
- 1 (tmot) Feldzeug Troop (3 LMGs)
- 1 (mot) Maintenance Company (4 LMGs)

Other
- 1 Mixed Butcher/Bakery/Administration Company (3 LMGs)

- 1 (mot) Medical Company (2 LMGs)
- 1 (mot) Medical Supply Company
- 1 Veterinary Company (4 LMGs)
- 1 (mot) Field Post Office

Note: Apparently this used the same organization as a Volks Grenadier Division.

Theoretical Organization
SS Cavalry Division
1/2/45

Division Staff
- 1 Divisional Staff (2 LMGs)
- 1 (mot) Mapping Detachment
- 1 (tmot) Military Police Detachment (3 LMGs)

3 Cavalry Regiments, each with
- 1 Cavalry Regimental Staff & (mot) Staff Company
- 1 Staff Platoon (1 LMG)
- 1 Pioneer Platoon (3 LMGs)
- 1 Siganls Platoon
- 4 Squadrons (1 LMG ea)
- 1 Machine Gun Squadron (8 HMGs & 6 80mm mortars)
- 1 Support Squadron
  - 1 (mot) Pioneer Platoon (4 LMGs & 6 flamethrowers)
  - 1 (motZ) Panzerjäger Platoon (3 75mm PAK & 3 LMGs)
  - 1 (motZ) Panzerjäger Platoon (4 37mm PAK & 2 LMGs)
  - 1 (motZ) Flak Battery (4 20mm flak guns)

Panzerjäger Battalion
- 1 Battalion Staff & (mot) Staff Platoon (1 LMG)
- 1 Sturmgeschütz Company (14 StuG & 16 LMGs)
- 1 (motZ) Panzerjäger Company (9 75mm PAK & 12 LMGs)
- 1 (motZ) Flak Company (9 37mm flak & 4 LMGs)

Fusilier Battalion
- 3 (bicycle) Fusilier Companies (2 HMGs & 13 LMGs)
- 1 Heavy Company (6 HMGs, 3 LMGs, 4 120mm mortars & 6 80mm mortars)

Cavalry Artillery Regiment
- 1 Regimental Staff & (mot) Staff Battery (1 LMG)
1st, 2nd & 3rd Battalions, each with
- 1 Battalion Staff & Staff Battery

- 3 Horse Batteries (4 105mm leFH & 2 LMGs ea)

Pioneer Battalion
- 1 Battalion Staff (4 LMGs & 2 flamethrowers)
- 2 Pioneer Companies (2 HMGs, 9 LMGs, 6 flamethrowers, & 2 80mm mortars ea)
- 1 Pioneer Company (2 HMGs, 9 LMGs, 6 flamethrowers, & 2 80mm mortars)

Signals Battalion
- 1 (tmot) Telephone Company (5 LMGs)
- 1 (mot) Radio Company (5 LMGs)
- 1 (tmot) Supply Column (2 LMGs)

Feldersatz Battalion
- 1 Supply Company
- 2–5 Companies

Supply Troop
- 1 (mot) 120 ton Transportation Company (4 LMGs)
- 3 50 ton Transportation Company (2 LMGs ea)
- 1 Supply Platoon (2 LMGs)
- 1 (tmot) Feldzeug Troop
- 1 (mot) Maintenance Company (1 LMG)

Other
- 1 (mot) Butcher Company
- 1 (mot) Bakery Company
- 1 (mot) Divisional Administration Company
- 1 Medical Company (2 LMGs)
- 2 (mot) Medical Supply Companies
- 2 Veterinary Companies (2 LMGs ea)
- 1 (mot) Field Post Office

Theoretical Organization
SS Panzer Division
3/1/45

Division Staff
1 Divisional Staff
1 (mot) Mapping Detachment
1 (mot) Escort Company
  1 Machine Gun Platoon (4 HMGs & 6 LMGs)
  1 Motorcycle Platoon (6 LMGs)
  1 Self Propelled Flak Battery (4 20mm flak guns)
1 (mot) Military Police Detachment (9 LMGs)

1 SS Panzer Regiment
1 Panzer Regimental Staff & Staff Company
  1 Panzer Signals Platoon
  1 Panzer Platoon
  1 Panzer Flak Battery (4 37mm & 4 20mm flak guns)

1st Battalion
1 Panzer Battalion Staff (1 LMG)
1 Panzer Battalion Staff Company (11 LMGs & 3 20mm Flak guns)
4 Panzer Companies (17 Panther Mk V Tanks ea)
1 (mot) Supply Company (4 LMGs)

1st Battalion
1 Panzer Battalion Staff (1 LMG)
1 Panzer Battalion Staff Company (11 LMGs & 3 20mm Flak guns)
4 Panzer Companies (17 Mk IV Tanks ea)
1 (mot) Supply Company (4 LMGs)

1 Panzergrenadier Regiment
1 Panzergrenadier Regimental Staff & Staff Company
  1 Signals Platoon
  1 Motorcycle Platoon (4 LMGS)

1st & 2nd (mot) Battalions each with
1 Battalion Staff
1 (mot) Supply Company (3 LMGs)
3 (mot) Panzergrenadier Companies (12 LMGs & 1 Sturm Platoon)
1 (mot) Panzergrenadier Machine Gun Company
  3 Machine Gun Platoons (4 HMGs ea)
  1 Panzerjäger Platoon (3 LMGs & 3 75mm PAK)
1 (mot) Panzergrenadier Mortar Company
  2 Medium Mortar Platoons (4 80mm mortars ea)
  2 Heavy Mortar Platoons (2 120mm mortars ea)
1 Self Propelled Infantry Gun Company (6 150mm sIG & 2 LMGS)
1 Self Propelled Flak Company (12 20mm & 2 LMGs)
1 (mot) Pioneer Company (12 LMGS & 18 flamethrowers)

2nd Panzergrenadier Regiment
1 Panzergrenadier Regimental Staff & Staff Company
  1 Signals Platoon
  1 Motorcycle Platoon (4 LMGS)

1st (half track) Battalion
1 Battalion Staff
1 (halftrack) Supply Company (3 LMGs)
3 (halftrack) Panzergrenadier Companies (3 HMGs, 30 LMGS, 2 80mm mortars, 7 20mm & 2 75mm guns)
1 (halftrack) Panzergrenadier Machine Gun Company
  2 Mortar Platoons (2 120mm mortars ea)
  2 Infantry Gun Platoons (3 75mm & 2 LMGS ea)

2nd (mot) Battalion
same as motorized battalions of first regiment
1 Self Propelled Infantry Gun Company (6 150mm sIG & 2 LMGS)
1 Self Propelled Flak Company (12 20mm & 2 LMGs)
1 (mot) Pioneer Company
  1 Staff Platoon (1 LMG)
  1 (halftrack) Platoon (6 LMGs & 6 flamethrowers)
  1 (halftrack) Platoon (12 LMGs, 1 20mm & 6 flamethrowers)
  1 Platoon (12 flamethrowers & 8 LMGs)
  1 Platoon (2 HMGs & 2 80mm mortars)

Panzerjäger Battalion
1 Battalion Staff & Staff Platoon (3 jagdpanzers)
2 Jagdpanzer Companies (13 Jagdpanzer IV ea)
1 (motZ) Panzerjäger Company (12 75mm PAK & 12 LMGs)
1 (mot) Supply Company (4 LMGs)

1 Panzer Reconnaissance Battalion
1 Panzer Reconnaissance Battalion Staff (2 LMGs)
1 (mot) Reconnaissance Battalion Staff Company
  1 (mot) Signals Platoon (3 LMGS)
1 Armored Car Company (16 20mm & 25 LMGs)
1 Half Track Reconnaissance Company (2 75mm, 4 LMGs & 2 80mm mortars)
1 Half Track Reconnaissance Company (2 75mm, 7 20mm 2 80mm mortars, 3 HMGs & 30 LMGs)
1 Half Track Reconnaissance Company
  1 Staff Platoon (1 LMG)
  1 Panzerjäger Platoon (6 75mm & 2 LMGs)
  1 Mortar Platoon (2 LMGs & 6 80mm Mortars)
  1 Pioneer Platoon (13 LMG)

1 (mot) Supply Company (4 LMGs)

(mot) Flak Battalion
1 Staff & (mot) Staff Battery (2 LMGs)
2 (motZ) Heavy Flak Companies (6 88mm, 3 20mm & 3 LMGs ea)
1 (motZ) Medium Flak Companies (9 37mm & 4 LMGs ea)
1 Self Propelled Flak Battery (3 quad 20mm guns)

Panzer Artillery Regiment
1 Regimental Staff & (mot) Staff Battery (2 LMGs)
1 Self Propelled Flak Battery (4 quad 20mm guns)

1st Battalion
1 Battalion Staff & (mot) Staff Battery (2 LMGs)
1 Flak Battery (2 mountain 20mm flak guns)
1 Self Propelled Battery (6 150mm sFH Hummels SdKfz 165 & 4 LMGs ea)
2 Self Propelled Batteries (6 105mm leFH Wespe SdKfz 124 & 4 LMGs ea)

2nd Battalion
1 Battalion Staff & (mot) Staff Battery (2 LMGs)
1 Flak Battery (2 mountain 20mm flak guns)
3 (motZ) Batteries (6 105mm leFH & 4 LMGs ea)

3rd Battalion
1 Battalion Staff & (mot) Staff Battery (2 LMGs)
1 Flak Battery (2 mountain 20mm flak guns)
1 (motZ) Battery (6 105mm leFH & 4 LMGs)
2 (motZ) Batteries (6 150mm sFH & 4 LMGs ea)

Panzer Pioneer Battalion
1 Battalion Staff
1 (halftrack) Battalion Staff Company (9 LMGs)

1 (halftrack) Reconnaissance Platoon (8 LMGs)
2 (halftrack) Pioneer Platoons (2 HMGs, 43 LMGs, 2 80mm mortars, & 6 flamethrowers)
2 (mot) Pioneer Companies (2 HMGs, 18 LMGs, 2 80mm mortars & 6 flamethrowers ea)

Panzer Signals Troop
1 Panzer Telephone Company (11 LMGs)
1 Panzer Radio Company (19 LMGs)
1 (mot) Supply Platoon (2 LMGs)

Feldersatz Battalion
2–5 Companies

Supply Troop
1 (mot) Supply Battalion Staff
1 (mot) Supply Battalion Staff Company
3 (mot) 120 ton Transportation Companies (4 LMGs ea)
2 (horse drawn) 60 ton Transportation Company (4 LMGs ea)
1 (mot) Maintenance Platoon

Maintenance Troops
2 (mot) Maintenance Companies (3 LMGs ea)
1 (mot) Heavy Maintenance Supply Column

Other
1 (mot) Butcher Company (2 LMGs)
1 (mot) Bakery Company (4 LMGs)
1 (mot) Divisional Administration company (2 LMGs)
1 (mot) Medical Company (2 LMGs)
1 (mot) Medical Supply Company (1 LMG)
1 (mot) Field Post Office

Theoretical Organization
SS Panzergrenadier Division
3/1/45

Headquarters
1 Divisional Headquarters (2 LMGs)
1 (mot) Mapping Detachment
1 (mot) Military Police Troop (2 LMGs)

Panzer Battalion
1 Panzer Battalion Staff (1 LMG)
1 Panzer Battalion Staff Company (11 LMGs)
1 Sturmgeschütz Platoon (3 StuG)
1 Self Propelled Flak Battery (3 quad 20mm flak guns)
3 Sturmgeschütz Companies (14 StuGs)
1 (mot) Supply Company (3 LMGs)
1 Panzer Maintenance (2 LMGs)

1 Panzergrenadier Regiment
1 Panzergrenadier Regiment Staff

1 (mot) Panzergrenadier Regiment Staff Company
1 Signals Platoon
1 Motorcycle Platoon (6 LMGs)

1st Panzergrenadier Battalion
1 Panzergrenadier Battalion Staff
1 (mot) Supply Company (4 LMGs)
3 (mot) Panzergrenadier Companies (4 HMGs, 18 LMGs & 2 80mm mortars)
1 (mot) Machine Gun (12 HMG, 3 75mm, & 3 20mm flak)
1 (mot) Mortar Company
1 Heavy Mortar Platoon (8 80mm mortars & 4 LMGs)
1 Medium Mortar Platoon (4 120mm mortars & 2 LMGs)

2nd Panzergrenadier Battalion
same as 1st Battalion

3rd Panzergrenadier Battalion
1 Panzergrenadier Battalion Staff
1 Supply Company (4 LMGs)
3 Panzergrenadier Companies (4 HMGs, 18 LMGs & 2 80mm mortars) (1 on bicycles)
1 Machine Gun (12 HMG, 3 75mm, & 3 20mm flak)
1 Mortar Company
    1 Heavy Mortar Platoon (8 80mm mortars & 4 LMGs)
    1 Medium Mortar Platoon (4 120mm mortars & 2 LMGs)
1 Self Propelled Flak Company (12 20mm & 2 LMGs)
1 (motZ) Panzerjäger Company (6 75mm PAK & 3 LMGs)
1 (mot) Pioneer Company (12 LMGs & 18 flamethrowers)

2nd Panzergrenadier Regiment
same as the 1st Panzergrenadier Regiment

Panzerjäger Battalion
1 Battalion Staff & Staff Company (1 Jagdpanzer)
2 Jagdpanzer Companies (14 Jagdpanzer IV ea)
1 (motZ) Panzerjäger Company (12 75mm & 12 LMGs)
1 (mot) Supply Company (4 LMGs)

1 (mot) Reconnaissance Battalion
1 Battalion Staff & Staff Company
    1 Signals Platoon
    1 Armored Car Platoon (3 75mm, 13 20mm & 16 LMGs)
3 (mot) Reconnaissance Companies (2 80mm mortars, 4 HMGs & & 9 LMGs)
1 (mot) Reconnaissance Pioneer Company
    1 Pioneer Platoon (4 LMGs & 6 flamethrowers)
    1 Mortar Platoon (6 80mm mortars)

(mot) Flak Battalion
1 Staff & (mot) Staff Battery (2 LMGs)
2 (motZ) Heavy Flak Companies (6 88mm, 3 20mm & 3 LMGs ea)
1 (motZ) Medium Flak Companies (9 37mm & 4 LMGs ea)
1 Self Propelled Flak Battery (3 quad 20mm guns)

Panzer Artillery Regiment
1 Regimental Staff & (mot) Staff Battery (2 LMGs)
1 Self Propelled Flak Battery (4 quad 20mm guns)
1st Battalion
1 Battalion Staff & (mot) Staff Battery (2 LMGs)
1 Staff Flak Battery (2 mountain 20mm flak guns)
3 (motZ) Batteries (4 105mm leFH & 4 LMGs ea)

2nd Battalion
same as 1st Battalion
3rd Battalion
1 Battalion Staff & (mot) Staff Battery (2 LMGs)
1 Flak Battery (2 mountain 20mm flak guns)
1 (motZ) Battery (4 100mm K18 & 4 LMGs)
2 (motZ) Batteries (4 150mm sFH & 4 LMGs ea)

(mot) Pioneer Battalion
1 Battalion Staff (3 LMGs)
1 (mot) Supply Company (2 LMGs)
3 (mot) Pioneer Companies (6 flamethrowers, 2 80mm mortars,
1 (mot Light Panzer Bridging Train (3 LMGs)

Feldersatz Battalion
2–5 companies

(mot) Signals Battalion;
1 (mot) Supply Platoon (2 LMGs)
1 (mot) Radio Company (6 LMGs)
1 (mot) Telephone Company (5 LMGs)

Supply Troop
1 (mot) Supply Battalion Staff
1 (mot) Supply Battalion Staff Company
3 (mot) 120 ton Transportation Companies (4 LMGs ea)
1 (horse drawn) 60 ton Transportation Company (4 LMGs)
1 (mot) Maintenance Platoon

Maintenance Troops
2 (mot) Maintenance Companies (3 LMGs ea)
1 (mot) Heavy Maintenance Supply Column

Other
1 (mot) Butcher Company (2 LMGs)
1 (mot) Bakery Company (4 LMGs)
1 (mot) Divisional Administration company (2 LMGs)
1 (mot) Medical Company (2 LMGs)
1 (mot) Medical Supply Company (1 LMG)
1 (mot) Field Post Office

APPENDIX 2

History of the SS Totenkopf Regiments, SS Polizei Regiments, and SS Wach-Battalions

SS Totenkopf Regiments

1st SS Totenkopfstandarte "Oberbayern"
prewar	stationed Dachau; not part of the Waffen-SS
10-27-39	renamed SS Totenkopf Rekruten Standarte
04-27-40	broken up; I=II/7 SSTk; II=III/6 SSTk; III=formed 16 SSTk Standarte; IV=III/14 SSTk

1st SS Totenkopf Infanterie Regiment
10-16-39	formed at Dachau from levies of old SS Totenkopf standarten; assigned to SS Totenkopf Division
winter 41/42	I/1 lost; replaced by III/2 SSTk Infantry Regiment
12- -42	formed into Schützen Regt "Thule"; then Panzer Grenadier Regiment "Thule"; then 1st SS Panzer Grenadier Regiment "Thule"
10-22-43	renamed 5th SS Panzergrenadier Regiment "Thule"

2nd SS Totenkopfstandarte "Brandenberg"
prewar	formed at Oranienburg; not part of the Waffen-SS
09-12-39	divided into 2nd & 5th SS Totenkopf Standarten levies to 2nd SS Totenkopf Infantry Regiment

2nd SS Totenkopf Infanterie Regiment
10-16-39	formed at Dachau from levies of old SS Totenkopf standarten; assigned to SS Totenkopf Division
winter 41/42	lost; III/2 became I/1st SSTk Infantry Regiment, rest formed Totenkopf Motorcycle Bn

3rd SS Totenkopfstandarte "Thüringen"
prewar	stationed Buchenwald; not part of the Waffen-SS
11-11-39	renamed 10th SS Totenkopf-Standarte

3rd SS Infanterie Regiment
10-16-39	formed at Dachau from levies of old SS Totenkopf-standarten; assigned to SS Totenkopf Division
02-09-43	named SS Panzergrenadier Regiment "Theodor Eicke"; then 3rd SS Panzergrenadier Regiment "Theodor Eicke"
10-22-43	6th SS Panzergrenadier Regiment "Theodor Eicke"

4th SS Totenkopfstandarte "Ostmark"
08-17-38	formed at Steyr
09- -39	mobilized as 4th SS Totenkopf-Standarte
02-25-41	renamed 4th SS Infanterie Regiment RFSS assigned to 2nd SS Infantry Brigade
12- -41	reassigned to SS Das Reich Divivision
04-22-42	joined SS Das Reich Division
04-20-42	renamed "Langemarck" Schnelle Regiment"; renamed "Langemarck" Schützen Regiment
- -43	"Langemarck" Schützen Regiment lost

5th SS Totenkopfstandarte "Brandenburg"
09-12-39	formed from 2nd SS Totenkopfstandarte
11- -39	I/5 formed 13th SS Totenkopfstandarte new I/5 formed
06-04-40	III/5 formed Sonder-Bataillonn Reitz which was assigned to SS Standarte "K" (Kirkenes) new III/5 formed
09-12-40	renamed 5th SS Totenkopf Infanterie Regiment (mot)
02-25-41	renamed 5th SS Infanterie Regiment RFS
09-01-41	lost; remnants built SS Ersatz Bataillon Ost

6th SS Totenkopf-Standarte
09-12-39	formed in Prague from old SS Totenkopfstandarten

| 10- -39 | renamed and became 9th SS Totenkopf-Standarte |
| - -39 | rebuilt as regiment |

04-27-40	III/6 became 14th SS Totenkopf-Standarte
	new III/6 from II/SS Totenkopf Rekruten Standarte
09-12-40	became motorized
02-25-41	renamed 6th SS Infanterie Regiment (mot)
06-04-42	renamed 6th SS Inf Regt "Reinhard Heydrich" (mot)
09- -42	reorganized as 6th SS Gebirgsjäger Regiment "Reinhard Heydrich"; II/6,III/6 lost; new II/6 from IV SS Gebirgs-Jäger Bataillon; new III/6 from III/7 SS Infantry Regiment
10-23-43	renamed 11th SS Gebirgsjäger Regiment "Reinhard Heydrich"

7th SS Totenkopf-Standarte

09-12-39	formed in Brünn from old SS Totenkopfstandarten
04-27-40	II/7 became II/9th SS Totenkopf-Standarte
	new II from I/SS Totenkopf Rekruten Standarte
09-12-40	became motorized
02-25-41	renamed 7th SS Infanterie Regiment (mot)
09- -42	reorganized as 7th SS Gebirgsjäger Regiment from SS I, II, III Geb-Jg Bns; ex I/7 became Schützen Battalion SS Gebirgs-Division Nord; ex II/7 lost; ex III/7 became III/6th SS Gebirgsjäger Regt
10-22-43	renamed 12th SS Gebirgsjäger Regt

8th SS Totenkopfstandarte

11-11-39	formed in Krakau from levies of 4th SSTk Standarte
09-12-40	became motorized
02-25-41	renamed 8th SS Infanterie Regiment;
06-06-41	assigned to 1st SS Infantry Brigade RFSS
09-01-43	renamed 8th SS Grenadier Regiment
11-12-43	renamed 39th SS Grenadier Regiment
01-25-44	renamed 39th SS Panzergrenadier Regiment

9th SS Totenkopf-Standarte

11-11-39	formed in Danzig from part of 6th SSTk Standarte
04-24-40	II/9 to 14th SSTk Standarte
04-27-40	new II/9 formed from II/7th SSTk Standarte
08-15-40	III/12th SSTk absorbed into Standarte
09-12-40	became motorized
11-15-40	lost; troops built SS Wach-Bataillon Prag
11-20-40	staff became Staff/SS Totenkopf-Standarte "K"
02-18-41	rebuilt by renaming SS T-Standarte "K"(Kirkenes)
02-25-41	renamed 9th SS Infanterie Regiment ; new III/9 formed
08- -42	lost; Staff/,III/9th SS Infantery Regiment became Staff/,II/SS Regt (mot) "Thule"

10th SS Totenkopf-Standarte

11-11-39	formed at Buchenwald by renaming 2nd SS Totenkopf standarte
09-12-40	became motorized
02-25-41	renamed 10th SS Infanterie Regiment
06-06-41	assigned to 1st SS Inf Bde RFSS
10-01-42	ordered reassigned to 2nd SS Infantry Brigade RFSS; never transferred
09-01-43	renamed 10th SS Grenadier Regiment
10-22-43	renamed 40th SS Grenadier Regiment
01-25-44	renamed 40th SS Panzergrenadier Regiment

11th SS Totenkopf-Standarte

11-11-39	formed at Brünn from 4th & 7th SS T-Standarten
09-19-40	became motorized
02-25-41	renamed 11th SS Infanterie Regiment (mot)
- -41	reassigned to SS Das Reich Division
- -42	lost

12th SS Totenkopf-Standarte
11-11-39	formed at Posen from 5th & 7th SS T-Standarten
08-15-40	lost; 2 companies to SSTk "K"; III/12 to 9th SSTk Standarte; detachment to 4th SSTk Standarte

13th SS Totenkopf-Standarte
11-11-39	formed from part of 5th SSTk Standarte
07-29-40	lost

14th SS Totenkopf-Standarte
04-24-40	formed at Buchenwald from II/9 SSTk, III/6 SSTk, IV/SS Tk-Rekruten Standarte
09-12-40	became motorized
02-25-41	renamed 14th SS Infanterie Regiment (mot); assigned to 2nd SS Infanterie Brigade RFSS
06-30-41	lost; divided among 2nd SS Infanterie Brigade RFSS
	I/14 became Sonder-Bataillon RFSS

15th SS Totenkopf-Standarte
03-01-40	formed at Plock I/15 only
10-10-40	II/15 formed
09-12-40	became motorized
11-15-40	lost; I/15 became Wach-Bataillon Oranienberg

16th SS Totenkopf-Standarte
04-24-40	formed at Prague from III/SSTk-Rekruten Standarte
08-15-40	lost

SS Totenkopf Standarte "K" (Kirkenes)
06-04-40	formed I/SSTk "K" from Sonder-Bataillon Reitz
09-01-40	fromed I/SSTk "K" from 2 companies ex 12th SSTk Standarte; Co of Ersatz Bn "SS Der Führer" Regiment
12-11-40	formed Staff/SSTk "K" from Staff/9th SSTk Standarte
02-18-41	renamed 9th SS Totenkopf Standarte

SS Totenkopf-Reiter-Standarte
11-15-39	formed in Poland
05-21-40	divided into 1st & 2nd SS Totenkopf-Reiter-Standarten

1st SS Totenkopf-Reiter-Standarte
05-21-40	formed by dividing SS Totenkopf-Reiter-Standarte
02-25-41	renamed 1st SS Kavallerie Regiment; assigned to SS Kavallerie Brigade
10-22-43	renamed 15th SS Kavallerie Regiment

2nd SS Totenkopf-Reiter-Standarte
05-21-40	formed by dividing SS Totenkopf-Reiter-Standarte
02-25-41	renamed 2nd SS Kavallerie Regiment; assigned SS Kavallerie Brigade
10-22-43	renamed 16th SS Kavallerie Regiment

SS Polizei Regiments

1st Polizei Schützen Regiment
10-01-39	formed from Ordnungspolizei
	assigned to SS Polizei Division
02-24-42	renamed 1st SS Polizei Schützen Regiment
10-15-42	renamed 1st SS Polizei Infanterie Regiment
02-01-43	renamed 1st SS Polizei Grenadier Regiment
06-06-43	renamed 1st SS Polizei Panzergrenadier Regiment
10-22-43	renamed 7th SS Panzergrenadier Regiment

2nd Polizei Schützen Regiment
10-01-39	formed from Ordnungspolizei
	assigned to SS Polizei Division

02-24-42	renamed 2nd SS Polizei Schützen Regiment
10-15-42	renamed 2nd SS Polizei Infanterie Regiment
02-01-43	renamed 2nd SS Polizei Grenadier Regiment
06-06-43	renamed 2nd SS Polizei Panzergrenadier Regiment
10-22-43	renamed 8th SS Panzergrenadier Regiment

3rd Polizei Schützen Regiment
10-01-39	formed from Ordnungspolizei
	assigned to SS Polizei Division
02-24-42	renamed 3rd SS Polizei Schützen Regiment
10-15-42	renamed 3rd SS Polizei Infanterie Regiment
02-01-43	renamed 3rd SS Polizei Grenadier Regiment
10-22-43	to be renamed 9th SS Panzergrenadier Regiment
11-12-43	Staff/, I/lost; II/3 became I/8th SS Panzer
	Grenadier Regiment III/3 became 1/7th SS Panzer
	Grenadier Regiment

1st SS Polizei Regiment
07- -42	formed as 1st Polizei Regiment from Ordnungspolizei
02-24-43	renamed 1st SS Polizei Regiment

2nd SS Polizei Regiment
07- -42	formed as 2nd Polizei Regiment from Ordnungspolizei
03-24-43	renamed 2nd SS Polizei Regiment

3rd SS Polizei Regiment
07- -42	formed as 1st Polizei Regiment from Ordnungspolizei
02-24-43	renamed 1st SS Polizei Grenadier Regiment

4th SS Polizei Regiment
07- -42	formed as 4th Polizei Regiment from Ordnungspolizei
02-14-43	renamed 4th SS Polizei Regiment

5th SS Polizei Regiment
07- -42	formed as 5th Polizei Regiment from Ordnungspolizei
02-14-43	renamed 5th SS Polizei Regiment

6th SS Polizei Regiment
07- -42	formed as 6th Polizei Regiment from Ordnungspolizei
02-24-43	renamed 6th SS Polizei Regiment

7th SS Polizei Regiment
07- -42	formed as 7th Polizei Regiment from Ordnungspolizei
02-24-43	renamed 7th SS Polizei Regiment

8th SS Polizei Regiment
07- -42	formed as 8th Polizei Regiment from Ordnungspolizei
02-24-43	renamed 8th SS Polizei Regiment

9th SS Polizei Regiment
07- -42	formed as 9th Polizei Regiment from Ordnungspolizei
02-24-43	renamed 9th SS Polizei Regiment

10th SS Polizei Regiment
07- -42	formed as 10th Polizei Regiment from Ordnungspolizei
02-22-43	renamed 10th SS Polizei Regiment

11th SS Polizei Regiment
07- -42	formed as 11th Polizei Regiment from Ordnungspolizei
02-22-43	renamed 11th SS Polizei Regiment

12th SS Polizei Regiment
07- -42	formed as 12th Polizei Regiment from Ordnungspolizei
02-24-43	renamed 12th SS Polizei Regiment

13th SS Polizei Regiment
07- -42	formed as 13th Polizei Regiment from Ordnungspolizei
02-24-43	renamed 13th SS Polizei Regiment

14th SS Polizei Regiment
07- -42	formed as 14th Polizei Regiment from Ordnungspolizei
02-24-43	renamed 14th SS Polizei Regiment
04-06-45	renamed 91st SS Polizei Grenadier Regiment

15th SS Polizei Regiment
| 07- -42 | formed as 15th Polizei Regiment from Ordnungspolizei |
| 02-24-43 | renamed 15th SS Polizei Regiment |

16th SS Polizei Regiment
| 07- -42 | formed as 16th Polizei Regiment from Ordnungspolizei |
| 02-24-43 | renamed 16th SS Polizei Regiment |

17th SS Polizei Regiment
| 07- -42 | formed as 17th Polizei Regiment from Ordnungspolizei |
| 02-24-43 | renamed 17th SS Polizei Regiment |

18th SS Polizei Gebirgsjäger Regiment
| 07- -42 | formed as 18th Polizei Gebirgsjäger Regiment from Ordnungspolizei |
| 02-24-43 | renamed 18th SS Polizei Gebirgsjäger Regiment |

19th SS Polizei Regiment
| 07- -42 | formed as 19th Polizei Regiment from Ordnungspolizei |
| 02-24-43 | renamed 19th SS Polizei Regiment |

20th SS Polizei Regiment
| 07- -42 | formed as 20th Polizei Regiment from Ordnungspolizei |
| 02-24-43 | renamed 20th SS Polizei Regiment |

21st SS Polizei Regiment
| 07- -42 | formed as 21st Polizei Regiment from Ordnungspolizei |
| 02-24-43 | renamed 21st SS Polizei Regiment |

22nd SS Polizei Regiment
| 07- -42 | formed as 22nd Polizei Regiment from Ordnungspolizei |
| 02-24-43 | renamed 22nd SS Polizei Regiment |

23rd SS Polizei Regiment
| 07- -42 | formed as 23rd Polizei Regiment from Ordnungspolizei |
| 02-24-43 | renamed 23rd SS Polizei Regiment |

24th SS Polizei Regiment
| 07- -42 | formed as 24th Polizei Regiment from Ordnungspolizei |
| 02-24-43 | renamed 24th SS Polizei Regiment |

25th SS Polizei Regiment
| 07- -42 | ormed as 25th Polizei Regiment from Ordnungspolizei |
| 02-24-43 | renamed 25th SS Polizei Regiment |

26th SS Polizei Regiment
| 07- -42 | formed as 26th Polizei Regiment from Ordnungspolizei |
| 02-24-43 | renamed 26th SS Polizei Regiment |

27th SS Polizei Regiment
| 07- -42 | formed as 27th Polizei Regiment from Ordnungspolizei |
| 02-24-43 | renamed 27th SS Polizei Regiment |

28th SS Polizei Regiment "Todt"
| 11- -42 | formed as 28th Polizei Regiment "Todt" from Ordnungspolizei |
| 02-24-43 | renamed 28th SS Polizei Regiment "Todt" |

29th SS Polizei Regiment
- -4?	formed as 1st Polizei Regiment z.b.V. of Bde Wirth from Ordnungspolizei
03-26-45	renamed 29th SS Polizei Regiment
04-06-45	renamed 89th SS Polizei Grenadier Regiment

30th SS Polizei Regiment
- -4?	formed as 2nd Polizei Regiment z.b.V. of Bde Wirth from Ordnungspolizei
03-16-45	renamed 30th SS Polizei Regiment
04-06-45	renamed 90th SS Polizei Grenadier Regiment

SS Wach-Battalions

SS Wach-Battalion Berlin (1st SS Wach-Bataillon)
-    -   formed
12-01-43   renamed 1st SS Wach-Bataillon
SS Wach-Battalion Prag (2nd SS Wach-Bataillon)
-    -   formed
12-01-43   renamed 2nd SS Wach-Bataillon
SS Wach-Battalion Böhmen-Mähren
07-30-40   formed
06-14-41   became 3rd Co SS Wach-Bataillon Prag
SS Wach-Battalion Oranienberg
11-15-40   formed from I/15th SSTk Standarte
02-   -41   moved to Debica
09-01-41   reduced to Kompanie
SS Wach-Battalion Nordwest (3rd SS Wach Bataillon)
01-01-42'   formed in the Hague
12-01-43   renamed 3rd SS Wach-Bataillon
04-15-44   moved to Amersfoort
4th SS Wach-Battalion
11-   -44   formed at Truppenübungsplatz Plock
11-   -44   lost
5th SS Wach-Battalion
12-01-43   formed at Truppenübungsplatz Westpreussen
10-15-44   lost
SS Wach-Battalion Oslo (6th SS Wach-Bataillon)
-    -   formed
12-01-43   renamed 6th SS Wach-Bataillon

APPENDIX 3
Theoretical Organization
Fallschirmjäger Division
16 February 1945

Division Staff
  1 Division Staff (6 LMGs)
  1 (mot) Reconnaissance Company (7 LMGS)
  1 Fallschirmjäger Motorcycle Platoon (12 LMGs)
  1 (mot) Military Police Detachment (3 LMGs)
3 Fallschirmjäger Regiments, each with
  1 Fallschirmjäger Regimental Staff (3 LMGs)
  1 (mot) Fallschirmjäger Signals Platoon (2 LMGs)
  1 Fallschirmjäger Bicycle Platoon (2 LMGs)
3 Fallschirmjäger Battalions, each with
  1 Fallschirmjäger Battalion Staff (2 LMGs)
  1 (mot) Fallschirmjäger Signals Platoon (2 LMGs)
  1 Self Propelled Flak Platoon (4 20mm flak guns)
  3 (mot) Companies (20 LMGs & 3 80mm mortars)
  1 (mot) Heavy Company (8 HMGs, 2 LMGS, 2 75mm leIG & 4 80mm mortars)
13th (mot) Fallschirmjäger Mortar Company
  (9 120mm mortars & 6 LMGs)
14th (mot) Fallschirmjäger Panzerjäger Company
  (12 75mm PAK & 12 LMGs)
15th (mot) Fallschirmjäger Pioneer Company
  (2 HMGs, 1 LMGs, 2 80mm mortars)
Other
  1 (mot) Fallschirmjäger Supply Column
  1 Self Propelled Flak Platoon (3 37mm guns)
Fallschirmjäger Mortar Battalion
  Fallschirmjäger Mortar Battalion Staff
  Fallschirmjäger Mortar Battalion Staff Battery (4 LMGs)
  3 (mot) Fallschirmjäger Mortar Companies (12 120mm mortars & 14 LMGs)
Fallschirmjäger Panzerjäger Battalion
  1 Fallschirmjäger Panzerjäger Battalion Staff
  1 Fallschirmjäger Radio Platoon (2 LMGs)
  3 (motZ) Fallschirmjäger Companies (12 75mm PAK & 12 LMGs)
Fallschirmjäger Artillery Regiment
  1 Fallschirmjäger Artillery Regimental Staff
  1 Fallschirmjäger Artillery Regimental Staff Battery (2 LMGs)
  2 Fallschirmjäger Artillery Battalions, each with
  1 Fallschirmjäger Artillery Battalion Staff

1 (mot) Fallschirmjäger Artillery Battalion Staff Battery (2 LMGs)
  3 (motZ) Fallschirmjäger Batteries (4 105mm leFH 18 & 5 LMGS)
  1 Self Propelled Flak Platoon (3 20mm guns)
  1 (mot) Supply Column
1 Fallschirmjäger Artillery Battalion
  1 Fallschirmjäger Artillery Battalion Staff
  1 (mot) Fallschirmjäger Artillery Battalion Staff Battery (2 LMGs)
  3 (motZ) Fallschirmjäger Batteries (4 150mm sFH 18 & 5 LMGS)
  1 Self Propelled Flak Platoon (3 20mm guns)
  1 (mot) Supply Column
9th Fallschirmjäger Flak Battalion
  1 Fallschirmjäger Flak Battalion Staff (4 LMGs)
  1 Fallschirmjäger Signals Platoon
  1 Self Propelled Flak Platoon (3 20mm guns)
  3 (motZ) Heavy Flak Batteries (6 88mm, 3 20mm & 4 LMGS ea)
  1 Self Propelled Medium Flak Battery (12 37mm & 6 LMGs)
  1 Self Propelled Fallschirmjäger Light Flak Battery (12 20mm & 6 LMGs)
  1 (mot) 60 ton Flak Supply Column
9th Fallschirmjäger Pioneer Battalion
  1 Fallschirmjäger Pioneer Battalion Staff
  1 (mot) Fallschirmjäger Signals Platoon (2 LMGs)
  1 Self Propelled Flak Platoon (3 20mm guns)
  4 (mot) Fallschirmjäger Pioneer Companies (2 HMGs, 11 LMGs & 2 80mm mortars)
9th Fallschirmjäger Signals Battalion
  1 Fallschirmjäger Signals Battalion Staff
  1 Self Propelled Flak Platoon (3 20mm guns)
  1 (mot) Signals Company
  1 (mot) Radio Company (5 LMGs)
9th Fallschirmjäger Feldersatz Battalion
  4 Companies
9th Fallschirmjäger Supply Troop
  1 Fallschirmjäger Supply Troop Staff
  1 (horse drawn) (90 ton) Transportation Company

2 (mot) Transportation Companies (9 LMGs & 3 self propelled 20mm)

1 (mot) Supply Company (10 LMGs & 3 self propelled 20mm)

1 (mot) Maintenance Company (5 LMGs & 3 self propelled 20mm)

1 (mot) Maintenance Platoon (2 LMGs)

1 (mot) Bakery Company (3 LMGs & 3 self propelled 20mm)

1 (mot) Butcher Company (1 LMG & 3 self propelled 20mm)

1 (mot) Administration Platoon

1 (mot) Field Post Office

Fallschirmjäger Medical Battalion

2 (mot) Medical Companies (9 LMGs ea)

1 (mot) Field Hospital (6 LMGs)

3 Ambulances

Bibliography

Waffen SS

Brandt, A., *The Last Knight of Flanders*. Atglen, PA: Schiffer Publishing Ltd, 1998.

Fosten, D.S.V. & Marrion, R.J., *Waffen-SS, Its Uniforms, Insignia, and Equipment, 1938–1945*. London: Almark Publishing, 1972.

Green, J., *Mare Nostrum, The War in the Mediterranean*. Watonsville, CA: J.Green, 1990.

Jentz, T.L., *Panzer Truppen*. Atglen, PA: Schiffer Military History, 1996.

Kaltenegger, R., *Mountain Troups of the Waffen-SS, 1941–1945*. Atglen, PA: Schiffer Military History, 1995.

Keilig, W., *Das Deutsche Heer 1939–1945*. Bad Neuheim: Verlag Hans-Henning Podzun, 1956.

Kleitmann, Dr. K.G., *Die Waffen-SS, eine Dokumentation*. Osnabrück: Verlag "Der Freiwillige", 1986.

Landwehr, R., *Italian Volunteers of the Waffen-SS, 24. Waffen-Gebirgs-(Karstjäger) Division der SS and 29. Waffen-Grenadier-Division der SS (italienische Nr. 1)*. Glendale, OR: Siegrunen, 1987.

Lehmann, R., *The Liebstandarte, I, II, & III* , Osnabruck: J.J.Fedorowicz Publishing, 1987.

Lepre, G., *Himmler's Bosnian Division: The Waffen-SS Handschar Division, 1943–1945*. Atglen, PA: Schiffer Military History, 1997.

Littlejohn, D., *Foreign Legions of the Third Reich*. San Jose, CA.: R.James Bender Publishing, 1987.

Logusz, M.O., *Galica Division, the Waffen-SS 14th Grenadier Division 1943–1945*. Atglen, PA: Schiffer Publishing Ltd, 1997.

Lucas, J., *Das Reich, The Military Role of the 2nd SS Division*. London: Arm and Armour Press, 1991.

Mueller-Hillebrand, B., *Das Heer 1933–1945. Vol I & II, Verband der Truppen der deutschen Wehrmacht und Waffen SS 1939–1945*. Frankfurt am Main: date unknown.

Tessin, G., *Verbänd und Truppen der detuschen Wehrmacht und Waffen-SS im Zweiten Weltkrieg 1939–1945*. Osnabruck: Biblo Verlag, 1977.

Records of Headquarters, German Army High Command, American Historical Association Committee for the Study of War Documents, Washington, DC., 1960

National Archives

Microcopy No. T-78, Rolls 397, 398, 404, 405, 409, 411, 412, & 430

Microcopy No. T-311, Rolls 4 & 18

Microcopy No. T-312, Roll 268

Microcopy No. T-313, Roll 355

Microcopy No. T-314, Rolls 746, 747, & 1568

Microcopy No. T-341, Rolls 142, 143, & 146

Microcopy No. T-354, Roll 149

Microcopy No. T-501, Roll 269

US War Department Technical Manual TM–E30–451 *Handbook on German Military Forces, 15 March 1945*. Washington DC: US War Department, 1945.

Weidinger, O., *Division Das Reich*. Osnabruck: Munen Verlag, 1967

Yerger, M.C., *Riding East, The SS Cavalry Brigade in Poland and Russia 1939–1942*. Atglen, PA: Schiffer Miltary History, 1996.

Luftwaffe, Naval, and Mountain Division

Bender, R.J., & Peterson, G.A., *"Hermann Göring" from Regiment to Fallschirmpanzerkorps*. San Jose, CA: R. James Bender Publishing.

Böhmler, R., & Haupt, W., *Fallschirmjäger Paratrooper, Bildband und Chronik, A History in Words and Pictures*. Dorheim: Verlag Hans-Henning Podzun, 1985.

Denzel, E., *Die Luftwaffen Feldivisionen, 1942–1945*. Neckargemünd: Kurt Vowinckel Verlag, 1986.

Green, J., *Mare Nostrum, The War in the Mediterranean*. Watonsville, CA: J.Green, 1990.

Histories of Two Hundred and Fifty-One Divisions of the German Army Which Participated in the War (1914–1918). Washington, DC: Government Printing Office, 1920.

Keilig, W., *Das Deutsche Heer 1939–1945*. Bad Neuheim: Verlag Hans-Henning Podzun, 1956.

Lucas, J., *Hitler's Mountain Troops*. London: Arms and Armour Press, 1992.

————, *Alpine Elite, German Mountain Troops of WWII*. London: Jane's, 1980.

Mueller-Hillebrand, B., *Das Heer l933–1945*. Vol I & II, *Verband der Truppen der deutschen Wehrmacht und Waffen SS l939–l945*. Frankfurt am Main: date unknown.

Tessin, G., *Verbänd und Truppen der deutschen Wehrmacht und Waffen-SS im Zweiten Weltkrieg 1939–1945*. Osnabruck: Biblo Verlag, 1977.

Records of Headquarters, German Army High Command, American Historical Association Committee for the Study of War Documents, Washington, DC, 1960

National Archives

Microcopy No. T-78, Rolls 343, 397, 398,404, 405, 409, 410, 411, & 417

Microcopy No. T-311, Rolls 4, 18, & 51

Microcopy No. T-312, Roll 427, 668, & 1391

Microcopy No. T-313, Roll 355

Microcopy No. T-314, Rolls 746, 747, & 1568

Microcopy No. T-341, Rolls 142, 143, & 146

Microcopy No. T-501, Roll 296

US War Department Technical Manual TM–E30–451 *Handbook on German Military Forces, 15 March 1945*. Washington DC: US War Department, 1945.

Whiting, C., *Hunters from the Sky, The German Parachute Corps, 1940–1945*. London: Leo Cooper, 1974.

Foreign Division

Kliment, C.K., & Nakládal, B., *Germany's First Ally: Armed Forces of the Slovak State, 1939–1945*. Atglen, PA: Schiffer Publishing Ltd., 1997.

Littlejohn, D., *Foreign Legions of the Third Reich*, Vol. 3, *Albania, Czechoslovakia, Greece, Hungary and Yugoslavia*. Vol. 4, *Poland, the Ukraine, Bulgaria, Romania, Free India, Estonia, Latvia, Lithuania, Finland and Russia*. San Jose, CA: R.J.Bender Publishing, 1987.

Records of Headquarters, German Army High Command, National Archives, American Historical Association Committee for the Study of War Documents, Washington, DC., 1960, Microcopy Nos. T-78, Rolls 412, 413, 416, 418

Records of Headquarters, German Army High Command, National Archives, American Historical Association Committee for the Study of War Documents, Washington, DC., 1960, Microcopy Nos. T-312, Roll 51.

Newland, S.J., *Cossacks in the German Army*. London: Frank Cass, 1991.

Schmitz, P., Thies, K.J., Wegmann, G., & Zweng, C., *Die deutschen Divisionen 1939–1945. Vol. 1*. Osnabrück: Biblo Verlag, 1993.